The Complete Coding Interview Guide in Java

An effective guide for aspiring Java developers to ace their programming interviews

Anghel Leonard

BIRMINGHAM—MUMBAI

The Complete Coding Interview Guide in Java

Copyright © 2020 Packt Publishing

All rights reserved. No part of this book may be reproduced, stored in a retrieval system, or transmitted in any form or by any means, without the prior written permission of the publisher, except in the case of brief quotations embedded in critical articles or reviews.

Every effort has been made in the preparation of this book to ensure the accuracy of the information presented. However, the information contained in this book is sold without warranty, either express or implied. Neither the author, nor Packt Publishing or its dealers and distributors, will be held liable for any damages caused or alleged to have been caused directly or indirectly by this book.

Packt Publishing has endeavored to provide trademark information about all of the companies and products mentioned in this book by the appropriate use of capitals. However, Packt Publishing cannot guarantee the accuracy of this information.

Commissioning Editor: Kunal Chaudhari
Acquisition Editor: Alok Dhuri
Senior Editor: Rohit Singh
Content Development Editor: Kinnari Chohan
Technical Editor: Gaurav Gala
Copy Editor: Safis Editing
Project Coordinator: Deeksha Thakkar
Proofreader: Safis Editing
Indexer: Rekha Nair
Production Designer: Joshua Misquitta

First published: August 2020

Production reference: 2030321

Published by Packt Publishing Ltd.
Livery Place
35 Livery Street
Birmingham
B3 2PB, UK.

ISBN 978-1-83921-206-2

www.packt.com

Packt.com

Subscribe to our online digital library for full access to over 7,000 books and videos, as well as industry leading tools to help you plan your personal development and advance your career. For more information, please visit our website.

Why subscribe?

- Spend less time learning and more time coding with practical eBooks and videos from over 4,000 industry professionals
- Improve your learning with Skill Plans designed especially for you
- Get a free eBook or video every month
- Fully searchable for easy access to vital information
- Copy and paste, print, and bookmark content

Did you know that Packt offers eBook versions of every book published, with PDF and ePub files available? You can upgrade to the eBook version at packt.com and, as a print book customer, you are entitled to a discount on the eBook copy. Get in touch with us at customercare@packtpub.com for more details.

At www.packt.com, you can also read a collection of free technical articles, sign up for a range of free newsletters, and receive exclusive discounts and offers on Packt books and eBooks.

Contributors

About the author

Anghel Leonard is a chief technology strategist with more than 20 years' experience in the Java ecosystem. In his daily work, he is focused on architecting and developing Java-distributed applications that empower robust architectures, clean code, and high performance. He is also passionate about coaching, mentoring, and technical leadership.

> *I would like to thank the Packt team for making this book possible.*

About the reviewer

Tejaswini Mandar Jog is a passionate and enthusiastic Java trainer. She has more than 12 years' experience in the IT training field, specializing in Java, J2EE, Spring, Spring Cloud, microservices, and relevant technologies.

She has worked with many renowned corporate companies on training and skill enhancement programs. She is also involved in the development of projects using Java, Spring, and Hibernate and is the author of three books related to Spring, reactive programming, and modular programming.

Packt is searching for authors like you

If you're interested in becoming an author for Packt, please visit authors.packtpub.com and apply today. We have worked with thousands of developers and tech professionals, just like you, to help them share their insight with the global tech community. You can make a general application, apply for a specific hot topic that we are recruiting an author for, or submit your own idea.

Table of Contents

Preface

Section 1: The Non-Technical Part of an Interview

1
Where to Start and How to Prepare for the Interview

The novice interview roadmap	4
Know yourself	4
Know the market	8
It's all about getting the right experience	11
Start something	11
It's time to shine online	12
Time to write your resume	**18**
What resume screeners are looking for	18
How long the resume should be	18
How to list your employment history	19
List the most relevant projects (top five)	19
Nominate your technical skills	20
LinkedIn resume	21
The job application process	**22**
Finding companies that are hiring	22
Submitting the resume	23
I got an interview! Now what?	**23**
The phone screening stage	23
Going to in-person interviews	24
Avoiding common mistakes	24
Summary	**25**

2
What Interviews at Big Companies Look Like

Interviews at Google	28
Interviews at Amazon	28
Interviews at Microsoft	29
Interviews at Facebook	29
Interviews at Crossover	30
Summary	31

3

Common Non-Technical Questions and How To Answer Them

What is the purpose of non-technical questions?	34	Why are you looking to change jobs?	37
What is your experience?	35	What is your salary history?	38
What is your favorite programming language?	35	Why should we hire you?	38
What do you want to do?	36	How much money do you want to make?	38
What are your career goals?	36	Do you have a question for me?	40
What's your working style?	36	Summary	40

4

How to Handle Failures

Accepting or rejecting an offer	42	the mismatches	44
Failure is an option	42	Don't form an obsession for a company	44
A company can reject you for a lot of reasons	43	Don't lose confidence in yourself – sometimes, they don't deserve you!	44
Getting feedback after the interview	43	Summary	45
Objectively identifying and eliminating			

5

How to Approach a Coding Challenge

Technical quiz	48
Coding challenge	50
The problems specific to coding challenges are meant to be difficult	50
Tackling a coding challenge problem	52
Summary	59

Section 2: Concepts

6
Object-Oriented Programming

Technical requirements	64
Understanding OOP concepts	64
What is an object?	65
What is a class?	66
What is abstraction?	67
What is encapsulation?	70
What is inheritance?	73
What is polymorphism?	75
What is association?	79
What is aggregation?	81
What is composition?	83
Getting to know the SOLID principles	**86**
What is S?	86
What is L?	93
What is I?	98
What is D?	102
Popular questions pertaining to OOP, SOLID, and GOF design patterns	**105**
What is method overriding in OOP (Java)?	105
What is method overloading in OOP (Java)?	106
What is covariant method overriding in Java?	107
What are the main restrictions in terms of working with exceptions in overriding and overloading methods?	109
How can the superclass overridden method be called from the subclass overriding method?	110
Can we override or overload the main() method?	110
Can we override a non-static method as static in Java?	110
What are the main differences between interfaces with default methods and abstract classes?	114
What is the main difference between abstract classes and interfaces?	115
Can we have an abstract class without an abstract method?	115
Can we have a class that is both abstract and final at the same time?	115
What is the difference between polymorphism, overriding, and overloading?	115
What are the main differences between static and dynamic binding?	116
What is method hiding in Java?	116
Can we write virtual methods in Java?	118
What is the difference between polymorphism and abstraction?	118
Do you consider overloading an approach for implementing polymorphism?	118
Which OOP concept serves the Decorator design pattern?	119
When should the Singleton design pattern be used?	119
What is the difference between the Strategy and State design patterns?	119
What is the difference between the Proxy and Decorator patterns?	120
What is the difference between the Facade and Decorator patterns?	120

What is the key difference between the Builder and Factory patterns?	121	Example 4: Parking lot	133
		Example 5: Online reader system	139
What is the key difference between the Adapter and Bridge patterns?	122	Example 6: Hash table	145
		Example 7: File system	148
Coding challenges	**123**	Example 8: Tuple	149
Example 1: Jukebox	123	Example 9: Cinema with a movie ticket booking system	149
Example 2: Vending machine	126		
Example 3: Deck of cards	129	**Summary**	**150**

7
Big O Analysis of Algorithms

Analogy	**152**	Example 13 – identifying O(1) loops	169
Big O complexity time	**153**	Example 14 – looping half of the array	170
The best case, worst case, and expected case	**154**	Example 15 – reducing Big O expressions	170
Big O examples	**154**	Example 16 – looping with O(log n)	171
Example 1 – O(1)	155	Example 17 – string comparison	172
Example 2 – O(n), linear time algorithms	155	Example 18 – factorial Big O	173
Example 3 – O(n), dropping the constants	156	Example 19 – using n notation with caution	174
Example 6 – different steps are summed or multiplied	160	Example 21 – the number of iteration counts in Big O	175
Example 7 – log n runtimes	161	Example 22 – digits	175
Example 9 – in-order traversal of a binary tree	164	Example 23 – sorting	176
Example 10 – n may vary	165	**Key hints to look for in an interview**	**177**
Example 11 – memoization	166	**Summary**	**178**

8
Recursion and Dynamic Programming

Technical requirements	**180**	Memoization (or Top-Down Dynamic Programming)	182
Recursion in a nutshell	**180**		
Recognizing a recursive problem	180	Tabulation (or Bottom-Up Dynamic Programming)	184
Dynamic Programming in a nutshell	**181**	**Coding challenges**	**185**

Coding challenge 1 – Robot grid (I)	186	permutations	208
Coding challenge 3 – Josephus	191	Coding challenge 11 – Knight tour	214
Coding challenge 6 – Five towers	198	Coding challenge 12 – Curly braces	217
Coding challenge 8 – The falling ball	204	Coding challenge 13 – Staircase	219
Coding challenge 9 – The highest colored tower	206	Coding challenge 14 – Subset sum	220
Coding challenge 10 – String		Coding challenge 15 – Word break (this is a famous Google problem)	227

9
Bit Manipulation

Technical requirements	**236**	in code	256
Bit manipulation in a nutshell	**236**	Coding challenge 12 – Replacing bits	257
Obtaining the binary representation of a Java integer	236	Coding challenge 13 – Longest sequence of 1	259
Bitwise operators	237	Coding challenge 14 – Next and previous numbers	262
Bit shift operators	239	Coding challenge 15 – Conversion	266
Tips and tricks	241	Coding challenge 16 – Maximizing expressions	267
Coding challenges	**242**	Coding challenge 17 – Swapping odd and even bits	269
Coding challenge 1 – Getting the bit value	242	Coding challenge 18 – Rotating bits	270
Coding challenge 2 – Setting the bit value	243	Coding challenge 19 – Calculating numbers	272
Coding challenge 3 – Clearing bits	245	Coding challenge 20 – Unique elements	273
Coding challenge 4 – Summing binaries on paper	246	Coding challenge 21 – Finding duplicates	277
Coding challenge 5 – Summing binaries in code	247	Coding challenge 22 – Two non-repeating elements	278
Coding challenge 6 – Multiplying binaries on paper	249	Coding challenge 23 – Power set of a set	281
Coding challenge 7 – Multiplying binaries in code	250	Coding challenge 24 – Finding the position of the only set bit	283
Coding challenge 8 – Subtracting binaries on paper	252	Coding challenge 25 – Converting a float into binary and vice versa	284
Coding challenge 9 – Subtracting binaries in code	253	**Summary**	**285**
Coding challenge 10 – Dividing binaries on paper	254		
Coding challenge 11 – Dividing binaries			

Section 3: Algorithms and Data Structures

10
Arrays and Strings

Technical requirements	289
Arrays and strings in a nutshell	290
Coding challenges	290
Coding challenge 1 – Unique characters (1)	292
Coding challenge 2 – Unique characters (2)	294
Coding challenge 3 – Encoding strings	296
Coding challenge 4 – One edit away	297
Coding challenge 5 – Shrinking a string	299
Coding challenge 6 – Extracting integers	301
Coding challenge 7 – Extracting the code points of surrogate pairs	302
Coding challenge 8 – Is rotation	305
Coding challenge 9 – Rotating a matrix by 90 degrees	306
Coding challenge 10 – Matrix containing zeros	309
Coding challenge 11 – Implementing three stacks with one array	313
Coding challenge 12 – Pairs	318
Coding challenge 13 – Merging sorted arrays	321
Coding challenge 14 – Median	324
Coding challenge 15 – Sub-matrix of one	330
Coding challenge 16 – Container with the most water	334
Coding challenge 17 – Searching in a circularly sorted array	339
Coding challenge 18 – Merging intervals	342
Coding challenge 19 – Petrol bunks circular tour	348
Coding challenge 20 – Trapping rainwater	351
Coding challenge 21 – Buying and selling stock	356
Coding challenge 22 – Longest sequence	367
Coding challenge 23 – Counting game score	369
Coding challenge 24 – Checking for duplicates	370
Coding challenge 25 – Longest distinct substring	374
Coding challenge 26 – Replacing elements with ranks	374
Coding challenge 27 – Distinct elements in every sub-array	375
Coding challenge 28 – Rotating the array k times	375
Coding challenge 29 – Distinct absolute values in sorted arrays	375
Summary	376

11
Linked Lists and Maps

Technical requirements	378
Linked lists in a nutshell	378
Maps in a nutshell	379
Coding challenges	380

Coding challenge 1 – Map put, get, and remove	381	intersection	401
Coding challenge 2 – Map the key set and values	384	Coding challenge 11 – Swap adjacent nodes	403
Coding challenge 3 – Nuts and bolts	385	Coding challenge 12 – Merge two sorted linked lists	406
Coding challenge 4 – Remove duplicates	386	Coding challenge 13 – Remove the redundant path	411
Coding challenge 5 – Rearranging linked lists	389	Coding challenge 14 – Move the last node to the front	413
Coding challenge 6 – The nth to last node	391	Coding challenge 15 – Reverse a singly linked list in groups of k	415
Coding challenge 7 – Loop start detection	393	Coding challenge 16 – Reverse a doubly linked list	417
Coding challenge 8 – Palindromes	397	Coding challenge 17 – LRU cache	418
Coding challenge 9 – Sum two linked lists	399	**Summary**	**423**
Coding challenge 10 – Linked lists			

12

Stacks and Queues

Technical requirements	**426**	Coding challenge 6 – Queue via stacks	446
Stacks in a nutshell	**426**	Coding challenge 7 – Stack via queues	448
Queues in a nutshell	**429**	Coding challenge 8 – Max histogram area	452
Coding challenges	**432**	Coding challenge 9 – Smallest number	455
Coding challenge 1 – Reverse string	432	Coding challenge 10 – Islands	457
Coding challenge 2 – Stack of curly braces	433	Coding challenge 11 – Shortest path	461
Coding challenge 3 – Stack of plates	435	**Infix, postfix, and prefix expressions**	**464**
Coding challenge 4 – Stock span	438	**Summary**	**465**
Coding challenge 5 – Stack min	442		

13

Trees and Graphs

Technical requirements	**467**	Complete binary tree	477
Trees in a nutshell	**468**	Full binary tree	478
General tree	469	Perfect binary tree	478
Binary Search Tree	473	Binary Heaps	479
Balanced and unbalanced binary trees	474	**Graphs in a nutshell**	**481**

Adjacency matrix	482	Coding challenge 15 – Handling duplicates in BSTs	524
Adjacency list	483		
Graph traversal	484	Coding challenge 16 – Isomorphism of binary trees	526

Coding challenges — 486

Coding challenge 1 – Paths between two nodes	486	Coding challenge 17 – Binary tree right view	529
Coding challenge 2 – Sorted array to minimal BST	487	Coding challenge 18 – k^{th} largest element	531
		Coding challenge 19 – Mirror binary tree	533
Coding challenge 3 – List per level	489	Coding challenge 20 – Spiral-level order traversal of a binary tree	535
Coding challenge 4 – sub-tree	491		
Coding challenge 5 – Landing reservation system	494	Coding challenge 21 – Nodes at a distance k from leafs	539
Coding challenge 6 – Balanced binary tree	499	Coding challenge 22 – Pair for a given sum	541
Coding challenge 7 – Binary tree is a BST	502	Coding challenge 23 – Vertical sums in a binary tree	546
Coding challenge 8 – Successor node	504		
Coding challenge 9 – Topological sort	507	Coding challenge 23 – Converting a max heap into a min heap	548
Coding challenge 10 – Common ancestor	509	Coding challenge 24 – Finding out whether a binary tree is symmetric	551
Coding challenge 11 – Chess knight	511		
Coding challenge 12 – Printing binary tree corners	514	Coding challenge 25 – Connecting n ropes at the minimum cost	554
Coding challenge 13 – Max path sum	516	**Advanced topics**	**556**
Coding challenge 14 – Diagonal traversal	519	**Summary**	**557**

14
Sorting and Searching

Technical requirements	**559**	Coding challenge 1 – Merging two sorted arrays	580
Sorting algorithms	**560**		
Heap Sort	561	Coding challenge 2 – Grouping anagrams together	583
Merge Sort	564		
Quick Sort	567	Coding challenge 3 – List of unknown size	587
Bucket Sort	570		
Radix Sort	575	Coding challenge 4 – Merge sorting a linked list	589
Searching algorithms	**577**	Coding challenge 5 – Strings interspersed with empty strings	593
Coding challenges	**580**		
		Coding challenge 6 – Sorting a queue	

with the help of another queue	595	Coding challenge 12 – First position of first one	613
Coding challenge 7 – Sorting a queue without extra space	599	Coding challenge 13 – Maximum difference between two elements	614
Coding challenge 8 – Sorting a stack with the help of another stack	602	Coding challenge 14 – Stream ranking	616
		Coding challenge 15 – Peaks and valleys	619
Coding challenge 9 – Sorting a stack in place	604	Coding challenge 16 – Nearest left smaller number	622
Coding challenge 10 – Searching in a full sorted matrix	608	Coding challenge 17 – Word search	624
		Coding challenge 18 – Sorting an array based on another array	625
Coding challenge 11 – Searching in a sorted matrix	610	Summary	627

15
Mathematics and Puzzles

Technical requirements	**630**	Coding challenge 13 – Clock angle	657
Tips and suggestions	**630**	Coding challenge 14 – Pythagorean triplets	659
Coding challenges	**631**		
Coding challenge 1 – FizzBuzz	631	Coding challenge 15 – Scheduling one elevator	662
Coding challenge 2 – Roman numerals	632		
Coding challenge 3 – Visiting and toggling 100 doors	635	**Summary**	**667**
Coding challenge 4 – 8 teams	638		
Coding challenge 5 – Finding the kth number with the prime factors 3, 5, and 7	639		
Coding challenge 6 – Count decoding a digit's sequence	640		
Coding challenge 7 – ABCD	643		
Coding challenge 8 – Rectangles overlapping	644		
Coding challenge 9 – Multiplying large numbers	648		
Coding challenge 10 – Next greatest number with the same digits	651		
Coding challenge 11 – A number divisible by its digits	654		
Coding challenge 12 – Breaking chocolate	655		

Section 4: Bonus – Concurrency and Functional Programming

16
Concurrency

Technical Requirements	672	Runnable	680
Java concurrency (multithreading) in a nutshell	672	Coding challenge 12 – wait() versus sleep()	681
		Coding challenge 14 – ThreadLocal	682
Questions and coding challenges	674	Coding challenge 15 – submit() versus execute()	682
Coding challenge 1 – Thread life cycle states	674	Coding challenge 16 – interrupted() and isInterrupted()	682
Coding challenge 2 – Deadlocks	676	Coding challenge 18 – sharing data between threads	684
Coding challenge 3 – Race conditions	677	Coding challenge 20 – Producer-Consumer	684
Coding challenge 5 – Executor and ExecutorService	678	Producer-Consumer via wait() and notify()	685
Coding challenge 7 – Starvation	679		
Coding challenge 10 – Thread versus			

17
Functional-Style Programming

Java functional-style programming in a nutshell	690	Coding challenge 5 – The flatMap() function	697
Key concepts of functional-style programming	690	Coding challenge 6 – map() versus flatMap()	697
		Coding challenge 7 – The filter() function	699
Questions and coding challenges	693	Coding challenge 8 – Intermediate versus terminal operations	700
Coding challenge 1 – Lambda parts	693	Coding challenge 9 – The peek() function	700
Coding challenge 2 – Functional interface	695	Coding challenge 10 – Lazy streams	701
Coding challenge 3 – Collections versus streams	696	Coding challenge 11 – Functional interfaces versus regular interfaces	701
Coding challenge 4 – The map() function	696	Coding challenge 12 – Supplier versus Consumer	701

Coding challenge 13 – Predicates	702	Coding challenge 18 – The default method	705
Coding challenge 14 – findFirst() versus findAny()	702	Coding challenge 19 – Iterator versus Spliterator	705
Coding challenge 15 – Converting arrays to streams	703	Coding challenge 20 – Optional	706
Coding challenge 16 – Parallel streams	704	Coding challenge 21 – String::valueOf	707
Coding challenge 17 – The method reference	704	**Summary**	**707**

18
Unit Testing

Technical Requirements	**709**	Coding challenge 8 – Mocking and stubbing	717
Unit testing in a nutshell	**710**	Coding challenge 9 – Test suite	717
Questions and coding challenges	**712**	Coding challenge 10 – Ignoring test methods	719
Coding challenge 1 – AAA	712	Coding challenge 11 – Assumptions	719
Coding challenge 2 – FIRST	713	Coding challenge 12 – @Rule	721
Coding challenge 3 – Test fixtures	713	Coding challenge 13 – Method test return type	721
Coding challenge 4 – Exception testing	714	Coding challenge 14 – Dynamic tests	721
Coding challenge 5 – Developer or tester	716	Coding challenge 15 – Nested tests	722
Coding challenge 6 – JUnit extensions	716	**Summary**	**724**
Coding challenge 7 – @Before* and @After* annotations	717		

19
System Scalability

Scalability in a nutshell	**726**	Coding challenge 6 – Load balancing	729
Questions and coding challenges	**727**	Coding challenge 7 – Sticky session	730
		Coding challenge 8 – Sharding	731
Coding challenge 1 – Scaling types	727	Coding challenge 9 – Shared-nothing architecture	732
Coding challenge 2 – High availability	728	Coding challenge 10 – Failover	732
Coding challenge 3 – Low latency	728	Coding challenge 11 – Session replication	732
Coding challenge 4 – Clustering	728	Coding challenge 12 – The CAP theorem	733
Coding challenge 5 – Latency, bandwidth, and throughput	729	Coding challenge 13 – Social networks	733

Practicing is the key to success 735

Designing bitly, TinyURL, and goo.gl (a service for shorting URLs) 735
Designing Netflix, Twitch, and YouTube (a global video streaming service) 736
Designing WhatsApp and Facebook Messenger (a global chat service) 736
Designing Reddit, HackerNews, Quora, and Voat (a message board service and social network) 736
Designing Google Drive, Google Photos, and Dropbox (a global file storage and sharing service) 737
Designing Twitter, Facebook, and Instagram (an extremely large social media service) 737
Designing Lyft, Uber, and RideAustin (a ride-sharing service) 737
Designing a type-ahead and web crawler (a search engine related service) 737
Designing an API rate limiter (for example, GitHub or Firebase) 738
Designing nearby places/friends and Yelp (a proximity server) 738

Summary 739

Other Books You May Enjoy
Index

Preface

Java is a very popular language, featuring in a high number of IT job offers across a wide range of fields and industries. Since Java empowers billions of devices all over the world, it's become a very appealing technology to learn. However, learning Java is one thing; starting to develop a career in the Java field is something else. This book is dedicated to people who want to develop a Java career and want to ace Java-centric interviews.

With this book, you'll learn how to do the following:

- Solve the 220+ most popular Java coding interview problems in a contretemps fashion encountered in a wide range of companies, including top firms such as Google, Amazon, Microsoft, Adobe, and Flipkart.
- Collect the best techniques for solving a wide range of Java coding problems.
- Tackle brain-teasing algorithms meant to develop strong and fast logic abilities.
- Iterate the common non-technical interview questions that can make the difference between success and failure.
- Get an overall picture of what employers want from a Java developer.

By the end of this book, you will have a solid informational foundation for solving Java coding interview problems. The knowledge achieved from this book will give you high confidence in yourself to obtain your Java-centric dream job.

Who this book is for

The Complete Coding Interview Guide in Java is a comprehensive resource for those who are looking for a Java developer (or related) job and need to tackle coding problems in a contretemps fashion. It is especially dedicated to entry- and middle-level candidates.

What this book covers

Chapter 1, Where to Start and How to Prepare for the Interview, is a comprehensive guide that tackles the preparation process for a Java interview from zero to hire. More precisely, we want to highlight the main checkpoints that can ensure a smooth and successful career path ahead.

Chapter 2, What Interviews at Big Companies Look Like, talks about how interviews are conducted in the main Big Tech firms of Google, Amazon, Microsoft, Facebook, and Crossover.

Chapter 3, Common Non-Technical Questions and How To Answer Them, tackles the main aspects of the non-technical questions. This part of the interview is commonly carried out by a hiring manager or even an HR person.

Chapter 4, How to Handle Failures, discusses a delicate aspect of the interview – handling failures. The main purpose of this chapter is to show you how to identify the causes of failure and how to mitigate them in the future.

Chapter 5, How to Approach a Coding Challenge, covers the technical quizzes and coding challenge topics that are commonly referred to as the technical interview.

Chapter 6, Object-Oriented Programming, explains the most popular questions and problems concerning object-oriented programming encountered at Java interviews, including the SOLID principles and coding challenges such as Jukebox, Parking Lot, and Hash Table.

Chapter 7, Big O Analysis of Algorithms, provides the most popular metric for analyzing the efficiency and scalability of algorithms, the Big O notation, in the context of a technical interview.

Chapter 8, Recursion and Dynamic Programming, covers one of the favorite topics of interviewers – recursion and Dynamic Programming. Both of these topics work hand in hand with each other, so you have to be able to cover both.

Chapter 9, Bit Manipulation, explains the most important aspects of bit manipulation that you should know in a technical interview. Such problems are often encountered in interviews and they are not easy. In this chapter, you have 25 such coding challenges.

Chapter 10, Arrays and Strings, covers 29 popular problems involving strings and arrays.

Chapter 11, Linked Lists and Maps, teaches you the 17 most famous coding challenges that involve maps and linked lists encountered in interviews.

Chapter 12, *Stacks and Queues,* explains the 11 most popular interview coding challenges involving stacks and queues. Mainly, you have to learn how to provide a stack/queue implementation from scratch and how to tackle coding challenges via the Java built-in implementations.

Chapter 13, *Trees and Graphs,* covers one of the most tricky topics in interviews – trees and graphs. While there are tons of problems related to these two topics, only a handful of them are actually encountered in interviews. It is therefore very important to give a high priority to the most popular problems concerning trees and graphs.

Chapter 14, *Sorting and Searching,* covers the most popular sorting and searching algorithms encountered in technical interviews. We will cover sorting algorithms such as Merge Sort, Quick Sort, Radix Sort, Heap Sort, and Bucket Sort, and searching algorithms such as Binary Search. By the end of this chapter, you should be able to tackle a wide range of problems that involve sorting and searching algorithms.

Chapter 15, *Mathematics and Puzzles,* talks about a controversial topic in interviews: mathematics and puzzle problems. A significant number of companies consider that these kinds of problems should not be part of a technical interview, while other companies still regard this topic as relevant for interviews.

Chapter 16, *Concurrency,* covers the most popular questions about Java concurrency (multithreading) that occur in general interviews involving the Java language.

Chapter 17, *Functional-Style Programming,* examines the most popular questions about Java functional-style programming. We cover key concepts, lambdas, and streams.

Chapter 18, *Unit Testing,* talks about unit-testing interview problems that you may encounter if you apply for a position such as a developer or software engineer. Of course, if you are looking for a tester (manual/automation) position, then this chapter may represent just another perspective on testing. Therefore, do not expect to see questions here specific to manual/automation tester positions.

Chapter 19, *System Scalability,* provides the widest range of scalability interview questions you may be asked during a junior/middle-level interview for a position such as a web application software architect, Java architect, or software engineer.

To get the most out of this book

All you need is Java (preferably Java 8+) and your favorite IDE (NetBeans, IntelliJ IDEA, Eclipse, and so on).

I also strongly recommend that readers consult the *Java Coding Problems* book, also from Packt, to improve your skills further.

Download the example code files

You can download the example code files for this book from your account at `www.packt.com`. If you purchased this book elsewhere, you can visit `www.packtpub.com/support` and register to have the files emailed directly to you.

You can download the code files by following these steps:

1. Log in or register at `www.packt.com`.
2. Select the **Support** tab.
3. Click on **Code Downloads**.
4. Enter the name of the book in the **Search** box and follow the onscreen instructions.

Once the file is downloaded, please make sure that you unzip or extract the folder using the latest version of:

- WinRAR/7-Zip for Windows
- Zipeg/iZip/UnRarX for Mac
- 7-Zip/PeaZip for Linux

The code bundle for the book is also hosted on GitHub at `https://github.com/PacktPublishing/The-Complete-Coding-Interview-Guide-in-Java`. In case there's an update to the code, it will be updated on the existing GitHub repository.

We also have other code bundles from our rich catalog of books and videos available at `https://github.com/PacktPublishing/`. Check them out!

Download the color images

We also provide a PDF file that has color images of the screenshots/diagrams used in this book. You can download it here: `https://static.packt-cdn.com/downloads/9781839212062_ColorImages.pdf`

Conventions used

There are a number of text conventions used throughout this book.

`Code in text`: Indicates code words in text, database table names, folder names, filenames, file extensions, pathnames, dummy URLs, user input, and Twitter handles. Here is an example: "The `Triangle`, `Rectangle`, and `Circle` classes implement the `Shape` interface and override the `draw()` method to draw the corresponding shape."

A block of code is set as follows:

```
public static void main(String[] args) {

    Shape triangle = new Triangle();
    Shape rectangle = new Rectangle();
    Shape circle = new Circle();

    triangle.draw();
    rectangle.draw();
    circle.draw();
}
```

When we wish to draw your attention to a particular part of a code block, the relevant lines or items are set in bold:

```
public static void main(String[] args) {

    Shape triangle = new Triangle();
    Shape rectangle = new Rectangle();
    Shape circle = new Circle();

    triangle.draw();
    rectangle.draw();
    circle.draw();
}
```

Bold: Indicates a new term, an important word, or words that you see on screen. For example, words in menus or dialog boxes appear in the text like this. Here is an example: "However, this approach does not work for the third case, 339809 (10100**10111101**100001)."

> Tips or important notes
> Appear like this.

Get in touch

Feedback from our readers is always welcome.

General feedback: If you have questions about any aspect of this book, mention the book title in the subject of your message and email us at `customercare@packtpub.com`.

Errata: Although we have taken every care to ensure the accuracy of our content, mistakes do happen. If you have found a mistake in this book, we would be grateful if you would report this to us. Please visit `www.packtpub.com/support/errata`, selecting your book, clicking on the Errata Submission Form link, and entering the details.

Piracy: If you come across any illegal copies of our works in any form on the internet, we would be grateful if you would provide us with the location address or website name. Please contact us at `copyright@packt.com` with a link to the material.

If you are interested in becoming an author: If there is a topic that you have expertise in, and you are interested in either writing or contributing to a book, please visit `authors.packtpub.com`.

Reviews

Please leave a review. Once you have read and used this book, why not leave a review on the site that you purchased it from? Potential readers can then see and use your unbiased opinion to make purchase decisions, we at Packt can understand what you think about our products, and our authors can see your feedback on their book. Thank you!

For more information about Packt, please visit `packt.com`.

Section 1: The Non-Technical Part of an Interview

The objective of this section consists of covering the non-technical part of an interview. This includes interview idioms and the patterns of big companies, such as Amazon, Microsoft, Google, and so on. You will become familiar with the main non-technical interview questions and their meaning (how the interviewer interprets the answers).

This section comprises the following chapters:

- *Chapter 1, Where to Start and How to Prepare for the Interview*
- *Chapter 2, What Interviews at Big Companies Look Like*
- *Chapter 3, Common Non-Technical Questions and How To Answer Them*
- *Chapter 4, How to Handle Failures*
- *Chapter 5, How to Approach a Coding Challenge*

1
Where to Start and How to Prepare for the Interview

This chapter is a comprehensive guide that tackles the preparation process for a Java interview from the very start, to getting hired. More precisely, we want to highlight the main checkpoints that can ensure a smooth and successful career road ahead. Of course, at the time you read this book, you might find yourself at any of these checkpoints:

- Start your interview preparation as early as possible
- Get the right experience
- Show your work to the world
- Prepare your resume
- Take the interview

By the end of this chapter, you'll have a clear picture of how to achieve the preceding checkpoints depending on your current status. So, let's start by covering the first checkpoint and take a look at the novice interview roadmap.

The novice interview roadmap

Let's start from a fundamental truth that is absolutely necessary, but not sufficient, to become a successful developer: the best Java developers are passionate about their work, and, in time, true passions become professions. Over the long term, passion is priceless and it will make you stand out of the crowd of skilled but dispassionate people.

Since you bought this book, you want to invest some time and money in a Java software development career. Mainly, you want to become part of the amazing Java ecosystem! You already feel the power and the energy that comes from focusing on working with Java, therefore, even if you haven't yet actively thought about it, you've already started to prepare yourself for a Java interview.

Most probably, you are a student or you've just got a bachelor's degree in IT, computer science, or you've simply discovered your propensity for the Java language. Nevertheless, since you are here, you have a lot of questions and doubts about how to get the dream job in the Java ecosystem.

It is time to bake a plan for success! The following flowchart represents the interview roadmap for a student or Java novice who wants to be part of the Java ecosystem:

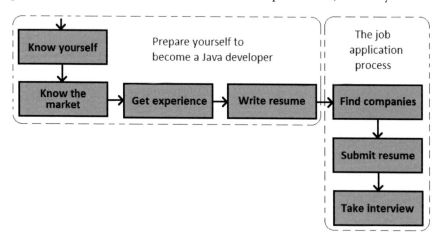

Figure 1.1 – Novice interview roadmap

In this chapter, we will cover each item of the preceding diagram. Let's get started with the first item, *Know yourself*.

Know yourself

Before searching for a job, it is important to know yourself. This means that you should know what kind of developer you are and what kind of job you want.

This is crucial to getting the right experience, evolving your package of skills, and finding the right employer. Most probably, you can cover a wide range of Java programming tasks, but do you find all of them equally engaging? Doing something that you don't like for a short period of time is OK, but it will not work for the long term.

Ideally, in the long term, you must focus on what you like to do the most! This way, you maximize your chances of becoming a top Java developer. But, doing what you like the most should be considered in the context of what the IT market offers (in both the short term, and most importantly, the long term). Some Java technologies are widely covered by job offers, while others may require a lot of time to find a job or must make some really unpleasant trade-offs (for example, relocation). It is strongly advisable to periodically consult and participate (every vote counts) in the most relevant Java surveys conducted by websites such as `blogs.oracle.com`, `snyk.io`, `jaxenter.com`, `codeburst.io`, `jetbrains.com`, and `dzone.com`. Having a wide range of companies to choose from statistically maximizes the chances of finding the right company for you. This is half of the problem, while the other half is to prepare yourself to make sure that the company with the job you want will want you.

Now, let's examine 10 questions that will help you to identify what kind of developer you plan to become. Look inside yourself and try to overlap your personality and skills in considering the following questions and explanations:

1. **Are you interested in developing user interfaces or the heavy business logic that is executed behind the scenes?** Developing great user interfaces is an extremely important aspect of a graphical interface. After all, the graphical interface is what the end user sees and interacts with. It requires creativity, innovation, vision, and psychology (for example, developing multi-device interfaces is quite challenging). It requires knowledge of Java AWT, Swing, JavaFX, Vaadin, and so on. On the other hand, the business logic that is executed behind the scenes and answers to end user actions is the engine behind the interface, but, for the end user, most of the time it is a black box. The business logic requires strong coding skills and solid knowledge of algorithms, data structures, frameworks (such as Spring Boot, Jakarta EE, and Hibernate), databases, and so on. Most Java developers opt for coding the business logic behind the scenes (for desktop and web applications).

2. **What kind of applications do you find most engaging** (desktop, mobile, web, or others)? Each type of application has specific challenges and dedicated suites of tools. Today, companies target as many consumers as possible, therefore, modern applications should be available for multi-platform devices. Most of all, you should be able to code in the knowledge that the application will be exposed on different devices and will interact with other systems.

3. **Are you especially interested in testing, debugging, and/or code review?** Having strong skills in writing valuable tests, finding bugs, and reviewing the code are the most important skills for guaranteeing a high-quality final product. Of these three areas, we should focus on testing, as almost any Java developer job description requires the candidate to have strong skills in writing unit tests and integration tests (the most commonly preferred tools are JUnit, TestNG, Mockito, and Cucumber-JVM). Nevertheless, trying to find a dedicated Java tester job or Java code reviewer is quite challenging and is usually encountered in big companies (especially in companies that provide remote jobs, such as Upstack or Crossover). Most companies prefer *pair code review* and each Java developer should write meaningful tests that provide high coverage for the code that they wrote. So you have to be able do both: write astonishing code, and write the tests for that code.

4. **Are you interested in applications that interact with databases or do you try to avoid such applications?** Most Java applications use a database (a relational database or a NoSQL database). A wide range of Java developer jobs will imperatively require you to have strong knowledge of coding against a database via Object Relational Mapping frameworks (such as Hibernate), JPA implementations (such as Hibernate JPA or Eclipse Link), or SQL-centric libraries (such as jOOQ). Most Java applications interact with a relational database such as MySQL, PostgreSQL, Oracle, or SQL Server. But NoSQL databases such as MongoDB, Redis, or Cassandra are also encountered in a significant number of applications. Trying to avoid developing applications that interact with a database may seriously limit the range of jobs on offer. If this is your case, then you should reconsider this aspect starting today.

5. **Do you have a predilection for code optimization and performance?** Caring about the performance of your code is a highly appreciated skill. Such actions will catalog you as a perfectionist with great attention to detail. Having solutions that optimize the code and increase its performances will place you pretty quickly in the position of getting involved in designing and architecting the solutions of functional requirements. But at the interview (the code challenge stage), don't focus on code optimizations and performance! Simply focus on delivering a working solution and, as much as possible, clean code.

6. **What is more appealing to you: a coding-focused job or being a software architect?** At the beginning of your career as a Java developer, you will be focused on coding and taking implementation design decisions at code level. In time, some developers discover their abilities and interest in architecting large applications. This means that it's time to evolve from a Java developer to a Java architect, or even a Java chief architect. While coding is still part of your job, as an architect you will wear different hats on the same day. You have to split your time between meetings, architecting, and coding. If you feel that you have the aptitude for designing and architecting different pieces of a project, then it is advisable to consider some training in software architecture as well. Moreover, during your coding-focused job, challenge yourself to see what solutions you can find and compare them with those implemented by the current architect of the application.

7. **Are you aiming for a small or a big company?** Choosing between a small or a big company is a matter of trade-offs. Ideally, a big company (a brand) will give stability, a career path, and a good salary plan. But you may feel stifled by the bureaucracy, lack of communication and rivalry between departments, and a cold and rigid environment. In a small company, you have the chance to feel more intensely that you are part of the success and will get a nice, warm feeling of being part of a small community (even a family). However, small companies may fail fast and you might be fired in a year or two, most likely without any compensation package.

8. **Do you target a software company (working on a wide range of projects) or a certain industry (for example, the oil industry, medicine, the automobile industry, and so on)?** A software company manages projects from a variety of fields (for example, a software company might develop a website for a Hollywood star, a financial application, and an airline traffic control application at the same time). From a developer's perspective, this means that you need versatile thinking and to be capable of quickly adapting to understand the requirements of different business domains without diving into those domains. On the other hand, big industries (for example, the oil industry) prefer to create their own IT departments that develop and maintain applications specific to that company field. In such cases, you would most likely receive some training in the given company's field as well. You will have the advantage of becoming an expert at developing applications specific to a certain domain.

9. **Do you prefer a remote job?** In the past few years, a significant number of companies have decided to hire remote developers. Moreover, new companies such as Upwork, Remote|OK, X-Team, and Crossover are 100% remote companies recruiting only for remote positions. The advantage of working from any corner of the world with a flexible program is quite appealing. These companies offer jobs for junior, middle, and senior developers, and some of them (for example, Crossover) offer remote management positions as well. But, you have to be aware of some of the other aspects of this arrangement as well: it is possible that you will be monitored via webcam (for example, with snapshots every 10 minutes); you need to work in a completely remote team with members from different time zones (it may be challenging to participate in meetings at night, for example); you will have to be familiar with tools including JIRA, GitHub, Zoom, Slack, Meetup, and in-house marketplace platforms; you may face a lot of friction (tons of emails) and a lack of communication; you need to pay your taxes, and last but not least, you may need to achieve unreal metrics to the detriment of quality to maintain your position.

10. **Does management interest you?** Commonly, reaching a managerial position is a goal that requires leadership skills. In other words, you should be able to take important decisions at both the technical and human levels. From this perspective, you need to avoid companies that offer a solid technical career path but don't provide opportunities to get promoted to the ranks of management.

> **Important note**
> Knowing yourself is one of the hardest parts required in order to make the best decisions in life. Sometimes, asking the opinion of other people is the best way to eliminate your subjective view of yourself. Most of the time, asking your teachers, parents, and friends will help you to better understand what your skills are and where you fit the best. Making important decisions alone is risky.

Once you know yourself, it is time to get to know the market.

Know the market

Knowing what you want is great, but is not enough. As the next step, you should research what the market wants from you. The goal is to obtain the perfect cocktail of what you want and what the market offers.

> **Important note**
> Developing marketable skills is an important aspect of getting a job in the near future.

First, you must check which Java technologies have been most popular over the last few years and what the future trends look likely to be. Technologies that maintain relatively stable popularity over time are the most used in companies.

Take your time to read several surveys from the last 2-3 years from important websites such as `blogs.oracle.com`, `snyk.io`, `jaxenter.com`, `codeburst.io`, `jetbrains.com`, and `dzone.com`. Primarily, you can search on Google for *java technologies survey 2019* or similar combinations of keywords. Also, don't neglect the financial part, so make sure to search for *java salaries survey 2019* as well.

You will find a variety of surveys that nicely summarize the most popular technologies, as you can see in the following two figures. The first one shows the popularity of application servers:

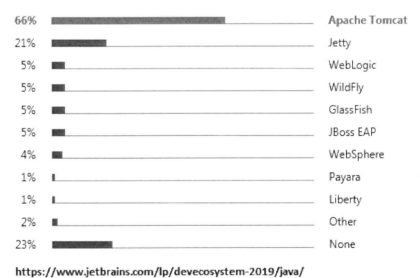

Figure 1.2 – The application servers that are used

The following figure shows which frameworks developers prefer:

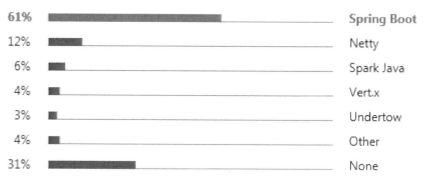

Figure 1.3 – The frameworks that developers prefer to use

While reading, make a list and note down what Java technologies are the most popular and what technologies don't deserve your attention at this moment. It will be a list similar to the following:

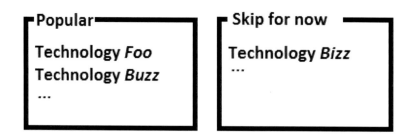

Figure 1.4 – Splitting technologies by popularity

This way, you can quickly filter the technologies that are most required by the market. Learning popular technologies maximizes your chances of getting a job in the near future.

Further, take the pulse of the market toward the technologies that you added to the *Popular* column via the following means:

- **Social networks**: A significant number of social networks contain posts about technologies and what's trending in the IT industry. Some major players are LinkedIn, Stack Overflow, Twitter, Reddit, and Facebook.
- **Bookstores**: Book publishers strive to satisfy the interest of the programming community by covering the most popular technologies. They carry out serious research campaigns for filtering the topics that deserve to be covered in their books. A new book or a significant number of books on a certain topic or technology is a good indicator of programming community interest in that topic. Nevertheless, pay attention to technologies that are suddenly going mainstream. Most of the time, such technologies are not adopted by companies immediately. It may take years until they are adopted, or they may remain in the shadows forever.
- **Courses and training**: Besides colleges and universities, tons of websites strive to provide courses and training for popular and hot topics.

It's all about getting the right experience

You know what you want and what the market offers. This is cool! Now it's time to get the right experience! Without experience, there is no resume, and without a resume, there is no interview, therefore, this is a major and laborious step. The following subsections will help you to achieve two main goals:

- Accumulate a lot of technical knowledge and skills.
- Gain trust and visibility across the Java ecosystem.

Pay attention – these two goals won't materialize overnight! It takes time and requires perseverance, but there is a clear and guaranteed result – you'll become a top Java developer. So, let's start something!

Start something

For a student or a recent graduate, it is pretty hard to decide where to start from in order to gain experience and write a resume. You are aware that you should *start something*, but you cannot decide what that *something* should be. Well, that *something* should be **code**. Before you have any formal work, get involved in school projects, internships, programming, volunteering work, and any kind of practical experience.

It's time to shine online

It is mandatory to get online and show the world what you can do as early as possible (for example, from school). Companies and programming communities are looking forward to seeing how you grow online. But just before you jump in, ensure that you follow the next two golden rules:

- **It is very important to pay attention to the identity used to expose your work online.** Don't use dummy credentials, avatars, nicknames, emails, passwords, and so on. Most likely, the accounts that you will create now (on GitHub, Stack Overflow, LinkedIn, YouTube, Twitter, and so on) will be shared all over the internet and will make you famous. Always use your complete name (for example, Mark Janel, Joana Nimar), use a relevant photo of yourself for your profile (as in the following figure), and use your name in accounts (for example, @markjanel, joananimar) and in emails addresses (for example, mark.janel@gmail.com). It is more difficult for dummy names, emails, and nicknames to become associated with you and with your work:

Figure 1.5 – Using a relevant photo

- **Always accept criticism and be polite.** Exposing your work online is going to attract critics. An extremely small percent of what you receive will be really malicious comments with no logical arguments. The best practice, in this case, is to ignore such comments. But most critics will be positive and constructive. Always answer to such comments with arguments and always be polite. **Common sense is the most important skill!** Be open and stay open to other opinions!

Do not get disappointed or frustrated. And never give up!

Contribute to open source projects

Contributing to open source projects is a supersonic approach for measuring your skills and quickly gaining experience and visibility to companies looking for candidates. Don't underestimate yourself! Small contributions count as well. Even reading and understanding the code of an open source project is a great opportunity to gain coding experience and learn coding techniques.

A lot of open source projects encourage and support developers to contribute. For example, check out the Hibernate ORM open source project in the following screenshot:

Figure 1.6 – Contributing to an open source project

You have the chance to add your footprint to the code that you will use later in your daily work! And it is also used by millions of developers. How cool is that!?

Start your own GitHub account

Besides contributing to open source projects, it is advisable to start your own GitHub account. Employers will evaluate the content of your GitHub profile before they meet you. Don't neglect any aspect! Take your time and clean up your GitHub profile so it reflects your best code. Keep in mind that the worst kind of GitHub account is an empty account or an account that shows low activity on a long-term basis, as shown on the left in the following screenshot:

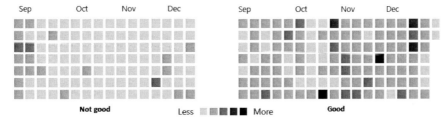

Figure 1.7 – GitHub contributions over four months

Demonstrate a preference for clean code and meaningful `README.md` files and avoid periods of low activity on a long-term basis, as shown in the previous screenshot.

Start your own Stack Overflow account

Stack Overflow is the next stop for companies that evaluate your work. Your questions and answers on Stack Overflow will appear in Google searches, therefore, you have to pay extra attention to what you post (questions and answers). As a rule of thumb, your questions may reveal your level of knowledge, therefore, *don't* post simple questions, questions that have easy answers in the documentation, questions that sit behind trivial programming challenges, and so on. On the other hand, make sure to provide valuable answers and don't repeat other people's answers. Provide content that will bring you badges, not downvotes. Link your GitHub profile to your answers to provide complete solutions.

Start your own YouTube channel

Besides entertainment, YouTube is also a huge source of technical knowledge. On YouTube, you can post complete coding solutions that show people how to program and how to become better programmers. You can quickly increase your YouTube subscribers if you do the following:

- Don't go for long videos (stick to 10-20-minute lessons)!
- Ensure that you have a good webcam and microphone. A good webcam has at least 1080p resolution, and a good microphone is the Snowball ICE; for recording use free or low-cost tools such as Free2X Webcam Recorder (`free2x.com/webcam-recorder`) and Loom (`loom.com`); Camtasia Studio is also awesome (`techsmith.com/video-editor.html`).
- Demonstrate excellent English skills (English is used most commonly on YouTube).
- Introduce yourself (but do it quickly).
- Be enthusiastic (show people that you enjoy your work, but don't exaggerate).
- Be practical (people love live coding).
- Take the chance to prove your speaking skills (this opens you the door to technical conferences).
- Promote your work (add links and hints for more videos, source code, and so on).
- Respond to people's feedback/questions (don't ignore what people say about your video).
- Accept criticism and be polite.

Link your GitHub and Stack Overflow accounts to your YouTube videos to get more exposure and followers.

Start your technical blog

Your awesome work on GitHub, Stack Overflow, and YouTube can easily be promoted in stories on a technical blog. Write about programming topics, especially about programming problems that you solved, and write tutorials, tips and tricks, and so on. Constant posting and high-quality content will increase your traffic and will index your blog on search engines. Someday, this valuable content can be exploited to write an astonishing book or develop a great video on Udemy (`udemy.com`) or PluralSight (`learn.pluralsight.com`).

There are a lot of blogging platforms such as Blogger (`blogger.com`), WordPress (`wordpress.org`), and Medium (`medium.com`). Choose the one that you prefer and get started.

Write articles and attract huge traffic and/or get paid

If you want to post technical articles and earn money or attract a huge amount of traffic to your work, then a personal blog will not be very useful, at least not for a significant amount of time (1-2 years). But you can write technical articles for websites that register huge amounts of daily traffic themselves. For example, DZone (`dzone.com`) is a great technical platform where you can write for free or you can join different programs where you are paid for your work. By simply creating a free DZone account, you can immediately start publishing technical articles via their online editor. In 1-5 days, they will review your work and publish it online. Almost instantly, thousands of people will read your articles. Besides DZone, other great technical platforms will pay you to write for them (commonly between $10-$150 per article depending on length, topic, internal policies, and so on). Some of these platforms include InformIT (`informit.com`), InfoQ (`infoq.com`), Mkyong (`mkyong.com`), developer.com (`developer.com`), Java Code Geeks (`javacodegeeks.com`), GeeksForGeeks (`geeksforgeeks.org`), and SitePoint (`sitepoint.com`).

Promote yourself and your work (portfolio)

It's important to work, but it is also important to show people what you've done and get their feedback.

> **Important note**
>
> *Managing your online profile is very important.* Recruiters use online profiles to find desirable candidates, to get to know you better, and to prepare in-depth or custom interview questions.

Along with GitHub, Stack Overflow, and so on, recruiters will search your name on Google and will check your personal website and social network profiles.

Personal websites

A personal website (or portfolio) is a website that shows off your work. Simply add the screenshots of applications that you've made/contributed to and give brief descriptions of your work. Explain your role in each project and provide a link to the project. Pay attention to not expose private and proprietary company information. You can quickly get inspiration from the internet (for example, `codeburst.io/10-awesome-web-developer-portfolios-d266b32e6154`)

For building your personal website, you can rely on free or low-cost website builders such as Google Sites (`sites.google.com`) and Wix (`wix.com`).

Social network profiles

One of the most important social networks is Twitter. On Twitter, you can promote your work in front of the best Java developers in the world. Right from day 1, search and follow the best Java developers, and soon they will follow you too! As a tip, start to follow as many Java Champions (an exclusive community of the best Java developers in the world) you can find. There is a huge and valuable community of Java developers on Twitter. Get to know them as fast as you can!

Other social networks such as Facebook and Instagram are also scanned by recruiters. Pay attention to the content of your posts. Obviously, radicalism, racism, fanaticism, trivial or sexual content, political content, slogans and incitement to violence, defamatory and offensive content, and so on will cause the recruiter to take a step back.

CodersRank matters

CodersRank (`codersrank.io/`) is a platform that harvests information about your work (for example, it harvests information from GitHub, Stack Overflow, Bitbucket, HakerRank, and so on) and tries to rank you against millions of other developers from around the world. In the following screenshot, you can see a developer's profile page:

Figure 1.8 – CodersRank profile summary

This is another important barometer for recruiters.

Learn, code, learn, code...

Once you become a developer, you must follow the *Learn->Code* practice in order to get on top and stay there. Never stop learning and never stop coding! As a rule of thumb, the *Learn->Code* practice can be applied via the *learning by example* or *teaching is my way of learning* approaches, or any other approach that fits you best.

How about certifications?

Once you access `education.oracle.com/certification`, you can see that Oracle provides a suite of Java certifications. While there's nothing wrong with getting certifications (from Oracle or an other party), they are not required in job descriptions. Taking these certifications requires a significant amount of money and time, and most of the time they don't pay off the effort. You can use this time more wisely and get involved in projects (side projects, school projects, open source projects, and so on). This is a better way to impress employers. So, certificates have limited value and it takes a lot of resources to obtain them. Moreover, certificates are perishable. Think how useful it is today, in 2020, to be Java 6 certified, or in 2030 to be Java 12 certified!

But if you really want to consider certifications, then here are the top certifications on offer (for more information, search on Google for them since links can break over time):

- OCAJP (Oracle Certified associate, Java Programmer 1) and OCPJP (Oracle Certified Professional, Java Programmer 2)
- Spring Professional Certification
- OCEWCD (Oracle Certified Expert, Java EE 6 Web Component Developer)
- Apache Spark Cert HDPCD (HDP Certified Developer)
- Professional Scrum Master
- Project Management (PMP)
- AWS Solutions Architect
- Oracle Certified Master

Having experience and visibility (fans) all over the internet is a tremendous plus in your career. But you still need a useful resume for applying to Java jobs. So, it's time to write your resume.

Time to write your resume

Writing an impressive resume is not easy. There are tons of platforms that promise you that your resume will be amazing if you let them do it for you. There are also tons of resume templates, most of them quite complex and cumbersome. On the other hand, a resume is something personal, and it is better to do it yourself. Bearing the following points in mind will be enough to produce an appealing resume for recruiters. Let's see these points and how to approach them.

What resume screeners are looking for

First, resume screeners want to find out whether you are a good coder and you are smart. Second, they want to find out if you are a good fit for a certain available position (they check your experience against certain technologies and tools required for that position).

Strive to highlight that you are a good coder and are intelligent. This means being as technical as possible in a concentrated form. Pay attention: too many words dilute the essence of your resume and lead to loss of focus. **Be technical, clear, and concise**.

How long the resume should be

To answer how long a resume should be, you must answer another question: how long do you think a recruiter spends reading a resume? Most likely, around 10-20 seconds. In other words, recruiters read between the lines, trying to quickly identify what interests them.

In general, a resume should not be longer than a page. If you have 10+ year's experience, then you can go with 2 pages.

You may think that it is impossible to condense your vast experience in 1-2 pages, but this is not true. First, prioritize content, and second, add this content until you cover 1-2 pages. Skip the remaining content. Don't worry that the recruiters will not know everything you've done! They will be impressed by your resume highlights and will be happy to discover the rest of your experience in the interview.

> **Write a resume that fits on one page.**
> If you have 10+ years of experience, then consider two pages. Keep in mind that some recruiters may skip long resumes without reading a single line. They want to find the most impressive items right away. Adding less important items and/or too many words will distract the recruiter and makes them waste time.

How to list your employment history

If you have a short employment history (2-4 roles), then add all of it to the resume. Don't go for your complete employment history if you have a long list of roles (4+ roles). Just choose 4 roles that are the most impressive (roles in important companies, leading roles, roles where you have achieved great results and/or made significant contributions).

For each role, follow the *Achievement->Action->Effect* model. Always start with the achievement! This will act as a magnet for the recruiter. Once they read the achievement, you've got their attention to continuing reading.

For example, let's imagine that you worked at the company *Foo* and you've managed to increase the performance of the connection pool by 30% by tuning its parameters. Now the application can accommodate a transaction throughput of 15% extra. Add this achievement in the resume in a single statement as follows:

Increased the connection pool performance by 30% by tuning its parameters, leading to a transaction throughput boost of 15%.

List the most relevant roles via Achievement->Action->Effect statements. Always try to measure the benefits you created. Don't say, *I reduced the memory footprint by compressing ...*, and say, *I reduced the memory footprint by 5% by compressing ....*

List the most relevant projects (top five)

Some recruiters prefer to jump in directly into the *My Projects* section of your resume. They follow the *No Fluff, Just Stuff* statement. You don't have to list all your projects! Make a top five and add only those. Don't add all five from the same category. Choose one or two independent projects, one or two open source contributions, and so on. An independent project with a high GitHub star rating is what will really impress recruiters.

List the top projects with their relevant details. This is the right place to lose the modesty and do your best to impress.

Nominate your technical skills

The *Technical Skills* section is mandatory. Here, you have to list the programming languages, software, and tools you know. It doesn't have to be like a nomenclature, but it doesn't have to be a short and slim section either. It has to be relevant and in harmony with the listed projects. The following list mentions the main criteria to follow in writing the *Technical Skills* section:

- **Don't list all Java flavors**: Don't add a list such as Spring MVC, Spring Data, Spring Data REST, Spring Security, and so on. Just say Spring. Or, if you are Java EE guy, then don't add a list of JPA, EJB, JSF, JAX-RX, JSON-B, JSON-P, JASPIC, and so on. Just say Java EE, Jakarta EE. Or, if you see them listed that way in the job description, then you can add them between brackets. For example: *Spring (MVC, Data including Data REST, Security)* or *Java EE (JPA, EJB, JSF, JAX-RX, JSON-B, JSON-B, JASPIC)*.

- **Do not add software versions**: Avoid things like Java 8, Spring Boot 2, or Hibernate 5. If such details are necessary, then the interviewer will ask you about them.

- **Don't list utility technologies**: Avoid listing utility libraries that are commonly used in projects. For example, don't add Apache Commons, Google Guava, Eclipse Collections, and so on. It is possible that recruiters have not heard of them. Or, if they have, they will smile ironically.

- **Don't list the technologies that you have only lightly touched**: It's quite risky to list technologies that you've used only rarely and/or superficially. At the interview, you may get asked questions about them that will put you in a difficult situation.

- **For each technology, add your experience**: For example, write *Java (expert), Spring Boot (advanced), Jakarta EE (proficient), Hibernate (expert)*.

- **Do not measure your experience with a technology in years**: Most of the time, it's not relevant. This metric doesn't say much to the recruiter. Your experience is shown by your projects.

- **Avoid common technologies**: Don't list operating systems, Microsoft Office, Gmail, Slack, and so on. Listing such things is just noise for the recruiter.

- **Double-check your English**: A recruiter can throw away a resume if it has typos. If you are a non-native English speaker, then find a native English speaker to proofread your resume.

- **Don't list a single programming language**: Ideally, you should list two to three programming languages (for example, *Java (expert), C++ (medium), Python (prior experience)*), but don't say that you are an expert in all of them. Nobody will believe you! On the other hand, a single programming language can be interpreted as meaning that you are not open to learning new technologies.
- **Split technologies into categories**: Don't add the technologies as a long, comma-separated list. For example, avoid something like *Java, Ruby, C++, Java EE, Spring Boot, Hibernate, JMeter, JUnit, MySQL, PostgreSQL, AWS, Ocean, and Vue.js*. Split them into categories and sort them by experience, as in the following example:

  a. **Programming languages**: Java (expert), Ruby (intermediate), and C++ (beginner)

  b. **Frameworks**: Java EE (expert), Spring Boot (advanced)

  c. **Object Relation Mapping (ORM)**: Hibernate (expert)

  d. **Testing**: JMeter (expert), JUnit (advanced)

  e. **Databases**: MySQL (expert), PostgreSQL (intermediate)

  f. **Cloud**: AWS (expert), Ocean (beginner)

  g. **JavaScript frameworks**: Vue.js (intermediate)

LinkedIn resume

Most likely, your LinkedIn profile will be the first stop for recruiters. Moreover, a significant number of e-job platforms require your LinkedIn account whenever you try to apply for a job. There are even cases where this account is mandatory.

LinkedIn is a social network dedicated to tracking professional connections. Essentially, LinkedIn is an online resume on steroids. On LinkedIn, you can create job alerts, and colleagues, customers, and friends can endorse you or your work, which can be quite valuable.

> **Important note**
> Pay attention to keeping your LinkedIn resume in sync with your paper resume. Also, pay attention if you are looking for a job via LinkedIn since all your contacts receive notifications about your updates. These contacts include people at your current company, and most likely, you don't want them to know you're looking for a new job. The solution is to disable these notifications before you make your updates.

Now, we can discuss the job application process.

The job application process

Technical companies prefer multi-step interviews. But, before getting invited to an interview, you have to find companies that are hiring, apply for their jobs, and then finally meet them.

Finding companies that are hiring

Surveys from the past few years (2017+) estimate that 70%-85% of all jobs are filled via networking (`linkedin.com/pulse/new-survey-reveals-85-all-jobs-filled-via-networking-lou-adler/`). Technical jobs (especially in the IT field) represent the leading segment that takes advantage of networking.

In almost any country, there are several e-jobs platforms. Let's call them *local* e-jobs platforms. Commonly, the *local* e-jobs platforms list job offers from companies active in that country, or companies that recruit globally.

Worldwide, we have *global* e-jobs platforms. These platforms include several major players (all these websites allow you to upload your resume or create one online):

- **LinkedIn** (`linkedin.com`): With more than 610 million users covering more than 200 countries worldwide, this is the world's largest professional network and social recruiting platform.
- **Indeed** (`indeed.com`): This is a leading job site with millions of jobs harvested from thousands of websites.
- **CareerBuilder** (`careerbuilder.com`): This is another huge platform that posts tons of jobs from all around the globe.
- **Stack Overflow** (`stackoverflow.com/jobs`): This is the largest, most trusted online community for developers to learn, share their programming knowledge, and build their careers.
- **FlexJobs** (`flexjobs.com`) and **Upwork** (`upwork.com`): These are platforms dedicated to freelancers that offer premium, flexible remote jobs.

Other platforms that provide services useful for finding a job include the following:

- **Dice** (`dice.com`): This is the leading career destination for tech experts at every stage of their careers.
- **Glassdoor** (`glassdoor.com`): This is a complex platform including company-specific ratings and reviews.

In addition to these platforms, there are many others that you will discover by yourself.

Submitting the resume

Once you've found the companies you want to apply to, it's time to submit your resume.

First, look at the company's website. This can help you to find out the following:

- See if you can apply directly via the company website (by bypassing the placement agency, you can speed up the process and the company can hire you directly without paying commission to the placement agency).
- You can register in the company database to be contacted whenever a suitable position is opened.
- You have the chance to find out more about the company history, vision, projects, culture, and so on.
- You can find out contacts of relevant people at the company (for example, you can find a phone number for details and support).

Second, double-check your resume and online profile. Most likely, if your resume impresses the recruiter, they will search your name on Google and will inspect your networking activity. From technical content to social media, everything will be scanned before sending you an interview offer.

Third, don't send the exact same resume to all companies! For each company, make adjustments to the resume so it is as relevant to the job description as possible.

I got an interview! Now what?

If you followed the roadmap so far, then it is just a matter of days until you will receive an e-mail or a phone call to invite you to an interview. Oh, wait... you are saying that you've already got an interview? Cool! It's time to prepare yourself!

The phone screening stage

Most IT companies prefer to start the multi-step interview process with a *phone screen*. A phone screen is usually accomplished via Skype, Zoom, or Meetup (or similar platforms), and you'll need to share your webcam. A microphone and a set of headphones are needed as well. Phone screens are very popular if you opt for a remote position, but lately, they are used for all kinds of positions.

Commonly, there are two approaches used by companies:

- **Phone screen with a human resources or placement agency person**: This is an optional, non-technical interview of 15-30 minutes meant to detail the offer terms, expose your personality, concerns, both your and their expectations, and so on. This can take place before or after the technical phone screen.
- **Technical phone screen first**: Some companies will invite you directly to a technical phone screen. In such cases, you can expect several technical questions, maybe a quiz, and one or more coding challenge sessions (tackling coding challenges is the main focus of this book). If you pass the technical phone screen, then, most probably, a non-technical one will follow.

Going to in-person interviews

Unless you opt for a remote position, the next step will consist of a face-to-face interview. There are cases when there is no phone screen, and this is the first step of the interview. In such cases, you may be interviewed by HR people, followed by a technical interview. But, if you had a phone screen, then you may or may not be contacted. This depends on how the company evaluates the phone screen. If they decide to not proceed with the next stage of the interview, then it is possible you will receive some feedback covering what was good and what was less good about your phone screen performance. Don't ignore the feedback, read it carefully and in an objective manner. It might help you to avoid repeating the same mistakes. Speaking about mistakes...

Avoiding common mistakes

Pay attention to the following common mistakes that may sit behind the failure of an interview:

- **Ignoring the power of information**: There are cases where after failing an interview, we meet a friend to tell them how it went. At that moment, your friend may say: *My friend, I know a person who had a successful interview at this company 2 months ago! Why you did not tell me before? I'm sure he could have given you some insights!* Obviously, it's too late to do that now! Avoid such cases and try to obtain as much information as possible. **See if you or your friends have contacts in the company, ask on social media, and so on.** This way it's possible to obtain extremely useful information.
- **Lacking clarity and coherence in answers**: Your answers should be technical, crystal clear, meaningful, expressive, and always on topic. **Answer the questions thoughtfully**. Stammering, incomplete answers, interjections, and so on are not appreciated by interviewers.

- **Considering that image doesn't matter**: Don't ignore your image! Dress professionally, go to the barbershop, and smell nice! All these aspects are part of the first impression. **If you look sloppy, then maybe your code looks the same. If you dress professionally, then the interviewers will treat you as if you're a cut above the rest.** However, dressing professionally doesn't mean you should be opulent.

- **Not selling yourself well**: The interviewer must see your value. Nobody can communicate your value to them better than you can. Tell them about a problem that you had (at a previous company, in a certain project, and so on) and explain how you solved it with your team or independently. Employers want people who are excellent team players but are capable of working independently as well. Follow the *Situation|Action|Result (SAR)* approach. Start by describing the situation. Continue by explaining the actions you took, and finally, describe the result.

- **Not practicing coding challenges**: At some point, you will be scheduled for at least one coding challenge. Most of the time, general coding skills are not enough! These challenges are specific to interviews and you have to practice them before the interview. As a rule of thumb, solving coding challenges (problems) follows the *Approach->Break down->Craft* solution pattern. Obviously, you cannot memorize solutions, therefore you need to practice as much as possible. Later in this book, we will discuss the best approaches for solving coding challenges.

Once the interview is complete, it's time to wait for the response. Most companies will tell you how much time they need to provide a final answer and will commonly provide an answer representing the offer, rejection, next interview step, or just the status of your application. Keep your fingers crossed!

Summary

This chapter summarized the best practices that should be followed to obtain a job in the Java ecosystem. We talked about choosing a proper job and our eligibility, getting experience, working on resumes, and so on. Most of this advice was addressed to students or people who have just graduated. Of course, do not consider these pieces of advice as an exhaustive list or a list that should be applied integrally. These practices will help you pick up the fruits that you consider appealing and allow you to add your own touch to the process.

Next, let's see how big companies conduct their interviews.

2
What Interviews at Big Companies Look Like

Interviews at big companies are relatively long processes with progressively increasing complexity of technical questions and coding challenges (such an interview process can take a month or even more). Most companies prefer one or more technical phone screens, on-site technical challenges, and in-person interviews before making an offer. Commonly, one of these interviews will be non-technical (known as a *lunch interview*).

Let's get an overview of how interviews are conducted in several leading IT companies. Generally speaking, all these companies are looking for smart, passionate, and excellent coders.

We will talk about how interviews are conducted in the following companies:

- Google
- Amazon
- Microsoft

- Facebook
- Crossover

Let's get started!

Interviews at Google

The Google interview starts with a technical phone screen (technical questions and coding challenges). There will be 4-5 people involved in these technical phone screens. One of the phone screens will be non-technical. At this moment, feel free to ask anything you want.

During these interview stages, you will be scored for your analytical ability, coding, experience, and communication skills.

The interviewers submit their feedback to the **Hiring Committee (HC)**. The HC is responsible for making an offer or rejecting you. If the HC considers that you are the right person for the job, then they forward the offer proposal to other committees. The final decision is taken by the executive management committee.

The main technical focus is on analytical algorithms, brain-teasing algorithms, system design, and scalability.

Most probably, you'll need to wait several weeks for a response.

It is advisable to search *interview at Google* on YouTube and watch the most relevant testimonials and roadmap videos. Also, search for *Google's most asked interview questions*.

Interviews at Amazon

The Amazon interview starts with a technical phone screen conducted by a team from Amazon. If some interviewers are not convinced after this phone screen, then it is possible that they will ask for another one to clarify the issues.

If you pass the technical phone screen(s), then you will be invited to several face-to-face interviews. A team of interviewers from different areas of the business will individually conduct an interview and evaluate your technical skills (including coding). One of them is also known as the *bar raiser* guy. Commonly, this guy is the most experienced, and his questions and coding challenges will be harder. They will evaluate you against other candidates as well, and they will decide whether to make an offer or not.

The main focus is on **Object-Oriented Programming (OOP)** and scalability.

If you don't get any feedback after a week, then you should trigger a friendly follow-up e-mail to Amazon contacts. Most probably, they will quickly reply to your e-mail and explain the current status of your interview.

It is advisable to search *interview at Amazon* on YouTube and watch the most relevant testimonials and roadmap videos. Also, search for *Amazon's most asked interview questions*.

Interviews at Microsoft

The Microsoft interview starts with several technical phone screens or they might require you to travel to one of their working branches. You will have 4-5 technical interviews with different teams.

The final decision belongs to the hiring manager. Commonly, this hiring manager is contacted only if you passed all the technical interview stages.

The main focus is on algorithms and data structures.

If you did not get any feedback after a week, then you should trigger a friendly follow-up e-mail to Microsoft contacts. Sometimes, it takes just a day until they provide a decision, but it can take a week, a month, or even more.

It is advisable to search *interview at Microsoft* on YouTube and watch the most relevant testimonials and roadmap videos. Also, search for *Microsoft's most asked interview questions*.

Interviews at Facebook

The Facebook interview starts with several technical and non-technical phone screens involving questions (technical and non-technical) and coding challenges. Commonly, the interviews are conducted by a team of software engineers and hiring managers.

Facebook uses three types of interviews covering the following areas:

- Your ability to adapt to the Facebook culture, along with some technical skills – known as the *behavioral* or *Jedi* interview
- Your coding and algorithms skill (these are common problems that we'll cover later, starting with *Chapter 6, Object-Oriented Programming*) – known as the *Ninja* interview
- Your design and architecture skills – known as the *Pirate* interview

You can expect a combination of these types of interviews. Commonly, one Jedi and two Ninja are enough. For positions that require higher experience, there will be Pirate interviews as well.

If you pass these technical phone screens, then you will receive some homework including technical questions and coding challenges. This time, you have to provide elegant and clean coding solutions.

The main focus is on your capabilities to build something fast in any language. You can expect to code in PHP, Java, C++, Python, Erlang, and so on.

The team of interviewers will take the decision to hire you or not.

It is advisable to search *interview at Facebook* on YouTube and watch the most relevant testimonials and roadmap videos. Also, search for *Facebook's most asked interview questions*.

Interviews at Crossover

Crossover is a remote company. They recruit remotely via their platform and have an exclusive on-site interview process. Their on-site interview adheres to the following roadmap:

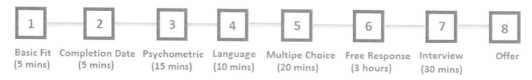

Figure 2.1 – Crossover interview roadmap

All steps are important, which means your responses at each step must pass their internal playbooks. If a step doesn't pass their internal playbooks, then it can lead to a sudden closure of the interview. But, the most important steps are steps 3, 5, 6, and 7. Step 3 represents an eliminatory **Criteria Cognitive Aptitude Test** (**CCAT**). For example, you have to answer 50 questions in 15 minutes. You have to answer correctly 25+ questions to have a chance to advance to the next step. If you are not familiar with CCAT tests, then it is strongly recommended to practice (there are books and websites dedicated to CCAT tests). Without serious practice, it will be quite challenging to pass it. If you are not a native English speaker, then you have to pay extra attention to practice the questions that require serious English skills.

At step 5, you'll get a quiz with technical questions. There are 30+ questions with 5 answer variants (one or more answers are correct). No coding is required at this step.

If you reach step 6, then you'll receive technical homework that should be completed in 3 hours and submitted (uploaded) to the platform. This homework can consist of one or more Java applications starting from a stub application provided via download.

At step 7, you'll finally meet a person via a phone screen. This is usually a mix of technical and non-technical questions.

The technical questions will cover a wide range of Java topics (collections, concurrency, I/O, exceptions, and so on).

Commonly, you'll receive the final response by e-mail in less than a week. Depending on the position, the offer will start with 1 month of paid boot camp experience. Note that after boot camp, you can still be rejected or required to apply again. During boot camp and after it, you'll have to maintain your position via weekly metrics that measure your performance. You'll have to work 40 hours/week with webcam screenshots every 10 minutes. And, you are responsible for arranging to pay your own taxes. Salaries are fixed and public on their website.

It is advisable to read the job description and testimonials on their website carefully. They also have brand ambassadors whom you can contact to find out more about the company culture, expectations, interview flow, and so on.

Other remote companies follow a three-step interview process. For example, Upstack follows this pattern:

1. Initial interview: Non-technical phone screen
2. Technical interview: Technical phone screen containing coding challenge
3. Offer: Sending you an offer and signing the agreement

Of course, there are many other big companies that are not listed here. But as a rule of thumb, the companies and their processes outlined here should give you some important insights into what you should expect from a big player in the IT industry.

Summary

In this chapter, we had an overview of how interviews are conducted in several leading IT companies. Most IT companies follow the same practices presented in this chapter, with their own different combinations and flavors.

Next, let's see what the most common non-technical questions are, and how to answer them.

3
Common Non-Technical Questions and How To Answer Them

In this chapter, we will tackle the main aspects of the non-technical interview questions. This part of the interview is commonly carried out by a hiring manager or even an HR person. To prepare for this interview means getting familiar with the following questions:

- What is the purpose of non-technical questions?
- What is your experience?
- What's your favorite programming language?
- What do you want to do?
- What are your career goals?
- What's your working style?
- Why are you looking to change jobs?

- What is your salary history?
- Why we should hire you?
- How much money do you want to make?
- Do you have a question for me?

We will discuss each question in its own specific section. Let's start.

What is the purpose of non-technical questions?

The non-technical interview questions are meant to measure the match between your experience, character, and personality, and your ability to fit in with other employees and teams. **Being a good fit in the existing team(s) is a must.** These questions are also useful for creating a human connection between you and the company and seeing whether there is any compatibility or chemistry between their ideal candidate and your education, beliefs, ideas, expectations, culture, and so on. Moreover, non-technical questions cover the practical and pragmatic aspects of the job as well, such as salary, relocation, medical insurance, work schedule, willingness to do overtime, and so on.

There are companies that reject candidates based on this non-technical interview, even if they were initially minded to make an offer.

Some companies hold this interview before the technical one. These companies try to determine right from the start whether your experience and goals make you a good candidate for the job in question. It is like saying that the human part has priority over the technical part.

Other companies hold this interview after the technical one. These companies try to determine what is the best offer for you. This is like saying that the technical part has priority over the human part.

Non-technical questions don't have right or wrong answers! In these situations, the best answers are sincere answers. As a rule of thumb, answer as you feel; don't try to say what the interviewer wants to hear. It's like a negotiation – there will be trade-offs. Don't forget to be polite and respectful.

Further, let's see the most common non-technical questions and some answer suggestions. Don't learn/copy these answers! Try to come up with your own answers and focus on what you want to highlight. Shape and repeat the answers at home and be prepared when you come in front of the interviewer. Don't rely on your spontaneity; rely on sincerity and balance the trade-offs.

What is your experience?

Most probably, after the formal introduction, you'll be asked about your experience. If you don't have an answer prepared for this question, then you are in trouble. Let's highlight several important aspects meant to help you to prepare an appropriate answer:

- **Don't detail your experience as a boring list of chronological facts**: Choose the most representative projects and achievements and talk about them with enthusiasm. Talk about your work with enthusiasm (but don't look desperate and don't exaggerate), and place your achievements in the context of the team/project. For example, avoid saying,... *and I did this and that on my own!* It is better to say,... *and I helped my team by doing this and that*. Don't say,...*I was the only one capable of doing that*. Prefer saying...*I was nominated by the team to accomplish this delicate task*. If you are in your first job, then talk about your school projects (think of your colleagues as your team) and about your independent projects. If you have participated in programming contests, then talk about your results and experience.

- **Don't highlight only the positive things**: Experiences can be positive and negative. Talk about what went right, but also about what went wrong. Most of the time, the truly valuable lessons come from negative experiences. These kinds of experiences force us to go beyond our limits to find solutions. Moreover, such experiences are proof of resistance to stress, tenacity, and power of concentration. Of course, balance positive and negative experiences and highlight what you've learned from both sides.

- **Don't provide too short or too long an answer**: Calibrate your answer to fit in 1-2 minutes.

What is your favorite programming language?

Since we are talking about a Java position, it's obvious that your favorite language is Java. But if such a question arises, then it is meant to reveal whether you are Java-addicted or an open-minded person. In other words, the interviewer considers that it's hard to work with rigid people who are addicted to one programming language and want to use it exclusively in all situations. Being a Java developer doesn't mean that you should consider Java for all your tasks and ignore everything else. So, a good answer might be, *Obviously, I am a big fan of Java, but I also consider it important to pick the best tool for the job. It is absurd to believe that Java is the answer to all problems.*

What do you want to do?

This is a hard question and your answer can have a lot of interpretations. Be sincere and tell the interviewer exactly what you want to do. You read the job description; therefore, you know that you want this job. Explain to the interviewer the main reasons behind your decision. For example, you could say, *I want to become an excellent Java backend developer and your projects are quite challenging in this area. I want to be part of the team that works on these projects.* Or, you could say, *I want to be part of a major start-up in an important company and this looks like a great opportunity for me. I heard that a new team is being formed and I would be very excited to be part of it.* Don't omit saying something about working in a great team! Most probably, you won't be working alone, and being a team player is a major aspect of working in almost any company.

What are your career goals?

Via this question (or its sister, *Where do you see yourself in five years?*), the interviewer is trying to see whether this position fits with your career goals. They seek to understand if you see this position as part of your career path, or if you have other reasons (apart from the money) for doing it. It is hard to describe a detailed career path, but you could give an answer that shows your commitment and motivation to do your job right. For example, you could say, *My current goal is to work as a Java backend developer on challenging projects that will help me to accumulate more experience. In several years, I see myself involved in architecting complex Java applications. Beyond that is too far away to think of right now.*

What's your working style?

This kind of question should ring a bell to you. Most of the time, this question is specific to companies that have an uncommon working style. For example, they often work overtime or they work on weekends. Maybe they work long shifts or they have metrics or deadlines that are hard to achieve. Or, they put a lot of pressure and responsibilities on this position. Explain to the interviewer your working style and underline indirectly the things that you do not agree with. For example, you could point out that you are not open to doing night shifts by saying, *I like to start working in the morning with the most difficult tasks, and in the second part of the day, I will deal with the planning of the next day.* Or, you could point out that you are not open to working on weekends by saying, *I like to work hard for 40 hours/week from Monday to Friday. I like to spend weekends with my friends.*

If you are asked directly about a specific aspect, then provide a clear answer. For example, the interviewer may say, *You know, if you work on weekends, then you'll be paid double. What do you say about this?*. Well, think twice, and answer as you feel but without leaving room for interpretation.

Why are you looking to change jobs?

Of course, if you are at your first job then you will not get such a question (or its sister, *How and why did you leave your last job?*). But if you had a previous role (or you plan the change your current role), then the interviewer will want to know why you took this decision. The key here is to detail clear and solid arguments without saying anything bad or offensive about your previous company, bosses, coworkers, and so on – follow the principle that *if you can't say anything nice about someone, don't say anything at all*.

Here are some tips that will help you with this question (pay attention to how this question is interleaved with the previous one – if the working style of this company relates nicely to the style of your current or ex-company, then most likely, the same reasons for leaving that job will apply to avoiding this job as well):

- **Don't cite money as the first argument**: Money is often a good reason to change jobs but citing it as the first argument is a dangerous route to take. The interviewer may think that all you care about is money. Or, they may think that your current employer didn't raise your salary because you were not valuable enough. Sooner or later, they might think, you will want more money and you'll proceed with the approach of looking elsewhere if they cannot offer you the desired raise.

- **Invoke a factor out of your control**: Invoking a factor out of your control keeps you in the secure zone. For example, you could say, *My team was assigned to a project that required relocation*. Or, you could say, *I was moved... to the night shift and I couldn't adapt my life to this schedule*.

- **Invoke a major change in the environment**: For example, you could say: *My company does mass layoffs and I don't want this risk*. Or, you could say, *I worked for 5 years in a small company, and now I want to put my experience to use in a big company*.

- **Invoke an aspect that you don't like and is known by the interviewer**: You could say, *I was hired as a Java backend programmer, but I spent a lot of time helping the frontend guys. As you saw in my resume, my experience is rooted in backend technologies*.

What is your salary history?

Obviously, this question is meant to determine a landmark for the new offer. If you are satisfied by your current salary, then you can give a number. Otherwise, is better to be polite and say that *I don't want to mess things up, and I am expecting compensation that is proper for the new position and its requirements.*

Why should we hire you?

This is a pertinent and slightly offensive question. In most cases, this is a trap question meant to reveal your reaction to criticism. If it comes at the beginning of the interview, then you should consider it as a misleading formulation of the question, *What's your experience?*.

If it comes at the end of the interview, then it is quite obvious that the interviewer knows very well why the company should hire you, therefore, he doesn't expect to hear a strong argument based on your resume or experience. In this case, stay calm and positive and mention why you like this company, why you want to work in this company, and what you know about it. Showing your interest (for example, showing that you've researched the company and visited their website) should be flattering for the interviewer, who can then quickly pass to the next question.

How much money do you want to make?

This question occurs right at the start (for example, in the non-technical phone screen) or at the end, when the company is ready to prepare an offer for you. When it occurs at the start, it means that whether the interview will continue will be based on your answer. If your expectations are beyond the potential offer, then most probably the interview will stop here. It is wise to postpone a clear answer as much as possible by saying something like, *I don't have a clear number in my head. Of course, money is important, but there are other important things as well. Let's see first if my value meets your expectations, and we can negotiate after that.* Or, if you must give an answer, then it's better to give a range of salaries. You should know the common salary range for this position (because you've done your homework and you've researched on the internet before the interview), therefore, provide a range that fits your expectations and respects your research.

Ideally, this question occurs at the end of the interview process. This is a clear signal that the company wants you and is prepared to make you an offer.

Now, you start the art of negotiation!

Don't jump into saying numbers! At this point, you should be pretty aware of how you did in the interview and how badly you want this job. Start by asking the interviewer about the range of the offer, what other bonuses are available, and what is included in the total compensation package. There are several scenarios you have to consider further:

- **In a very happy scenario, the offer will be higher than your expectations**: Accept it!

- **More likely, the offer is near your expectations**: Try to squeeze a little bit more. For example, if you got a range between $60,000 - $65,000, then say something like, *I had in mind something pretty similar – more precisely, I will be very satisfied if we can go for $65,000 - $70,000*. This will probably help you to obtain around $63,000 - $68,000.

- **Getting an evasive answer**: Instead of getting a range, you can receive an evasive answer such as, *We customize the salary depending on the applicant, therefore, I need to know your expectations*. In such a scenario, say the higher number you have in mind. Most probably, you will not get this offer, but it gives you room to negotiate. Be short and direct; for example, say, *I'm expecting to $65,000 a year*. You should get around $60,000 or an answer that will disappoint you like, *Sorry, but we had a much lower number in mind*. This leads to the next section.

- **Getting a disappointing offer**: In this scenario, try to be very prompt and start by expressing your disappointment like, *I have to say that I am very disappointed with this offer*. Continue by reiterating your strong skills and experience. Try to make clear arguments that support the requested number and underline that you do not want anything outlandish. If you are not open to accepting this job with these conditions, then finish your response with an ultimatum like, *If this is your final word, I cannot accept such an offer*. If the company was impressed by you, it's possible they'd require more time and get back to you with another offer. If you're thinking about accepting the offer, then ask for a written agreement for renegotiation in six months for now. Moreover, try to squeeze other benefits out of the negotiations, such as flexible hours, bonuses, and so on.

> **Important note**
> As a rule of thumb, try to keep in mind the following aspects:
> - Don't get shy or embarrassed when talking about salaries (novices often do).
> - Don't start from low numbers that don't give you room for negotiation.
> - Don't underestimate yourself and sell yourself short.
> - Don't lose time trying to negotiate non-negotiable things.

Do you have a question for me?

Almost any interview ends with this question. The interviewer wants to clarify any remaining doubts that you may have. You can ask whatever you want, but pay attention not to ask something stupid or something that requires a long answer. You can ask details about something that the interviewer said but that was not very clear, or you can ask for their personal opinion about you. Or, you could ask something like, *How did you come to this company? What has been most challenging for you?* If you have nothing to ask, then don't ask. Simply say something like, *Well, I have to say that you've answered all my important questions. Thank you for your time!*.

Summary

In this chapter, we covered the most common non-technical questions that you can face in an interview. These questions should be seriously trained for before the interview because they represent an important part of a successful interview. It's true that great answers to these questions will not bring you an offer alone, without a solid demonstration of the required technical knowledge, but they can impact your salary offer, your daily job expectations, your working style, and career goals. Therefore, don't go unprepared to such an interview.

In the next chapter, we'll see how to face the delicate situations when we don't manage to obtain the desired job.

4
How to Handle Failures

This chapter discusses a delicate aspect of interviews—handling failures. The main purpose of this chapter is to show you how to identify the causes of failure and how to mitigate them in the future.

However, before discussing handling failures, let's quickly tackle the proper way to accept or decline an offer. At the end of an interview, or at some point during the interview, you may find yourself in a position to accept or decline an offer. This is not about giving a simple and dry yes or no answer.

Our agenda for this chapter includes the following:

- Accepting or rejecting an offer
- Considering that failure is an option
- Understanding that a company can reject you for a lot of reasons
- Objectively identifying and eliminating the mismatches
- Not forming an obsession for a company

Let's get started with the first topic.

Accepting or rejecting an offer

Accepting an offer is quite simple. You need to inform the company that you accept the offer and discuss details such as the starting date (especially if you need to work a notice period at your current workplace), paperwork, reallocation (if it is the case), and so on.

Declining an offer is a bit more of a delicate situation. It must be done in a way that allows you to remain in good relations with everyone. The company has invested time and resources in the interview, and so you have to decline their offer politely. You may also, after a while, consider applying to the company again. For example, you can say something like *I want to thank you for the offer. I was impressed with your company and I enjoyed the interview process, but I've decided it's not the right choice for me right now. Thank you again, and maybe someday we will meet again.*

There are some cases when you need to manage multiple offers. While you accept an offer, you have to decline another. In the IT industry, it is very important to build contacts and maintain them over time. People frequently change their jobs and positions, and in this dynamic environment, it is important to not squander any contacts. Therefore, don't forget to call the hiring managers (or the contact person) that made you an offer and inform them about your decision. You can use the same phrase given previously. If you cannot call, then send an email or go to the office to meet them in person.

Failure is an option

In movies, we often hear the expression "failure is not an option." But those are just movies! An interview always ends with an offer or a rejection, and so failure is an option. It is our task to mitigate failures.

Handling failures is not easy, especially when they come one after the other. Each of us reacts to failure in a different and human way. From feeling disappointed and resigned to having a nervous reaction or saying things that you'll later be sorry about, these all are normal human reactions. However, it is important that you control these reactions and act professionally. This means applying a set of steps that will mitigate failures in the near future. To begin with, it is important to understand why you have been rejected.

A company can reject you for a lot of reasons

Well, maybe the problem starts exactly with this powerful word: reject. Is it correct to say or think that company X rejected you? I would say that this formulation is toxic and sounds like the company has something personal against you. This formulation of thoughts should be cut off right from the start. Instead, you should try to find out what went wrong.

How about saying or thinking that between you and the company, there are mismatches in skills and/or expectations? Most probably, this is much closer to reality. There are two parties in an interview (you and the interviewer), and both parties try to identify the matches or compatibilities that allow them to collaborate with a subjective approach. Once you think like this, you will not blame yourself and you'll try to find out what went wrong.

Getting feedback after the interview

If you've been informed by the company that you didn't make the cut, it is time to call them and ask for their feedback. You can say something like *Thanks for interviewing me. I'm trying to improve my interviewing skills, so it would be awesome if you could provide me any kind of feedback that you consider useful for me.*

Getting proper feedback is very important. It represents the starting point for fixing and eliminating the mismatches, and so you can start mitigating failures. The mismatches are commonly as follows:

- **Performance**: The candidate doesn't reach or maintain the expected performance during the interview process.
- **Expectations**: The candidate doesn't meet the interviewer's expectations (for example, their salary expectations are beyond the company's expectations).
- **Lack of skills/experience**: The candidate doesn't meet the skill level for the job (for example, lack of experience).
- **Communication**: The candidate has the technical skills but does not articulate them properly.
- **Interviewer's bias**: The candidate's conduct is not appropriate for the job/company.

Let's now have a look at how to identify and eliminate the mismatches.

Objectively identifying and eliminating the mismatches

While the feedback represents the starting point for fixing and eliminating the mismatches, you have to be aware that it can be pretty subjective. It is important to read the feedback carefully, and as you recall the phases of the interview, overlap their feedback with your memory of it with an objective approach.

Once you have identified the objective mismatches, it is time to eliminate them.

Don't form an obsession for a company

Some people struggle to get hired by a certain company. Even after two or three attempts, they don't stop. Is continuing to try perseverance or obsession? Has their dream job become an obsession or they should continue to try? These are extremely personal questions, but, as a rule of thumb, obsessions are always toxic and they don't lead to anything good. If you find yourself in this situation, or you know somebody that is, then it is time to change your attitude and think that maybe the following is the proper way to think.

Don't lose confidence in yourself – sometimes, they don't deserve you!

This title sounds like a sterile slogan of encouragement meant to make you feel better. However, that's not true! It happens all the time and in many contexts. For example, a singer at the beginning of her career went on a famous singing show and didn't win any prizes; she didn't even place among the ones who were considered to be good. She didn't try out for the contest again (as in the section title), but a few years later, she won her first Grammy award.

There are tons of examples like this in real life. The singer didn't lose her confidence in her skills and she were right! That famous singing show didn't deserve her. After years, the show organizer invited the singer to sing again (this time as a guest) and the organizer apologized for what had happened.

So, don't lose confidence in yourself – sometimes, they don't deserve you!

Summary

This chapter provided a brief overview of an important aspect that we must tackle wisely during a job search—failures. They are a part of life, and we must know how to handle them in a healthy and professional way. Don't get too emotional, and try to have a professional, cold, realistic, and objective approach of each failure.

In the next chapter, we'll cover the climax of a technical interview: the coding challenge.

5
How to Approach a Coding Challenge

This chapter covers *technical quizzes* and *coding challenges*, which are commonly used in technical interviews.

The coding challenge is the most important part of an interview. This part can consist of a single session or multiple sessions. Some companies prefer to split the technical interview into two parts: the first part consists of a technical quiz, while the second part consists of one or more coding challenges. In this chapter, we'll tackle these two topics in detail:

- Technical quiz
- Coding challenge

By the end of this chapter, you should be able to sketch a plan of your own to approach the technical interview. You'll know how to deal with the key moments during the interview, what the interviewer is expecting to see and hear from you, and how to deal with blocking moments when you don't have a clue about the answer/solution.

Technical quiz

The technical quiz can take on a question-answer format with the technical interviewer, or it can be an on-site quiz. Commonly, it contains 20-40 questions and takes less than an hour.

When the technical interviewer conducts the process, you will have to provide free answers and the duration may vary (for example, between 30-45 minutes). It is important to be crystal clear, concise, and always on topic.

Usually, when a technical interviewer conducts the interview, the questions are formulated as scenarios that require you to make a decision or choice. For example, a question may sound like this: *We need a space-efficient algorithm capable of searching millions of records extremely quickly with a decent number of false positives. What do you recommend for us?* Most probably, the expected answer is something like, *I will consider algorithms from the Bloom filters family*. If you came across a similar case in your previous projects, then you may say it like this: *We had the same scenario in a project about streaming data, and we decided to go with the Bloom filter algorithm.*

Another category of questions is meant to simply check your technical knowledge. These questions are not in the context of a scenario or project; for example, *Can you tell me what the life cycle states of a thread in Java are?* The expected answer is, *At any moment, a Java thread can be in one of the following states:* **NEW, RUNNABLE, RUNNING, BLOCKED, SLEEP, WAITING/TIMED/WAITING,** *or* **TERMINATED**.

Typically, answering technical questions is a three-step approach, as shown in the following diagram. First, you should understand the question. If you have any doubts, then ask for clarification. Second, you must know that the interviewer expects you to identify several keywords or key points in your answer. This is like a checklist. This means that you must know about the key things that should be highlighted in the answer. Third, you just need to wrap the keywords/key points in a logical and meaningful answer:

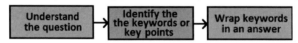

Figure 5.1 – The process of tackling a technical quiz

You will see plenty of examples from *Chapter 6, Object-Oriented Programming*, onward.

As a rule of thumb, your answers should be technical, articulated in a concise but comprehensive way, and communicated with confidence in yourself. A common mistake of shy people is to provide an answer that sounds like a question. Their tone is like they're asking for confirmation for every word. When your answer sounds like a question, the interviewer will probably tell you to just give the answer without asking him.

> **Important note**
>
> When you can only partially answer a question, don't rush to answer or say you don't know. Try to ask the interviewer for more details and/or a 20-second thinking time period. Sometimes, this will help you provide an incomplete but decent answer. For example, the interviewer may ask you, *What is the main difference between checked and unchecked exceptions in Java?* If you don't know the difference, then you can give an answer such as, *The checked exceptions are subclasses of Exception, while the unchecked exceptions are subclasses of RuntimeException.* You didn't actually answer the question, but it is better than saying, *I don't know!* Alternatively, you could formulate a question such as, *Are you referring to the exceptions that we are forced to catch?* By doing this, you may get more details from the interviewer. Pay attention and don't ask it like, *Are you referring to the exceptions that we are forced to catch and to the exceptions that we are not forced to catch?* You will probably receive a short answer, such as *Yes*. This doesn't help you!
>
> On the other hand, if you really have no clue about the answer/solution, then it is better to say, *I don't know*. This is not necessarily a strike against you, while trying to baffle the interviewer with too much gobbledygook will definitely be against you.

There are companies that prefer an on-site multiple choice quiz. In this case, there is no human assistance, and you'll have to finish the quiz in a fixed period of time (for example, in 30 minutes). It is important to try to answer as many questions as possible. If you don't know a question, then move on to the next one. The clock is ticking! At the end (the last 2-3 minutes), you can come back and try to provide an answer to those questions that you passed on.

Nevertheless, there are platforms that don't allow you to navigate backward and forward between the questions. In such a case, when you don't know the answer to a question, you are forced to risk it and try to guess an answer. Spending a lot of time answering a single question will result in a poor score at the end. Ideally, you should try to spend the same amount of time on each question. For example, if you have 20 questions to answer in 30 minutes, then you can allocate 30/20 = 1.5 minutes to each question.

One of the best techniques to approaching a technical quiz (no matter what type of quiz) is to perform several *mock* interviews. Grab a friend and ask him to act as the interviewer. Put the questions in a bowl and ask him to randomly choose them one by one. Answer the questions and act exactly as if you were in front of the real interviewer.

Coding challenge

The coding challenge is the climax of any technical interview. This is the moment where you can show all your coding skills. It's time to demonstrate that you can do this job. Having working and clean code can help you make a great impression.
A great impression may fill in the gaps that you left open during any other stage of the interview.

The coding challenge is a double-edged sword that may radically change the final result of the interview. One edge can cut you off from the scheme, while the other edge can bring you an offer in spite of other shortcomings.

However, the problems specific to these coding challenges are really hard for a variety of reasons. These will be covered in the next section.

The problems specific to coding challenges are meant to be difficult

Have you ever seen a problem specific to the coding challenge stage and found it weird, silly, or maybe pointless and nothing to do with real problems? If so, then you've seen an excellent problem specific to the coding challenge stage.

To better understand how to prepare for such problems, it is important to know their characteristics and requirements. So, let's have a look at them:

- **They are not real-world problems**: Commonly, real-world problems need a lot of time to be coded, so they are not a good candidate for coding challenges. The interviewer will ask you to solve problems that can be explained and coded in a reasonable amount of time, and such problems are usually not real-world problems.

- **They can be quite silly**: It is not uncommon to see problems that are quite silly and look like they have been invented just to complicate your life. They don't seem to be useful for something or serve a goal. This is normal since, most of the time, they are not real-world problems.

- **They are fairly complex**: Even if they can be solved pretty quickly, they are not easy! Most probably, you'll be asked to code a method or a class, but this doesn't mean that it will be easy. Commonly, they require all kinds of tricks, they are brain-teasing, and/or they exploit less well-known features of the programming languages (for example, working with bits).

- **The solution is not obvious**: Since they are fairly complex, the solutions to these problems are not obvious. Don't expect to find a solution immediately! Almost nobody does! These questions are specially designed to see how you handle a situation where you cannot immediately see the solution. This is why you may have couple of hours to solve it (most commonly, between 1 and 3 hours).

- **Prohibit the common solving paths**: Most of the time, such problems have clear clauses that prohibit the usage of common solving paths. For example, you may receive a problem that sounds like this: *Write a method that extracts a substring of a string between the given positions without using a built-in method such as String#substring()*. There are countless examples like this one. Simply choose one or more built-in Java methods (for example, utility methods) that can be implemented in a relatively short amount of time and formulate it; for example, *Write a method that does X without using a built-in solution such as Y*. Exploring API source code, participating in open source projects, and practicing such problems is quite useful for solving such problems.

- **They are meant to place you in an exclusive range of candidates that receive offers**: The difficulty of these coding challenges is calibrated to place you in an exclusive percentage of candidates. Some companies are making offers to less than 5% of candidates. If a certain problem can be easily solved by most candidates, then it will be replaced.

> **Important note**
> The problems specific to coding challenges are meant to be difficult and are usually asked in ascending order of difficulty. Most probably, to pass these coding challenges, your experience and coding skills will not be enough. So, don't get frustrated if, in spite of your knowledge, you cannot see a solution right away. Many such problems are meant to test your ability to find solutions to uncommon scenarios and test your coding skills. They might have ridiculous clauses and/or obscure solutions that exploit uncommon features of a programming language. They might contain silly requirements and/or dummy cases. Focus only on how to solve them and always do it by the rules.

A single coding challenge session is, most of the time, enough for the interviewers. Nevertheless, there are cases where you'll have to pass two or even three such challenges. The key is to practice as much as possible. The next section shows you how to handle, in general, a coding challenge problem.

Tackling a coding challenge problem

Before we discuss the process of tackling a coding challenge problem, let's quickly set up a possible environment for a coding challenge. Mainly, there are two coordinates that define this environment: the presence of the interviewer during the coding challenge and the paper-pen versus computer approach.

The interviewer's presence during the coding challenge

Most commonly, the interviewer is present (by phone screen or in-person) during the coding challenge. They will evaluate your final result (code), but they are not there just for this reason. Measuring just your coding ability doesn't require their presence and is usually encountered in programming contests. An interview coding challenge is not a programming contest. The interviewer wants to see you during the entire process in order to analyze your behavior and communication skills. They want to see whether you have a plan to solve the problem, whether you act in an organized or chaotic way, whether you write ugly code, whether you are willing to communicate your actions, or whether you are introverted. Moreover, they want to assist and guide you. Of course, you need to strive for no guidance or as little as possible, but a proper reaction to guidance is also appreciated. However, striving for no guidance doesn't mean that you should not interact with the interviewer.

Keep talking!

Interaction with the interviewer is an important factor. The following list explains several aspects of the interactivity plan:

- **Explain your solution before coding**: Before you start coding, it is important to squeeze some valuable information from the interviewer. Describe to them how you want to solve the problem, what steps you want to follow, and what you'll use. For example, you could say, *I think that a HashSet is the proper choice here because the order of insertion is not relevant and we don't need duplicate values.* You'll get a thumbs up or some guidance or advice that will help you obtain the expected results.

- **Explain what you are doing while coding**: While you're coding, explain it to the interviewer. For example, you could say, *First, I will create an instance of ArrayList,* or, *Here, I load the file from the local folder into memory.*

- **Ask the proper questions**: As long as you know and respect the limits, you can ask questions that can save you time. For example, it is OK to ask, *I can't remember – what is the default MySQL port, 3308 or 3306?* However, don't exaggerate with these questions!
- **Mention the aspects that matter**: If you know additional information related to the problem, then share it with the interviewer. This is a good chance to expose your programming knowledge, your thoughts, and your ideas around the problem.

If you encounter a problem that you already know (maybe you've solved it while practicing such problems), then don't blurt 'it' out. This will not impress the interviewer, and you will probably get another coding challenge. It is better to follow the same process that you'd follow for any other problem. Before we cover this process, let's tackle one more aspect of the interview environment.

Paper-pen versus computer approach

If the coding challenge takes place via a phone screen, then the interviewer will ask you to share your screen and code in your favorite **Integrated Development Environment** (**IDE**). This way, the interviewer can see how you take advantage of IDE help as well (for example, they can see if you use the IDE to generate getters and setters or if you write them by hand).

> **Important note**
> Avoid running the application after each line of code. Instead, run the application after each logical block of code. Make the corrections and run it again. Take advantage of the IDE debugging tool.

If you meet the interviewer in person, then you could be asked to use paper or a whiteboard for coding. This time, coding can be in Java or even pseudocode. Since your code cannot be compiled and executed, you have to test it manually. It is important to show that your code works by taking an example and passing it through your code.

> **Important note**
> Avoid excessive write-delete code cycles in a chaotic approach. Think twice and write once! Otherwise, you will give the interviewer a headache.

Now, let's take a look at the general steps that are meant to provide a methodological and logical approach to solving a problem.

The process of tackling a coding challenge problem

The process of tackling a coding challenge problem can be done in a suite of steps that should be applied sequentially. The following diagram shows these steps:

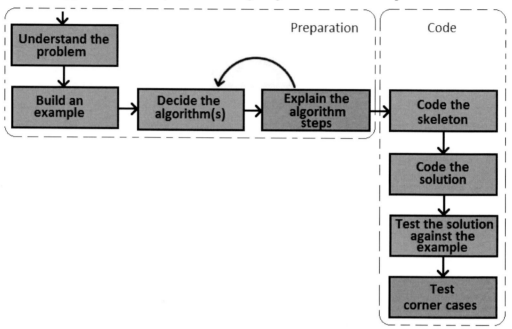

Figure 5.2 – The process of tackling a coding challenge problem

Now, let's detail each of these steps. While applying this problem-solving process, don't forget the interactivity component.

Understand the problem

It is very important to understand the problem. Don't start solving the problem based on assumptions or a partial understanding of the problem. Read the problem at least twice! Don't rely on a single read since, in most cases, these problems contain hidden and obscure requirements or details that are easy to miss.

Don't hesitate to ask your interviewer questions about the problem. There are cases when details are intentionally forgotten to test your ability to discover the underlying problem.

> **Important note**
> Only if you understand the problem will you have a chance of solving it.

Next, it is time to build an example. If you manage to build an example, then this is a clear signal that you have understood the problem.

Build an example

As they say, *A picture's worth a thousand words*, but we can say the same thing about an example.

Sketching the problem and building an example will clarify any remaining misunderstandings. It will give you the chance to discover the problem in detail via a methodological approach (step by step). Once you have a working example, you should start seeing the overall solution. This is also useful for testing your final code.

> **Important note**
> A sketch and an example are useful for solidifying your understanding of the problem.

Now, it is time to think about the overall solution and decide on the algorithm(s) to use.

Deciding on the algorithm(s) to use and explaining them

At this point, you have understood the problem and even built an example. Now, it is time to shape an overall solution and split it into steps and algorithms.

This is a time-consuming process. At this point, it is important to apply the *Communicate What You Think* approach. If you don't say anything, then the interviewer doesn't know if you are clueless or if you are in a brainstorm. For example, you could say, *I think I can use a List for storing the emails, ... hmmm ... no, this is not OK because a List accepts duplicates.* While you are talking (even if it looks like you are talking to yourself), the interviewer can judge the correctness of your reasoning, can see your knowledge level, and can provide you with some tips. The interviewer may reply with something like, *Yes, that is a good point, but nevertheless, do not forget that you need to maintain the order of insertion.*

Most of the time, the problem requires some form of data (strings, numbers, bits, objects, and so on) manipulation, such as sorting, ordering, filtering, reversing, flattening, searching, computing, and so on. Where there is data, there are data structures as well (arrays, lists, sets, maps, trees, and so on). The trick is to find the proper matches between the data manipulations that you need and the data structures. Usually, a proper match means the following:

- You can easily apply certain manipulations to the data structure.
- You can obtain good performance (Big O – see *Chapter 7, Big O Analysis of Algorithms*).
- You can maintain harmony between the used data structure(s). This means that you don't need heavy or complex algorithms, nor do you need to perform conversion to move/exploit the data between data structures.

These are the big pieces of the puzzle. Managing to identify the proper matches is half of the job. The other half is to bring these pieces together to shape the solution. In other words, you need to bring logic into the equation.

It is very tempting to start coding immediately after you read the problem or after you've understood it and shaped the big picture of the solution in your mind. *Don't do that!* Often, this will lead to a chain of failures that will make you lose your temper. Very soon, all your ideas will be surrounded by a dense mist of distrust and you will start to code hastily, even with ridiculous mistakes.

> **Important note**
> Take your time and think about the solution deeply before starting to code.

Now, it's time to start coding your solution and impress the interviewer with your coding skills.

Coding the skeleton

Start coding the solution with a skeleton. More precisely, define your classes, methods, and interfaces without implementation (behavior/actions). You will fill them up with code in the next step. This way, you're showing the interviewer that your coding stage follows a clear road. Don't jump into the code too hastily? Moreover, respect the fundamental principles of programming, such as **Single responsibility, Open–closed, Liskov substitution, Interface segregation, Dependency inversion** (**SOLID**) and **Don't Repeat Yourself** (**DRY**). Most probably, the interviewer will watch out for these principles.

> **Important note**
> Coding the skeleton of your solution helps the interviewer follow you easily and better understand your reasoning.

At this point, you have the attention of the interviewer. Now, it's time to bring your skeleton to life.

Coding the solution

Now, it's time to code the solution. While you're doing so, explain the main code lines that you write to the interviewer. Pay attention and respect the well-known Java coding style (for example, follow the *Google Java Style Guide* at `google.github.io/styleguide/javaguide.html`).

> **Important note**
> Following a well-known Java coding style and communicating your actions to the interviewer will be a big plus for the final result.

Once you've done the core implementation of your solution, it is time to increase the robustness of your code. So, as a final touch, don't ignore exceptions handling and validations (for example, validating the arguments of methods). Also, ensure that you've covered all the requirements of the problem and that you've employed the right data types. Finally, it is time to keep your fingers crossed that your code will pass the testing step.

Testing the solution is the final step of this process.

Testing the solution

In the second step of this process, you built an example. Now, it is time to show the interviewer that your code works by passing the example through it. *It is very important to demonstrate that your code works at least for this example.* It may go to the first key or run successfully after you've repaired some minor bugs, but in the end, it is just important that it works.

Don't relax! You have won the current battle, but not the war! Often, the interviewer will want to see your code working for corner cases or special cases as well. Usually, such special cases involve dummy values, boundaries values, improper inputs, actions that force exceptions, and so on. If your code is not robust and it fails these attempts, then the interviewer will think that this is exactly how you'll code the production applications as well. On the other hand, if your code works, then the interviewer will be totally impressed.

> **Important note**
> Code that works should put a smile on your interviewer's face. At the very least, you will feel that they are a little bit more friendly toward you and relaxed.

If you made a good impression, then the interviewer may want to ask you some extra questions. You should expect to be asked about the code's performance and alternative solutions. Of course, you can provide such information without being asked. The interviewer will be pleased to see that you can tackle a problem in multiple ways and that you understand the pros and cons of each solution and decision.

Getting stuck makes you freeze

First of all, it is normal to get stuck. Don't panic! Don't get frustrated! Don't quit!

If you get stuck, then others taking the interview will probably get stuck as well. The main problem is how to handle such a blockage, not the blockage itself. You have to stay calm and try to do the following:

- **Get back to your example**: Sometimes, it is helpful to detail your example, or to take a look at one more example. Having two examples can help you shape the general case in your mind and understand the pillars of the problem.

- **Isolate the problem in the example**: Every example has a suite of steps. Identify the step where you got stuck and focus on it as a separate problem. Sometimes, pulling out the issue from its context allows you to understand it better and solve it.

- **Try a different approach**: Sometimes, the solution is to tackle the issue from different angles. A different perspective can give you a new view. Maybe another data structure, a hidden feature of Java, a brute-force approach, and so on can help. An ugly solution is better than no solution!

- **Mock or postpone the issue**: Struggling for a long time to solve a step may lead to the unpleasant situation of you not being able to finish the problem on time. Sometimes, it is better to mock or postpone the step that causes you trouble and continue with the other steps. It is possible that, in the end, when you come back to this step, you will have a much clearer picture of it and will know how to code it.

- **Ask for guidance**: This should be your last resort, but in a crisis, you must apply desperate solutions. You can ask something such as, *I am confused about this aspect because...* (and explain; try to justify your confusion). *Can you please give me a tip about what I am missing here?*

The interviewer is aware of the difficulty of the step(s), so they will not be surprised that you got stuck. They will appreciate your perseverance, analytical capabilities, and calmness in trying to find a solution, even if you don't find it. The interviewer knows that you'll encounter similar situations in your daily job and that the most important thing in such scenarios is to stay calm and search for solutions.

Summary

In this chapter, we talked about the process of tackling a coding challenge problem. Besides the steps we enumerated earlier – understand the problem, build an example, decide and explain the algorithm(s), code the skeleton, and code and test the solution – there is one more step that will become the objective of the chapters that follow: practice a lot of problems! In the next chapter, we will start with the fundamental concepts of programming.

Section 2: Concepts

This section covers questions regarding concepts. Providing excellent knowledge in this area is a great indicator that you have the fundamental skills required, which means you have a solid and healthy technical foundation to answer questions at the interview stage. Companies look for such people as possible candidates that can be trained to solve very specific and complex tasks.

This section comprises the following chapters:

- *Chapter 6, Object-Oriented Programming*
- *Chapter 7, Big O Analysis of Algorithms*
- *Chapter 8, Recursion and Dynamic Programming*
- *Chapter 9, Bit Manipulation*

6
Object-Oriented Programming

This chapter covers the most popular questions and problems relating to **Object-Oriented Programming** (**OOP**) that are encountered at Java interviews.

Please bear in mind that my goal is not to teach you about OOP or, in more general terms, the aim of this book is not to teach you about Java. My goal is to teach you how to answer questions and solve problems in the context of an interview. In such a context, the interviewer wants a clear and concise answer; you'll not have the time for dissertations and tutorials. You have to be able to express your ideas lucidly and cogently. Your answers should be meaningful and you have to convince the interviewer that you really understand what you are saying and that you are not just reciting a number of sterile definitions. Most of the time, you should be able to express an article of several pages or a chapter of a book in one or several key paragraphs.

By the end of this chapter, you'll know how to answer 40+ questions and problems that cover the fundamental aspects of OOP. Being fundamental aspects, you have to know them in detail. There is no excuse in the event that you don't know the correct and concise answers to these problems. A lack of knowledge in this area can severely affect your chances of success at interview.

So, let's summarize our agenda as follows:

- OOP concepts
- SOLID principles
- GOF design patterns
- Coding challenges

Let's start with questions relating to OOP concepts.

Technical requirements

You can find all the codes present in this chapter on GitHub. Please visit the following link: `https://github.com/PacktPublishing/The-Complete-Coding-Interview-Guide-in-Java/tree/master/Chapter06`

Understanding OOP concepts

The OOP model is based on several concepts. These concepts must be familiar to any developer who is planning to design and program applications relying on objects. Therefore, let's start by enumerating them as follows:

- Object
- Class
- Abstraction
- Encapsulation
- Inheritance
- Polymorphism
- Association
- Aggregation
- Composition

Commonly, when these concepts are wrapped in questions, they are prefixed by *What is ...?* For example, *What is an object?*, or *What is polymorphism?*

> **Important note**
> The correct answers to these questions are a combination of technical knowledge and real-world analogies or examples. Avoid cold answers with super-technical details and no examples (for example, don't talk about the internal representation of an object). Pay attention to what you're saying because the interviewer may extract questions directly from your answers. If your answer has mentioned a notion in passing, then the next question may refer to that notion. In other words, don't add to your answer any aspects that you are unfamiliar with.

So, let's answer the questions relating to OOP concepts in an interview context. Notice that we apply what we've learned in *Chapter 5, How to Approach a Coding Challenge*. More precisely, we follow the **Understand the question|Nominate the key words/key points|Wrap an answer** technique. To begin with, in order to become familiar with this technique, I'll extract the key points as a bulleted list, and I will italicize them in the answer.

What is an object?

The key points that you should encapsulate in your answer are the following:

- An object is one of the core concepts of OOP.
- An object is a real-world entity.
- An object has state (fields) and behaviors (methods).
- An object represents an instance of a class.
- An object takes up some space in memory.
- An object can communicate with other objects.

Now, we can present an answer as follows:

An object is one of the core concepts of OOP. An object is a real-world entity, such as a car, table, or cat. During its life cycle, an object *has state and behaviors.* For example, a cat's state can be color, name, and breed, while its behaviors can be playing, eating, sleeping, and meowing. In Java, an object is an instance of a class usually built via the `new` keyword, and *it has state stored in fields and exposes its behavior through methods. Each instance takes some space in memory and can communicate with other objects.* For example, a boy, which is another object, can caress a cat and it sleeps.

If further details are required, then you may want to talk about the fact that objects can have different access modifiers and visibility ranges, can be mutable, unmodifiable, or immutable, and are collected via the garbage collector.

What is a class?

The key points that you should encapsulate in your answer are the following:

- A class is one of the core concepts of OOP.
- A class is a template or a blueprint for creating objects.
- A class doesn't consume memory.
- A class can be instantiated multiple times.
- A class does one, and only one, thing.

Now, we can present an answer as follows:

A class is one of the core concepts of OOP. A class is a set of instructions that are required to build a specific type of object. We can *think of a class as a template, a blueprint,* or a recipe that tells us how to create objects of that class. *Creating an object of that class is a process called instantiation* and is usually done via the `new` keyword. *We can instantiate as many objects as we wish. A class definition doesn't consume memory* being saved as a file on the hard drive. One of the best practices that a class should follow is the **Single Responsibility Principle (SRP)**. While conforming to this principle, *a class should be designed and written to do one, and only one, thing.*

If further details are required, then you may want to talk about the fact that classes can have different access modifiers and visibility ranges, support different types of variables (local, class, and instance variables), and can be declared as `abstract`, `final`, or `private`, nested in another class (inner class), and so on.

What is abstraction?

The key points that you should encapsulate in your answer are the following:

- Abstraction is one of the core concepts of OOP.
- Abstraction is the concept of exposing to the user only those things that are relevant to them and hiding the remainder of the details.
- Abstraction allows the user to focus on what the application does instead of how it does it.
- Abstraction is achieved in Java via abstract classes and interfaces.

Now, we can present an answer as follows:

Einstein claims that *Everything should be made as simple as possible, but not simpler*. Abstraction is one of the main OOP concepts that strive to make things as simple as possible for the user. In other words, *abstraction exposes the user only to the things that are relevant to them and hides the remainder of the details*. In OOP terms, we say that an object should expose to its users only a set of high-level operations, while the internal implementation of those operations is hidden. So, *abstraction allows the user to focus on what the application does instead of how it does it*. This way, abstraction reduces the complexity of exposing the things, increases code reusability, avoids code duplications, and sustains low coupling and high cohesion. Moreover, it maintains the security and discretion of the application by exposing only the important details.

Let's consider a real-life example: a man driving a car. The man knows what each pedal does and what the steering wheel does, but he doesn't know how these things are done internally by the car. He doesn't know about the inner mechanisms that empower these things. This is what abstraction is. *In Java, abstraction can be achieved via abstract classes and interfaces*.

If further details are required, then you may share the screen or use paper and a pen and code your example.

So, we said that a man is driving a car. The man can speed up or slow down the car via the corresponding pedals. He also can turn left and right with the aid of the steering wheel. All these actions are grouped in an interface named `Car`:

```java
public interface Car {

    public void speedUp();
    public void slowDown();
    public void turnRight();
```

```
    public void turnLeft();
    public String getCarType();
}
```

Next, each type of car should implement the `Car` interface and override these methods to provide the implementation of these actions. This implementation is hidden from the user (the man driving the car). For example, the `ElectricCar` class appears as follows (in reality, in place of `System.out.println`, we have complex business logic):

```
public class ElectricCar implements Car {

    private final String carType;

    public ElectricCar(String carType) {
        this.carType = carType;
    }

    @Override
    public void speedUp() {
        System.out.println("Speed up the electric car");
    }

    @Override
    public void slowDown() {
        System.out.println("Slow down the electric car");
    }

    @Override
    public void turnRight() {
        System.out.println("Turn right the electric car");
    }

    @Override
    public void turnLeft() {
        System.out.println("Turn left the electric car");
    }
```

```java
    @Override
    public String getCarType() {
        return this.carType;
    }
}
```

The user of this class has access to these `public` methods without being aware of the implementation:

```java
public class Main {

    public static void main(String[] args) {

        Car electricCar = new ElectricCar("BMW");

        System.out.println("Driving the electric car: "
            + electricCar.getCarType() + "\n");

        electricCar.speedUp();
        electricCar.turnLeft();
        electricCar.slowDown();
    }
}
```

The output is listed as follows:

```
Driving the electric car: BMW
Speed up the electric car
Turn left the electric car
Slow down the electric car
```

So, this was an example of abstraction via an interface. The complete application is named *Abstraction/AbstractionViaInterface*. In the code bundled to this book, you can find the same scenario implemented via an abstract class. The complete application is named *Abstraction/AbstractionViaAbstractClass*.

Moving on, let's talk about encapsulation.

What is encapsulation?

The key points that you should encapsulate in your answer are the following:

- Encapsulation is one of the core concepts of OOP.
- Encapsulation is the technique whereby the object state is hidden from the outer world and a set of public methods for accessing this state are exposed.
- Encapsulation is achieved when each object keeps its state private, inside a class.
- Encapsulation is known as the *data-hiding* mechanism.
- Encapsulation has a number of important advantages associated with it, such as loosely coupled, reusable, secure, and easy-to-test code.
- In Java, encapsulation is implemented via the access modifiers – `public`, `private`, and `protected`.

Now, we can present an answer as follows:

Encapsulation is one of the core concepts of OOP. Mainly, encapsulation binds together the code and data in a single unit of work (a class) and acts as a defensive shield that doesn't allow external code to access this data directly. Mainly, *it is the technique of hiding the object state from the outer world and exposing a set of* `public` *methods for accessing this state. When each object keeps its state* `private` *inside a class, we can say that encapsulation was achieved. This is why encapsulation is also referenced as the* **data-hiding** *mechanism.* The code that takes advantage of encapsulation is loosely coupled (for example, we can change the names of the class variables without breaking the client code), reusable, secure (the client is not aware of how data is manipulated inside the class), and easy to test (it is easier to test methods than fields). In Java, encapsulation can be achieved via the access modifiers, `public`, `private`, and `protected`. Commonly, when an object manages its own state, its state is declared via `private` variables and is accessed and/or modified via `public` methods. Let's consider an example: a `Cat` class can have its state represented by fields such as `mood`, `hungry`, and `energy`. While the code external to the `Cat` class cannot modify any of these fields directly, it can call `public` methods, such as `play()`, `feed()`, and `sleep()` that modify the `Cat` state internally. The `Cat` class may also have `private` methods that are not accessible outside the class, such as `meow()`. This is encapsulation.

If further details are required, then you may share the screen or use paper and a pen and code your example.

So, the Cat class from our example can be coded as indicated in the following code block. Notice that the state of this class was encapsulated via `private` fields, and is therefore not directly accessible from outside the class:

```java
public class Cat {

    private int mood = 50;
    private int hungry = 50;
    private int energy = 50;

    public void sleep() {
        System.out.println("Sleep ...");
        energy++;
        hungry++;
    }

    public void play() {
        System.out.println("Play ...");
        mood++;
        energy--;
        meow();
    }

    public void feed() {
        System.out.println("Feed ...");
        hungry--;
        mood++;
        meow();
    }

    private void meow() {
        System.out.println("Meow!");
    }

    public int getMood() {
        return mood;
    }
```

```
    public int getHungry() {
        return hungry;
    }

    public int getEnergy() {
        return energy;
    }
}
```

The only way to modify the state is via the public methods, `play()`, `feed()`, and `sleep()`, as in the following example:

```
public static void main(String[] args) {

    Cat cat = new Cat();

    cat.feed();
    cat.play();
    cat.feed();
    cat.sleep();

    System.out.println("Energy: " + cat.getEnergy());
    System.out.println("Mood: " + cat.getMood());
    System.out.println("Hungry: " + cat.getHungry());
}
```

The output will be as follows:

```
Feed ...Meow!Play ...Meow!Feed ...Meow!Sleep ...

Energy: 50
Mood: 53
Hungry: 49
```

The complete application is named *Encapsulation*. Now, let's have a rundown on inheritance.

What is inheritance?

The key points that you should encapsulate in your answer are the following:

- Inheritance is one of the core concepts of OOP.
- Inheritance allows an object to be based on another object.
- Inheritance sustains code reusability by allowing an object to reuse the code of another object and adds its own logic as well.
- Inheritance is known as an **IS-A** relationship, also referenced as a parent-child relationship.
- In Java, inheritance is achieved via the `extends` keyword.
- The inherited object is referenced as the superclass, and the object that inherits the superclass is referenced as the subclass.
- In Java, multiple classes cannot be inherited.

Now, we can present an answer as follows:

Inheritance is one of the core concepts of OOP. It allows an object to be based on another object, which is useful when different objects are pretty similar and share some common logic, but they are not identical. *Inheritance sustains code reusability by allowing an object to reuse the code of another object while it adds its own logic as well.* So, in order to achieve inheritance, we reuse the common logic and extract the unique logic in another class. *This is known as an IS-A relationship, also referenced as a parent-child relationship.* It is just like saying `Foo` IS-A `Buzz` type of thing. For example, cat IS-A feline, and train IS-A vehicle. An IS-A relationship is the unit of work used to define hierarchies of classes. *In Java, inheritance is accomplished via the `extends` keyword by deriving the child from its parent.* The child can reuse the fields and methods of its parent and add its own fields and methods. *The inherited object is referenced as the superclass, or the parent class, and the object that inherits the superclass is referenced as the subclass, or the child class. In Java, inheritance cannot be multiple*; therefore, a subclass or child class cannot inherit fields and methods of more than one superclass or parent class. For example, an `Employee` class (parent class) can define the common logic of any employee in a software company, while another class (child class), named `Programmer`, can extend the `Employee` to use this common logic and add logic specific to a programmer. Other classes can extend the `Programmer` or `Employee` classes as well.

If further details are required, then you may share the screen or use paper and a pen and code your example.

The `Employee` class is quite simple. It wraps the name of the employee:

```java
public class Employee {
    
    private String name;
    
    public Employee(String name) {
        this.name = name;
    }
    
    // getters and setters omitted for brevity
}
```

Then, the `Programmer` class extends the `Employee`. As any employee, a programmer has a name, but they are also assigned to a team:

```java
public class Programmer extends Employee {
    
    private String team;
    
    public Programmer(String name, String team) {
        super(name);
        this.team = team;
    }
    
    // getters and setters omitted for brevity
}
```

Now, let's test inheritance by creating a `Programmer` and calling `getName()`, inherited from the `Employee` class, and `getTeam()`, inherited from the `Programmer` class:

```java
public static void main(String[] args) {
    
    Programmer p = new Programmer("Joana Nimar", "Toronto");
    
    String name = p.getName();
    String team = p.getTeam();
    
    System.out.println(name + " is assigned to the "
```

```
               + team + " team");
    }
```

The output will be as follows:

```
Joana Nimar is assigned to the Toronto team
```

The complete application is named *Inheritance*. Moving on, let's talk about polymorphism.

What is polymorphism?

The key points that you should encapsulate in your answer are the following:

- Polymorphism is one of the core concepts of OOP.
- Polymorphism means *many forms* in Greek.
- Polymorphism allows an object to behave differently in certain cases.
- Polymorphism can be shaped via method overloading (known as Compile-Time Polymorphism) or via method overriding in the case of an IS-A relationship (known as Runtime Polymorphism).

Now, we can present an answer as follows:

Polymorphism is one of the core concepts of OOP. Polymorphism is a word composed of two Greek words: *poly*, which means *many*, and *morph*, which means *forms*. Therefore, *polymorphism means many forms*.

More precisely, in the OOP context, *polymorphism allows an object to behave differently in certain cases* or, in other words, allows an action to be accomplished in different ways (approaches). *One way to implement polymorphism is via method overloading. This is known as Compile-Time Polymorphism* because the compiler can identify at compile time which form of an overloaded method to call (multiple methods with the same name but different arguments). So, depending on which form of the overloaded method is called, the object behaves differently. For example, a class named `Triangle` can define multiple methods named `draw()` with different arguments.

Another way to implement polymorphism is via method overriding, and this is the common approach when we have an IS-A relationship. It is known as Runtime Polymorphism, or Dynamic Method Dispatch. Typically, we start with an interface containing a bunch of methods. Next, each class implements this interface and overrides these methods to provide a specific behavior. This time, polymorphism allows us to use any of these classes exactly like its parent (the interface) without any confusion of their types. This is possible because, at runtime, Java can distinguish between these classes and knows which one is used. For example, an interface named `Shape` can declare a method named `draw()`, and the `Triangle`, `Rectangle`, and `Circle` classes implement the `Shape` interface and override the `draw()` method to draw the corresponding shape.

If further details are required, then you may share the screen or use paper and a pen and code your example.

Polymorphism via method overloading (compile time)

The `Triangle` class contains three `draws()` methods, as follows:

```java
public class Triangle {

    public void draw() {
        System.out.println("Draw default triangle ...");
    }

    public void draw(String color) {
        System.out.println("Draw a triangle of color "
            + color);
    }

    public void draw(int size, String color) {
        System.out.println("Draw a triangle of color " + color
            + " and scale it up with the new size of " + size);
    }
}
```

Next, notice how the corresponding `draw()` method is called:

```
public static void main(String[] args) {

    Triangle triangle = new Triangle();
    triangle.draw();
    triangle.draw("red");
    triangle.draw(10, "blue");
}
```

The output will be as follows:

```
Draw default triangle ...
Draw a triangle of color red
Draw a triangle of color blue and scale it up
with the new size of 10
```

The complete application is named *Polymorphism/CompileTime*. Moving on, let's look at an example of implementing runtime polymorphism.

Polymorphism via method overriding (runtime)

This time, the `draw()` method is declared in an interface, as follows:

```
public interface Shape {

    public void draw();
}
```

The `Triangle`, `Rectangle`, and `Circle` classes implement the `Shape` interface and override the `draw()` method to draw the corresponding shape:

```
public class Triangle implements Shape {

    @Override
    public void draw() {
        System.out.println("Draw a triangle ...");
    }
}
```

```java
public class Rectangle implements Shape {

    @Override
    public void draw() {
        System.out.println("Draw a rectangle ...");
    }
}

public class Circle implements Shape {

    @Override
    public void draw() {
        System.out.println("Draw a circle ...");
    }
}
```

Next, we create a triangle, a rectangle, and a circle. For each of these instances, let's call the `draw()` method:

```java
public static void main(String[] args) {

    Shape triangle = new Triangle();
    Shape rectangle = new Rectangle();
    Shape circle = new Circle();

    triangle.draw();
    rectangle.draw();
    circle.draw();
}
```

The output reveals that, at runtime, Java called the proper `draw()` method:

```
Draw a triangle ...
Draw a rectangle ...
Draw a circle ...
```

The complete application is named *Polymorphism/Runtime*. Moving on, let's talk about association.

> **Important note**
> There are people who consider polymorphism as the most important concept in OOP. Moreover, there are voices that consider runtime polymorphism as the only genuine polymorphism, while compile-time polymorphism is not actually a form of polymorphism. During an interview, initiating such a debate is not recommended. It is better to act as a mediator and present both sides of the coin. We will discuss soon how to tackle such situations.

What is association?

The key points that you should encapsulate in your answer are the following:

- Association is one of the core concepts of OOP.
- Association defines the relation between two classes that are independent of one another.
- Association has no owner.
- Association can be one-to-one, one-to-many, many-to-one, and many-to-many.

Now, we can present an answer as follows:

Association is one of the core concepts of OOP. The association goal is to define the relation between two classes independent of one another and is also referenced as the multiplicity relation between objects. *There is no owner of the association.* The objects involved in an association can use one another (bidirectional association), or only one uses the other one (unidirectional association), but they have their own life span. *Association can be unidirectional/bidirectional, one-to-one, one-to-many, many-to-one, and many-to-many.* For example, between the `Person` and `Address` objects, we may have a bidirectional many-to-many relationship. In other words, a person can be associated with multiple addresses, while an address can belong to multiple people. However, people can exist without addresses, and vice versa.

If further details are required, then you may share the screen or use paper and a pen and code your example.

The `Person` and `Address` classes are very simple:

```java
public class Person {

    private String name;

    public Person(String name) {
        this.name = name;
    }

    // getters and setters omitted for brevity
}

public class Address {

    private String city;
    private String zip;

    public Address(String city, String zip) {
        this.city = city;
        this.zip = zip;
    }

    // getters and setters omitted for brevity
}
```

The association between `Person` and `Address` is accomplished in the `main()` method, as shown in the following code block:

```java
public static void main(String[] args) {

    Person p1 = new Person("Andrei");
    Person p2 = new Person("Marin");

    Address a1 = new Address("Banesti", "107050");
    Address a2 = new Address("Bucuresti", "229344");

    // Association between classes in the main method
```

```
        System.out.println(p1.getName() + " lives at address "
                + a2.getCity() + ", " + a2.getZip()
                + " but it also has an address at "
                + a1.getCity() + ", " + a1.getZip());
        System.out.println(p2.getName() + " lives at address "
                + a1.getCity() + ", " + a1.getZip()
                + " but it also has an address at "
                + a2.getCity() + ", " + a2.getZip());
}
```

The output is listed as follows:

```
Andrei lives at address Bucuresti, 229344 but it also has an
address at Banesti, 107050
Marin lives at address Banesti, 107050 but it also has an
address at Bucuresti, 229344
```

The complete application is named *Association*. Moving on, let's talk about aggregation.

What is aggregation?

The key points that you should encapsulate in your answer are the following:

- Aggregation is one of the core concepts of OOP.
- Aggregation is a special case of unidirectional association.
- Aggregation represents a HAS-A relationship.
- Two aggregated objects have their own life cycle, but one of the objects is the owner of the HAS-A relationship.

Now, we can present an answer as follows:

Aggregation is one of the core concepts of OOP. Mainly, aggregation is a special case of unidirectional association. While an association defines the relationship between two classes independent of one another, *aggregation represents a HAS-A relationship between these two classes.* In other words, *two aggregated objects have their own life cycle, but one of the objects is the owner of the HAS-A relationship.* Having their own life cycle means that ending one object will not affect the other object. For example, a `TennisPlayer` has a `Racket`. This is a unidirectional association since a `Racket` cannot have a `TennisPlayer`. Even if the `TennisPlayer` dies, the `Racket` is not affected.

> **Important note**
>
> Notice that, when we define the notion of aggregation, we also have a statement regarding what an association is. Follow this approach whenever two notions are tightly related and one of them is a special case of the other one. The same practice is applied next for defining composition as a special case of aggregation. The interviewer will notice and appreciate that you have an overview of things and that you can provide a meaningful answer that didn't overlook the context.

If further details are required, then you may share the screen or use paper and a pen and code your example.

We start with the `Rocket` class. This is a simple representation of a tennis racket:

```java
public class Racket {

    private String type;
    private int size;
    private int weight;

    public Racket(String type, int size, int weight) {
        this.type = type;
        this.size = size;
        this.weight = weight;
    }

    // getters and setters omitted for brevity
}
```

A `TennisPlayer` HAS-A `Racket`. Therefore, the `TennisPlayer` class must be capable of receiving a `Racket` as follows:

```java
public class TennisPlayer {

    private String name;
    private Racket racket;

    public TennisPlayer(String name, Racket racket) {
        this.name = name;
        this.racket = racket;
```

```
    }

    // getters and setters omitted for brevity
}
```

Next, we create a `Racket` and a `TennisPlayer` that uses this `Racket`:

```
public static void main(String[] args) {

    Racket racket = new Racket("Babolat Pure Aero", 100, 300);
    TennisPlayer player = new TennisPlayer("Rafael Nadal",
        racket);

    System.out.println("Player " + player.getName()
        + " plays with " + player.getRacket().getType());
}
```

The output is as follows:

```
Player Rafael Nadal plays with Babolat Pure Aero
```

The complete application is named *Aggregation*. Moving on, let's talk about composition.

What is composition?

The key points that you should encapsulate in your answer are the following:

- Composition is one of the core concepts of OOP.
- Composition is a more restrictive case of aggregation.
- Composition represents a HAS-A relationship that contains an object that cannot exist on its own.
- Composition sustains code reuse and the visibility control of objects.

Now, we can present an answer as follows:

Composition is one of the core concepts of OOP. Primarily, composition is a more restrictive case of aggregation. While aggregation represents a HAS-A relationship between two objects having their own life cycle, *composition represents a HAS-A relationship that contains an object that cannot exist on its own.* In order to highlight this coupling, the HAS-A relationship can be named PART-OF as well. For example, a Car has an Engine. In other words, the engine is PART-OF the car. If the car is destroyed, then the engine is destroyed as well. Composition is said to be better than inheritance because *it sustains code reuse and the visibility control of objects.*

If further details are required, then you may share the screen or use paper and a pen and code your example.

The Engine class is quite simple:

```java
public class Engine {

    private String type;
    private int horsepower;

    public Engine(String type, int horsepower) {
        this.type = type;
        this.horsepower = horsepower;
    }

    // getters and setters omitted for brevity
}
```

Next, we have the Car class. Check out the constructor of this class. Since Engine is part of Car, we create it with the Car:

```java
public class Car {

    private final String name;
    private final Engine engine;

    public Car(String name) {
        this.name = name;
```

```
        Engine engine = new Engine("petrol", 300);
        this.engine=engine;
    }

    public int getHorsepower() {
        return engine.getHorsepower();
    }

    public String getName() {
        return name;
    }
}
```

Next, we can test composition from the `main()` method as follows:

```
public static void main(String[] args) {

    Car car = new Car("MyCar");

    System.out.println("Horsepower: " + car.getHorsepower());
}
```

And the output is as follows:

```
Horsepower: 300
```

The complete application is named *Composition*.

So far, we have covered the essential questions regarding OOP concepts. Keep in mind that such questions can occur in Java technical interviews for almost any position that involves coding or architecting applications. Especially if you have around 2–4 years of experience, the chances are high that you will be asked the preceding questions, and you must know the answers, otherwise this will be a black mark against you.

Now, let's continue with the SOLID principles. This is another fundamental area and a must-know topic alongside the OOP concepts. A lack of knowledge in this area will prove detrimental when it comes to a final decision regarding your interview.

Getting to know the SOLID principles

In this section, we will formulate answers to the questions corresponding to the five famous design patterns for writing classes – the SOLID principles. By way of a quick remainder, SOLID is an acronym of the following:

- **S**: Single Responsibility Principle
- **O**: Open Closed Principle
- **L**: Liskov's Substitution Principle
- **I**: Interface Segregation Principle
- **D**: Dependency Inversion Principle

In interviews, the most common questions pertaining to SOLID are of the *What is ...?* type. For example, *What is S?* or *What is D?* Typically, OOP-related questions are intentionally vague. This way, the interviewer tests your level of knowledge and wants to see whether you request further clarification. So, let's tackle each of these questions in turn and provide an awesome answer that will impress the interviewer.

What is S?

The key points that you should encapsulate in your answer are the following:

- S stands for the **Single Responsibility Principle** (SRP).
- S stands for *One class should have one, and only one, responsibility*.
- S tells us to write a class for only one goal.
- S sustains high maintainability and visibility control across the application modules.

Now, we can present an answer as follows:

First of all, SOLID is an acronym for the first five **Object-Oriented Design (OOD)** principles enunciated by Robert C. Martin, also known as Uncle Bob (*optional phrase*). S is the first principle from SOLID and is known as the **Single Responsibility Principle (SRP)**. *This principle translates to the fact that one class should have one, and only one, responsibility.* This is a very important principle that should be followed in any type of project for any type of class (model, service, controller, manager class, and so on). *As long as we write a class for only one goal, we will sustain high maintainability and visibility control across the application modules.* In other words, by *sustaining high maintainability*, this principle has a significant business impact, and by *providing visibility control across the application modules*, this principle sustains encapsulation.

If further details are required, then you may share the screen or use paper and a pen to code an example as the one presented here.

For example, you want to calculate the area of a rectangle. The dimensions of the rectangle are initially given in meters and the area is computed in meters as well, but we want to be able to convert the computed area to other units, such as inches. Let's see the approach that breaks the SRP.

Breaking the SRP

Implementing the preceding problem in a single class, `RectangleAreaCalculator`, can be done as follows. But this class does more than one thing: it breaks SRP. Keep in mind that, typically, when you use the word **and** to express what a class does, this is a sign that the SRP is broken. For example, the following class computes the area **and** converts it to inches:

```java
public class RectangleAreaCalculator {

    private static final double INCH_TERM = 0.0254d;

    private final int width;
    private final int height;

    public RectangleAreaCalculator(int width, int height) {
        this.width = width;
        this.height = height;
    }

    public int area() {
        return width * height;
    }

    // this method breaks SRP
    public double metersToInches(int area) {
        return area / INCH_TERM;
    }
}
```

Since this code contravenes the SRP, we must fix it in order to follow the SRP.

Following the SRP

The situation can be remedied by removing the `metersToInches()` method from `RectangleAreaCalculator`, as follows:

```java
public class RectangleAreaCalculator {

    private final int width;
    private final int height;

    public RectangleAreaCalculator(int width, int height) {
        this.width = width;
        this.height = height;
    }

    public int area() {
        return width * height;
    }
}
```

Now, `RectangleAreaCalculator` does only one thing (it computes the rectangle area), thereby observing the SRP.

Next, `metersToInches()` can be extracted in a separate class. Moreover, we can add a new method for converting from meters to feet as well:

```java
public class AreaConverter {

    private static final double INCH_TERM = 0.0254d;
    private static final double FEET_TERM = 0.3048d;

    public double metersToInches(int area) {
        return area / INCH_TERM;
    }

    public double metersToFeet(int area) {
        return area / FEET_TERM;
    }
}
```

This class also follows the SRP, hence our job is done. The complete application is named *SingleResponsabilityPrinciple*. Moving on, let's talk about the second SOLID principle, the Open Closed Principle.

What is O?

The key points that you should encapsulate in your answer are the following:

- O stands for the **Open Closed Principle** (OCP).
- O stands for *Software components should be open for extension, but closed for modification.*
- O sustains the fact that our classes should not contain constraints that will require other developers to modify our classes in order to accomplish their job – other developers should only extend our classes to accomplish their job.
- O sustains software extensibility in a versatile, intuitive, and non-harmful way.

Now, we can present an answer as follows:

First of all, SOLID is an acronym for the first five **Object-Oriented Design (OOD)** principles enunciated by Robert C. Martin, also known as Uncle Bob (*optional phrase*). O is the second principle from SOLID and is known as the **Open Closed Principle** (OCP). This principle stands for *Software components should be open for extension, but closed for modification*. This means that our classes should be designed and written in such a way that other developers can change the behavior of these classes by simply extending them. So, *our classes should not contain constraints that will require other developers to modify our classes in order to accomplish their job – other developers should only extend our classes to accomplish their job.*

While we *must sustain software extensibility in a versatile, intuitive, and non-harmful way,* we don't have to think that other developers will want to change the whole logic or the core logic of our classes. Primarily, if we follow this principle, then our code will act as a good framework that doesn't give us access to modify their core logic, but we can modify their flow and/or behavior by extending some classes, passing initialization parameters, overriding methods, passing different options, and so on.

If further details are required, then you may share the screen or use paper and a pen to code an example like the one presented here.

Now, for instance, you have different shapes (for example, rectangles, circles) and we want to sum their areas. First, let's see the implementation that breaks the OCP.

Breaking the OCP

Each shape will implement the `Shape` interface. Therefore, the code is pretty straightforward:

```
public interface Shape {
}


public class Rectangle implements Shape {

    private final int width;
    private final int height;

    // constructor and getters omitted for brevity
}


public class Circle implements Shape {

    private final int radius;

    // constructor and getter omitted for brevity
}
```

At this point, we can easily use the constructors of these classes to create rectangles and circles of different sizes. Once we have several shapes, we want to sum their areas. For this, we can define an `AreaCalculator` class as follows:

```
public class AreaCalculator {

    private final List<Shape> shapes;

    public AreaCalculator(List<Shape> shapes) {
        this.shapes = shapes;
    }

    // adding more shapes requires us to modify this class
    // this code is not OCP compliant
    public double sum() {
        int sum = 0;
```

```
        for (Shape shape : shapes) {
            if (shape.getClass().equals(Circle.class)) {
                sum += Math.PI * Math.pow(((Circle) shape)
                    .getRadius(), 2);
            } else
            if(shape.getClass().equals(Rectangle.class)) {
                sum += ((Rectangle) shape).getHeight()
                    * ((Rectangle) shape).getWidth();
            }
        }

        return sum;
    }
}
```

Since each shape has its own formula for area, we require an `if-else` (or `switch`) structure to determine the type of shape. Furthermore, if we want to add a new shape (for example, a triangle), we have to modify the `AreaCalculator` class to add a new `if` case. This means that the preceding code breaks the OCP. Fixing this code to observe the OCP imposes several modifications in all classes. Hence, be aware that fixing code that doesn't follow the OCP can be quite tricky, even in the case of a simple example.

Following the OCP

The main idea is to extract from `AreaCalculator` the area formula of each shape in the corresponding `Shape` class. Hence, the rectangle will compute its area, the circle as well, and so on. To enforce the fact that each shape must calculate its area, we add the `area()` method to the `Shape` contract:

```
public interface Shape {

    public double area();
}
```

Next, `Rectangle` and `Circle` implements `Shape` as follows:

```
public class Rectangle implements Shape {

    private final int width;
```

```java
    private final int height;

    public Rectangle(int width, int height) {
        this.width = width;
        this.height = height;
    }

    public double area() {
        return width * height;
    }
}

public class Circle implements Shape {

    private final int radius;

    public Circle(int radius) {
        this.radius = radius;
    }

    @Override
    public double area() {
        return Math.PI * Math.pow(radius, 2);
    }
}
```

Now, the `AreaCalculator` can loop the list of shapes and sum the areas by calling the proper `area()` method:

```java
public class AreaCalculator {

    private final List<Shape> shapes;

    public AreaCalculator(List<Shape> shapes) {
        this.shapes = shapes;
    }
```

```
    public double sum() {
        int sum = 0;
        for (Shape shape : shapes) {
            sum += shape.area();
        }

        return sum;
    }
}
```

The code is OCP-compliant. We can add a new shape and there is no need to modify the `AreaCalculator`. So, `AreaCalculator` is closed for modifications and, of course, is open for extension. The complete application is named the *OpenClosedPrinciple*. Moving on, let's talk about the third SOLID principle, Liskov's Substitution Principle.

What is L?

The key points that you should encapsulate in your answer are the following:

- L stands for **Liskov's Substitution Principle (LSP)**.
- L stands for *Derived types must be completely substitutable for their base types*.
- L sustains the fact that objects of subclasses must behave in the same way as the objects of superclasses.
- L is useful for runtime-type identification followed by the cast.

Now, we can present an answer as follows:

First of all, SOLID is an acronym for the first five **Object-Oriented Design (OOD)** principles enunciated by Robert C. Martin, also known as Uncle Bob (optional phrase). *L* is the third principle from SOLID and is known as **Liskov's Substitution Principle (LSP)**. This principle stands for *Derived types must be completely substitutable for their base types*. This means that the classes that extend our classes should be usable across the application without causing failures. More precisely, *this principle sustains the fact that objects of subclasses must behave in the same way as the objects of superclasses*, so every subclass (or derived class) should be capable of substituting their superclass without any issues. Most of the time, *this is useful for runtime-type identification followed by the cast*. For example, consider `foo(p)`, where `p` is of the type `T`. Then, `foo(q)` should work fine if `q` is of the type `S` and `S` is a subtype of `T`.

If further details are required, then you may share the screen or use paper and a pen to code an example like the one presented here.

We have a chess club that accepts three types of members: Premium, VIP, and Free. We have an abstract class named `Member` that acts as the base class, and three subclasses – `PremiumMember`, `VipMember`, and `FreeMember`. Let's see whether each of these member types can substitute the base class.

Breaking the LSP

The `Member` class is abstract, and it represents the base class for all members of our chess club:

```java
public abstract class Member {

    private final String name;

    public Member(String name) {
        this.name = name;
    }

    public abstract void joinTournament();

    public abstract void organizeTournament();
}
```

The `PremiumMember` class can join chess tournaments or organize such tournaments as well. So, its implementation is quite simple:

```java
public class PremiumMember extends Member {

    public PremiumMember(String name) {
        super(name);
    }


    @Override
    public void joinTournament() {
        System.out.println("Premium member joins tournament");
    }
```

```
    @Override
    public void organizeTournament() {
        System.out.println("Premium member organize
            tournament");
    }
}
```

The `VipMember` class is roughly the same as `PremiumMember`, so we can skip it and focus on the `FreeMember` class. The `FreeMember` class can join tournaments, but cannot organize tournaments. This is an issue that we need to tackle in the `organizeTournament()` method. We can throw an exception with a meaningful message or we can display a message as follows:

```
public class FreeMember extends Member {

    public FreeMember(String name) {
        super(name);
    }

    @Override
    public void joinTournament() {
        System.out.println("Classic member joins tournament
            ...");
    }

    // this method breaks Liskov's Substitution Principle
    @Override
    public void organizeTournament() {
        System.out.println("A free member cannot organize
            tournaments");
    }
}
```

But throwing an exception or displaying a message doesn't mean that we follow LSP. Since a free member cannot organize tournaments, it cannot be a substitute for the base class, therefore it breaks the LSP. Check out the following list of members:

```
List<Member> members = List.of(
    new PremiumMember("Jack Hores"),
    new VipMember("Tom Johns"),
    new FreeMember("Martin Vilop")
);
```

The following loop reveals that our code is not LSP-compliant because when the `FreeMember` class has to substitute the `Member` class, it cannot accomplish its job since `FreeMember` cannot organize chess tournaments:

```
for (Member member : members) {
    member.organizeTournament();
}
```

This situation is a showstopper. We cannot continue the implementation of our application. We must redesign our solution to obtain a code that is LSP-compliant. So let's do this!

Following the LSP

The refactoring process starts by defining two interfaces meant to separate the two actions, joining and organizing chess tournaments:

```
public interface TournamentJoiner {

    public void joinTournament();
}

public interface TournamentOrganizer {

    public void organizeTournament();
}
```

Next, the abstract base class implements these two interfaces as follows:

```java
public abstract class Member
    implements TournamentJoiner, TournamentOrganizer {

    private final String name;

    public Member(String name) {
        this.name = name;
    }
}
```

`PremiumMember` and `VipMember` remain untouched. They extend the `Member` base class. However, the `FreeMember` class, which cannot organize tournaments, will not extend the `Member` base class. It will implement the `TournamentJoiner` interface only:

```java
public class FreeMember implements TournamentJoiner {

    private final String name;

    public FreeMember(String name) {
        this.name = name;
    }

    @Override
    public void joinTournament() {
        System.out.println("Free member joins tournament ...");
    }
}
```

Now, we can define a list of members who can join chess tournaments as follows:

```java
List<TournamentJoiner> members = List.of(
    new PremiumMember("Jack Hores"),
    new PremiumMember("Tom Johns"),
    new FreeMember("Martin Vilop")
);
```

Looping this list and substituting the `TournamentJoiner` interface with each type of member works as expected and observes the LSP:

```
// this code respects LSP
for (TournamentJoiner member : members) {
    member.joinTournament();
}
```

Following the same logic, a list of members who can organize chess tournaments can be written as follows:

```
List<TournamentOrganizer> members = List.of(
    new PremiumMember("Jack Hores"),
    new VipMember("Tom Johns")
);
```

`FreeMember` doesn't implement the `TournamentOrganizer` interface. Therefore, it cannot be added to this list. Looping this list and substituting the `TournamentOrganizer` interface with each type of member works as expected and follows the LSP:

```
// this code respects LSP
for (TournamentOrganizer member : members) {
    member.organizeTournament();
}
```

Done! Now we have an LSP-compliant code. The complete application is named *LiskovSubstitutionPrinciple*. Moving on, let's talk about the fourth SOLID principle, the Interface Segregation Principle.

What is I?

The key points that you should encapsulate in your answer are the following:

- I stands for the **Interface Segregation Principle (ISP)**.
- I stands for *Clients should not be forced to implement unnecessary methods that they will not use.*
- I splits an interface into two or more interfaces until clients are not forced to implement methods that they will not use.

Now, we can present an answer as follows:

First of all, SOLID is an acronym for the first five **Object-Oriented Design (OOD)** principles enunciated by Robert C. Martin, also known as Uncle Bob (optional phrase). It is the fourth principle from SOLID, and is known as the **Interface Segregation Principle (ISP)**. This principle stands for *Clients should not be forced to implement unnecessary methods that they will not use*. In other words, *we should split an interface into two or more interfaces until clients are not forced to implement methods that they will not use*. For example, consider the `Connection` interface, which has three methods: `connect()`, `socket()`, and `http()`. A client may want to implement this interface only for connections via HTTP. Therefore, they don't need the `socket()` method. Most of the time, the client will leave this method empty, and this is a bad design. In order to avoid such situations, simply split the `Connection` interface into two interfaces; `SocketConnection` with the `socket()` method, and `HttpConnection` with the `http()` method. Both interfaces will extend the `Connection` interface that remains with the common method, `connect()`.

If further details are required, then you may share the screen or use paper and a pen to code an example like the one presented here. Since we've described the preceding example, let's jump into the section about breaking the ISP.

Breaking the ISP

The `Connection` interface defines three methods as follows:

```
public interface Connection {

    public void socket();
    public void http();
    public void connect();
}
```

`WwwPingConnection` is a class that pings different websites via HTTP; hence, it requires the `http()` method, but doesn't need the `socket()` method. Notice the dummy `socket()` implementation – since `WwwPingConnection` implements `Connection`, it is forced to provide an implementation to the `socket()` method as well:

```
public class WwwPingConnection implements Connection {

    private final String www;
```

```java
    public WwwPingConnection(String www) {
        this.www = www;
    }

    @Override
    public void http() {
        System.out.println("Setup an HTTP connection to "
            + www);
    }

    @Override
    public void connect() {
        System.out.println("Connect to " + www);
    }

    // this method breaks Interface Segregation Principle
    @Override
    public void socket() {
    }
}
```

Having an empty implementation or throwing a meaningful exception from methods that are not needed, such as `socket()`, is a really ugly solution. Check the following code:

```
WwwPingConnection www
    = new WwwPingConnection 'www.yahoo.com');

www.socket(); // we can call this method!
www.connect();
```

What do we expect to obtain from this code? A working code that does nothing, or an exception caused by the `connect()` method because there is no HTTP endpoint? Or, we can throw an exception from `socket()` of the type: *Socket is not supported!*. Then, why is it here?! Hence, it is now time to refactor the code to follow the ISP.

Following the ISP

In order to comply with the ISP, we need to segregate the `Connection` interface. Since the `connect()` method is required by any client, we leave it in this interface:

```
public interface Connection {

    public void connect();
}
```

The `http()` and `socket()` methods are distributed in to separate interfaces that extend the `Connection` interface as follows:

```
public interface HttpConnection extends Connection {

    public void http();
}


public interface SocketConnection extends Connection {

    public void socket();
}
```

This time, the `WwwPingConnection` class can implement only the `HttpConnection` interface and use the `http()` method:

```
public class WwwPingConnection implements HttpConnection {

    private final String www;

    public WwwPingConnection(String www) {
        this.www = www;
    }

    @Override
    public void http() {
        System.out.println("Setup an HTTP connection to "
            + www);
    }
```

```java
    @Override
    public void connect() {
        System.out.println("Connect to " + www);
    }
}
```

Done! Now, the code follows the ISP. The complete application is named *InterfaceSegregationPrinciple*. Moving on, let's talk about the last SOLID principle, the Dependency Inversion Principle.

What is D?

The key points that you should encapsulate in your answer are the following:

- *D* stands for the **Dependency Inversion Principle (DIP)**.
- *D* stands for *Depend on abstractions, not on concretions.*
- *D* sustains the use of abstract layers to bind concrete modules together instead of having concrete modules that depend on other concrete modules.
- *D* sustains the decoupling of concrete modules.

Now, we can present an answer as follows:

First of all, SOLID is an acronym for the first five **Object-Oriented Design (OOD)** principles enunciated by Robert C. Martin, also known as Uncle Bob (*optional phrase*). D is the last principle from SOLID and is known as the **Dependency Inversion Principle (DIP)**. This principle stands for *Depend on abstractions, not on concretions.* This means that we should *rely on abstract layers to bind concrete modules together instead of having concrete modules that depend on other concrete modules.* To accomplish this, all concrete modules should expose abstractions only. This way, the concrete modules allow extension of the functionality or plug-in in another concrete module while retaining the decoupling of concrete modules. Commonly, high coupling occurs between high-level concrete modules and low-level concrete modules.

If further details are required, then you may share the screen or use paper and a pen to code an example.

A database JDBC URL, `PostgreSQLJdbcUrl`, can be a low-level module, while a class that connects to the database may represent a high-level module, such as `ConnectToDatabase#connect()`.

Breaking the DIP

If we pass to the `connect()` method an argument of the `PostgreSQLJdbcUrl` type, then we have violated the DIP. Let's look at the code of `PostgreSQLJdbcUrl` and `ConnectToDatabase`:

```java
public class PostgreSQLJdbcUrl {

    private final String dbName;

    public PostgreSQLJdbcUrl(String dbName) {
        this.dbName = dbName;
    }

    public String get() {
        return "jdbc:// ... " + this.dbName;
    }
}

public class ConnectToDatabase {

    public void connect(PostgreSQLJdbcUrl postgresql) {
        System.out.println("Connecting to "
            + postgresql.get());
    }
}
```

If we create another type of JDBC URL (for example, `MySQLJdbcUrl`), then we cannot use the preceding `connect(PostgreSQLJdbcUrl postgreSQL)` method. So, we have to drop this dependency on concrete and create a dependency on abstraction.

Following the DIP

The abstraction can be represented by an interface that should be implemented by each type of JDBC URL:

```java
public interface JdbcUrl {

    public String get();
}
```

Next, `PostgreSQLJdbcUrl` implements `JdbcUrl` to return a JDBC URL specific to PostgreSQL databases:

```java
public class PostgreSQLJdbcUrl implements JdbcUrl {

    private final String dbName;

    public PostgreSQLJdbcUrl(String dbName) {
        this.dbName = dbName;
    }

    @Override
    public String get() {
        return "jdbc:// ... " + this.dbName;
    }
}
```

In precisely the same manner, we can write `MySQLJdbcUrl`, `OracleJdbcUrl`, and so on. Finally, the `ConnectToDatabase#connect()` method is dependent on the `JdbcUrl` abstraction, so it can connect to any JDBC URL that implements this abstraction:

```java
public class ConnectToDatabase {

    public void connect(JdbcUrl jdbcUrl) {
        System.out.println("Connecting to " + jdbcUrl.get());
    }
}
```

Done! The complete application is named *DependencyInversionPrinciple*.

So far, we've covered the OOP fundamental concepts and the popular SOLID principles. If you plan to apply for a Java position that includes the design and architecture of applications, then it is recommended that you take a look at the **General Responsibility Assignment Software Principles (GRASP)** as well (`https://en.wikipedia.org/wiki/GRASP_(object-oriented_design)`). This is not a popular topic in interviews, but you never know!

Moving on, we will scan a bunch of popular questions that combine these notions. Now that you are familiar with the **Understand the Question | Nominate key points | Answer** technique, I will only highlight the key points in the answer without extracting them as a list beforehand.

Popular questions pertaining to OOP, SOLID, and GOF design patterns

In this section, we will tackle some more difficult questions that require a true understanding of OOP concepts, SOLID design principles, and **Gang of Four (GOF)** design patterns. Note that this book doesn't cover GOF design patterns, but there are great books and videos out there that are dedicated to this topic. I recommend that you try *Learn Design Patterns with Java*, by Aseem Jain (`https://www.packtpub.com/application-development/learn-design-patterns-java-video`).

What is method overriding in OOP (Java)?

*Method overriding is an object-oriented programming technique that allows the developer to write two methods (***non-static, non-private and non-final***) with the same name and signature but different behavior.* Method overriding can be used in the presence of **Inheritance** or **Runtime Polymorphism**.

In the presence of inheritance, we have a method in the superclass (referenced as the overridden method) and we override it in the subclass (referenced as the overriding method). In Runtime Polymorphism, we have a method in an interface and the classes that implements this interface are overriding this method.

Java decides at runtime the actual method that should be called, depending upon the type of object. Method overriding sustains flexible and extensible code, or, in other words, *it sustains the addition of new functionality with minimal code changes.*

If further details are required, then you can list the main rules that govern method overriding:

- The name and signature (including the same return type or subtype) of the method is the same in the superclass and subclass, or in the interface and implementations.
- We cannot override a method in the same class (but we can overload it in the same class).
- We cannot override `private`, `static`, and `final` methods.

- The overriding method cannot reduce the accessibility of the overridden method, but the opposite is possible.
- The overriding method cannot throw checked exceptions that are higher in the exception hierarchy than the checked exception thrown by the overridden method.
- Always use the `@Override` annotation for the overriding method.

An example of overriding methods in Java is available in the code bundled to this book under the name *MethodOverriding*.

What is method overloading in OOP (Java)?

Method overloading is an object-oriented programming technique that allows the developer to write two methods (both static or non-static) with the same name, but a different signature and different functionalities. By different signature, we understand a different number of arguments, different types of arguments, and/or a different order of arguments list. *The return type is not part of the method signature*. Therefore, the case when two methods have identical signatures, but different return types, is not a valid case of method overloading. So, this is a powerful technique that allows us to write methods (both static or non-static) having the same name but with different inputs. The *compiler bind overloaded method calls to the actual method; therefore, no binding is done during runtime*. A famous example of method overloading is `System.out.println()`. The `println()` method has several overloading flavors.

Hence, there are four main rules that govern method overloading:

- Overloading is accomplished by changing the method signature.
- The return type is not part of the method signature.
- We can overload `private`, `static`, and `final` methods.
- We can overload a method in the same class (but we cannot override it in the same class).

If further details are required, you can try to code an example. An example of overloading methods in Java is available in the code bundled to this book under the name *MethodOverloading*.

> **Important note**
>
> Besides the two aforementioned questions, you may need to answer some other related questions, including *What rules govern method overloading and overriding* (see above)?, *What are the main differences between method overloading and overriding* (see above)?, *Can we override a static or a private method* (the short answer is *No*, see above)?, *Can we override a final method* (the short answer is *No*, see above)?, *Can we overload a static method* (the short answer is *Yes*, see above)?, *Can we change the argument list of an overriding method* (the short answer is *No*, see above)? So, it is advisable to extract and prepare the answers to such questions. All the information required is available in the preceding section.
>
> Also, pay attention to questions such as *Is it true that we can only prevent overriding a method via the final modifier*? This type of wording is meant to confuse the candidate because the answer requires an overview of the notion involved. The answer here can be formulated as *This is not true, because we can prevent overriding a method by marking it as private or static as well. Such methods cannot be overridden.*

Moving on, let's examine several other questions related to overriding and overloading methods.

What is covariant method overriding in Java?

Covariant method overriding is a less known feature introduced in Java 5. By means of this feature, *an overriding method can return a subtype of its actual return type*. This means that a client of the overriding method doesn't need an explicit type casting of the returned type. For example, the Java `clone()` method returns `Object`. This means that, when we override this method to return a clone, we get back an `Object` that must be explicitly casted to the actual subclass of `Object` that we need. However, if we take advantage of the Java 5 covariant method overriding feature, then the overriding `clone()` method can return the requisite subclass directly instead of `Object`.

Almost always, a question such as this requires an example as part of the answer, so let's consider the `Rectangle` class that implements the `Cloneable` interface. The `clone()` method can return `Rectangle` instead of `Object` as follows:

```
public class Rectangle implements Cloneable {

    ...

    @Override
    protected Rectangle clone()
            throws CloneNotSupportedException {

        Rectangle clone = (Rectangle) super.clone();

        return clone;
    }
}
```

Calling the `clone()` method doesn't require an explicit cast:

```
Rectangle r = new Rectangle(4, 3);
Rectangle clone = r.clone();
```

The complete application is named *CovariantMethodOverriding*. Pay attention to less direct questions regarding covariant method overriding. For example, it can be formulated like this: *Can we modify the return type of method to subclass while overriding?* The answer to this question is the same as *What is covariant method overriding in Java?*, discussed here.

> **Important note**
>
> Knowing the answer to questions that target less known features of Java can be a big plus at the interview. This demonstrates to the interviewer that you have a deep level of knowledge and that you are up to date with the Java evolution. If you require a supersonic update of all JDK 8 to JDK 13 features via tons of examples and minimum theory, then you will love my book entitled *Java Coding Problems*, published by Packt (`packtpub.com/au/programming/java-coding-problems`).

What are the main restrictions in terms of working with exceptions in overriding and overloading methods?

First, let's discuss the overriding methods. *If we talk about unchecked exceptions, then we must say that there are no restrictions on using them in overriding methods.* Such methods can throw an unchecked exception, hence, any `RuntimeException`. On the other hand, *in the case of checked exceptions, the overriding methods can throw only the checked exception of the overridden method or a subclass of that checked exception.* In other words, an overriding method cannot throw a checked exception that has a broader scope than the checked exception thrown by the overridden method. For example, if the overridden method throws `SQLException`, then the overriding method can throw subclasses such as `BatchUpdateException`, but it cannot throw super classes such as `Exception`.

Second, let's discuss the overloading methods. *Such methods do not impose any kind of restrictions.* This means that we can modify the `throw` clause as required.

> **Important note**
>
> Pay attention to questions that are worded along the lines of *What are the main ...?, Can you enumerate the certain ...?, Can you nominate the...?, Can you highlight the ...?*, and so on. Commonly, when the question contains words such as *main, certain, nominate,* and *highlight*, the interviewer expects a clear and concise answer that should sound like a bullet list. The best practice for answering such questions is to jump into the response directly and enumerate each item as a compressed and meaningful statement. Don't make the common mistake of embarking on a story or dissertation of the notions involved before giving the expected answer. The interviewer wants to see your ability to synthesize and sanitize things and extract the essence while checking your level of knowledge.

If more detail is required, then you can code an example like those from the code bundled to this book. Consider checking the *OverridingException* and *OverloadingException* applications. Now, let's continue with some more questions.

How can the superclass overridden method be called from the subclass overriding method?

We can call the superclass overridden method from the subclass overriding method via the Java `super` *keyword.* For example, consider a superclass, `A`, that contains a method, `foo()`, and a subclass of `A` named `B`. If we override the `foo()` method in subclass `B`, and we call `super.foo()` from the overriding method, `B#foo()`, then we call the overridden method, `A#foo()`.

Can we override or overload the main() method?

We must keep in mind that the `main()` method is static. This means that we can overload it. However, we cannot override it because the static methods are resolved at compile time, while the methods that we can override are resolved at runtime depending upon the type of object.

Can we override a non-static method as static in Java?

No. *We cannot override a non-static method as static.* Moreover, the reverse is not possible either. Both lead to compilation errors.

> **Important note**
>
> Questions that are to the point, like the last two aforementioned questions, deserve a short and concise answer. Interviewers trigger such flashlight questions to measure your ability to analyze a situation and make a decision. Mainly, the answer is brief, but you need some time to say *Yes* or *No*. Such questions don't carry a high score, but they may have a significant negative impact if you don't know the answer. If you know the answer, the interviewer might say in his mind, *Well, OK, this was an easy question anyway!* But, if you don't know the answer, then he might say, *He missed an easy one! There is a serious shortcoming in her/his basic knowledge.*

Next, let's look at some more questions related to other OOP concepts.

Can we have a non-abstract method inside a Java interface?

Until Java 8, we could not have a non-abstract method in a Java interface. All methods from an interface were implicitly public and abstract. However, starting with Java 8, we have new types of methods that can be added to an interface. *In practical terms, starting with Java 8, we can add methods that have implementations directly in interfaces. This can be done by using the* `default` *and* `static` *keywords. The* `default` *keyword was introduced in Java 8 for including in interfaces the methods known as* **default, defender, or extension methods**. Their main goal is to allow us to evolve the existing interfaces while ensuring backward compatibility. JDK itself uses default methods to evolve Java by adding new features without breaking the existing code. *On the other hand,* `static` *methods in interfaces are quite similar to the default methods, the only difference being that we cannot override* `static` *methods in the classes that implement these interfaces.* Since `static` methods are not bound to an object, they can be called by using the interface name preceded by a dot and the method name. Moreover, `static` methods can be called within other `default` and `static` methods.

If further details are required, then you can try to code an example. Consider that we have an interface for shaping a vehicle like a steam car (this is an old car type exactly like old code):

```
public interface Vehicle {

    public void speedUp();
    public void slowDown();
}
```

Obviously, different kinds of steam cars have been built by means of the following `SteamCar` class:

```
public class SteamCar implements Vehicle {

    private String name;

    // constructor and getter omitted for brevity

    @Override
    public void speedUp() {
        System.out.println("Speed up the steam car ...");
```

```
    }

    @Override
    public void slowDown() {
        System.out.println("Slow down the steam car ...");
    }
}
```

Since the `SteamCar` class implements the `Vehicle` interface, it overrides the `speedUp()` and `slowDown()` methods. After a while, petrol cars are invented, and people start to care about horsepower and fuel consumption. So, our code must evolve to provide support for petrol cars as well. To compute the level of consumption, we can evolve the `Vehicle` interface by adding the `computeConsumption()` default method as follows:

```
public interface Vehicle {

    public void speedUp();

    public void slowDown();

    default double computeConsumption(int fuel,
            int distance, int horsePower) {
        // simulate the computation
        return Math.random() * 10d;
    }
}
```

Evolving the `Vehicle` interface doesn't break `SteamCar` compatibility. Furthermore, electric cars have been invented. Computing the consumption of an electric car is not the same as in the case of a petrol car, but the formula relies on the same terms: the fuel, distance, and horsepower. This means that `ElectricCar` will override `computeConsumption()` as follows:

```
public class ElectricCar implements Vehicle {

    private String name;
    private int horsePower;
```

```
    // constructor and getters omitted for brevity

    @Override
    public void speedUp() {
        System.out.println("Speed up the electric car ...");
    }

    @Override
    public void slowDown() {
        System.out.println("Slow down the electric car ...");
    }

    @Override
    public double computeConsumption(int fuel,
            int distance, int horsePower) {

        // simulate the computation
        return Math.random()*60d / Math.pow(Math.random(), 3);
    }
}
```

So, we can override a `default` method, or we can use the implicit implementation. Finally, we have to add a description to our interface since now it serves steam, petrol, and electric cars. We can do this by adding to `Vehicle` a `static` method named `description()`, as follows:

```
public interface Vehicle {

    public void speedUp();

    public void slowDown();

    default double computeConsumption(int fuel,
            int distance, int horsePower) {

        return Math.random() * 10d;
```

```
        }

        static void description() {
            System.out.println("This interface control
                steam, petrol and electric cars");
        }
    }
```

This `static` method is not bound to any type of car and it can be called directly via `Vehicle.description()`. The complete code is named *Java8DefaultStaticMethods*.

Next, let's continue with other questions. So far, you should be pretty familiar with the **Understand the Question|Nominate key points|Answer** technique, so I will stop highlighting the key points. From now on, it is your job to spot them.

What are the main differences between interfaces with default methods and abstract classes?

Among the differences between Java 8 interfaces and abstract classes, we can mention the fact that an abstract class can have a constructor while an interface doesn't support constructors. So, an abstract class can have a state while an interface cannot have a state. Moreover, interfaces remain the first citizens of full abstraction, with the main purpose of being implemented, while abstract classes are meant for partial abstraction. Interfaces are still designed to target completely abstract things that don't do anything by themselves, but specify contracts about how things will work at implementation. The default methods represent an approach for adding additional features to the interfaces without affecting the client code and without changing the state. They shouldn't be used for other purposes. In other words, another difference consists of the fact that it is perfectly fine to have an abstract class with no abstract methods, but it is an anti-pattern to have an interface only with default methods. This means that we have created the interface as a utility class substitute. This way, we defeat the main purpose of an interface, which is to be implemented.

> **Important note**
> When you have to enumerate a bunch of differences or similarities between two notions, pay attention to limit your answer to the coordinates settled by the question. For example, in the case of the preceding question, do not say that one difference lies in the fact that interfaces sustain multiple inheritance while abstract classes don't. This is a general variation between interfaces and classes, and not specifically between Java 8 interfaces and abstract classes.

What is the main difference between abstract classes and interfaces?

Until Java 8, the main difference between abstract classes and interfaces consisted of the fact that an abstract class can contain non-abstract methods, while an interface cannot contain such methods. Starting with Java 8, the main difference consists of the fact that an abstract class can have constructors and state while an interface cannot have either of these.

Can we have an abstract class without an abstract method?

Yes, we can. By adding the `abstract` keyword to a class, it becomes abstract. It cannot be instantiated, but it can have constructors and only non-abstract methods.

Can we have a class that is both abstract and final at the same time?

A final class cannot be sub-classed or inherited. An abstract class is meant to be extended in order to be used. Therefore, final and abstract are opposite notions. This means that they cannot be applied to the same class at the same time. The compiler will throw an error.

What is the difference between polymorphism, overriding, and overloading?

In the context of this question, the overloading technique is known as **Compiled-Time Polymorphism**, while the overriding technique is known as **Runtime Polymorphism**. Overloading involves the use of static (or early) binding, while overriding uses dynamic (or late) binding.

The next two questions constitute add-ons to this one, but they can be formulated as standalone as well.

What is a binding operation?

A binding operation determines the method (or variable) to be called as a result of its references in the code lines. In other words, the process of associating a method call to the method body is known as a binding operation. Some references are bound at compile time, while other references are bound at runtime. Those that are bound at runtime depend upon the type of object. The references resolved at compile time are known as static binding operations, while those resolved at runtime are known as dynamic binding operations.

What are the main differences between static and dynamic binding?

First of all, static binding occurs at compile time, while dynamic binding occurs at runtime. The second thing to consider involves the fact that private, static, and final members (methods and variables) use static binding, while virtual methods are bonded at runtime based upon the type of object. In other words, static binding is accomplished via `Type` (class in Java) information, while dynamic binding is accomplished via `Object`, meaning that a method relying on static binding is not associated with an object, but is instead called on `Type` (class in Java), while a method relying on dynamic binding is associated with an `Object`. The execution of methods that rely on static binding is marginally faster than those that rely on dynamic binding. Static and dynamic binding are used in polymorphism as well. Static binding is used by compile-time polymorphism (overloading methods), while dynamic binding is used in runtime polymorphism (overriding methods). Static binding adds overhead in terms of performance at compile time, while dynamic binding adds overhead in terms of performance at runtime, meaning that static binding is preferable.

What is method hiding in Java?

Method hiding is specific to static methods. More precisely, if we declare two static methods with the same signature and name in the superclass and in the subclass, then they will hide each other. Calling the method from the superclass will call the static method from the superclass, and calling the same method from the subclass will call the static method from the subclass. Hiding is not the same thing with overriding because static methods cannot be polymorphic.

If further details are required, then you can write an example. Consider the `Vehicle` superclass having the `move()` static method:

```java
public class Vehicle {

    public static void move() {
        System.out.println("Moving a vehicle");
    }
}
```

Now, consider the `Car` subclass having the same static method:

```java
public class Car extends Vehicle {

    // this method hides Vehicle#move()
    public static void move() {
        System.out.println("Moving a car");
    }
}
```

Now, let's call these two static methods from the `main()` method:

```java
public static void main(String[] args) {

    Vehicle.move(); // call Vehicle#move()
    Car.move();     // call Car#move()
}
```

The output reveals that these two static methods are hiding one another:

```
Moving a vehicle
Moving a car
```

Notice that we call static methods via the class name. Calling static methods on instances is a very bad practice, so avoid doing this during an interview!

Can we write virtual methods in Java?

Yes, we can! Actually, in Java, all non-static methods are, by default, virtual methods. We can write a non-virtual method by marking it with the `private` and/or `final` keyword. In other words, the methods that can be inherited for polymorphic behavior are virtual methods. Or, if we turn the logic of this statement on its head, the methods that cannot be inherited (marked as `private`) and the methods that cannot be overridden (marked as `final`) are non-virtual.

What is the difference between polymorphism and abstraction?

Abstraction and polymorphism represent two fundamental OOP concepts that are interdependent. Abstraction allows the developer to design general solutions that are reusable and customizable, while polymorphism allows the developer to defer choosing the code that should be executed at runtime. While abstraction is implemented via interfaces and abstract classes, polymorphism relies on overriding and overloading techniques.

Do you consider overloading an approach for implementing polymorphism?

This is a controversial topic. Some people do not regard overloading as polymorphism; therefore, they do not accept the idea of compile-time polymorphism. Such voices maintain that the only overriding method is genuine polymorphism. The argument behind this statement says that only overriding allows code to behave differently depending on the runtime conditions. In other words, exhibiting polymorphic behavior is the privilege of method overriding. I consider that as long as we understand the premises of overloading and overriding, we also understand how both variants sustain polymorphic behavior.

> **Important note**
>
> Questions that tackle controversial topics are delicate and hard to approach correctly. Therefore, it is advisable to jump into the answer directly with this statement *This is a controversial topic*. Of course, the interviewer is interested to hear your opinion as well, but he will be pleased to see that you know both sides of the coin. As a rule of thumb, try to answer in an objective manner and don't approach one side of a coin with radicalism or with a poor arsenal of arguments. Controversial things remain controversial after all, and this is not the proper time and place to demystify them.

OK, now let's continue with some questions based on the SOLID principles and the famous and indispensable **Gang Of Four (GOF)** design patterns. Note that this book doesn't cover GOF design patterns, but there are great books and videos out there that are dedicated to this topic. I recommend that you try *Learn Design Patterns with Java*, by Aseem Jain (`https://www.packtpub.com/application-development/learn-design-patterns-java-video`).

Which OOP concept serves the Decorator design pattern?

The OOP concept that serves the Decorator design pattern is **Composition**. Via this OOP concept, the Decorator design pattern provides new functionalities without modifying the original class.

When should the Singleton design pattern be used?

The Singleton design pattern seems to be the proper choice when we need just one application-level (global) instance of a class. Nevertheless, a Singleton should be used with precaution because it increases the coupling between classes and can become a bottleneck during development, testing, and debugging. As the famous *Effective Java* points out, using Java enums is the best way of implementing this pattern. It is a common scenario to rely on a Singleton pattern for global configurations (for example, loggers, `java.lang.Runtime`), hardware access, database connections, and so on.

> **Important note**
> Whenever you can cite or mention famous references, do so.

What is the difference between the Strategy and State design patterns?

The State design pattern is meant to do a certain thing depending upon the *state* (it exhibits certain behaviors in different *states* without changing the class). The Strategy design pattern, on the other hand, is meant to be used for switching between a range of algorithms without modifying the code that uses it (the client uses algorithms interchangeably via composition and runtime delegation). Moreover, in State, we have a clear order of *state* transition (the flow is created by linking each *state* to another *state*), while in Strategy, the client can choose the algorithm that it wants in any order. For example, the State pattern can define the *states* of sending a package to a client.

The package starts from the *ordered state*, and continues with the *delivered state* and so on until it passes through each *state* and reaches the final *state* when the client has *received* the package. On the other hand, the Strategy pattern defines different strategies for accomplishing each *state* (for example, we may have different strategies for delivering the package).

What is the difference between the Proxy and Decorator patterns?

The Proxy design pattern is useful for providing an access control gateway to something. Commonly, this pattern creates proxy objects that stand in place of the real object. Each request for the real object must pass through the proxy objects, which decides how and when to forward it to the real object. The Decorator design pattern never creates an object, it just decorates an existing object at runtime with new functionality. While chaining proxies is not an advisable practice, chaining decorators in a certain order exploits this pattern in the right way. For example, while the Proxy pattern can represent a proxy server for the internet, the Decorator pattern can be used to decorate the proxy server with different custom settings.

What is the difference between the Facade and Decorator patterns?

While the Decorator design pattern is meant to add new functionalities to an object (in other words, to decorate the object), the Facade design pattern doesn't add new functionalities at all. It just facades the existing functionalities (hides the complexities of a system) and calls them behind the scenes via a *friendly face* exposed to the client. The Facade pattern can expose a simple interface that calls individual components to accomplish complex tasks. For example, the Decorator pattern can be used to build a car by decorating a chassis with an engine, a gearbox, and so on, while the Facade pattern can hide the complexity of building the car by exposing a simple interface for command industrial robots that know the building process details.

What is the key difference between the Template Method and the Strategy pattern?

The Template Method and Strategy patterns encapsulate domain-specific sets of algorithms into objects, but they don't do it in the same way. The key difference consists of the fact that the Strategy pattern is meant to decide at runtime between different strategies (algorithms) based on the requirements, while the Template Method pattern is meant to follow a fixed skeleton (predefined sequence of steps) implementation of an algorithm. Some steps are fixed, while other steps can be modified for different uses. For example, the Strategy pattern may decide between different payment strategies (for example, a credit card or PayPal), while the Template Method can describe the predefined sequence of steps for paying with a certain strategy (for example, payment via PayPal requires a fixed sequence of steps).

What is the key difference between the Builder and Factory patterns?

The Factory pattern creates an object in a single method call. We have to pass in this call all the necessary parameters and the factory will return the object (commonly, by invoking a constructor). On the other hand, the Builder pattern is designed for building complex objects via chains of setter methods that allow us to shape any combination of parameters. At the end of the chain, the Builder method exposes a `build()` method that signals that the list of parameters is set, and it is time to build the object. In other words, Factory acts as a wrapper of a constructor, while Builder is much granular, acting as a wrapper of all the possible parameters you might want to pass into a constructor. Via Builder, we avoid the telescopic constructor used to expose all the possible combinations of parameters. For example, think back to the `Book` object. A book is characterized by a hand of fixed parameters such as the author, title, ISBN, and format. Most probably, you will not be juggling with the number of these parameters when creating books, and therefore the factory pattern will be a good fit for factoring books. But how about a `Server` object? Well, a server is a complex object with tons of optional parameters, and so the Builder pattern is much more appropriate here, or even a combination of these patterns where Factory relies internally on Builder.

What is the key difference between the Adapter and Bridge patterns?

The Adapter pattern strives to provide compatibility between an existing code that we cannot modify (for example, third-party code) and a new system or interface. On the other hand, the Bridge pattern is implemented upfront and is meant to decouple an abstraction from implementation in order to avoid an insane number of classes. So, Adapter strives to provide compatibility between things after they were designed (think along the lines of *A comes from After*), while Bridge is built upfront to let the abstraction and the implementation vary independently (think along the lines of *B comes from Before*). While Adapter acts as the **middle man** between two systems that work fine independently but cannot communicate with one another (they don't have compatible input/output), the Bridge pattern enters the scene when our problem can be solved via orthogonal class hierarchy, but we get stuck with scalability issues and limited extension. For example, consider two classes, `ReadJsonRequest` and `ReadXmlRequest`, which are capable of reading from several devices, such as `D1`, `D2`, and `D3`. `D1` and `D2` produce only JSON requests, while `D3` produces XML requests only. Via Adapter, we can convert between JSON and XML, meaning that these two classes can communicate with all three devices. On the other hand, via the Bridge pattern, we can avoid ending with many classes such as `ReadXMLRequestD1`, `ReadXMLRequestD2`, `ReadXMLRequestD3`, `ReadJsonRequestD1`, `ReadJsonRequestD2`, and `ReadJsonRequestD3`.

We can continue to compare design patterns until we finish all the possible combinations. The final few of these questions have covered the most popular questions of the type **Design Pattern 1 versus Design Pattern 2**. It is strongly advisable to challenge yourself with these types of questions and try to identify similarities and differences between two or more given design patterns. Most of the time, these questions use two design patterns from the same category (for example, two structural or two creational patterns), but they can be from different categories as well. In such a case, this is the first statement that the interviewer expects to hear. So, in such cases, start by saying to which category each of the design patterns involved belongs.

Notice that we skipped all simple questions of the type, *What is an interface?*, *What is an abstract class?*, and so on. Typically, such questions are avoided since they don't say much about your understanding level, being more about reciting some definitions. The interviewer can ask *What is the main difference between abstract classes and interfaces?*, and he can deduce from your answer whether you know what an interface and an abstract class is. Always be prepared to give examples. The inability to shape an example reveals a serious lack of understanding of the essence of things.

Having OOP knowledge is just half of the problem. The other half is represented by having the vision and agility to put this knowledge into designing applications. This is what we will do in the next 10 examples. Keep in mind that we are focused on design, not on implementation.

Coding challenges

Next, we will tackle several coding challenges regarding object-oriented programming. For each problem, we will follow Figure 5.2 from *Chapter 5, How to Approach a Coding Challenge*. Mainly, we will start by asking the interviewer a question such as *What are the design constraints?* Commonly, coding challenges that orbit OOD are expressed by the interviewer in a general way. This is done intentionally to make you ask details about design constraints.

Once we have a clear picture of the constraints, we can try an example (which can be a sketch, a step-by-step runtime visualization, a bullet list, and suchlike). Then, we figure out the algorithm(s)/solution(s), and finally, we provide the design skeleton.

Example 1: Jukebox

Amazon, **Google**

Problem: Design the main classes of the jukebox musical machine.

What to ask: What is the jukebox playing – CDs, MP3s? What should I design – the jukebox building process, how it works, or something else? It is a free jukebox or is money required?

Interviewer: Is a free jukebox playing only CDs? Design its main functionalities, and therefore design how it works.

Solution: In order to understand what classes should be involved in our design, we can try to visualize a jukebox and identify its main parts and functionalities. Sketching a diagram along the lines of the one here also helps the interviewer to see how you think. I suggest that you always take the approach of visualizing the problem in a written form – a sketch is a perfect start:

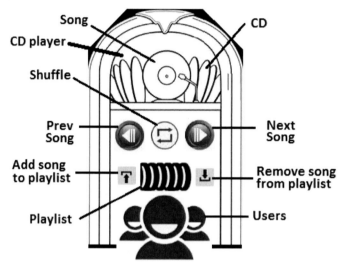

Figure 6.1 – Jukebox

So, we can identify the two main parts of a jukebox: a CD player (or a specific jukebox-playing mechanism) and an interface with commands for the users. The CD player is capable of managing a playlist and playing those songs. We can think of the interface of commands as a Java interface implemented by a Jukebox as shown in the next code. Along with the following code, you can use the UML diagram from here: https://github.com/PacktPublishing/The-Complete-Coding-Interview-Guide-in-Java/blob/master/Chapter06/Jukebox/JukeboxUML.png

```
public interface Selector {

    public void nextSongBtn();
    public void prevSongBtn();
    public void addSongToPlaylistBtn(Song song);
    public void removeSongFromPlaylistBtn(Song song);
    public void shuffleBtn();
}

public class Jukebox implements Selector {
```

```java
    private final CDPlayer cdPlayer;

    public Jukebox(CDPlayer cdPlayer) {
        this.cdPlayer = cdPlayer;
    }

    @Override
    public void nextSongBtn() {...}

    // rest of Selector methods omitted for brevity
}
```

The `CDPlayer` is the heart of the jukebox. Via `Selector`, we control the `CDPlayer` behavior. `CDPlayer` must have access to the set of available CDs and to the playlist:

```java
public class CDPlayer {

    private CD cd;

    private final Set<CD> cds;
    private final Playlist playlist;

    public CDPlayer(Playlist playlist, Set<CD> cds) {
        this.playlist = playlist;
        this.cds = cds;
    }

    protected void playNextSong() {...}
    protected void playPrevSong() {...}
    protected void addCD(CD cd) {...}
    protected void removeCD(CD cd) {...}

    // getters omitted for brevity
}
```

Next, the `Playlist` manages a list of `Song`:

```java
public class Playlist {

    private Song song;

    private final List<Song> songs; // or Queue

    public Playlist(List<Song> songs) {
        this.songs = songs;
    }

    public Playlist(Song song, List<Song> songs) {
        this.song = song;
        this.songs = songs;
    }

    protected void addSong(Song song) {...}
    protected void removeSong(Song song) {...}
    protected void shuffle() {...}
    protected Song getNextSong() {...};
    protected Song getPrevSong() {...};

    // setters and getters omitted for brevity
}
```

The `User`, `CD`, and `Song` classes are skipped for now, but you can find them all in the complete application named *Jukebox*. This kind of problem can be implemented in a wide variety of ways, so feel free to try your own designs as well.

Example 2: Vending machine

Amazon, **Google**, **Adobe**

Problem: Design the main classes that sustain the implementation of the functionalities of a typical vending machine.

What to ask: Is this a vending machine with different types of coins and items? Does it expose functionalities, such as checking an item price, buying an item, a refund, and resetting?

Interviewer: Yes, exactly! For coins, you can consider a penny, a nickel, a dime, and a quarter.

Solution: In order to understand what classes should be involved in our design, we can try to sketch a vending machine. There are a wide range of vending machine types. Simply sketch one that you know (like the one in the following diagram):

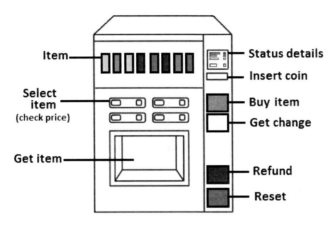

Figure 6.2 – Vending machine

First of all, we immediately notice that items and coins are good candidates for Java enums. We have four types of coins and several types of items, so we can write two Java enums as follows. Along with the following code, you can use the UML diagram from here: https://github.com/PacktPublishing/The-Complete-Coding-Interview-Guide-in-Java/blob/master/Chapter06/VendingMachine/VendingMachineUML.png

```
public enum Coin {
    PENNY(1), NICKEL(5), DIME(10), QUARTER(25);
    ...
}

public enum Item {
    SKITTLES("Skittles", 15), TWIX("Twix", 35) ...
    ...
}
```

The vending machine needs an internal inventory to track the items and status of the coins. We can shape this generically as follows:

```
public final class Inventory<T> {

    private Map<T, Integer> inventory = new HashMap<>();

    protected int getQuantity(T item) {...}
    protected boolean hasItem(T item) {...}
    protected void clear() {...}
    protected void add(T item) {...}
    protected void put(T item, int quantity) {...}
    protected void deduct(T item) {...}
}
```

Next, we can focus on the buttons used by a client to interact with the vending machine. As you saw in the previous example as well, it is common practice to extract these buttons to an interface as follows:

```
public interface Selector {

    public int checkPriceBtn(Item item);
    public void insertCoinBtn(Coin coin);
    public Map<Item, List<Coin>> buyBtn();

    public List<Coin> refundBtn();
    public void resetBtn();
}
```

Finally, the vending machine can be shaped to implement the `Selector` interface and provide a bunch of private methods used to accomplish the internal tasks:

```
public class VendingMachine implements Selector {

    private final Inventory<Coin> coinInventory
        = new Inventory<>();
    private final Inventory<Item> itemInventory
        = new Inventory<>();
```

```
        private int totalSales;
        private int currentBalance;

        private Item currentItem;

        public VendingMachine() {
            initMachine();
        }

        private void initMachine() {
            System.out.println("Initializing the
                vending machine with coins and items ...");
        }

        // override Selector methods omitted for brevity
}
```

The complete application is named *VendingMachine*. By following the two aforementioned examples, you can try to design an ATM, a washing machine, and similar things.

Example 3: Deck of cards

Amazon, **Google**, **Adobe**, **Microsoft**

Problem: Design the main classes of a generic deck of cards.

What to ask: Since a card can be almost anything, can you define *generic*?

Interviewer: A card is characterized by a symbol (suit) and a value. For example, think of a standard 52-card set.

Solution: In order to understand what classes should be involved in our design, we can quickly sketch a card and a deck of cards for the standard 52-card set, as shown in Figure 6.3:

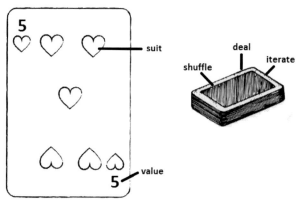

Figure 6.3 – A deck of cards

Since every card has a suit and a value, we will need a class that encapsulates these fields. Let's call this class `StandardCard`. A suit for `StandardCard` contains a *Spade, Heart, Diamond,* or *Club*, so this suit is a good candidate for a Java enum. A `StandardCard` value can be between 1 and 13.

A card can live as a standalone or be a part of a pack of cards. Multiple cards form a pack of cards (for example, a standard 52-card set forms a pack of cards). The number of cards in a pack is usually obtained as a Cartesian product between the possible suits and values (for example, 4 suits x 13 values = 52 cards). So, 52 `StandardCard` objects form `StandardPack`.

Finally, a deck of cards should be a class capable of performing some actions with this `StandardPack`. For example, a deck of cards can shuffle the cards, can deal a hand or a card, and so on. This means that a `Deck` class is also needed.

So far, we have settled on having a Java `enum` and the `StandardCard`, `StandardPack`, and `Deck` classes. If we add the abstraction layers needed to avoid high coupling between these concrete layers, then we obtain the following implementation. Along with the following code, you can use the UML diagram from here: https://github.com/PacktPublishing/The-Complete-Coding-Interview-Guide-in-Java/blob/master/Chapter06/DeckOfCards/DeckOfCardsUML.png

- For standard card implementation:

```
public enum StandardSuit {
    SPADES, HEARTS, DIAMONDS, CLUBS;
```

```
}

public abstract class Card {

    private final Enum suit;
    private final int value;

    private boolean available = Boolean.TRUE;

    public Card(Enum suit, int value) {
        this.suit = suit;
        this.value = value;
    }

    // code omitted for brevity
}

public class StandardCard extends Card {

    private static final int MIN_VALUE = 1;
    private static final int MAX_VALUE = 13;

    public StandardCard(StandardSuit suit, int value) {
        super(suit, value);
    }

    // code omitted for brevity
}
```

- Standard pack of cards implementation gives the following code:

```
public abstract class Pack<T extends Card> {

    private List<T> cards;

    protected abstract List<T> build();
```

```java
    public int packSize() {
        return cards.size();
    }

    public List<T> getCards() {
        return new ArrayList<>(cards);
    }

    protected void setCards(List<T> cards) {
        this.cards = cards;
    }
}

public final class StandardPack extends Pack {

    public StandardPack() {
        super.setCards(build());
    }

    @Override
    protected List<StandardCard> build() {

        List<StandardCard> cards = new ArrayList<>();

        // code omitted for brevity

        return cards;
    }
}
```

- Deck of cards implementation provides the following:

```java
public class Deck<T extends Card> implements Iterable<T> {

    private final List<T> cards;

    public Deck(Pack pack) {
```

```
        this.cards = pack.getCards();
    }

    public void shuffle() {...}
    public List<T> dealHand(int numberOfCards) {...}
    public T dealCard() {...}
    public int remainingCards() {...}
    public void removeCards(List<T> cards) {...}

    @Override
    public Iterator<T> iterator() {...}
}
```

A demo of the code can be quickly written as follows:

```
// create a single classical card
Card sevenHeart = new StandardCard(StandardSuit.HEARTS, 7);

// create a complete deck of standards cards
Pack cp = new StandardPack();
Deck deck = new Deck(cp);

System.out.println("Remaining cards: "
    + deck.remainingCards());
```

Furthermore, you can easily add more types of cards by extending the Card and Pack classes. The complete code is named *DeckOfCards*.

Example 4: Parking lot

Amazon, Google, Adobe, Microsoft

Problem: Design the main classes of a parking lot.

What to ask: Is it a single-level or multi-level parking lot? Are all parking space spots the same? What type of vehicles should we park? Is it free parking? Do we use parking tickets?

Interviewer: It is a synchronous automatic multi-level free parking lot. All parking spots are the same size, but we expect cars (1 spot needed), vans (2 spots needed) and trucks (5 spots needed). Other types of vehicles should be added without modifying the code. The system releases a parking ticket that can be used later to unpark the vehicle. But if the driver introduces only the vehicle information (assuming a lost ticket), the system should still work and locate the vehicle in the parking lot and unpark it.

Solution: In order to understand what classes should be involved in our design, we can quickly sketch a parking lot to identify the main actors and behaviors as in Figure 6.4:

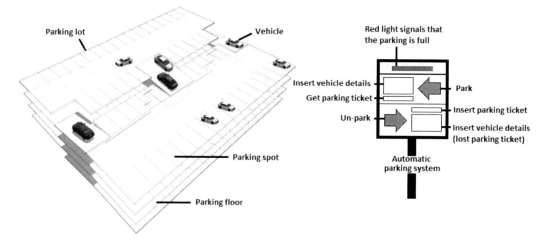

Figure 6.4 – A parking lot

The diagram reveals two major actors: the parking lot and the automatic parking system.

First, let's focus on the parking lot. The main purpose of a parking lot is to park vehicles; therefore, we need to shape the accepted vehicles (car, van, and truck). This looks like a typical case for an abstract class (`Vehicle`) and three subclasses (`Car`, `Van`, and `Truck`). But this is not true! The driver provides information about their vehicle. They don't effectively push the vehicle (the object) into the parking system, so our system does not need dedicated objects for cars, vans, trucks, and so on. Think from the perspective of a parking lot. It needs the vehicle license plate and the free spots required for parking. It doesn't care about the characteristics of a van or a truck. So, we can shape a `Vehicle` as follows. Along with the following code, you can use the UML diagram from here: https://github.com/PacktPublishing/The-Complete-Coding-Interview-Guide-in-Java/blob/master/Chapter06/ParkingLot/ParkingLotUML.png

```
public enum VehicleType {
    CAR(1), VAN(2), TRUCK(5);
```

```
}

public class Vehicle {

    private final String licensePlate;
    private final int spotsNeeded;
    private final VehicleType type;

    public Vehicle(String licensePlate,
            int spotsNeeded, VehicleType type) {
        this.licensePlate = licensePlate;
        this.spotsNeeded = spotsNeeded;
        this.type = type;
    }

    // getters omitted for brevity

    // equals() and hashCode() omitted for brevity
}
```

Next, we have to design the parking lot. Mainly, a parking lot has several floors (or levels) and each floor has parking spots. Among others, a parking lot should expose methods for parking/unparking a vehicle. These methods will delegate the parking/unparking tasks to each floor (or to a certain floor) until it succeeds or there is no floor to scan:

```
public class ParkingLot {

    private String name;
    private Map<String, ParkingFloor> floors;

    public ParkingLot(String name) {
        this.name = name;
    }

    public ParkingLot(String name,
            Map<String, ParkingFloor> floors) {
        this.name = name;
```

```java
            this.floors = floors;
    }

    // delegate to the proper ParkingFloor
    public ParkingTicket parkVehicle(Vehicle vehicle) {...}

    // we have to find the vehicle by looping floors
    public boolean unparkVehicle(Vehicle vehicle) {...}

    // we have the ticket, so we have the needed information
    public boolean unparkVehicle
            ParkingTicket parkingTicket) {...}

    public boolean isFull() {...}

    protected boolean isFull(VehicleType type) {...}

    // getters and setters omitted for brevity
}
```

A parking floor controls the parking/unparking process on a certain floor. It has its own registry of parking tickets and is capable of managing its parking spots. Mainly, each parking floor acts as an independent parking lot. This way, we can shut down a complete floor while the remainder of the floors are not affected:

```java
public class ParkingFloor {

    private final String name;
    private final int totalSpots;
    private final Map<String, ParkingSpot>
            parkingSpots = new LinkedHashMap<>();

    // here, I use a Set, but you may want to hold the parking
    // tickets in a certain order to optimize search
    private final Set<ParkingTicket>
            parkingTickets = new HashSet<>();
```

```java
    private int totalFreeSpots;

    public ParkingFloor(String name, int totalSpots) {
        this.name = name;
        this.totalSpots = totalSpots;

        initialize(); // create the parking spots
    }

    protected ParkingTicket parkVehicle(Vehicle vehicle) {...}

    //we have to find the vehicle by looping the parking spots
    protected boolean unparkVehicle(Vehicle vehicle) {...}

    // we have the ticket, so we have the needed information
    protected boolean unparkVehicle(
        ParkingTicket parkingTicket) {...}

    protected boolean isFull(VehicleType type) {...}
    protected int countFreeSpots(
        VehicleType vehicleType) {...}

    // getters omitted for brevity

    private List<ParkingSpot> findSpotsToFitVehicle(
        Vehicle vehicle) {...}
    private void assignVehicleToParkingSpots(
        List<ParkingSpot> spots, Vehicle vehicle) {...}
    private ParkingTicket releaseParkingTicket(
        Vehicle vehicle) {...}
    private ParkingTicket findParkingTicket(
        Vehicle vehicle) {...}
    private void registerParkingTicket(
        ParkingTicket parkingTicket) {...}
    private boolean unregisterParkingTicket(
        ParkingTicket parkingTicket) {...}
```

```java
        private void initialize() {...}
}
```

Finally, a parking spot is an object that holds information about its name (label or number), availability (whether it is free) and vehicle (whether a vehicle is parked on that spot). It also has methods for assigning/removing a vehicle to/from this spot:

```java
public class ParkingSpot {

    private boolean free = true;
    private Vehicle vehicle;

    private final String label;
    private final ParkingFloor parkingFloor;

    protected ParkingSpot(ParkingFloor parkingFloor,
            String label) {
        this.parkingFloor = parkingFloor;
        this.label = label;
    }

    protected boolean assignVehicle(Vehicle vehicle) {...}
    protected boolean removeVehicle() {...}

    // getters omitted for brevity
}
```

At this moment, we have all the major classes of the parking lot. Next, we are going to focus on the automatic parking system. This can be shaped as a single class that acts as a dispatcher of the parking lot:

```java
public class ParkingSystem implements Parking {

    private final String id;
    private final ParkingLot parkingLot;

    public ParkingSystem(String id, ParkingLot parkingLot) {
        this.id = id;
```

```
            this.parkingLot = parkingLot;
    }

    @Override
    public ParkingTicket parkVehicleBtn(
            String licensePlate, VehicleType type) {...}

    @Override
    public boolean unparkVehicleBtn(
            String licensePlate, VehicleType type) {...}

    @Override
    public boolean unparkVehicleBtn(
            ParkingTicket parkingTicket) {...}

    // getters omitted for brevity
}
```

The complete application containing a partial implementation as well is named *ParkingLot*.

Example 5: Online reader system

Problem: Design the main classes of an online reader system.

What to ask: What are the required functionalities? How many books can be read simultaneously?

Interviewer: The system should be capable of managing readers and books. Your code should be able to add/remove a reader/book and to display a reader/book. The system can serve a single reader and a single book at a time.

Solution: In order to understand what classes should be involved in our design, we can think about sketching something as in Figure 6.5:

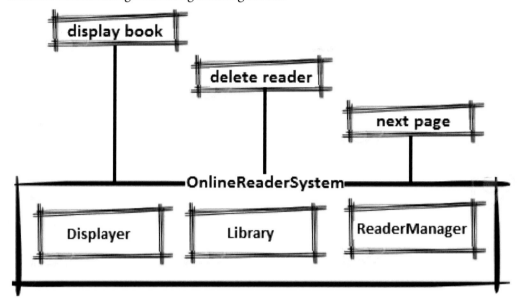

Figure 6.5 – An online reader system

In order to manage readers and books, we need to have such objects. This is a small and easy part, and starting with such parts in an interview is very helpful for breaking the ice and accommodating the problem at hand. When we design objects in an interview, there is no need to come up with a full version of an object. For example, a reader having a name and email, and a book having an author, title, and ISBN is more than sufficient. Let's see them in the following code. Along with the following code, you can use the UML diagram from here: `https://github.com/PacktPublishing/The-Complete-Coding-Interview-Guide-in-Java/blob/master/Chapter06/OnlineReaderSystem/OnlineReaderSystemUML.png`

```
public class Reader {

    private String name;
    private String email;

    // constructor omitted for brevity

    // getters, equals() and hashCode() omitted for brevity
}
```

```java
public class Book {

    private final String author;
    private final String title;
    private final String isbn;

    // constructor omitted for brevity

    public String fetchPage(int pageNr) {...}

    // getters, equals() and hashCode() omitted for brevity
}
```

Next, if we consider that books are usually managed by a library, then we can wrap several functionalities, such as adding, finding, and removing a book, in a class as follows:

```java
public class Library {

    private final Map<String, Book> books = new HashMap<>();

    protected void addBook(Book book) {
        books.putIfAbsent(book.getIsbn(), book);
    }

    protected boolean remove(Book book) {
        return books.remove(book.getIsbn(), book);
    }

    protected Book find(String isbn) {
        return books.get(isbn);
    }
}
```

Readers can be managed by a similar class named `ReaderManager`. You can find this class in the complete application. To read a book, we require a displayer. The `Displayer` should display the reader and the book details and should be capable of navigating through the books pages:

```java
public class Displayer {

    private Book book;
    private Reader reader;
    private String page;
    private int pageNumber;

    protected void displayReader(Reader reader) {
        this.reader = reader;
        refreshReader();
    }

    protected void displayBook(Book book) {
        this.book = book;
        refreshBook();
    }

    protected void nextPage() {
        page = book.fetchPage(++pageNumber);
        refreshPage();
    }

    protected void previousPage() {
        page = book.fetchPage(--pageNumber);
        refreshPage();
    }

    private void refreshReader() {...}
    private void refreshBook() {...}
    private void refreshPage() {...}
}
```

Finally, all we have to do is to wrap `Library`, `ReaderManager`, and `Displayer` in the `OnlineReaderSystem` class. This class is listed here:

```java
public class OnlineReaderSystem {

    private final Displayer displayer;
    private final Library library;
    private final ReaderManager readerManager;

    private Reader reader;
    private Book book;

    public OnlineReaderSystem() {
        displayer = new Displayer();
        library = new Library();
        readerManager = new ReaderManager();
    }

    public void displayReader(Reader reader) {
        this.reader = reader;
        displayer.displayReader(reader);
    }

    public void displayReader(String email) {
        this.reader = readerManager.find(email);
        if (this.reader != null) {
            displayer.displayReader(reader);
        }
    }

    public void displayBook(Book book) {
        this.book = book;
        displayer.displayBook(book);
    }

    public void displayBook(String isbn) {
        this.book = library.find(isbn);
```

```java
            if (this.book != null) {
                displayer.displayBook(book);
            }
        }

        public void nextPage() {
            displayer.nextPage();
        }

        public void previousPage() {
            displayer.previousPage();
        }

        public void addBook(Book book) {
            library.addBook(book);
        }

        public boolean deleteBook(Book book) {
            if (!book.equals(this.book)) {
                return library.remove(book);
            }

            return false;
        }

        public void addReader(Reader reader) {
            readerManager.addReader(reader);
        }

        public boolean deleteReader(Reader reader) {
            if (!reader.equals(this.reader)) {
                return readerManager.remove(reader);
            }

            return false;
        }
```

```
    public Reader getReader() {
        return reader;
    }

    public Book getBook() {
        return book;
    }
}
```

The complete application is named *OnlineReaderSystem*.

Example 6: Hash table

Amazon, Google, Adobe, Microsoft

Problem: Design a hash table (this is a very popular problem in interviews).

What to ask: What are the required functionalities? What technique should be applied to solve index collisions? What is the data type of the key-value pairs?

Interviewer: Speaking about the functionalities, I don't want anything special. I only want the typical `add()` and `get()` operations. For solving index collisions, I suggest you use the *chaining* technique. The key-value pairs should be generic.

A brief overview of a hash table: A hash table is a type of data structure that stores key-value pairs. Commonly, an array holds all the key-value entries in the table and the size of this array is set to accommodate the amount of data anticipated. The key of each key-value is passed through a hash function (or several hash functions) that outputs a hash value or a hash. Mainly, the hash value represents the index of the key-value pair in the hash table (for example, if we use an array to store all key-value pairs, then the hash function returns the index of this array that should hold the current key-value pair). Passing the same key through the hash function should produce the same index every time – this is useful for finding a value via its key.

When a hash function generates two identical indexes for different keys, we face an index collision. The most frequently used techniques for solving an index collision problem are *linear probing* (this technique searches linearly for the next free slot in the table – trying to find in the array a slot (an index) that doesn't hold a key-value pair) and *chaining* (this technique represents a hash table implemented as an array of linked lists – collisions are stored at the same array index as linked list nodes). The following diagram is a hash table for storing *name-phone* pairs. It has *chaining* capabilities (check the *Marius-0838234* entry, which is chained to *Karina-0727928*, because their keys, *Marius* and *Karina*, lead to the same array index, *126*):

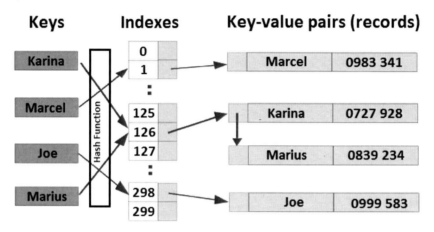

Figure 6.6 – A hash table

Solution: First, we need to shape a hash table entry (`HashEntry`). As you can see in the preceding diagram, a key-value pair has three main parts: the key, the value, and a link to the next key-value pair (this way, we implement *chaining*). Since a hash table entry should be accessed only via dedicated methods, such as `get()` and `put()`, we encapsulate it as follows:

```
public class HashTable<K, V> {

    private static final int SIZE = 10;

    private static class HashEntry<K, V> {

        K key;
        V value;

        HashEntry <K, V> next;
```

```
    HashEntry(K k, V v) {
        this.key = k;
        this.value = v;
        this.next = null;
    }
}
...
```

Next, we define the array that holds `HashEntry`. For testing purposes, a size of `10` elements is enough and it allows us to test *chaining* easily (having a small size is prone to collisions). In reality, such an array is much bigger:

```
private final HashEntry[] entries
    = new HashEntry[SIZE];
...
```

Next, we add the `get()` and `put()` methods. Their code is quite intuitive:

```
public void put(K key, V value) {

    int hash = getHash(key);

    final HashEntry hashEntry = new HashEntry(key, value);

    if (entries[hash] == null) {
        entries[hash] = hashEntry;
    } else { // collision => chaining
        HashEntry currentEntry = entries[hash];
        while (currentEntry.next != null) {
            currentEntry = currentEntry.next;
        }

        currentEntry.next = hashEntry;
    }
}

public V get(K key) {
```

```java
            int hash = getHash(key);

            if (entries[hash] != null) {
                HashEntry currentEntry = entries[hash];

                // Loop the entry linked list for matching
                // the given 'key'
                while (currentEntry != null) {

                    if (currentEntry.key.equals(key)) {
                        return (V) currentEntry.value;
                    }

                    currentEntry = currentEntry.next;
                }
            }

            return null;
        }
```

Finally, we add a dummy hash function (in reality, we use hash functions such as Murmur 3 – https://en.wikipedia.org/wiki/MurmurHash):

```java
        private int getHash(K key) {
            return Math.abs(key.hashCode() % SIZE);
        }
    }
```

Done! The complete application is named *HashTable*.

For the following four examples, we skipped the source code from the book. Take your time and dissect each example. Being able to understand an existing design is just another tool that you can use to shape your design skills. Of course, you can try your own approach before looking into the book's code and compare the results in the end.

Example 7: File system

Problem: Design the main classes of a file system.

What to ask: What are the required functionalities? What are the pieces of the file system?

Interviewer: Your design should support the addition, deletion, and renaming of directories and files. We are talking about a hierarchical structure of directories and files, like most operating systems have.

Solution: The complete application is named *FileSystem*. Please visit the following link to check the UML: `https://github.com/PacktPublishing/The-Complete-Coding-Interview-Guide-in-Java/blob/master/Chapter06/FileSystem/FileSystemUML.png`

Example 8: Tuple

Amazon, **Google**

Problem: Design a tuple data structure.

What to ask: A tuple can have from 1 to *n* elements. So, what kind of tuple do you expect? What data types should be stored in the tuple?

Interviewer: I am expecting a tuple with two generic elements. The tuple is also known as a *pair*.

Solution: The complete application is named *Tuple*.

Please visit the following link to check the UML: `https://github.com/PacktPublishing/The-Complete-Coding-Interview-Guide-in-Java/tree/master/Chapter06/Tuple`

Example 9: Cinema with a movie ticket booking system

Amazon, **Google**, **Adobe**, **Microsoft**

Problem: Design a cinema with a movie ticket booking system.

What to ask: What is the main structure of the cinema? Does it have multiple cinema rooms? What types of tickets do we have? How do we play a movie (only in a room, just once a day)?

Interviewer: I am expecting a cinema with multiple identical rooms. A movie can run in multiple rooms at the same time and can run multiple times in a day in the same room. There are three types of tickets, simple, silver, and gold, based on the seat type. A movie can be added/removed in a very versatile way (for example, we can remove a movie from certain rooms at certain start times, or we can add a movie to all rooms).

Solution: The complete application is named *MovieTicketBooking*. Please visit the following link to check the UML: `https://github.com/PacktPublishing/The-Complete-Coding-Interview-Guide-in-Java/blob/master/Chapter06/MovieTicketBooking/MovieTicketBookingUML.png`

Example 10: Circular byte buffer

Amazon, **Google**, **Adobe**

Problem: Design a circular byte buffer.

What to ask: It should be resizable?

Interviewer: Yes, it should be resizable. Mainly, I expect you to design the signatures of all methods that you consider necessary.

Solution: The complete application is named *CircularByteBuffer*.

Please visit the following link to check the UML: `https://github.com/PacktPublishing/The-Complete-Coding-Interview-Guide-in-Java/tree/master/Chapter06/CircularByteBuffer`

So far so good! I suggest you try your own designs for the preceding 10 problems as well. Do not consider that the solutions presented are the only ones that are correct. Practice as much as you can by varying the context of the problem and challenge yourself with other problems as well.

The source code bundle for this chapter is available under the name *Chapter06*.

Summary

This chapter covered the most popular questions about OOP fundamentals and 10 design coding challenges that are very popular in interviews. In the first part, we began with OOP concepts (object, class, abstraction, encapsulation, inheritance, polymorphism, association, aggregation, and composition), continued with the SOLID principles, and finished with an amalgam of questions combining OOP Concepts, SOLID principles, and design pattern knowledge. In the second part, we tackled 10 carefully crafted design coding challenges, including designing a jukebox, a vending machine, and the famous hash table.

Practicing these questions and problems will give you the ability to tackle any OOP problem encountered in an interview.

In the next chapter, we will tackle Big O notation and time.

7
Big O Analysis of Algorithms

This chapter covers the most popular metric for analyzing the efficiency and scalability of algorithms—Big O notation—in the context of a technical interview.

There are plenty of articles dedicated to this topic. Some of them are purely mathematical (academic), while others try to explain it with a more friendly approach. The pure mathematical approach is quite hard to digest and not very useful during an interview, so we will go for a more friendly approach that will be much more familiar to interviewers and developers.

Even so, this is not an easy mission because besides being the most popular metric for measuring the efficiency and scalability of algorithms, Big O notation can often also be the thing that you've never been motivated enough to learn about, despite knowing that it's going to show up in every single interview. From juniors to senior warriors, Big O notation is probably the biggest Achilles heel for everyone. However, let's make an effort to turn this Achilles heel into a strong point for our interviews.

We will quickly go over Big O notation and highlight the things that matter the most. Next, we'll jump into examples that have been carefully crafted to cover a wide range of problems, and so by the end of this chapter, you'll be able to determine and express Big O for almost any given snippet of code. Our agenda includes the following:

- Analogy
- Big O complexity time
- The best case, worst case, and expected case
- Big O examples

So, let's start our Big O journey!

Analogy

Imagine a scenario where you've found one of your favorite movies on the internet. You can order it or download it. Since you want to see it as soon as possible, which is the best way to proceed? If you order it, then it will take a day to arrive. If you download it, then it will take half a day to download. So, it is faster to download it. That's the way to go!

But wait! Just when you get ready to download it, you spot the *Lord of the Rings Master Collection* at a great price, and so you think about downloading it as well. Only this time, the download will take 2 days. However, if you place an order, then it will still only take a single day. So, placing an order is faster!

Now, we can conclude that no matters how many items we order, the shipping time remains constant. We call this O(1). This is a constant runtime.

Moreover, we conclude that the download time is directly proportional to the file sizes. We call this O(n). This is an asymptotic runtime.

From day-to-day observations, we can also conclude that online ordering scales better than online downloading.

This is exactly what Big O time means: an asymptotic runtime measurement or an asymptotic function.

As an asymptotic measurement, we are talking about Big O complexity time (this can be complexity space as well).

Big O complexity time

The following diagram reveals that, at some moment in time, O(n) surpasses O(1). So, until O(n) surpasses O(1), we can say that O(n) performs better than O(1):

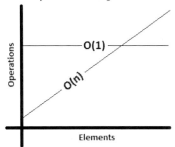

Figure 7.1 – The asymptotic runtime (Big O time)

Besides the O(1)—constant time—and O(n)—linear time runtimes—we have many other runtimes, such as O(log n), O(n log n)—logarithmic time—O(n^2)—quadratic time, O(2^n)— exponential time, and O(n!)—factorial time. These are the most common runtimes, but many more also exist.

The following diagram represents the Big O complexity chart:

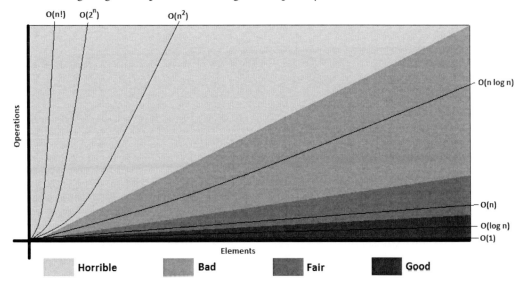

Figure 7.2 – Big O complexity chart

As you can see, not all O times perform the same. O(n!), O(2^n), and O(n^2) are considered **horrible** and we should strive to write algorithms that perform outside this area. O(n log n) is better than O(n!) but is still **bad**. O(n) is considered **fair**, while O(log n) and O(1) are **good**.

Sometimes, we need multiple variables to express the runtime performance. For example, the time for mowing the grass on a soccer field can be expressed as O(*wl*), where *w* is the width of the soccer field and *l* is the length of the soccer field. Or, if you have to mow *p* soccer fields, then you can express it as O(*wlp*).

However, it is not all about time. We care about space as well. For example, building an array of *n* elements needs O(n) space. Building a matrix of *n* x *n* elements needs O(n^2) space.

The best case, worst case, and expected case

If we simplify things, then we can think of the efficiency of our algorithms in terms of *best case*, *worst case*, and *expected case*. The best case is when the input of our algorithms meets some extraordinary conditions that allow it to perform the best. The worst case is at the other extreme, where the input is in an unfavorable shape that makes our algorithm reveal its worst performances. Commonly, however, these amazing or terrible situations won't happen. So, we introduce the expected performance.

Most of the time, we care about the worst and expected cases, which, in the case of most algorithms, are usually the same. The best case is an idealistic performance, and so it remains idealistic. Mainly, for almost any algorithm, we can find a special input that will lead to the O(1) best-case performance.

For more details about Big O, I strongly recommended you read the Big O cheat sheet (https://www.bigocheatsheet.com/).

Now, let's tackle a bunch of examples.

Big O examples

We will try to determine Big O for different snippets of code exactly as you will see at interviews, and we will go through several relevant lessons that need to be learned. In other words, let's adopt a *learning-by-example* approach.

The first six examples will highlight the fundamental rules of Big O, listed as follows:

- Drop constants
- Drop non-dominant terms
- Different input means different variables
- Different steps are summed or multiplied

Let us begin with trying out the examples.

Example 1 – O(1)

Consider the following three snippets of code and compute Big O for each of them:

```
// snippet 1
return 23;
```

Since this code returns a constant, Big O is O(1). Regardless of what the rest of the code does, this line of code will execute at a constant rate:

```
// snippet 2 - 'cars' is an array
int thirdCar = cars[3];
```

Accessing an array by index is accomplished with O(1). Regardless of how many elements are in the array, getting an element from a specific index is a constant operation:

```
// snippet 3 - 'cars' is a 'java.util.Queue'
Car car = cars.peek();
```

The `Queue#peek()` method retrieves but does not remove, the head (first element) of this queue. It doesn't matter how many elements follows the head, the time to retrieve the head via the `peek()` method is O(1).

So, all three snippets in the preceding code block have the O(1) complexity time. Similarly, inserting and removing from a queue, pushing and popping from a stack, inserting a node in a linked list, and retrieving the left/right child of a node of a tree stored in an array are also cases of O(1) time.

Example 2 – O(n), linear time algorithms

Consider the following snippet of code and compute Big O:

```
// snippet 1 - 'a' is an array
for (int i = 0; i < a.length; i++) {
    System.out.println(a[i]);
}
```

In order to determine the Big O value for this snippet of code, we have to answer the following question: *how many times does this `for` loop iterate?* The answer is `a.length` times. We cannot say exactly how much time this means, but we can say that the time will grow linearly with the size of the given array (which represents the input). So, this snippet of code will have an O(`a.length`) time and is known as linear time. It is denoted as O(n).

Example 3 – O(n), dropping the constants

Consider the following snippet of code and compute Big O:

```
// snippet 1 - 'a' is an array
for (int i = 0; i < a.length; i++) {

    System.out.println("Current element:");
    System.out.println(a[i]);
    System.out.println("Current element + 1:");
    System.out.println(a[i] + 1);
}
```

Even if we added more instructions to the loop, we would still have the same runtime as in *Example 2*. The runtime will still be linear in the size of its input, a.length. As in *Example 2* we had a single line of code in a loop, while here we have four lines of code in a loop, you might expect Big O to be O(n + 4) or something like that. However, this kind of reasoning is not precise or accurate—it's just wrong! Big O here is still O(n).

> **Important note**
> Keep in mind that Big O doesn't depend on the number of code lines. It depends on the runtime rate of increase, which is not modified by constant-time operations.

Just to reinforce this scenario, let's consider the following two snippets of code, which compute the minimum and maximum of the given array, a:

```
// snippet 1                                // snippet 2
int min = Integer.MAX_VALUE;                int min = Integer.MAX_VALUE;
int max = Integer.MIN_VALUE;                int max = Integer.MIN_VALUE;
for (int i = 0; i < a.length; i++) {        for (int i = 0; i < a.length; i++) {
    if (a[i] < min) {                           if (a[i] < min) {
        min = a[i];                                 min = a[i];
    }                                           }
    if (a[i] > max) {                       }
        max = a[i];
    }                                       for (int i = 0; i < a.length; i++) {
}                                               if (a[i] > max) {
                                                    max = a[i];
                                                }
                                            }
```

7.3 – Code Comparison

Now, which one of these two code snippets runs faster?

The first code snippet uses a single loop, but it has two `if` statements, while the second code snippet uses two loops, but it has one `if` statement per loop.

Thinking like this opens the door to insanity! Counting the statements can continue at a deeper level. For example, we can continue to count the statements (operations) at the compiler level, or we might want to take into consideration the compiler optimizations. Well, that's not what Big O is about!

> **Important note**
> Big O is not about counting the code statements. Its goal is to express the runtime growth for input sizes and express how the runtime scales. In short, Big O just describes the runtime rate of increase.

Moreover, don't fall into the trap of thinking that because the first snippet has one loop, Big O is O(n), while in the case of the second snippet, because it has two loops, Big O is O(2n). Simply remove 2 from *2n* since 2 is a constant!

> **Important note**
> As a rule of thumb, when you express Big O, drop the constants in runtime.

So, both of the preceding snippets have a Big O value of O(n).

Example 4 – dropping the non-dominant terms

Consider the following snippet of code and compute Big O (a is an array):

```
for (int i = 0; i < a.length; i++) {
    System.out.println(a[i]);
}
```
O(n)

```
for (int i = 0; i < a.length; i++) {
    for (int j = 0; j < a.length; j++) {
        System.out.println(a[i] + a[j]);
    }
}
```
O(n^2)

7.4 – Code snippet executed in O(n)

The first `for` loop is executed in O(n), while the second `for` loop is executed in O(n^2). So, we may think that the answer to this problem is O(n) + O(n^2) = O(n + n^2). But this is not true! The rate of increase is given by n^2, while n is a non-dominant term. If the size of the array is increased, then n^2 affects the rate of increase much more than n, and so n is not relevant. Consider a few more examples:

- O(2^n + 2n) -> drop constants and non-dominant terms -> O(2^n).
- O(n + log n) -> drop non-dominant terms -> O(n).
- O(3*n^2 + n + 2*n) -> drop constants and non-dominant terms -> O(n^2).

> **Important note**
> As a rule of thumb, when you express Big O, drop the non-dominant terms.

Next, let's focus on two examples that are a common source of confusion for candidates.

Example 5 – different input means different variables

Consider the following two snippets of code (a and b are arrays). How many variables should be used to express Big O?

```
// snippet 1
for (int i=0; i<a.length; i++) {
}


for (int i=0; i<a.length; i++) {
}
```

```
// snippet 2
for (int i=0; i<a.length; i++) {
}


for (int i=0; i<b.length; i++) {
}
```

7.5 – Code snippets 1 and 2

In the first snippet, we have two `for` loops that loop the same array, a (we have the same input for both loops), and so Big O can be expressed as O(n), where *n* refers to a. In the second code snippet, we also have two `for` loops, but they loop different arrays (we have two inputs, a and b). This time, Big O is not O(n)! What does *n* refer to – a or b? Let's say that *n* refers to a. If we increase the size of b, then O(n) doesn't reflect the runtime rate of increase. Therefore, Big O is the sum of these two runtimes (the runtime of a plus the runtime of b). This means that Big O must refer to both runtimes. For this, we can use two variables that refer to a and to b. So, Big O is expressed as O(a + b). This time, if we increase the size of a and/or b, then O(a + b) captures the runtime rate increase.

> **Important note**
> As a rule of thumb, different inputs mean different variables.

Next, let's see what happens when we add and multiply the algorithm steps.

Example 6 – different steps are summed or multiplied

Consider the following two snippets of code (a and b are arrays). How do you express Big O for each of these snippets?

```
// snippet 1
for (int i=0;i<a.length;i++){
   System.out.println(a[i]);
}

for (int j=0;j<b.length;j++){
   System.out.println(b[j]);
}
```

```
// snippet 2
for (int i=0;i<a.length;i++){
   for (int j=0;j<b.length;j++){
      System.out.println(a[i]+b[j]);
   }
}
```

7.6 – Code snippet a and b

We already know from the previous example that, in the case of the first snippet, Big O is O(a + b). We sum up the runtimes since their work is not interweaved as in the case of the second snippet. So, in the second snippet, we cannot sum up the runtimes since, for each case of a[i], the code loops the b array, and so Big O is O(a * b).

Think twice before deciding between summing and multiplying the runtimes. This is a common mistake made in interviews. Also, it is quite common to not notice that there is more than one input (here, there are two) and to mistakenly express Big O using a single variable. That would be wrong! Always pay attention to how many inputs are present. For each input that affects the runtime rate of increase, you should have a separate variable (see *Example 5*).

> **Important note**
>
> As a rule of thumb, different steps can be summed or multiplied. The runtimes should be summed or multiplied based on the following two statements:
>
> If you describe your algorithm as **it foos and when it's done, it buzzes**, then sum the runtimes.
>
> If you describe your algorithm as **for each time it foos, it buzzes**, then multiply the runtimes.

Now, let's discuss *log n* runtimes.

Example 7 – log n runtimes

Write a snippet of pseudo-code that has Big O as O(log n).

In order to understand the O(log n) runtimes, let's start with the Binary Search algorithm. The Binary Search algorithm details and implementation is available in *Chapter 14, Sorting and Searching*. This algorithm describes the steps for looking for element x in an array, a. Consider a sorted array, a, of 16 elements, such as the following:

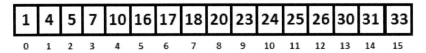

Figure 7.7 – Ordered array of 16 elements

First, we compare x with the midpoint of the array, p. If they are equal, then we return the corresponding array index as the final result. If x > p, then we search on the right side of the array. If x < p, then we search on the left side of the array. The following is a graphical representation of the binary search algorithm for finding the number 17:

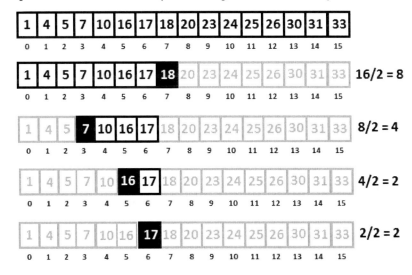

Figure 7.8 – The binary search algorithm

Notice that we start with 16 elements and end with 1. After the first step, we are down to 16/2 = 8 elements. At the second step, we are down to 8/2 = 4 elements. At the third step, we are down to 4/2 = 2 elements. Then, at the last step, we find the searched number, 17. If we translate this algorithm into pseudo-code, then we obtain something as follows:

```
search 17 in {1, 4, 5, 7, 10, 16, 17, 18, 20,
              23, 24, 25, 26, 30, 31, 33}
```

```
        compare 17 to 18 -> 17 < 18
      search 17 in {1, 4, 5, 7, 10, 16, 17, 18}
            compare 17 to 7 -> 17 > 7
           search 17 in {7, 10, 16, 17}
               compare 17 to 16 -> 17 > 16
                  search 17 in {16, 17}
                    compare 17 to 17
                       return
```

Now, let's express Big O for this pseudo-code. We can observe that the algorithm consists of a continuous half-life of the array until only one element remains. So, the total runtime is dependent on how many steps we need in order to find a certain number in the array.

In our example, we had four steps (we halved the array 4 times) that can be expressed as following:

$$16 * \frac{1}{2} = 8; \; 8 * \frac{1}{2} = 4; \; 4 * \frac{1}{2} = 2; \; 2 * \frac{1}{2} = 1$$

Or, if we condense it then we get:

$$16 * \left(\frac{1}{2}\right)^4 = 1$$

One step further, and we can express it for general case as (n is the size of the array, k is the number of steps to reach the solution):

$$n * \left(\frac{1}{2}\right)^k = 1 \equiv n * \frac{1}{2^k} = 1 \equiv 2^k * \frac{n}{2^k} = 2^k \equiv 2^k = n$$

But, $2^k = n$ is exactly what logarithm means - *A quantity representing the power to which a fixed number (the base) must be raised to produce a given number.* So, we can write the follows:

$$2^k = n \; -> \; log_2 n = k$$

In our case, $2^k = n$ means $2^4 = 16$, which is $log_2 16 = 4$.

So, Big O for the Binary Search algorithm is O(log n). However, where is the logarithm base? The short answer is that the logarithm base is not needed for expressing Big O because logs of different bases are only different by a constant factor.

> **Important note**
>
> As a rule of thumb, when you have to express Big O for an algorithm that halves its input at each step/iteration, there are big chances of it being a case of O(log n).

Next, let's talk about evaluating Big O for recursive runtimes.

Example 8 – recursive runtimes

What is Big O for the following snippet of code?

```
int fibonacci(int k) {
    if (k <= 1) {
        return k;
    }

    return fibonacci(k - 2) + fibonacci(k - 1);
}
```

On our first impression, we may express Big O as $O(n^2)$. Most likely, we will reach this result because we are misled by the two calls of the `fibonacci()` method from `return`. However, let's give value to *k* and quickly sketch the runtime. For example, if we call `fibonacci(7)` and we represent the recursive calls as a tree, then we obtain the following diagram:

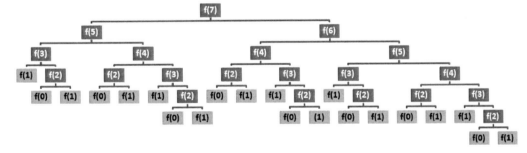

Figure 7.9 – Tree of calls

We almost immediately notice that the depth of this tree is equal to 7, and so the depth of the general tree is equal to *k*. Moreover, with the exception of the terminal levels, each node has two children, and so almost every level has twice the number of calls as the one above it. This means that we can express Big O as $O(branches^{depth})$. In our case, this is $O(2^k)$, denoted $O(2^n)$.

In an interview, just saying $O(2^n)$ should be an acceptable answer. If we want to be more accurate, then we should take into account the terminal levels, especially the last level (or the bottom of the call stack), which can sometimes contain a single call. This means that we don't always have two branches. A more accurate answer would be $O(1.6^n)$. Mentioning that the real value is less than 2 should be enough for any interviewer.

If we want to express Big O in terms of space complexity, then we obtain $O(n)$. Do not be fooled by the fact that the runtime complexity is $O(2^n)$. At any moment, we cannot have more than k numbers. If we look in the preceding tree, we can only see numbers from 1 to 7.

Example 9 – in-order traversal of a binary tree

Consider a given perfect binary search tree. If you need a quick remainder of binary trees then consider the *Nutshell* section of *Chapter 13, Trees and Graphs*. What is Big O for the following snippet of code?

```
void printInOrder(Node node) {
    if (node != null) {
        printInOrder(node.left);
        System.out.print(" " + node.element);
        printInOrder(node.right);
    }
}
```

A perfect binary search tree is a binary search tree whose internal nodes have exactly two children and all the leaf nodes are on the same level or depth. In the following diagram, we have a typical perfect binary search tree (again, visualizing the runtime input is very useful):

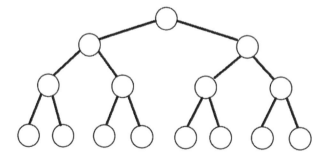

Figure 7.10 – Height-balanced binary search tree

We know from experience (more precisely, from the previous example) that when we face a recursive problem with branches, we can have an O(branches ^{depth}) case. In our case, we have two branches (each node has two children), and so we have O(2^{depth}). Having an exponential time looks weird, but let's see what the relationship between the number of nodes and the depth is. In the preceding diagram, we have 15 nodes and the depth is 4. If we had 7 nodes, then the depth would be 3, and if we had 31 nodes, then the depth would be 5. Now, if we don't already know from the theory that the depth of a perfect binary tree is logarithmic, then maybe we can observe the following:

- For 15 nodes, we have a depth of 4; therefore, we have $2^4 = 16$, equivalent to $\log_2 16 = 4$.
- For 7 nodes, we have a depth of 3; therefore, we have $2^3 = 8$, equivalent to $\log_2 8 = 3$.
- For 31 nodes, we have a depth of 5; therefore, we have $2^5 = 32$, equivalent to $\log_2 32 = 5$.

Based on the preceding observations, we can conclude that we can express Big O as O($2^{\log n}$) since the depth is roughly *log n*. So, we can write the following:

$$2^{\log n} = X \equiv log_2 X = \log n \equiv X = n \equiv O(X) = O(n)$$

Figure 7.11 – Big O expression

So, Big O in this case is O(n). We could reach the same conclusion if we recognized that this code is in fact the In-Order traversal of a binary tree, and in this traversal (exactly as in case of Pre-Order and Post-Order traversals), each node is visited a single time. Moreover, for each traversed node, there is a constant amount of work, and so Big O is O(n).

Example 10 – n may vary

What is Big O for the following snippet of code?

```
void printFibonacci(int k) {
    for (int i = 0; i < k; i++) {
        System.out.println(i + ": " + fibonacci(i));
    }
}

int fibonacci(int k) {
```

```
        if (k <= 1) {
            return k;
        }

        return fibonacci(k - 2) + fibonacci(k - 1);
}
```

From *Example 8*, we already know that the Big O value of the `fibonacci()` method is $O(2^n)$. `printFibonacci()` calls `fibonacci()` *n* times, so it is very tempting to express the total Big O value as $O(n)*O(2^n) = O(n2^n)$. However, is this true or have we rushed to give an apparently easy answer?

Well, the trick here is that *n* varies. For example, let's visualize the runtime:

$$
\begin{aligned}
i = 0 &\to \text{fibonacci}(0) \to 2^0 \text{ steps} \\
i = 1 &\to \text{fibonacci}(1) \to 2^1 \text{ steps} \\
i = 2 &\to \text{fibonacci}(2) \to 2^2 \text{ steps} \\
&\ldots \\
i = k-1 &\to \text{fibonacci}(k) \to 2^{k-1} \text{ steps}
\end{aligned}
\right\} = 2^0 + 2^1 + 2^2 + \ldots + 2^{k-1} \text{ steps}
$$

We cannot say that we execute the same code *n* times, so this is $O(2^n)$.

Example 11 – memoization

What is Big O for the following snippet of code?

```
void printFibonacci(int k) {
        int[] cache = new int[k];
        for (int i = 0; i < k; i++) {
                System.out.println(i + ": " + fibonacci(i, cache));
        }
}

int fibonacci(int k, int[] cache) {
        if (k <= 1) {
            return k;
        } else if (cache[k] > 0) {
            return cache[k];
```

```
        }

        cache[k] = fibonacci(k - 2, cache)
            + fibonacci(k - 1, cache);

    return cache[k];
}
```

This code computes the Fibonacci number via recursion. However, this code uses a technique known as *Memoization*. Mainly, the idea is to cache the return value and use it to reduce recursive calls. We already know from *Example 8* that Big O of the `fibonacci()` method is $O(2^n)$. Since *Memoization* should reduce recursive calls (it introduces an optimization), we can guess that Big O of this code should do better than $O(2^n)$. However, this is just an intuition, so let's visualize the runtime for $k = 7$:

```
Calling fibonacci(0):
Result of fibonacci(0) is 0

Calling fibonacci(1):
Result of fibonacci(1) is 1

Calling fibonacci(2):
    fibonacci(0)
    fibonacci(1)
    fibonacci(2) is computed and cached at cache[2]
Result of fibonacci(2) is 1

Calling fibonacci(3):
    fibonacci(1)
    fibonacci(2) is fetched from cache[2] as: 1
    fibonacci(3) is computed and cached at cache[3]
Result of fibonacci(3) is 2

Calling fibonacci(4):
    fibonacci(2) is fetched from cache[2] as: 1
    fibonacci(3) is fetched from cache[3] as: 2
    fibonacci(4) is computed and cached at cache[4]
Result of fibonacci(4) is 3
```

```
Calling fibonacci(5):
    fibonacci(3) is fetched from cache[3] as: 2
    fibonacci(4) is fetched from cache[4] as: 3
    fibonacci(5) is computed and cached at cache[5]
Result of fibonacci(5) is 5

Calling fibonacci(6):
    fibonacci(4) is fetched from cache[4] as: 3
    fibonacci(5) is fetched from cache[5] as: 5
    fibonacci(6) is computed and cached at cache[6]
Result of fibonacci(6) is 8
```

Each `fibonacci(k)` method is computed from the cached `fibonacci(k-1)` and `fibonacci(k-2)` methods. Fetching the computed values from the cache and summing them is a constant time work. Since we do this work *k* times, this means that Big O can be expressed as O(n).

Besides *Memoization*, we can use another approach, known as *Tabulation*. More details are available in *Chapter 8, Recursion and Dynamic Programming*.

Example 12 – looping half of the matrix

What is Big O for the following two snippets of code (a is an array)?

```
// snippet 1                              // snippet 2
for (int i=0;i<a.length;i++){             for (int i=0;i<a.length;i++){
  for (int j=0;j<a.length;j++){             for (int j=i+1;j<a.length;j++){
    System.out.println(a[i]+a[j]);            System.out.println(a[i]+a[j]);
  }                                         }
}                                         }
```

7.12 – Code snippets for Big O

These snippets of code are almost identical, except that in the first snippet, `j` starts from 0, while in the second snippet, it starts from `i+1`.

We can easily give value to the array size and visualize the runtime of these two snippets of code. For example, let's consider that the array size is 5. The left-hand matrix is the runtime of the first snippet of code, while the right-hand matrix corresponds to the runtime of the second snippet of code:

                            a.length = 5

(0, 0) (0, 1) (0, 2) (0, 3) (0, 4)	(0, 1) (0, 2) (0, 3) (0, 4)
(1, 0) (1, 1) (1, 2) (1, 3) (1, 4)	(1, 2) (1, 3) (1, 4)
(2, 0) (2, 1) (2, 2) (2, 3) (2, 4)	(2, 3) (2, 4)
(3, 0) (3, 1) (3, 2) (3, 3) (3, 4)	(3, 4)
(4, 0) (4, 1) (4, 2) (4, 3) (4, 4)	

Figure 7.13 – Visualizing the runtime

The matrix corresponding to the first snippet of code reveals an $n*n$ size, while the matrix corresponding to the second snippet of code roughly reveals an $n*n/2$ size. So, we can write the following:

- Snippet 1 runtime is: $n * n = n^2 \equiv O(n^2)$.
- Snippet 2 runtime is: $\frac{n*n}{2} = \frac{n^2}{2} = n^2 * \frac{1}{2} \equiv O(n^2)$ since we eliminate constants.

So, both snippets of code have $O(n^2)$.

Alternatively, you can think of it like this:

- For the first snippet, the inner loop doesn't work and it is run n times by the outer loop, and so $n*n = n^2$, results in $O(n^2)$.
- For the second snippet, the inner loop does roughly $n/2$ work and it is run n times by the outer loop, so $n*n/2 = n^2/2 = n^2 * 1/2$, which results in (after removing the constants) $O(n^2)$.

Example 13 – identifying O(1) loops

What is Big O for the following snippet of code (a is an array)?

```
for (int i = 0; i < a.length; i++) {
    for (int j = 0; j < a.length; j++) {
        for (int q = 0; q < 1_000_000; q++) {
            System.out.println(a[i] + a[j]);
        }
    }
}
```

If we ignore the third loop (the q loop), then we already know that Big O is O(n²). So, how does the third loop influence the total Big O value? The third loop iterates from 0 to 1 million, independent of the array size, and so Big O for this loop is O(1), which is a constant. Since the third loop doesn't depend on how the input size varies, we can write it as follows:

```
for (int i = 0; i < a.length; i++) {
    for (int j = 0; j < a.length; j++) {
        // O(1)
    }
}
```

Now, it is clear that Big O for this example is O(n²).

Example 14 – looping half of the array

What is Big O for the following snippet of code (a is an array)?

```
for (int i = 0; i < a.length / 2; i++) {
    System.out.println(a[i]);
}
```

Confusion here can be caused by the fact that this snippet loops only half of the array. Don't make the common mistake of expressing Big O as O(n/2). Remember that constants should be removed, and so Big O is O(n). Iterating only half of the array doesn't impact the Big O time.

Example 15 – reducing Big O expressions

Which of the following can be expressed as O(n)?

- O(n + p)
- O(n + log n)

The answer is that O(n + log n) can be reduced to O(n) because *log n* is a non-dominant term and it can be removed. On the other hand, O(n + p) cannot be reduced to O(n) because we don't know anything about *p*. Until we establish what *p* is and what the relationship between *n* and *p* is, we have to keep both of them.

Example 16 – looping with O(log n)

What is Big O for the following snippet of code (a is an array)?

```
for (int i = 0; i < a.length; i++) {
    for (int j = a.length; j > 0; j /= 2) {
        System.out.println(a[i] + ", " + j);
    }
}
```

Let's just focus on the outer loop. Based on the experiences from the previous examples, we can quickly express Big O as O(n).

How about the inner loop? We can notice that j starts from the array length and, at each iteration, it is halved. Remember the important note from *Example 7* that say: *When you have to express Big O for an algorithm that halves its input at each step, there are big chances to be in a O(log n) case.*

> **Important note**
> Whenever you think that there are big chances of it being a case of O(log n), it is advised that you use test numbers that are powers of the divisor. If the input is divided by 2 (it is halved), then use numbers that are a power of 2 (for example, $2^3 = 8$, $2^4 = 16$, $2^5 = 32$, and so on). If the input is divided by 3, then use numbers that are a power of 3 (for example, $3^2 = 9$, $3^3 = 27$, and so on). This way, it is easy to count the number of divisions.

So, let's give value to a.length and visualize the runtime. Let's say that a.length is 16. This means that j will take the 12, 8, 4, 2, and 1 values. We have divided j by 2 exactly four times, so we have the following:

$$2^4 = 16 \equiv log_2 16 = 4$$

Figure 7.14 – Loop with O (log n)

So, Big O for the inner loop is O(log n). To compute the total Big O, we consider that the outer loop is executed *n* times, and within that loop, another loop is executed *log n* times. So, the total Big O result is O(n)* O (log n) = O(n log n).

As a tip, a lot of sorting algorithms (for example, Merge Sort and Heap Sort) have the O(n log n) runtime. Moreover, a lot of O(n log n) algorithms are recursive. Generally speaking, algorithms that are classified under the **Divide and Conquer** (**D&C**) category of algorithms are O(n log n). Hopefully, keeping these tips in mind will be very handy in interviews.

Example 17 – string comparison

What is Big O for the following snippet of code? (note that a is an array, and be sure to carefully read the comments):

```
String[] sortArrayOfString(String[] a) {
    for (int i = 0; i < a.length; i++) {
        // sort each string via O(n log n) algorithm
    }

    // sort the array itself via O(n log n) algorithm

    return a;
}
```

sortArrayOfString() receives an array of String and performs two major actions. It sorts each string from this array and the array itself. Both sorts are accomplished via algorithms whose runtime is expressed as O(n log n).

Now, let's focus on the for loop and see the wrong answer that is commonly given by candidates. We already know that sorting a single string gives us O(n log n). Doing this for each string means O(n) * (n log n) = O(n*n log n) = O(n^2 log n). Next, we sort the array itself, which is also given as O(n log n). Putting all of the results together, the total Big O value is O(n^2 log n) + O(n log n) = O(n^2 log n + n log n), which is O(n^2 log n) since *n log n* is a non-dominant term. However, is this correct? The short answer is no! But why not?! There are two major mistakes that we've done: we've used *n* to represent two things (the size of the array and the length of the string) and we assumed that comparing String requires a constant time as is the case for fixed-width integers.

Let's detail the first problem. So, sorting a single string gives us O(n log n), where *n* represents the length of that string. We sort a.length strings, so *n* now represents the size of the array. This is where the confusion comes from, because when we say that the for loop is O(n^2 log n), to which *n* are we referring to? Since we are working with two variables, we need to denote them differently. For example, we can consider the following:

- *s*: The length of the longest String.
- *p*: The size of the array of String.

In these terms, sorting a single string is O(s log s), and doing this *p* times results in O(p)*O(s log s) = O(p*s log s).

Now, let's tackle the second problem. In our new terms, sorting the array is O(p log p) – I've just replaced *n* with *p*. However, does the comparison of String require a constant time as is the case of fixed-width integers? The answer is no! String sorting changes O(p log p) because the String comparison itself has a variable cost. The length of String varies, and so the comparison time varies as well. So, in our case, each String comparison takes O(s), and since we have O(p log p) comparisons, it results that sorting the array of strings is O(s) * O(p log p) = O(s*p log p).

Finally, we have to add O(p*s log s) to O(s*p log p) = O(s*p(log s + log p)). Done!

Example 18 – factorial Big O

What is Big O for the following snippet of code?

```
long factorial(int num) {
    if (num >= 1) {
        return num * factorial(num - 1);
    } else {
        return 1;
    }
}
```

It is obvious that this snippet of code is a recursive implementation of computing factorials. Don't do the common mistake of thinking that Big O is O(n!). This is not true! Always analyze the code carefully without prior assumption.

The recursive process traverses the sequence *n*–1, *n*–2, ... 1 times; therefore, this is O(n).

Example 19 – using n notation with caution

What is Big O for the following two snippets of code?

```
int multiply(int x, int y) {         int powerxy(int x, int y) {
    int result = 1;                      if (y < 0) {
    for (int i=1; i<=y; i++) {               return 0;
        result *= x;                     } else if (y == 0) {
    }                                        return 1;
                                         } else {
    return result;                           return x*powerxy(x, y-1);
}                                        }
                                     }
```

7.15 – Code snippets

The first snippet (on the left-side hand) does constant work for y times. The x input doesn't affect the runtime rate of increase, and so Big O can be expressed as O(y). Pay attention to the fact that we don't say O(n) since n can be confused with x as well.

The second snippet (on the right-side hand) recursively traverses y-1, y-2, ..., 0. Each y input is traversed a single time, so Big O can be expressed as O(y). Again, the x input doesn't affect the runtime rate of increase. Moreover, we avoid saying O(n) since there is more than one input and O(n) will create confusion.

Example 20 – the sum and count

What is Big O for the following snippet of code (x and y are positive)?

```
int div(int x, int y) {
    int count = 0;
    int sum = y;
    while (sum <= x) {
        sum += y;
        count++;
    }

    return count;
}
```

Let's give values to x and y and watch the count variable, which counts the number of iterations. Consider that x=10 and y=2. For this scenario, count will be 5 (10/2 = 5). Following the same logic, we have x=14, y=4, count=3 (14/4 = 3.5), or x=22, y=3, or count=7 (22/3 = 7.3). We can notice that in the worst-case scenario, count is x/y, and so Big O can be expressed as O(x/y).

Example 21 – the number of iteration counts in Big O

The following snippet of code tries to guess the square root of a number. What is Big O?

```
int sqrt(int n) {
    for (int guess = 1; guess * guess <= n; guess++) {
        if (guess * guess == n) {
            return guess;
        }
    }
    return -1;
}
```

Let's consider that the number (n) is a perfect square root, such as 144, and we already know that sqrt(144) = 12. Since the guess variable starts from 1 and stops at guess*guess <= n with step 1, it is quite simple to compute that guess will take the values 1, 2, 3, ... , 12. When guess is 12, we have 12*12 = 144, and the loop stops. So, we had 12 iterations, which is exactly sqrt(144).

We follow the same logic for a non-perfect square root. Let's consider that n is 15. This time, guess will take the 1, 2, and 3 values. When guess=4, we have 4*4 > 15 and the loop stops. The returned value is -1. So, we had 3 iterations.

In conclusion, we have sqrt(n) iterations, so Big O can be expressed as O(sqrt(n)).

Example 22 – digits

The following snippet of code sum up the digits of an integer What is Big O?

```
int sumDigits(int n) {
    int result = 0;
    while (n > 0) {
        result += n % 10;
        n /= 10;
```

```
        }

        return result;
}
```

At each iteration, n is divided by 10. This way, the code isolates a digit in the right-side of the number (for example, 56643/10 = 5664.3). To traverse all the digits, the `while` loop needs a number of iterations equal to the number of digits (for example, for 56,643 it needs 5 iterations to isolate 3, 4, 6, 6, and 5).

However, a number with 5 digits can be up to 10^5 = 100,000, which means 99,999 iterations. Generally speaking, this means a number (n) with *d* digits can be up to 10^d. So, we can say the following:

$$10^d = n \equiv log_2 n = d \equiv O(\log n)$$

Figure 7.16 – Digits relationship

Example 23 – sorting

What is Big O for the following snippet of code?

```
boolean matching(int[] x, int[] y) {
    mergesort(y);

    for (int i : x) {
        if (binarySearch(y, i) >= 0) {
            return true;
        }
    }

    return false;
}
```

In *Example 16*, we said that a lot of sorting algorithms (including Merge Sort) have a runtime of O(n log n). This means that `mergesort(y)` has a runtime of O(y log y).

In *Example 7*, we said that the Binary Search algorithm has a runtime of O(log n). This means that `binarySearch(y, i)` has a runtime of O(log y). In the worst-case scenario, the `for` loop will iterate the whole x array, and so the binary search algorithm will be executed `x.length` times. The `for` loop will have a runtime of O(x log y).

So, the total Big O value can be expressed as O(y log y) + O(x log y) = O(y log y + x log y).

Done! This was the last example presented here. Next, let's try to extract several key hints that can help you in interviews to determine and express Big O.

Key hints to look for in an interview

During an interview, time and stress are serious factors that can affect concentration. Having the capacity to identify templates, recognize certain cases, guess the correct answer, and so on gives you a major advantage. As we stated in *Chapter 5, How to Approach a Coding Challenge,* in *figure 5.2,* building an example (or a use case) is the second step to tackling a coding challenge. Even if the code is given by the interviewer, building an example is still quite useful for determining Big O.

As you probably noticed, in almost every non-trivial example that we covered, we preferred to visualize the runtime for one or several concrete cases. That way, you can really understand the details of the code, identify the inputs, determine the static (constant) and dynamic (variable) parts of the code, and get a general view of how the code works.

The following is a non-exhaustive list of key hints that can help you in an interview:

- **If the algorithm does constant work, then the Big O is O(1)**: This kind of example uses the inputs to perform constant work (for example, take three integers, x, y, and w, and do some computations, such as x-y and y*w). In some cases, to create confusion, it adds repetitive statement as well (for example, the computations are done in for(int i=0; i<10; i++)). So, it is very important to settle right from the start whether the inputs of the algorithm affect its runtime or not.

- **If the algorithm loops the entire array or list, then O(n) may be involved in the total Big O value**: Commonly, the code snippets contain one or more repetitive statements that loop the whole input, which is usually an array or list (for example, for(int i=0; i<a.length; i++), where a is an array). Typically, these structures have a runtime of O(n). In some cases, to create confusion, the repetitive structure adds a condition that validates a break statement. Remember that Big O is about the worst-case scenario, so you should evaluate the runtime keeping in mind that the condition that validates the break statement may never happen and Big O is still O(n).

- **If, at each iteration, the algorithm halves the input data, then O(log n) may be involved in the total Big O value**: As you saw in *Example 7,* the Binary Search algorithm is a famous case of O(log n). Typically, you can identify similar cases by trying to visualize the runtime.

- **A recursive problem of having branches is a good signal that O(branches ^{depth}) might be part of the total Big O value**: The most common case where O(2^{depth}) is encountered is in snippets of code that manipulate binary trees. Pay attention to how you determine the *depth* as well. As you saw in *Example 9*, the *depth* can influence the final result. In that case, O($2^{\log n}$) was reduced to O(n).

- **Recursive algorithms that use Memoization or Tabulation are good candidates for having O(n) as their total Big O value**: Typically, recursive algorithms expose exponential runtimes (for example, O(2^n)) but optimizations such as *Memoization* and *Tabulation* may reduce the runtime to O(n).

- **Sort algorithms commonly introduce O(n log n) in the total Big O value**: Keep in mind that a lot of sorting algorithms (for example, Heap Sort, Merge Sort, and so on) have a runtime of O(n log n).

I hope these hints help you as we have covered some very tried and tested examples.

Summary

In this chapter, we covered one of the most predominant topics in an interview, Big O. Sometimes, you'll have to determine Big O for a given code, while other times, you'll have to determine it for your own code. In other words, there is little chance of bypassing Big O in an interview. No matter how hard you train, Big O always remains a hard topic that can put even the best developers in trouble. Fortunately, the cases covered here are the most popular in interviews and they represent perfect templates for a lot of derived problems.

In the next chapter, we will tackle other favored topics in interviews: recursion and Dynamic Programming.

8
Recursion and Dynamic Programming

This chapter covers one of the favorite topics of interviewers: Recursion and Dynamic Programming. Both work hand in hand, so you must be able to cover both. Commonly, the interviewer expects to see a plain recursive solution. However, they may ask you to provide some optimization hints or even to code an optimized version of your code. In other words, your interviewer will want to see Dynamic Programming at work.

In this chapter, we will cover the following topics:

- Recursion in a nutshell
- Dynamic Programming in a nutshell
- Coding challenges

By the end of this chapter, you will be able to implement a wide range of recursive algorithms. You'll have a significant number of recursive patterns and approaches you can use to recognize and implement recursive algorithms in minutes in your toolbelt. Let's start with the first topic of our agenda: recursion.

Technical requirements

You will find all the code presented in this chapter on GitHub at https://github.com/PacktPublishing/The-Complete-Coding-Interview-Guide-in-Java/tree/master/Chapter08.

Recursion in a nutshell

A method that calls itself directly/indirectly is called recursion. This method is known as a recursive method. The famous Fibonacci numbers problem can be implemented recursively, as follows:

```
int fibonacci(int k) {

    // base case
    if (k <= 1) {
        return k;
    }

    // recursive call
    return fibonacci(k - 2) + fibonacci(k - 1);
}
```

There are two important parts in this code:

- **Base case**: Returns a value without subsequent recursive calls. For special input(s), the function can be evaluated without recursion.
- **Recursive call**: Since the `fibonacci()` method calls itself, we have a recursive method.

Recognizing a recursive problem

Before we try to solve a problem via a recursive algorithm, we must recognize it as a good candidate for such an algorithm. Most of the recursive problems used in interviews are famous, so we recognize them by name. For example, problems such as Fibonacci numbers, summing a list of numbers, greatest common divisor, the factorial of a number, recursive Binary Search, reversing a string, and so on are well-known recursive problems.

But what do all these problems have in common? Once we know the answer to this question, we will be able to recognize other recursive problems as well. The answer is quite simple: all these problems can be built off of sub-problems. In other words, we say that we can express the value returned by a method in terms of other values returned by that method.

> **Important Note**
> When a problem can be built off sub-problems, it is a good candidate for being solved recursively. Typically, such problems include the words *list top/last n ...*, *compute the nth or all...*, *count/find all solutions that ...*, *generate all cases that ...*, and so on. In order to compute *the nth...*, we must compute n^{th-1}, n^{th-2}, and so on so that we can divide the problem into sub-problems. In other words, computing f(n) requires computing f(n-1), f(n-2), and so on.
>
> *Practice* is the keyword in recognizing and solving recursive problems. Solving a lot of recursive problems will help you recognize them just as easily as you blink.

Next, we'll highlight the main aspects of Dynamic Programming and learn how to optimize plain recursion via Dynamic Programming.

Dynamic Programming in a nutshell

When we talk about optimizing recursion, we talk about Dynamic Programming. This means that solving recursive problems can be done using plain recursive algorithms or Dynamic Programming.

Now, let's apply Dynamic Programming to the Fibonacci numbers, starting with the plain recursive algorithm:

```
int fibonacci(int k) {
    if (k <= 1) {
        return k;
    }

    return fibonacci(k - 2) + fibonacci(k - 1);
}
```

The plain recursive algorithm for the Fibonacci numbers has a runtime of $O(2^n)$ and a space complexity of $O(n)$ – you can find the explanation in *Chapter 7, Big O Analysis of Algorithms*. If we set *k*=7 and represent the call stack as a tree of calls, then we obtain the following diagram:

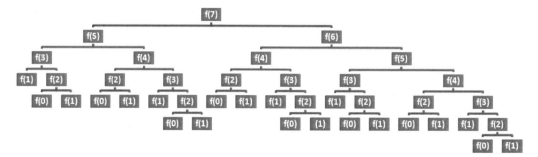

Figure 8.1 – Tree of calls (plain recursion)

If we check the Big O chart from *Chapter 7, Big O Analysis of Algorithms*, then we'll notice that $O(2^n)$ is far from being efficient. Exponential runtimes fit the **Horrible** area of the Big O chart. Can we do this better? Yes, via the *Memoization* approach.

Memoization (or Top-Down Dynamic Programming)

When a recursive algorithm has repeated calls for the same inputs, this indicates that it performs duplicate work. In other words, a recursive problem may have overlapping sub-problems, so the road to the solution involves solving the same sub-problem multiple times. For example, if we redraw the tree of calls for Fibonacci numbers and we highlight the overlapping problems, then we obtain the following diagram:

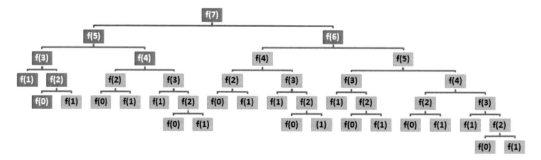

Figure 8.2 – Tree of calls (duplicate work)

It is obvious that more than half of the calls are duplicate calls.

Memoization is a technique that's used to remove duplicate work in a method. It guarantees that a method is called for the same input only once. To achieve this, *Memoization* caches the results of the given inputs. This means that, when the method should be called to compute an input that has already been computed, *Memoization* will avoid this call by returning the result from the cache.

The following code uses *Memoization* to optimize the plain recursive algorithm for the Fibonacci numbers (the cache is represented by the `cache` array):

```
int fibonacci(int k) {
    return fibonacci(k, new int[k + 1]);
}

int fibonacci(int k, int[] cache) {

    if (k <= 1) {
        return k;
    } else if (cache[k] > 0) {
        return cache[k];
    }

    cache[k] = fibonacci(k - 2, cache)
        + fibonacci(k - 1, cache);

    return cache[k];
}
```

If we redraw the tree of calls from the preceding code, then we obtain the following diagram:

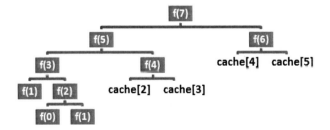

Figure 8.3 – Tree of calls (Memoization)

Here, it is obvious that *Memoization* has drastically reduced the number of recursive calls. This time, the `fibonacci()` method take advantage of cached results. The runtime was reduced from $O(2^n)$ to $O(n)$, so from exponential to polynomial.

> **Important note**
>
> *Memoization* is also referred to as a *Top-Down* approach. The *Top-Down* approach is not very intuitive because we start developing the final solution immediately by explaining how we develop it from smaller solutions. This is like saying the following:
>
> *I wrote a book. How? I wrote its chapters. How? I wrote the sections of each chapter. How? I wrote the paragraphs of each section.*

The space complexity remains $O(n)$. Can we improve it? Yes, via the *Tabulation* approach.

Tabulation (or Bottom-Up Dynamic Programming)

Tabulation, or the *Bottom-Up* approach, is more intuitive than *Top-Down*. Essentially, a recursive algorithm (often) starts from the end and works backward, while a *Bottom-Up* algorithm starts right from the beginning. The *Bottom-Up* approach avoids recursion and improves space complexity.

> **Important note**
>
> *Tabulation* is commonly referred to as a *Bottom-Up* approach. Going bottom-up is an approach that avoids recursion and is quite natural. It's like saying the following:
>
> *I wrote the paragraphs of each section. And? And I wrote the sections of each chapter. And? And I wrote all the chapters. And? And I wrote a book.*
>
> *Bottom-Up* reduces the memory cost imposed by recursion when it builds up the call stack, which means that *Bottom-Up* eliminates the vulnerability of getting stack overflow errors. This may happen if the call stack gets too large and runs out of space.

For example, when we compute `fibonacci(k)` via the recursive approach, we start with *k* and continue with *k-1*, *k-2*, and so on until 0. With the *Bottom-Up* approach, we start with 0 and continue with 1, 2, and so on until *k*. As shown in the following code, this is an iterative approach:

```
int fibonacci(int k) {

    if (k <= 1) {
```

```
        return k;
    }

    int first = 1;
    int second = 0;
    int result = 0;

    for (int i = 1; i < k; i++) {
        result = first + second;
        second = first;
        first = result;
    }

    return result;
}
```

The runtime of this algorithm is still O(n), but the space complexity was brought down from O(n) to O(1). So, to recap the Fibonacci numbers algorithms, we have that the following:

- The **plain recursion** algorithm has a runtime of $O(2^n)$ and a space complexity of O(n).
- The **Memoization recursion** algorithm has a runtime of O(n) and a space complexity of O(n).
- The **Tabulation** algorithm has a runtime of O(n) and a space complexity of O(1).

Now, it's time to practice some coding challenges.

Coding challenges

In the following 15 coding challenges, we will exploit recursion and Dynamic Programming. These problems have been carefully crafted to help you understand and cover a wide range of problems from this category. By the end of this coding challenge session, you should be able to recognize and solve recursive problems in the context of an interview.

Coding challenge 1 – Robot grid (I)

Adobe, Microsoft

Problem: We have an *m* x *n* grid. A robot is placed at the top-left corner of this grid. The robot can only move either right or down at any point in time, but it is not allowed to move in certain cells. The robot's goal is to find a path from the top-left corner to the bottom-right corner of the grid.

Solution: First, we need to set some conventions of the *m* x *n* grid. Let's assume that the bottom-right corner has the coordinates (0, 0), while the top-left corner has the coordinates (*m*, *n*), where *m* is the row and *n* is the column of the grid. So, the robot starts from (*m*, *n*) and must find a path to (0, 0). If we try to sketch an example for a 6x6 grid, then we can obtain something like the following:

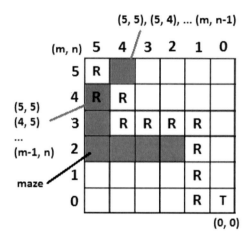

Figure 8.4 – Determining the moving pattern

Here, we can see that the robot can go from one cell (*m*, *n*) to an adjacent cell, which can be (*m*-1, *n*) or (*m*, *n*-1). For example, if the robot is placed at (5, 5), then it can go to (4, 5) or (5, 4). Furthermore, from (4, 5), it can go to (3, 5) or (4, 4), while from (5, 4), it can go to (5, 3) or (4, 4).

So, we have a problem that can be divided into sub-problems. We must find the final path for the cells (the problem), which we can do if we are able to find the path to an adjacent cell (sub-problem). This sounds like a recursive algorithm. In recursion, we approach the problem from top to down, so we start from (*m*, *n*) and move back to the origin (0, 0), as shown in the preceding diagram. This means that from cell (*m*, *n*), we try to go into (*m*, *n*-1) or (*m*-1, *n*).

Putting this into code can be done as follows (the `maze[][]` matrix is a `boolean` matrix that has values of `true` for cells that we are not allowed to go in – for example, `maze[3][1] = true` means that we are not allowed in cell (3,1)):

```
public static boolean computePath(int m, int n,
    boolean[][] maze, Set<Point> path) {

    // we fell off the grid so we return
    if (m < 0 || n < 0) {
        return false;
    }

    // we cannot step at this cell
    if (maze[m][n]) {
        return false;
    }

    // we reached the target
    // (this is the bottom-right corner)
    if (((m == 0) && (n == 0))
        // or, try to go to the right
        || computePath(m, n - 1, maze, path)
        // or, try to go to down
        || computePath(m - 1, n, maze, path)) {

        // we add the cell to the path
        path.add(new Point(m, n));

        return true;
    }

    return false;
}
```

The returned path is stored as a `LinkedHashSet<Point>`. Each path contains *m+n* steps and there are only two valid choices we can make at each step; therefore, the runtime is $O(2^{m+n})$. But we can reduce this runtime to O(mn) if we cache the cells that failed (returned `false`). This way, the *Memoization* approach saves the robot from trying to go in a failed cell multiple times. The complete application is called *RobotGridMaze*. It also contains the *Memoization* code.

Another popular problem of using a robot is as follows. Let's say we have an *m* x *n* grid. A robot is placed at the top-left corner of this grid. The robot can only move either right or down at any point in time. The robot's goal is to find all the unique paths from the top-left corner to the bottom-right corner of the grid.

The plain recursive solution and *Bottom-Up* approach are available in the *RobotGridAllPaths* application.

Coding challenge 2 – Tower of Hanoi

Problem: This is a classical problem that can occur in an interview at any time. The Tower of Hanoi is a problem with three rods (*A, B,* and *C*) and *n* disks. Initially, all the disks are placed in ascending order on a single rod (the largest disk is on the bottom (disk *n*), a smaller one sitting on it (*n-1*), and so on (*n-2, n-3, ...*) until the smallest disk is on the top (disk 1). The aim is to move all the disks from this rod to another rod while respecting the following rules:

- Only one disk can be moved at a time.
- A move means to slide the upper disk from one rod to another rod.
- A disk cannot be placed on top of a smaller disk.

Solution: Trying to solve such problems means that we need to visualize some cases. Let's consider that we want to move the disks from rod *A* to rod *C*. Now, let's put *n* disks on rod *A*:

For *n*=1: Having a single disk, we need to move one disk from rod *A* to *C*.

For *n*=2: We know how to move a single disk. To move two, we need to complete the following steps:

1. Move disk 1 from *A* to *B* (rod *B* acts as an intermediate for disk 1).
2. Move disk 2 from *A* to *C* (disk 2 goes directly in its final place).
3. Move disk 1 from *B* to *C* (disk 1 can be moved on top of disk 2 on rod *C*).

For *n*=3: Let's get some help from the following diagram:

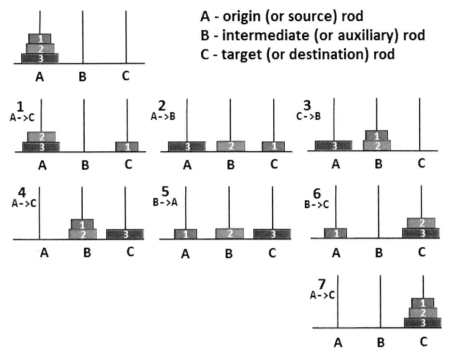

Figure 8.5 – Tower of Hanoi (three disks)

Due to *n*=2, we know how to move the top two disks from *A* (origin) to *C* (target). In other words, we know how to move the top two disks from one rod to another rod. Let's move them from *A* to *B*, as follows:

1. Move disk 1 from *A* to *C* (this time, we use *C* as the intermediate).
2. Move disk 2 from *A* to *B*.
3. Move disk 1 from *C* to *B*.

OK, so this is something that we've done before. Next, we can move disks 2 and 3 onto *C*, as follows:

4. Move disk 3 from *A* to *C*.
5. Move disk 1 from *B* to *A* (we use *A* as the intermediate).
6. Move disk 2 from *B* to *C*.
7. Finally, move disk 3 from *A* to *C*.

Continuing with this logic, we can intuit that we can move four disks because we know how to move three, we can move five disks because we know how to move four, and so on. With rod *A* as the origin, rod *B* as the intermediate, and rod *C* as the target, we can conclude that we can move *n* disks by doing the following:

- Move the top *n* - 1 disks from the origin to the intermediate, using the target as an intermediate.

- Move the top *n* - 1 disks from the intermediate to the target, using the origin as an intermediate.

At this point, it is clear that we have a problem that can be divided into sub-problems. Based on the preceding two bullets, we can code this as follows:

```java
public static void moveDisks(int n, char origin,
    char target, char intermediate) {

    if (n <= 0) {
        return;
    }

    if (n == 1) {
        System.out.println("Move disk 1 from rod "
            + origin + " to rod " + target);
        return;
    }

    // move top n - 1 disks from origin to intermediate,
    // using target as a intermediate
    moveDisks(n - 1, origin, intermediate, target);

    System.out.println("Move disk " + n + " from rod "
            + origin + " to rod " + target);

    // move top n - 1 disks from intermediate to target,
    // using origin as an intermediate
    moveDisks(n - 1, intermediate, target, origin);
}
```

The complete application is called *HanoiTowers*.

Coding challenge 3 – Josephus

Amazon, Google, Adobe, Microsoft, Flipkart

Problem: Consider a group of *n* men arranged in a circle (1, 2, 3, ..., *n*). Every k^{th} man will be killed around the circle until only one survivor remains. Write an algorithm that finds the *k* position of this survivor. This is known as the Josephus problem.

Solution: Remember that we had a note previously saying that when a problem contains the words *compute the nth* and similar expressions, then it is possibly a good candidate for being solved via recursion. Here, we have *find the k position*, which is a problem that can be divided into sub-problems and be solved via recursion.

Let's consider *n*=15 and *k*=3. So, there are 15 men and every third man will be eliminated from the circle until only one remains. Let's visualize this via the following diagram (this is very useful for figuring out the pattern of killings):

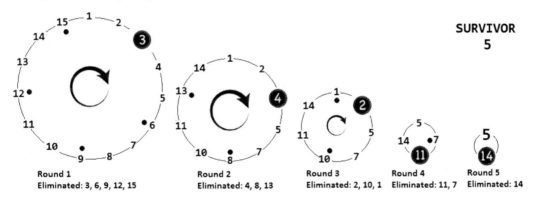

Figure 8.6 – Josephus for n=15 and k=3

So, we have five rounds until we find the survivor, as follows:

- Round 1: The first elimination is position 3; next, 6, 9, 12, and 15 are eliminated.
- Round 2: The first elimination is position 4 (1 and 2 are skipped, since position 15 was the last eliminated in round 1); next, 8 and 13 are eliminated.
- Round 3: The first elimination is position 2 (14 and 1 are skipped, since position 13 was the last eliminated in round 2); next, 10 and 1 are eliminated.
- Round 4: The first elimination position is 11, followed by position 7.
- Round 5: 14 is eliminated and 5 is the survivor.

Trying to identify a pattern or a recursive call can be done based on the following observations. After the first man (k^{th}) is eliminated, n-1 men are left. This means that we call `josephus(n - 1, k)` to get the position of the n-1th man. However, notice that the position returned by `josephus(n - 1, k)` will take into account the position starting from $k\%n + 1$. In other words, we have to adjust the position returned by `josephus(n - 1, k)` to obtain `(josephus(n - 1, k) + k - 1) % n + 1`. The recursive method is shown here:

```
public static int josephus(int n, int k) {
    if (n == 1) {
        return 1;
    } else {
        return (josephus(n - 1, k) + k - 1) % n + 1;
    }
}
```

If you find this approach quite tricky, then you can try an iterative approach based on a queue. First, fill up the queue with *n* men. Next, loop the queue and, for each man, retrieve and remove the head of this queue (`poll()`). If the retrieved man is not the kth, then insert this man back in the queue (`add()`). If this is the kth man, then break the loop and repeat this process until the queue's size is 1. The code for this is as follows:

```
public static void printJosephus(int n, int k) {
    
    Queue<Integer> circle = new ArrayDeque<>();
    
    for (int i = 1; i <= n; i++) {
        circle.add(i);
    }
    
    while (circle.size() != 1) {
        for (int i = 1; i <= k; i++) {
            int eliminated = circle.poll();
            
            if (i == k) {
                System.out.println("Eliminated: "
                    + eliminated);
                break;
            }
```

```
            circle.add(eliminated);
        }
    }

    System.out.println("Using queue! Survivor: "
        + circle.peek());
}
```

The complete application is called *Josephus*.

Coding challenge 4 – Color spots

Amazon, Google, Adobe, Microsoft, Flipkart

Problem: Consider an *r* x *c* grid where *r* stands for rows and *c* stands for columns. Each cell has a color represented by a number *k* (for example, for three colors, *k*=3). We define the connected set of a cell (or a color spot) as the total cells in which we can go from the respective cell by successive displacements on the row or the column, thus keeping the color. The goal is to determine the color and the number of cells of the maximum connected set. In other words, we need to determine the biggest color spot.

Solution: Let's consider a 5x5 grid and three colors, where we have *r*=*c*=5 and *k*=3. Next, let's represent the grid as shown in the following diagrams:

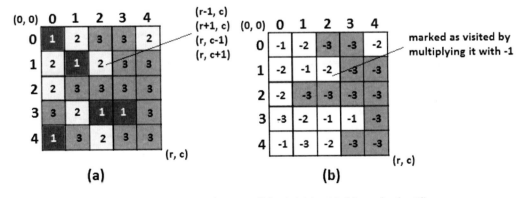

Figure 8.7 – Biggest color spot ((a) – initial grid, (b) – solved grid)

Let's focus on image (a). Here, we can see that moving from a cell to another cell can be done in a maximum of four directions (up, down, left, and right). This means that, from a cell (r,c), we can try to go to (r-1, c), (r+1, c), (r, c-1), and (r, c+1). We cannot perform a move if we risk falling from the grid or the targeted cell has another color than the current cell. So, by iterating each cell ((0, 0), (0, 1), ... (r, c)), we can determine the size of the connected set of that cell (the size of the color spot) by visiting each allowed cell and counting it. In image (a), we have four spots that are color 1 whose sizes are 1, 1, 1, and 2. We also have six spots that are color 2 whose sizes are 1, 1, 2, 1, 1, and 1. Finally, we have three spots that are color 3 whose sizes are 11, 1, and 1.

From this, we can conclude that the biggest color spot has a size of 11 and a color of 3. Mainly, we can consider that the color spot of the first cell is the maximum spot and that each time we find a color spot bigger than this one, we replace this one with the one we found.

Now, let's focus on image (b). Why do we have negative values? Because when we visit a cell, we switch its *color* value to *-color*. This is a convenient convention that's used to avoid computing the same connected set of a cell multiple times. It is like saying that we mark this cell as visited. By convention, we cannot move in a cell that has a negative value for a color, so we will not compute the size of the same color spot twice.

Now, gluing these observations together to make a recursive method leads to the following code:

```java
public class BiggestColorSpot {

    private int currentColorSpot;

    void determineBiggestColorSpot(int cols,
            int rows, int a[][]) {
        ...
    }

    private void computeColorSpot(int i, int j,
            int cols, int rows, int a[][], int color) {

        a[i][j] = -a[i][j];
        currentColorSpot++;

        if (i > 1 && a[i - 1][j] == color) {
```

```
            computeColorSpot(i - 1, j, cols,
                rows, a, color);
        }

        if ((i + 1) < rows && a[i + 1][j] == color) {
            computeColorSpot(i + 1, j, cols, rows, a, color);
        }

        if (j > 1 && a[i][j - 1] == color) {
            computeColorSpot(i, j - 1, cols,
                rows, a, color);
        }

        if ((j + 1) < cols && a[i][j + 1] == color) {
            computeColorSpot(i, j + 1, cols,
                rows, a, color);
        }
    }
}
```

While the preceding recursive method, `computeColorSpot()`, can compute the size of a color spot, starting from the given cell, the following method determines the biggest color spot:

```
void determineBiggestColorSpot(int cols,
        int rows, int a[][]) {

    int biggestColorSpot = 0;
    int color = 0;

    for (int i = 0; i < rows; i++) {
        for (int j = 0; j < cols; j++) {

            if (a[i][j] > 0) {
                currentColorSpot = 0;

                computeColorSpot(i, j, cols,
```

```
                    rows, a, a[i][j]);

                if (currentColorSpot > biggestColorSpot) {
                    biggestColorSpot = currentColorSpot;
                    color = a[i][j] * (-1);
                }
            }
        }
    }

    System.out.println("\nColor: " + color
        + " Biggest spot: " + biggestColorSpot);
}
```

The complete application is called *BiggestColorSpot*.

Coding challenge 5 – Coins

Google, Adobe, Microsoft

Problem: Consider an amount of *n* cents. Count the ways you can change this amount using any number of quarters (25 cents), dimes (10 cents), nickels (5 cents), and pennies (1 cent).

Solution: Let's imagine that we have to change 50 cents. Right from the start, we can see that changing 50 cents is a problem that can be solved via sub-problems. For example, we can change 50 cents using 0, 1, or 2 quarters. Or we can do it using 0, 1, 2, 3, 4, or 5 dimes. We can also do it using 0, 1, 2, 3, 4, 5, 6, 7, 8, 9, or 10 nickels. Finally, we can do it using 0, 1, 2, 3, ..., 50 pennies. Let's assume that we have 1 quarter, 1 dime, 2 nickels, and 5 pennies. We can use our quarter to say the following:

calculateChange(50) = **1 quarters + ...**

But this is like saying the following:

calculateChange(25) = **0 quarters + ...**

We don't have more quarters; therefore, we add a dime:

calculateChange(25) = **0 quarters + 1 dimes + ...**

This can be reduced, as follows:

calculateChange(15) = **0 quarters + 0 dimes + ...**

We don't have any more dimes. We add the nickels:

calculateChange(15) = **0 quarters + 0 dimes + 2 nickel + ...**

This can be reduced to the following:

calculateChange(5) = **0 quarters + 0 dimes + 0 nickel + ...**

Finally, since we don't have more nickels, we add the pennies:

calculateChange(5) = **0 quarters + 0 dimes + 0 nickel + 5 pennies**

This can be reduced to the following:

calculateChange(0) = **0 quarters + 0 dimes + 0 nickel + 0 pennies**

If we try to represent all the possible reductions, we obtain the following diagram:

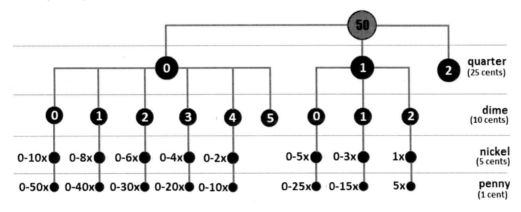

Figure 8.8 – Changing n cents into quarters, dimes, nickels, and pennies

Implementing this reducible algorithm can be done via recursion, as shown in the following code. Notice that we are using *Memoization* to avoid changing the same amount multiple times:

```
public static int calculateChangeMemoization(int n) {
    int[] coins = {25, 10, 5, 1};
    int[][] cache = new int[n + 1][coins.length];

    return calculateChangeMemoization(n, coins, 0, cache);
}

private static int calculateChangeMemoization(int amount,
        int[] coins, int position, int[][] cache) {
```

```
        if (cache[amount][position] > 0) {
            return cache[amount][position];
        }

        if (position >= coins.length - 1) {
            return 1;
        }

        int coin = coins[position];
        int count = 0;
        for (int i = 0; i * coin <= amount; i++) {
            int remaining = amount - i * coin;
            count += calculateChangeMemoization(remaining,
                coins, position + 1, cache);
        }

        cache[amount][position] = count;

        return count;
    }
```

The complete application is called *Coins*. It also contains the plain recursive approach (without *Memoization*).

Coding challenge 6 – Five towers

Problem: Consider a 5x5 grid with five defensive towers spread across the grid. To provide an optimal defense for the grid, we have to build a tower on each row of the grid. Find all the solutions for building these towers so that none of them share the same column and diagonal.

Solution: We know that, on each row, we must build a tower and that it is not important in what order we build them on the grid. Let's sketch a solution and a failure, as follows:

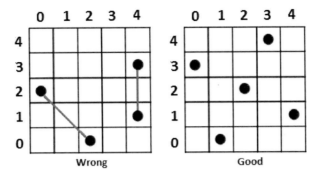

Figure 8.9(a) – Failure and solution

Let's focus on the solution and start from the first row: row 0. We can build a tower on this row in any column; therefore, we can say the following:

- Try to build the first tower at (0, 0), (0,1), (0, 2), (0, 3) or (0,4)
- The first tower can be build at (0, 0), (0,1), (0, 2), (0, 3) or (0,4)
- The first tower was built at (0,2)

Figure 8.9(b): Part 1 of the logic to build the towers

If we continue with the same logic, then we can say the following:

First row:
- Try to build the first tower at (0, 0), (0,1), (0, 2), (0, 3) or (0,4)
- The first tower can be build at (0, 0), (0,1), (0, 2), (0, 3) or (0,4)
  - The first tower was built at (0, 2)
    Second row:
    - Try to build the second tower at (1, 0), (1,1), (1, 2), (1, 3) or (1,4)
    - The second tower can be build at (1, 3) or (1, 4)
    - The second tower was built at (1, 4)
      Third row:
      - Try to build the third tower at (2, 0), (2,1), (2, 2), (2, 3) or (2,4)
      - The third tower can be build at (2, 0) or (2, 2)
      - The third tower was built at (2, 2)
      ...

Figure 8.9(c). Part 2 of the logic to build the towers

So, we start from the first row and build the first tower on (0,0). We go to the second row and try to build the second tower so that we don't share the column or diagonal with the first tower. We go to the third row and try to build the third tower so that we don't share the column or diagonal with the first two towers. We follow the same logic for the fourth and fifth towers. This is our solution. Now, we repeat this logic – we build the first tower at (0,1) and continue building until we find the second solution. Next, we build the first tower at (0, 2), (0, 3) and finally at (0,4) while we repeat the process. We can write this recursive algorithm as follows:

```java
protected static final int GRID_SIZE = 5; // (5x5)

public static void buildTowers(int row, Integer[] columns,
        Set<Integer[]> solutions) {

    if (row == GRID_SIZE) {
        solutions.add(columns.clone());
    } else {
        for (int col = 0; col < GRID_SIZE; col++) {

            if (canBuild(columns, row, col)) {

                // build this tower
                columns[row] = col;

                // go to the next row
                buildTowers(row + 1, columns, solutions);
            }
        }
    }
}

private static boolean canBuild(Integer[] columns,
    int nextRow, int nextColumn) {

    for (int currentRow=0; currentRow<nextRow;
            currentRow++) {
        int currentColumn = columns[currentRow];
```

```
            // cannot build on the same column
            if (currentColumn == nextColumn) {
                return false;
            }

            int columnsDistance
                    = Math.abs(currentColumn - nextColumn);
            int rowsDistance = nextRow - currentRow;

            // cannot build on the same diagonal
            if (columnsDistance == rowsDistance) {
                return false;
            }
        }

        return true;
    }
```

The complete application is called *FiveTowers*.

Coding challenge 7 – Magic index

Adobe, Microsoft

Problem: Consider a sorted array of *n* elements that allows duplicates. An index *k* is magic if *array*[*k*] = *k*. Write a recursive algorithm that finds the first magic index.

Solution: First, let's quickly draw two sorted arrays containing 18 elements, as shown in the following diagram. The array at the top of the image contains no duplicates, while the array at the bottom contains duplicates. This way, we can observe the influence of these duplicates:

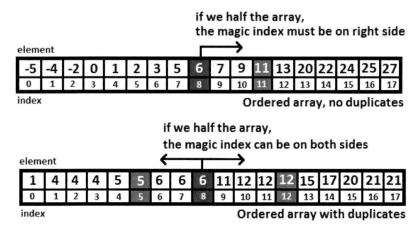

Figure 8.10 – Sorted array of 18 elements

If we halve the array with no duplicates, then we can conclude that the magic index must be on the right-hand side because *array*[8] < 8. This is true since the magic index is 11, so *array*[11] = 11.

If we halve the array with duplicates, we cannot get the same conclusion we received previously. The magic index can be on both sides. Here, we have *array*[5] = 5 and *array*[12] = 12. We must find the first magic index, so we should search the left-hand side first.

But how do we find it? The most obvious approach consists of looping the array and checking if *array*[i] = i. While this works for any ordered array, it will not impress the interviewer since it is not recursive, so we need another approach.

In *Chapter 7, Big O Analysis of Algorithms*, you saw an example of searching in a sorted array via the Binary Search algorithm. This algorithm can be implemented via recursion since, at each step, we halve the previous array and create a sub-problem. Since the indexes of an array are ordered, we can adapt the Binary Search algorithm. The main issue that we face is that duplicated elements complicate the search. When we halve the array, we cannot say that the magic index is on the left or the right, so we have to search in both directions, as shown in the following code (first, we search the left-hand side):

```
public static int find(int[] arr) {
    return find(arr, 0, arr.length - 1);
}
```

```
private static int find(int[] arr,
        int startIndex, int endIndex) {

    if (startIndex > endIndex) {
        return -1; // return an invalid index
    }

    // halved the indexes
    int middleIndex = (startIndex + endIndex) / 2;

    // value (element) of middle index
    int value = arr[middleIndex];

    // check if this is a magic index
    if (value == middleIndex) {
        return middleIndex;
    }

    // search from middle of the array to the left
    int leftIndex = find(arr, startIndex,
            Math.min(middleIndex - 1, value));
    if (leftIndex >= 0) {
        return leftIndex;
    }

    // search from middle of the array to the right
    return find(arr, Math.max(middleIndex + 1,
        value), endIndex);
    }
}
```

The complete application is called *MagicIndex*.

Coding challenge 8 – The falling ball

Problem: Consider an *m* x *n* grid where each (*m*, *n*) cell has an elevation represented by a number between 1 and 5 (5 is the highest elevation). A ball is placed in a cell of the grid. This ball can fall into another cell, as long as that cell has a smaller elevation than the ball cell. The ball can fall in four directions: north, west, east, and south. Display the initial grid, as well as the grid after the ball falls on all possible paths. Mark the paths with 0.

Solution: Always pay attention to the problem requests. Notice that we must display the solved grid, not list the paths or count them. The easiest way to display a grid is to use two loops, as shown in the following code:

```
for (int i = 0; i < rows; i++) {
    for (int j = 0; j < cols; j++) {
        System.out.format("%2s", elevations[i][j]);
    }

    System.out.println();
}
```

Now, let's sketch a 5x5 grid and view an input and its output. The following image shows the initial grid in the form of a 3D model, along with a possible path and the solved grid:

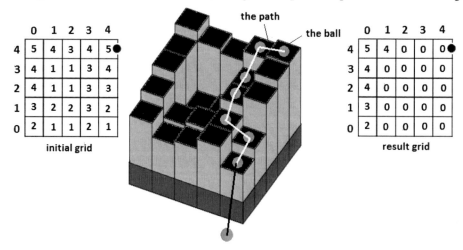

Figure 8.11 – The falling ball

I think we have enough experience to intuit that this problem can be solved via recursion. Mainly, we move the ball in all acceptable directions and mark each visited cell with 0. When we have the ball in the (*i*, *j*) cell, we can go in (*i*-1, *j*), (*i*+1, *j*), (*i*, *j*-1), and (*i*, *j*+1) directions, as long those cells have smaller elevations. In terms of code, we have the following:

```java
public static void computePath(
        int prevElevation, int i, int j,
        int rows, int cols, int[][] elevations) {

    // ensure the ball is still on the grid
    if (i >= 0 && i <= (rows-1) && j >= 0 && j <= (cols-1)) {

        int currentElevation = elevations[i][j];
        // check if the ball can fall
        if (prevElevation >= currentElevation
                && currentElevation > 0) {

            // store the current elevation
            prevElevation = currentElevation;

            // mark this cell as visited
            elevations[i][j] = 0;

            // try to move the ball
            computePath(prevElevation,i,j-1,
                rows,cols,elevations);
            computePath(prevElevation,i-1,
                j,rows,cols,elevations);
            computePath(prevElevation,i,j+1,
                rows,cols,elevations);
            computePath(prevElevation,i+1,j,
                rows,cols,elevations);
        }
    }
}
```

The complete application is called *TheFallingBall*.

Coding challenge 9 – The highest colored tower

Adobe, Microsoft, Flipkart

Problem: Consider n boxes of different widths ($w_{1...n}$), heights ($h_{1...n}$), and colors ($c_{1...n}$). Find the highest tower of boxes that respects the following conditions:

- You cannot rotate the boxes.
- You cannot place two successive boxes of the same color.
- Each box is strictly larger than the box above it in terms of their width and height.

Solution: Let's try to visualize this, as follows:

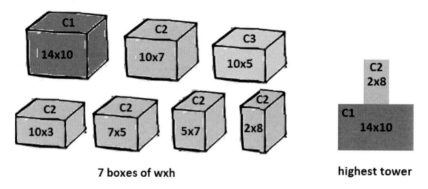

7 boxes of wxh   highest tower

Figure 8.12(a) – The highest colored tower

We have seven boxes of different sizes and colors. We can imagine that the highest tower will contain all these boxes, $b_1...b_7$. But we have several constraints that don't allow us to simply stack the boxes. We can choose one of the boxes as the base box and place another allowed box on top of it, as follows:

- Choose the 14x10 box as the base box
    - On top of 14x10 box we can add the 10x7 box
        - On top of 10x7 box we cannot add another box; the total high is 17
    - On top of 14x10 box we can add the 10x5 box
        - On top of 10x5 we cannot add another box; the total high is 15, therefore we can ignore it since is less than 17
    ...
    - On top of 14x10 box we can add the 2x8
        - On top of 2x8 we cannot add another box; the total high is 18, therefore we update the high to 18, and this is the final result

Figure 8.12(b) The logic to select the boxes to build the highest tower

So, we identified a pattern. We choose a box as the base, and we try to see which of the remaining boxes can go on top as the second level. We do the same for the third level and so on. When we are done (we cannot add more boxes or no boxes are left), we store the size of the highest tower. Next, we repeat this scenario with another base box.

Since every box must be larger in terms of width and height than the box above it, we can sort the boxes by width or height in descending order (it is not important which one we choose). This way, for any tower of $b_0,...b_k$, $k < n$ boxes, we can find the next valid box by searching the $b_{k+1}...n$ interval.

Moreover, we can avoid recalculating the best solution for the same base box by caching the best solutions via *Memoization*:

```java
// Memoization
public static int buildViaMemoization(List<Box> boxes) {

    // sorting boxes by width (you can do it by height as well)
    Collections.sort(boxes, new Comparator<Box>() {
        @Override
        public int compare(Box b1, Box b2) {
            return Integer.compare(b2.getWidth(),
                b1.getWidth());
        }
    });

    // place each box as the base (bottom box) and
    // try to arrange the rest of the boxes
    int highest = 0;
    int[] cache = new int[boxes.size()];
    for (int i = 0; i < boxes.size(); i++) {
        int height = buildMemoization(boxes, i, cache);
        highest = Math.max(highest, height);
    }

    return highest;
}

// Memoization
private static int buildMemoization(List<Box> boxes,
```

```
            int base, int[] cache) {

    if (base < boxes.size() && cache[base] > 0) {
        return cache[base];
    }

    Box current = boxes.get(base);

    int highest = 0;
    // since the boxes are sorted we don't
    // look in [0, base + 1)
    for (int i = base + 1; i < boxes.size(); i++) {
        if (boxes.get(i).canBeNext(current)) {

            int height = buildMemoization(boxes, i, cache);
            highest = Math.max(height, highest);
        }
    }

    highest = highest + current.getHeight();
    cache[base] = highest;

    return highest;
}
```

The complete application is called *HighestColoredTower*. The code also contains the plain recursion approach to this problem (without *Memoization*).

Coding challenge 10 – String permutations

Amazon, Google, Adobe, Microsoft, Flipkart

Problem: Write an algorithm that computes all the permutations of a string and accommodates the following two conditions:

- The given string can contain duplicates.
- The returned list of permutations should not contain duplicates.

Solution: Like in any recursive problem, the key consists of recognizing the relationship and patterns between the different sub-problems. Right away, we can intuit that permuting a string with duplicates should be more complicated than permuting a string with unique characters. This means that we must understand the permutations of a string with unique characters first.

The most natural way of permuting the characters of a string can follow a simple pattern: each character of the string will become the first character of the string (swap their positions) and then permute all the remaining letters using a recursive call. Let's delve into the general case. For a string containing a single character, we have a single permutation:

$P(c_1) = c_1$

If we add another character, then we can express the permutations as follows:

$P(c_1c_2) = c_1c_2$ and c_2c_1

If we add another character, then we must express the permutations using c_1c_2. Each permutation of $c_1c_2c_3$ represents an ordering of c_1c_2, as follows:

$c_1c_2 \rightarrow c_1c_2c_3, c_1c_3c_2, c_3c_1c_2$

$c_2c_1 \rightarrow c_2c_1c_3, c_2c_3c_1, c_3c_2c_1$

Let's replace $c_1c_2c_3$ with ABC. Next, we represent P(ABC) as a diagram:

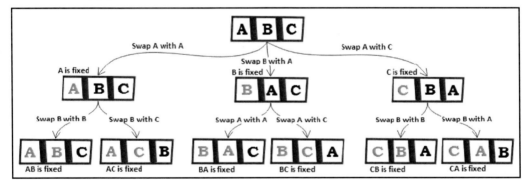

Figure 8.13 – Permuting ABC

If we add another character, then we must express the permutations using $c_1c_2c_3c_4$. Each permutation of $c_1c_2c_3c_4$ represents an ordering of $c_1c_2c_3$, as follows:

$c_1c_2c_3 \to c_1c_2c_3c_4, c_1c_2c_4c_3, c_1c_4c_2c_3, c_4c_1c_2c_3$

$c_1c_3c_2 \to c_1c_3c_2c_4, c_1c_3c_4c_2, c_1c_4c_3c_2, c_4c_1c_3c_2$

$c_3c_1c_2 \to c_3c_1c_2c_4, c_3c_1c_4c_2, c_3c_4c_1c_2, c_4c_3c_1c_2$

$c_2c_1c_3 \to c_2c_1c_3c_4, c_2c_1c_4c_3, c_2c_4c_1c_3, c_4c_2c_1c_3$

$c_2c_3c_1 \to c_2c_3c_1c_4, c_2c_3c_4c_1, c_2c_4c_3c_1, c_4c_2c_3c_1$

$c_3c_2c_1 \to c_3c_2c_1c_4, c_3c_2c_4c_1, c_3c_4c_2c_1, c_4c_3c_2c_1$

We can continue like this forever, but I think it is quite clear what pattern can be used for generating $P(c_1, c_2, ..., c_n)$.

So, this is the right moment to take our logic a step further. Now, it is time to ask the following questions: if we know how to compute all the permutations for strings of k-1 characters ($c_1c_2...c_{k-1}$), then how we can use this information to compute all the permutations for strings of k characters ($c_1c_2...c_{k-1}c_k$)? For example, if we know how to compute all the permutations for the $c_1c_2c_3$ string, then how we can express all the permutations of the $c_1c_2c_3c_4$ string using $c_1c_2c_3$ permutations? The answer is to take each character from the $c_1c_2...c_k$ string and append the $c_1c_2...c_{k-1}$ permutation to it, as follows:

$P(c_1c_2c_3c_4) = [c_1 + P(c_2c_3c_4)] + [c_2 + P(c_1c_3c_4)] + [c_3 + P(c_1c_2c_4)] + [c_4 + P(c_1c_2c_3)]$

$[c_1 + P(c_2c_3c_4)] \to c_1c_2c_3c_4, c_1c_2c_4c_3, c_1c_3c_2c_4, c_1c_3c_4c_2, c_1c_4c_2c_3, c_1c_4c_3c_2$

$[c_2 + P(c_1c_3c_4)] \to c_2c_1c_3c_4, c_2c_1c_4c_3, c_2c_3c_1c_4, c_2c_3c_4c_1, c_2c_4c_1c_3, c_2c_4c_3c_1$

$[c_3 + P(c_1c_2c_4)] \to c_3c_1c_2c_4, c_3c_1c_4c_2, c_3c_2c_1c_4, c_3c_2c_4c_1, c_3c_4c_1c_2, c_3c_4c_2c_1$

$[c_4 + P(c_1c_2c_3)] \to c_4c_1c_2c_3, c_4c_1c_3c_2, c_4c_2c_1c_3, c_4c_2c_3c_1, c_4c_3c_1c_2, c_4c_3c_2c_1$

We can continue to add another character and repeat this logic so that we have a recursive pattern that can be expressed in terms of code as follows:

```java
public static Set<String> permute(String str) {
    return permute("", str);
}

private static Set<String> permute(String prefix, String str) {

    Set<String> permutations = new HashSet<>();

    int n = str.length();

    if (n == 0) {
        permutations.add(prefix);
    } else {
        for (int i = 0; i < n; i++) {
            permutations.addAll(permute(prefix + str.charAt(i),
                str.substring(i + 1, n) + str.substring(0, i)));
        }
    }

    return permutations;
}
```

This code will work fine. Because we use a Set (not a List), we respect the requirement stating that *the returned list of permutations should not contain duplicates*. However, we do generate duplicates. For example, if the given string is *aaa*, then we generate six identical permutations, even if there is only one. The only difference is that they are not added to the result since a Set doesn't accept duplicates. This is far from being efficient.

We can avoid generating duplicates in several ways. One approach starts by counting the characters of a string and storing them in a map. For example, for the given string *abcabcaa*, the key-value map can be *a*=4, *b*=2, and *c*=2. We can do this via a simple helper method, as follows:

```
private static Map<Character, Integer> charactersMap(
                String str) {
    Map<Character, Integer> characters = new HashMap<>();

    BiFunction<Character, Integer, Integer> count = (k, v)
            -> ((v == null) ? 1 : ++v);

    for (char c : str.toCharArray()) {
        characters.compute(c, count);
    }

    return characters;
}
```

Next, we choose one of these characters as the first character and find all the permutations of the remaining characters. We can express this as follows:

P(*a*=4,*b*=2,*c*=2) = [*a* + P(*a*=3,*b*=2,*c*=2)] + [*b* + P(*a*=4,*b*=1,*c*=1)] + [*c* + P(*a*=4,*b*=2,*c*=1)]

P(*a*=3,*b*=2,*c*=2) = [*a* + P(*a*=2,*b*=2,*c*=2)] + [*b* + P(*a*=3,*b*=1,*c*=1)] + [*c* + P(*a*=3,*b*=2,*c*=1)]
P(*a*=4,*b*=1,*c*=1) = [*a* + P(*a*=3,*b*=1,*c*=1)] + [*b* + P(*a*=4,*b*=0,*c*=1)] + [*c* + P(*a*=4,*b*=1,*c*=0)]
P(*a*=4,*b*=2,*c*=1) = [*a* + P(*a*=3,*b*=2,*c*=1)] + [*b* + P(*a*=4,*b*=1,*c*=1)] + [*c* + P(*a*=4,*b*=2,*c*=0)]

P(*a*=2,*b*=2,*c*=2) = [*a* + P(*a*=1,*b*=2,*c*=2)] + [*b* + P(*a*=2,*b*=1,*c*=2)] + [*c* + P(*a*=2,*b*=2,*c*=1)]
P(*a*=3,*b*=1,*c*=1) = ...

We can continue writing until there are no remaining characters. Now, it should be quite simple to put this into lines of code:

```
public static List<String> permute(String str) {
    return permute("", str.length(), charactersMap(str));
}

private static List<String> permute(String prefix,
        int strlength, Map<Character, Integer> characters) {
    List<String> permutations = new ArrayList<>();

    if (strlength == 0) {
        permutations.add(prefix);
    } else {
        // fetch next char and generate remaining permutations
        for (Character c : characters.keySet()) {

            int count = characters.get(c);

            if (count > 0) {
                characters.put(c, count - 1);
                permutations.addAll(permute(prefix + c,
                    strlength - 1, characters));
                characters.put(c, count);
            }
        }
    }

    return permutations;
}
```

The complete application is called *Permutations*.

Coding challenge 11 – Knight tour

Amazon, Google

Problem: Consider a chessboard (an 8x8 grid). Place a knight on this board and print all its unique movements.

Solution: As you've already seen, the best way to tackle such problems is to take a piece of paper and a pen and sketch the scenario. A picture is worth a thousand words:

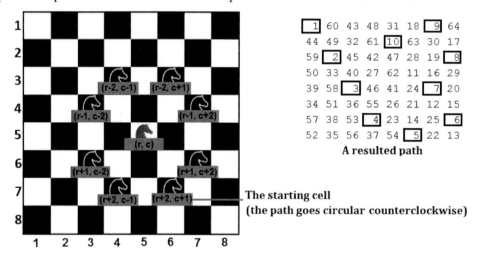

Figure 8.14 – Knight tour

As we can see, a knight can move from a (r, c) cell into a maximum of eight other valid cells; that is, $(r+2, c+1)$, $(r+1, c+2)$, $(r-1, c+2)$, $(r-2, c+1)$, $(r-2, c-1)$, $(r-1, c-2)$, $(r+1, c-2)$, and $(r+2, c-1)$. So, in order to obtain the path from 1 to 64 (as shown in the right-hand side of the preceding diagram), we can start from a given location and recursively try to visit each valid movement. If the current path doesn't represent a solution or we've tried all eight cells, then we backtrack.

To be as efficient as possible, we consider the following aspects:

- We start from a corner of the chessboard: This way, the knight can initially go in only two directions instead of eight.

- We check for valid cells in a fixed sequence: Maintaining a circular path will help us find a new move faster than picking one randomly. The counterclockwise circular path from (r, c) is $(r+2, c+1)$, $(r+1, c+2)$, $(r-1, c+2)$, $(r-2, c+1)$, $(r-2, c-1)$, $(r-1, c-2)$, $(r+1, c-2)$, and $(r+2, c-1)$.

- We compute the circular path using two arrays: We can move from (r, c) to $(r + ROW[i], c + COL[i])$ with i in $[0, 7]$:

  $COL[] = \{1,2,2,1,-1,-2,-2,-1,1\}$;

  $ROW[] = \{2,1,-1,-2,-2,-1,1,2,2\}$;

- We avoid cycles in paths and duplicate work (for example, visiting the same cell multiple times) by storing the visited cells in an $r \times c$ matrix.

By gluing everything together in terms of code, we obtain the following recursive approach:

```java
public class KnightTour {

    private final int n;

    // constructor omitted for brevity

    // all 8 possible movements for a knight
    public static final int COL[]
        = {1,2,2,1,-1,-2,-2,-1,1};
    public static final int ROW[]
        = {2,1,-1,-2,-2,-1,1,2,2};

    public void knightTour(int r, int c,
            int cell, int visited[][]) {

        // mark current cell as visited
        visited[r][c] = cell;

        // we have a solution
        if (cell >= n * n) {
            print(visited);
            // backtrack before returning
            visited[r][c] = 0;
            return;
        }

        // check for all possible movements (8)
```

```java
            // and recur for each valid movement
            for (int i = 0; i < (ROW.length - 1); i++) {

                int newR = r + ROW[i];
                int newC = c + COL[i];

                // check if the new position is valid un-visited
                if (isValid(newR, newC)
                        && visited[newR][newC] == 0) {
                    knightTour(newR, newC, cell + 1, visited);
                }
            }

            // backtrack from current cell
            // and remove it from current path
            visited[r][c] = 0;
        }

        // check if (r, c) is valid chess board coordinates
        private boolean isValid(int r, int c) {
            return !(r < 0 || c < 0 || r >= n || c >= n);
        }

        // print the solution as a board
        private void print(int[][] visited) {
            ...
        }
    }
```

The complete application is called *KnightTour*.

Coding challenge 12 – Curly braces

Amazon, Google, Adobe, Microsoft, Flipkart

Problem: Print all the valid combinations of n pairs of curly braces. A valid combination is when the curly braces are properly opened and closed. For $n=3$, the valid combinations are as follows:

{{{}}}, {{}{}}, {{}}{}, {}{{}}, {}{}{}

Solution: The valid combination for $n=1$ is {}.

For $n=2$, we immediately see the combination as {}{}. However, another combination consists of adding a pair of curly braces to the previous combination; that is, {{}}.

Going one step further, for $n=3$, we have the trivial combination {}{}{}. Following the same logic, we can add a pair of curly braces to combinations for $n=2$, so we obtain {{{}}}, {{}}{}, {}{{}}, {}{}{}.

Actually, this is what we obtain after we remove or ignore duplicates. Let's sketch the case for the $n=3$ build based on $n=2$, as follows:

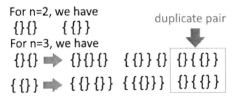

Figure 8.15 – Curly braces duplicate pairs

So, if we add a pair of curly braces inside each existing pair of curly braces and we add the trivial case ({}{}...{}) as well, then we obtain a pattern that can be implemented via recursion. However, we have to deal with a significant number of duplicate pairs, so we need additional checks to avoid having duplicates in the final result.

So, let's consider another approach, starting with a simple observation. For any given n, a combination will have $2*n$ curly braces (not pairs!). For example, for $n=3$, we have six curly braces (three left curly braces ({{{) and three right curly braces (}}})) arranged in different, valid combinations. This means that we can try to build the solution by starting with zero curly braces and add left/right curly braces to it, as long as we have a valid expression. Of course, we keep track of the number of added curly braces so that we don't exceed the maximum number, $2*n$. The rules that we must follow are as follows:

- We add all left curly braces in a recursive manner.
- We add the right curly braces in a recursive manner, as long as the number of right curly braces doesn't exceed the number of left curly braces.

In other words, the key to this approach is to track the number of left and right curly braces that are allowed. As long as we have left curly braces, we insert a left curly brace and call the method again (recursion). If there are more right curly braces remaining than there are left curly braces, then we insert a right curly brace and call the method (recursion). So, let's get coding:

```java
public static List<String> embrace(int nr) {

    List<String> results = new ArrayList<>();
    embrace(nr, nr, new char[nr * 2], 0, results);

    return results;
}

private static void embrace(int leftHand, int rightHand,
        char[] str, int index, List<String> results) {

    if (rightHand < leftHand || leftHand < 0) {
        return;
    }

    if (leftHand == 0 && rightHand == 0) {

        // result found, so store it
        results.add(String.valueOf(str));
    } else {
        // add left brace
        str[index] = '{';
        embrace(leftHand - 1, rightHand, str, index + 1,
            results);

        // add right brace
        str[index] = '}';
        embrace(leftHand, rightHand - 1, str, index + 1,
            results);
    }
}
```

The complete application is called *Braces*.

Coding challenge 13 – Staircase

Amazon, Adobe, Microsoft

Problem: A person walks up a staircase. They can hop either one step, two steps, or three steps at a time. Count the number of possible ways they can reach the top of the staircase.

Solution: First, let's set what hopping one, two, or three steps means. Consider that hopping one step means to go up the staircase step by step (we land on each step). To hop two steps means to jump over a step and land on the next one. Finally, to hop three steps means to jump over two steps and land on the third one.

For example, if we consider a staircase with three steps, then we can go from step 0 (or, no step) to step 3 in four ways: step by step (we land on each step), we jump over step 1 and land on step 2 and walk on step 3, we walk on step 1 and jump over step 2, thereby landing on step 3, or we jump directly on step 3, as shown in the following diagram:

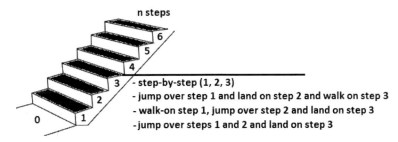

Figure 8.16 – Staircase (how to reach step 3)

By going one step further in our logic, we may ask ourselves how to reach step *n*. Mainly, the nth step can be reached if we do the following:

- *n*-1 step and hop 1 step
- *n*-2 step and hop 2 steps
- *n*-3 step and hop 3 steps

However, reaching any of these steps – *n*-1, *n*-2, or *n*-3 – is possible if we follow the preceding bullets. For example, we can reach the *n*-1 step if we are on *n*-2 and hop 1 step, we are on *n*-3 step and hop 2 steps, or we are on *n*-4 step and hop 3 steps.

So, to reach the nth step, we have three possible paths. To reach step $n-1^{th}$, we also have three possible paths. So, to reach both steps, we must have 3+3=6 paths. Do not say 3*3=9 paths! This is wrong!

Now, we can conclude that adding all the paths in a recursive manner should give us the expected answers. Moreover, we can use our experience to add *Memoization* as well. This way, we avoid calling the method with the same inputs many times (exactly as in the case of the Fibonacci numbers):

```java
public static int countViaMemoization(int n) {

    int[] cache = new int[n + 1];
    return count(n, cache);
}

private static int count(int n, int[] cache) {
    if (n == 0) {
        return 1;
    } else if (n < 0) {
        return 0;
    } else if (cache[n] > 0) {
        return cache[n];
    }

    cache[n] = count(n - 1, cache)
        + count(n - 2, cache) + count(n - 3, cache);

    return cache[n];
}
```

The complete application is called *Staircase*. It also contains the plain recursion approach (without *Memoization*).

Coding challenge 14 – Subset sum

Amazon, Adobe, Microsoft, Flipkart

Problem: Consider a given set (*arr*) of positive integers and a value, *s*. Write a snippet of code that finds out if there is a subset in this array whose sum is equal to the given *s*.

Solution: Let's consider the array, *arr* = {3, 2, 7, 4, 5, 1, 6, 7, 9}. If *s*=7, then a subset can contain the elements 2, 4, and 1, as shown in the following diagram:

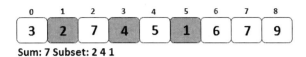

Figure 8.17 – Subset of sum 7

The subset containing the elements 2, 4, and 1 is just one of the possible subsets. All possible subsets include (3, 4), (2, 4, 1), (2, 5), (7), (1, 6), and (7).

Recursive approach

Let's try to find a solution via recursion. If we add the subset *arr*[0]=3, then we have to find the subset for *s* = *s*-*arr*[0] = 7-3 = 4. Finding a subset for *s*=4 is a sub-problem that can be solved based on the same logic, which means we can add *arr*[1]=2 in the subset, and the next sub-problem will consist of finding the subset for *s* = *s*-*arr*[1] = 4-2 = 2.

Alternatively, we can think like this: start with *sum*=0. We add *arr*[0]=3 to this *sum* as *sum*=*sum*+*arr*[0] = 3. Next, we check if *sum* = *s* (for example, if 3 = 7). If so, we found a subset. If not, we add the next element, *arr*[1]=2, to the *sum* as *sum* = *sum*+*arr*[1] = 3+2 =5. We recursively continue to repeat this process until there are no more elements to add. At this point, we recursively remove elements from *sum* and check if *sum* = *s* upon each removal. In other words, we build every possible subset and check if its *sum* is equal to *s*. When we have this equality, we print the current subset.

So far, it is clear that if we recursively solve each and every sub-problem, then it will lead us to the result. For each element from *arr* we must make a decision. Mainly, we have two options: include the current element in the subset or not include it. Starting from these statements, we can create the following algorithm:

1. Define a subset as an array of the same length as the given *arr*. This array takes only values of 1 and 0.

2. Recursively add each element from *arr* to the subset by setting a value of 1 at that particular index. Check for the solution (*current sum = given sum*).

3. Recursively remove each element from the subset by setting a value of 0 at that particular index. Check for the solution (*current sum = given sum*).

Let's see the code:

```
/* Recursive approach */
public static void findSumRecursive(int[] arr, int index,
        int currentSum, int givenSum, int[] subset) {

    if (currentSum == givenSum) {
```

```java
            System.out.print("\nSubset found: ");
            for (int i = 0; i < subset.length; i++) {
                if (subset[i] == 1) {
                    System.out.print(arr[i] + " ");
                }
            }
        } else if (index != arr.length) {

            subset[index] = 1;
            currentSum += arr[index];
            findSumRecursive(arr, index + 1,
                    currentSum, givenSum, subset);

            currentSum -= arr[index];
            subset[index] = 0;

            findSumRecursive(arr, index + 1,
                    currentSum, givenSum, subset);
        }
    }
```

The time complexity of this code is $O(n2^n)$, so it's far from being efficient. Now, let's try an iterative approach via Dynamic Programming. This way, we avoid solving the same problem repeatedly.

Dynamic Programming approach

Via Dynamic Programming, we can solve this problem in $O(s*n)$. More precisely, we can rely on the *Bottom-Up* approach and a `boolean` bidimensional matrix of dimension $(n+1)$ x $(s+1)$, where n is the size of the set (*arr*).

To understand this implementation, you have to understand how this matrix is filled up and how it is read. If we consider that the given *arr* is {5, 1, 6, 10, 7, 11, 2} and $s=9$, then this `boolean` matrix starts from an initial state, as shown in the following diagram:

Coding challenges

		0	1	2	3	4	5	6	7	8	9
		0	1	2	3	4	5	6	7	8	9
0	0	T	F	F	F	F	F	F	F	F	F
1	5	T									
2	1	T									
3	6	T									
4	10	T									
5	7	T									
6	11	T									
7	2	T									

Figure 8.18 – Initial matrix

So, we have $s+1 = 9+1 = 10$ columns and $n+1 = 7+1 = 8$ rows. As you can see, we have filled up row and column 0. These are the *base cases* and can be interpreted as follows:

- Initialize the first row (row 0) of the matrix (*matrix*[0][]) with 0 (or `false`, F) except *matrix*[0][0], which is initialized with 1 (or `true`, T). In other words, if the given sum is not 0, then there is no subset to satisfy this sum. However, if the given sum is 0, then there is a subset containing only 0. So, the subset containing a 0 can form a single sum equal to 0.

- Initialize the first column (column 0) of matrix (*matrix*[][0]) with 1 (or `true`, T) because, for any set, a subset is possible with 0 sum.

Next, we take each row (5, 1, 6, ...) and we try to fill it up with F or T. Let's consider the second row, which contains the element 5. Now, for each column, let's answer the following question: can we form a sum of *column number* with a 5? Let's see the output:

		0	1	2	3	4	5	6	7	8	9
		0	1	2	3	4	5	6	7	8	9
0	0	T	F	F	F	F	F	F	F	F	F
1	5	T	F	F	F	F	T	F	F	F	F
2	1	T									
3	6	T									
4	10	T									
5	7	T									
6	11	T									
7	2	T									

Figure 8.19 – Filling up the second row

224   Recursion and Dynamic Programming

- Can we form a sum of 1 with a 5? No, so false (F).
- Can we form a sum of 2 with a 5? No, so false (F).

...

- Can we form a sum of 5 with a 5? Yes, so true (T).
- Can we form a sum of 6 with a 5? No, so false (F).

...

- Can we form a sum of 9 with a 5? No, so false (F).

We can try to apply this question to each of the remaining rows, but the more we advance, the harder it will be. Moreover, we cannot implement this question in code without an algorithm. Fortunately, we can employ an algorithm that can be applied to each (*row, column*) cell. This algorithm contains the following steps:

1. While the element of the current row (*i*) is greater than the value of the current column (*j*), we just copy the preceding value (*i-1, j*), in the current (*i, j*) cell.

2. If the element of the current row (*i*) is smaller than or equal to the value of the current column (*j*), then we look to the (*i-1, j*) cell and do the following:

   a. If cell (*i-1, j*) is T, then we fill up the (*i, j*) cell with T as well.

   b. If cell (*i-1, j*) is F, then we fill up the (*i, j*) cell with the value at (*i-1, j-element_at_this_row*).

If we apply this algorithm to the second row (containing the element 5), then we obtain the same result shown in the following diagram:

			0	1	2	3	4	5	6	7	8	9
			0	1	2	3	4	5	6	7	8	9
0	0		T	F	F	F	F	F	F	F	F	F
1	5		T	F	F	F	F	T	F	F	F	F
2	1		T									
3	6		T									
4	10		T									
5	7		T									
6	11		T									
7	2		T									

Figure 8.20 – Applying the algorithm to the second row

Conforming to *step 1*, for 5 < 1, 5 < 2, 5 < 3, and 5 < 4, we copy the value from the preceding cell. When we reach cell (1, 5), we have 5=5, so we need to apply *step 2*. More precisely, we apply *step 2b*. The cell (1-1, 5-5) is the cell (0, 0) that has the value T. So, the cell (1, 5) is filled up with T. The same logic applies to the remaining cells. For example, cell (1, 6) is filled up with F since F is the value at (0, 5); the cell at (1, 7) is filled up with F since F is the value at (0, 6), and so on.

If we apply this algorithm to all the rows, then we obtain the following filled matrix:

		0	1	2	3	4	5	6	7	8	9
		0	1	2	3	4	5	6	7	8	9
0	0	T	F	F	F	F	F	F	F	F	F
1	5	T	F	F	F	F	T	F	F	F	F
2	1	T	T	F	F	F	T	T	F	F	F
3	6	T	T	F	F	F	T	T	T	F	F
4	10	T	T	F	F	F	T	T	T	F	F
5	7	T	T	F	F	F	T	T	T	T	F
6	11	T	T	F	F	F	T	T	T	T	F
7	2	T	T	T	T	F	T	T	T	T	**T**

Figure 8.21 – Complete matrix

Notice that we highlighted the last cell at (7, 9). If the right-bottom cell has the value T, then we say that there is at least a subset that satisfies the given sum. If it is F, then there is no such subset.

So, in this case, there is a subset whose sum is equal to 9. Can we identify it? Yes, we can, via the following algorithm:

1. Start from the right-bottom cell, which is T (let's say that this cell is at (i, j)).

    a. If the cell above this one, $(i-1, j)$, is F, then write down the element at this row (this element is part of the subset) and go to cell $(i-1, j-element\_at\_this\_row)$.

    b. While the cell above this one, $(i-1, j)$, is T, we go up the cell $(i-1, j)$.

    c. Repeat this from *step 1a* until the entire subset is written down.

Let's draw the path of the subset in our case:

	0	1	2	3	4	5	6	7	8	9
		0	1	2	3	4	5	6	7	8	9
0	0	T	F	F	F	F	F	F	F	F	F
1	5	T	F	F	F	F	T	F	F	F	F
2	1	T	T	F	F	F	T	T	F	F	F
3	6	T	T	F	F	F	T	T	T	F	F
4	10	T	T	F	F	F	T	T	T	F	F
5	7	T	T	F	F	F	T	T	T	T	F
6	11	T	T	F	F	F	T	T	T	T	F
7	2	T	T	T	T	F	T	T	T	T	T

9 = 2 + 6 + 1, so a subset is {2, 6, 1}

Figure 8.22 – Subset solution path

So, we start from the bottom-right cell, which is at (7, 9) and has the value T. Because this cell is T, we can attempt to find the subset that has the sum 9. Next, we apply *step 1a*, so we write down the element at row 7 (which is 2) and go to cell (7-1, 9-2) = (6, 7). So far, the subset is {2}.

Next, we apply *step 1b*, so we land in cell (3, 7). The cell above (3, 7) has the value F, so we apply *step 1a*. First, we write down the element at row 3, which is 6. Then, we go to cell (3-1, 7-6) = (2, 1). So far, the subset is {2, 6}.

The cell above (2, 1) has the value F, so we apply *step 1a*. First, we write down the element at row 2, which is 1. Then, we go to cell (2-1, 1-1) = (1, 0). Above cell (1,0), we have only T, so we stop. The current and final subset is {2, 6, 1}. Obviously, 2+6+1 = 9.

The following code will clarify any other details (this code can tell if the given sum at least has a corresponding subset):

```
/* Dynamic Programming (Bottom-Up) */
public static boolean findSumDP(int[] arr, int givenSum) {

    boolean[][] matrix
            = new boolean[arr.length + 1][givenSum + 1];

    // prepare the first row
    for (int i = 1; i <= givenSum; i++) {
        matrix[0][i] = false;
    }
```

```java
    // prepare the first column
    for (int i = 0; i <= arr.length; i++) {
        matrix[i][0] = true;
    }

    for (int i = 1; i <= arr.length; i++) {
        for (int j = 1; j <= givenSum; j++) {

            // first, copy the data from the above row
            matrix[i][j] = matrix[i - 1][j];

            // if matrix[i][j] = false compute
            // if the value should be F or T
            if (matrix[i][j] == false && j >= arr[i - 1]) {
                matrix[i][j] = matrix[i][j]
                    || matrix[i - 1][j - arr[i - 1]];
            }
        }
    }

    printSubsetMatrix(arr, givenSum, matrix);
    printOneSubset(matrix, arr, arr.length, givenSum);

    return matrix[arr.length][givenSum];
}
```

The `printSubsetMatrix()` and `printOneSubset()` methods can be found in the complete code named *SubsetSum*.

Coding challenge 15 – Word break (this is a famous Google problem)

Amazon, Google, Adobe, Microsoft, Flipkart

Problem: Consider that you're given a dictionary of words and a string, *str*. Write a snippet of code that returns `true` if the given string (*str*) can be segmented into a space-separated sequence of dictionary words.

Solution: This problem is common to Google and Amazon and at the time of writing, it is adopted by a lot of medium-large companies. If we type a string that doesn't make sense into Google, then Google attempts to break it down into words and asks us if that is what we actually tried to type. For example, if we type "thisisafamousproblem", then Google will ask us if we wanted to type "this is a famous problem".

Plain recursion-based solution

So, if we assume that the given string is *str*="thisisafamousproblem" and the given dictionary is {"this" "is" "a" "famous" "problem"}, then we can form the result; that is, "this is a famous problem".

So, how can we obtain this? How can we check if the given string can be segmented into a space-separated sequence of dictionary words?

Let's start with an observation. If we start from the first character of the given string, then we notice that "t" is not a word in the given dictionary. We can continue by appending the second character to "t", so we get "th". Since "th" is not a word in the given dictionary, we can append the third character, "i". Obviously, "thi" is not a word in the dictionary, so we append the fourth character, "s". This time, we found a word because "this" is a word in the dictionary. This word becomes part of the result.

Taking this logic further, if we found "this", then the initial problem is reduced to a smaller problem that consists of finding the remaining words. So, by appending every character, the problem reduces to a smaller problem but essentially remains the same. This sounds like an ideal case for a recursive implementation.

If we elaborate on the recursive algorithm, then we have the following steps that we must perform:

1. Iterate the given string, *str*, from the first character (*index* 0).

2. Take each substring from the given string (by substring, we understand substring from *index* to 1, substring from *index* to 2, ...substring from *index* to *str.length*). In other words, as long as the current substring is not a word in the given dictionary, we continue to add a character from the given string, *str*.

3. If the current substring is a word in the given dictionary, then we update the index so that it's the length of this substring and rely on recursion by checking the remaining string from *index* to *str.length*.

4. If *index* reaches the length of the string, we return `true`; otherwise, we return `false`.

The code for this is as follows:

```
private static boolean breakItPlainRecursive(
        Set<String> dictionary, String str, int index) {

    if (index == str.length()) {
        return true;
    }

    boolean canBreak = false;
    for (int i = index; i < str.length(); i++) {
        canBreak = canBreak
            || dictionary.contains(str.substring(index, i + 1))
                && breakItPlainRecursive(dictionary, str, i + 1);
    }

    return canBreak;
}
```

There is no surprise that the runtime of this code is exponential. Now, it is time to deploy Dynamic Programming.

Bottom-up solution

We can avoid recursion and deploy Dynamic Programming instead. More precisely, we can use the *Bottom-Up* solution shown here:

```
public static boolean breakItBottomUp(
        Set<String> dictionary, String str) {

    boolean[] table = new boolean[str.length() + 1];
    table[0] = true;

    for (int i = 0; i < str.length(); i++) {
        for (int j = i + 1; table[i] && j <= str.length(); j++) {
            if (dictionary.contains(str.substring(i, j))) {
                table[j] = true;
            }
```

```
        }
    }
    
    return table[str.length()];
}
```

This code still runs in exponential time $O(n^2)$.

Trie-based solution

The most efficient solution to solve this problem relies on Dynamic Programming and the Trie data structure since it provides the best time complexity. You can find a detailed implementation of the Trie data structure in the book *Java Coding Problems*: (https://www.amazon.com/gp/product/B07Y9BPV4W/).

Let's consider the problem of breaking a given string into a set of components representing its words. If *p* is a prefix of *str* and *q* is the suffix of *str* (the remaining characters), then *pq* is *str* (the concatenation of *p* with *q* is *str*). And, if we can break *p* and *q* into words via recursion, then we can break *pq* = *str* by merging the two sets of words.

Now, let's continue this logic in the context of a Trie representing the given dictionary of words. We can assume that *p* is a word from the dictionary, and we must find a way to construct it. This is exactly where the Trie comes in. Because *p* is considered a word from the dictionary and *p* is a prefix of *str*, we can say that *p* must be found in the Trie via a path consisting of the first few letters of *str*. To accomplish this via Dynamic Programming, we use an array, let's denote it as *table*. Every time we find an appropriate *q*, we signal it in the *table* array by setting a solution at |*p*| + 1, where |*p*| is the length of the prefix, *p*. This means that we can continue by checking the last entry to determine if the whole string can be broken up. Let's see the code for this:

```
public class Trie {

    // characters 'a'-'z'
    private static final int CHAR_SIZE = 26;
    private final Node head;
    
    public Trie() {
        this.head = new Node();
    }
    
    // Trie node
```

```java
    private static class Node {

        private boolean leaf;
        private final Node[] next;

        private Node() {
            this.leaf = false;
            this.next = new Node[CHAR_SIZE];
        }
    };

    // insert a string in Trie
    public void insertTrie(String str) {

        Node node = head;

        for (int i = 0; i < str.length(); i++) {
            if (node.next[str.charAt(i) - 'a'] == null) {
                node.next[str.charAt(i) - 'a'] = new Node();
            }

            node = node.next[str.charAt(i) - 'a'];
        }

        node.leaf = true;
    }

    // Method to determine if the given string can be
    // segmented into a space-separated sequence of one or
    // more dictionary words
    public boolean breakIt(String str) {

        // table[i] is true if the first i
        // characters of str can be segmented
        boolean[] table = new boolean[str.length() + 1];
        table[0] = true;
```

```
                for (int i = 0; i < str.length(); i++) {
                    if (table[i]) {
                        Node node = head;
                        for (int j = i; j < str.length(); j++) {
                            if (node == null) {
                                break;
                            }
                            node = node.next[str.charAt(j) - 'a'];
                            // [0, i]: use our known decomposition
                            // [i+1, j]: use this String in the Trie
                            if (node != null && node.leaf) {
                                table[j + 1] = true;
                            }
                        }
                    }
                }
                // table[n] would be true if
                // all characters of str can be segmented
                return table[str.length()];
            }
        }
```

Apparently, because we have two nested loops, the runtime of this solution is $O(n^2)$. Actually, the inner loop breaks if the node is null. And, in the worst-case scenario, this happens after k steps, where k is the deepest path in the Trie. So, for a dictionary that contains the longest word of size z, we have $k=z+1$. This means that the time complexity of the inner loop is $O(z)$ and that the total time complexity is $O(nz)$. The extra space is O(*space of the Trie + str.length*).

The complete application is called *WordBreak*. This application also contains a method that prints all the strings that can be generated for the given string. For example, if the given string is "thisisafamousproblem" and the dictionary is { "this", "th", "is", "a", "famous", "f", "a", "m", "o", "u", "s", "problem"}, then the output will contain four sequences:

- th is is a f a m o u s problem
- th is is a famous problem
- this is a f a m o u s problem
- this is a famous problem

Done! Now, it's time to summarize this chapter.

Summary

In this chapter, we covered one of the most popular topics in interviews: recursion and Dynamic Programming. Mastering this topic requires a lot of practice. Fortunately, this chapter provided a comprehensive set of problems that covered the most common recursive patterns. From permutations to grid-based problems, from classical problems such as Tower of Hanoi to tricky problems such as generating curly braces, this chapter has covered a wide range of recursive cases.

Don't forget that the key to solving recursive problems consists of drawing a meaningful sketch and practicing several cases. This way, you can identify patterns and recursive calls.

In the next chapter, we will discuss problems that require bit manipulation.

9
Bit Manipulation

This chapter covers the most important aspects of bit manipulation that you should know about when it forms part of a technical interview. Such problems are often encountered in interviews and they are not easy. The human mind was not designed to manipulate bits; computers were designed for that. This means that manipulating bits is quite hard and extremely prone to mistakes. Hence, it is advisable to always double-check every bit operation.

Two things are extremely important for mastering these kinds of problems, as follows:

- You must understand the theory of bits very well (for example, bit operators)
- You must practice bit manipulation as much as possible

We need to keep these two statements in mind as we tackle the following topics:

- Understanding bit manipulation
- Coding challenges

Let's start with the theoretical part. It is strongly recommended that you extract the diagrams from this section. They will be your best friends in the second part of this chapter.

Technical requirements

All the code present in this chapter can be found on GitHub at https://github.com/PacktPublishing/The-Complete-Coding-Interview-Guide-in-Java/tree/master/Chapter09.

Bit manipulation in a nutshell

In Java, we can manipulate bits of the following data types: `byte` (8-bit), `short` (16-bit), `int` (32-bit), `long` (64-bit), and `char` (16-bit).

For example, let's use the positive number, 51. In this situation, we have the following statements:

- The binary representation of 51 is 110011.
- Because 51 is an `int`, it is represented as a 32-bit value; that is, 32 values of 1 or 0 (from 0 to 31).
- All the positions to the left of 110011 are actually filled with zeros, up to 32 bits in total.
- This means that 51 is 00000000 00000000 00000000 00110011 (we render it as 110011 since the additional zeros are usually not needed for displaying the binary representation).

Obtaining the binary representation of a Java integer

How do we know that 110011 is the binary representation of 51? How can we compute the binary representation of 112 or any other Java integer? A simple approach consists of successively dividing the number by 2 until the quotient is less than 1 and interpret the remainder as 0 or 1. A remainder of 0 is interpreted as 0, while a remainder greater than 0 is interpreted as 1. For example, let's apply this to 51:

1. 51/2 = 25.5 has a quotient of 25 and a remainder of 5 -> store 1
2. 25/2 = 12.5 has a quotient of 12 and a remainder of 5 -> store 1
3. 12/2 = 6 has a quotient of 6 and a remainder of 0 -> store 0
4. 6/2 = 3 has a quotient of 3 and a remainder of 0 -> store 0
5. 3/2 = 1.5 has a quotient of 1 and a remainder of 5 -> store 1
6. 1/2 = 0.5 has a quotient of 0 and a remainder of 5 -> store 1

So, we stored 110011, which is the binary representation of 51. The rest of the 26 bits are zeros (00000000 00000000 00000000 00**110011**). The reverse process starts from right to left and involves adding powers of 2 where the bits are equal to 1. So here, $51 = 2^0+2^1+2^4+2^5$. The following diagram can help us understand this:

```
00000000 00000000 00000000 00110011
                     ...  2⁷2⁶2⁵2⁴2³2²2¹2⁰
                                      51
```

Figure 9.1 – Binary to decimal (32-bit integer)

In Java, we can quickly see the binary representation of a number via `Integer#toString(int i, int radix)` or `Integer#toBinaryString(int i)`. For example, a radix of 2 means binary:

```java
// 110011
System.out.println("Binary: " + Integer.toString(51, 2));
System.out.println("Binary: " + Integer.toBinaryString(51));
```

The reverse process (from binary to decimal) can be obtained via `Integer#parseInt(String nr, int radix)`:

```java
System.out.println("Decimal: "
  + Integer.parseInt("110011", 2));   //51
```

Next, let's tackle bitwise operators. These operators allow us to manipulate bits, so it is very important to understand them.

Bitwise operators

Manipulating bits involves several operators. These operators are as follows:

- **Unary bitwise complement operator** [~]: Being unary, this operator needs a single operand that is placed before the number. This operator takes every bit of the number and flips its value, so 1 becomes 0 and vice versa; for example, 5 = 101, ~5 = 010.

- **Bitwise AND** [&]: This operator needs two operands and is placed between two numbers. This operator compares the bits of both numbers one by one. It acts as the logical AND (&&), meaning that it returns 1 only if the compared bits are equal to 1; for example, 5 = 101, 7 = 111, 5 & 7 = 101 & 111 = 101 = 5.

- **Bitwise OR [|]**: This operator needs two operands and is placed between two numbers. This operator compares the bits of both numbers one by one. It acts as the logical OR (||), meaning that it returns 1 if at least one of the compared bits is 1 (or both). Otherwise, it returns 0; for example, 5 = 101, 7 = 111, 5 | 7 = 101 | 111 = 111 = 7.

- **Bitwise Exclusive OR (XOR) [^]**: This operator needs two operands and is placed between two numbers. This operator compares the bits of both numbers one by one. It returns 1 only if the compared bits have a different value. Otherwise, it returns 0; for example, 5 = 101, 7 = 111, 5 ^ 7 = 101 | 111 = 010 = 2.

The following diagram is a handy tool that you should keep close when you need to deal with bits. Basically, it summarizes how bit operators work (I suggest you keep this table close when you read through the *Coding challenges* section):

X	Y	X&Y	X|Y	X^Y	~(X)
0	0	0	0	0	1
0	1	0	1	1	1
1	0	0	1	1	0
1	1	1	1	0	0

Figure 9.2 – Bitwise operators

Moreover, the following diagram represents several tips that are quite useful for manipulating bits. The 0s notation represents a sequence of zeros, while the 1s notation represents a sequence of ones:

X | 0s = X	X ^ 0s = X	X & 0s = 0
X | 1s = X	X ^ 1s = ~X	X & 1s = X
X | X = X	X ^ X = 0	X & X = X

Figure 9.3 – Bitwise tips

Take your time and explore each of these tips. Take a paper and a pen and go through each of them. Moreover, try to discover other tips as well.

Bit shift operators

Shifting is a common operation when working on bits. Here, we have **Signed Left Shift** [<<], **Signed Right Shift** [>>], and **Unsigned Right Shift** [>>>]. Shifting works for `byte` (8-bit), `short` (16-bit), `int` (32-bit), `long` (64-bit), and `char` (16-bit); bit shift operators don't throw exceptions.

Signed Left Shift [<<]

Signed Left Shift, or shortly Left Shift, takes two operands. Left Shift gets the bit pattern of the first operand (left-hand side operand) and shifts it to the left by the number of positions given by the second operand (right-hand operand).

For example, the following is the result of left shifting 23 by 3 positions, 23 << 3:

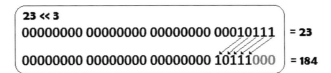

Figure 9.4 – Signed Left Shift

As we can see, every bit of the integer 12 (10111) is shifted 3 positions to the left, while all the positions to the right are automatically padded with zeros.

> **Important note**
>
> Here are two hints that can be quite useful in certain scenarios:
>
> 1. Left shifting a number by n positions is equivalent to multiplying by 2^n (for example, 23 << 3 is equal to 184, which is equivalent to $184 = 23 * 2^3$).
>
> 2. The number of positions to shift is automatically reduced to modulo 32; that is, 23 << 35 is equivalent to 23 << (35 % 32), which is equivalent to 23 << 3.

Negative integers in Java

First of all, it is important to keep in mind that the binary representation itself doesn't tell us whether a number is negative. This means that computers need some rules for representing negative numbers. Commonly, computers store integers in what is known as the *two's complement* representation. Java uses this representation as well.

In short, the *two's complement* representation takes the binary representation of a negative number and flips (negates) all its bits. After that, it adds 1 and appends it to the left of the bit sign. If the leftmost bit is 1, then the number is negative. Otherwise, it is positive.

Let's look at the 4-bit integer, -5, as an example. We have one bit for the sign and three bits for the value. We know that 5 (positive number) is represented as 101, while -5 (negative number) is represented as **1**011. This is obtained by flipping 101 so that it becomes 010, adding 1 to obtain 011 and appending it to the left of the sign bit (**1**) to obtain **1**011. The 1 in bold is the sign bit. So, we have one bit for sign and three bits for value.

Another way to do this is to know that the binary representation of -Q (negative Q) as an *n*-bit number is obtained by concatenating 1 with $2^{n-1} - Q$.

Signed Right Shift [>>]

Signed Right Shift, or Arithmetic Right Shift [>>], takes two operands. Signed Right Shift gets the bit pattern of the first operand (left-hand side operand) and shifts it to the right by the number of positions given by the second operand (right-hand operand) by preserving the sign.

For example, the following is the result of -75 >> 1 (-75 is an 8-bit integer where the sign bit is the **Most Significant Bit (MSB)**):

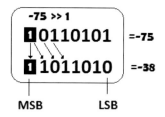

Figure 9.5 – Signed Right Shift

As we can see, every bit of -75 (10110101) is shifted by 1 position to the right (notice that the **Least Significant Bit (LSB)** has changed) and the bit sign is preserved.

> **Important note**
>
> Here are three hints that can be quite useful in certain scenarios:
>
> Right shifting a number by n positions is equivalent to dividing by 2^n (for example, 24 >> 3 is equal to 3, which is equivalent to $3 = 24/2^3$).
>
> The number of positions to shift is automatically reduced to modulo 32; that is, 23 >> 35 is equivalent to 23 >> (35 % 32), which is equivalent to 23 >> 3.
>
> A sequence of all 1s in (signed) binary terms represents -1 in decimal form.

Unsigned Right Shift [>>>]

Unsigned Right Shift, or Logical Right Shift [>>>], takes two operands. Unsigned Right Shift gets the bit pattern of the first operand (left-hand side operand) and shifts it to the right by the number of positions given by the second operand (right-hand operand). The MSB is set to 0. That means that, for positive numbers, the Signed and Unsigned Right Shift return the same result, while negative numbers always become positives.

For example, the following is the result of -75 >>> 1 (-75 is an 8-bit integer where the sign bit is the MSB):

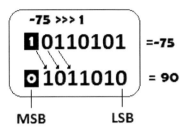

Figure 9.6 – Unsigned Right Shift

> **Important note**
> The number of positions to shift is automatically reduced to modulo 32; that is, 23 >>> 35 is equivalent to 23 >>> (35 % 32), which is equivalent to 23 >>> 3.

Now that you have an idea of what bit shift operators are, it's time to tackle more tips and tricks.

Tips and tricks

Manipulating bits involves great skill when working with bits operators and knowing some tips and tricks. You already saw several tips earlier in this chapter. Now, let's add some more as a bullet point list:

- If we XOR[^] a number with itself for an even number of times, then the result is 0 (x ^ x = 0; x ^ x ^ x ^ x = (x ^ x) ^ (x ^ x) = 0 ^ 0 = 0).
- If we XOR[^] a number with itself for an odd number of times, then the result is that number (x ^ x ^ x = (x ^ (x ^ x)) = (x ^ 0) = x; x ^ x ^ x ^ x ^ x = (x ^ (x ^ x) ^ (x ^ x)) = (x ^ 0 ^ 0) = x).

- We can compute the value of the expression $p \% q$ with $p > 0$, $q > 0$, where q is a power of 2; that is, $p \& (q - 1)$. A simple application where you can see this is *ComputeModuloDivision*.
- For a given positive integer p, we say that it is odd if $((p \& 1) \neq 0)$ and even if $((p \& 1) == 0)$. A simple application where you can see this is *OddEven*.
- For two given numbers p and q, we can say that p is equal to q if $((p \wedge q) == 0)$. A simple application where you can see this is *CheckEquality*.
- For two given integers p and q, we can swap them via $p = p \wedge q \wedge (q = p)$. A simple application where you can see this is *SwapTwoIntegers*.

Ok, it is time to tackle some coding challenges.

Coding challenges

In the next 25 coding challenges, we will exploit different aspects of bit manipulations. Since these kinds of problems are really brain-teasing, they are preferred in interviews. Understanding a snippet of code that manipulates bits is not an easy task, so take your time and dissect each problem and snippet of code. This is the only way to obtain some patterns and templates in order to solve these kinds of problems.

The following figure contains a set of four bit-mask that are important to have in your toolbelt:

Expression	Bit-mask	Example
1 << k	0000...10000000...	k=5, 000...100000
~(1 << k)	111111...01111111...	k=5, 111...011111
(1 << k) - 1	000000...111111...	k=5, 000...11111
-1 << (k + 1)	11111...000000...	k=5, 111...000000

Figure 9.7 – Bit-masks

They can be useful for solving a variety of problems where you need to manipulate bits.

Coding challenge 1 – Getting the bit value

Problem: Consider a 32-bit integer, n. Write a snippet of code that returns the bit value of n at the given position, k.

Solution: Let's consider that *n*=423. Its binary representation is 110100111. How can we say what the value of the bit at position *k*=7 is (the bold bit at position 7 has a value of 1)? A solution will consist of right shifting the given number by *k* positions ($n >> k$). This way, the kth bit becomes the bit at position 0 (110100111 >> 7 = 000000011). Next, we can apply the AND [&] operator as 1 & ($n >> k$):

$$\begin{array}{cccccccc} 0 & 0 & 0 & 0 & 0 & 0 & 1 & \mathbf{1} \\ & & & & & & & \underline{1} \\ & & & & & & & 1 \end{array} \&$$

Figure 9.8 – Binary representation

If the value of the bit at position 0 is 1, then the AND[&] operator will return 1; otherwise, it will return 0. In terms of code, we have the following:

```
public static char getValue(int n, int k) {

    int result = n & (1 << k);

    if (result == 0) {
        return '0';
    }

    return '1';
}
```

Another approach consists of replacing the expression 1 & ($n >> k$) with the expression n & (1 << k). Take your time and try to dissect it. The complete application is called *GetBitValue*.

Coding challenge 2 – Setting the bit value

Amazon, Google, Adobe, Microsoft, Flipkart

Problem: Consider a 32-bit integer, *n*. Write a snippet of code that sets the bit value of *n* at the given position, *k* to 0 or 1.

Solution: Let's consider that $n=423$. Its binary representation is 1**1**0100111. How can we set the bit from position $k=7$, which is now 1, to 0? Having the bitwise operators table in front of us helps us see that the AND[&] operator is the only operator with two operands that allows us to write that 1 & 0 = 0 or the 7th bit & 0 = 0. Moreover, we have 1 & 1 = 1, 0 & 1 = 0 and 0 & 0 = 0, so we can take a bit-mask as 1...101111111 and write the following:

$$\begin{array}{c}1\ \mathbf{1}\ 0\ 1\ 0\ 0\ 1\ 1\ 1 \\ 1\ \mathbf{0}\ 1\ 1\ 1\ 1\ 1\ 1\ 1 \\ \hline 1\ \mathbf{0}\ 0\ 1\ 0\ 0\ 1\ 1\ 1 \end{array} \&$$

Figure 9.9 – Binary representation

This is exactly what we want. We want to turn the 7th bit from 1 into 0 and leave the rest untouched. But how do we obtain the 1...101111... mask? Well, there are two bit-masks that you need to know about. First, a bit-mask, that has a 1 and the rest are 0s (10000...). This can be obtained by left shifting 1 by k positions (for example, the bit mask 1000 can be obtained as 1 << 3, though if we represent it as a 32-bit mask, we get 00000000 00000000 00000000 000**1**000). The other bit-mask contains a 0, while the remainder are 1s (01111...). This can be obtained by applying the unary bitwise complement operator [~] to the bit-mask 10000.... (for example, ~(1000) = 0111, though if we represent it as a 32-bit mask, we get 11111111 11111111 11111111 111**0**111). So, we can obtain the 1...101111... bit-mask as ~(1 << k). Finally, all we have to do is use the AND[&] operator, as shown in the following code:

```
public static int setValueTo0(int n, int k) {

    return n & ~(1 << k);
}
```

If we take $k=3$, 4, or 6, then we get 0 & 0 = 0.

Let's consider that $n=295$. Its binary representation is 1**0**0100111. How can we set the bit from position $k=7$, which is now 0, to 1? Having the bitwise operators table in front of us helps us see that the OR[|] and XOR[^] operators are the operators with two operands that allow us to write that 0 | 1 = 1 or 0 ^ 1 = 1, respectively.

Or, we can write that 7th | 1 = 1 and 7th ^ 1 = 1.

By going one step further, we can see that in the case of the OR[|] operator, we can write the following:

1 | 1 = 1, while in the case of the XOR[^] operator, we write 1 ^ 1 = 0.

Since we want to turn the 7th bit value from 0 to 1, we can use either of these two operators. However, if *k* indicates a bit with an initial value of 1, then 1 ^ 1 = 0 doesn't help us anymore, while 1 | 1 = 1 is exactly what we want. So here, we should use the 10000... bit-mask, as shown here:

$$
\begin{array}{cccccccc}
1 & 0 & 0 & 1 & 0 & 0 & 1 & 1 & 1 \\
  &   & 1 & 0 & 0 & 0 & 0 & 0 & 0 \\
\hline
1 & 1 & 0 & 1 & 0 & 0 & 1 & 1 & 1
\end{array} \Big|
$$

Figure 9.10 – Binary representation

In terms of code, we have the following:

```
public static int setValueTo1(int n, int k) {

    return n | (1 << k);
}
```

If we take *k*=0, 1, 2, 5, or 8, then we get 1 | 1 = 1.

The complete application is called *SetBitValue*.

Coding challenge 3 – Clearing bits

Amazon, **Google**, **Adobe**

Problem: Consider a 32-bit integer, *n*. Write a snippet of code that clears the bits of *n* (sets their value to 0) between the MSB and the given *k*.

Solution: Let's consider that *n*=423. Its binary representation is **110**100111. How can we clear the bits between MSB and position *k*=6 so that there are 110 bits? Having the bitwise operators table in front of us helps us see that we need a bit-mask of type 00011111. Let's see what happens if we apply the AND[&] operator between *n* and this bit-mask:

$$
\begin{array}{cccccccc}
1 & 1 & 0 & 1 & 0 & 0 & 1 & 1 & 1 \\
0 & 0 & 0 & 1 & 1 & 1 & 1 & 1 & 1 \\
\hline
0 & 0 & 0 & 1 & 0 & 0 & 1 & 1 & 1
\end{array} \&
$$

Figure 9.11 – Binary representation

So, we cleared the bits between MSB and *k*=6. Generally speaking, we need a bit-mask that contains 0s between the MSB and *k* (inclusive) and 1s between *k* (exclusive) and LSB. We can do this by left shifting the bits of 1 with *k* positions (for example, for *k*=6, we obtain 1000000) and subtracting 1. This way, we obtain the needed bit-mask, 0111111. So, in terms of code, we have the following:

```
public static int clearFromMsb(int n, int k) {

    return n & ((1 << k) - 1);
}
```

How about clearing the bits between the given *k* and the LSB? Let me show you the code:

```
public static int clearFromPosition(int n, int k) {

    return n & ~((1 << k) - 1);
}
```

Now, take your time and dissect this solution. Moreover, we can replace this solution with this one: n & (-1 << ($k + 1$)).

Again, use a paper and a pen and take it step by step. The complete application is called *ClearBits*.

Coding challenge 4 – Summing binaries on paper

Problem: Consider several positive 32-bit integers. Take a pen and some paper and show me how you sum up their binary representation.

Note: This is not quite a coding challenge, but it is important to know about.

Solution: Summing binary numbers can be done in several ways. A simple approach is to do the following:

1. Sum all the bits of the current column (the first column is the column of LSB).
2. Convert the result into binary (for example, via successive divisions by 2).
3. Keep the rightmost bit as the result.
4. Carry the remains bits into the remaining columns (one bit per column).
5. Go to the next column and repeat from *step 1*.

An example will clarify things. Let's add 1 (1) + 9 (1001) + 29 (011101) + 124 (1111100) = 163 (10100011).

The following diagram represents the result of summing these numbers:

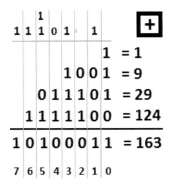

Figure 9.12 – Summing binary numbers

Now, let's see this step by step (the bold sections are carried):

- Sum bits on column 0: 1 + 1 + 1 + 0 = 3   = **1**1   1
- Sum bits on column 1: **1** + 0 + 0 + 0 = 1   = 1   1
- Sum bits on column 2: 0 + 1 + 1 = 2   = **1**0   0
- Sum bits on column 3: **1** + 1 + 1 + 1 = 4   = **10**0   0
- Sum bits on column 4: **0** + 1 + 1 = 2   = **1**0   0
- Sum bits on column 5: **1** + **1** + 0+1 = 3 = **1**1   1
- Sum bits on column 6: **1** + 1 = 2   = **1**0   0
- Sum bits on column 7: **1** = 1   = 1   1

So, the result is 10100011.

Coding challenge 5 – Summing binaries in code

Problem: Consider two 32-bit integers, q and p. Write a snippet of code that computes $q + p$ using their binary representation.

Solution: We can try an implementation of the algorithm presented in the previous coding challenge, or we can try another approach. This approach introduces an equation that is useful to know:

$$p + q = 2 * (p \& q) + (p \wedge q)$$

Notice the presence of the AND[&] and XOR[^] bitwise operators. If we denote $p \& q$ with *and*, and $p \wedge q$ with *xor*, then we can write that as follows:

$$p + q = 2 * and + xor$$

If p and q have no common bits, then we can reduce this to the following:

$$p + q = xor$$

For example, if p = 1010 and q = 0101, then $p \& q$ = 0000. Since 2*0000 = 0, we remain with $p + q = xor$, or $p + q$ = 1111.

However, if p and q have common bits, then we must deal with the addition of *and* and *xor*. So, *and* + *xor* can be solved if we force the *and* expression to return 0. This can be done via recursion.

Through recursion, we can write the first step of recursion as:

$$p + q = 2 * (2 * and \& xor) + (2 * and \wedge xor)$$

Alternatively, if we denote $and\{1\} = 2 * and \& xor$, and $xor\{1\} = 2 * and \wedge xor$ where $\{1\}$ means one step of recursion, then we can write this:

$$step\ 1\ of\ recursion: p + q = 2 * and\{1\} + xor\{1\}$$
$$step\ 2\ of\ recursion: p + q = 2 * and\{2\} + xor\{2\}$$
$$...$$
$$step\ n\ of\ recursion: p + q = 2 * and\{n\} + xor\{n\}$$

But when does this recursion stop? Well, it should stop when the intersection between the two bit sequences (p and q) in the $and\{n\}$ expression returns 0. So, here, we forced the *and* expression to return 0.

In terms of code, we have the following:

```
public static int sum(int q, int p) {
    int xor;
    int and;
    int t;
```

```
    and = q & p;
    xor = q ^ p;

    // force 'and' to return 0
    while (and != 0) {

      and = and << 1; // this is multiplication by 2

      // prepare the next step of recursion
      t = xor ^ and;
      and = and & xor;
      xor = t;
    }

    return xor;
}
```

The complete application is called *SummingBinaries*.

Coding challenge 6 – Multiplying binaries on paper

Problem: Consider two positive 32-bit integers, q and p. Take some paper and a pen and show me how you multiply the binary representation of these two numbers ($q*p$).

Note: This is not quite a coding challenge, but it is important to know about.

Solution: When we multiply binary numbers, we must keep in mind that multiplying a binary number by 1 gives us back exactly the same binary number, while multiplying a binary number by 0 gives us back 0. The steps for multiplying two binary numbers are as follows:

1. Multiply every bit of the second binary number by every bit of the first binary number, starting from the rightmost column (column 0).
2. Sum up the results.

Let's do 124 (1111100) * 29 (011101) = 3596 (111000001100).

The following diagram represents the result of our computation:

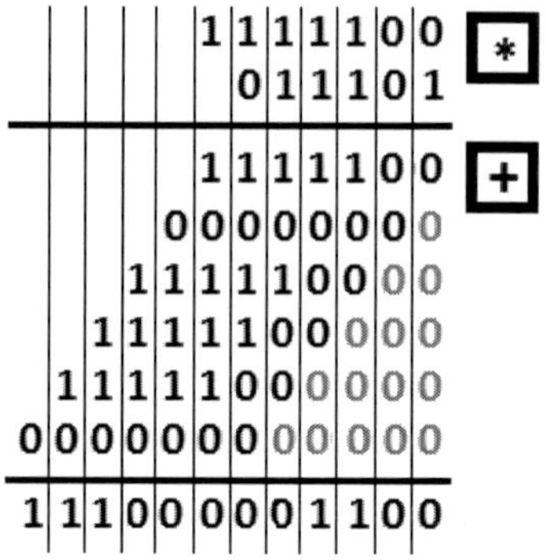

Figure 9.13 – Multiplying binary numbers

So, we multiply every bit of 29 with every bit of 124. Next, we sum up those binaries, as you saw earlier in the *Coding challenge 4 – Summing binaries on paper* section.

Coding challenge 7 – Multiplying binaries in code

Amazon, Google, Adobe

Problem: Consider two 32-bit integers, q and p. Write a snippet of code that computes $q * p$ using their binary representation.

Solution: We can try an implementation of the algorithm presented in the previous coding challenge, or we can try another approach. This approach starts by assuming that $p=1$, so here, we have $q*1=q$. We know that any q multiplied by 1 is q, so we can say that $q*1$ follows the next sum (we go from 0 to 30, so we ignore the signed bit on position 31):

$$q * 1 = \sum_{i=0}^{30} q_{30} * 2^{30} + q_{29} * 2^{29} + \ldots + q_0 * 2^0$$

Figure 9.14 – Multiplying binaries in a code

For example, if $q=5$ (101), then $5 * 1 = 0*2^{30} + 0*2^{29} + \ldots 1*2^2 + 0*2^1 + 1*2^0 = 5$.

So, $5 * 1 = 5$.

So far, this is not such a big deal, but let's continue with $5 * 2$; that is, with 101 * 10. If we think that $5 * 2 = 5 * 0 + 10 * 1$, then this means that 101 * 10 = 101 * 0 + 1010 * 1. So, we left shifted 5 by one position and we right shifted 2 by one position.

Let's continue with $5 * 3$. This is 101 * 011. However, $5 * 3 = 5 * 1 + 10 * 1$. Hence it is like 101 * 1 + 1010 * 1.

Let's continue with 5 * 4. This is 101 * 100. However, 5 * 4 = 5 * 0 + 10 * 0 + 20 * 1. Thus, it is like 101 * 0 + 1010 * 0 + 10100 * 1.

Now, we can start to see a pattern that follows these steps (initially, *result*=0):

1. If the LSB of *p* is 1, then we write the following:

$$result = result + \sum_{i=0}^{30} q_{30} * 2^{30} + q_{29} * 2^{29} + \ldots + q_0 * 2^0$$

Figure 9.15 – LSB of p is 1

2. We left shift *q* by one position and logical right shift *p* by one position.
3. We repeat from *step 1* until *p* is 0.

If we put these three steps into code, then we obtain the following output:

```
public static int multiply(int q, int p) {

    int result = 0;

    while (p != 0) {

        // we compute the value of q only when the LSB of p is 1
        if ((p & 1) != 0) {
            result = result + q;
        }

        q = q << 1; // q is left shifted with 1 position
        p = p >>> 1; // p is logical right shifted with 1 position
    }

    return result;
}
```

The complete application is called *MultiplyingBinaries*.

Coding challenge 8 – Subtracting binaries on paper

Problem: Consider two positive 32-bit integers, q, and p. Take some paper and a pen and show me how you subtract the binary representation of these two numbers ($q-p$).

Note: This is not quite a coding challenge, but it is important to know about.

Solution: Subtracting binary numbers can be reduced in order to compute 0 minus 1. Mainly, we know that 1 minus 1 is 0, 0 minus 0 is 0, and 1 minus 0 is 1. To compute 0 minus 1, we must follow these steps:

1. From the current column, we search the left column(s) until we find a bit of 1.
2. We borrow this bit and put it in the preceding column as two values of 1.
3. We then borrow one of these two values of 1 from the preceding column as other two of 1.
4. Repeat *step 3* for each column until we reach the current column.
5. Now, we can perform the computation.
6. If we encounter another 0 minus 1, then we repeat this process from *step 1*.

Let's do 124 (1111100) - 29 (011101) = 95 (1011111).

The following diagram represents the result of our computation:

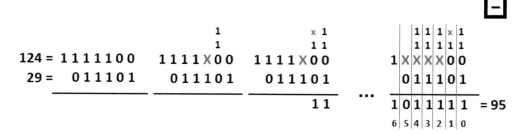

Figure 9.16 – Subtracting binary numbers

Now, let's see this step by step:

1. Start from column 0, so from 0 minus 1. We search in the left column(s) until we find a bit of 1. We find it at column 2 (this bit corresponds to $2^2=4$). We borrow this bit in column 1 and use it as two values of 1 (in other words, two of 2 is 2^1+2^1). We borrow one of these two values of 1 (this is $2^1=2$) in column 0 and use them as two other two values of 1 (in other words, two of 1 is 2^0+2^0). Now, we can do the computation as 2 minus 1 equals 1. We write down 1 and move on to column 1.

2. We continue with column 1, so with 1 minus 0 equals 1. We write down 1 and we move to column 2.

3. We then continue with column 2, so with 0 minus 1. We search in the left column(s) until we find a bit of 1. We find it at column 3 (this bit corresponds to $2^3=8$). We borrow this bit from column 2 and use it as two values of 1 (in other words, two of 2 is 2^2+2^2). Now, we can do the computation as 2 minus 1 equals 1. We write down 1 and we move to column 3.

4. We continue with column 3, so with 0 minus 1. We search in the left column(s) until we find a bit of 1. We find it at column 4 (this bit corresponds to $2^4=16$). We borrow this bit in column 3 and use it as two values of 1 (in other words, two of 2 is 2^3+2^3). Now, we can do the computation as 2 minus 1 equals 1. We write down 1 and we move to column 4.

5. We continue with column 4, so with 0 minus 1. We search in the left column(s) until we find a bit of 1. We find it at column 5 (this bit corresponds to $2^5=32$). We borrow this bit in column 4 and use it as two values of 1 (in other words, two of 2 is 2^4+2^4). Now, we can do the computation as 2 minus 1 equals 1. We write down 1 and we move to column 5.

6. We continue with column 5, so with 0 minus 0. We write down 0 and we move to column 6.

7. We continue with column 6, so with 1 minus 0. We write down 1 and then we're done.

So, the result is 1011111.

Coding challenge 9 – Subtracting binaries in code

Problem: Consider two 32-bit integers, q and p. Write a snippet of code that computes $q - p$ using their binary representation.

Solution: We already know from the previous coding challenge that subtracting binary numbers can be reduced to compute 0 minus 1. Moreover, we know how to solve 0 minus 1 by using the *borrowing* technique. Besides the borrowing technique, it is important to notice that $|q - p| = q \wedge p$; for example:

$|1 - 1| = 1 \wedge 1 = 0, |1 - 0| = 1 \wedge 0 = 1, |0 - 1| = 0 \wedge 1 = 1$ and $|0 - 0| = 0 \wedge 0 = 0$.

Based on these two statements, we can implement the subtraction of two binaries, as follows:

```
public static int subtract(int q, int p) {

  while (p != 0) {

    // borrow the unset bits of q AND set bits of p
    int borrow = (~q) & p;

    // subtraction of bits of q and p
    // where at least one of the bits is not set
    q = q ^ p;

    // left shift borrow by one position
    p = borrow << 1;
  }

  return q;
}
```

The complete application is called *SubtractingBinaries*.

Coding challenge 10 – Dividing binaries on paper

Problem: Consider two positive 32-bit integers, q and p. Take some paper and a pen and show me how you divide the binary representation of these two numbers (q/p).

Note: This is not quite a coding challenge, but it is important to know about.

Solution: In binary division, there are only two possibilities: either 0 or 1. Division involves the *dividend* (q), the *divisor* (p), the *quotient*, and the *remainder*. For example, we know that 11(dividend) / 2(divisor) = 5(quotient) 1(remainder). Or, in binary representation, we have 1011(dividend) / 10 (divisor) = 101(quotient) 1(remainder)

We start by comparing the divisor with the MSB of the dividend (let's call this the *sub-dividend*) and do the following:

a. If the divisor doesn't fit into the sub-dividend (divisor > sub-dividend), then we append 0 to the quotient.

    a.a) We append the next bit of the dividend to the sub-dividend and continue from *step a*).

b. If the divisor fits into the sub-dividend (divisor <= sub-dividend), then we append 1 to the quotient.

    b.a) We subtract the divisor from the current sub-dividend.

    b.b) We append the next bit of the dividend to the result of the subtraction (this is the new sub-dividend) and we repeat from *step a*).

c. When we've processed all the bits of the dividend, we should have the quotient and the remainder, which is the result of the division.

    c.a) We can stop here and express the result in terms of the obtained quotient and the remainder.

    c.b) We can append a dot (".") to the quotient and a 0 to the current remainder (this is the new sub-dividend) and continue from *step a* until the remainder is 0 or we are satisfied by the result.

The following diagram represents the 11/2 division:

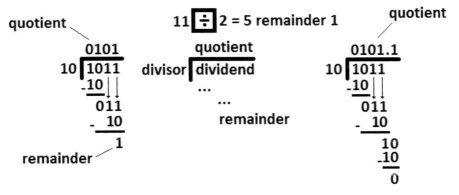

Figure 9.17 – Dividing binary numbers

Now, let's see this step by step (focus on the left-hand side of the preceding diagram):

- Sub-dividend = 1, 10 > 1 since 2 > 1, therefore we append 0 to the quotient.
- Sub-dividend = 10, 10 = 10 since 2 = 2, therefore we append 1 to the quotient.
- Do subtraction, 10 - 10 = 0.
- Sub-dividend = 01, 10 > 01 since 2 > 1, therefore we append 0 to the quotient.
- Sub-dividend = 011, 10 < 011 since 2 < 3, therefore we append 1 to the quotient.
- Do subtraction, 011 - 10 = 1.
- There are no more bits to process from the dividend, so we can say that 11/2 has the quotient 101 (which is 5) and that the remainder is 1.

If you look at the right-hand side of the preceding diagram, then you will see that we can continue the computation until the remainder is 0 by applying the *step c.b* given.

Coding challenge 11 – Dividing binaries in code

Amazon, Google, Adobe

Problem: Consider two 32-bit integers, q and p. Write a snippet of code that computes q/p using their binary representation.

Solution: There are several approaches we can use to divide two binaries. Let's focus on implementing a solution that computes only the quotient, which means we skip the remainder.

This approach is quite straightforward. We know that a 32-bit integer contains the bits that count for us between 31 and 0. All we have to do is left shift the divisor (p) by i positions (i=31, 30, 29, ..., 2, 1, 0) and check if the result is less than the dividend (q). Each time we find such a bit, we update the ith bit position. We accumulate the result and pass it to the next position. The following code speaks for itself:

```
private static final int MAX_BIT = 31;
...
public static long divideWithoutRemainder(long q, long p) {

    // obtain the sign of the division
    long sign = ((q < 0) ^ (p < 0)) ? -1 : 1;

    // ensure that q and p are positive
```

```
q = Math.abs(q);
p = Math.abs(p);

long t = 0;
long quotient = 0;

for (int i = MAX_BIT; i >= 0; --i) {

    long halfdown = t + (p << i);

    if (halfdown <= q) {

        t = t + p << i;
        quotient = quotient | 1L << i;
    }
}

return sign * quotient;
}
```

The complete application is called *DividingBinaries*. It also contains the implementation that computes the remainder.

Coding challenge 12 – Replacing bits

Amazon, Google, Adobe

Problem: Consider two positive 32-bit integers, q and p, and two bit positions, i and j. Write a snippet of code that replaces the bits from q between positions i and j with the bits of p. You can assume that, between i and j, there is enough space to fit all bits of p.

Solution: Let's consider that $q=4914$ (in binary, 1001100110010), $p=63$ (in binary, 111111), $i=4$, and $j=9$. The following diagram shows what we have and what we want to obtain:

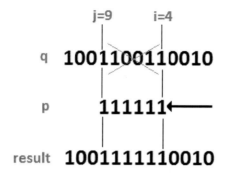

Figure 9.18 – Replacing the bits between i and j

As we can see, the solution should accomplish three main steps. First, we need to clear the bits of q between i and j. Second, we need to left shift p by i positions (this way, we place p in the right position). Finally, we merge p and q in the final result.

In order to clear the bits of q between i and j (set those bits to 0, no matter their initial value), we can use the AND[&] operator. We know that only 1 & 1 return 1, so if we have a bit-mask that contains 0s between i and j, then q & *bit mask* will result in a sequence of bits containing only 0s between i and j since 1 & 0 and 0 & 0 are 0. Moreover, between the MSB and j (exclusive), and i (exclusive) and the LSB of the bit mask, we should have only values of 1. This way, q & *bit mask* will preserve the q bits since 1 & 1 = 1 and 0 & 1 = 0. So, our bit mask should be 1110000001111. Let's see it at work:

```
1 0 0 1 1 0 0 1 1 0 0 1 0
1 1 1 0 0 0 0 0 0 1 1 1 1  &
1 0 0 0 0 0 0 0 0 0 0 1 0
```

Figure 9.19 – Bit-mask (a)

But how can we obtain this mask? We can obtain it via the OR[|] operator, as follows:

```
1 1 1 0 0 0 0 0 0 0 0 0
0 0 0 0 0 0 0 0 0 1 1 1  |
1 1 1 0 0 0 0 0 0 1 1 1
```

Figure 9.20 – Bit-mask (b)

The 1110000000000 bit mask can be obtained by left shifting -1 by *j*+1 positions, while the 0000000001111 bit mask can be obtained by left shifting 1 by *i* positions and subtracting 1.

Here, we solved the first two steps. Finally, we need to put *p* in the right position. This is easy: we just left shift *p* by *i* positions. Finally, we apply the OR(|) operator between *q* with cleared bits between *i* and *j*, and the shifted *p*:

```
1 0 0 0 0 0 0 0 0 0 1 0
0 0 0 1 1 1 1 1 0 0 0 0    |
1 0 0 1 1 1 1 1 0 0 1 0
```

Figure 9.21 – Binary representation

We're done! Now, let's put this into code:

```
public static int replace(int q, int p, int i, int j) {

    int ones = ~0; // 11111111 11111111 11111111 11111111

    int leftShiftJ = ones << (j + 1);
    int leftShiftI = ((1 << i) - 1);

    int mask = leftShiftJ | leftShiftI;

    int applyMaskToQ = q & mask;
    int bringPInPlace = p << i;

    return applyMaskToQ | bringPInPlace;
}
```

The complete application is called *ReplaceBits*.

Coding challenge 13 – Longest sequence of 1

Amazon, **Adobe**, **Microsoft**, **Flipkart**

Problem: Consider a 32-bit integer, *n*. A sequence of 101 can be considered 111. Write a snippet of code that computes the length of the longest sequence of 1.

Solution: We will look at several examples (the following three columns represent the integer number, its binary representation, and the length of the longest sequence of 1):

67534	10000**011111**001110	5
67	1000**011**	2
339809	10100**101111**0**11**00001	9

Figure 9.22 – Three examples

The solution to this problem is quite easy to implement if we know that n & $1 = 1$ if the LSB of n is 1 and n & $0 = 0$ if the LSB of n is 0. Let's focus on the first example, 67534 (10000**011111**001110). Here, we do the following:

- Initialize the longest sequence = 0.
- Apply AND[&]:10000**011111**001110 & 1 = 0, longest sequence = 0.
- Right shift and apply AND[&]:1000001111100111 & 1 = 1, longest sequence = 1.
- Right shift and apply AND[&]:100000111110011 & 1 = 1, longest sequence = 2.
- Right shift and apply AND[&]:10000011111001 & 1 = 1, longest sequence = 3.
- Right shift and apply AND[&]:1000001111100 & 1 = 0, longest sequence = 0
- Right shift and apply AND[&]:100000111110 & 1 = 0, longest sequence = 0.
- Right shift and apply AND[&]:10000011111 & 1 = 1, longest sequence = 1.
- Right shift and apply AND[&]:1000001111 & 1 = 1, longest sequence = 2.
- Right shift and apply AND[&]:100000111 & 1 = 1, longest sequence = 3.
- Right shift and apply AND[&]:10000011 & 1 = 1, longest sequence = 4.
- Right shift and apply AND[&]:1000001 & 1 = 1, longest sequence = 5.
- Right shift and apply AND[&]:100000 & 1 = 0, longest sequence = 0.

So, as long as we don't have any 0s interleaved in the longest sequence of 1, we can implement the preceding approach. However, this approach does not work for the third case, 339809 (10100**10111101**100001). Here, we need to do some additional checks; otherwise, the longest sequence will have a length equal to 4. But since 101 can be treated as 111, the correct answer is 9. This means that when we have *n* & 1 = 0, we must perform the following checks (mainly, we check that the current bit of 0 is guarded by two bits of 1 as 101):

- Check that the next bit is 1 or 0, (*n* & 2) == 1 or 0
- If the next bit is 1, then check whether the previous bit was 1

We can put this into code as follows:

```
public static int sequence(int n) {

  if (~n == 0) {
    return Integer.SIZE; // 32
  }

  int currentSequence = 0;
  int longestSequence = 0;
  boolean flag = true;

  while (n != 0) {
    if ((n & 1) == 1) {
      currentSequence++;
      flag = false;
    } else if ((n & 1) == 0) {
      currentSequence = ((n & 0b10) == 0) // 0b10 = 2
        ? 0 : flag
        ? 0 : ++currentSequence;
      flag = true;
    }

    longestSequence = Math.max(
      currentSequence, longestSequence);

    n >>>= 1;
```

```
    }

    return longestSequence;
}
```

The complete application is called *LongestSequence*.

Coding challenge 14 – Next and previous numbers

Adobe, Microsoft

Problem: Consider a 32-bit integer, n. Write a snippet of code that returns the next largest number that contains exactly the same number of 1 bits.

Solution: Let's consider that $n=124344$ (11110010110111000). To obtain another number with the same number of 1 bits, we have to flip a bit of 1 to turn it into 0 and another bit of 0 to turn it into 1. The resulting number will be different from the given one and will contain the same number of 1 bits. Now, if we want this number to be bigger than the given one, then the bit that was flipped from 0 to 1 should be at the left of the bit that was flipped from 1 to 0. In other words, having two bit positions, i and j, and flipping the bit at position i from 1 to 0 and the bit at position j from 0 to 1, this will result in the new number being smaller than the given number if $i > j$, while bigger if $i < j$, respectively.

This means that we must find the first bit of 0 that doesn't contain only zeros on its right (in other words, the first bit of non-trailing zero). This way, if we flip this bit from 0 to 1, then we know that there is at least one bit of 1 in the right of this bit that can be flipped from 1 to 0. This means that we obtain a bigger number with the same number of 1 bits. The following diagram shows these numbers in pictorial form:

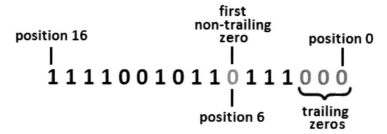

Figure 9.23 – The non-trailing zero

So, for our number, the first non-trailing zero is at bit 6. If we flip this bit from 0 to 1, then the resulting number is bigger than the given number. But now, we must choose a bit, from the right of this bit, that will flip from 1 to 0. Basically, we must choose between the bits from positions 3, 4, and 5. However, is this the proper logic? Remember that we must return the next largest number, NOT any number larger than the given one. Flipping the bit at position 5 is better than flipping the bit from position 3 or 4, but this is not the next largest number. Check out the following relationships (the subscript is the decimal value corresponding to the binary representation):

$11110010110111000_{124344}$ < $11110010111111000_{124408}$ (flip to 1 the bit at position 6)

$11110010111111000_{124408}$ > $11110010111011000_{124376}$ (flip to 0 the bit at position 5)

$11110010111011000_{124376}$ < $11110010111101000_{124392}$ (flip to 0 the bit at position 4)

$11110010111101000_{124392}$ < $11110010111110000_{124400}$ (flip to 0 the bit at position 3)

Figure 9.24 – Several relationships

So far, we can conclude that $11110010111011000_{124376}$ looks like the proper choice. However, we should also take note of the following:

$11110010111011000_{124376}$ > $11110010111000011_{124355}$

So, the next largest number is obtained if we count the number of bits of 1 between positions 6 (exclusive) and 0 (let's denote it with $k=3$), clear all the bits between positions 6 (exclusive) and 0 (set them to 0), and set $k-1$ bits to 1 between positions $k-1$ and 0.

OK; so far, so good! Now, let's put this algorithm into code. First, we need to find the position of the first bit of non-trailing zero. This means we need to sum the count of trailing zeros with the count of 1s until we get the first 0. Counting the trailing zeros can be done as follows (we are working on a copy of n since we don't want to shift the bits of the given number):

```
int copyn = n;
int zeros = 0;
while ((copyn != 0) && ((copyn & 1) == 0)) {
    zeros++;
    copyn = copyn >> 1;
}
```

Counting the 1s until the first 0 can be done like so:

```
int ones=0;
while ((copyn & 1) == 1) {
  ones++;
  copyn = copyn >> 1;
}
```

Now, `marker = zeros + ones` gives us the searched position. Next, we flip the bit from this position from 0 to 1 and clear all the bits between this position (exclusive) and 0:

```
n = n | (1 << marker);
```

In our case, `marker=6`. The effect of this line produces the following output:

```
  1 1 1 0 0 1 0 1 1 0 1 1 1 0 0 0
  0 0 0 0 0 0 0 0 0 1 0 0 0 0 0 0
  1 1 1 0 0 1 0 1 1 1 1 1 1 0 0 0   |
```

Figure 9.25 – Output (1)

```
n = n & (-1 << marker);
```

```
  1 1 1 0 0 1 0 1 1 1 1 1 0 0 0
  1 1 1 1 1 1 1 1 1 0 0 0 0 0 0
  1 1 1 0 0 1 0 1 1 1 0 0 0 0 0 0   &
```

Figure 9.26 – Output (2)

Finally, we set the bits between (`ones` - 1) and 0 to 1:

```
n = n | (1 << (ones - 1)) - 1;
```

In our case, `ones=3`. The effect of this line produces the following output:

```
  1 1 1 0 0 1 0 1 1 1 0 0 0 0 0 0
  0 0 0 0 0 0 0 0 0 0 0 0 0 0 1 1
  1 1 1 0 0 1 0 1 1 1 0 0 0 0 1 1   |
```

Figure 9.27 – Output (3)

So, the final result is 11110010111000011, which is 124355. So, the final method looks as follows:

```
public static int next(int n) {

  int copyn = n;

  int zeros = 0;
  int ones = 0;

  // count trailing 0s
  while ((copyn != 0) && ((copyn & 1) == 0)) {
    zeros++;
    copyn = copyn >> 1;
  }

  // count all 1s until first 0
  while ((copyn & 1) == 1) {
    ones++;
    copyn = copyn >> 1;
  }

  // the 1111...000... is the biggest number
  // without adding more 1
  if (zeros + ones == 0 || zeros + ones == 31) {
    return -1;
  }

  int marker = zeros + ones;

  n = n | (1 << marker);
  n = n & (-1 << marker);
  n = n | (1 << (ones - 1)) - 1;

  return n;
}
```

The complete application is called *NextNumber*. It also contains a method that returns the next smallest number that contains exactly the same number of 1 bits. Take up the challenge and try to provide a solution by yourself. When you're done, just confront your solution with the one from the bundled code. As a hint, you will need the number of trailing 1s (let's denote this with *k*) and the number of 0s immediately to the left of the trailing 1s until you reach the first 1. Summing up these values will give you the position of the bit that should be flipped from 1 to 0. Next, clear up all the bits to the right of this position and set (*k* + 1) bits to 1 immediately to the right of this position.

Coding challenge 15 – Conversion

Amazon, Google, Adobe

Problem: Consider two positive 32-bit integers, *q* and *p*. Write a snippet of code that counts the number of bits that we should flip in *q* in order to convert it into *p*.

Solution: The solution to this problem becomes clear if we observe that the XOR[^] operator only returns 1 when the operands are different. Let's consider *q* = 290932 (1000111000001110100) and *p* = 352345 (1010110000001011001). Let's apply the XOR[^] operator:

```
1 0 0 0 1 1 1 0 0 0 0 0 1 1 1 0 1 0 0
1 0 1 0 1 1 0 0 0 0 0 0 1 0 1 1 0 0 1  ^
0 0 1 0 0 0 1 0 0 0 0 0 0 1 0 1 1 0 1
```

Figure 9.28 – Conversion

In other words, if we denote *q* ^ *p* with *xor* (*xor* = *q* ^ *p*), then all we have to do is count the number of bits of 1 in *xor* (in our example, we have six of 1). This can be done using the AND[&] operator, which only returns 1 for 1 & 1 = 1, so we can count *xor* & 1 for each bit in *xor*. After each comparison, we right shift *xor* by one position. The code speaks for itself:

```
public static int count(int q, int p) {

    int count = 0;

    // each 1 represents a bit that is
    // different between q and p
    int xor = q ^ p;

    while (xor != 0) {
```

```
    count += xor & 1; // only 1 & 1 = 1
    xor = xor >> 1;
  }

  return count;
}
```

The complete application is called *Conversion*.

Coding challenge 16 – Maximizing expressions

Problem: Consider two positive 32-bit integers, q and p, where $q \neq p$. What is the relationship between q and p that maximizes the expression (q AND s) * (p AND s), where AND is the logical operator [&]?

Solution: This is the kind of problem that sounds hard but is extremely simple. Let's start with a simple $a * b$. When is $a * b$ at its maximum? Well, let's consider that $b = 4$. When is $a * 4$ at its maximum? Let's write some test cases:

$a = 1, 1 * 4 = 4$

$a = 2, 2 * 4 = 8$

$a = 3, 3 * 4 = 12$

$a = 4, 4 * 4 = 16$

So, when $a = b$, we have reached the maximum value, 16. However, a can be 5 and 5 * 4 = 20 > 16. This is correct, but this means that b can be 5 as well, so 5 * 5 =, 25 > 20. This is far away from a mathematical demonstration, but we can notice that $a * b$ is at its maximum if $a = b$.

For those interested in the mathematical demonstration, let's say that we have the following:

$$(a - b)^2 \geq 0 \rightarrow (a + b)^2 - 4 * a * b \geq 0 \rightarrow a * b \leq \frac{(a + b)^2}{4}$$

Figure 9.29 – Maximizing expressions (1)

This means that we have the following:

$$a * b = \frac{(a+b)^2}{4} \rightarrow 4 * a * b = a + 2 * a * b + b^2$$

Figure 9.30 – Maximizing expressions (2)

Furthermore, this means that we have the following:

$$a^2 - 2 * a * b + b^2 = 0 \rightarrow (a-b)^2 = 0 \rightarrow \boldsymbol{a = b}$$

Figure 9.31 – Maximizing expressions (3)

Now, if we say that $a * b$ is the maximum when $a = b$, then let's denote $a = (q$ AND $s)$ and $b = (p$ AND $s)$. So, $(q$ AND $s) * (p$ AND $s)$ is at its maximum when $(q$ AND $s) = (p$ AND $s)$.

Let's consider that $q = 822$ (1100110110) and $p = 663$ (1010010111). The LSB of q is 0, while the LSB of p is 1, so we can write the following:

(1 AND s) = (0 AND s) → s = 0 → (1 & 0) = (0 & 0) = 0

If we right shift q and p by 1 position, then we find that the LSB of q is 1 and that the LSB of p is 1:

(1 AND s) = (1 AND s) → s = 0 or 1
→ s = 0 → (1 & 0) = (1 & 0) = 0
→ s = 1 → (1 & 1) = (1 & 1) = 1 (we choose s=1 to maximize)

Figure 9.32 – Right shifting q and p by 1 position

Here, we have two more cases that can be intuited as follows:

(0 AND s) = (1 AND s) → s = 0 → (0 & 0) = (1 & 0) = 0
(0 AND s) = (0 AND s) → s = 0 or 1
→ s = 0 → (0 & 0) = (0 & 0) = 0 (we choose s=0 since they are the same)
→ s = 1 → (0 & 1) = (0 & 1) = 0

Figure 9.33 – Two cases

Here, we can see that the answer to our problem is $q \& p = s$. Let's see this at work:

$$
\begin{array}{c}
1\ 1\ 0\ 0\ 1\ 1\ 0\ 1\ 1\ 0 \\
1\ 0\ 1\ 0\ 0\ 1\ 0\ 1\ 1\ 1 \\
\hline
1\ 0\ 0\ 0\ 0\ 1\ 0\ 1\ 1\ 0
\end{array} \&
$$

Figure 9.34 – Answer

The answer is 1000010110, which is 534. This means that (822 AND 534) = (663 AND 534).

Coding challenge 17 – Swapping odd and even bits

Adobe, Microsoft, Flipkart

Problem: Consider a positive 32-bit integer, n. Write a snippet of code that swaps the odd and even bits of this integer.

Solution: Let's consider that $n = 663$ (1010010111). If we perform the swap manually, then we should obtain 0101101011. We can do this in two steps:

1. We take the odd bits and shift them to the right by one position.
2. We take the even bits and shift them to the left by one position.

But how we can do this?

We can take the odd bits via the AND[&] operator and a bit-mask that contains bits of 1 in the odd positions: 10101010101010101010101010101010. Let's see this in action:

$$
\begin{array}{c}
1\ 0\ 1\ 0\ 1\ 0\ 1\ 0\ 1\ 0\ 1\ 0\ 1\ 0\ 1\ 0\ 1\ 0\ 1\ 0\ 1\ 0\ 1\ 0\ 1\ 0\ 1\ 0\ 1\ 0 \\
1\ 0\ 1\ 0\ 0\ 1\ 0\ 1\ 1\ 1 \\
\hline
1\ 0\ 1\ 0\ 0\ 0\ 0\ 0\ 1\ 0
\end{array} \&
$$

Figure 9.35 – Swapping odd and even bits (1)

The result reveals that 1010010111 contains the odd bits of 1 at positions 1, 7, and 9. Next, we shift the result, 1010000010, to the right by one position. This results in 0101000001.

We can take the even bits via the AND[&] operator and a bit-mask that contains bits of 1 in the even positions: 1010101010101010101010101010101. Let's see this in action:

$$\begin{array}{r} 1\,0\,1\,0\,1\,0\,1\,0\,1\,0\,1\,0\,1\,0\,1\,0\,1\,0\,1\,0\,1\,0\,1\,0\,1\,0\,1\,0\,1 \\ 1\,0\,1\,0\,0\,1\,0\,1\,1\,1 \\ \hline 0\,0\,0\,0\,0\,1\,0\,1\,0\,1 \end{array} \&$$

Figure 9.36 – Swapping odd and even bits (2)

The result reveals that 1010010111 contains the even bits of 1 at positions 0, 2, and 4. Next, we shift the result, 0000010101, to the left by one position. This results in 0000101010.

To obtain the final result, we just need to apply the OR[|] operator to these two results:

$$\begin{array}{r} 0\,1\,0\,1\,0\,0\,0\,0\,0\,1 \\ 0\,0\,0\,0\,1\,0\,1\,0\,1\,0 \\ \hline 0\,1\,0\,1\,1\,0\,1\,0\,1\,1 \end{array} |$$

Figure 9.37 – Final result

The final result is 0101101011. The implementation follows these steps *ad litteram*, so this is straightforward:

```
public static int swap(int n) {

  int moveToEvenPositions
    = (n & 0b10101010101010101010101010101010) >>> 1;

  int moveToOddPositions
    = (n & 0b01010101010101010101010101010101) << 1;

  return moveToEvenPositions | moveToOddPositions;
}
```

The complete application is called *SwapOddEven*.

Coding challenge 18 – Rotating bits

Amazon, Google, Adobe, Microsoft, Flipkart

Problem: Consider a positive 32-bit integer, n. Write a snippet of code that rotates k bits to the left or the right. By rotation, we understand that the bits that fall off at one end of the binary representations are sent to the other end. So, in the left rotation, the bits that fall off the left end are sent to the right end, while in the right rotation, the bits that fall off the right end are sent to the left end.

Solution: Let's focus on the left rotation (typically, the right rotation solution is a mirrored left rotation solution). We already know that by shifting *k* bits to the left, we move the bits to the left and the empty spots are padded with zeros. However, in place of these zeros, we have to put the bits that fell off the left end.

Let's consider that *n*= 423099897 (00011001001101111111110111111001) and *k*=10, so we rotate 10 bits to the left. The following diagram highlights the falling bits and the final result:

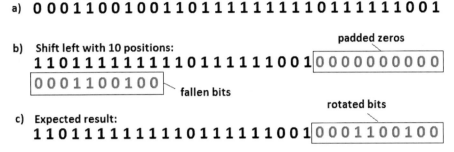

Figure 9.38 – Left rotating bits

The preceding diagram gives us the solution. If we look carefully at points b) and c), we will see that the fallen bits appear in the final result. This result can be obtained by right shifting the fallen bits by 32-10 = 22 positions.

So, if we left shift *n* by 10 positions, we obtain a binary representation padded with zeros on the right-hand side (as in point b) of the preceding diagram or the dividend of the next division). If we right shift *n* by 22 positions, we obtain a binary representation padded with zeros on the left-hand side (as the divisor of the next division). At this point, the OR(|) operator enters the scene, as shown in the following example:

```
n ≪ 10   11011111111101111110010000000000
n ≫ 22   00000000000000000000000001100100
         11011111111101111110010001100100
```

Figure 9.39 – Applying the OR(|) operator

The final result of the left rotation is 11011111111101111110010001100100. Now, we can easily put this into code, as follows:

```java
public static int leftRotate(int n, int bits) {

    int fallBits = n << bits;
    int fallBitsShiftToRight = n >> (MAX_INT_BITS - bits);
```

```
        return fallBits | fallBitsShiftToRight;
}
```

Now, challenge yourself by implementing the right rotation.

For the right rotation, the code will look as follows (you should be able to follow this solution with no issues):

```
public static int rightRotate(int n, int bits) {

  int fallBits = n >> bits;
  int fallBitsShiftToLeft = n << (MAX_INT_BITS - bits);

  return fallBits | fallBitsShiftToLeft;
}
```

The complete application is called *RotateBits*.

Coding challenge 19 – Calculating numbers

Problem: Consider two positions, i and j ($j > i$), representing the positions of two bits in a binary representation. Write a snippet of code that returns a 32-bit integer containing 1s (set) between i (inclusive) and j (inclusive) and where the rest of the bits are 0s (unset).

Solution: Let's consider that $i=3$ and $j=7$. We know that the required 32-bit integer is 248, or, in binary representation, 11111000 (or with all 0s, 00000000000000000000000011111000).

If you paid attention to *Coding challenge 8 – Subtracting binaries on paper*, then you should know that 0 minus 1 is an operation that can be accomplished by *borrowing* a bit from the left of the current bit. The *borrowing* technique is propagated to the left until a bit of 1 is found. Moreover, if we remember that 1 minus 0 is 1, then we can write the following subtraction:

$$
\begin{array}{r}
0\,0\,0\,1\,0\,0\,0\,0\,0\,0\,0\,0 \\
\underline{0\,0\,0\,0\,0\,0\,0\,0\,1\,0\,0\,0} \\
0\,0\,0\,0\,1\,1\,1\,1\,1\,0\,0\,0
\end{array}
$$

Figure 9.40 – Subtraction

Look at the result of this subtraction. The 1s are exactly between positions *i*=3 (inclusive) and *j*=7 (inclusive). This is exactly the number that we are looking for: 248. The dividend and the divisor are obtained by left shifting 1 by (*j*+1) positions and by *i* positions, respectively.

With these statements in place, it is very easy to put them into code:

```
public static int setBetween(int left, int right) {

  return (1 << (right + 1)) - (1 << left);
}
```

The complete application is called *NumberWithOneInLR*.

Coding challenge 20 – Unique elements

Amazon, **Google**, **Adobe**, **Microsoft**, **Flipkart**

Problem: Consider a given array of integers, *arr*. Every element from this array occurs exactly three times, except for one element, which occurs only once. This makes it unique. Write a snippet of code that finds this unique element in O(n) complexity time and O(1) extra space.

Solution: Let's consider that the given array is *arr*={4, 4, 3, 1, 7, 7, 7, 1, 1, 4}, so 3 is the unique element. If we write the binary representation of these numbers, we obtain the following: 100, 100, 011, 001, 111, 111, 111, 001, 001, 100. Now, let's sum up the bits at the same positions and check whether the resulting sums are multiples of 3, as follows:

- Sum of first bits % 3 = 0+0+1+1+1+1+1+1+1+0 = 7 % 3 = 1
- Sum of second bits % 3 = 0+0+1+0+1+1+1+0+0+0 = 4 % 3 = 1
- Sum of third bits % 3 = 1+1+0+0+1+1+1+0+0+1 = 6 % 3 = 0

The unique number is 011 = 3.

Let's take a look at another example. This time, *arr*={51, 14, 14, 51, 98, 7, 14, 98, 51, 98}, so 7 is the unique element. Let's apply the same logic we used previously to the binary representation: 110011, 1110, 1110, 110011, 1100010, 111, 1110, 1100010, 110011, 1100010. This time, let's use a diagram since this makes things clearer:

1. The given array
[51, 14, 14, 51, 98, 7, 14, 98, 51, 98]

2. Sum bits:

							3. Compute % 3	4. Result
	1	1	0	0	1	1 (51)	3 % 3 = 0	0000111 = 7
			1	1	1	0 (14)	6 % 3 = 0	
			1	1	1	0 (14)	3 % 3 = 0	
	1	1	0	0	1	1 (51)	3 % 3 = 0	
1	1	0	0	0	1	0 (98)	4 % 3 = 1	
				1	1	1 (7)	10 % 3 = 1	
			1	1	1	0 (14)	4 % 3 = 1	
1	1	0	0	0	1	0 (98)		
	1	1	0	0	1	1 (51)		
1	1	0	0	0	1	0 (98)		
3	6	3	3	4	10	4		

Figure 9.41 – Finding the unique element in the given array

So, based on these two examples, we can elaborate the following algorithm:

1. Sum up the bits on the same positions.
2. For each *sum*, compute the modulus 3.
3. If *sum* % 3 = 0 (*sum* is a multiple of 3), this means that the bit is set in the elements that appear thrice among the given elements.
4. If *sum* % 3 ! = 0 (*sum* is not a multiple of 3), this means that the bit is set in the element that appears once (**but it is not sure if that bit is unset or set in the elements that appear thrice**).
5. We have to repeat *steps 1*, *2*, and *3* for all the given elements and for all the positions of the bits. By doing this, we will get the element that appears only once, exactly as you saw in the preceding diagram.

The code for this is as follows:

```java
private static final int INT_SIZE = 32;

public static int unique(int arr[]) {

  int n = arr.length;
  int result = 0;

  int nr;
  int sumBits;

  // iterate through every bit
  for (int i = 0; i < INT_SIZE; i++) {

    // compute the sum of set bits at
    // ith position in all array
    sumBits = 0;
    nr = (1 << i);
    for (int j = 0; j < n; j++) {
      if ((arr[j] & nr) == 0) {
        sumBits++;
      }
    }

    // the sum not multiple of 3 are the
    // bits of the unique number
    if ((sumBits % 3) == 0) {
      result = result | nr;
    }
  }

  return result;
}
```

This was one approach to solving this problem. Another approach starts from the fact that the XOR[^] operator, when applied to the same number twice, returns 0. Moreover, the XOR[^] operator is associative (gives the same result, regardless of grouping: 1 ^ 1 ^ 2 ^ 2 = 1 ^ 2 ^ 1 ^ 2 = 0) and commutative (independent of order: 1 ^ 2 = 2 ^ 1). However, if we XOR[^] the same number three times, then the result will be the same number, so using XOR[^] on all the numbers will not be helpful here. However, we can employ the following algorithm:

Use a variable to note that the variable appeared for the first time.

1. For each new element, put the XOR[^] of it in a variable, oneAppearance.

2. If the element appears a second time, then it will be removed from oneAppearance and we put the XOR[^] of it in another variable, twoAppearances.

3. If the element appears a third time, then it will be removed from oneAppearance and twoAppearances. The oneAppearance and twoAppearances variables become 0 and we start looking for a new element.

4. For all the elements that appear three times, the oneAppearance and twoAppearances variables will be 0. On the other hand, for the element that appears only once, the oneAppearance variable will be set with that value.

In terms of code, this looks as follows:

```
public static int unique(int arr[]) {

  int oneAppearance = 0;
  int twoAppearances = 0;

  for (int i = 0; i < arr.length; i++) {
    twoAppearances = twoAppearances
        | (oneAppearance & arr[i]);
    oneAppearance = oneAppearance ^ arr[i];
    int neutraliser = ~(oneAppearance & twoAppearances);
    oneAppearance = oneAppearance & neutraliser;
    twoAppearances = twoAppearances & neutraliser;
  }
}
```

```
        return oneAppearance;
}
```

The runtime of this code is O(n) with O(1) extra time. The complete application is called *OnceTwiceThrice*.

Coding challenge 21 – Finding duplicates

Amazon, Google, Adobe, Microsoft, Flipkart

Problem: Consider that you're given an array of integers ranging from 1 to *n*, where *n* can be, at most, 32,000. The array may contain duplicates and you don't know the value of *n*. Write a snippet of code that prints all the duplicates from the given array using only 4 kilobytes (KB) of memory.

Solution: The solution should start from the fact that 4 KB of memory is the equivalent to $4 * 8 * 2^{10}$ bits. Since $4 * 8 * 2^{10}$ is greater than 32,000, we can create a vector of 32,000 bits and represent each integer as 1 bit. There is no need to write our own implementation for a vector of bits; we can simply use Java's built-in `BitSet` class (this class implements a vector of bits that grows as needed).

With a `BitSet`, we can iterate the given array and, for each traversed element, flip the bit from the corresponding index from 0 to 1. If we attempt to flip a bit that is already 1, then we find and print a duplicate. The code for this is quite simple:

```
private static final int MAX_N = 32000;

public static void printDuplicates(int[] arr) {

    BitSet bitArr = new BitSet(MAX_N);

    for (int i = 0; i < arr.length; i++) {

        int nr = arr[i];
        if (bitArr.get(nr)) {
            System.out.println("Duplicate: " + nr);
        } else {
            bitArr.set(nr);
        }
    }
}
```

The complete application is called *FindDuplicates*.

Coding challenge 22 – Two non-repeating elements

Amazon, Google, Adobe

Problem: Consider that you're given an array of integers containing $2n+2$ elements. The $2n$ elements are n elements repeated once. So, each element in $2n$ appears twice in the given array. The remaining two elements appear only once. Write a snippet of code that finds these two elements.

Solution: Let's consider that the given array is *arr*={2, 7, 1, 5, 9, 4, 1, 2, 5, 4}. The two numbers that we are looking for are 7 and 9. These two numbers appear only once in the array, while 2, 1, 5, and 4 appear twice.

If we consider the brute-force approach, then it is quite intuitive to iterate the array and check the number of occurrences for each element. But the interviewer will not be impressed by this solution since its runtime is $O(n^2)$.

Another approach consists of sorting the given array. This way, the repeated elements are grouped together so that we can count the number of occurrences for each group. The group of size 1 represents a non-repeated value. It is good to mention this approach during the process of finding a better solution.

A better solution relies on *hashing*. Create a `Map<Element, Count>` and fill it with elements and the number of occurrences (for example, for our data, we will have the following pairs: (2, 2), (7, 1), (1, 2), (5, 2), (9, 1), and (4, 2)). Now, traverse the map and locate the elements whose count is 1. It is good to mention this approach during the process of finding a better solution.

In this chapter, we are dealing with bits, so the best solution should rely on bit manipulation. This solution relies on the XOR[^] operator and a tip that we mentioned in the *Tips and tricks* section:

- If we XOR[^] a number with itself for an even number of times, then the result is as follows 0 ($x \wedge x = 0$; $x \wedge x \wedge x \wedge x = (x \wedge x) \wedge (x \wedge x) = 0 \wedge 0 = 0$)

On the other hand, if we apply the XOR[^] operator to two different numbers, p and q, then the result is a number that contains the set of bits (bits of 1) at the places where p and q differ. This means that if we apply XOR[^] to all the elements in the array (*xor* = $arr[0]\wedge arr[1]\wedge arr[2] \wedge ... \wedge arr[arr.length-1]$), then all the repeating elements would nullify each other.

So, if we take any set bit (for example, the rightmost bit) of the result of XOR[^] and divide the elements of the array into two sets, then one set will contain elements with the same bit set and the other set will contain elements with the same bit not set. In other words, we divide the elements into two sets by comparing the rightmost set bit of XOR[^] with the bit at the same position in each element. By doing so, we will get p in one set and q in the other set.

Now, if we apply the XOR[^] operator to all the elements in the first set, then we will get the first non-repeating element. Doing the same in the other set will get the second non-repeating element.

Let's apply this flow to our data, arr={2, 7, 1, 5, 9, 4, 1, 2, 5, 4}. So, 7 and 9 are the non-repeating values. First, we apply the XOR[^] operator to all the numbers:

xor = 2 ^ 7 ^ 1 ^ 5 ^ 9 ^ 4 ^ 1 ^ 2 ^ 5 ^ 4 = 0010 (2) ^ 0111 (7) ^ 0001 (1) ^ 0101 (5) ^ 1001 (9) ^ 0100 (4) ^ 0001 (1) ^ 0010 (2) ^ 0101 (5) ^ 0100 (4) = 1110 = 7 ^ 9 = 0111 & 1001 = 1110 = 14.

So, 7 ^ 9 ! = 0 if 7 ! = 9. Hence, there will be at least one set bit (at least one bit of 1). We can take any set bit, but it is quite simple to take the rightmost bit as xor & ~(xor-1). So, we have 1110 & ~(1101) = 1110 & 0010 = 0010. Feel free to take any other set bit.

So far, we found this set bit (0010) in XOR[^] of these two numbers (7 and 9), so this bit must be present in 7 or 9 (in this case, it is present in 7). Next, let's divide the elements into two sets by comparing the rightmost set bit of XOR[^] with the bit at the same position in each element. We obtain the first set, containing the elements {2, 7, 2}, and the second set, containing the elements {1, 5, 9, 4, 1, 5, 4}. Since 2, 7, and 2 contain the set bit, they are in the first set, while 1, 5, 9, 4, 1, 5, and 4 don't contain the set bit, which means they are part of the second set.

With that, we've isolated the first non-repeated element (7) in a set and put the second non-repeated element (9) in the other set. Moreover, each repeated element will be in the same set of bit representations (for example, {2, 2} will always be in the same set).

Finally, we apply XOR[^] to each set. So, we have xor_first_set = 2 ^ 7 ^ 2 = 010 ^ 111 ^ 010 = 111 = 7 (the first non-repeated element).

For the second set, we have:

xor_second_set = 1 ^ 5 ^ 9 ^ 4 ^ 1 ^ 5 ^ 4 = 0001 ^ 0101 ^ 1001 ^ 0100 ^ 0001 ^ 0101 ^ 0100 = 1001 = 9 (the second non-repeated element).

Done!

In terms of code, we have the following:

```java
public static void findNonRepeatable(int arr[]) {

  // get the XOR[^] of all elements in the given array
  int xor = arr[0];
  for (int i = 1; i < arr.length; i++) {
    xor ^= arr[i];
  }

  // get the rightmost set bit (you can use any other set bit)
  int setBitNo = xor & ~(xor - 1);

  // divide the elements in two sets by comparing the
  // rightmost set bit of XOR[^] with the bit at the same
  // position in each element
  int p = 0;
  int q = 0;
  for (int i = 0; i < arr.length; i++) {
    if ((arr[i] & setBitNo) != 0) {
      // xor of the first set
      p = p ^ arr[i];
    } else {
      // xor of the second set
      q = q ^ arr[i];
    }
  }

  System.out.println("The numbers are: " + p + " and " + q);
}
```

The runtime of this code is O(n) with an O(1) auxiliary space (*n* is the number of elements from the given array). The complete application is called *TwoNonRepeating*.

Coding challenge 23 – Power set of a set

Amazon, Google, Adobe

Problem: Consider a given set, S. Write a snippet of code that returns the Power Set of S. A Power Set, P(S), of a set, S, is the set of all possible subsets of S, including the empty set and S itself.

Solution: Consider that the given S is {a, b, c}. If so, the Power Set includes {}, {a}, {b}, {c}, {a, b}, {a, c}, {a, c} and {a, b, c}. Notice that for a set containing three elements, the Power Set contains $2^3=8$ elements. For a set containing four elements, the Power Set contains $2^4=16$ elements. Generally speaking, for a set of n elements, the Power Set contains 2^n elements.

Now, if we generate all the binary numbers from 0 to 2^n-1, then we obtain something similar to the following (this example is for 2^3-1):

2^0=000, 2^1=001, 2^2=010, 2^3=011, 2^4=100, 2^5=101, 2^6=110, 2^7=111

Next, if we list these binaries and we consider that the first set bit (rightmost bit) is associated with a, the second set bit is associated with b, and the third set bit (the leftmost bit) is associated with c, then we obtain the following:

$2^0 = 000 = \{\}$

$2^1 = 001 = \{a\}$

$2^2 = 010 = \{b\}$

$2^3 = 011 = \{a, b\}$

$2^4 = 100 = \{c\}$

$2^5 = 101 = \{a, c\}$

$2^6 = 110 = \{b, c\}$

$2^7 = 111 = \{a, b, c\}$

Notice that if we replace the bits of 1 with a, b, and c, then we obtain the Power Set of the given set. Based on these statements, we can create the following pseudo-code for the given set, S:

```
Compute the Power Set size as 2 size of S
Iterate via i from 0 to Power Set size
    Iterate via j from 0 to size of S
        If jth bit in i is set then
```

```
                    Add jth element from set to current subset
        Add the resulted subset to subsets
Return all subsets
```

So, a solution to this problem can be written as follows:

```java
public static Set<Set<Character>> powerSet(char[] set) {

  // total number of subsets (2^n)
  long subsetsNo = (long) Math.pow(2, set.length);

  // store subsets
  Set<Set<Character>> subsets = new HashSet<>();

  // generate each subset one by one
  for (int i = 0; i < subsetsNo; i++) {
    Set<Character> subset = new HashSet<>();

    // check every bit of i
    for (int j = 0; j < set.length; j++) {
      // if j'th bit of i is set,
      // add set[j] to the current subset
      if ((i & (1 << j)) != 0) {
        subset.add(set[j]);
      }
    }

    subsets.add(subset);
  }

  return subsets;
}
```

The complete code is called *PowerSetOfSet*.

Coding challenge 24 – Finding the position of the only set bit

Adobe, **Microsoft**

Problem: Consider a positive integer, *n*. The binary representation of this number has a single bit set (a single bit of 1). Write a snippet of code that returns the position of this bit.

Solution: The problem itself give us an important detail or constraint: the given number contains a single bit of 1. This means that the given number must be a power of 2. Only $2^0, 2^1, 2^2, 2^3, 2^4, 2^5, ..., 2^n$ have binary representations containing a single bit of 1. All other numbers contain 0 or multiple values of 1.

An *n* & (*n*-1) formula can tell us whether the given number is a power of two. Check out the following diagram:

n	n	n-1	n&(n-1)
0	0000	0000	0000
1	0001	0000	0000
2	0010	0001	0000
3	0011	0010	0010
4	0100	0011	0000
5	0101	0100	0100
...			
8	1000	0111	0000
9	1001	1000	1000
...			
15	1111	1110	1110
16	10000	1111	0000
...			

Figure 9.42 – The n & (n-1) formula gives us the powers of two

So, the numbers 0, 1, 2, 8, 16, ... have their binary representation of *n* & (*n*-1) as 0000. So far, we can say that the given number is a power of two. If it is not, then we can return -1 since there is no bit of 1 or there are multiple bits of 1.

Next, we can shift *n* to the right as long as *n* is not 0 while tracking the number of shifts. When *n* is 0, this means we've shifted the single bit of 1, so we can stop and return the counted shifts. Based on these statements, the code for this is quite simple:

```
public static int findPosition(int n) {

  int count = 0;

  if (!isPowerOfTwo(n)) {
    return -1;
```

```
    }

    while (n != 0) {
      n = n >> 1;
      ++count;
    }

    return count;
}

private static boolean isPowerOfTwo(int n) {

    return (n > 0) && ((n & (n - 1)) == 0);
}
```

The complete code is called *PositionOfFirstBitOfOne*.

Coding challenge 25 – Converting a float into binary and vice versa

Problem: Consider a Java `float` number, *n*. Write a snippet of code that converts this `float` into an IEEE 754 single-precision binary floating-point (binary-32) and vice versa.

Solution: To solve this problem, it is important to know that Java uses IEEE 754 single-precision binary floating-point representation for `float` numbers. The IEEE 754 standard specifies a binary-32 as having the sign bit (1 bit), exponent width (8 bits that can represent 256 values), and significant precision (24 bits (23 explicitly stored)), also known as the mantissa.

The following diagram represents a binary-32 in the IEEE 754 standard:

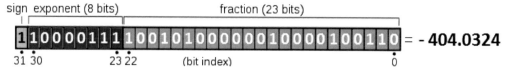

Figure 9.43 – IEEE 754 single-precision binary floating-point (binary 32)

The float value, when represented by the 32-bit binary data with a given sign, biased exponent, *e*, (the 8-bit unsigned integer), and a 23-bit fraction, is as follows:

$$v = -1^{sign} \times 2^{(e-127)} \times \left(1 + \sum_{i=1}^{23} b_{23-i} 2^{-i}\right)$$

Figure 9.44 – Float value

The exponent stored on 8 bits uses values from 0 to 127 to represent negative exponents (for example, 2^{-3}) and uses the values from 128-255 for positive exponents. A negative exponent of 10^{-7} would have a value of -7+127=120. The 127 value is known as the exponent bias.

With this information, you should be able to convert a float number into the IEEE 754 binary-32 representation and vice versa. Before checking the source code for this, called *FloatToBinaryAndBack*, try using your own implementation.

This was the last coding challenge of this chapter. Let's quickly summarize it!

Summary

Since this chapter is a comprehensive resource for bit manipulation, then if you got this far, you've seriously boosted your bit manipulation skills. We covered the main theoretical aspects and solved 25 coding challenges in order to help you learn patterns and templates for solving bit manipulation problems.

In the next chapter, we'll continue our journey with arrays and strings.

Section 3: Algorithms and Data Structures

One of the climaxes of a technical interview is represented by the questions that are meant to discover your skills in the field of algorithms and data structures. Commonly, special attention is given to the problems in this area. This is perfectly understandable since algorithms and data structures are used in the various daily tasks of a Java developer.

This section comprises the following chapters:

- *Chapter 10, Arrays and Strings*
- *Chapter 11, Linked Lists and Maps*
- *Chapter 12, Stacks and Queues*
- *Chapter 13, Trees and Graphs*
- *Chapter 14, Sorting and Searching*
- *Chapter 15, Mathematics and Puzzles*

10
Arrays and Strings

This chapter covers a wide range of problems involving strings and arrays. Since Java strings and arrays are common topics for developers, I will briefly introduce them via several headlines that you must remember. However, if you need to deep dive into this topic, then consider the official Java documentation (`https://docs.oracle.com/javase/tutorial/java/`).

By the end of this chapter, you should be able to tackle any problem involving Java strings and/or arrays. It is highly likely that they will show up in a technical interview. So, the topics that will be covered in this chapter are pretty short and clear:

- Arrays and strings in a nutshell
- Coding challenges

Let's start with a quick recap of strings and arrays.

Technical requirements

All the code present in this chapter can be found on GitHub at `https://github.com/PacktPublishing/The-Complete-Coding-Interview-Guide-in-Java/tree/master/Chapter10`.

Arrays and strings in a nutshell

In Java, arrays are objects and are dynamically created. Arrays can be assigned to variables of the `Object` type. They can have a single dimension (for example, `m[]`) or multiple dimensions (for example, as a three-dimensional array, `m[][][]`). The elements of an array are stored starting with index 0, so an array of length *n* stores its elements between indexes 0 and *n-1* (inclusive). Once an array object is created, its length never changes. Arrays cannot be immutable except for the useless array of length 0 (for example, `String[] immutable = new String[0]`).

In Java, strings are immutable (`String` is immutable). A string can contain **ASCII characters** (unprintable control codes between 0-31, printable characters between 32-127, and extended ASCII codes between 128-255) and **Unicode characters**. Unicode characters less than 65,535 (0xFFFF) are represented in Java using the 16-bit `char` data type (for example, calling `charAt(int index)` works as expected – `index` is the index varying from 0 to *string length* - 1). Unicode characters that exceed 65,535 until 1,114,111 (0x10FFFF) don't fit into 16 bits (Java `char`). They are stored as 32-bit integer values (known as *code points*). This aspect is detailed in the *Coding challenge 7 – Extracting code points of surrogate pairs* section.

A very useful class for manipulating strings is `StringBuilder` (and the thread-safe `StringBuffer`).

Now, let's look at some coding challenges.

Coding challenges

In the following 29 coding challenges, we'll tackle a set of popular problems encountered in Java technical interviews done by medium to large companies (including Google, Amazon, Flipkart, Adobe, and Microsoft). Besides these 29 coding challenges (discussed in this book), you may like to check out the following non-exhaustive list of strings and arrays coding challenges that you can find in my other book, *Java Coding Problems* (https://www.amazon.com/gp/product/1789801419/), published by Packt as well:

- Counting duplicate characters
- Finding the first non-repeated character
- Reversing letters and words
- Checking whether a string contains only digits
- Counting vowels and consonants

- Counting the occurrences of a certain character
- Removing white spaces from a string
- Joining multiple strings with a delimiter
- Checking whether a string is a palindrome
- Removing duplicate characters
- Removing a given character
- Finding the character with the most appearances
- Sorting an array of strings by length
- Checking that a string contains a substring
- Counting substring occurrences in a string
- Checking whether two strings are anagrams
- Declaring multiline strings (text blocks)
- Concatenating the same string *n* times
- Removing leading and trailing spaces
- Finding the longest common prefix
- Applying indentation
- Transforming strings
- Sorting an array
- Finding an element in an array
- Checking whether two arrays are equal or mismatched
- Comparing two arrays lexicographically
- Minimum, maximum, and average of an array
- Reversing an array
- Filling and setting an array
- Next greater element
- Changing array size

The 29 coding challenges tackled in this chapter are not covered in the preceding challenges and vice versa.

Coding challenge 1 – Unique characters (1)

Google, Adobe, Microsoft

Problem: Consider a string that can contain ASCII and Unicode characters ranging between 0-65,535. Write a snippet of code that returns true if this string contains unique characters. The whitespaces can be ignored.

Solution: Let's consider the following three valid given strings:

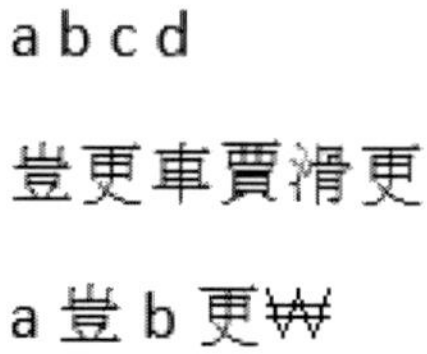

a b c d

豈更車賈滑更

a 豈 b 更 ₩

Figure 10.1 – Strings

First of all, it is important to know that we can fetch any character between 0 and 65,535 via the charAt(int index) method (index is the index varying from 0 to *string length* – 1) because these characters are represented in Java using the 16-bit char data type.

A simple solution to this problem consists of using a Map<Character, Boolean>. While we loop the characters of the given string via the charAt(int index) method, we try to put the character from index into this map and flip the corresponding boolean value from false to true. The Map#put(K k, V v) method returns null if there was no mapping for the given key (character). If there is a mapping for the given key (character), then Map#put(K k, V v) returns the previous value (in our case, true) associated with this key. So, when the returned value is not null, we can conclude that at least one character is duplicated, so we can say that the given string doesn't contain unique characters.

Moreover, before trying to put a character in the map, we ensure that its code ranges between 0 and 65,535 via `String#codePointAt(index i)`. This method returns the Unicode character at the specified `index` as an `int`, which is known as the *code point*. Let's see the code:

```java
private static final int MAX_CODE = 65535;
...
public static boolean isUnique(String str) {

  Map<Character, Boolean> chars = new HashMap<>();

  // or use, for(char ch : str.toCharArray()) { ... }
  for (int i = 0; i < str.length(); i++) {

    if (str.codePointAt(i) <= MAX_CODE) {

      char ch = str.charAt(i);
      if (!Character.isWhitespace(ch)) {
        if (chars.put(ch, true) != null) {
          return false;
        }
      }
    } else {
      System.out.println("The given string
        contains unallowed characters");
      return false;
    }
  }

  return true;
}
```

The complete application is called *UniqueCharacters*.

Coding challenge 2 – Unique characters (2)

Google, Adobe, Microsoft

Problem: Consider a string that can contain only characters from *a-z*. Write a snippet of code that returns `true` if this string contains unique characters. The whitespaces can be ignored.

Solution: The solution presented in the preceding coding challenge covers this case as well. However, let's try to come up with a solution specific to this case. The given string can contain only characters from *a-z*, so it can only contain ASCII codes from 97(*a*) to 122(*z*). Let's consider that the given string is *afghnqrsuz*.

If we recall our experience from *Chapter 9, Bit Manipulation*, then we can think of a bit mask that covers *a-z* letters with bits of 1, as shown in the following figure (the bits of 1 correspond to the letters of our string, *afghnqrsuz*):

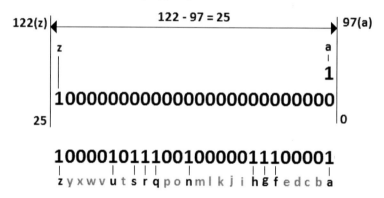

Figure 10.2 – Unique characters bit mask

If we represent each letter from *a-z* as a bit of 1, then we obtain a bit mask of the unique characters, similar to the one shown in the preceding image. Initially, this bit mask contains only 0s (since no letter has been processed, we have all bits equal to 0 or they're unset).

Next, we peek at the first letter from the given string and we compute the subtraction between its ASCII code and 97 (the ASCII code of *a*). Let's denote this with *s*. Now, we create another bit mask by left shifting 1 by *s* positions. This will result in a bit mask that has the MSB of 1 followed by *s* bits of 0 (1000...). Next, we can apply the AND[&] operator between the bit mask of unique characters (which is initially 0000...) and this bit mask (1000...). The result will be 0000... since 0 & 1 = 0. This is the expected result since this is the first processed letter, so there are no letters being flipped in the bit mask of unique characters.

Next, we update the unique character's bit mask by flipping the bit from position *s* from 0 to 1. This is done via the OR[|] operator. Now, the bit mask of unique characters is 1000.... There is a single bit of 1 since we flipped a single bit; that is, the one corresponding to the first letter.

Finally, we repeat this process for each letter of the given string. If you encounter a duplicate, then the AND[&] operation between the bit mask of unique characters and the 1000... mask corresponding to the currently processed letter will return 1 (1 & 1 = 1). If this happens, then we have found a duplicate, so we can return it.

In terms of code, we have the following:

```
private static final char A_CHAR = 'a';
...
public static boolean isUnique(String str) {

  int marker = 0;
  for (int i = 0; i < str.length(); i++) {

    int s = str.charAt(i) - A_CHAR;
    int mask = 1 << s;

    if ((marker & mask) > 0) {
      return false;
    }

    marker = marker | mask;
  }

  return true;
}
```

The complete application is called *UniqueCharactersAZ*.

Coding challenge 3 – Encoding strings

Problem: Consider a string given as a `char[]`, *str*. Write a snippet of code that replaces all whitespaces with a sequence, *%20*. The resulting string should be returned as a `char[]`.

Solution: Consider that the given `char[]` represents the following string:

```
char[] str = "  String   with spaces  ".toCharArray();
```

The expected result is *%20%20String%20%20%20with%20spaces%20%20*.

We can solve this problem in three steps:

1. We count the number of whitespaces in the given `char[]`.
2. Next, create a new `char[]` that's the size of the initial `char[]`, *str*, plus the number of whitespaces multiplied by 2 (a single whitespace occupies one element in the given `char[]`, while the *%20* sequences will occupy three elements in the resulting `char[]`).
3. Lastly, we loop the given `char[]` and create the resulting `char[]`.

In terms of code, we have the following:

```
public static char[] encodeWhitespaces(char[] str) {

  // count whitespaces (step 1)
  int countWhitespaces = 0;
  for (int i = 0; i < str.length; i++) {
    if (Character.isWhitespace(str[i])) {
      countWhitespaces++;
    }
  }

  if (countWhitespaces > 0) {

    // create the encoded char[] (step 2)
    char[] encodedStr = new char[str.length
        + countWhitespaces * 2];

    // populate the encoded char[] (step 3)
```

```
        int index = 0;
        for (int i = 0; i < str.length; i++) {
          if (Character.isWhitespace(str[i])) {
            encodedStr[index] = '0';
            encodedStr[index + 1] = '2';
            encodedStr[index + 2] = '%';
            index = index + 3;
          } else {
            encodedStr[index] = str[i];
            index++;
          }
        }

        return encodedStr;
    }

    return str;
}
```

The complete application is called *EncodedString*.

Coding challenge 4 – One edit away

Google, **Microsoft**

Problem: Consider two given strings, *q* and *p*. Write a snippet of code that determines whether we can obtain two identical strings by performing a single edit in *q* or *p*. More precisely, we can insert, remove, or replace a single character in *q* or in *p*, and *q* will become equal to *p*.

Solution: To better understand the requirements, let's consider several examples:

- *tank, tanc*   One edit: Replace *k* with *c* (or vice versa)
- *tnk, tank*   One edit: Insert *a* in *tnk* between *t* and *n* or remove *a* from *tank*
- *tank, tinck*   More than one edit is needed!
- *tank, tankist*   More than one edit is needed!

By inspecting these examples, we can conclude that we are one edit away if the following occurs:

- The difference in length between *q* and *p* is not bigger than 1
- *q* and *p* are different in a single place

We can easily check the difference in length between *q* and *p* as follows:

```
if (Math.abs(q.length() - p.length()) > 1) {
   return false;
}
```

To find out whether *q* and *p* are different in a single place, we have to compare each character from *q* with each character from *p*. If we find more than one difference, then we return `false`; otherwise, we return `true`. Let's see this in terms of code:

```
public static boolean isOneEditAway(String q, String p) {

   // if the difference between the strings is bigger than 1
   // then they are at more than one edit away
   if (Math.abs(q.length() - p.length()) > 1) {
      return false;
   }

   // get shorter and longer string
   String shorter = q.length() < p.length() ? q : p;
   String longer = q.length() < p.length() ? p : q;

   int is = 0;
   int il = 0;
   boolean marker = false;
   while (is < shorter.length() && il < longer.length()) {

      if (shorter.charAt(is) != longer.charAt(il)) {

         // first difference was found
         // at the second difference we return false
         if (marker) {
            return false;
```

```
            }

            marker = true;

            if (shorter.length() == longer.length()) {
                is++;
            }
        } else {
            is++;
        }
        il++;
    }

    return true;
}
```

The complete application is called *OneEditAway*.

Coding challenge 5 – Shrinking a string

Problem: Consider a given string containing only letters *a-z* and whitespaces. This string contains a lot of consecutive repeated characters. Write a snippet of code that shrinks this string by counting the consecutive repeated characters and creating another string that appends each character and the number of consecutive occurrences. The whitespaces should be copied in the resulting string as they are (don't shrink the whitespaces). If the resulting string is not shorter than the given string, then return the given string.

Solution: Consider that the given string is *abbb vvvv s rttt rr eeee f*. The expected result will be *a1b3 v4 s1 r1t3 r2 e4 f1*. To count the consecutive characters, we need to loop this string character by character:

- If the current character and the next character are the same, then we increment a counter.
- If the next character is different from the current character, then we append the current character and the counter value to the final result, and we reset the counter to 0.

- In the end, after processing all the characters from the given string, we compare the length of the result with the length of the given string and we return the shortest string.

In terms of code, we have the following:

```java
public static String shrink(String str) {

  StringBuilder result = new StringBuilder();

  int count = 0;
  for (int i = 0; i < str.length(); i++) {

    count++;

    // we don't count whitespaces, we just copy them
    if (!Character.isWhitespace(str.charAt(i))) {

      // if there are no more characters
      // or the next character is different
      // from the counted one
      if ((i + 1) >= str.length()
          || str.charAt(i) != str.charAt(i + 1)) {

        // append to the final result the counted character
        // and number of consecutive occurrences
        result.append(str.charAt(i))
              .append(count);

        // reset the counter since this
        // sequence was appended to the result
        count = 0;
      }
    } else {
      result.append(str.charAt(i));
      count = 0;
    }
```

```
    }

    // return the result only if it is
    // shorter than the given string
    return result.length() > str.length()
            ? str : result.toString();
}
```

The complete application is called *StringShrinker*.

Coding challenge 6 – Extracting integers

Problem: Consider a given string containing whitespaces and *a-z* and *0-9* characters. Write a snippet of code that extracts integers from this string. You can assume that any sequence of consecutive digits forms a valid integer.

Solution: Consider that the given string is *cv dd 4 k 2321 2 11 k4k2 66 4d*. The expected result will contain the following integers: 4, 2321, 2, 11, 4, 2, 66, and 4.

A straightforward solution will loop the given string character by character and concatenate sequences of consecutive digits. A digit contains ASCII code between 48 (inclusive) and 97 (inclusive). So, any character whose ASCII code is in the range [48, 97] is a digit. We can also use the Character#isDigit(char ch) method. When a sequence of consecutive digits is interrupted by a non-digit character, we can convert the harvested sequence into an integer and append it as a list of integers. Let's see this in terms of code:

```
public static List<Integer> extract(String str) {

  List<Integer> result = new ArrayList<>();
  StringBuilder temp = new StringBuilder(
    String.valueOf(Integer.MAX_VALUE).length());

  for (int i = 0; i < str.length(); i++) {

    char ch = str.charAt(i);

    // or, if (((int) ch) >= 48 && ((int) ch) <= 57)
    if (Character.isDigit(ch)) {
      temp.append(ch);
```

```
      } else {
        if (temp.length() > 0) {
          result.add(Integer.parseInt(temp.toString()));
          temp.delete(0, temp.length());
        }
      }
    }

    return result;
}
```

The complete application is called *ExtractIntegers*.

Coding challenge 7 – Extracting the code points of surrogate pairs

Problem: Consider a given string containing any kind of characters, including Unicode characters, that are represented in Java as *surrogate pairs*. Write a snippet of code that extracts the *code points* of the *surrogate pairs* in a list.

Solution: Let's consider that the given string contains the Unicode characters shown in the following image (the first three Unicode characters are represented in Java as *surrogate pairs*, while the last one is not):

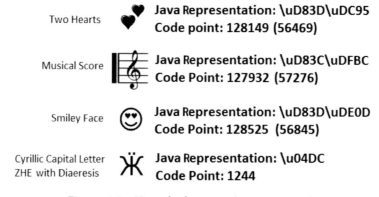

Figure 10.3 – Unicode characters (surrogate pairs)

In Java, we can write such a string as follows:

```java
char[] musicalScore = new char[]{'\uD83C', '\uDFBC'};
char[] smileyFace = new char[]{'\uD83D', '\uDE0D'};
char[] twoHearts = new char[]{'\uD83D', '\uDC95'};
char[] cyrillicZhe = new char[]{'\u04DC'};

String str = "is" + String.valueOf(cyrillicZhe) + "zhe"
    + String.valueOf(twoHearts) + "two hearts"
    + String.valueOf(smileyFace) + "smiley face and, "
    + String.valueOf(musicalScore) + "musical score";
```

To solve this problem, we must know several things, as follows (it is advisable to keep the following statements in mind since they are vital for solving problems that involve Unicode characters):

- Unicode characters that exceed 65,535 until 1,114,111 (0x10FFFF) don't fit into 16 bits, and so 32-bit values (known as *code points*) were considered for the UTF-32 encoding scheme.

  Unfortunately, Java doesn't support UTF-32! Nevertheless, Unicode has come up with a solution for still using 16 bits to represent these characters. This solution implies the following:

  - 16-bit *high surrogates*: 1,024 values (U+D800 to U+DBFF)
  - 16-bit *low surrogates*: 1,024 values (U+DC00 to U+DFFF)

- Now, a *high surrogate* followed by a *low surrogate* defines what is known as a *surrogate pair*. These *surrogate pairs* are used to represent values between 65,536 (0x10000) and 1,114,111 (0x10FFFF).

- Java takes advantage of this representation and exposes it via a suite of methods, such as `codePointAt()`, `codePoints()`, `codePointCount()`, and `offsetByCodePoints()` (take a look at the Java documentation for details).

- Calling `codePointAt()` instead of `charAt()`, `codePoints()` instead of `chars()`, and so on helps us write solutions that cover ASCII and Unicode characters as well.

For example, the well-known two-hearts symbol (first symbol in the preceding image) is a Unicode surrogate pair that can be represented as a `char[]` containing two values: \uD83D and \uDC95. The *code point* of this symbol is 128149. To obtain a `String` object from this code point, call the following:

```
String str = String.valueOf(Character.toChars(128149));
```

Counting the code points in `str` can be done by calling `str.codePointCount(0, str.length())`, which returns 1, even if the `str` length is 2. Calling `str.codePointAt(0)` returns 128149, while calling `str.codePointAt(1)` returns 56469. Calling `Character.toChars(128149).length` returns 2 since two characters are needed to represent this *code point* as a Unicode *surrogate pair*. For ASCII and Unicode 16-bit characters, it will return 1.

Based on this example, we can identify a *surrogate pair* quite easily, as follows:

```
public static List<Integer> extract(String str) {

   List<Integer> result = new ArrayList<>();

   for (int i = 0; i < str.length(); i++) {

     int cp = str.codePointAt(i);
     if (i < str.length()-1
        && str.codePointCount(i, i+2) == 1) {
       result.add(cp);
       result.add(str.codePointAt(i+1));
       i++;
     }
   }

   return result;
}
```

Or, like this:

```
public static List<Integer> extract(String str) {

   List<Integer> result = new ArrayList<>();
```

```
  for (int i = 0; i < str.length(); i++) {

    int cp = str.codePointAt(i);
    // the constant 2 means a suroggate pair
    if (Character.charCount(cp) == 2) {
      result.add(cp);
      result.add(str.codePointAt(i+1));
      i++;
    }
  }

  return result;
}
```

The complete application is called *ExtractSurrogatePairs*.

Coding challenge 8 – Is rotation

Amazon, Google, Adobe, Microsoft

Problem: Consider two given strings, *str1* and *str2*. Write a single line of code that tell us whether *str2* is a rotation of *str1*.

Solution: Let's consider that *str1* is *helloworld* and *str2* is *orldhellow*. Since *str2* is a rotation of *str1*, we can say that *str2* is obtained by cutting *str1* into two parts and rearranging them. The following image shows these words:

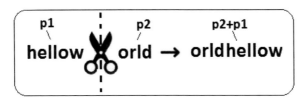

Figure 10.4 – Cutting str1 into two parts and rearranging them

So, based on this image, let's denote the left-hand side of the scissor as *p1* and the right-hand side of the scissor as *p2*. With these notations, we can say that *p1* = *hellow* and *p2* = *orld*. Moreover, we can say that *str1* = *p1+p2* = *hellow* + *orld* and *str2* = *p2+p1* = *orld* + *hellow*. So, no matter where we perform the cut of *str1*, we can say that *str1* = *p1+p2* and *str2*=*p2+p1*. However, this means that *str1+str2* = *p1+p2+p2+p1* = *hellow* + *orld* + *orld* + *hellow* = *p1+p2+p1+p2* = *str1* + *str1*, so *p2+p1* is a substring of *p1*+**p2+p1**+*p2*. In other words, *str2* must be a substring of *str1+str1*; otherwise, it cannot be a rotation of *str1*. In terms of code, we can write the following:

```
public static boolean isRotation(String str1, String str2) {
    return (str1 + str1).matches("(?i).*"
        + Pattern.quote(str2) + ".*");
}
```

The complete code is called *RotateString*.

Coding challenge 9 – Rotating a matrix by 90 degrees

Amazon, **Google**, **Adobe**, **Microsoft**, **Flipkart**

Problem: Consider a given *n* x *n* matrix of integers, *M*. Write a snippet of code that rotates this matrix by 90 degrees in a counterclockwise direction without using any extra space.

Solution: There are at least two solutions to this problem. One solution relies on the transpose of a matrix, while the other one relies on rotating the matrix ring by ring.

Using the matrix transpose

Let's tackle the first solution, which relies on finding the transpose of the matrix, *M*. The transpose of a matrix is a notion from linear algebra that means we need to flip a matrix over its main diagonal, which results in a new matrix denoted as M^T. For example, having the matrix *M* and indices *i* and *j*, we can write the following relationship:

$$[M^T]_{ij} = [M]_{ji}$$

Figure 10.5 – Matrix transpose relationship

Once we've obtained the transpose of *M*, we can reverse the columns of the transpose. This will give us the final result (the matrix *M* rotated by 90 degrees counterclockwise). The following image clarifies this relationship for a 5x5 matrix:

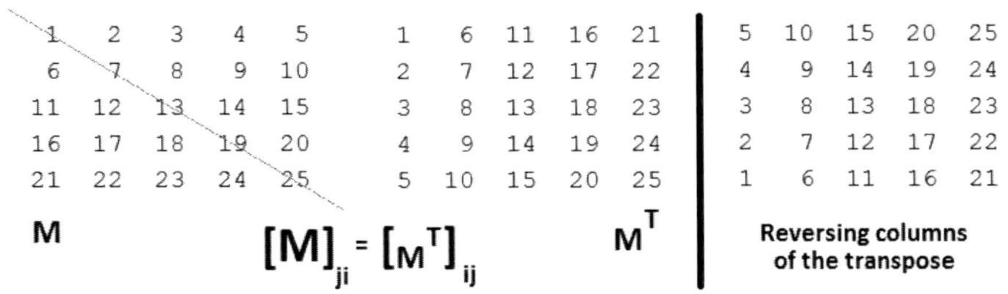

```
 1  2  3  4  5        1  6 11 16 21        5 10 15 20 25
 6  7  8  9 10        2  7 12 17 22        4  9 14 19 24
11 12 13 14 15        3  8 13 18 23        3  8 13 18 23
16 17 18 19 20        4  9 14 19 24        2  7 12 17 22
21 22 23 24 25        5 10 15 20 25        1  6 11 16 21

      M              $[M]_{ji} = [M^T]_{ij}$    $M^T$    Reversing columns
                                                         of the transpose
```

Figure 10.6 – The transpose of a matrix on the left and the final result on the right

To obtain the transpose (M^T), we can swap $M[j][i]$ with $M[i][j]$ via the following method:

```
private static void transpose(int m[][]) {

  for (int i = 0; i < m.length; i++) {
    for (int j = i; j < m[0].length; j++) {
      int temp = m[j][i];
      m[j][i] = m[i][j];
      m[i][j] = temp;
    }
  }
}
```

Reversing the columns of M^T can be done like so:

```
public static boolean rotateWithTranspose(int m[][]) {

  transpose(m);

  for (int i = 0; i < m[0].length; i++) {
    for (int j = 0, k = m[0].length - 1; j < k; j++, k--) {
      int temp = m[j][i];
      m[j][i] = m[k][i];
      m[k][i] = temp;
    }
  }

  return true;
}
```

This solution has a time complexity of $O(n^2)$ and a space complexity of $O(1)$, so we respect the problem requirements. Now, let's look at another solution to this problem.

Rotating the matrix ring by ring

If we think of a matrix as a set of concentric rings, then we can try to rotate each ring until the entire matrix is rotated. The following image is a visualization of this process for a 5x5 matrix:

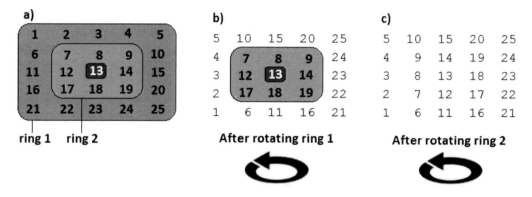

Figure 10.7 – Rotating a matrix ring by ring

We can start from the outermost ring and eventually work our way inward. To rotate the outermost ring, we swap index by index, starting from the top, (0, 0). This way, we move the right edge in place of the top edge, the bottom edge in place of the right edge, the left edge in place of the bottom edge, and the top edge in place of the left edge. When this process is done, the outermost ring is rotated by 90 degrees counterclockwise. We can continue with the second ring, starting from index (1, 1), and repeat this process until we rotate the second ring. Let's see this in terms of code:

```java
public static boolean rotateRing(int[][] m) {

    int len = m.length;

    // rotate counterclockwise
    for (int i = 0; i < len / 2; i++) {
        for (int j = i; j < len - i - 1; j++) {

            int temp = m[i][j];

            // right -> top
```

```
            m[i][j] = m[j][len - 1 - i];

            // bottom -> right
            m[j][len - 1 - i] = m[len - 1 - i][len - 1 - j];

            // left -> bottom
            m[len - 1 - i][len - 1 - j] = m[len - 1 - j][i];

            // top -> left
            m[len - 1 - j][i] = temp;
        }
    }

    return true;
}
```

This solution has a time complexity of O(n²) and a space complexity of O(1), so we have respected the problem's requirements.

The complete application is called *RotateMatrix*. It also contains the solution for rotating the matrix 90 degrees clockwise. Moreover, it contains the solution for rotating the given matrix in a separate matrix.

Coding challenge 10 – Matrix containing zeros

Google, Adobe

Problem: Consider a given $n \times m$ matrix of integers, M. If $M(i, j)$ is equal to 0, then the entire row, i, and column, j, should contain only zeros. Write a snippet of code that accomplishes this task without using any extra space.

Solution: A naive approach consists of looping the matrix and for each $(i, j) = 0$, setting the row, i, and column, j, to zero. The problem is that when we traverse the cells of this row/column, we will find zeros and apply the same logic again. There is a big chance that we will end up with a matrix of zeros.

To avoid such naive approaches, it is better to take an example and try to visualize the solution. Let's consider a 5x8 matrix, as shown in the following image:

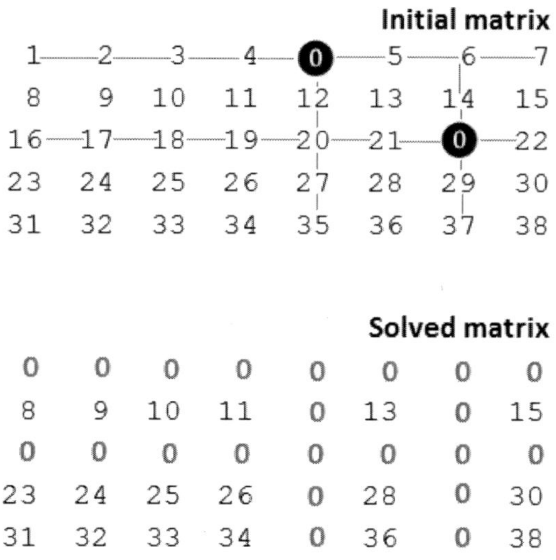

Initial matrix

1	2	3	4	**0**	5	6	7
8	9	10	11	12	13	14	15
16	17	18	19	20	21	**0**	22
23	24	25	26	27	28	29	30
31	32	33	34	35	36	37	38

Solved matrix

0	0	0	0	0	0	0	0
8	9	10	11	0	13	0	15
0	0	0	0	0	0	0	0
23	24	25	26	0	28	0	30
31	32	33	34	0	36	0	38

Figure 10.8 – Matrix containing zeros

The initial matrix has a 0 at (0, 4) and another one at (2, 6). This means that the solved matrix should contains only zeros on rows 0 and 2 and on columns 4 and 6.

An easy-to-implement approach would be storing the locations of the zeros and, at a second traversal of the matrix, set the corresponding rows and columns to zero. However, storing the zeros means using some extra space, and this is not allowed by the problem.

> **Tip**
> With a little trick and some work, we can keep the space complexity set to O(1). The trick consists of using the first row and column of the matrix to mark the zeros found in the rest of the matrix. For example, if we find a zero at cell (i, j) with $i \neq 0$ and $j \neq 0$, then we set $M[i][0] = 0$ and $M[0][j] = 0$. Once we've done that for the entire matrix, we can loop the first column (column 0) and propagate each zero that's found on the row. After that, we can loop the first row (row 0) and propagate each zero that's found on the column.

But how about the potential initial zeros of the first row and column? Of course, we have to tackle this aspect as well, so we start by flagging whether the first row/column contains at least one 0:

```
boolean firstRowHasZeros = false;
boolean firstColumnHasZeros = false;
```

```
// Search at least a zero on first row
for (int j = 0; j < m[0].length; j++) {
  if (m[0][j] == 0) {
    firstRowHasZeros = true;
    break;
  }
}

// Search at least a zero on first column
for (int i = 0; i < m.length; i++) {
  if (m[i][0] == 0) {
    firstColumnHasZeros = true;
    break;
  }
}
```

Furthermore, we apply what we've just said. To do this, we loop the rest of the matrix, and for each 0, we mark it on the first row and column:

```
// Search all zeros in the rest of the matrix
for (int i = 1; i < m.length; i++) {
  for (int j = 1; j < m[0].length; j++) {
    if (m[i][j] == 0) {
      m[i][0] = 0;
      m[0][j] = 0;
    }
  }
}
```

Next, we can loop the first column (column 0) and propagate each zero that was found on the row. After that, we can loop the first row (row 0) and propagate each zero that was found on the column:

```
for (int i = 1; i < m.length; i++) {
  if (m[i][0] == 0) {
    setRowOfZero(m, i);
  }
}
```

```
}
```

```
for (int j = 1; j < m[0].length; j++) {
   if (m[0][j] == 0) {
      setColumnOfZero(m, j);
   }
}
```

Finally, if the first row contains at least one 0, then we set the entire row to 0. Also, if the first column contains at least one 0, then we set the entire column to 0:

```
if (firstRowHasZeros) {
   setRowOfZero(m, 0);
}
```

```
if (firstColumnHasZeros) {
   setColumnOfZero(m, 0);
}
```

setRowOfZero() and setColumnOfZero() are quite simple:

```
private static void setRowOfZero(int[][] m, int r) {
   for (int j = 0; j < m[0].length; j++) {
      m[r][j] = 0;
   }
}
```

```
private static void setColumnOfZero(int[][] m, int c) {
   for (int i = 0; i < m.length; i++) {
      m[i][c] = 0;
   }
}
```

The application is called *MatrixWithZeros*.

Coding challenge 11 – Implementing three stacks with one array

Amazon, Google, Adobe, Microsoft, Flipkart

Problem: Write an implementation of three stacks using a single array. The implementation should expose three methods: push(), pop(), and printStacks().

Solution: There are two main approaches to providing the required implementation. The approach that we'll address here is based on interleaving the elements of these three stacks. Check out the following image:

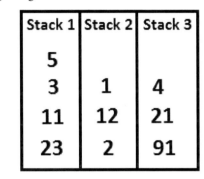

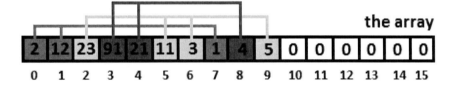

Figure 10.9 – Interleaving the nodes of the stacks

As you can see, there is a single array that holds the nodes of these three stacks, denoted as *Stack 1*, *Stack 2*, and *Stack 3*. The key to our implementation relies on the fact that each node that's pushed onto the stack (the array, respectively) has a backward link to its previous node. The bottom of each stack has a link to -1. For example, for *Stack 1*, we know that value 2 at index 0 has a backward link to the dummy index -1, value 12 at index 1 has a backward link to the index 0, and that value 1 at index 7 has a backward link to the index 1.

So, a stack node holds two pieces of information – the value and the backward link:

```
public class StackNode {

    int value;
```

```
    int backLink;

    StackNode(int value, int backLink) {
      this.value = value;
      this.backLink = backLink;
    }
  }
```

On the other hand, the array manages a link to the next free slot. Initially, when the array is empty, we can only create free slots, so the links are shaped as follows (notice the `initializeSlots()` method):

```
public class ThreeStack {

  private static final int STACK_CAPACITY = 15;

  // the array of stacks
  private final StackNode[] theArray;

  ThreeStack() {
    theArray = new StackNode[STACK_CAPACITY];
    initializeSlots();
  }
  ...
  private void initializeSlots() {
    for (int i = 0; i < STACK_CAPACITY; i++) {
      theArray[i] = new StackNode(0, i + 1);
    }
  }
}
```

Now, when we push a node into one of the stacks, we need to find a free slot and mark it as not free. This is done by the following code:

```
public class ThreeStack {

  private static final int STACK_CAPACITY = 15;
```

```java
    private int size;

    // next free slot in array
    private int nextFreeSlot;

    // the array of stacks
    private final StackNode[] theArray;

    // maintain the parent for each node
    private final int[] backLinks = {-1, -1, -1};
    ...
    public void push(int stackNumber, int value)
            throws OverflowException {

      int stack = stackNumber - 1;
      int free = fetchIndexOfFreeSlot();
      int top = backLinks[stack];
      StackNode node = theArray[free];

      // link the free node to the current stack
      node.value = value;
      node.backLink = top;

      // set new top
      backLinks[stack] = free;
    }

    private int fetchIndexOfFreeSlot()
            throws OverflowException {

      if (size >= STACK_CAPACITY) {
        throw new OverflowException("Stack Overflow");
      }

      // get next free slot in array
      int free = nextFreeSlot;
```

```
        // set next free slot in array and increase size
        nextFreeSlot = theArray[free].backLink;
        size++;

        return free;
    }
}
```

When we pop a node from a stack, we must free that slot. This way, this slot can be reused by a future push. The relevant code is listed here:

```
public class ThreeStack {

  private static final int STACK_CAPACITY = 15;

  private int size;

  // next free slot in array
  private int nextFreeSlot;

  // the array of stacks
  private final StackNode[] theArray;

  // maintain the parent for each node
  private final int[] backLinks = {-1, -1, -1};
  ...
    public StackNode pop(int stackNumber)
              throws UnderflowException {

      int stack = stackNumber - 1;
      int top = backLinks[stack];

      if (top == -1) {
        throw new UnderflowException("Stack Underflow");
      }
```

```
        StackNode node = theArray[top]; // get the top node

    backLinks[stack] = node.backLink;
    freeSlot(top);

    return node;
}

private void freeSlot(int index) {

    theArray[index].backLink = nextFreeSlot;
    nextFreeSlot = index;

    size--;
    }
}
```

The complete code, including the usage of `printStacks()`, is called *ThreeStacksInOneArray*.

Another approach to solving this problem is splitting the array of stacks into three distinct zones:

- The first zone is assigned to the first stack and lies at the left-hand side of the array endpoint (while we push into this stack, it grows in the right direction).
- The second zone is assigned to the second stack and lies at the right-hand side of the array endpoint (while we push into this stack, it grows in the left direction).
- The third zone is assigned to the third stack and lies in the middle of the array (while we push into this stack, it may grow in any direction).

The following image will help you clarify these points:

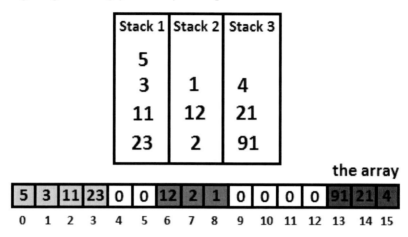

Figure 10.10 – Splitting the array into three zones

The main challenge of this approach consists of avoiding stack collisions by shifting the middle stack accordingly. Alternatively, we can divide the array into three fixed zones and allow the individual stack to grow in that limited space. For example, if the array size is *s*, then the first stack can be from 0 (inclusive) to *s*/3 (exclusive), the second stack can be from *s*/3 (inclusive) to 2**s*/3 (exclusive), and the third stack can be from 2**s*/3 (inclusive) to *s* (exclusive). This implementation is available in the bundled code as *ThreeStacksInOneArrayFixed*.

Alternatively, the middle stack could be implemented via an alternating sequence for subsequent pushes. This way, we also mitigate shifting but we are decreasing homogeneity. However, challenge yourself and implement this approach as well.

Coding challenge 12 – Pairs

Amazon, **Adobe**, **Flipkart**

Problem: Consider an array of integers (positive and negative), *m*. Write a snippet of code that finds all the pairs of integers whose sum is equal to a given number, *k*.

Solution: As usual, let's consider an example. Let's assume we have an array of 15 elements, as follows: -5, -2, 5, 4, 3, 7, 2, 1, -1, -2, 15, 6, 12, -4, 3. Also, if *k*=10, then we have four pairs whose sum is 10: (-15 + 5), (-2 + 12), (3 + 7), and (4 + 6). But how do we find these pairs?

There are different approaches to solving this problem. For example, we have the brute-force approach (usually, interviewers don't like this approach, so use it only as a last resort – while the brute-force approach can be a good start for understanding the details of the problem, it is not accepted as the final solution). Conforming to brute force, we take each element from the array and try to make a pair with each of the remaining elements. As with almost any brute-force-based solution, this one has an unacceptable complexity time as well.

We can find a better approach if we consider sorting the given array. We can do this via the Java built-in `Arrays.sort()` method, which has a runtime of O(n log n). Having a sorted array allows us to use two pointers that scan the whole array based on the following steps (this technique is known as *two-pointers* and you'll see it at work in several problems during this chapter):

1. One pointer starts from index 0 (left pointer; let's denote it as *l*) and the other pointer starts from (*m.length* - 1) index (right pointer; let's denote it as *r*).
2. If $m[l] + m[r] = k$, then we have a solution and we can increment the *l* position and decrement the *r* position.
3. If $m[l] + m[r] < k$, then we increment *l* and keep *r* in place.
4. If $m[l] + m[r] > k$, then we decrement *r* and keep *l* in place.
5. We repeat *steps 2-4* until $l >= r$.

The following image will help you implement these steps:

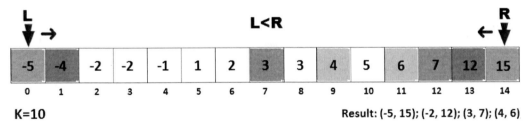

Figure 10.11 – Finding all pairs whose sum is equal to the given number

Keep an eye on this image while we see how it works for *k*=10:

- $l = 0, r = 14 \rightarrow sum = m[0] + m[14] = -5 + 15 = 10 \rightarrow sum = k \rightarrow l++, r--$
- $l = 1, r = 13 \rightarrow sum = m[1] + m[13] = -4 + 12 = 8 \rightarrow sum < k \rightarrow l++$
- $l = 2, r = 13 \rightarrow sum = m[2] + m[13] = -2 + 12 = 10 \rightarrow sum = k \rightarrow l++, r--$
- $l = 3, r = 12 \rightarrow sum = m[3] + m[12] = -2 + 7 = 5 \rightarrow sum < k \rightarrow l++$

- $l = 4, r = 12 \rightarrow sum = m[4] + m[12] = -1 + 7 = 6 \rightarrow sum < k \rightarrow l$++
- $l = 5, r = 12 \rightarrow sum = m[5] + m[12] = 1 + 7 = 8 \rightarrow sum < k \rightarrow l$++
- $l = 6, r = 12 \rightarrow sum = m[6] + m[12] = 2 + 7 = 9 \rightarrow sum < k \rightarrow l$++
- $l = 7, r = 12 \rightarrow sum = m[7] + m[12] = 3 + 7 = 10 \rightarrow sum = k \rightarrow l$++, r--
- $l = 8, r = 11 \rightarrow sum = m[8] + m[11] = 3 + 6 = 9 \rightarrow sum < k \rightarrow l$++
- $l = 9, r = 11 \rightarrow sum = m[9] + m[11] = 4 + 6 = 10 \rightarrow sum = k \rightarrow l$++, r--
- $l = 10, r = 10 \rightarrow$ STOP

If we put this logic into code, then we obtain the following method:

```java
public static List<String> pairs(int[] m, int k) {

  if (m == null || m.length < 2) {
    return Collections.emptyList();
  }

  List<String> result = new ArrayList<>();

  java.util.Arrays.sort(m);

  int l = 0;
  int r = m.length - 1;

  while (l < r) {

    int sum = m[l] + m[r];

    if (sum == k) {
      result.add("(" + m[l] + " " + m[r] + ")");
      l++;
      r--;
    } else if (sum < k) {
      l++;
    } else if (sum > k) {
      r--;
```

```
        }
    }
    return result;
}
```

The complete application is called *FindPairsSumEqualK*.

Coding challenge 13 – Merging sorted arrays

Amazon, Google, Adobe, Microsoft, Flipkart

Problem: Imagine that you have *k* sorted arrays of different lengths. Write an application that merges these arrays into O(nk log n), where *n* is the length of the longest array.

Solution: Let's assume that the given arrays are the following five arrays denoted with *a*, *b*, *c*, *d*, and *e*:

a: {1, 2, 32, 46}   *b*: {-4, 5, 15, 18, 20}   *c*: {3}   *d*: {6, 8}   *e*: {-2, -1, 0}

The expected result will be as follows:

{-4, -2, -1, 0, 1, 2, 3, 5, 6, 8, 15, 18, 20, 32, 46}

The simplest approach consists of copying all the elements from these arrays into a single array. This will take O(nk), where *n* is the length of the longest array and *k* is the number of arrays. Next, we sort this array via an O(n log n) time complexity algorithm (for example, via Merge Sort). This will result in O(nk log nk). However, the problem requires us to write an algorithm that can perform in O(nk log n).

There are several solutions that perform in O(nk log n), and one of them is based on a Binary Min Heap (this is detailed in *Chapter 13, Trees and Graphs*). In a nutshell, a Binary Min Heap is a complete binary tree. A Binary Min Heap is typically represented as an array (let's denote it as *heap*) whose root is at *heap*[0]. More importantly, for *heap*[*i*], we have the following:

- *heap*[(*i* - 1) / 2]: Returns the parent node
- *heap*[(2 * *i*) + 1]: Returns the left child node
- *heap*[(2 * *i*) + 2]: Returns the right child node

Now, our algorithm follows these steps:

1. Create the resulting array of size *n*k*.
2. Create a Binary Min Heap of size *k* and insert the first element of all the arrays into this heap.
3. Repeat the following steps *n*k* times:

    a. Get the minimum element from the Binary Min Heap and store it in the resulting array.

    b. Replace the Binary Min Heap's root with the next element from the array that the element was extracted from (if the array doesn't have any more elements, then replace the root element with infinite; for example, with `Integer.MAX_VALUE`).

    c. After replacing the root, *heapify* the tree.

The code is too big to be listed in this book, so the following is just the end of its implementation (the heap structure and the `merge()` operation):

```java
public class MinHeap {

    int data;
    int heapIndex;
    int currentIndex;

    public MinHeap(int data, int heapIndex,
            int currentIndex) {
        this.data = data;
        this.heapIndex = heapIndex;
        this.currentIndex = currentIndex;
    }
}
```

The following code is for the `merge()` operation:

```java
public static int[] merge(int[][] arrs, int k) {

    // compute the total length of the resulting array
    int len = 0;
    for (int i = 0; i < arrs.length; i++) {
        len += arrs[i].length;
```

```
    }

    // create the result array
    int[] result = new int[len];

    // create the min heap
    MinHeap[] heap = new MinHeap[k];

    // add in the heap first element from each array
    for (int i = 0; i < k; i++) {
      heap[i] = new MinHeap(arrs[i][0], i, 0);
    }

    // perform merging
    for (int i = 0; i < result.length; i++) {

      heapify(heap, 0, k);

      // add an element in the final result
      result[i] = heap[0].data;

      heap[0].currentIndex++;
      int[] subarray = arrs[heap[0].heapIndex];
      if (heap[0].currentIndex >= subarray.length) {
        heap[0].data = Integer.MAX_VALUE;
      } else {
        heap[0].data = subarray[heap[0].currentIndex];
      }
    }

    return result;
}
```

The complete application is called *MergeKSortedArr*.

Coding challenge 14 – Median

Amazon, Google, Adobe, Microsoft, Flipkart

Problem: Consider two sorted arrays, q and p (they can have different lengths). Write an application that computes the median value of these two arrays in logarithmic runtime.

Solution: A median value separates the higher half of a data sample (for example, an array) from the lower half. For example, the following image shows the median value of an array with an odd number of elements (left-hand side) and with an even number of elements (right-hand side), respectively:

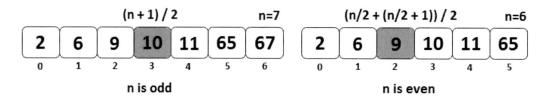

Figure 10.12 – Median values for odd and even arrays

So, for an array with n number of elements, we have the following two formulas:

- If n is odd, then the median value is given by $(n+1)/2$
- If n is even, then the median value is given by $[(n/2+(n/2+1)]/2$

It is quite easy to compute the median of a single array. But how do we compute it for two arrays of different lengths? We have two sorted arrays and we must find something out from them. Having the experience of a candidate that knows how to prepare for an interview should be enough to intuit that the well-known Binary Search algorithm should be considered. Typically, having sorted arrays is something you should take into consideration when implementing the Binary Search algorithm.

We can roughly intuit that finding the median value of two sorted arrays can be reduced to finding the proper conditions that must be respected by this value.

Since the median value divides input into two equal parts, we can conclude that the first condition imposes that the median value of the q array should be at the middle index. If we denote this middle index as *qPointer*, then we obtain two equal parts: [0, *qPointer*] and [*qPointer*+1, *q.length*]. If we apply the same logic to the p array, then the median value of the p array should be at the middle index as well. If we denote this middle index as *pPointer*, then we obtain two equal parts: [0, *pPointer*] and [*pPointer*+1, *p.length*]. Let's visualize this via the following diagram:

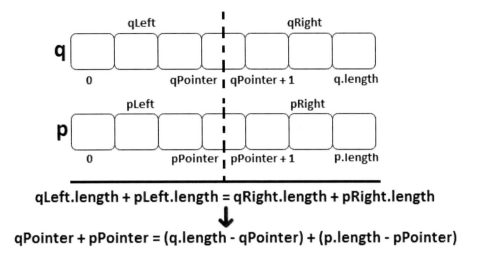

Figure 10.13 – Splitting arrays into two equal parts

We can conclude from this diagram that the first condition that the median value should respect is *qLeft* + *pLeft* = *qRight* + *pRight*. In other words, *qPointer* + *pPointer* = (*q.length*-*qPointer*) + (*p.length* - *pPointer*).

However, since our arrays aren't the same length (they can be equal, but this is just a special case that should be covered by our solution as well), we cannot simply halve both of them. What we can do is assume that $p >= q$ (if they are not given like this, then we just swap them to force this assumption). Furthermore, under the umbrella of this assumption, we can write the following:

qPointer + *pPointer* = (*q.length*- *qPointer*) + (*p.length* - *pPointer*) →

2 * *pPointer* = *q.length* + *p.length* - 2 * *qPointer* →

pPointer = (*q.length* + *p.length*)/2 - *qPointer*

So far, *pPointer* can fall in the middle and we can avoid this by adding 1, which means we have the following starting pointers:

- *qPointer* = ((*q.length* - 1) + 0)/2
- *pPointer* = (*q.length* + *p.length* + 1)/2 - *qPointer*

If $p>=q$, then the minimum (*q.length* + *p.length* + 1)/2 - *qPointer* will always lead to *pPointer* as a positive integer. This will eliminate array-out-of-bounds exceptions and respects the first condition as well.

However, our first condition is not enough because it doesn't guarantee that all the elements in the left array are less than the elements in the right array. In other words, the maximum of the left part must be less than the minimum of the right part. The maximum of the left part can be *q[qPointer-1]* or *p[pPointer-1]*, while the minimum of the right part can be *q[qPointer]* or *p[pPointer]*. So, we can conclude that the following conditions should be respected as well:

- *q[qPointer-1]* <= *p[pPointer]*
- *p[pPointer-1]* <= *q[qPointer]*

Under these conditions, the median value of *q* and *p* will be as follows:

- *p.length + q.length* is even: The average of the maximum of the left part and the minimum of the right part
- *p.length + q.length* is odd: The maximum of the left parts, max(*q[qPointer-1]*, *p[pPointer-1]*).

Let's try to summarize this in an algorithm with three steps and an example. We start with *qPointer* as the middle of *q* (so as, [(*q.length* - 1) + 0)/2] and with *pPointer* as (*q.length* + *p.length* + 1)/2 - *qPointer*. Let's go through the following steps:

1. If *q[qPointer-1]* <= *p[pPointer]* and *p[pPointer-1]* <= *q[qPointer]*, then we have found the perfect *qPointer* (the perfect index).

2. If *p[pPointer-1]* > *q[qPointer]*, then we know that *q[qPointer]* is too small, so *qPointer* must be increased and *pPointer* must be decreased. Since the arrays are sorted, this action will result in a bigger *q[qPointer]* and a smaller *p[pPointer]*. Moreover, we can conclude that *qPointer* can only be in the right part of *q* (from *middle*+1 to *q.length*). Go back to *step 1*.

3. If *q[qPointer-1]* > *p[pPointer]*, then we know that *q[qPointer-1]* is too big. We must decrease *qPointer* to get *q[qPointer-1]* <= *p[pPointer]*. Moreover, we can conclude that *qPointer* can be only in the left part of *q* (from 0 to *middle*-1). Go to *step 2*.

Now, let's consider that *q*={ 2, 6, 9, 10, 11, 65, 67} and *p*={ 1, 5, 17, 18, 25, 28, 39, 77, 88}, and let's apply the previous steps.

Conforming to our preceding statements, we know that *qPointer* = (0 + 6) / 2 = 3 and *pPointer* = (7 + 9 + 1) / 2 - 3 = 5. The following image speaks for itself:

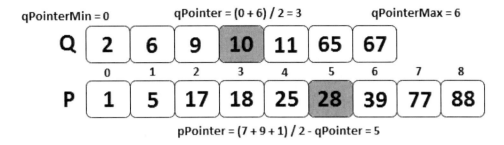

Figure 10.14 – Computing the median value (step 1)

Step 1 of our algorithm specifies that q[qPointer-1] <= p[pPointer] and p[pPointer-1] <= q[qPointer]. Obviously, 9 < 28, but 25 > 10, so we apply *step 2* and afterward, go back to *step 1*. We increase *qPointer* and decrease *pPointer*, so *qPointerMin* becomes *qPointer* + 1. The new *qPointer* will be (4 + 6) / 2 = 5 and the new *pPointer* will be (7 + 9 + 1)/2 - 5 = 3. The following image will help you visualize this scenario:

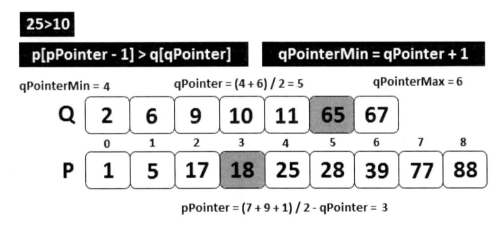

Figure 10.15 – Computing the median value (step 2)

Here, you can see that the new *qPointer* and new *pPointer* respect *step 1* of our algorithm since q[qPointer-1], which is 11, is less than p[pPointer], which is, 18; and p[pPointer-1], which is 17, is less than q[qPointer], which is 65. With this, we found the perfect *qPointer* to be 5.

Finally, we have to find the maximum of the left-hand side and the minimum of the right-hand side and, based on the odd or even length of the two arrays, return the maximum of the left-hand side or the average of the maximum of the left-hand side and the minimum of the right-hand side. We know that the maximum of the left-hand side is max(q[qPointer-1], p[pPointer-1]), so max(11, 17) = 17. We also know that the minimum of the right-hand side is min(q[qPointer], p[pPointer]), so min(65, 18) = 18. Since the sum of lengths is 7 + 9 = 16, we compute that the median value is the average of these two, so avg(17, 18) = 17.5. We can visualize this as follows:

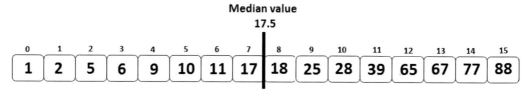

Figure 10.16 – Median value (final result)

Putting this algorithm into code results in the following output:

```
public static float median(int[] q, int[] p) {

    int lenQ = q.length;
    int lenP = p.length;

    if (lenQ > lenP) {
        swap(q, p);
    }

    int qPointerMin = 0;
    int qPointerMax = q.length;
    int midLength = (q.length + p.length + 1) / 2;

    int qPointer;
    int pPointer;

    while (qPointerMin <= qPointerMax) {

        qPointer = (qPointerMin + qPointerMax) / 2;
        pPointer = midLength - qPointer;
```

```java
    // perform binary search
    if (qPointer < q.length
            && p[pPointer-1] > q[qPointer]) {
      // qPointer must be increased
      qPointerMin = qPointer + 1;
    } else if (qPointer > 0
            && q[qPointer-1] > p[pPointer]) {
      // qPointer must be decreased
      qPointerMax = qPointer - 1;
    } else { // we found the poper qPointer

      int maxLeft = 0;

      if (qPointer == 0) { // first element on array 'q'?
        maxLeft = p[pPointer - 1];
      } else if (pPointer == 0) { // first element
                                  // of array 'p'?
        maxLeft = q[qPointer - 1];
      } else { // we are somewhere in the middle -> find max
        maxLeft = Integer.max(q[qPointer-1], p[pPointer-1]);
      }

      // if the length of 'q' + 'p' arrays is odd,
      // return max of left
      if ((q.length + p.length) % 2 == 1) {
        return maxLeft;
      }

      int minRight = 0;

      if (qPointer == q.length) { // last element on 'q'?
        minRight = p[pPointer];

      } else if (pPointer == p.length) { // last element
                                         // on 'p'?
        minRight = q[qPointer];
      } else { // we are somewhere in the middle -> find min
```

```
            minRight = Integer.min(q[qPointer], p[pPointer]);
        }

        return (maxLeft + minRight) / 2.0f;
    }
}

    return -1;
}
```

Our solution performs in O(log(max(*q.length*, *p.length*))) time. The complete application is called *MedianOfSortedArrays*.

Coding challenge 15 – Sub-matrix of one

Amazon, Microsoft, Flipkart

Problem: Consider that you've been given a matrix, *m* x *n*, containing only 0 and 1 (binary matrix). Write a snippet of code that returns the maximum size of the square sub-matrix so that it contains only elements of 1.

Solution: Let's consider that the given matrix is the one in the following image (5x7 matrix):

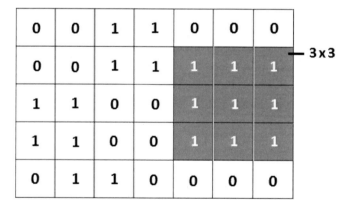

Figure 10.17 – The given 5 x 7 binary matrix

As you can see, the square sub-matrix only containing elements of 1 has a size of 3. The brute-force approach, or the naive approach, would be to find all the square sub-matrices containing all 1s and determine which one has the maximum size. However, for an *m* x *n* matrix that has $z=\min(m, n)$, the time complexity will be $O(z^3mn)$. You can find the brute-force implementation in the code bundled with this book. Of course, challenge yourself before checking the solution.

For now, let's try to find a better approach. Let's consider that the given matrix is of size *n* x *n* and study several scenarios of a 4x4 sample matrix. In a 4x4 matrix, we can see that the maximum square sub-matrix of 1s can have a size of 3x3, so in a matrix of size *n* x *n*, the maximum square sub-matrix of 1s can have a size of *n*-1 x *n*-1. Moreover, the following image reveals two base cases that are true for an *m* x *n* matrix as well:

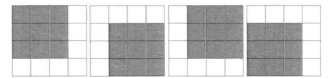

Figure 10.18 – Maxim sub-matrix of 1s in a 4 x 4 matrix

These cases are explained as follows:

- If the given matrix contains only one row, then cells with 1's in them will be the maximum size of the square sub-matrix. Therefore, the maximum size is 1.
- If the given matrix contains only one column, then cells with 1's in them will be the maximum size of the square sub-matrix. Therefore, the maximum size is 1.

Next, let's consider that *subMatrix*[*i*][*j*] represents the maximum size of the square sub-matrix, with all 1s ending at cell (*i,j*):

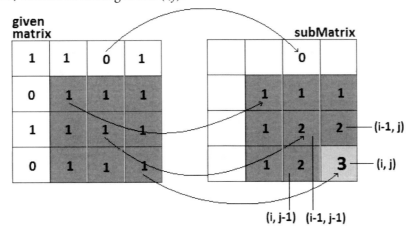

Figure 10.19 – Overall recurrence relation

The preceding figure allows us to establish a recurrence relation between the given matrix and an auxiliary *subMatrix* (a matrix that's the same size as the given matrix that should be filled in based on the recurrence relation):

- It is not easy to intuit this, but we can see that if $matrix[i][j] = 0$, then $subMatrix[i][j] = 0$
- If $matrix[i][j] = 1$, then $subMatrix[i][j]$

$= 1 + \min(subMatrix[i - 1][j], subMatrix[i][j - 1], subMatrix[i - 1][j - 1])$

If we apply this algorithm to our 5 x 7 matrix, then we obtain the following result:

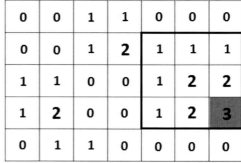

Figure 10.20 – Resolving our 5 x 7 matrix

Gluing together the preceding base cases and the recurrence relations results in the following algorithm:

1. Create an auxiliary matrix (*subMatrix*) of the same size as the given matrix.
2. Copy the first row and first column from the given matrix to this auxiliary *subMatrix* (these are the base cases).
3. For each cell from the given matrix (starting at (1, 1)), do the following:

    a. Fill up the *subMatrix* conforming to the preceding recurrence relations.

    b. Track the maximum element of *subMatrix* since this element gives us the maximum size of the sub-matrix containing all 1's.

The following implementation clarifies any remaining details:

```
public static int ofOneOptimized(int[][] matrix) {

    int maxSubMatrixSize = 1;
    int rows = matrix.length;
```

```java
        int cols = matrix[0].length;

        int[][] subMatrix = new int[rows][cols];

        // copy the first row
        for (int i = 0; i < cols; i++) {
            subMatrix[0][i] = matrix[0][i];
        }

        // copy the first column
        for (int i = 0; i < rows; i++) {
            subMatrix[i][0] = matrix[i][0];
        }

        // for rest of the matrix check if matrix[i][j]=1
        for (int i = 1; i < rows; i++) {
            for (int j = 1; j < cols; j++) {
                if (matrix[i][j] == 1) {
                    subMatrix[i][j] = Math.min(subMatrix[i - 1][j - 1],
                        Math.min(subMatrix[i][j - 1],
                            subMatrix[i - 1][j])) + 1;

                    // compute the maximum of the current sub-matrix
                    maxSubMatrixSize = Math.max(
                        maxSubMatrixSize, subMatrix[i][j]);
                }
            }
        }

        return maxSubMatrixSize;
    }
```

Since we iterate $m*n$ times to fill the auxiliary matrix, the overall complexity of this solution is O(mn). The complete application is called *MaxMatrixOfOne*.

Coding challenge 16 – Container with the most water

Google, **Adobe**, **Microsoft**

Problem: Consider that you've been given n positive integers, $p_1, p_2, ..., p_n$, where each integer represents a point at coordinate (i, p_i). Next, n vertical lines are drawn so that the two endpoints of line i are at (i, p_i) and $(i, 0)$. Write a snippet of code that finds two lines that, together with the X-axis, form a container that contains the most water.

Solution: Let's consider that the given integers are 1, 4, 6, 2, 7, 3, 8, 5, and 3. Following the problem statements, we can sketch the n vertical lines (line 1: {(0, 1), (0, 0)}, line 2: {(1, 4), (1,0)}, line 3: {(2, 6), (2, 0)}, and so on). This can be seen in the following graph:

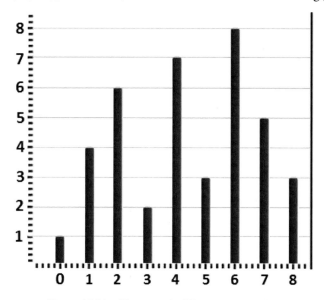

Figure 10.21 – The n vertical line representation

First of all, let's see how we should interpret the problem. We have to find the container that contains the most water. This means that, in our 2D representation, we have to find the rectangle that has the maximum area. In a 3D representation, this container will have the maximum volume, so it will contain the most water.

Thinking about the solution in terms of the brute-force approach is quite straightforward. For each line, we compute the areas showing the rest of the lines while tracking the largest area found. This requires two nested loops, as shown here:

```
public static int maxArea(int[] heights) {
  int maxArea = 0;
```

```
    for (int i = 0; i < heights.length; i++) {
      for (int j = i + 1; j < heights.length; j++) {
        // traverse each (i, j) pair
        maxArea = Math.max(maxArea,
            Math.min(heights[i], heights[j]) * (j - i));
      }
    }

    return maxArea;
}
```

The problem with this code is that its runtime is $O(n^2)$. A better approach consists of employing a technique known as *two-pointers*. Don't worry – it is a pretty simple technique that it is quite useful to have in your toolbelt. You never know when you'll need it!

We know that we are looking for the maximum area. Since we are talking about a rectangular area, this means that the maximum area must accommodate the best report between the *biggest width* and the *biggest height* as much as possible. The biggest width is from 0 to *n-1* (in our example, from 0 to 8). To find the biggest height, we must adjust the biggest width while tracking the maximum area. For this, we can start from the biggest width, as shown in the following graph:

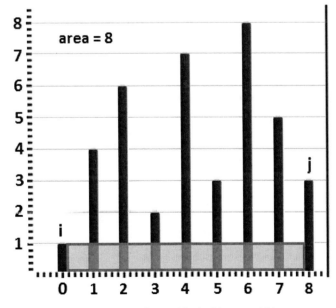

Figure 10.22 – Area with the biggest width

So, if we demarcate the boundaries of the biggest width with two pointers, we can say that $i=0$ and $j=8$ (or n-1). In this case, the container that holds the water will have an area of $p_i *$ $8 = 1 * 8 = 8$. The container cannot be higher than $p_i = 1$ because the water will flow out. However, we can increment i ($i=1$, $p_i=4$) to obtain a higher container, and potentially a bigger container, as shown in the following graph:

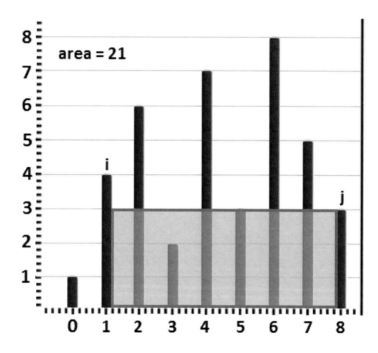

Figure 10.23 – Increasing i to obtain a bigger container

Generally speaking, if $p_i \leq p_j$, then we increment i; otherwise, we decrement j. By successively increasing/decreasing i and j, we can obtain the maximum area. From left to right and from top to bottom, the following image shows this statement at work for the next six steps:

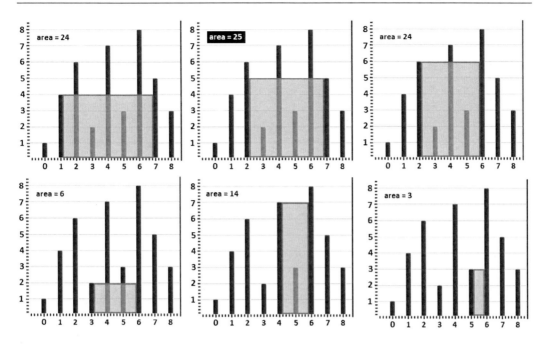

Figure 10.24 – Computing areas while increasing/decreasing i and j

The steps are as follows:

1. In the top-left corner image, we decreased j since $p_i > p_j$, $p_1 > p_8$ (4 > 3).
2. In the top-middle image, we increased i since $p_i < p_j$, $p_1 < p_7$ (4 < 5).
3. In the top-right corner image, we decreased j since $p_i > p_j$, $p_2 > p_7$ (6 > 5).
4. In the bottom-left corner image, we increased i since $p_i < p_j$, $p_2 < p_6$ (6 < 8).
5. In the bottom-middle image, we increased i since $p_i < p_j$, $p_3 < p_6$ (2 < 8).
6. In the bottom-right corner image, we increased i since $p_i < p_j$, $p_4 < p_6$ (7 < 8).

Done! If we increase i or decrease j one more time, then $i=j$ and the area is 0. At this point, we can see that the maximum area is 25 (top-middle image). Well, this technique is known as *two-pointers* and can be implemented in this case with the following algorithm:

1. Start with the maximum area as 0, $i=0$ and $j=n-1$
2. While $i < j$, do the following:

    a. Compute the area for the current i and j.

    b. Update the maximum area accordingly (if needed).

    c. If $p_i \leq p_j$, then i++; else, j--.

In terms of code, we have the following:

```java
public static int maxAreaOptimized(int[] heights) {

    int maxArea = 0;

    int i = 0; // left-hand side pointer
    int j = heights.length - 1; // right-hand side pointer

    // area cannot be negative,
    // therefore i should not be greater than j
    while (i < j) {

        // calculate area for each pair
        maxArea = Math.max(maxArea, Math.min(heights[i],
            heights[j]) * (j - i));

        if (heights[i] <= heights[j]) {
            i++; // left pointer is small than right pointer
        } else {
            j--; // right pointer is small than left pointer
        }
    }

    return maxArea;
}
```

The runtime of this code is O(n). The complete application is called *ContainerMostWater*.

Coding challenge 17 – Searching in a circularly sorted array

Amazon, **Google**, **Adobe**, **Microsoft**, **Flipkart**

Problem: Consider that you've been given a circularly sorted array of integers with no duplicates, m. Write a program that searches for the given x in O(log n) complexity time.

Solution: If we could solve this problem in O(n) complexity time, then the brute-force approach is the simplest solution. A linear search in the array will give the index of the searched x. However, we need to come up with an O(log n) solution, so we need to tackle the problem from another perspective.

We have enough hints that point us to the well-known Binary Search algorithm, which we discussed in *Chapter 7, Big O Analysis of Algorithms* and in *Chapter 14, Sorting and Searching*. We have a sorted array, we need to find a certain value, and we need to do it in O(log n) complexity time. So, there are three hints that point us to the Binary Search algorithm. Of course, the big issue is represented by the circularity of the sorted array, so we cannot apply a plain Binary Search algorithm.

Let's consider that $m = \{11, 14, 23, 24, -1, 3, 5, 6, 8, 9, 10\}$ and $x = 14$, and we expected the output to be index 1. The following image introduces several notations and serves as guidance in solving the problem at hand:

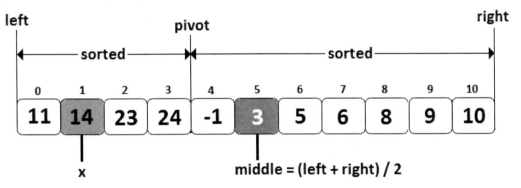

Figure 10.25 – Circularly sorted array and Binary Search algorithm

Since the sorted array is circular, we have a *pivot*. This is an index pointing to the head of the array. The elements from the left of the pivot have been rotated. When the array is not rotated, it will be {-1, 3, 5, 6, 8, 9, 10, **11, 14, 23, 24**}. Now, let's see the steps for the solution based on the Binary Search algorithm:

1. We apply the Binary Search algorithm, so we start by computing the *middle* of the array as (*left* + *right*) / 2.

2. We check whether $x = m[middle]$. If so, we return the *middle*. If not, we continue with the next step.

3. Next, we check whether the right-half of the array is sorted. All the elements from the range [*middle*, *right*] are sorted if $m[middle] <= m[right]$:

    a. If $x > m[middle]$ and $x <= m[right]$, then we ignore the left-half, set *left* = *middle* + 1, and repeat from *step 1*.

    b. If $x <= m[middle]$ or $x > m[right]$, then we ignore the right-half, set *right* = *middle* - 1, and repeat from *step 1*.

4. If the right-half of the array is not sorted, then the left-half must be sorted:

    a. If $x >= m[left]$ and $x < m[middle]$, then we ignore the right-half, set *right* = *middle* - 1, and repeat from *step 1*.

    b. If $x < m[left]$ or $x >= m[middle]$, then we ignore the left-half, set *left* = *middle* + 1, and repeat from *step 1*.

We repeat *steps 1-4* as long as we didn't find x or *left* <= *right*.

Let's apply the preceding algorithm to our case.

So, *middle* is (*left* + *right*) / 2 = (0 + 10) / 2 = 5. Since $m[5] \neq 14$ (remember that 14 is x), we continue with *step 3*. Since $m[5] < m[10]$, we conclude that the right-half is sorted. However, we notice that $x > m[right]$ (14 > 10), so we apply *step 3b*. Basically, we ignore the right-half and we set *right* = *middle* - 1 = 5 - 1 = 4. We apply *step 1* again.

The new *middle* is (0 + 4) / 2 = 2. Since $m[2] \neq 14$, we continue with *step 3*. Since $m[2] > m[4]$, we conclude that the left-half is sorted. We notice that $x > m[left]$ (14 > 11) and $x < m[middle]$ (14 < 23), so we apply *step 4a*. We ignore the right-half and we set *right* = *middle* - 1 = 2 - 1 = 1. We apply *step 1* again.

The new *middle* is (0 + 1) / 2 = 0. Since *m*[0]≠14, we continue with *step 3*. Since *m*[0]<*m*[1], we conclude that the right-half is sorted. We notice that $x > m[middle]$ (14 > 11) and $x = m[right]$ (14 = 14), so we apply *step 3a*. We ignore the left-half and we set *left* = *middle* + 1 = 0 + 1 = 1. We apply *step 1* again.

The new *middle* is (1 + 1) / 2 = 1. Since *m*[1]=14, we stop and return 1 as the index of the array where we found the searched value.

Let's put this into code:

```
public static int find(int[] m, int x) {

  int left = 0;
  int right = m.length - 1;

  while (left <= right) {

    // half the search space
    int middle = (left + right) / 2;

    // we found the searched value
    if (m[middle] == x) {
      return middle;
    }

    // check if the right-half is sorted (m[middle ... right])
    if (m[middle] <= m[right]) {

      // check if n is in m[middle ... right]
      if (x > m[middle] && x <= m[right]) {
        left = middle + 1;   // search in the right-half
      } else {
        right = middle - 1;  // search in the left-half
      }
    } else { // the left-half is sorted (A[left ... middle])
      // check if n is in m[left ... middle]
      if (x >= m[left] && x < m[middle]) {
        right = middle - 1; // search in the left-half
```

```
            } else {
                left = middle + 1; // search in the right-half
            }
        }
    }

    return -1;
}
```

The complete application is called *SearchInCircularArray*. Similar problems will ask you to find the maximum or the minimum value in a circularly sorted array. While both applications are available in the bundled code as *MaximumInCircularArray* and *MinimumInCircularArray*, it is advisable to use what you've learned so far and challenge yourself to find a solution.

Coding challenge 18 – Merging intervals

Amazon, Google, Adobe, Microsoft, Flipkart

Problem: Consider that you've been given an array of intervals of the [*start, end*] type. Write a snippet of code that merges all the intervals that are overlapping.

Solution: Let's consider that the given intervals are [12,15], [12,17], [2,4], [16,18], [4,7], [9,11], and [1,2]. After we merge the overlapping intervals, we obtain the following result: [1, 7], [9, 11] [12, 18].

We can start with the brute-force approach. It is quite intuitive that we take an interval (let's denote it as p_i) and compare its end (p_{ei}) with the starts of the rest of the intervals. If the start of an interval (from the rest of the intervals) is less than the end of p, then we can merge these two intervals. The end of the merged interval becomes the maximum of the ends of these two intervals. But this approach will perform in O(n^2), so it will not impress the interviewer.

Coding challenges 343

However, the brute-force approach can give us an important hint for attempting a better implementation. At any moment of time, we must compare the end of p with the start of another interval. This is important because it can lead us to the idea of sorting the intervals by their starts. This way, we seriously reduce the number of comparisons. Having the sorted intervals allows us to combine all the intervals in a linear traversal.

Let's try and use a graphical representation of our sample intervals sorted in ascending order by their starts ($p_{si} < p_{si+1} < p_{si+2}$). Also, each interval is always forward-looking ($p_{ei} > p_{si}$, $p_{ei+1} > p_{si+1}$, $p_{ei+2} > p_{si+2}$, and so on). This will help us understand the algorithm that we'll cover soon:

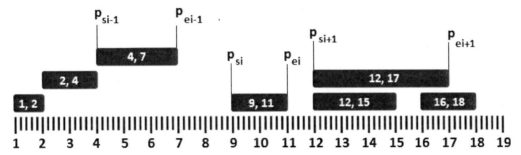

Figure 10.26 – Sorting the given intervals

Based on the preceding image, we can see that if the start of p is greater than the end of the previous p, ($p_{si} > p_{ei-1}$), then the start of the next p is greater than the end of the previous p, ($p_{si+1} > p_{ei-1}$), so there is no need to compare the previous p with the next p. In other words, if p_i doesn't overlap with p_{i-1}, then p_{i+1} cannot overlap with p_{i-1} because the start of p_{i+1} must be greater than or equal to p_i.

If p_{si} is less than p_{ei-1}, then we should update p_{ei-1} with the maximum between p_{ei-1} and p_{ei} and move to p_{ei+1}. This can be done via a stack, as follows:

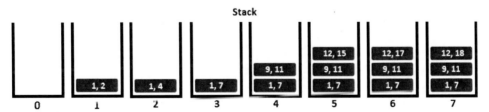

Figure 10.27 – Using a stack to solve the problem

These are the steps that occur:

Step 0: We start with an empty stack.

Step 1: Since the stack is empty, we push the first interval ([1, 2]) into the stack.

Step 2: Next, we focus on the second interval ([2, 4]). The start of [2, 4] is equal to the end of the interval from the top of the stack, [1, 2], so we don't push [2, 4] into the stack. We continue to compare the end of [1, 2] with the end of [2, 4]. Since 2 is less than 4, we update the interval [1, 2] to [1, 4]. So, we merged [1, 2] with [2, 4].

Step 3: Next, we focus on interval [4, 7]. The start of [4, 7] is equal to the end of the interval from the top of the stack, [1, 4], so we don't push [4, 7] into the stack. We continue to compare the end of [1, 4] with the end of [4, 7]. Since 4 is less than 7, we update the interval [1, 4] to [1, 7]. So, we merged [1, 4] with [4, 7].

Step 4: Next, we focus on interval [9, 11]. The start of [9, 11] is greater than the end of the interval from the top of the stack, [1, 7], so intervals [1, 7] and [9, 11] don't overlap. This means that we can push interval [9, 11] into the stack.

Step 5: Next, we focus on interval [12, 15]. The start of [12, 15] is greater than the end of the interval from the top of the stack, [9, 11], so intervals [9, 11] and [12, 15] don't overlap. This means that we can push interval [12, 15] into the stack.

Step 6: Next, we focus on interval [12, 17]. The start of [12, 17] is equal to the end of the interval from the top of the stack, [12, 15], so we don't push [12, 17] into the stack. We continue and compare the end of [12, 15] with the end of [12, 17]. Since 15 is less than 17, we update interval [12, 15] to [12, 17]. So, here, we merged [12, 15] with [12, 17].

Step 7: Finally, we focus on interval [16, 18]. The start of [16, 18] is less than the end of the interval from the top of the stack, [12, 17], so intervals [16, 18] and [12, 17] are overlapping. This time, we have to update the end of the interval from the top of the stack with the maximum between the end of this interval and [16, 18]. Since 18 is greater than 17, the interval from the top of the stack becomes [12, 17].

Now, we can pop the content of the stack to see the merged intervals, [[12, 18], [9, 11], [1, 7]], as shown in the following image:

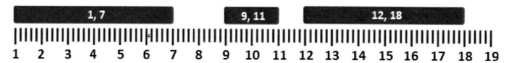

Figure 10.28 – The merged intervals

Based on these steps, we can create the following algorithm:

1. Sort the given intervals in ascending order based on their starts.
2. Push the first interval into the stack.

3. For the rest of intervals, do the following:

   a. If the current interval does not overlap with the interval from the top of the stack, then push it into the stack.

   b. If the current interval overlaps with the interval from the top of the stack and the end of the current interval is greater than that of the stack top, then update the top of the stack with the end of the current interval.

4. At the end, the stack contains the merged intervals.

In terms of code, this algorithm looks as follows:

```java
public static void mergeIntervals(Interval[] intervals) {

    // Step 1
    java.util.Arrays.sort(intervals,
            new Comparator<Interval>() {
        public int compare(Interval i1, Interval i2) {
            return i1.start - i2.start;
        }
    });

    Stack<Interval> stackOfIntervals = new Stack();

    for (Interval interval : intervals) {

        // Step 3a
        if (stackOfIntervals.empty() || interval.start
                > stackOfIntervals.peek().end) {
            stackOfIntervals.push(interval);
        }

        // Step 3b
        if (stackOfIntervals.peek().end < interval.end) {
            stackOfIntervals.peek().end = interval.end;
        }
    }
}
```

```
        // print the result
        while (!stackOfIntervals.empty()) {
            System.out.print(stackOfIntervals.pop() + " ");
        }
    }
}
```

The runtime of this code is O(n log n) with an auxiliary space of O(n) for the stack. While the interviewer should be satisfied with this approach, he/she may ask you for optimization. More precisely, can we drop the stack and obtain a complexity space of O(1)?

If we drop the stack, then we must perform the merge operation in-place. The algorithm that can do this is self-explanatory:

1. Sort the given intervals in ascending order based on their starts.
2. For the rest of the intervals, do the following:

    a. If the current interval is not the first interval and it overlaps with the previous interval, then merge these two intervals. Do the same for all the previous intervals.

    b. Otherwise, add the current interval to the output array of intervals.

Notice that, this time, the intervals are sorted in descending order of their starts. This means that we can check whether two intervals are overlapping by comparing the start of the previous interval with the end of the current interval. Let's see the code for this:

```
public static void mergeIntervals(Interval intervals[]) {

    // Step 1
    java.util.Arrays.sort(intervals,
            new Comparator<Interval>() {
        public int compare(Interval i1, Interval i2) {
            return i2.start - i1.start;
        }
    });

    int index = 0;

    for (int i = 0; i < intervals.length; i++) {

        // Step 2a
```

```java
        if (index != 0 && intervals[index - 1].start
                <= intervals[i].end) {
            while (index != 0 && intervals[index - 1].start
                    <= intervals[i].end) {

                // merge the previous interval with
                // the current interval
                intervals[index - 1].end = Math.max(
                    intervals[index - 1].end, intervals[i].end);
                intervals[index - 1].start = Math.min(
                    intervals[index - 1].start, intervals[i].start);
                index--;
            }
        // Step 2b
        } else {
            intervals[index] = intervals[i];
        }

        index++;
    }

    // print the result
    for (int i = 0; i < index; i++) {
        System.out.print(intervals[i] + " ");
    }
}
```

The runtime of this code is O(n log n) with an auxiliary space of O(1). The complete application is called *MergeIntervals*.

Coding challenge 19 – Petrol bunks circular tour

Amazon, Google, Adobe, Microsoft, Flipkart

Problem: Consider that you've been given *n* petrol bunks along a circular route. Every petrol bunk contains two pieces of data: the amount of fuel (*fuel*[]) and the distance from that current petrol bunk to the next petrol bunk (*dist*[]). Next, you have a truck with an unlimited gas tank. Write a snippet of code that calculates the first point from where the truck should start in order to complete a full tour. You begin the journey with an empty tank at one of the petrol bunks. With 1 liter of petrol, the truck can go 1 unit of distance.

Solution: Consider that you've been given the following data: *dist* = {5, 4, 6, 3, 5, 7}, *fuel* = {3, 3, 5, 5, 6, 8}.

Let's use the following images to get a better understanding of the context of this problem and to support us in finding a solution:

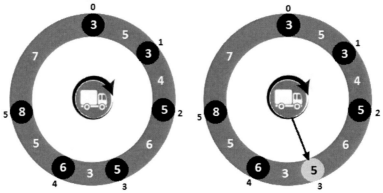

Figure 10.29 – Truck circular tour sample

From 0 to 5, we have six petrol bunks. On the left-hand side of the image, you can see a sketch of the given circular route and the distribution of the petrol bunks. The first petrol bunk has 3 liters of petrol, and the distance to the next petrol bunk is 5 units. The second petrol bunk has 3 liters of petrol, and the distance to the next petrol bunk is 4 units. The third petrol bunk has 5 liters of petrol, and the distance to the next petrol bunk is 6 units, and so on. Obviously, a vital condition if we wish to go from petrol bunk *X* to petrol bunk *Y* is that the distance between *X* and *Y* is less than or equal to the amount of fuel in the tank of the truck. For example, if the truck starts the journey from petrol bunk 0, then it cannot go to petrol bunk 1 since the distance between these two petrol bunks is 5 units and the truck can have only 3 liters of petrol in the tank. On the other hand, if the truck starts the journey from petrol bunk 3, then it can go to petrol bunk 4 because the truck will have 5 liters of petrol in the tank. Actually, as shown on the right-hand side of the image, the solution to this case is to start from petrol bunk 3 with 5 liters of petrol in the tank – take your time and complete the tour using some paper and a pen.

The brute-force (or naive) approach can rely on a straightforward statement: we start from each petrol bunk and try to make the complete tour. This is simple to implement but its runtime will be O(n^2). Challenge yourself to come up with a better implementation.

To solve this problem more efficiently, we need to understand and use the following facts:

- If the *sum of fuel* ≥ *the sum of distances*, then the tour can be completed.
- If petrol bunk X cannot reach petrol bunk Z in the sequence of X → Y → Z, then Y cannot make it either.

While the first bullet is a commonsense notion, the second bullet requires some extra proof. Here is the reasoning behind the second bullet:

If *fuel*[X] < *dist*[X], then X cannot even reach Y
  So to reach Z from X, *fuel*[X] must be ≥ *dist*[X].

Given that X cannot reach Z, we have *fuel*[X] + *fuel*[Y] < *dist*[X] + *dist*[Y], and *fuel*[X] ≥ *dist*[X].
  Therefore, *fuel*[Y] < *dist*[Y] and Y cannot reach Z.

Based on these two points, we can come up with the following implementation:

```java
public static int circularTour(int[] fuel, int[] dist) {

    int sumRemainingFuel = 0; // track current remaining fuel
    int totalFuel = 0;        // track total remaining fuel
    int start = 0;

    for (int i = 0; i < fuel.length; i++) {

        int remainingFuel = fuel[i] - dist[i];

        //if sum remaining fuel of (i-1) >= 0 then continue
        if (sumRemainingFuel >= 0) {
            sumRemainingFuel += remainingFuel;

        //otherwise, reset start index to be current
        } else {
            sumRemainingFuel = remainingFuel;
            start = i;
        }
```

```
        totalFuel += remainingFuel;
    }

    if (totalFuel >= 0) {
        return start;
    } else {
        return -1;
    }
}
```

To understand this code, try to pass the given set of data through the code using some paper and a pen. Also, you may wish to try the following sets:

```
// start point 1
int[] dist = {2, 4, 1};
int[] fuel = {0, 4, 3};

// start point 1
int[] dist = {6, 5, 3, 5};
int[] fuel = {4, 6, 7, 4};

// no solution, return -1
int[] dist = {1, 3, 3, 4, 5};
int[] fuel = {1, 2, 3, 4, 5};

// start point 2
int[] dist = {4, 6, 6};
int[] fuel = {6, 3, 7};
```

The runtime of this code is O(n). The complete application is called *PetrolBunks*.

Coding challenge 20 – Trapping rainwater

Amazon, Google, Adobe, Microsoft, Flipkart

Problem: Consider that you've been given a set of bars that are different heights (non-negative integers). The width of a bar is equal to 1. Write a snippet of code that computes the amount of water that can be trapped within the bars.

Solution: Let's consider that the given set of bars is an array, as follows: *bars* = { 1, 0, 0, 4, 0, 2, 0, 1, 6, 2, 3}. The following image is a sketch of these bars' heights:

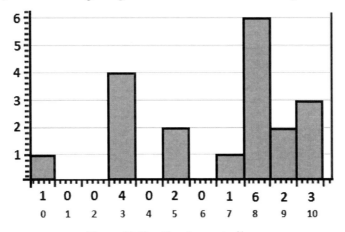

Figure 10.30 – The given set of bars

Now, rain is filling up between the spaces of these bars. So, after the rain has fallen, we will have something like the following:

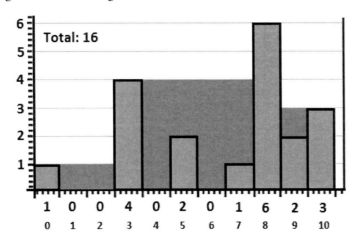

Figure 10.31 – The given bars after rain

So, here, we have a maximum amount of water equal to 16. The solution to this problem depends on how we look at the water. For example, we can look at the water between the bars or at the water on top of each bar. The second view is exactly what we want.

Check out the following image, which has some additional guidance regarding how to isolate the water on top of each bar:

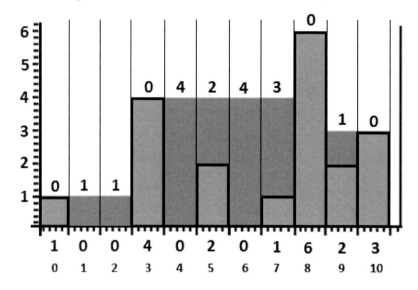

Figure 10.32 – Water on top of each bar

So, above bar 0, we have no water. Above bar 1, we have 1 unit of water. Above bar 2, we have 1 unit of water, and so on and so forth. If we sum up these values, then we get $0 + 1 + 1 + 0 + 4 + 2 + 4 + 3 + 0 + 1 + 0 = 16$, which is the precise amount of water we have. However, to determine the amount of water on top of bar x, we must know the minimum between the highest bars on the left- and right-hand sides. In other words, for each of the bars, that is, 1, 2, 3 ... 9 (notice that we don't use bars 0 and 10 since they are the boundaries), we have to determine the highest bars on the left- and right-hand sides and compute the minimum between them. The following image reveals our computations (the bar in the middle ranges from 1 to 9):

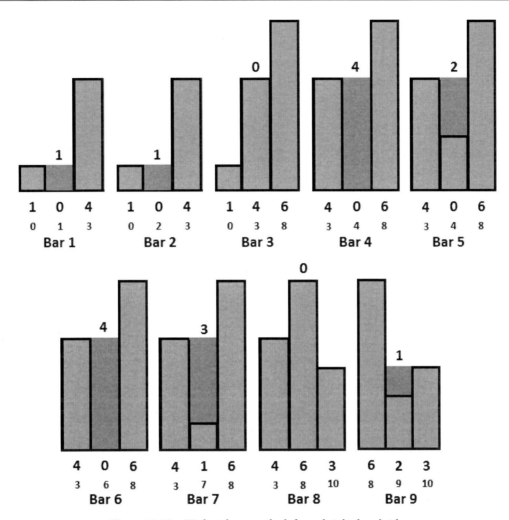

Figure 10.33 – Highest bars on the left- and right-hand sides

Hence, we can conclude that a simple solution would be to traverse the bars to find the highest bars on the left- and right-hand sides. The minimum of these two bars can be exploited as follows:

- If the minimum is smaller than the height of the current bar, then the current bar cannot hold water on top of it.
- If the minimum is greater than the height of the current bar, then the current bar can hold an amount of water equal to the difference between the minimum and the height of the current bar on top of it.

So, this problem can be addressed by computing the highest bars on the left- and right-hand sides of every bar. An efficient implementation of these statements consists of pre-computing the highest bars on the left- and right-hand sides of every bar in O(n) time. Then, we need to use the results to find the amount of water on the top of each bar. The following code should clarify any other details:

```java
public static int trap(int[] bars) {

  int n = bars.length - 1;
  int water = 0;

  // store the maximum height of a bar to
  // the left of the current bar
  int[] left = new int[n];
  left[0] = Integer.MIN_VALUE;

  // iterate the bars from left to right and
  // compute each left[i]
  for (int i = 1; i < n; i++) {
    left[i] = Math.max(left[i - 1], bars[i - 1]);
  }

  // store the maximum height of a bar to the
  // right of the current bar
  int right = Integer.MIN_VALUE;

  // iterate the bars from right to left
  // and compute the trapped water
  for (int i = n - 1; i >= 1; i--) {

    right = Math.max(right, bars[i + 1]);

    // check if it is possible to store water
    // in the current bar
    if (Math.min(left[i], right) > bars[i]) {
      water += Math.min(left[i], right) - bars[i];
    }
```

```
    }

    return water;
}
```

The runtime of this code is O(n) with an auxiliary space of O(n) for the *left*[] array. A similar Big O can be obtained by using an implementation based on a stack (the bundled code contains this implementation as well). How about writing an implementation that has O(1) space?

Well, instead of maintaining an array of size *n* to store all the left maximum heights, we can use two variables to store the maximum until that bar (this technique is known as *two-pointers*). As you may recall, you observed this in some of the previous coding challenges. The two pointers are `maxBarLeft` and `maxBarRight`. The implementation is as follows:

```
public static int trap(int[] bars) {

    // take two pointers: left and right pointing
    // to 0 and bars.length-1
    int left = 0;
    int right = bars.length - 1;

    int water = 0;

    int maxBarLeft = bars[left];
    int maxBarRight = bars[right];

    while (left < right) {
        // move left pointer to the right
        if (bars[left] <= bars[right]) {
            left++;
            maxBarLeft = Math.max(maxBarLeft, bars[left]);
            water += (maxBarLeft - bars[left]);
        // move right pointer to the left
        } else {
            right--;
            maxBarRight = Math.max(maxBarRight, bars[right]);
```

```
            water += (maxBarRight - bars[right]);
        }
    }

    return water;
}
```

The runtime of this code is O(n) with an O(1) space. The complete application is called *TrapRainWater*.

Coding challenge 21 – Buying and selling stock

Amazon, **Microsoft**

Problem: Consider that you've been given an array of positive integers representing the price of a stock on each day. So, the ith element of the array represents the price of the stock on day *i*. As a general rule, you may not perform multiple transactions (a buy-sell sequence is known as a transaction) at the same time and you must sell the stock before you buy again. Write a snippet of code that returns the maximum profit in one of the following scenarios (usually, the interviewer will give you one of the following scenarios):

- You are allowed to buy and sell the stock only once.
- You are allowed to buy and sell the stock only twice.
- You are allowed to buy and sell the stock unlimited times.
- You are allowed to buy and sell the stock only *k* times (*k* is given).

Solution: Let's consider that the given array of prices is *prices*={200, 500, 1000, 700, 30, 400, 900, 400, 550}. Let's tackle each of the preceding scenarios.

Buying and selling the stock only once

In this scenario, we must obtain the maximum profit by buying and selling the stock only once. This is quite simple and intuitive. The idea is to buy the stock when it is at its cheapest and sell it when it is at its most expensive. Let's identify this statement via the following price-trend graph:

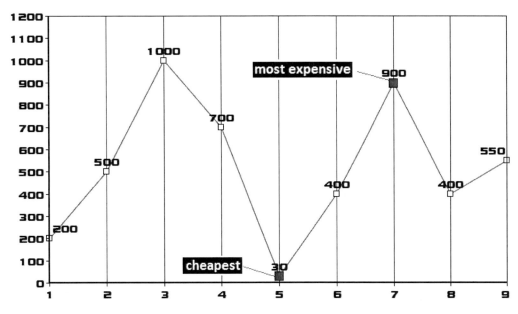

Figure 10.34 – Price-trend graph

Conforming to the preceding graphic, we should buy the stock at a price of 30 on day 5 and sell it at a price of 900 on day 7. This way, the profit will be at its maximum (870). To determine the maximum profit, we can employ a simple algorithm, as follows:

1. Consider the *cheapest price* at day 1 and no profit (*maximum profit* is 0).
2. Iterate the rest of the days (2, 3, 4, ...) and do the following:

    a. For each day, update the *maximum profit* as the max(*current maximum profit, (today's price - cheapest price)*).

    b. Update the *cheapest price* as the min(*current cheapest price, today's price*).

Let's apply this algorithm to our data. So, we consider the *cheapest price* as 200 (price at day 1) and the *maximum profit* is 0. The following image reveals the computations day by day:

	Day 1	Day 2	Day 3	Day 4	Day 5	Day 6	Day 7	Day 8	Day 9
Price	200	500	1000	700	30	400	900	400	550
Min price (from day 1 till today)	200	200	200	200	30	30	30	30	30
Price - Min price	0	300	800	500	0	370	870	370	520
Max profit max(Max profit, Price - Min Price)	200	300	800	800	800	800	870	870	870

maximum profit

Figure 10.35 – Computing the maximum profit

Day 1: The *minimum price* is 200; the *price on day 1 - minimum price* = 0; therefore, the *maximum profit* so far is 200.

Day 2: The *minimum price* is 200 (since 500 > 200); the *price on day 2 - minimum price* = 300; therefore, the *maximum profit* so far is 300 (since 300 > 200).

Day 3: The *minimum price* is 200 (since 1000 > 200); the *price on day 3 - minimum price* = 800; therefore, the *maximum profit* so far is 800 (since 800 > 300).

Day 4: The *minimum price* is 200 (since 700 > 200); the *price on day 4 - minimum price* = 500; therefore, the *maximum profit* so far is 800 (since 800 > 500).

Day 5: The *minimum price* is 30 (since 200 > 30); the *price on day 5 - minimum price* = 0; therefore, the *maximum profit* so far is 800 (since 800 > 0).

Day 6: The *minimum price* is 30 (since 400 > 30); the *price on day 6 - minimum price* = 370; therefore, the *maximum profit* so far is 800 (since 800 > 370).

Day 7: The *minimum price* is 30 (since 900 > 30); the *price on day 7 - minimum price* = 870; therefore, the *maximum profit* so far is 870 (since 870 > 800).

Day 8: The *minimum price* is 30 (since 400 > 30); the *price on day 8 - minimum price* = 370; therefore, the *maximum profit* so far is 870 (since 870 > 370).

Day 9: The *minimum price* is 30 (since 550 > 30); the *price on day 9 - minimum price* = 520; therefore, the *maximum profit* so far is 870 (since 870 >520).

Finally, the *maximum profit* is 870.

Let's see the code:

```
public static int maxProfitOneTransaction(int[] prices) {

    int min = prices[0];
    int result = 0;
    for (int i = 1; i < prices.length; i++) {
        result = Math.max(result, prices[i] - min);
        min = Math.min(min, prices[i]);
    }

    return result;
}
```

The runtime of this code is O(n). Let's tackle the next scenario.

Buying and selling the stock only twice

In this scenario, we must obtain the maximum profit by buying and selling the stock only twice. The idea is to buy the stock when it is as its cheapest and sell it when it is at its most expensive. We do this twice. Let's identify this statement via the following price-trend graph:

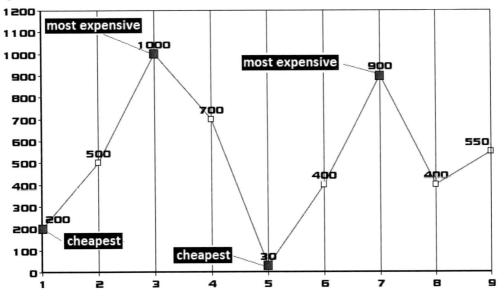

Figure 10.36 – Price-trend graph

Conforming to the preceding graph, we should buy the stock at a price of 200 on day 1 and sell it at a price of 1,000 on day 3. This transaction brings a profit of 800. Next, we should buy the stock at a price of 30 on day 5 and sell it at a price of 900 on day 7. This transaction brings a profit of 870. So, the maximum profit is 870+800=1670.

To determine the *maximum profit*, we must find the two most profitable transactions. We can do this via dynamic programming and the *divide and conquer* technique. We *divide* the algorithm into two parts. The first part of the algorithm contains the following steps:

1. Consider the *cheapest price* at day 1.
2. Iterate the rest of the days (2, 3, 4, ...) and do the following:

    a. Update the *cheapest price* as the min(*current cheapest price, today's price*).

    b. Track the *maximum profit* for today as the max(*maximum profit of the previous day*, (*today price - cheapest price*)).

At the end of this algorithm, we will have an array (let's denote it as *left*[]) representing the maximum profit that can be obtained before each day (inclusive of that day). For example, until day 3 (inclusive of day 3), the maximum profit is 800 since you can buy at a price of 200 on day 1 and sell at a price of 1,000 on day 3, or until day 7 (inclusive of day 7), where the maximum profit is 870 since you can buy at a price of 30 on day 5 and sell at a price of 900 on day 7, and so on.

This array is obtained via *step 2b*. We can represent it for our data as follows:

	Day 1	Day 2	Day 3	Day 4	Day 5	Day 6	Day 7	Day 8	Day 9
Price	200	500	1000	700	30	400	900	400	550
left[day] maximum profit till this day	0	300	800	800	800	800	870	870	870
	left[0]	left[1]	left[2]	left[3]	left[4]	left[5]	left[6]	left[7]	left[8]

Figure 10.37 – Computing the maximum profit before each day, starting from day 1

The *left*[] array is useful for after we've covered the second part of the algorithm. Next, the second part of the algorithm goes as follows:

1. Consider the *most expensive price* on the last day.
2. Iterate the rest of the days from (*last-1*) to the *first* day(*last-1, last-2, last-3, ...*) and do the following:

    a. Update the *most expensive price* as the max(*current most expensive price, today's price*).

b. Track the *maximum profit* for today as the max(*maximum profit of the next day, (most expensive price - today price)*).

At the end of this algorithm, we will have an array (let's denote it as *right*[]) representing the maximum profit that can be obtained after each day (inclusive of that day). For example, after day 3 (inclusive of day 3), the maximum profit is 870 since you can buy at a price of 30 on day 5 and sell at a price of 900 on day 7, or after day 7 the maximum profit is 150 since you can buy at a price of 400 on day 8 and sell at a price of 550 on day 9, and so on. This array is obtained via *step 2b*. We can represent it for our data as follows:

	Day 1	Day 2	Day 3	Day 4	Day 5	Day 6	Day 7	Day 8	Day 9
Price	200	500	1000	700	30	400	900	400	550
right[day] maximum profit after this day	870	870	870	870	870	500	150	150	0
	right[0]	right[1]	right[2]	right[3]	right[4]	right[5]	right[6]	right[7]	right[8]

Figure 10.38 – Computing the maximum profit after each day, starting from the previous day

So far, we have accomplished the *divide* part. Now, it's time for the *conquer* part. The *maximum profit* that can be accomplished in two transactions can be obtained as the max(*left*[*day*]+*right*[*day*]). We can see this in the following image:

	Day 1	Day 2	Day 3	Day 4	Day 5	Day 6	Day 7	Day 8	Day 9
Price	200	500	1000	700	30	400	900	400	550
transaction 1, left[day]	0	300	800	800	800	800	870	870	870
transaction2, right[day]	870	870	870	870	870	500	150	150	0
max(left[day]+right[day])	870	1170	**1670**	1670	1670	1300	1020	1020	870

maximum profit

Figure 10.39 – Computing the final maximum profit of transactions 1 and 2

Now, let's see the code:

```
public static int maxProfitTwoTransactions(int[] prices) {

    int[] left = new int[prices.length];
    int[] right = new int[prices.length];

    // Dynamic Programming from left to right
    left[0] = 0;
    int min = prices[0];
```

```
    for (int i = 1; i < prices.length; i++) {
      min = Math.min(min, prices[i]);
      left[i] = Math.max(left[i - 1], prices[i] - min);
    }

    // Dynamic Programming from right to left
    right[prices.length - 1] = 0;
    int max = prices[prices.length - 1];
    for (int i = prices.length - 2; i >= 0; i--) {
      max = Math.max(max, prices[i]);
      right[i] = Math.max(right[i + 1], max - prices[i]);
    }

    int result = 0;
    for (int i = 0; i < prices.length; i++) {
      result = Math.max(result, left[i] + right[i]);
    }

    return result;
}
```

The runtime of this code is O(n). Now, let's tackle the next scenario.

Buying and selling the stock an unlimited amount of times

In this scenario, we must obtain the maximum profit by buying and selling the stock an unlimited amount of times. You can identify this statement via the following price-trend graph:

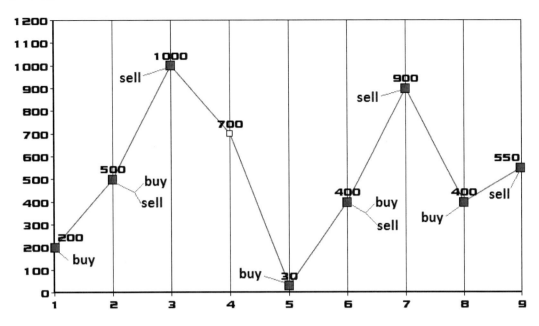

Figure 10.40 – Price-trend graph

Conforming to the preceding graphic, we should buy the stock at a price of 200 on day 1 and sell it at a price of 500 on day 2. This transaction brings in a profit of 300. Next, we should buy the stock at a price of 500 on day 2 and sell it at a price of 1000 on day 3. This transaction brings in a profit of 500. Of course, we can merge these two transactions into one by buying at a price of 200 on day 1 and selling at a price of 1000 on day 3. The same logic can be applied until day 9. The final maximum profit will be 1820. Take your time and identify all the transactions from day 1 to day 9.

By studying the preceding price-trend graphic, we can see that this problem can be viewed as an attempt to find all the ascending sequences. The following graph highlights the ascending sequences for our data:

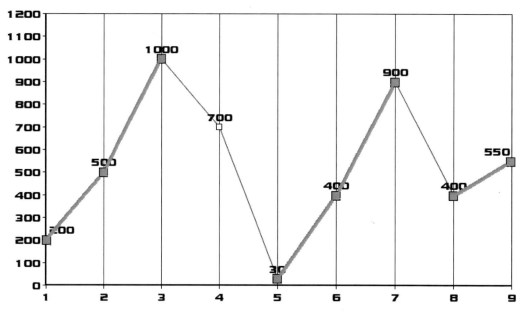

Figure 10.41 – Ascending sequences

Finding all the ascending sequences is a simple task based on the following algorithm:

1. Consider the *maximum profit* as 0 (no profit).
2. Iterate all the days, starting from day 2, and do the following:

    a. Compute the difference between the *today price* and the *preceding day price* (for example, at the first iteration, compute (the price of day 2 - the price of day 1), so 500 - 200).

    b. If the computed difference is positive, then increment the *maximum profit* by this difference.

At the end of this algorithm, we will know the final *maximum profit*. If we apply this algorithm to our data, then we'll obtain the following output:

	Day 1	Day 2	Day 3	Day 4	Day 5	Day 6	Day 7	Day 8	Day 9
Price	200	500	1000	700	30	400	900	400	550
Max profit	0	300	800	800	800	1170	1670	1670	1820

maximum profit

Figure 10.42 – Computing the final maximum profit

Day 1: The *maximum profit* is 0.

Day 2: The *maximum profit* is 0 + (500 - 200) = 0 + 300 = 300.

Day 3: The *maximum profit* is 300 + (1000 - 500) = 300 + 500 = 800.

Day 4: The *maximum profit* remains 800 since 700 - 1000 < 0.

Day 5: The *maximum profit* remains 800 since 30 - 700 < 0.

Day 6: The *maximum profit* is 800 + (400 - 30) = 800 + 370 = 1170.

Day 7: The *maximum profit* is 1170 + (900 - 400) = 1170 + 500 = 1670.

Day 8: The *maximum profit* remains 1670 since 400 - 900 < 0.

Day 9: The *maximum profit* is 1670 + (550 - 400) = 1670 + 150 = 1820.

The final *maximum profit* is 1820.

In terms of code, this looks as follows:

```
public static int maxProfitUnlimitedTransactions(
          int[] prices) {

  int result = 0;
  for (int i = 1; i < prices.length; i++) {
    int diff = prices[i] - prices[i - 1];
    if (diff > 0) {
      result += diff;
    }
  }

  return result;
}
```

The runtime of this code is O(n). Next, let's tackle the last scenario.

Buying and selling the stock only k times (k is given)

This scenario is the generalized version of the *Buying and selling the stock only twice.* scenario. Mainly, by solving this scenario, we also solve the *Buying and selling the stock only twice* scenario for *k=2*.

Based on our experience from the previous scenarios, we know that solving this problem can be done via Dynamic Programming. More precisely, we need to track two arrays:

- The first array will track the *maximum profit* of *p* transactions when the last transaction is on the qth day.
- The second array will track the *maximum profit* of *p* transactions until the qth day.

If we denote the first array as `temp` and the second array as `result`, then we have the following two relations:

1.

```
temp[p] = Math.max(result[p - 1]
        + Math.max(diff, 0), temp[p] + diff);
```

2.

```
result[p] = Math.max(temp[p], result[p]);
```

For a better understanding, let's put these relations into the context of code:

```
public static int maxProfitKTransactions(
        int[] prices, int k) {

    int[] temp = new int[k + 1];
    int[] result = new int[k + 1];

    for (int q = 0; q < prices.length - 1; q++) {
        int diff = prices[q + 1] - prices[q];
        for (int p = k; p >= 1; p--) {
            temp[p] = Math.max(result[p - 1]
                    + Math.max(diff, 0), temp[p] + diff);
            result[p] = Math.max(temp[p], result[p]);
```

```
        }
    }

    return result[k];
}
```

The runtime of this code is O(kn). The complete application is called *BestTimeToBuySellStock*.

Coding challenge 22 – Longest sequence

Amazon, Adobe, Microsoft

Problem: Consider that you've been given an array of integers. Write a snippet of code that finds the longest sequence of integers. Notice that a sequence contains only consecutive distinct elements. The order of the elements in the given array is not important.

Solution: Let's consider that the given array is { 4, 2, 9, 5, 12, 6, 8}. The longest sequence contains three elements and it is formed from 4, 5, and 6. Alternatively, if the given array is {2, 0, 6, 1, 4, 3, 8}, then the longest sequence contains five elements and it is formed from 2, 0, 1, 4, and 3. Again, notice that the order of the elements in the given array is not important.

The brute-force or naive approach consists of sorting the array in ascending order and finding the longest sequence of consecutive integers. Since the array is sorted, a gap breaks a sequence. However, such an implementation will have a runtime of O(n log n).

A better approach consists of employing a *hashing* technique. Let's use the following image as support for our solution:

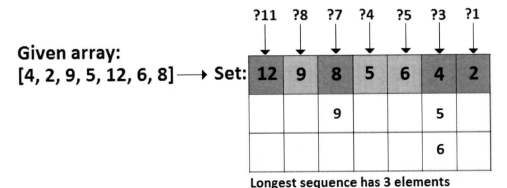

Figure 10.43 – Sequence set

First, we build a set from the given array {4, 2, 9, 5, 12, 6, 8}. As the preceding image reveals, the set doesn't maintain the order of insertion, but this is not important for us. Next, we iterate the given array and, for each traversed element (let's denote it as *e*), we search the set for *e*-1. For example, when we traverse 4, we search the set for 3, when we traverse 2, we search for 1, and so on. If *e*-1 is not in the set, then we can say that *e* represents the start of a new sequence of consecutive integers (in this case, we have sequences starting with 12, 8, 4, and 2); otherwise, it is already part of an existing sequence. When we have the start of a new sequence, we continue to search the set for the consecutive elements: *e*+1, *e*+2, *e*+3, and so on. As long as we find consecutive elements, we count them. If *e*+*i* (1, 2, 3, ...) cannot be found, then the current sequence is complete, and we know its length. Finally, we compare this length with the longest length we've found so far and proceed accordingly.

The code for this is quite simple:

```java
public static int findLongestConsecutive(int[] sequence) {

    // construct a set from the given sequence
    Set<Integer> sequenceSet = IntStream.of(sequence)
        .boxed()
        .collect(Collectors.toSet());

    int longestSequence = 1;

    for (int elem : sequence) {

        // if 'elem-1' is not in the set then
        // start a new sequence
        if (!sequenceSet.contains(elem - 1)) {

            int sequenceLength = 1;

            // lookup in the set for elements
            // 'elem + 1', 'elem + 2', 'elem + 3' ...
            while (sequenceSet.contains(elem + sequenceLength)) {
                sequenceLength++;
            }

            // update the longest consecutive subsequence
```

```
            longestSequence = Math.max(
                longestSequence, sequenceLength);
        }
    }

    return longestSequence;
}
```

The runtime of this code is O(n) with an auxiliary space of O(n). Challenge yourself and print the longest sequence. The complete application is called *LongestConsecutiveSequence*.

Coding challenge 23 – Counting game score

Amazon, Google, Microsoft

Problem: Consider a game where a player can score 3, 5, or 10 points in a single move. Moreover, consider that you've been given a total score, *n*. Write a snippet of code that returns the number of ways to reach this score.

Solution: Let's consider that the given score is 33. There are seven ways to reach this score:

(10+10+10+3) = 33

(5+5+10+10+3) = 33

(5+5+5+5+10+3) = 33

(5+5+5+5+5+5+3) = 33

(3+3+3+3+3+3+3+3+3+3+3) = 33

(3+3+3+3+3+3+5+5+5) = 33

(3+3+3+3+3+3+5+10) = 33

We can solve this problem with the help of Dynamic Programming. We create a table (an array) whose size is equal to *n*+1. In this table, we store the counts of all scores from 0 to *n*. For moves 3, 5, and 10, we increment the values in the array. The code speaks for itself:

```java
public static int count(int n) {

  int[] table = new int[n + 1];

  table[0] = 1;

  for (int i = 3; i <= n; i++) {
    table[i] += table[i - 3];
  }

  for (int i = 5; i <= n; i++) {
    table[i] += table[i - 5];
  }

  for (int i = 10; i <= n; i++) {
    table[i] += table[i - 10];
  }

  return table[n];
}
```

The runtime of this code is O(n) with O(n) extra space. The complete application is called *CountScore3510*.

Coding challenge 24 – Checking for duplicates

Amazon, Google, Adobe

Problem: Consider that you've been given an array of integers, *arr*. Write several solutions that return `true` if this array contains duplicates.

Solution: Let's assume that the given integer is $arr=\{1, 4, 5, 4, 2, 3\}$, so 4 is a duplicate. The brute-force approach (or the naive approach) will rely on nested loops, as shown in the following trivial code:

```java
public static boolean checkDuplicates(int[] arr) {

  for (int i = 0; i < arr.length; i++) {
    for (int j = i + 1; j < arr.length; j++) {
      if (arr[i] == arr[j]) {
        return true;
      }
    }
  }

  return false;
}
```

This code is very simple but it performs in $O(n^2)$ and $O(1)$ auxiliary space. We can sort the array before checking for duplicates. If the array is sorted, then we can compare adjacent elements. If any adjacent elements are equal, we can say that the array contains duplicates:

```java
public static boolean checkDuplicates(int[] arr) {

  java.util.Arrays.sort(arr);

  int prev = arr[0];
  for (int i = 1; i < arr.length; i++) {
    if (arr[i] == prev) {
      return true;
    }

    prev = arr[i];
  }

  return false;
}
```

This code performs in O(n log n) (since we sort the array) and O(1) auxiliary space. If we want to write an implementation that performs in O(n) time, we must also consider an auxiliary O(n) space. For example, we can rely on *hashing* (if you are not familiar with the concept of hashing, then please read *Chapter 6, Object-Oriented Programming*, the *Hash table* problem). In Java, we can use hashing via the built-in `HashSet` implementation, so there is no need to write a hashing implementation from scratch. But how is this `HashSet` useful? While we iterate the given array, we add each element from the array to `HashSet`. But if the current element is already present in `HashSet`, this means we found a duplicate, so we can stop and return:

```java
public static boolean checkDuplicates(int[] arr) {

    Set<Integer> set = new HashSet<>();

    for (int i = 0; i < arr.length; i++) {
      if (set.contains(arr[i])) {
        return true;
      }

      set.add(arr[i]);
    }

    return false;
}
```

So, this code performs in O(n) time and auxiliary O(n) space. But we can simplify the preceding code if we remember that `HashSet` doesn't accept duplicates. In other words, if we insert all the elements of the given array into `HashSet` and this array contains duplicates, then the size of `HashSet` will differ from the size of the array. This implementation and a Java 8-based implementation that has an O(n) runtime and an O(n) auxiliary space can be found in the code bundled with this book.

How about an implementation that has an O(n) runtime and an O(1) auxiliary space? This is possible if we take two important constraints of the given array into consideration:

- The given array doesn't contain negative elements.
- The elements lies in the range [0, *n*-1], where *n=arr.length*.

Under the umbrella of these two constraints, we can employee the following algorithm.

1. We iterate over the given array and for each *arr[i]*, we do the following:

    a. If *arr*[abs(*arr*[*i*])] is greater than 0, then we make it negative.

    b. If *arr*[abs(*arr*[*i*])] is equal to 0, then we make it -(*arr.length*-1).

    c. Otherwise, we return `true` (there are duplicates).

Let's consider our array, *arr*={1, 4, 5, 4, 2, 3}, and apply the preceding algorithm:

- *i*=0, since *arr*[abs(*arr*[0])] = *arr*[1] = 4 > 0 results in *arr*[1] = -*arr*[1] = -4.
- *i*=1, since *arr*[abs(*arr*[1])] = *arr*[4] = 2 > 0 results in *arr*[4] = -*arr*[4] = -2.
- *i*=2, since *arr*[abs(*arr*[5])] = *arr*[5] = 3 > 0 results in *arr*[5] = -*arr*[5] = -3.
- *i*=3, since *arr*[abs(*arr*[4])] = *arr*[4] = -2 < 0 returns `true` (we found a duplicate)

Now, let's look at *arr*={1, 4, 5, 3, 0, 2, 0}:

- *i*=0, since *arr*[abs(*arr*[0])] = *arr*[1] = 4 > 0 results in *arr*[1] = -*arr*[1] = -4.
- *i*=1, since *arr*[abs(*arr*[1])] = *arr*[4] = 0 = 0 results in *arr*[4] = -(*arr.length*-1) = -6.
- *i*=2, since *arr*[abs(*arr*[2])] = *arr*[5] = 2 > 0 results in *arr*[5] = -*arr*[5] = -2.
- *i*=3, since *arr*[abs(*arr*[3])] = *arr*[3] = 3 > 0 results in *arr*[3] = -*arr*[3] = -3.
- *i*=4, since *arr*[abs(*arr*[4])] = *arr*[6] = 0 = 0 results in *arr*[6] = -(*arr.length*-1) = -6.
- *i*=5, since *arr*[abs(*arr*[5])] = *arr*[2] = 5 > 0 results in *arr*[2] = -*arr*[2] = -5.
- *i*=6, since *arr*[abs(*arr*[6])] = *arr*[6] = -6 < 0 returns `true` (we found a duplicate).

Let's put this algorithm into code:

```java
public static boolean checkDuplicates(int[] arr) {

    for (int i = 0; i < arr.length; i++) {

        if (arr[Math.abs(arr[i])] > 0) {
            arr[Math.abs(arr[i])] = -arr[Math.abs(arr[i])];
        } else if (arr[Math.abs(arr[i])] == 0) {
            arr[Math.abs(arr[i])] = -(arr.length-1);
        } else {
            return true;
        }
```

```
    }

    return false;
}
```

The complete application is called *DuplicatesInArray*.

For the following five coding challenges, you can find the solutions in the code bundled with this book. Take your time and challenge yourself to come up with a solution before checking the bundled code.

Coding challenge 25 – Longest distinct substring

Problem: Consider you've been given a string, *str*. The accepted characters of *str* belong to the extended ASCII table (256 characters). Write a snippet of code that finds the longest substring of *str* containing distinct characters.

Solution: As a hint, use the *sliding window* technique. If you are not familiar with this technique, then consider reading *Sliding Window Technique* by Zengrui Wang (https://medium.com/@zengruiwang/sliding-window-technique-360d840d5740) before continuing. The complete application is called *LongestDistinctSubstring*. You can visit the following link to check the code: https://github.com/PacktPublishing/The-Complete-Coding-Interview-Guide-in-Java/tree/master/Chapter10/LongestDistinctSubstring

Coding challenge 26 – Replacing elements with ranks

Problem: Consider you've been given an array without duplicates, *m*. Write a snippet of code that replaces each element of this array with the element's rank. The minimum element in the array has a rank of 1, the second minimum has a rank of 2, and so on.

Solution: As a hint, you can use a `TreeMap`. The complete application is called *ReplaceElementWithRank*. You can visit the following link to check the code: https://github.com/PacktPublishing/The-Complete-Coding-Interview-Guide-in-Java/tree/master/Chapter10/ReplaceElementWithRank

Coding challenge 27 – Distinct elements in every sub-array

Problem: Consider you've been given an array, *m*, and an integer, *n*. Write a snippet of code that counts the number of distinct elements in every sub-array of size *n*.

Solution: As a hint, use a `HashMap` to store the frequency of the elements in the current window whose size is *n*. The complete application is called *CountDistinctInSubarray*. You can visit the following link to check the code: `https://github.com/PacktPublishing/The-Complete-Coding-Interview-Guide-in-Java/tree/master/Chapter10/CountDistinctInSubarray`

Coding challenge 28 – Rotating the array k times

Problem: Consider you've been given an array, *m*, and an integer, *k*. Write a snippet of code that rotates the array to the right *k* times (for example, array {1, 2, 3, 4, 5}, when rotated three times, results in {3, 4, 5, 1, 2}).

Solution: As a hint, rely on the modulo (%) operator. The complete application is called *RotateArrayKTimes*. You can visit the following link to check the code: `https://github.com/PacktPublishing/The-Complete-Coding-Interview-Guide-in-Java/tree/master/Chapter10/RotateArrayKTimes`.

Coding challenge 29 – Distinct absolute values in sorted arrays

Problem: Consider you've been given a sorted array of integers, *m*. Write a snippet of code that counts the distinct absolute values (for example, -1 and 1 are considered a single value).

Solution: As a hint, use the *sliding window* technique. If you are not familiar with this technique, then consider reading *Sliding Window Technique* by Zengrui Wang (`https://medium.com/@zengruiwang/sliding-window-technique-360d840d5740`) before continuing. The complete application is called *CountDistinctAbsoluteSortedArray*. You can visit the following link to check the code: `https://github.com/PacktPublishing/The-Complete-Coding-Interview-Guide-in-Java/tree/master/Chapter10/CountDistinctAbsoluteSortedArray`

Summary

The goal of this chapter was to help you master various coding challenges involving strings and/or arrays. Hopefully, the coding challenges in this chapter have provided various techniques and skills that will be very useful in tons of coding challenges that fall under this category. Don't forget that you can enrich your skills even more via the book *Java Coding Problems* (`https://www.amazon.com/gp/product/1789801419/`), which is published by Packt as well. *Java Coding Problems* comes with 35+ strings and arrays problems that were not tackled in this book.

In the next chapter, we will discuss linked lists and maps.

11
Linked Lists and Maps

This chapter covers the most popular coding challenges involving maps and linked lists that you will encounter in coding interviews. Since singly linked lists are preferred in technical interviews, most of the problems in this chapter will exploit them. However, you can challenge yourself and try to solve each such problem in the context of a doubly linked list as well. Commonly, the problems become easier to solve for a doubly linked list because a doubly linked list maintains two pointers for each node and allows us to navigate back and forth within the list.

By the end of this chapter, you'll know all of the popular problems involving linked lists and maps, and you'll have enough knowledge and understanding of numerous techniques to help you to tackle any other problem in this category. Our agenda is quite simple; we'll cover the following topics:

- Linked lists in a nutshell
- Maps in a nutshell
- Coding challenges

Technical requirements

All of the code files in this chapter are available on GitHub and can be accessed at `https://github.com/PacktPublishing/The-Complete-Coding-Interview-Guide-in-Java/tree/master/Chapter11`.

However, before going into the coding challenges, let's first learn about linked lists and maps.

Linked lists in a nutshell

A linked list is a linear data structure that represents a sequence of nodes. The first node is commonly referred to as the **head**, while the last node is commonly referred to as the **tail**. When each node points to the next node, we have a *singly linked list*, as shown in the following diagram:

Figure 11.1 – A singly linked list

When each node points to the next node and to the previous node, we have a *doubly linked list*, as shown in the following diagram:

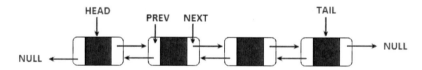

Figure 11.2 – A doubly linked list

Let's consider a singly linked list. If the tail points to the head, then we have a *circular singly linked list*. Alternatively, let's consider a doubly linked list. If the tail points to the head and the head points to the tail, then we have a *circular doubly linked list*.

In a singly linked list, a node holds the data (for example, an integer or an object) and the pointer to the next node. The following code represents the node of a singly linked list:

```
private final class Node {

    private int data;
    private Node next;
}
```

A doubly linked list also requires the pointer to the previous node:

```
private final class Node {

  private int data;
  private Node next;
  private Node prev;
}
```

Unlike an array, a linked list doesn't provide constant time to access the nth element. We have to iterate n-1 elements to obtain the nth element. We can insert, remove, and update nodes in constant time from the beginning of a linked list (singly and doubly). If our implementation manages the tail of the doubly linked list (known as a two-head doubly linked list), then we can insert, remove, and update nodes in constant time from the end of the linked list as well; otherwise, we need to iterate the linked list until the last node. If our implementation manages the tail of the singly linked list (known as a two-head singly linked list), then we can insert nodes in constant time at the end of the linked list; otherwise, we need to iterate the linked list until the last node.

The code bundle for this book comes with the following applications (each application exposes the `insertFirst()`, `insertLast()`, `insertAt()`, `delete()`, `deleteByIndex()`, and `print()` methods):

- *SinglyLinkedList*: Implementation of a two-head singly linked list
- *SinglyLinkedListOneHead*: Implementation of a single-head singly linked list
- *DoublyLinkedList*: Implementation of a two-head doubly linked list
- *DoublyLinkedListOneHead*: Implementation of a single-head doubly linked list

It is highly recommended that you dissect, to the bone, each of these applications on your own. Each of them is heavily commented to help you to understand each step. The following coding challenges rely on these linked list implementations.

Maps in a nutshell

Imagine that you are looking for a word in a dictionary. The word itself is unique and can be considered a *key*. The meaning of this word can be considered the *value*. Therefore, the word and its meaning form a *key-value pair*. Similarly, in computing, a key-value pair accommodates a piece of data in which the value can be found by searching with the key. In other words, we know the key and we can use it to find the value.

A map is an **Abstract Data Type** (**ADT**) that manages key-value pairs (known as entries) via an array. The characteristics of a map include the following:

- Keys are unique (that is, no duplicate keys are allowed).
- We can view the list of keys, the list of values, or both.
- The most common methods to work with a map are `get()`, `put()`, and `remove()`.

Now that we've briefly overviewed the notions of linked lists and maps, let's begin our coding challenges.

Coding challenges

In the following 17 coding challenges, we will cover a number of problems involving maps and linked lists. Since linked lists are a more popular topic in technical interviews, we will allocate a higher number of problems to them. However, to master the concept of map data structures, especially built-in Java map implementations, I strongly recommend that you buy the book *Java Coding Problems*, which is also published by Packt Publishing (`https://www.packtpub.com/programming/java-coding-problems`). Besides being an awesome companion to this book, *Java Coding Problems* contains the following problems with maps (note that this is not a complete list):

- Creating unmodifiable/immutable collections
- Mapping a default value
- Computing whether a value is absent/present in a `Map`
- Removal from a `Map`
- Replacing entries from a `Map`
- Comparing two maps
- Sorting a `Map`
- Copying a `HashMap`
- Merging two maps
- Removing all the elements of a collection that match a predicate

Now that we have a basic idea of what linked lists and maps are, let's take a look at the most popular problems in interviews to do with maps and linked lists.

Coding challenge 1 – Map put, get, and remove

Problem: Write a basic implementation of a map data structure that allows you to put, get, and remove values. You should have one method named put(K k, V v), one method named get(K k), and one method named remove(K k).

Solution: As you know, a map is a key-value pair data structure. Each key-value pair is an entry to the map. Therefore, we cannot implement a map's functionalities until we materialize an entry. Since an entry holds two pieces of information, we need to define a class that wraps the key and the value in a generic approach.

The code is quite simple:

```java
private final class MyEntry<K, V> {

  private final K key;
  private V value;

  public MyEntry(K key, V value) {
    this.key = key;
    this.value = value;
  }

  // getters and setters omitted for brevity
}
```

Now that we have an entry, we can declare a map. A map is managed via an array of entries that have a default size, which is known as the map capacity. A map with an initial capacity of 16 elements is declared as follows:

```java
private static final int DEFAULT_CAPACITY = 16;
private MyEntry<K, V>[] entries
        = new MyEntry[DEFAULT_CAPACITY];
```

Next, we can focus on working with this array to act as a map for the client. Putting an entry into the map can only be done if the entry's key is unique across the map. If the given key exists, then we just update its value. In addition to this, we can add an entry as long as we haven't exceeded the map capacity. The typical approach in such a case is to double the size of the map. The code based on these statements is as follows:

```java
private int size;
public void put(K key, V value) {

  boolean success = true;

  for (int i = 0; i < size; i++) {
    if (entries[i].getKey().equals(key)) {
      entries[i].setValue(value);
      success = false;
    }
  }

  if (success) {
    checkCapacity();
    entries[size++] = new MyEntry<>(key, value);
  }
}
```

The following helper method is used to double the capacity of the map. Since a Java array cannot be resized, we need to tackle this issue by creating a copy of the initial array, but with a double the size of the initial array:

```java
private void checkCapacity() {

  if (size == entries.length) {
    int newSize = entries.length * 2;
    entries = Arrays.copyOf(entries, newSize);
  }
}
```

Getting a value is done using the key. If the given key is not found, then we return `null`. Getting a value doesn't remove the entry from the map. Let's take a look at the code:

```java
public V get(K key) {

  for (int i = 0; i < size; i++) {
    if (entries[i] != null) {
      if (entries[i].getKey().equals(key)) {
        return entries[i].getValue();
      }
    }
  }

  return null;
}
```

Finally, we need to remove an entry using the key. Removing an element from an array involves shifting the remaining elements by one position. After the elements are shifted, the penultimate and last elements are equal. You can avoid memory leaks by nullifying the last element of the array. It is a common mistake to forget this step:

```java
public void remove(K key) {

  for (int i = 0; i < size; i++) {
    if (entries[i].getKey().equals(key)) {
      entries[i] = null;

      size--;

      condenseArray(i);
    }
  }
}

private void condenseArray(int start) {

  int i;
  for (i = start; i < size; i++) {
```

```
        entries[i] = entries[i + 1];
    }

    entries[i] = null; // don't forget this line
}
```

The production implementation of a map is much more complicated than the one exposed here (for example, a map uses buckets). However, most probably, you won't need to know more than this implementation in an interview. Nevertheless, it is a good idea to mention this to the interviewer. That way, you can show them you understand the complexity of the problem and that you are aware of it.

Done! The complete application is named *Map*.

Coding challenge 2 – Map the key set and values

Problem: Consider the previous coding challenge as a basic implementation of a map data structure. Enrich this implementation with a method that returns a set of keys (`keySet()`) and a method that returns a collection of values (`values()`).

Solution: Returning a set of keys is a straightforward operation that involves looping the map's keys and adding them, one by one, to a `Set`. The following code speaks for itself:

```
public Set<K> keySet() {

    Set<K> set = new HashSet<>();
    for (int i = 0; i < size; i++) {
        set.add(entries[i].getKey());
    }

    return set;
}
```

To return a collection of values, we loop the map and add the values, one by one, to a `List`. We use a `List` since values can contain duplicates:

```
public Collection<V> values() {

    List<V> list = new ArrayList<>();
    for (int i = 0; i < size; i++) {
        list.add(entries[i].getValue());
```

```
    }

    return list;
}
```

Done! This was simple; a map implemented for production is far more complex than what is shown here. For example, the values are cached instead of being extracted every time. Mention this to the interviewer so she/he can see that you are aware of how a production map works. Take your time and check the Java built-in `Map` and `HashMap` source code.

The complete application is named *Map*.

Coding challenge 3 – Nuts and bolts

Google, **Adobe**

Problem: Given *n* nuts and *n* bolts, consider a one-to-one mapping between them. Write a snippet of code that finds all matches between the nuts and bolts with the minimum number of iterations.

Solution: Let's consider that the nuts and bolts are represented by the following two arrays:

```
char[] nuts = {'$', '%', '&', 'x', '@'};
char[] bolts = {'%', '@', 'x', '$', '&'};
```

The most intuitive solution relies on a brute-force approach. We can choose a nut and iterate the bolts to find its mate. For example, if we choose `nuts[0]`, we can find its mate with `bolts[3]`. Additionally, we can take `nuts[1]` and find its mate with `bolts[0]`. This algorithm is very simple to implement via two `for` statements and has a complexity time of $O(n^2)$.

Alternatively, we can consider sorting the nuts and bolts. This way, the matches between the nuts and bolts will automatically align. This will also work, but it will not include the minimum number of iterations.

In order to obtain a minimum number of iterations, we can use a hash map. In this hash map, first, we put each nut as a key and its position in the given array of nuts as a value. Next, we iterate the bolts, and we check whether the hash map contains each bolt as a key. If the hash map contains a key for the current bolt, then we have found a match (a pair); otherwise, there is no match for this bolt. Let's take a look at the code:

```java
public static void match(char[] nuts, char[] bolts) {

  // in this map, each nut is a key and
  // its position is as value
  Map<Character, Integer> map = new HashMap<>();
  for (int i = 0; i < nuts.length; i++) {
    map.put(nuts[i], i);
  }

  //for each bolt, search a nut
  for (int i = 0; i < bolts.length; i++) {
    char bolt = bolts[i];
    if (map.containsKey(bolt)) {
      nuts[i] = bolts[i];
    } else {
      System.out.println("Bolt " + bolt + " has no nut");
    }
  }

  System.out.println("Matches between nuts and bolts: ");
  System.out.println("Nuts: " + Arrays.toString(nuts));
  System.out.println("Bolts: " +Arrays.toString(bolts));
}
```

The runtime for this code is O(n). The complete code is named *NutsAndBolts*.

Coding challenge 4 – Remove duplicates

Amazon, **Google**, **Adobe**, **Microsoft**

Problem: Consider an unsorted singly linked list of integers. Write a snippet of code that removes duplicates.

Solution: A trivial solution consists of iterating the given linked list and storing the data of each node in a Set<Integer>. However, before adding the data of the current node into the Set, we check the data against the current contents of the Set. If the Set already contains that data, we remove the node from the linked list; otherwise, we just add its data to the Set. Removing a node from a singly linked list can be done by linking the previous node to the next node of the current node.

The following diagram illustrates this statement:

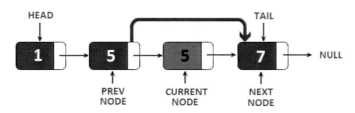

Figure 11.3 – Removing a node from a singly linked list

Since a singly linked list holds a pointer to only the next node, we cannot know the node previous to the current node. The trick is to track two consecutive nodes starting with the current node as the linked list head and the previous node as null. When the current node advances to the next node, the previous node advances to the current node. Let's look at the code that glues these statements together:

```
// 'size' is the linked list size
public void removeDuplicates() {

    Set<Integer> dataSet = new HashSet<>();

    Node currentNode = head;
    Node prevNode = null;
    while (currentNode != null) {
        if (dataSet.contains(currentNode.data)) {
            prevNode.next = currentNode.next;

            if (currentNode == tail) {
                tail = prevNode;
            }

            size--;
```

```
        } else {
            dataSet.add(currentNode.data);
            prevNode = currentNode;
        }

        currentNode = currentNode.next;
    }
}
```

This solution works in the time and space complexity of O(n), where *n* is the number of nodes in the linked list. We can try another approach that reduces space complexity to O(1). First, let's consider the following diagram as a guide for the next steps:

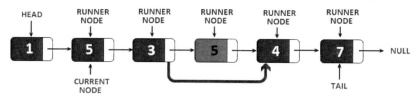

Figure 11.4 – Removing a node from a singly linked list

This approach uses two pointers:

1. The current node, which starts from the head of the linked list and traverses the linked list, node by node, until it reaches the tail (for example, in the preceding diagram, the current node is the second node).
2. The runner node, which starts from the same place as the current node, that is, the head of the linked list.

Additionally, the runner node iterates through the linked list and checks whether the data of each node is equal to the data of the current node. While the runner code iterates through the linked list, the current node's position remains fixed.

If the runner node detects a duplicate, then it removes it from the linked list. When the runner node reaches the tail of the linked list, the current node advances to the next node, and the runner node iterates through the linked list again starting from the current node. So, this is an $O(n^2)$ time complexity algorithm, but with an O(1) space complexity. Let's take a look at the code:

```
public void removeDuplicates() {

    Node currentNode = head;
```

```
    while (currentNode != null) {

        Node runnerNode = currentNode;

        while (runnerNode.next != null) {
            if (runnerNode.next.data == currentNode.data) {

                if (runnerNode.next == tail) {
                    tail = runnerNode;
                }

                runnerNode.next = runnerNode.next.next;
                size--;
            } else {
                runnerNode = runnerNode.next;
            }
        }

        currentNode = currentNode.next;
    }
}
```

The complete code is named *LinkedListRemoveDuplicates*.

Coding challenge 5 – Rearranging linked lists

Adobe, Flipkart, Amazon

Problem: Consider an unsorted singly linked list of integers and a given integer, *n*. Write a snippet of code that rearranges the nodes around *n*. In other words, by the end, the linked list will contain all of the values that are less than *n* followed by all of the nodes that are larger than *n*. The order of the nodes can be altered and *n* itself can be anywhere between the values that are larger than *n*.

Solution: Consider that the given linked list is 1 → 5 → 4 → 3 → 2 → 7 → null, and *n*=3. So, 3 is our pivot. The rest of the nodes should be rearranged around this pivot conforming to the problem requirement. One solution to this problem is to iterate the linked list node by node and each node that is smaller than the pivot is put at the head, while each node that is larger than the pivot is put at the tail. The following diagram helps us to visualize this solution:

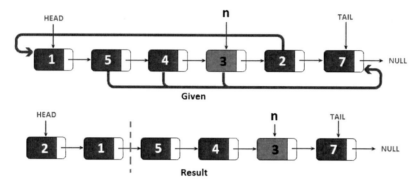

Figure 11.5 – Linked list rearranging

So, the nodes with the values of 5, 4, and 3 are moved to the tail, while the node with the value of 2 is moved to the head. By the end, all values smaller than 3 are on the left side of the dashed line, while all values larger than 3 are on the right side of the dashed line. We can put this algorithm into code as follows:

```
public void rearrange(int n) {

  Node currentNode = head;
  head = currentNode;
  tail = currentNode;

  while (currentNode != null) {

    Node nextNode = currentNode.next;

    if (currentNode.data < n) {
      // insert node at the head
      currentNode.next = head;
      head = currentNode;
    } else {
      // insert node at the tail
```

```
        tail.next = currentNode;
        tail = currentNode;
    }

    currentNode = nextNode;
}

tail.next = null;
}
```

The complete application is named *LinkedListRearranging*.

Coding challenge 6 – The nth to last node

Adobe, **Flipkart**, **Amazon**, **Google**, **Microsoft**

Problem: Consider a singly linked list of integers and a given integer, n. Write a snippet of code that returns the value of the nth to last node.

Solution: We have a bunch of nodes and we have to find the nth node that satisfies a given constraint. Based on our experience from *Chapter 8, Recursion and Dynamic Programming*, we can intuit that this problem has a solution involving recursion. But we can also solve it via an iterative solution. Since the iterative solution is more interesting, I will present it here, while the recursive solution is available in the bundled code.

Let's use the following diagram to present the algorithm (follow the diagram from top to bottom):

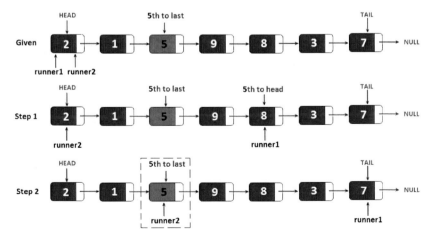

Figure 11.6 – The nth to last node

So, we are given a linked list, 2 → 1 → 5 → 9 → 8 → 3 → 7 → null, and we want to find the fifth to last node value, which is 5 (you can see this at the top of the preceding diagram). The iterative solution uses two pointers; let's denote them as *runner1* and *runner2*. Initially, both of them point to the head of the linked list. In step 1 (the middle of the preceding diagram), we move the *runner1* from the head to the 5th to head (or n^{th} to head) node. This is easy to accomplish in a `for` loop from 0 to 5 (or *n*). In step 2 (the bottom of the preceding diagram), we move *runner1* and *runner2* simultaneously until *runner1* is `null`. When *runner1* is `null`, *runner2* will point to the fifth from the head to last node (or n^{th} from the head to last). In code lines, we do it as follows:

```java
public int nthToLastIterative(int n) {

    // both runners are set to the start
    Node firstRunner = head;
    Node secondRunner = head;

    // runner1 goes in the nth position
    for (int i = 0; i < n; i++) {
        if (firstRunner == null) {
            throw new IllegalArgumentException(
                "The given n index is out of bounds");
        }

        firstRunner = firstRunner.next;
    }

    // runner2 run as long as runner1 is not null
    // basically, when runner1 cannot run further (is null),
    // runner2 will be placed on the nth to last node
    while (firstRunner != null) {
        firstRunner = firstRunner.next;
        secondRunner = secondRunner.next;
    }

    return secondRunner.data;
}
```

The complete application is named *LinkedListNthToLastNode*.

Coding challenge 7 – Loop start detection

Adobe, Flipkart, Amazon, Google, Microsoft

Problem: Consider a singly linked list of integers that contains a loop. In other words, the tail of the linked list points to one of the previous nodes defining a loop or a circularity. Write a snippet of code that detects the first node of the loop (that is, the node from which the loop starts).

Solution: If we manage the tail node of the linked list, then it is obvious that the searched node (the loop start) is at `tail.next`. If we don't manage the tail, then we can search for the node that has two nodes pointing to it. This is also quite easy to implement. If we know the size of the linked list, then we can iterate from 0 to size, and the last `node.next` points to the node that marks the loop start.

The Fast Runner/Slow Runner approach

However, let's try another algorithm that requires more imagination. This approach is called the Fast Runner/Slow Runner approach. It is important because it can be used in certain problems involving linked lists.

Primarily, the Fast Runner/Slow Runner approach involves using two pointers that start from the head of the linked list and iterate through the list simultaneously until a certain condition(s) is met. One pointer is named **Slow Runner** (**SR**) because it iterates through the list node by node. The other pointer is named **Fast Runner** (**FR**) because it iterates through the list by jumping over the next node at every move. The following diagram is an example of four moves:

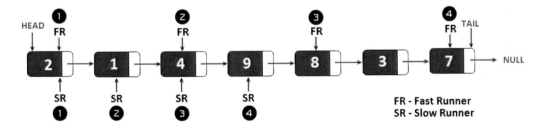

Figure 11.7 – Fast Runner/Slow Runner example

So, at the first move, *FR* and *SR* are pointing to the *head*. At the second move, *SR* points to the *head.next* node with value 1, while *FR* points to the *head.next.next* node with value 4. The moves continue following this pattern. When *FR* reaches the tail of the linked list, *SR* is pointing to the middle node.

As you will see in the next coding challenge, the Fast Runner/Slow Runner approach can be used to detect whether a linked list is a palindrome. However, for now, let's resume our problem. So, can we use this approach to detect whether a linked list has a loop and to find the start node of this loop? This question generates another question. If we apply the Fast Runner/Slow Runner approach to a linked list having a loop, do the *FR* and *SR* pointers collide or meet? The answer is yes, they will collide.

To explain this, let's assume that before starting the loop, we have q preceding nodes (these are the nodes that are outside the loop). For every q nodes traversed by *SR*, *FR* has traversed $2*q$ nodes (this is obvious since *FR* jumps over a node at every move). Therefore, when *SR* enters the loop (reaches the loop start node), *FR* has traversed $2*q$ nodes. In other words, *FR* is at $2*q-q$ nodes in the loop portion; therefore, it is at q nodes in the loop portion. Let's visualize this via the following test case:

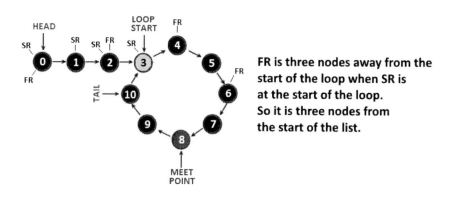

FR is three nodes away from the start of the loop when SR is at the start of the loop. So it is three nodes from the start of the list.

Figure 11.8 – Linked list with a loop

So, when *SR* enters the loop (reaches the fourth node), *FR* reaches the fourth node into the loop. Of course, we need to consider that q (the number of preceding non-loop nodes) might be much larger than the loop length; therefore, we should express $2*q-q$ as $Q=modulo(q, LOOP\_SIZE)$.

For example, consider $Q = modulo(3, 8) = 3$, where we have three non-loop nodes ($q=3$) and the loop size is eight ($LOOP\_SIZE=8$). In this case, we can apply $2*q-q$ as well since $2*3-3=3$. Hence, we can conclude that *SR* is at three nodes from the start of the list and *FR* is at three nodes from the start of the loop. However, if the linked list has 25 nodes that precede a loop of 7 nodes, then $Q = modulo(25, 7) = 4$ nodes, while $2*25-25=25$, which is wrong.

In addition to this, *FR* and *SR* are moving inside the loop. Since they are moving in a circle, it means that when *FR* moves away from *SR*, it also moves closer to *SR* and vice versa. The following diagram isolates the loop and shows how it continues moving *FR* and *SR* until they collide:

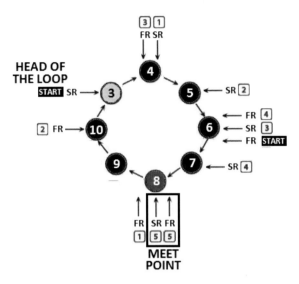

Figure 11.9 – FR and SR collision

Take your time tracking *SR* and *FR* until they reach the meet point. We know that *FR* is at *LOOP_SIZE* – *Q* nodes behind *FR* and that *SR* is *Q* nodes behind *FR*. In our test case, *FR* is 8-3=5 nodes behind *SR*, and *SR* is 3 nodes behind *FR*. By continuing to move *SR* and *FR*, we can see that *FR* catches up at a rate of 1 step per move.

So, where do they meet? Well, if *FR* catches up at a rate of 1 step per move and *FR* is *LOOP_SIZE* – *Q* nodes behind *SR*, then they will meet *Q* steps before the head of the loop. In our test case, they will meet 3 steps before the head of the loop at the node with a value of 8.

If the meet point is at *Q* nodes from the head of the loop, we can continue by recalling that the meet point is at *q* nodes from the head of the loop as well, since *Q=modulo(q, LOOP_SIZE)*. This means that we can develop the following four-step algorithm:

1. Start with *FR* and *SR* from the head of the linked list.
2. Move *SR* at a rate of 1 node and *FR* at a rate of 2 nodes.
3. When they collide (at the meet point), move *SR* to the head of the linked list and keep *FR* where it is.
4. Move *SR* and *FR* at a rate of 1 node until they collide (this is the node representing the head of the loop).

Let's put this into code:

```java
public void findLoopStartNode() {

  Node slowRunner = head;
  Node fastRunner = head;

  // fastRunner meets slowRunner
  while (fastRunner != null && fastRunner.next != null) {
    slowRunner = slowRunner.next;
    fastRunner = fastRunner.next.next;
    if (slowRunner == fastRunner) { // they met
      System.out.println("\nThe meet point is at
        the node with value: " + slowRunner);
      break;
    }
  }

  // if no meeting point was found then there is no loop
  if (fastRunner == null || fastRunner.next == null) {
    return;
  }

  // the slowRunner moves to the head of the linked list
  // the fastRunner remains at the meeting point
  // they move simultaneously node-by-node and
  // they should meet at the loop start
  slowRunner = head;
  while (slowRunner != fastRunner) {
    slowRunner = slowRunner.next;
    fastRunner = fastRunner.next;
  }

  // both pointers points to the start of the loop
  System.out.println("\nLoop start detected at
      the node with value: " + fastRunner);
}
```

As a quick note, don't expect that *FR* can jump over *SR*, so they will not meet. This scenario is not possible. Imagine that *FR* has jumped over *SR* and it is at node *a*, then *SR* must be at node *a*-1. This means that, at the previous step, *FR* was at node *a*-2 and *SR* was at node (*a*-1)-1=*a*-2; therefore, they have collided.

The complete application is named *LinkedListLoopDetection*. In this code, you'll find a method named `generateLoop()`. This method is called to generate random linked lists with loops.

Coding challenge 8 – Palindromes

Adobe, Flipkart, Amazon, Google, Microsoft

Problem: Consider a singly linked list of integers. Write a snippet of code that returns `true` if the linked list is a palindrome. The solution should involve the Fast Runner/Slow Runner approach (this approach was detailed in the previous coding challenge).

Solution: Just as a quick reminder, a palindrome (whether a string, a number, or a linked list) looks unchanged when it's reversed. This means that processing (reading) a palindrome can be done from both directions and the same result will be obtained (for example, the number 12321 is a palindrome, while the number 12322 is not).

We can intuit a solution that involves the Fast Runner/Slow Runner approach by thinking that when *FR* reaches the end of the linked list, *SR* is in the middle of the linked list.

If the first half of the linked list is the reverse of the second half, then the linked list is a palindrome. So, if, in a stack, we store all of the nodes traversed by *SR* until *FR* reaches the end of the linked list, the resulting stack will contain the first half of the linked list in reverse order. Let's visualize this via the following diagram:

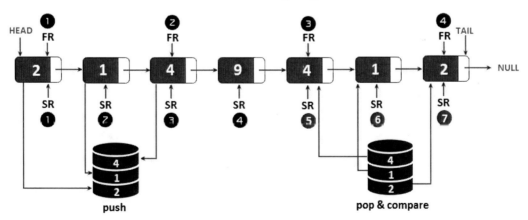

Figure 11.10 – Linked list palindrome using the Fast Runner/Slow Runner approach

So, when *FR* has reached the end of the linked list and *SR* has reached the fourth node (the middle of the linked list), the stack contains the values of 2, 1, and 4. Next, we can continue to move *SR* at a rate of 1 node until the end of the linked list. At each move, we pop a value from the stack, and we compare it with the current node value. If we find a mismatch, then the linked list is not a palindrome. In the code, we have the following:

```java
public boolean isPalindrome() {

  Node fastRunner = head;
  Node slowRunner = head;

  Stack<Integer> firstHalf = new Stack<>();

  // the first half of the linked list is added into the stack
  while (fastRunner != null && fastRunner.next != null) {

    firstHalf.push(slowRunner.data);

    slowRunner = slowRunner.next;
    fastRunner = fastRunner.next.next;
  }

  // for odd number of elements we to skip the middle node
  if (fastRunner != null) {
    slowRunner = slowRunner.next;
  }

  // pop from the stack and compare with the node by node of
  // the second half of the linked list
  while (slowRunner != null) {
    int top = firstHalf.pop();

    // a mismatch means that the list is not a palindrome
    if (top != slowRunner.data) {
      return false;
    }
```

```
    slowRunner = slowRunner.next;
  }

  return true;
}
```

The complete application is named *LinkedListPalindrome*.

Coding challenge 9 – Sum two linked lists

Adobe, Flipkart, Microsoft

Problem: Consider two positive integers and two singly linked lists. The first integer is stored in the first linked list digit by digit (the first digit is the head of the first linked list). The second integer is stored in the second linked list digit by digit (the first digit is the head of the second linked list). Write a snippet of code that adds the two numbers and returns the sum as a linked list having one digit per node.

Solution: Let's start with a visualization of a test case:

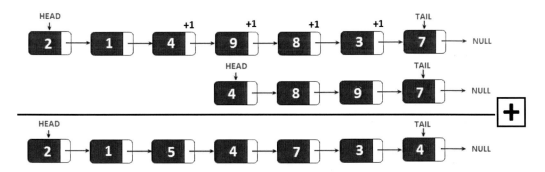

Figure 11.11 – Summing two numbers as linked lists

If we compute the sum from the preceding diagram step by step, we obtain the following:

We add 7 + 7 = 14, so we write down 4 and carry 1:

  The resulting linked list is 4 → ?

We add 3 + 9 + 1 = 13, so we write down 3 and carry 1:

  The resulting linked list is 4 → 3 → ?

We add 8 + 8 + 1 = 17, so we write down 7 and carry 1:

  The resulting linked list is 4 → 3 → 7 → ?

We add 9 + 4 + 1 = 14, so we write down 4 and carry 1

    The resulting linked list is 4 → 3 → 7 → 4 → ?

We add 4 + 1 = 5, so we write down 5 and carry nothing:

    The resulting linked list is 4 → 3 → 7 → 4 → 5 → ?

We add 1 + 0 = 1, so we write down 1 and carry nothing:

    The resulting linked list is 4 → 3 → 7 → 4 → 5 → 1 → ?

We add 2 + 0 = 2, so we write down 2 and carry nothing:

    The resulting linked list is 4 → 3 → 7 → 4 → 5 → 1 → 2

If we write the resulting linked list as a number, we obtain 4374512; therefore, we need to reverse it to 2154734. While the method for reversing the resulting linked list (which can be considered a coding challenge itself) can be found in the bundled code, the following method applies the preceding steps in a recursive approach (if you are not skilled in recursion problems, don't forget to cover *Chapter 8, Recursion and Dynamic Programming*). Essentially, the following recursion works by adding data node by node, carrying over any excess data to the next node:

```
private Node sum(Node node1, Node node2, int carry) {

  if (node1 == null && node2 == null && carry == 0) {
    return null;
  }

  Node resultNode = new Node();
  int value = carry;

  if (node1 != null) {
    value += node1.data;
  }

  if (node2 != null) {
    value += node2.data;
  }

  resultNode.data = value % 10;
```

```
    if (node1 != null || node2 != null) {
        Node more = sum(node1 == null
            ? null : node1.next, node2 == null
            ? null : node2.next, value >= 10 ? 1 : 0);

        resultNode.next = more;
    }

    return resultNode;
}
```

The complete application is named *LinkedListSum*.

Coding challenge 10 – Linked lists intersection

Adobe, Flipkart, Google, Microsoft

Problem: Consider two singly linked lists. Write a snippet of code that checks whether the two lists intersect. The intersection is based on reference, not on value, but you should return the value of the intersection node. So, check the intersection by reference and return the value.

Solution: If you are not sure what the *intersection of two linked lists* means, then we recommended that you sketch a test case and discuss the details with the interviewer. The following diagram shows such a case:

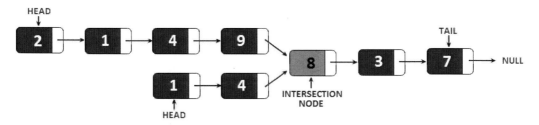

Figure 11.12 – The intersection of two lists

In this diagram, we have two lists that intersect at the node with value 8. Because we are talking about an intersection by reference, this means that the nodes with the value of 9, and value of 4, point to the memory address of the node with the value of 8.

The main issue is that the lists are not of the same size. If their sizes were equal, we could traverse both of them, node by node, from head to tail until they collide (until *node_list_1.next= node_list_2.next*). If we could skip the nodes with values of 2 and 1, our lists will be the same size (refer to the next diagram; since the first list is longer than the second list, we should start iterating from the node marked *virtual head*):

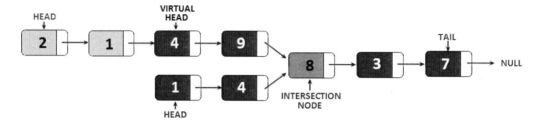

Figure 11.13 – Removing the first two nodes of the top list

Keeping this statement in mind, we can deduce the following algorithm:

1. Determine the sizes of the lists.

2. If the first list (let's denote it as *l1*) is longer than the second one (let's denote it as *l2*), then move the pointer of the first list to (*l1-l2*).

3. If the first list is shorter than the second one, then move the pointer of the second list to (*l2-l1*).

4. Move both pointers, node by node, until you reach the end or until they collide.

Putting these steps into code is straightforward:

```
public int intersection() {

  // this is the head of first list
  Node currentNode1 = {head_of_first_list};

  // this is the head of the second list
  Node currentNode2 = {head_of_second_list};

  // compute the size of both linked lists
  // linkedListSize() is just a helper method
  int s1 = linkedListSize(currentNode1);
  int s2 = linkedListSize(currentNode2);
```

```
    // the first linked list is longer than the second one
    if (s1 > s2) {
      for (int i = 0; i < (s1 - s2); i++) {
        currentNode1 = currentNode1.next;
      }
    } else {
      // the second linked list is longer than the first one
      for (int i = 0; i < (s2 - s1); i++) {
        currentNode2 = currentNode2.next;
      }
    }

    // iterate both lists until the end or the intersection node
    while (currentNode1 != null && currentNode2 != null) {

      // we compare references not values!
      if (currentNode1 == currentNode2) {
        return currentNode1.data;
      }

      currentNode1 = currentNode1.next;
      currentNode2 = currentNode2.next;
    }

    return -1;
}
```

The complete application is named *LinkedListsIntersection*. In the code, you will see a helper method named `generateTwoLinkedListWithInterection()`. This is used to generate random lists with an intersection point.

Coding challenge 11 – Swap adjacent nodes

Amazon, Google

Problem: Consider a singly linked list. Write a snippet of code that swaps the adjacent nodes so that a list such as 1 → 2 → 3 → 4 → null becomes 2 → 1 → 4 → 3 → null. Consider swapping the adjacent nodes, not their values!

Solution: We can reduce the problem of finding a solution to swap two consecutive nodes, *n1* and *n2*. A well-known technique to swap two values (for example, two integers, *v1* and *v2*) relies on an auxiliary variable and can be written as follows:

aux = v1; v1 = v2; v2 = aux;

However, we cannot apply this plain approach to nodes because we have to deal with their links. It is not enough to write the following:

aux = n1; n1 = n2; n2 = aux;

If we rely on this plain approach to swap *n1* with *n2*, then we will obtain something similar to the following diagram (notice that after swapping *n1* with *n2*, we have *n1.next = n3* and *n2.next = n1*, which is totally wrong):

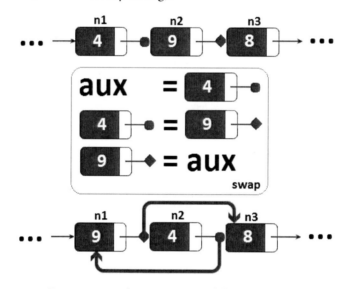

Figure 11.14 – Plain swapping with broken links (1)

But we can fix the links, right? Well, we can explicitly set *n1.next* to point to *n2*, and set *n2.next* to point to *n3*:

n1.next = n2

n2.next = n3

Now it should be good! We can swap two consecutive nodes. However, when we swap a pair of nodes, we also break the links between two consecutive pairs of nodes. The following diagram illustrates this issue (we swap and fix the links for the *n1-n2* pair and the *n3-n4* pair):

Coding challenges

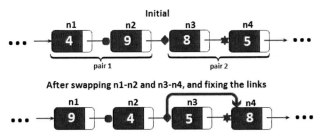

Figure 11.15 – Plain swapping with broken links (2)

Notice that after swapping these two pairs, *n2.next* points to *n4*, which is wrong. Hence, we must fix this link as well. For this, we can store *n2*, and, after swapping *n3-n4*, we can repair the link by setting *n2.next=n3*. Now, everything looks good and we can put it into code:

```
public void swap() {

  if (head == null || head.next == null) {
    return;
  }

  Node currentNode = head;
  Node prevPair = null;

  // consider two nodes at a time and swap their links
  while (currentNode != null && currentNode.next != null) {

    Node node1 = currentNode;                // first node
    Node node2 = currentNode.next;           // second node
    Node node3 = currentNode.next.next;      // third node

    // swap node1 node2
    Node auxNode = node1;
    node1 = node2;
    node2 = auxNode;

    // repair the links broken by swapping
    node1.next = node2;
    node2.next = node3;
```

```
      // if we are at the first swap we set the head
      if (prevPair == null) {
        head = node1;
      } else {
        // we link the previous pair to this pair
        prevPair.next = node1;
      }

      // there are no more nodes, therefore set the tail
      if (currentNode.next == null) {
        tail = currentNode;
      }

      // prepare the prevNode of the current pair
      prevPair = node2;

      // advance to the next pair
      currentNode = node3;
   }
}
```

The complete application is named *LinkedListPairwiseSwap*. Consider challenging yourself to swap sequences of *n* nodes.

Coding challenge 12 – Merge two sorted linked lists

Amazon, Google, Adobe, Microsoft, Flipkart

Problem: Consider two sorted singly linked lists. Write a snippet of code that merges these two lists without extra space.

Solution: So, we have two sorted lists, *list1*: 4 → 7 → 8 → 10 → null and *list2*: 5 → 9 → 11 → null, and we want to obtain the result, 4 → 5 → 7 → 8 → 9 → 10 → 11 → null. Moreover, we want to obtain this result without allocating new nodes.

Since we cannot allocate new nodes, we have to choose one of these lists to become the final result or the merged linked list. In other words, we can start with *list1* as the merged linked list and add nodes from *list2* at the appropriate place in *list1*. After processing each comparison, we move the pointer (*list1*) to the last node in the merged list.

For example, we start by comparing the heads of these two lists. If the head of *list1* is smaller than the head of *list2*, we choose the head of *list1* as the head of the merged list. Otherwise, if the head of *list1* is bigger than the head of *list2*, we swap the heads. The following diagram illustrates this step:

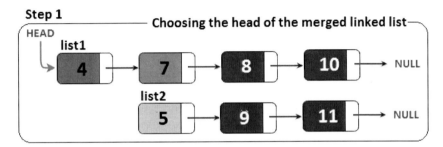

Figure 11.16 – Merging two sorted linked lists (step 1)

Since the head of *list1* is less than the head of *list2* (4 < 5), it becomes the head of the merged list. We said that *list1* will point to the last node of the merged list; therefore, the next node to compare should be *list1.next* (the node with value 7) and *list2* (the node with value 5). The following diagram reveals the result of this comparison:

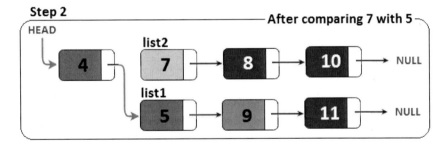

Figure 11.17 – Merging two sorted linked lists (step 2)

Because *list1* follows the merged list (the final result), we have to move *list1.next* to the node with value 5, but we cannot do it directly. If we say *list1.next=list2*, then we lose the rest of *list1*. Therefore, we have to perform a swap, as follows:

```
Node auxNode = list1.next;   // auxNode = node with value 7
list1.next = list2;          // list1.next = node with value 5
list2 = auxNode;             // list2 = node with value 7
```

Next, we move *list1* to *list1.next*, which is the node with value 9. We compare *list.next* with *list2*; therefore, we compare 9 with 7. The following diagram reveals the result of this comparison:

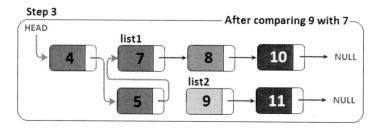

Figure 11.18 – Merging two sorted linked lists (step 3)

Because *list1* follows the merged list (the final result), we have to move *list1.next* to the node with value 7 (since 7 < 9), and we do it using the swap that we discussed earlier. Next, we move *list1* to *list1.next*, which is the node with value 8. We compare *list.next* with *list2*; therefore, we compare 8 with 9. The following diagram reveals the result of this comparison:

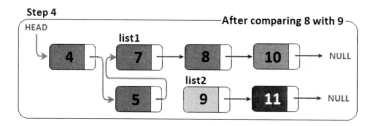

Figure 11.19 – Merging two sorted linked lists (step 4)

Since 8 < 9, no swap is needed. We move *list1.next* to the next node (the node with value 10) and compare 10 with 9. The next diagram reveals the result of this comparison:

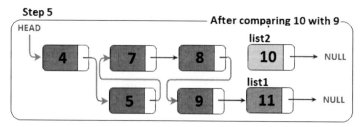

Figure 11.20 – Merging two sorted linked lists (step 5)

As *list1* follows the merged list (the final result), we have to move *list1.next* to the node with value 9 (since 9 < 10), and we do it using the swap that we discussed earlier. Next, we move *list1* to *list1.next*, which is the node with value 11. We compare *list.next* with *list2*; therefore, we compare 11 with 10. The next diagram reveals the result of this comparison:

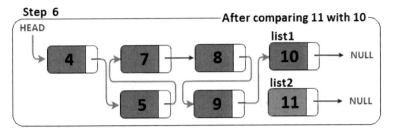

Figure 11.21 – Merging two sorted linked lists (step 6)

Because *list1* follows the merged list (the final result), we have to move *list1.next* to the node with value 10 (since 10 < 11), and we do it using the swap that we discussed earlier. Next, we move *list1* to *list1.next*, which is `null`; therefore, we copy the remaining part from *list2*. The next diagram reveals the result of this comparison:

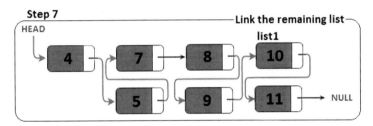

Figure 11.22 – Merging two sorted linked lists (last step)

At this point, the merged linked list is complete. It is time to reveal the code (this method is added to the well-known `SinglyLinkedList`):

```
public void merge(SinglyLinkedList sll) {

    // these are the two lists
    Node list1 = head;       // the merged linked list
    Node list2 = sll.head;   // from this list we add nodes at
                             // appropriate place in list1

    // compare heads and swap them if it is necessary
    if (list1.data < list2.data) {
```

```
      head = list1;
    } else {
      head = list2;
      list2 = list1;
      list1 = head;
    }

    // compare the nodes from list1 with the nodes from list2
    while (list1.next != null) {
      if (list1.next.data > list2.data) {

        Node auxNode = list1.next;
        list1.next = list2;
        list2 = auxNode;
      }

      // advance to the last node in the merged linked list
      list1 = list1.next;
    }

    // add the remaining list2
    if (list1.next == null) {
      list1.next = list2;
    }
}
```

The complete application is named *LinkedListMergeTwoSorted*. A similar problem may require you to merge two sorted linked lists via recursion. While you can find this application named as *LinkedListMergeTwoSortedRecursion*, I advise you to challenge yourself to try an implementation. Additionally, based on this recursive implementation, challenge yourself to merge *n*-linked lists. The complete application is named *LinkedListMergeNSortedRecursion*.

Coding challenge 13 – Remove the redundant path

Problem: Consider a singly linked list storing a path in a matrix. The data of a node is of type (*row, column*) or, in short, (*r, c*). The path can only be either horizontal (by *column*) or vertical (by *row*). The complete path is given by the end points of all of the horizontal and vertical paths; therefore, the middle points (or points in between) are redundant. Write a snippet of code that removes the redundant path.

Solution: Let's consider a linked list containing the following path: (0, 0) → (0, 1) → (0, 2) → (1, 2) → (2, 2) → (3, 2) → (3, 3) → (3, 4) → null. The redundant path includes the following nodes: (0, 1), (1, 2), (2, 2), and (3, 3). So, after removing the redundant path, we should remain with a list that contains four nodes: (0, 0) → (0, 2) → (3, 2) → (3, 4) → null. The following diagram represents the redundant path:

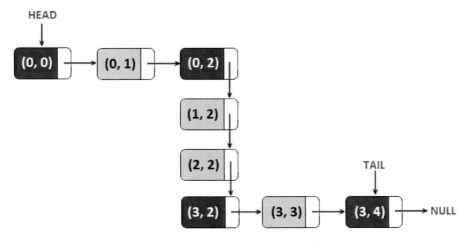

Figure 11.23 – The redundant path

After removing the redundant path, we obtain the following diagram:

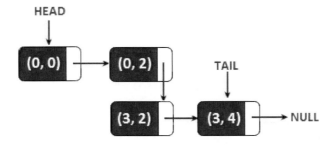

Figure 11.24 – The remaining path after removing the redundancy

The preceding diagrams should suggest a solution to this problem. Notice that the nodes that define a vertical path have the same column since we move only down/up on the rows, while the nodes that define a horizontal path have the same row since we move only left/right on the columns. This means that if we consider three consecutive nodes having the same value for the column or the row, then we can remove the middle node. Repeating this process for adjacent triplets will remove all redundant nodes. The code should be quite simple to follow:

```
public void removeRedundantPath() {

  Node currentNode = head;

  while (currentNode.next != null
          && currentNode.next.next != null) {

    Node middleNode = currentNode.next.next;

    // check for a vertical triplet (triplet with same column)
    if (currentNode.c == currentNode.next.c
            && currentNode.c == middleNode.c) {

      // delete the middle node
      currentNode.next = middleNode;

    } // check for a horizontal triplet
    else if (currentNode.r == currentNode.next.r
            && currentNode.r == middleNode.r) {

      // delete the middle node
      currentNode.next = middleNode;

    } else {
      currentNode = currentNode.next;
    }
  }
}
```

The complete application is named *LinkedListRemoveRedundantPath*.

Coding challenge 14 – Move the last node to the front

Problem: Consider a singly linked list. Write a snippet of code that moves the last node to the front via two approaches. So, the last node of the linked list becomes its head.

Solution: This is the kind of problem that sounds simple, and it is simple. The first approach will follow these steps:

1. Move a pointer to the second to last node (let's denote it as *currentNode*).
2. Store the *currentNode.next* (let's denote it as *nextNode* – this is the last node).
3. Set *currentNode.next* to `null` (so, the last node becomes the tail).
4. Set the new head as the stored node (so, the head becomes *nextNode*).

In code lines, we have the following:

```
public void moveLastToFront() {

  Node currentNode = head;

  // step 1
  while (currentNode.next.next != null) {
    currentNode = currentNode.next;
  }

  // step 2
  Node nextNode = currentNode.next;

  // step 3
  currentNode.next = null;

  // step 4
  nextNode.next = head;
  head = nextNode;
}
```

The second approach can be performed with the following steps:

1. Move a pointer to the second to last node (let's denote it as *currentNode*).
2. Convert the linked list into a circular list (link *currentNode.next.next* to the head).
3. Set the new head as *currentNode.next*.
4. Break the circularity by setting *currentNode.next* to `null`.

In code lines, we have the following:

```
public void moveLastToFront() {
  Node currentNode = head;

  // step 1
  while (currentNode.next.next != null) {
     currentNode = currentNode.next;
  }

  // step 2
  currentNode.next.next = head;

  // step 3
  head = currentNode.next;

  // step 4
  currentNode.next = null;
}
```

The complete application is named *LinkedListMoveLastToFront*.

Coding challenge 15 – Reverse a singly linked list in groups of k

Amazon, Google, Adobe, Microsoft

Problem: Consider a singly linked list and an integer, k. Write a snippet of code that reverses the linked list's nodes in *k* groups.

Solution: Let's consider that the given linked list is 7 → 4 → 3 → 1 → 8 → 2 → 9 → 0 → null and *k*=3. The result should be 3 → 4 → 7 → 2 → 8 → 1 → 0 → 9 → null.

Let's consider that the given *k* is equal to the size of the linked list. In this case, we reduced the problem to reversing the given linked list. For example, if the given list is 7 → 4 → 3 → null and *k*=3, then the result should be 3 → 4 → 7 → null. So, how can we obtain this result?

In order to reverse the nodes, we need the current node (*current*), the node next to the current node (*next*), and the node previous to the current node (*previous*), and we apply the following algorithm representing the rearrangement of nodes:

1. Start with a counter from 0.

2. As the *current* node (initially the head) is not `null` and we haven't reached the given *k*, the following occurs:

    a. The *next* node (initially `null`) becomes the node next to the *current* node (initially the head).

    b. The node next to the *current* node (initially the head) becomes the *previous* node (initially `null`).

    c. The *previous* node becomes the *current* node (initially the head).

    d. The *current* node becomes the *next* node (the node from *step 2a*).

    e. Increment the counter.

So, if we apply this algorithm, we can reverse the whole list. But we need to reverse it in the groups; therefore, we must solve the *k* subproblems of what we've done. If this sounds like recursion to you, then you are right. At the end of the preceding algorithm, the node set at *step 2a* (*next*) points to the node where the counter is pointing as well. We can say that we've reversed the first *k* nodes. Next, we continue with the next group of *k* nodes via recursion starting from the *next* node. The following diagram illustrates this idea:

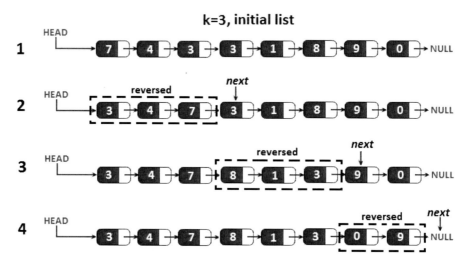

Figure 11.25 – Reversing the list in k groups (k=3)

And the following code implements this idea:

```
public void reverseInKGroups(int k) {

  if (head != null) {
    head = reverseInKGroups(head, k);
  }
}

private Node reverseInKGroups(Node head, int k) {

  Node current = head;
  Node next = null;
  Node prev = null;

  int counter = 0;
```

```
    // reverse first 'k' nodes of linked list
    while (current != null && counter < k) {

        next = current.next;
        current.next = prev;
        prev = current;
        current = next;

        counter++;
    }

    // 'next' points to (k+1)th node
    if (next != null) {
        head.next = reverseInKGroups(next, k);
    }

    // 'prev' is now the head of the input list
    return prev;
}
```

This code runs in O(n), where *n* is the number of nodes in the given list. The complete application is named *ReverseLinkedListInGroups*.

Coding challenge 16 – Reverse a doubly linked list

Microsoft, **Flipkart**

Problem: Consider a doubly linked list. Write a snippet of code that reverses its nodes.

Solution: Reversing a doubly linked list can take advantage of the fact that a doubly linked list maintains the link to the previous node. This means that we can simply swap the previous pointers and the next pointers for each node, as shown in the following code:

```
public void reverse() {

    Node currentNode = head;
    Node prevNode = null;
```

```
    while (currentNode != null) {

      // swap next and prev pointers of the current node
      Node prev = currentNode.prev;
      currentNode.prev = currentNode.next;
      currentNode.next = prev;

      // update the previous node before moving to the next node
      prevNode = currentNode;

      // move to the next node in the doubly linked list
      currentNode = currentNode.prev;
    }

    // update the head to point to the last node
    if (prevNode != null) {
      head = prevNode;
    }
  }
```

The complete application is named *DoublyLinkedListReverse*. To sort a singly and doubly linked list, please refer to *Chapter 14, Sorting and Searching*.

Coding challenge 17 – LRU cache

Amazon, Google, Adobe, Microsoft, Flipkart

Problem: Write a snippet of code to implement a fixed-size LRU cache. LRU cache stands for Least Recently Used Cache. This means that, when the cache is full, adding a new entry will instruct the cache to automatically evict the least recently used entry.

Solution: Any cache implementation must provide a fast and efficient way of retrieving data. This means that our implementation must respect the following constraints:

- **Fixed size**: The cache must use a limited amount of memory. Therefore, it needs to have some bounds (for example, a fixed size).
- **Fast access to data**: Inserting and searching operations should be fast; preferably, O(1) complexity time.
- **Fast eviction of data**: When the cache is full (it has reached its allocated bounds), the cache should empower an efficient algorithm to evict an entry.

In the context of the last bullet point, eviction from an LRU cache means evicting the least recently used data. To accomplish this, we have to keep track of the recently used entries and of the entries that have not been used for a long time. Moreover, we have to ensure O(1) complexity time for inserting and searching operations. There is no built-in data structure in Java that can give us this cache out of the box.

But we can start with a `HashMap` data structure. In Java, a `HashMap` allows us to insert and search (lookup) data by key in O(1) time. So, using a `HashMap` solves half of the problem. The other half, that is, keeping track of the recently used entries and of the entries that have not been used for a long time, cannot be accomplished with a `HashMap`.

However, if we imagine a data structure that provides fast insertions, updates, and deletions, then we have to think of a doubly linked list. Essentially, if we know the address of a node in a doubly linked list, then inserting, updating, and deleting can be performed in O(1).

This means that we can provide an implementation that relies on the symbiosis between a `HashMap` and a doubly linked list. Essentially, for each entry (key-value pair) in the LRU cache, we can store the key of the entry and the address of the associated linked list's node in the `HashMap`, while this node will store the value of the entry. The following diagram is a visual representation of this statement:

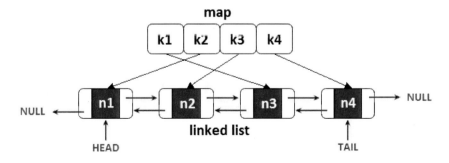

Figure 11.26 – An LRU cache using a HashMap and doubly linked list

But how does the doubly linked list help us to track the recently used entries? The secret relies on the following points:

- Inserting a new entry in the cache will result in adding the corresponding node to the head of the linked list (so, the head of the linked list holds the most recently used value).
- When an entry is accessed, we move its corresponding node to the head of the linked list.
- When we need to evict an entry, we evict the tail of the linked list (so, the tail of the linked list holds the least recently used value).

Well, based on these statements, we can provide the following straightforward implementation:

```java
public final class LRUCache {

  private final class Node {

    private int key;
    private int value;
    private Node next;
    private Node prev;
  }

  private final Map<Integer, Node> hashmap;

  private Node head;
  private Node tail;

  // 5 is the maximum size of the cache
  private static final int LRU_SIZE = 5;

  public LRUCache() {
    hashmap = new HashMap<>();
  }

  public int getEntry(int key) {
```

```java
    Node node = hashmap.get(key);

    // if the key already exist then update its usage in cache
    if (node != null) {
      removeNode(node);
      addNode(node);

      return node.value;
    }

    // by convention, data not found is marked as -1
    return -1;
  }

  public void putEntry(int key, int value) {

    Node node = hashmap.get(key);

    // if the key already exist then update
    // the value and move it to top of the cache
    if (node != null) {

      node.value = value;

      removeNode(node);
      addNode(node);

    } else {
      // this is new key
      Node newNode = new Node();
      newNode.prev = null;
      newNode.next = null;
      newNode.value = value;
      newNode.key = key;

      // if we reached the maximum size of the cache then
```

```
      // we have to remove the  Least Recently Used
      if (hashmap.size() >= LRU_SIZE) {

        hashmap.remove(tail.key);
        removeNode(tail);

         addNode(newNode);
      } else {
        addNode(newNode);
      }

      hashmap.put(key, newNode);
    }
  }

  // helper method to add a node to the top of the cache
  private void addNode(Node node) {
    node.next = head;
    node.prev = null;
    if (head != null) {
      head.prev = node;
    }
    head = node;
    if (tail == null) {
      tail = head;
    }
  }

  // helper method to remove a node from the cache
  private void removeNode(Node node) {

    if (node.prev != null) {
      node.prev.next = node.next;
    } else {
      head = node.next;
    }
```

```
        if (node.next != null) {
            node.next.prev = node.prev;
        } else {
            tail = node.prev;
        }
    }
}
```

The complete application is named *LRUCache*.

Well, this was the last coding challenge of the chapter. It's time to summarize the chapter!

Summary

This chapter brought your attention to the most common problems involving linked lists and maps. Among these problems, the ones that involve singly linked lists are preferred; therefore, this chapter was primarily focused on this category of coding challenges.

In the next chapter, we will tackle coding challenges related to stacks and queues.

12
Stacks and Queues

This chapter covers the most popular interview coding challenges involving stacks and queues. Mainly, you will learn how to provide a stack/queue implementation from scratch and how to tackle coding challenges via Java's built-in implementations, such as the `Stack` class, and the `Queue` interface implementations, especially `ArrayDeque`. Commonly, a coding challenge from this category will ask you to build a stack/queue or will ask you to solve a certain problem using Java's built-in implementations. Depending on the problem, it may explicitly disallow you to call certain built-in methods that will lead you to finding an easy solution.

By the end of this chapter, you'll have a deep insight into stacks and queues, you'll be able to exploit their capabilities, and also recognize and write solutions that depend on stacks and queues.

In this chapter, you'll learn about the following topics:

- Stacks in a nutshell
- Queues in a nutshell
- Coding challenges

Let's start by briefly covering the data structures of stacks.

Technical requirements

All the code files presented in this chapter are available on GitHub at `https://github.com/PacktPublishing/The-Complete-Coding-Interview-Guide-in-Java/tree/master/Chapter12`.

Stacks in a nutshell

A stack is a linear data structure that uses the **Last-In-First-Out** (**LIFO**) principle. Think of a stack of plates that needs to be washed. You take the first plate from the top (which was the last one to be added) and you wash it. Afterward, you take the next plate from the top and so on. This is exactly what a real-life stack is (for example, a stack of plates, a stack of books, a stack of CDs, and so on).

So, technically speaking, in a stack, the elements are only added (known as the **push** operation) and removed (known as the **pop** operation) to/from one end of it (known as the **top**).

The most common operations that are performed in a stack are as follows:

- `push(E e)`: Adds an element to the top of the stack
- `E pop()`: Removes the top element from the stack
- `E peek()`: Returns (but doesn't remove) the top element from the stack
- `boolean isEmpty()`: Returns `true` if the stack is empty
- `int size()`: Returns the size of the stack
- `boolean isFull()`: Returns `true` if the stack is full

Unlike an array, a stack does not provide access to the nth element in constant time. However, it does provide constant time for adding and removing elements. A stack can be implemented on top of an array or even on top of a linked list. The implementation that's being used here is based on an array and is named `MyStack`. The stub of this implementation is listed here:

```
public final class MyStack<E> {

    private static final int DEFAULT_CAPACITY = 10;

    private int top;
    private E[] stack;
```

```java
MyStack() {
   stack = (E[]) Array.newInstance(
           Object[].class.getComponentType(),
           DEFAULT_CAPACITY);

   top = 0; // the initial size is 0
}

public void push(E e) {}
public E pop() {}
public E peek() {}
public int size() {}
public boolean isEmpty() {}
public boolean isFull() {}
private void ensureCapacity() {}
}
```

Pushing an element into a stack means adding that element to the end of the underlying array. Before pushing an element, we have to ensure that the stack is not full. If it is full, then we can signal this via a message/exception, or we can increase its capacity, as shown here:

```java
// add an element 'e' in the stack
public void push(E e) {

   // if the stack is full, we double its capacity
   if (isFull()) {
     ensureCapacity();
   }

   // adding the element at the top of the stack
   stack[top++] = e;
}

// used internally for doubling the stack capacity
private void ensureCapacity() {
```

```
    int newSize = stack.length * 2;
    stack = Arrays.copyOf(stack, newSize);
}
```

As you can see, every time we reach the stack's capacity, we double its size. Popping an element from the stack means that we return the element that was last added to the underlying array. This element is removed from the underlying array by nullifying the last index, as shown here:

```
// pop top element from the stack
public E pop() {

    // if the stack is empty then just throw an exception
    if (isEmpty()) {
        throw new EmptyStackException();
    }

    // extract the top element from the stack
    E e = stack[--top];

    // avoid memory leaks
    stack[top] = null;

    return e;
}
```

Peeking an element from a stack means returning the element that was added last to the underlying array but without removing it from this array:

```
// return but not remove the top element in the stack
public E peek() {

    // if the stack is empty then just throw an exception
    if (isEmpty()) {
        throw new EmptyStackException();
    }
```

```
        return stack[top - 1];
    }
```

Since this implementation can represent the coding challenge you may face in an interview, it is advised that you take your time and dissect its code. The complete application is called *MyStack*.

Queues in a nutshell

A queue is a linear data structure that uses the **First-In-First-Out** (**FIFO**) principle. Think of people standing in a queue to buy stuff. You can also imagine ants that are walking in a queue formation.

So, technically speaking, the elements are removed from the queue in the same order that they are added. In a queue, the elements added at one end referred to as the rear (this operation is known as the enqueue operation) and removed from the other end referred to as the front (this operation is known as the dequeue or poll operation).

The common operations in a queue are as follows:

- `enqueue(E e)`: Adds an element to the rear of the queue
- `E dequeue()`: Removes and returns the element from the front of the queue
- `E peek()`: Returns (but doesn't remove) the element from the front of the queue
- `boolean isEmpty()`: Returns `true` if the queue is empty
- `int size()`: Returns the size of the queue
- `boolean isFull()` : Returns `true` if the queue is full

Unlike an array, a queue does not provide access to the nth element in constant time. However, it does provide constant time for adding and removing elements. A queue can be implemented on top of an array or even on top of a linked list or a stack (which is built on top of an array or a linked list). The implementation used here is based on an array and is named `MyQueue`. The stub of this implementation is listed here:

```
public final class MyQueue<E> {

    private static final int DEFAULT_CAPACITY = 10;

    private int front;
    private int rear;
```

```
    private int count;
    private int capacity;

    private E[] queue;

    MyQueue() {
      queue = (E[]) Array.newInstance(
              Object[].class.getComponentType(),
              DEFAULT_CAPACITY);

      count = 0; // the initial size is 0
      front = 0;
      rear = -1;

      capacity = DEFAULT_CAPACITY;
    }

    public void enqueue(E e) {}
    public E dequeue() {}
    public E peek() {}
    public int size() {}
    public boolean isEmpty() {}
    public boolean isFull() {}
    private void ensureCapacity() {}
}
```

Enqueuing an element into a queue means adding this element to the end of the underlying array. Before enqueuing an element, we have to ensure that the queue is not full. If it is full, then we can signal this via a message/exception, or we can increase its capacity, as follows:

```
// add an element 'e' in the queue
public void enqueue(E e) {

  // if the queue is full, we double its capacity
  if (isFull()) {
    ensureCapacity();
```

```java
    }

    // adding the element in the rear of the queue
    rear = (rear + 1) % capacity;
    queue[rear] = e;

    // update the size of the queue
    count++;
}

// used internally for doubling the queue capacity
private void ensureCapacity() {
    int newSize = queue.length * 2;
    queue = Arrays.copyOf(queue, newSize);

    // setting the new capacity
    capacity = newSize;
}
```

Dequeuing an element from a queue means returning the next element from the beginning of the underlying array. This element is removed from the array:

```java
// remove and return the front element from the queue
public E dequeue() {

    // if the queue is empty we just throw an exception
    if (isEmpty()) {
        throw new EmptyStackException();
    }

    // extract the element from the front
    E e = queue[front];
    queue[front] = null;

    // set the new front
    front = (front + 1) % capacity;
```

```
    // decrease the size of the queue
    count--;

    return e;
}
```

Peeking an element from a queue means returning the next element from the beginning of the underlying array without removing it from the array:

```
// return but not remove the front element in the queue
public E peek() {

    // if the queue is empty we just throw an exception
    if (isEmpty()) {
        throw new EmptyStackException();
    }

    return queue[front];
}
```

Since this implementation can represent the coding challenge you may face in an interview, it is advised that you take your time and dissect its code. The complete application is called *MyQueue*.

Coding challenges

In the next 11 coding challenges, we will cover the most popular problems involving stacks and queues that have appeared in interviews in the past few years in a wide range of companies that hire Java developers. One of the most common problems, *Implementing three stacks with one array*, was covered in *Chapter 10, Arrays and Strings*.

The solutions to the following coding challenges rely on the Java built-in `Stack` and `ArrayDeque` APIs. So, let's get started!

Coding challenge 1 – Reverse string

Problem: Consider you've been given a string. Use a stack to reverse it.

Solution: Reversing a string using a stack can be done as follows:

1. Loop the string from left to right and push each character into the stack.
2. Loop the stack and pop the characters one by one. Each popped character is put back into the string.

The code based on these two steps is as follows:

```
public static String reverse(String str) {

  Stack<Character> stack = new Stack();

  // push characters of the string into the stack
  char[] chars = str.toCharArray();
  for (char c : chars) {
    stack.push(c);
  }

  // pop all characters from the stack and
  // put them back to the input string
  for (int i = 0; i < str.length(); i++) {
    chars[i] = stack.pop();
  }

  // return the string
  return new String(chars);
}
```

The complete application is called *StackReverseString*.

Coding challenge 2 – Stack of curly braces

Amazon, Google, Adobe, Microsoft, Flipkart

Problem: Consider you've been given a `String` containing curly braces. Write a snippet of code that returns `true` if there are matching pairs of curly braces. If we can find a closing curly brace for an opening one in the proper order, then we can say that we have a matching pair. For example, a string containing matching pairs looks like this: {{{}}}{}{{}}.

Solution: Our solution should consider two major scenarios. First, if the number of opened curly braces is not equal to the number of closed curly braces, then we return `false`. Second, if their number is equal, then they must be in the proper order; otherwise, we return `false`. By the proper order, we understand that the last opened curly brace is the first one to be closed, the one prior to the last is the second to be closed, and so on. If we rely on a stack, then we can elaborate on the following algorithm:

1. For each character of the given string, take one of the following decisions:

   a. If the character is an opening curly brace, {, then put it on the stack.

   b. If the character is a closing curly brace, }, then do the following:

   i. Check the top of stack, and if it is {, pop and move it to the next character.

   ii. If it is not {, then return `false`.

2. If the stack is empty, return `true` (we found all pairs); otherwise, return `false` (the stack contains curly braces that do not match).

Putting these steps into code results in the following:

```
public static boolean bracesMatching(String bracesStr) {

  Stack<Character> stackBraces = new Stack<>();

  int len = bracesStr.length();
  for (int i = 0; i < len; i++) {

    switch (bracesStr.charAt(i)) {
      case '{':
        stackBraces.push(bracesStr.charAt(i));
        break;

      case '}':
        if (stackBraces.isEmpty()) { // we found a mismatch
          return false;
        }

        // for every match we pop the corresponding '{'
        stackBraces.pop();
        break;
```

```
        default:
            return false;
    }
}

return stackBraces.empty();
}
```

The complete application is called *StackBraces*. Challenge yourself by implementing a similar problem but for multiple types of parentheses (for example, allow () {} [] in the same given string).

Coding challenge 3 – Stack of plates

Amazon, **Google**, **Adobe**, **Microsoft**, **Flipkart**

Problem: Consider a stack of n plates. If the number of plates is bigger than n, then we need to arrange them in a new stack of n plates. So, each time the current stack exceeds the n capacity, a new stack of that capacity is created. Write a snippet of code that shapes these stacks so that they act as a single stack. In other words, the `push()` and `pop()` methods will work like there is a single stack. Additionally, write a `popAt(int stackIndex)` method that pops a value from the stack, as indicated via `stackIndex`.

Solution: We know how to deal with a single stack, but how do we link multiple stacks together? Well, since we have to *link*, how about a linked list? If the linked list contains a stack in each node, then the next pointer of a node will point to the next stack. The following diagram visualizes this solution:

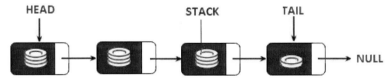

Figure 12.1 – Linked list of stacks

Whenever the current stack capacity is exceeded, we create a new node and append it to the linked list. Java's built-in linked list (`LinkedList`) gives us access to the last node via the `getLast()` method. In other words, via `LinkedList#getLast()`, we can easily operate on the current stack (for example, we can push or pop an element). Adding a new stack is quite simple via the `LinkedList#add()` method. Based on these statements, we can implement the `push()` method, as shown here:

```java
private static final int STACK_SIZE = 3;

private final LinkedList<Stack<Integer>> stacks
    = new LinkedList<>();

public void push(int value) {

  // if there is no stack or the last stack is full
  if (stacks.isEmpty() || stacks.getLast().size()
       >= STACK_SIZE) {

    // create a new stack and push the value into it
    Stack<Integer> stack = new Stack<>();
    stack.push(value);

    // add the new stack into the list of stacks
    stacks.add(stack);
  } else {
    // add the value in the last stack
    stacks.getLast().push(value);
  }
}
```

If we want to pop an element, then we have to do so from the last stack, so `LinkedList#getLast()` is very handy here. The corner-case here is represented by the moment we pop the last element from the last stack. When this happens, we must remove the last stack, in which case the one before the last (if any) will become the last. The following code speaks for itself:

```
public Integer pop() {

  // find the last stack
  Stack<Integer> lastStack = stacks.getLast();

  // pop the value from the last stack
  int value = lastStack.pop();

  // if last stack is empty, remove it from the list of stacks
  removeStackIfEmpty();

  return value;
}

private void removeStackIfEmpty() {
  if (stacks.getLast().isEmpty()) {
     stacks.removeLast();
  }
}
```

Finally, let's focus on implementing the `popAt(int stackIndex)` method. We can pop from the `stackIndex` stack by simply calling `stacks.get(stackIndex).pop()`. Once we've popped an element, we must shift the remaining elements. The bottom element of the next stack will become the top element of the stack being pointed to by `stackIndex` and so on. If the last stack contains a single element, then shifting the other elements will eliminate the last stack, and the one before it will become the last. Let's see this in terms of code:

```
public Integer popAt(int stackIndex) {

  // get the value from the correspondind stack
  int value = stacks.get(stackIndex).pop();
```

```
  // pop an element -> must shift the remaining elements
  shift(stackIndex);

  // if last stack is empty, remove it from the list of stacks
  removeStackIfEmpty();

  return value;
}

private void shift(int index) {

  for (int i = index; i<stacks.size() - 1; ++i) {
    Stack<Integer> currentStack = stacks.get(i);
    Stack<Integer> nextStack = stacks.get(i + 1);

    currentStack.push(nextStack.remove(0));
  }
}
```

The complete application is called *StackOfPlates*.

Coding challenge 4 – Stock span

Amazon, **Google**, **Adobe**, **Microsoft**, **Flipkart**

Problem: Consider you've been given an array of prices of a single stock for multiple consecutive days. A stock span is represented by the number of consecutive days prior to the current day (today) when the price of a stock was less than or equal to the price of the current day. For example, consider the prices of a stock covering 10 days; that is, {55, 34, 22, 23, 27, 88, 70, 42, 51, 100}. The resulting stock span is {1, 1, 1, 2, 3, 6, 1, 1, 2, 10}. Notice that, for the first day, the stock span is always 1. Write a snippet of code that computes the stock span for the given list of prices.

Solution: We can start from the given example and try to visualize it, as follows:

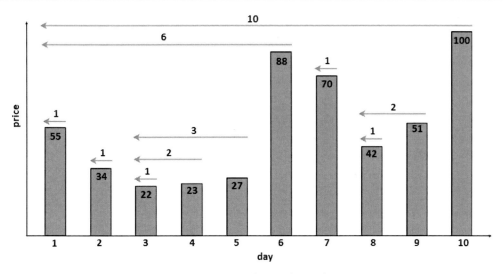

Figure 12.2 – Stock span for 10 days

From the preceding figure, we can observe the following:

- For the first day, the span is always 1.
- For day 2, the price is 34. Since 34 is less than the price of the prior day (55), the stock span of day 2 is also 1.
- For day 3, the price is 22. Since 22 is less than the price of the prior day (34), the stock span of day 3 is also 1. Days 7 and 8 fall under the same scenario.
- For day 4, the price is 23. Since 23 is greater than the price of the prior day (22), but is less than the price of day 2, the stock span is 2. Day 9 is similar to day 4.
- For day 5, the price is 27. Since this price is greater than the prices of days 3 and 4 but less than the price of day 2, the stock span is 3.
- For day 6, the price is 88. This is the biggest price so far, so the stock span is 6.
- For day 10, the price is 100. This is the biggest price so far, so the stock span is 10.

Notice that we compute the stock span of the current day as the difference between the index of the current day and the index of the day corresponding to the last biggest stock price. After tracking this scenario, the first idea that we have may sound like this: for each day, scan all days prior to it and increment the stock span until the price of the stock is bigger than the current day. In other words, we are using the brute-force approach. As I mentioned earlier in this book, the brute-force approach should be used as a last resort in an interview since it has a poor performance and the interviewers won't be impressed. In this case, the brute-force approach works in $O(n^2)$ complexity time.

However, let's try another perspective of thought. For each day, we want to find a prior day that has a bigger price than the current day. In other words, we are looking for the last price that is bigger than the price of the current day.

Here, we should choose a LIFO data structure that allows us to push the prices in descending order and pop the last pushed price. Once we have this in place, we can go through each day and compare the price at the top of the stack with the current day's price. Until the price on top of the stack is less than the current day's price, we can pop from the stack. But if the price at the top of the stack is bigger than the price of the current day, then we compute the stock span of the current day as the difference in days between the current day and the day for the price on top of the stack. This will work if we push the prices into the stack in descending order – the biggest price is at the top of the stack. However, since we can compute the stock span as the difference between the index of the current day and the index of the day corresponding to the last biggest stock price (let's denote it with `i`), we can simply store the `i` index in the stack; `stackPrices[i]` (let's denote the prices array as `stackPrices`) will return the price of the stock on the ith day.

This can be accomplished by the following algorithm:

1. The first day has a stock span of 1 and an index of 0 – we push this index into the stack (let's denote it as `dayStack`; therefore, `dayStack.push(0)`).
2. We loop the remaining days (day 2 has index 1, day 3 has index 2, and so on) and do the following:

    a. While `stockPrices[i] > stockPrices[dayStack.peek()]` and `!dayStack.empty()`, we pop from the stack (`dayStack.pop()`).
3. If `dayStack.empty()`, then the stock span in `i+1`.
4. If `stockPrices[i] <= stockPrices[dayStack.peek()]`, then the stock span is `i - dayStack.peek()`.
5. Push the index of the current day, `i`, into the stack (`dayStack`).

Let's see how this algorithm works for our test case:

1. The first day has a stock span of 1 and an index of 0 – we push this index into the stack, `dayStack.push(0)`.
2. For the second day, `stockPrices[1]=34` and `stockPrices[0]=55`. Since 34 < 55, the stock span of day 2 is `i - dayStack.peek() = 1 - 0 = 1`. We push in stack 1, `dayStack.push(1)`.

3. For the third day, `stockPrices[2]`=22 and `stockPrices[1]`=34. Since 22 < 34, the stock span of day 3 is 2 - 1 = 1. We push in stack 1, `dayStack.push(2)`.

4. For the fourth day, `stockPrices[3]`=23 and `stockPrices[2]`=22. Since 23 > 22 and the stack is not empty, we pop the top, so we pop the value 2. Since 23 < 34 (`stockPrices[1]`), the stock span of day 4 is 3 - 1 = 2. We push in stack 3, `dayStack.push(3)`.

5. For the fifth day, `stockPrices[4]`=27 and `stockPrices[3]`=23. Since 27 > 23 and the stack is not empty, we pop the top, so we pop the value 3. Next, 27 < 34 (remember that we popped the value 2 in the previous step, so the next top has the value 1), and the stock span of day 5 is 4 - 1 = 3. We push in stack 4, `dayStack.push(4)`.

6. For the sixth day, `stockPrices[5]`=88 and `stockPrices[4]`=27. Since 88 > 27 and the stack is not empty, we pop the top, so we pop the value 4. Next, 88 > 34 and the stack is not empty, so we pop the value 1. Next, 88 > 55 and the stack is not empty, so we pop the value 0. Next, the stack is empty and the stock span of day 6 is 5 + 1 = 6.

Well, I think you got the idea, so now, challenge yourself and continue until day 10. For now, we have enough information to put this algorithm into code:

```
public static int[] stockSpan(int[] stockPrices) {

  Stack<Integer> dayStack = new Stack();
  int[] spanResult = new int[stockPrices.length];

  spanResult[0] = 1; // first day has span 1
  dayStack.push(0);

  for (int i = 1; i < stockPrices.length; i++) {

    // pop until we find a price on stack which is
    // greater than the current day's price or there
    // are no more days left
    while (!dayStack.empty()
        && stockPrices[i] > stockPrices[dayStack.peek()]) {
      dayStack.pop();
```

```
        }

        // if there is no price greater than the current
        // day's price then the stock span is the numbers of days
        if (dayStack.empty()) {
            spanResult[i] = i + 1;
        } else {
            // if there is a price greater than the current
            // day's price then the stock span is the
            // difference between the current day and that day
            spanResult[i] = i - dayStack.peek();
        }

        // push current day onto top of stack
        dayStack.push(i);
    }

    return spanResult;
}
```

The complete application is called *StockSpan*.

Coding challenge 5 – Stack min

Amazon, Google, Adobe, Microsoft, Flipkart

Problem: Design a stack that computes the minimum value in constant time. The `push()`, `pop()`, and `min()` methods should operate in O(1) time.

Solution: The classical approach consists of declaring an instance variable that holds the minimum of the stack. When the value that's popped from the stack is equal to the minimum, we search through the stack for the new minimum. This works fine but not under the constraints of this problem, which require `push()` and `pop()` to run in O(1) time.

The solution that respects the problem's constraints requires an additional stack for tracking the minimum. Mainly, when the pushed value is smaller than the current minimum, we add this value to the auxiliary stack (let's denote it as `stackOfMin`) and the original stack. If the value that's popped from the original stack is the top of `stackOfMin`, then we pop it from `stackOfMin` as well. In terms of code, we have the following:

```java
public class MyStack extends Stack<Integer> {

  Stack<Integer> stackOfMin;

  public MyStack() {
    stackOfMin = new Stack<>();
  }

  public Integer push(int value) {

    if (value <= min()) {
      stackOfMin.push(value);
    }

    return super.push(value);
  }

  @Override
  public Integer pop() {

    int value = super.pop();
    if (value == min()) {
      stackOfMin.pop();
    }

    return value;
  }

  public int min() {
```

```
      if (stackOfMin.isEmpty()) {
         return Integer.MAX_VALUE;
      } else {
         return stackOfMin.peek();
      }
   }
}
```

Done! Our solution performed in O(1) complexity time. The complete application is called *MinStackConstantTime*. A problem related to this one requires you to implement the same functionality in constant time and space. The solution to this problem imposes several restrictions, as follows:

- The `pop()` method returns `void` to avoid returning incorrect values.
- The given value multiplied by 2 should not exceed the `int` data type domain.

In short, these restrictions are caused by the solution itself. We cannot use extra space; therefore, we will use the initial stack of values to store the minimum as well. Moreover, we need to multiply the given value by 2, so we should ensure that the `int` domain is not exceeded. Why do we need to multiply the given value by 2?

Let's bring some light to this subject! Let's assume that we need to push a value into a stack that has a certain minimum value. If this value is bigger than or equal to the current minimum value, then we can simply push it into the stack. But if it is smaller than the minimum, then we push 2*value-minimum, which should be smaller than the value itself. Then, we update the current minimum as value.

When we pop a value, we have to consider two aspects. If the popped value is bigger or equal to the minimum, then this is the real value that was pushed earlier. Otherwise, the popped value is not the pushed value. The real pushed value is stored in the minimum. After we pop the top of the stack (the minimum value), we have to restore the previous minimum. The previous minimum is obtained as 2*minimum - top. In other words, since the current top is 2*value - previous_minimum and the value is the current minimum, the previous minimum is 2*current_minimum - top. The following code illustrates this algorithm:

```
public class MyStack {

   private int min;
   private final Stack<Integer> stack = new Stack<>();
```

```java
  public void push(int value) {

    // we don't allow values that overflow int/2 range
    int r = Math.addExact(value, value);

    if (stack.empty()) {
      stack.push(value);
      min = value;
    } else if (value > min) {
      stack.push(value);
    } else {
      stack.push(r - min);
      min = value;
    }
  }

  // pop() doesn't return the value since this may be a wrong
  // value (a value that was not pushed by the client)!
  public void pop() {

    if (stack.empty()) {
      throw new EmptyStackException();
    }

    int top = stack.peek();
    if (top < min) {
      min = 2 * min - top;
    }
    stack.pop();
  }

  public int min() {
    return min;
  }
}
```

The complete application is called *MinStackConstantTimeAndSpace*.

Coding challenge 6 – Queue via stacks

Google, **Adobe**, **Microsoft**, **Flipkart**

Problem: Design a queue via two stacks.

Solution: In order to find the proper solution to this problem, we must start from the main difference between a queue and a stack. We know that a queue works on FIFO, while a stack works on LIFO. Next, we have to think of the main operations (push, pop, and peek) and identify the differences.

Both of them push new elements in the same way. When we push an element into a queue, we push it at one end (the rear of the queue). When we push an element into a stack, we push it from the new top of the stack, which can be considered the same as the rear of the queue.

When we pop or peek a value from a stack, we do so from the top. However, when we perform the same operations on a queue, we do so from the front. This means that, while popping or peeking an element, a reversed stack will act as a queue. The following diagram exemplifies this statement:

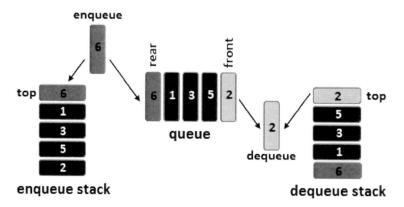

Figure 12.3 – Queue via two stacks

So, each new element is pushed into the *enqueue stack* as the new top. When we need to pop or peek a value, we use the *dequeue* stack, which is the reversed version of the *enqueue stack*. Notice that we don't have to reverse the *enqueue stack* at each pop/peek operation. We can let the elements sit in the *dequeue stack* until we absolutely must reverse the elements. In other words, for each pop/peek operation, we can check if the *dequeue stack* is empty. As long as the *dequeue stack* is not empty, we don't need to reverse the *enqueue stack* because we have at least one element to pop/peek.

Let's see this in terms of code:

```
public class MyQueueViaStack<E> {

  private final Stack<E> stackEnqueue;
  private final Stack<E> stackDequeue;

  public MyQueueViaStack() {
    stackEnqueue = new Stack<>();
    stackDequeue = new Stack<>();
  }

  public void enqueue(E e) {
    stackEnqueue.push(e);
  }

  public E dequeue() {
    reverseStackEnqueue();
    return stackDequeue.pop();
  }

  public E peek() {
    reverseStackEnqueue();
    return stackDequeue.peek();
  }

  public int size() {
    return stackEnqueue.size() + stackDequeue.size();
  }

  private void reverseStackEnqueue() {
    if (stackDequeue.isEmpty()) {
      while (!stackEnqueue.isEmpty()) {
        stackDequeue.push(stackEnqueue.pop());
```

                }
            }
        }
    }

The complete application is called *QueueViaStack*.

Coding challenge 7 – Stack via queues
Google, Adobe, Microsoft

Problem: Design a stack via two queues.

Solution: In order to find the proper solution to this problem, we must start from the main difference between a stack and a queue. We know that a stack is a LIFO, while a queue is a FIFO. Next, we have to think of the main operations (push, pop, and peek) and identify the differences.

Both of them push new elements in the same way. When we push an element into a stack, we push it from the new top of the stack. When we push an element into a queue, we push it from one end (the rear of the queue). The rear of the queue is like the top of the stack.

When we pop or peek a value from a queue, we do so from the front. However, when we perform the same operations on a stack, we do so from the top. This means that, while popping or peeking an element from a queue that acts as a stack, we need to poll all the elements except the last one. The last element is the one that we pop/peek. The following diagram exemplifies this statement:

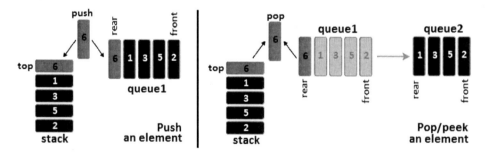

Figure 12.4 – Stack via two queues

As the left-hand side of the preceding diagram reveals, pushing an element into a stack and a queue is a simple operation. The right-hand side of the preceding diagram shows that problems occur when we want to pop/peek an element from the queue that acts as a stack. Mainly, before popping/peeking an element, we have to move the elements from the queue (denoted in the preceding diagram as *queue1*) between (*rear*-1) and *front* into another queue (denoted in the preceding diagram as *queue2*). In the preceding diagram, on the right-hand side, we poll the elements 2, 5, 3, and 1 from *queue1* and add them to *queue2*. Next, we pop/peek the last element from *queue1*. If we pop element 6, then *queue1* remains empty. If we peek element 6, then *queue1* remains with this element.

Now, the remaining elements are in *queue2*, so in order to perform another operation (push, peek, or pop), we have two options:

- Restore *queue1* by moving the remaining elements from *queue2* back.
- Use *queue2* as if it was *queue1*, which means using *queue1* and *queue2* alternatively.

In the case of the second option, we avoid the overhead of moving the elements from *queue2* back to *queue1*, with the purpose of performing the next operation on *queue1*. While you can challenge yourself to implement the first option, let's focus more on the second one.

Trying to use *queue1* and *queue2* alternatively can be done if we consider that the queue that we should use for the next operation is the one that is not empty. Since we move the elements between these two queues, one of them is always empty. Hence, a problem arises when we peek an element because the peek operation doesn't remove the element, so one of the queues remains with that element. Since none of the queues are empty, we don't know which queue should be used for the next operation. The solution is quite simple: we poll the last element, even for the peek operation, and we store it as an instance variable. Subsequent peek operations will return this instance variable. A push operation will push this instance variable back into the queue before pushing the given value and will set this instance variable to `null`. The pop operation will check if this instance variable is `null` or not. If it is not `null`, then this is the element to pop.

Let's see the code:

```
public class MyStackViaQueue<E> {

    private final Queue<E> queue1;
    private final Queue<E> queue2;
    private E peek;
    private int size;
```

```java
  public MyStackViaQueue() {
    queue1 = new ArrayDeque<>();
    queue2 = new ArrayDeque<>();
  }

  public void push(E e) {

    if (!queue1.isEmpty()) {
      if (peek != null) {
        queue1.add(peek);
      }
      queue1.add(e);
    } else {
      if (peek != null) {
        queue2.add(peek);
      }
      queue2.add(e);
    }

    size++;
    peek = null;
  }

  public E pop() {

    if (size() == 0) {
      throw new EmptyStackException();
    }

    if (peek != null) {
      E e = peek;
      peek = null;

      size--;

      return e;
```

```
    }

    E e;
    if (!queue1.isEmpty()) {
      e = switchQueue(queue1, queue2);
    } else {
      e = switchQueue(queue2, queue1);
    }

    size--;

    return e;
  }

  public E peek() {

    if (size() == 0) {
      throw new EmptyStackException();
    }

    if (peek == null) {
      if (!queue1.isEmpty()) {
        peek = switchQueue(queue1, queue2);
      } else {
        peek = switchQueue(queue2, queue1);
      }
    }

    return peek;
  }

  public int size() {
    return size;
  }

  private E switchQueue(Queue from, Queue to) {
```

```
    while (from.size() > 1) {
        to.add(from.poll());
    }

    return (E) from.poll();
}
```

The complete application is called *StackViaQueue*.

Coding challenge 8 – Max histogram area

Amazon, Google, Adobe, Microsoft, Flipkart

Problem: Consider you've been given the histogram shown in the following image:

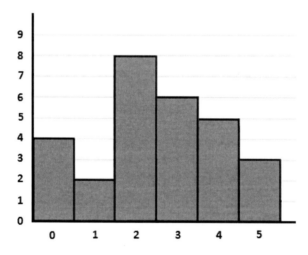

Figure 12.5 – Histogram with the class interval equal to 1

We define a histogram as a diagram of rectangular bars where the area is proportional to the frequency of a certain variable. The width of a bar is known as the histogram class interval. For example, the histogram in the preceding image has a class interval equal to 1. There are six bars whose widths are equal to 1 and whose heights are 4, 2, 8, 6, 5, and 3.

Consider you've been given these heights as an array of integers (this is the input of the problem). Write a snippet of code that uses a stack for computing the largest rectangular area in the histogram. For a better understanding of this, the following image highlights several rectangles (not all) that can be formed:

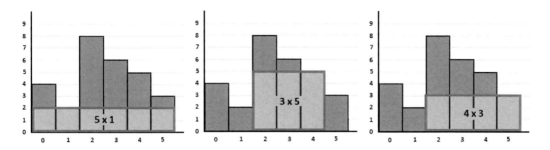

Figure 12.6 – Rectangles of a histogram

In the preceding image, the largest rectangular area (that is, the largest rectangle) is the one in the middle, 3 x 5 = 15.

Solution: This problem is harder than it may seem at first sight. First of all, we need to analyze the given image and formulate several statements. For example, it is very important to notice that a bar can only be part of a rectangular area if its height is less than or equal to the height of that area. Moreover, for each bar, we can say that all the bars from the left-hand side that are higher than the current bar can form a rectangular area with the current bar. Similarly, all the bars on the right-hand side that are higher than the current bar can form a rectangular area with the current bar.

This means that every rectangular area is delimited by a *left* and a *right* boundary, and (*right - left*) * *current_bar* give us the value of this area. We should compute all the possible areas and peek the highest area as the output of our implementation. The following image highlights the left and right boundaries of the 3 x 5 rectangle:

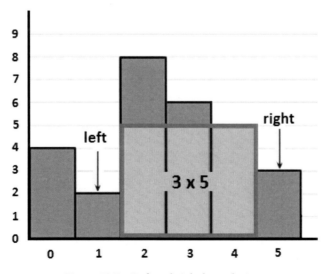

Figure 12.7 – Left and right boundaries

Remember that we must use a stack to solve this problem. Now that we have some statements that can lead us to the solution, it is time to bring the stack into the discussion. Mainly, we can use the stack to compute the left and right boundaries.

We start from the first bar and we push the index of it (index 0) into the stack. We continue with the remaining bars and do the following:

1. Repeat *steps 1a, 1b*, and *1c* as long as the current bar is smaller than the top of the stack and the stack is not empty:

   a. We pop the top of the stack.

   b. We compute the left boundary.

   c. We compute the width of the rectangular area that can be formed between the computed left boundary bar and the current bar.

   d. We compute the area as the computed width multiplied by the height of the bar that we popped in *step 1a*.

   e. If this area is bigger than the previous one, then we store this one.

2. Push the index of the current bar into the stack.

3. Repeat from *step 1* until every bar is processed.

Let's see this in terms of code:

```
public static int maxAreaUsingStack(int[] histogram) {

  Stack<Integer> stack = new Stack<>();

  int maxArea = 0;
  for (int bar = 0; bar <= histogram.length; bar++) {

    int barHeight;
    if (bar == histogram.length) {
      barHeight = 0; // take into account last bar
    } else {
      barHeight = histogram[bar];
    }

    while (!stack.empty()
           && barHeight < histogram[stack.peek()]) {
```

```
        // we found a bar smaller than the one from the stack
        int top = stack.pop();

        // find left boundary
        int left = stack.isEmpty() ? -1 : stack.peek();

        // find the width of the rectangular area
        int areaRectWidth = bar - left - 1;

        // compute area of the current rectangle
        int area = areaRectWidth * histogram[top];
        maxArea = Integer.max(area, maxArea);
    }

    // add current bar (index) into the stack
    stack.push(bar);
  }

  return maxArea;
}
```

The time complexity of this code is O(n). Moreover, the additional space complexity is O(n). The complete application is called *StackHistogramArea*.

Coding challenge 9 – Smallest number

Problem: Consider you've been given a string representing a number of n digits. Write a snippet of code that prints the smallest possible number after removing the given k digits.

Solution: Let's consider that the given number is n=4514327 and k=4. In this case, the smallest number after removing four digits is 127. If n=2222222, then the smallest number is 222.

The solution can be easily implemented via a Stack and the following algorithm:

1. Iterate the given number from left to right, digit by digit.

   a. While the given *k* is greater than 0, the stack is not empty and the top element in the stack is greater than the currently traversed digit:

   i. Pop out the top element from the stack.

   ii. Decrement *k* by 1.

   b. Push the current digit to the stack.

2. While the given *k* is greater than 0, do the following (to handle special cases such as 222222):

   a. Pop out elements from the stack.

   b. Decrement *k* by 1.

In terms of code, we have the following:

```
public static void smallestAfterRemove(String nr, int k) {

  int i = 0;
  Stack<Character> stack = new Stack<>();
  while (i < nr.length()) {
    // if the current digit is less than the previous
    // digit then discard the previous one
    while (k > 0 && !stack.isEmpty()
          && stack.peek() > nr.charAt(i)) {
      stack.pop();
      k--;
    }

    stack.push(nr.charAt(i));
    i++;
  }

  // cover corner cases such as '2222'
  while (k > 0) {
    stack.pop();
    k--;
```

```
    }

    System.out.println("The number is (as a printed stack; "
        + "ignore leading 0s (if any)): " + stack);
   }
  }
}
```

The complete application is called *SmallestNumber*.

Coding challenge 10 – Islands

Amazon, **Adobe**

Problem: Consider you've been given a matrix, *m*x*n*, containing only 0s and 1s. By convention, 1 means land and 0 means water. Write a snippet of code that counts the number of islands. An island is defined as a group of 1s surrounded by 0s.

Solution: Let's visualize a test case. The following is a 10x10 matrix that contains 6 islands, highlighted as 1, 2, 3, 4, 5, and 6:

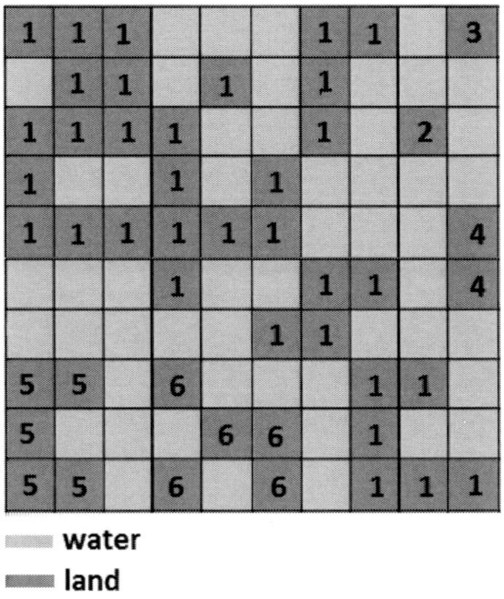

```
1, 1, 1, 0, 0, 0, 1, 1, 0, 1
0, 1, 1, 0, 1, 0, 1, 0, 0, 0
1, 1, 1, 1, 0, 0, 1, 0, 1, 0
1, 0, 0, 1, 0, 1, 0, 0, 0, 0
1, 1, 1, 1, 1, 1, 0, 0, 0, 1
0, 0, 0, 1, 0, 0, 1, 1, 0, 1
0, 0, 0, 0, 0, 1, 1, 0, 0, 0
1, 1, 0, 1, 0, 0, 0, 1, 1, 0
1, 0, 0, 0, 1, 1, 0, 1, 0, 0
1, 1, 0, 1, 0, 1, 0, 1, 1, 1
```

Figure 12.8 – Islands via a 10x10 matrix

In order to find the islands, we have to traverse the matrix. In other words, we have to traverse each cell of the matrix. Since a cell is characterized by a row (let's denote it as *r*) and a column (let's denote it as *c*), we observe that, from a cell (*r*, *c*), we can move in eight directions: (*r*-1, *c*-1), (*r*-1, *c*), (*r*-1, *c*+1), (*r*, *c*-1), (*r*, *c*+1), (*r*+1, *c*-1), (*r*+1, *c*), and (*r*+1, *c*+1). This means that from the current cell (*r*, *c*), we can move to (*r*+ROW[*k*], *c*+COL[*k*]) as long as ROW and COL are the below arrays and $0 \leq k \leq 7$:

```
// top, right, bottom, left and 4 diagonal moves
private static final int[] ROW = {-1, -1, -1, 0, 1, 0, 1, 1};
private static final int[] COL = {-1, 1, 0, -1, -1, 1, 0, 1};
```

Moving to a cell is valid as long as we do the following:

- Don't fall from the grid.
- Step on a cell representing land (a cell of 1).
- Haven't been in that cell before.

In order to ensure that we don't visit the same cell multiple times, we use a boolean matrix denoted as `flagged[][]`. Initially, this matrix contains only values of `false`, and each time we visit a cell (*r*, *c*), we flip the corresponding `flagged[r][c]` to `true`.

The following is the preceding three bullet points in code form:

```
private static booleanisValid(int[][] matrix,
        int r, int c, boolean[][] flagged) {

    return (r >= 0) && (r < flagged.length)
        && (c >= 0) && (c < flagged[0].length)
        && (matrix[r][c] == 1 && !flagged[r][c]);
}
```

So far, we know how to decide if a move from the current cell to another cell (from the eight possible movements) is valid or not. Furthermore, we have to define an algorithm to determine a movement pattern. We know that from a cell (*r*, *c*), we can move in eight directions in neighboring cells. So, the most convenient algorithm consists of trying to move from the current cell into all the valid neighbors, as follows:

1. Start with an empty queue.
2. Move to a valid cell (*r*, *c*), enqueue it, and mark it as flagged – the starting point should be cell (0, 0).

3. Dequeue the current cell and resolve all its eight neighboring cells – resolving a cell means to enqueue it if it is valid and mark it as flagged.
4. Repeat *step 3* until the queue is empty. When the queue is empty, this means we've found an island.
5. Repeat from *step 2* until there are no more valid cells.

In terms of code, we have the following:

```
private static class Cell {

  int r, c;

  public Cell(int r, int c) {
    this.r = r;
    this.c = c;
  }
}

// there are 8 possible movements from a cell
private static final int POSSIBLE_MOVEMENTS = 8;

// top, right, bottom, left and 4 diagonal moves
private static final int[] ROW = {-1, -1, -1, 0, 1, 0, 1, 1};
private static final int[] COL = {-1, 1, 0, -1, -1, 1, 0, 1};

public static int islands(int[][] matrix) {

  int m = matrix.length;
  int n = matrix[0].length;

  // stores if a cell is flagged or not
  boolean[][] flagged = new boolean[m][n];

  int island = 0;
  for (int i = 0; i < m; i++) {
    for (int j = 0; j < n; j++) {
```

```java
            if (matrix[i][j] == 1 && !flagged[i][j]) {
                resolve(matrix, flagged, i, j);
                island++;
            }
        }
    }

    return island;
}

private static void resolve(int[][] matrix,
        boolean[][] flagged, int i, int j) {

    Queue<Cell> queue = new ArrayDeque<>();
    queue.add(new Cell(i, j));

    // flag source node
    flagged[i][j] = true;

    while (!queue.isEmpty()) {

        int r = queue.peek().r;
        int c = queue.peek().c;
        queue.poll();

        // check for all 8 possible movements from current
        // cell and enqueue each valid movement
        for (int k = 0; k < POSSIBLE_MOVEMENTS; k++) {

            // skip this cell if the location is invalid
            if (isValid(matrix, r + ROW[k], c + COL[k], flagged)) {
                flagged[r + ROW[k]][c + COL[k]] = true;
                queue.add(new Cell(r + ROW[k], c + COL[k]));
            }
        }
```

```
        }
    }
```

The complete application is called *QueueIslands*.

Coding challenge 11 – Shortest path

Amazon, **Google**, **Adobe**

Problem: Consider you've been given a matrix, m x n, containing only 0s and 1s. By convention, 1 means safe land, while 0 represents unsafe land. More precisely, a 0 represents a sensor that should not be activated. Moreover, all eight adjacent cells can activate the sensor. Write a snippet of code that computes the shortest route from any cells of the first column to any cell of the last column. You can only move one step at a time; either left, right, up, or down. The resulting route (if its exists) should contain only values of 1.

Solution: Let's visualize a test case. The following is a 10 x 10 matrix.

On the left-hand side of the following image, you can see the given matrix. Notice the values of 0 representing sensors that should not be activated. On the right, you can see the matrix being used by the application and a possible solution. This matrix is obtained from the given matrix by expanding the sensor's coverage area. Remember that the eight adjacent cells of a sensor can activate the sensor as well. The solution starts from the first column (cell(4, 0)) and ends in the last column (cell (9, 9)) and contains 15 steps (from 0 to 14). You can see these steps in the following image:

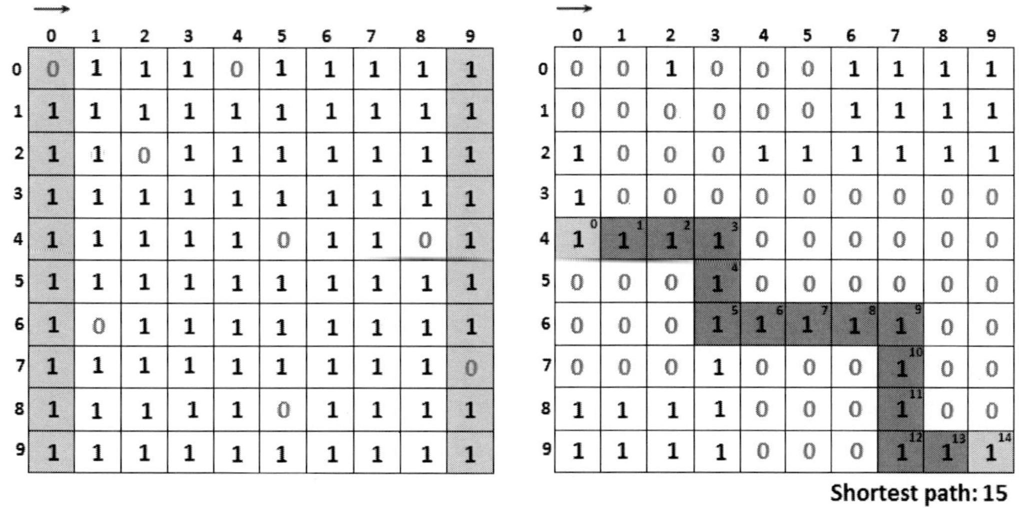

Figure 12.9 – The given matrix (left-hand side) and the resolved matrix (right-hand side)

From a safe cell of coordinates (r, c), we can move in four safe directions: (r-1, c), (r, c-1), (r+1, c), and (r, c+1). If we think of the possible movements as directions (edges) and the cells as vertices, then we can visualize this problem in the context of a graph. The edges are the possible moves, while the vertices are the possible cells where we can go. Each move holds the distance from the current cell to the start cell (a start cell is a cell from the first column). For each move, the distance is increased by 1. So, in the context of a graph, the problem reduces to finding the shortest path in a graph. Hence, we can use the **Breadth-first Search (BFS)** approach to solve this problem. In *Chapter 13, Trees and Graphs*, you were provided with a description of the BFS algorithm, and another problem was solved in the same manner as the one being solved here – the *Chess Knight* problem.

Now, based on the experience provided by the previous problem, we can elaborate on this algorithm:

1. Start with an empty queue.

2. Enqueue all the safe cells of the first column and set their distances to 0 (here, 0 represents the distance from each cell to itself). Moreover, these cells are marked as visited or flagged.

3. As long as the queue is not empty, do the following:

    a. Pop the cell representing the top of the queue.

    b. If the popped cell is the destination cell (that is, it is on the last column), then simply return its distance (the distance from the destination cell to the source cell on the first column).

    c. If the popped cell is not the destination then, for each of the four adjacent cells of this cell, enqueue each valid cell (safe and unvisited) into the queue with distance (+1) and mark it as visited.

    d. If we processed all the cells in the queue without reaching the destination, then there is no solution. Return -1.

Since we rely on the BFS algorithm, we know that all the cells whose shortest paths are 1 are visited first. Next, the visited cells are the adjacent cells who have the shortest paths as 1+1=2 and so on. So, the cell that has the shortest path is equal to the *shortest path of its parent* + 1. This means that, when we traverse the target cell for the first time, it gives us the final result. This is the shortest path. Let's see the most relevant part of the code for this:

```
private static int findShortestPath(int[][] board) {

  // stores if cell is visited or not
  boolean[][] visited = new boolean[M][N];

  Queue<Cell> queue = new ArrayDeque<>();

  // process every cell of first column
  for (int r1 = 0; r1 < M; r1++) {
    // if the cell is safe, mark it as visited and
    // enqueue it by assigning it distance as 0 from itself
    if (board[r1][0] == 1) {
      queue.add(new Cell(r1, 0, 0));
      visited[r1][0] = true;
    }
  }

  while (!queue.isEmpty()) {

    // pop the front node from queue and process it
    int rIdx = queue.peek().r;
    int cIdx = queue.peek().c;
    int dist = queue.peek().distance;

    queue.poll();

    // if destination is found then return minimum distance
    if (cIdx == N - 1) {
      return (dist + 1);
    }
```

```
        // check for all 4 possible movements from
        // current cell and enqueue each valid movement
        for (int k = 0; k < 4; k++) {
            if (isValid(rIdx + ROW_4[k], cIdx + COL_4[k])
                && isSafe(board, visited, rIdx + ROW_4[k],
                    cIdx + COL_4[k])) {

                // mark it as visited and push it into
                // queue with (+1) distance
                visited[rIdx + ROW_4[k]][cIdx + COL_4[k]] = true;
                queue.add(new Cell(rIdx + ROW_4[k],
                    cIdx + COL_4[k], dist + 1));
            }
        }
    }

    return -1;
}
```

The complete application is called *ShortestSafeRoute*.

Infix, postfix, and prefix expressions

Prefix, postfix, and infix expressions are not a very common interview topic these days, but it can be considered a topic that should be covered at least once by any developer. The following is a quick overview:

- **Prefix expressions**: This is a notation (algebraic expression) that's used for writing arithmetic expressions in which the operands are listed after their operators.
- **Postfix expressions**: This is a notation (algebraic expression) that's used for writing arithmetic expressions in which the operands are listed before their operators.
- **Infix expressions**: This is a notation (algebraic expression) that's typically used in arithmetic formulas or statements where the operators are written in between their operands.

If we have three operators, a, b, and c, we can write the expressions shown in the following image:

Infix	Postfix	Prefix
(a + b) * c	a b + c *	* + a b c
a + (b * c)	a b c * +	+ a * b c

Figure 12.10 – Infix, postfix, and prefix

The most common problems refer to evaluating prefix and postfix expressions and converting between prefix, infix, and postfix expressions. All these problems have solutions that rely on stacks (or binary trees) and are covered in any serious book dedicated to fundamental algorithms. Take your time and harvest some resources about this topic to get familiar with it. Since this topic is widely covered in dedicated books and is not a common topic in interviews, we will not cover it here.

Summary

This chapter covered the must-know stack and queue problems for any candidate that is preparing for a Java developer technical interview. Stacks and queues occur in many real applications, so mastering them is one of the top skills that an interviewer will test you on.

In the next chapter, *Trees, Tries, and Graphs*, you'll see that stacks and queues are frequently used for solving problems that involve trees and graphs as well, which means they also deserve your attention.

13
Trees and Graphs

This chapter covers one of the trickiest topics asked in interviews: trees and graphs. While there are tons of problems related to these two topics, only a handful of them are actually encountered in interviews. Therefore, it is very important to prioritize the most popular problems with trees and graphs.

In this chapter, we'll start with a brief overview of trees and graphs. Later, we'll tackle the most popular and challenging problems encountered in interviews at IT giants such as Amazon, Microsoft, Adobe, and other companies. By the end of this chapter, you'll know how to answer interview questions and solve coding challenges regarding trees and graphs in an efficient and comprehensive way.

This chapter covers the following topics:

- Trees in a nutshell
- Graphs in a nutshell
- Coding challenges

So, let's get started!

Technical requirements

All the code present in this chapter can be found on GitHub at `https://github.com/PacktPublishing/The-Complete-Coding-Interview-Guide-in-Java/tree/master/Chapter13`.

Trees in a nutshell

A tree is a non-linear data structure that organizes data hierarchically in nodes and cannot contain cycles. A tree has a specific terminology that may vary slightly, but commonly, the following notions are adopted:

- **Root** is the topmost node.
- **Edge** is the link or connection between two nodes.
- **Parent** is a node that has an edge to a child node.
- **Child** is a node that has a parent node.
- **Leaf** is a node that does not have a child node.
- **Height** is the length of the longest path to a leaf.
- **Depth** is the length of the path to its root.

The following diagram exemplifies these terms when used on a tree:

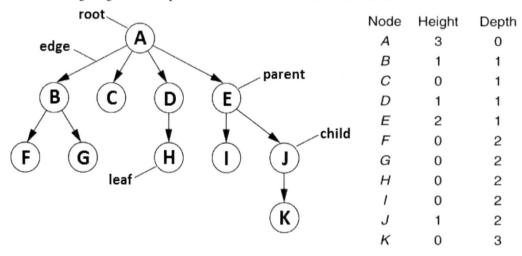

Figure 13.1 – Tree terminology

Typically, any tree can have a root. The nodes of the tree can respect a certain order (or not), can store any type of data, and may have links to their parents.

Tree coding challenges are rife with ambiguous details and/or incorrect assumptions. It is very important to clarify every single detail with the interviewer in order to eliminate ambiguity. One of the most important aspects refers to the type of tree. Let's take a look at the most common types of trees.

General tree

Roughly speaking, we can categorize trees into binary trees and the rest of the allowed trees. A binary tree is a tree in which each node has up to two children. In the following diagram, the left-hand side image is of a non-binary tree, while the right-hand side image is of a binary tree:

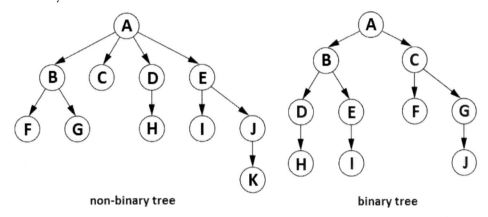

Figure 13.2 – Non-binary tree versus binary tree

In terms of code, a binary tree can be shaped as follows (this implementation is used later in the *Coding challenges* section, so keep this in mind):

```
private class Node {

  private Node left;
  private Node right;

  private final T element;

  public Node(T element) {
    this.element = element;
    this.left = null;
    this.right = null;
  }

  public Node(Node left, Node right, T element) {
    this.element = element;
    this.left = left;
    this.right = right;
```

```
    }

    // operations
}
```

As you can see, each Node keeps references to two other Node elements, as well as a generic data (element). The left and right nodes represent the children of the current node. Most tree coding challenges that are encountered in interviews use binary trees, so they deserve special attention. Binary trees can be categorized as follows.

Knowing binary tree traversal

Before attending a technical interview, you must know how to traverse a binary tree. Often, traversing a binary tree will not be a problem in itself, but you have to be comfortable with the **Breadth-first Search** (**BFS**) and the **Depth-first Search** (**DFS**) algorithms, along with their three variations: **Pre-Order**, **In-Order**, and **Post-Order**. The following diagram represents the result of each traversal type:

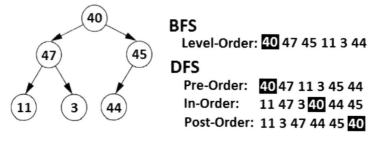

Figure 13.3 – Binary tree traversal

Let's have a brief overview of the BFS and DFS algorithms.

Breadth-first Search (BFS) for trees

BFS for trees is also referred as Level-Order traversal. The main idea is to maintain a queue of nodes that will ensure the order of traversal. Initially, the queue contains only the root node. The steps of the algorithm are as follows:

1. Pop the first node from the queue as the current node.
2. Visit the current node.
3. If the current node has a left node, then enqueue that left node.
4. If the current node has a right node, then enqueue that right node.
5. Repeat from *step 1* until the queue is empty.

In terms of code, we have the following:

```java
private void printLevelOrder(Node node) {

  Queue<Node> queue = new ArrayDeque<>();
  queue.add(node);

  while (!queue.isEmpty()) {
    // Step 1
    Node current = queue.poll();

    // Step 2
    System.out.print(" " + current.element);

    // Step 3
    if (current.left != null) {
      queue.add(current.left);
    }

    // Step 4
    if (current.right != null) {
      queue.add(current.right);
    }
  }
}
```

Next, let's focus on DFS.

Depth-first Search (DFS) for trees

DFS for trees has three variations: **Pre-Order**, **In-Order**, and **Post-Order**.

Pre-Order traversal visits the current node before its child nodes, as follows (**root | left sub-tree | right sub-tree**):

```java
private void printPreOrder(Node node) {
  if (node != null) {
    System.out.print(" " + node.element);
    printPreOrder(node.left);
```

```
      printPreOrder(node.right);
  }
}
```

In-Order traversal visits the left branch, then the current node, and finally, the right branch, as follows **(left sub-tree | root | right sub-tree)**:

```
private void printInOrder(Node node) {
  if (node != null) {
    printInOrder(node.left);
    System.out.print(" " + node.element);
    printInOrder(node.right);
  }
}
```

Post-Order visits the current node after its child nodes, as follows **(left sub-tree | right sub-tree | root)**:

```
private void printPostOrder(Node node) {
  if (node != null) {
    printPostOrder(node.left);
    printPostOrder(node.right);
    System.out.print(" " + node.element);
  }
}
```

The complete application is called *BinaryTreeTraversal*. Besides the preceding examples, the complete code also contains BFS and DFS implementations that return a `List` and an `Iterator`.

Binary Search Tree

A **Binary Search Tree** (**BST**) is a binary tree that follows an ordering rule. Typically, in a BST, the left descendants (all the elements on the left-hand side of the root) are smaller than or equal to the root element and, the right descendants (all the elements on the right-hand side of the root) are bigger than the root element. However, this order doesn't apply to just the root element. It applies to each node, n, so, in a BST, the *left descendants of n* $\leq n <$ *right descendants of n*. In the following diagram, the image on the left is of a binary tree, while the image on the right is of a BST:

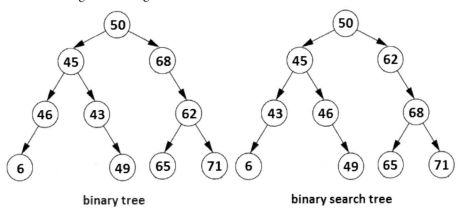

Figure 13.4 – Binary tree versus BST

Commonly, a BST doesn't accept duplicates, but when it does, they can be on one side (for example, only on the left-hand side) or on both sides. The duplicates can also be stored in a separated hash map, or directly in the structure of the tree via a counter. Pay attention and clarify these details with the interviewer. Handling duplicates in a BST is a problem encounter in interviews at Amazon, Flipkart, and Microsoft, which is why it will be tackled in the *Coding challenges* section.

In the code bundled with this book, you can find an application called *BinarySearchTreeTraversal* that exposes the following set of methods: `insert(T element)`, `contains(T element)`, `delete(T element)`, `min()`, `max()`, `root()`, `size()`, and `height()`. Moreover, it contains an implementation of BFS and DFS for printing nodes and for returning nodes as a `List` or an `Iterator`. Take your time and dissect the code.

Balanced and unbalanced binary trees

When a binary tree guarantees O(log n) times for insert and find operations, we can say that we have a *balanced* binary tree, but one that's not necessarily as balanced as it could be. When the difference between the heights of the left sub-tree and the right sub-tree for any node in the tree is no more than 1, then the tree is *height-balanced*. In the following diagram, the left-hand side tree is an unbalanced binary tree, the middle tree is a balanced binary tree but not height-balanced, and the right-hand side tree is a height-balanced tree:

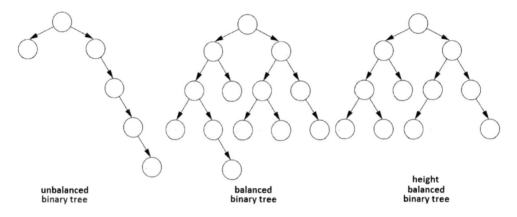

Figure 13.5 – Unbalanced binary tree versus balanced binary tree versus height-balanced binary tree

There are two types of balanced trees: Red-Black trees and AVL trees.

Red-Black tree

A Red-Black tree is a self-balancing BST where each node is under the incident of the following rules:

- Every node is either red or black
- The root node is always black
- Every leaf (NULL) is black
- Both children of a red node are black
- Every path from a node to a NULL node has the same number of black nodes

The following diagram represents a Red-Black tree:

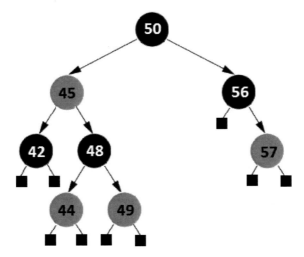

Figure 13.6 – Red-Black tree example

A Red-Black tree never gets terribly unbalanced. If all the nodes are black, then the tree becomes a *perfectly balanced tree*. The Red-Black tree becomes its maximum height when the nodes in its longest path are alternate black and red nodes. The height of a Black-Red tree is always less than or equal to $2\log_2(n+1)$, so its height is always in the order of O(log n).

Because of their complexity and time to implement, the problems that involve Red-Black trees are not a common topic in interviews. However, when they occur, the problem may ask you to implement the insert, delete, or find operations. In the code bundled with this book, you can find a Red-Black tree implementation that shows these operations at work. Take your time studying the code and getting familiar with the Red-Black tree concept. The application is called *RedBlackTreeImpl*.

More implementations that you may want to check out can be found at `github.com/williamfiset/data-structures/blob/master/com/williamfiset/datastructures/balancedtree/RedBlackTree.java` and `algs4.cs.princeton.edu/33balanced/RedBlackBST.java.html`. For a graphical visualization, please consider `www.cs.usfca.edu/~galles/visualization/RedBlack.html`.

If you need to deep dive into this topic, I strongly recommend that you read a book dedicated to data structures since this is a quite vast topic.

AVL tree

An **AVL** tree (named after their inventors, **A**delson-**V**elsky and **L**andis) is a self-balancing BST that respects the following rules:

- The height of a sub-tree can differ at most by 1.
- The balance factor (*BN*) of a node (*n*) is -1, 0, or 1 and is defined as the height (*h*) difference: $BN = h(right\_subtree(n)) - h(left\_subtree(n))$ or $BN = h(left\_subtree(n)) - h(right\_subtree(n))$.

The following diagram represents an AVL tree:

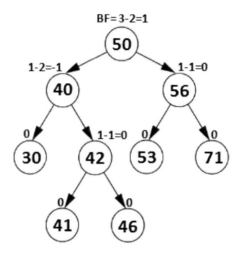

Figure 13.7 – AVL tree example

An AVL tree allows all operations (insert, delete, find min, find max, and so on) to perform in O(log n), where *n* is the number of nodes.

Because of their complexity and time to implement, the problems that involve AVL trees are not a common topic in interviews. However, when they occur, the problem may ask you to implement the insert, delete, or find operations. In the code bundled with this book, you can find an AVL tree implementation that shows these operations at work. Take your time studying the code and getting familiar with the AVL trees concept. The application is called *AVLTreeImpl*.

More implementations that you may want to check out can be found at `github.com/williamfiset/data-structures/blob/master/com/williamfiset/datastructures/balancedtree/AVLTreeRecursiveOptimized.java` and `algs4.cs.princeton.edu/code/edu/princeton/cs/algs4/AVLTreeST.java.html`. For a graphical visualization, please consider `www.cs.usfca.edu/~galles/visualization/AVLtree.html`.

If you need to deep dive into this topic, I strongly recommend that you read a book dedicated to data structures since this is a quite vast topic.

Complete binary tree

A complete binary tree is a binary tree in which every level, except possibly the last, is fully filled. Moreover, all the nodes are as far left as possible. In the following diagram, the left-hand side shows a non-complete binary tree, while the right-hand side shows a complete binary tree:

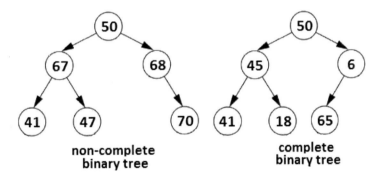

Figure 13.8 – A non-complete binary tree versus a complete binary tree

A complete binary tree must be filled from left to right, so the left-hand side tree shown in the preceding diagram is not complete. A complete binary tree with n nodes always has $O(\log n)$ height.

Full binary tree

A full binary tree is a binary tree in which every node has two children or none. In other words, a node cannot have only one child. In the following diagram, the left-hand side shows a non-full binary tree, while the right-hand side shows a full binary tree:

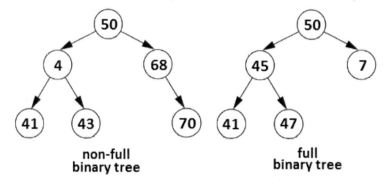

Figure 13.9 – A non-full binary tree versus a full binary tree

The left-hand side tree in the preceding diagram is not full because node 68 has one child.

Perfect binary tree

A perfect binary tree is complete and full at the same time. The following diagram shows one such tree:

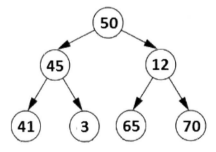

Figure 13.10 – Perfect binary tree

So, in a perfect binary tree, all the leaf nodes are at the same level. This means that the last level contains the maximum number of nodes. These kinds of tree are pretty rare in interviews.

> **Important note**
>
> Pay attention to problems that sound like this: *Consider you've been given a binary tree. Write a snippet of code that...* Do not make any assumptions about the given binary tree! Always ask the interviewer for more details, such as *Is this a balanced tree? Is it a full binary tree?, Is it a BST?*. In other words, don't base your solution on assumptions that may not be true for the given binary tree.

Now, let's discuss binary heaps in more detail.

Binary Heaps

In a nutshell, a Binary Heap is a complete binary tree that has a *heap property*. When the elements are in ascending order (the heap property says that the element of each node is greater than or equal to the element of its parent), we have a Min Binary Heap (the minimum element is the root element), while when they are in descending order (the heap property says that the element of each node is less than or equal to the element of its parent), we have a Max Binary Heap (the maximum element is the root element).

The following diagram shows a complete binary tree (left-hand side), a Min Binary Heap (in the middle), and a Max Binary Heap (right-hand side):

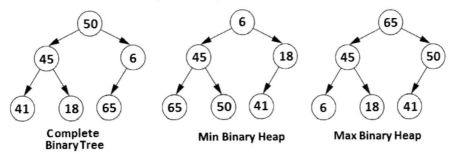

Figure 13.11 – Complete binary tree and min and max heaps

A Binary Heap is not sorted. It is partially ordered. There is no relationship between the nodes on any given level.

A Binary Heap is typically represented as an array (let's denote it as *heap*) whose root is at *heap*[0]. More importantly, for *heap*[*i*], we have that the following:

- *heap*[(*i* - 1) / 2]: Returns the parent node
- *heap*[(2 * *i*) + 1]: Returns the left child node
- *heap*[(2 * *i*) + 2]: Returns the right child node

A Max Binary Heap, when implemented via an array, looks as follows:

```java
public class MaxHeap<T extends Comparable<T>> {

  private static final int DEFAULT_CAPACITY = 5;

  private int capacity;
  private int size;
  private T[] heap;

  public MaxHeap() {

    capacity = DEFAULT_CAPACITY;
    this.heap = (T[]) Array.newInstance(
      Comparable[].class.getComponentType(),DEFAULT_CAPACITY);
  }

  // operations
}
```

The common operations that are used with a heap are `add()`, `poll()`, and `peek()`. After adding or polling an element, we must fix the heap so that it respects the heap property. This step is commonly referenced as *heapifying* the heap.

Adding an element to a heap is an O(log n) time operation. The new element is added at the end of the heap tree. If the new element is smaller than its parent, then we don't need to do anything. Otherwise, we have to traverse the heap upward to fix the violated heap property. This operation is known as *heapify-up*. The algorithm behind *heapify-up* has two steps:

1. Start from the end of the heap as the current node.
2. While the current node has a parent and the parent is less than the current node, swap these nodes.

Polling an element from a heap is also an O(log n) time operation. After we've polled the root element of the heap, we have to fix the heap so that it respects the heap property. This operation is known as *heapify-down*. The algorithm behind *heapify-down* has three steps:

1. Start from the root of the heap as the current node.
2. Determine the largest node between the children of the current node.
3. If the current node is less than its largest children, then swap these two nodes and repeat from *step 2*; otherwise, there is nothing else to do, so stop.

Finally, peeking is an O(1) operation that returns the root element of the heap.

In the code bundled with this book, you can find an application called *MaxHeap* that exposes the following set of methods: `add(T element)`, `peek()`, and `poll()`.

> **Important note**
> A special case of a tree is known as a Trie. Also known as a *digital tree* or a *prefix tree,* a Trie is an ordered tree structure used commonly for storing strings. Its name comes from the fact that Trie is a re*Trie*val data structure. Its performance is better than a binary tree. Trie is detailed in my book, *Java Coding Problems* (`https://www.packtpub.com/programming/java-coding-problems`), next to other data structures such as tuples, disjoint-set, binary indexed trees (Fenwick trees), and Bloom filters.

Next, let's have a brief overview of graphs.

Graphs in a nutshell

A graph is a data structure that's used to represent a collection of nodes that can be connected with edges. For example, a graph can be used to represent a network of members on a social media platform, so it is a great data structure for representing real-life connections. A tree (as detailed in the previous section) is a particular type of graph. In other words, a tree is a graph without cycles. In graph terms, a graph without cycles is called an *acyclic graph*.

The specific terminology for graphs involves two main terms:

- **Vertex** represents the information (for example, a member, a dog, or a value)
- **Edge** is the connection or the relationship between two vertices

The connection can be unidirectional (as in the case of binary trees) or bidirectional. When the connection is bidirectional (such as a two-way street), the graph is known as an *undirected graph* and it has *undirected edges*. When the connection is unidirectional (such as a one-way street), then the graph is known as a *directed graph* and it has *directed edges*.

The edges of a graph can carry information known as the weight (for example, the length of a road). In this case, the graphs are called *weighted graphs*. When a graph has a single edge that points to the same vertex, it is called a *self-loop graph*. The following diagram provides representations for each of these graph types:

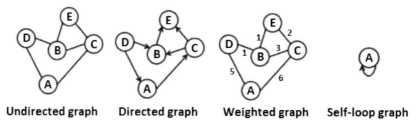

Figure 13.12 – Graph types

Unlike binary trees, representing graphs via node links is not practical. In computers, a graph is commonly represented via the adjacency matrix or adjacency list. Let's tackle the former; that is, the adjacency matrix.

Adjacency matrix

An adjacency matrix is represented by a boolean two-dimensional array (or an integer two-dimensional array that contains only 0s and 1s) of size *n* x *n*, where *n* is the number of vertices. If we denote this two-dimensional array as a *matrix*, then *matrix*[*i*][*j*] is true (or 1) if there is an edge from vertex *i* to vertex *j*; otherwise, it is false (or 0). The following diagram shows an example of an adjacency matrix for an undirected graph:

	A	B	C	D	E
A	0	0	1	1	0
B	0	0	1	1	1
C	1	1	0	0	1
D	1	1	0	0	0
E	0	1	1	0	0

Figure 13.13 – An adjacency matrix for an undirected graph

Graphs in a nutshell

In order to save space, a bit-matrix can be used as well.

In the case of weighted graphs, the adjacency matrix can store the weight of the edge, while 0 can be used to indicate the absence of the edge.

Implementing a graph based on the adjacency matrix can be done as follows (all we need is the list of vertices since the edges are passed to each method that has to traverse the graph as the adjacency matrix):

```java
public class Graph<T> {

  // the vertices list
  private final List<T> elements;

  public Graph() {
    this.elements = new ArrayList<>();
  }

  // operations
}
```

Another approach we can use to represent a graph in a computer is the adjacency list.

Adjacency list

An adjacency list is an array of lists whose size is equal to the number of vertices in the graph. Every vertex is stored in this array and it stores a list of adjacent vertices. In other words, the list at index *i* of the array contains the adjacent vertices of the vertex stored in the array at index *i*. The following diagram shows an example of an adjacency list for an undirected graph:

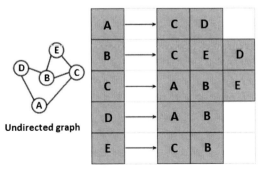

Figure 13.14 – An adjacency list for an undirected graph

Implementing a graph based on the adjacency list can be done as follows (here, we are using a `Map` to implement the adjacency list):

```
public class Graph<T> {

  // the adjacency list is represented as a map
  private final Map<T, List<T>> adjacencyList;

  public Graph() {
    this.adjacencyList = new HashMap<>();
  }

  // operations
}
```

Next, let's briefly cover the traversal of a graph.

Graph traversal

The two most common ways to traverse a graph are via **Depth-first Search** (**DFS**) and **Breadth-first Search** (**BFS**). Let's have a rundown of each. **BFS** is mainly used for graphs.

In the case of graphs, we must consider that a graph may have cycles. A plain BFS implementation (as you saw in the case of binary trees) doesn't take cycles into account, so we risk an infinite loop while traversing the BFS queue. Eliminating this risk can be done via an additional collection that holds the visited nodes. The steps for this algorithm are as follows:

1. Mark the start node (current node) as visited (add it to the collection of visited nodes) and add it to the BFS queue.
2. Pop the current node from the queue.
3. Visit the current node.
4. Get the adjacent nodes of the current node.

5. Loop the adjacent nodes. For each non-null and unvisited node, do the following:

   a. Mark it as visited (add it to the collection of visited nodes).

   b. Add it to the queue.

6. Repeat from *step 2* until the queue is empty.

Depth-first Search (DFS) for graphs

In the case of graphs, we can implement the DFS algorithm via recursion or iterative implementation.

DFS for graphs via recursion

The steps for implementing the DFS algorithm for graphs via recursion are as follows:

1. Start from the current node (the given node) and mark the current node as visited (add it to the collection of visited nodes).

2. Visit the current node.

3. Traverse the unvisited adjacent vertices via recursion.

DFS for graphs – iterative implementation

The iterative implementation of the DFS algorithm relies on a `Stack`. The steps are as follows:

1. Start from the current node (the given node) and push the current node into `Stack`.

2. While `Stack` is not empty, do the following:

   a. Pop the current node from `Stack`.

   b. Visit the current node.

   c. Mark the current node as visited (add it to the collection of visited nodes).

   d. Push the unvisited adjacent vertices into `Stack`.

In the code bundled with this book, you can find a graph implementation based on the adjacency matrix called *GraphAdjacencyMatrixTraversal*. You can also find one based on the adjacency list called *GraphAdjacencyListTraversal*. Both applications contain BFS and DFS implementations.

Coding challenges

Now that we have had a brief overview of trees and graphs, it is time to challenge ourselves with the 25 most popular coding problems encountered in interviews about these topics.

As usual, we have a mix of problems that are usually encountered by the top companies of the world, including IT giants such as Amazon, Adobe and Google. So, let's get started!

Coding challenge 1 – Paths between two nodes

Problem: Consider you've been given a directed graph. Write a snippet of code that returns `true` if there is a path (route) between two given nodes.

Solution: Let's consider the directed graph shown in the following diagram:

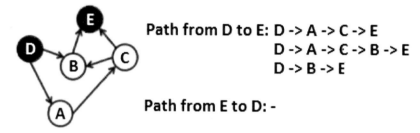

Figure 13.15 – Paths from D to E and vice versa

If we consider nodes *D* and *E*, then we can see that from *D* to *E*, there are three paths, while from *E* to *D*, there are none. So, if we start from *D* and traverse the graph (via BFS or DFS) then, at some point, we have to pass through node *E*, otherwise there will be no path between *D* and *E*. So, the solution to this problem consists of starting from one of the given nodes and traversing the graph until we reach the second given node or until there are no more valid moves. For example, we can do this via BFS as follows:

```
public boolean isPath(T from, T to) {

  Queue<T> queue = new ArrayDeque<>();
  Set<T> visited = new HashSet<>();

  // we start from the 'from' node
  visited.add(from);
  queue.add(from);
```

```java
    while (!queue.isEmpty()) {
      T element = queue.poll();

      List<T> adjacents = adjacencyList.get(element);
      if (adjacents != null) {

        for (T t : adjacents) {
          if (t != null && !visited.contains(t)) {
            visited.add(t);
            queue.add(t);

            // we reached the destination (the 'to' node)
            if (t.equals(to)) {
              return true;
            }
          }
        }
      }
    }

    return false;
  }
```

The complete application is called *DirectedGraphPath*.

Coding challenge 2 – Sorted array to minimal BST

Amazon, Google

Problem: Consider you've been given a sorted (ascending order) array of integers. Write a snippet of code that creates the minimal BST from this array. We define the minimal BST as the BST with the minimum height.

Solution: Consider the given array as {-2, 3, 4, 6, 7, 8, 12, 23, 90}. The minimal BST that can be created from this array looks as follows:

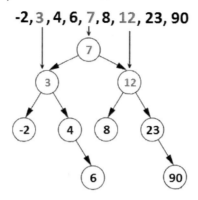

Figure 13.16 – Sorted array to minimal BST

In order to obtain a BST of minimal height, we must strive to distribute an equal number of nodes in the left and right sub-trees. With this statement in mind, note that we can choose the middle of the sorted array as the root. The elements of the array on the left-hand side of the middle are smaller than the middle, so they can form the left sub-tree. The elements of the array on the right-hand side of the middle are greater than the middle, so they can form the right sub-tree.

So, we can choose 7 as the root of the tree. Next, -2, 3, 4, and 6 should form the left sub-tree, while 8, 12, 23, and 90 should form the right sub-tree. However, we know that we cannot simply add these elements to the left or right sub-trees since we have to respect the BST property: in a BST, for each node, n, the *left descendants of $n \leq n <$ right descendants of n*.

However, we can simply follow the same technique. If we consider -2, 3, 4, and 6 as an array, then its middle is 3, and if we consider 8, 12, 24, and 90 as an array, then its middle is 12. So, 3 is the root of the left sub-sub-tree containing -2, and the right sub-sub-tree is the one that contains 4 and 6. Similarly, 12 is the root of the left sub-sub-tree containing 8, and the right sub-sub-tree is the one that contains 24 and 90.

Well, I think we have enough experience to intuit that the same technique can be applied until we've processed all the sub-arrays. Moreover, it is quite intuitive that this solution can be implemented via recursion (if you don't consider recursion one of your top skills, review *Chapter 8, Recursion and Dynamic Programming*). So, we can resume our algorithm in four steps:

1. Insert the middle element of the array into the tree.
2. Insert the elements of the left sub-array into the left sub-tree.

3. Insert the elements of the right sub-array into the right sub-tree.
4. Trigger the recursive call.

The following implementation puts these steps into code:

```
public void minimalBst(T m[]) {
  root = minimalBst(m, 0, m.length - 1);
}

private Node minimalBst(T m[], int start, int end) {

  if (end < start) {
    return null;
  }

  int middle = (start + end) / 2;
  Node node = new Node(m[middle]);

  nodeCount++;

  node.left = minimalBst(m, start, middle - 1);
  node.right = minimalBst(m, middle + 1, end);

  return node;
}
```

The complete application is called *SortedArrayToMinBinarySearchTree*.

Coding challenge 3 – List per level

Problem: Consider you've been given a binary tree. Write a snippet of code that creates a list of elements for each level of the tree (for example, if the tree has a depth of *d*, then you'll have *d* lists).

Trees and Graphs

Solution: Let's consider the binary tree shown in the following diagram:

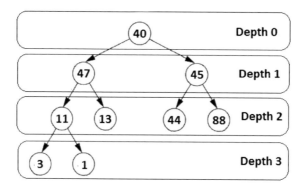

Figure 13.17 – List per level

So, we have a binary tree of depth 3. On depth 0, we have the root, 40. On depth 1, we have 47 and 45. On depth 2, we have 11, 13, 44, and 88. Finally, on depth 3, we have 3 and 1.

It is quite intuitive to think like this: if we traverse the binary tree level by level, then we can create a list of elements for each level. In other words, we can adapt the BFS algorithm (also known as Level-Order traversal) in such a way that we capture the elements at each traversed level. More precisely, we start by traversing the root (and create a list containing this element), continue by traversing level 1 (and create a list containing the elements from this level), and so on.

When we reach level *i*, we will have already fully visited all the nodes on the previous level, *i*-1. This means that to get the elements on level *i*, we must traverse all the children of the nodes of the previous level, *i*-1. The following solution runs in O(n) time:

```
public List<List<T>> fetchAllLevels() {

  // each list holds a level
  List<List<T>> allLevels = new ArrayList<>();

  // first level (containing only the root)
  Queue<Node> currentLevelOfNodes = new ArrayDeque<>();
  List<T> currentLevelOfElements = new ArrayList<>();

  currentLevelOfNodes.add(root);
  currentLevelOfElements.add(root.element);
```

```
    while (!currentLevelOfNodes.isEmpty()) {

      // store the current level as the previous level
      Queue<Node> previousLevelOfNodes = currentLevelOfNodes;

      // add level to the final list
      allLevels.add(currentLevelOfElements);

      // go to the next level as the current level
      currentLevelOfNodes = new ArrayDeque<>();
      currentLevelOfElements = new ArrayList<>();

      // traverse all nodes on current level
      for (Node parent : previousLevelOfNodes) {

        if (parent.left != null) {
          currentLevelOfNodes.add(parent.left);
          currentLevelOfElements.add(parent.left.element);
        }

        if (parent.right != null) {
          currentLevelOfNodes.add(parent.right);
          currentLevelOfElements.add(parent.right.element);
        }
      }
    }

    return allLevels;
}
```

The complete application is called *ListPerBinaryTreeLevel*.

Coding challenge 4 – sub-tree

Adobe, Microsoft, Flipkart

Problem: Consider you've been given two binary trees, *p* and *q*. Write a snippet of code that returns `true` if *q* is a sub-tree of *p*.

Solution: Consider the following diagram:

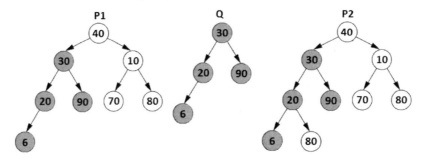

Figure 13.18 – Binary tree's sub-tree of another binary tree

As we can see, the binary tree in the middle, *q*, is a sub-tree of the *p1* binary tree (left-hand side) but is not a sub-tree of the *p2* binary tree (right-hand side).

Moreover, this diagram reveals two cases:

- If the root of *p* matches the root of *q* (*p.root.element == q.root.element*), then the problem reduces to check whether the right sub-tree of *q* is the same as the right sub-tree of *p*, or whether the left sub-tree of *q* is the same as the left sub-tree of *p*.

- If the root of *p* doesn't match the root of *q* (*p.root.element != q.root.element*), then the problem reduces to check whether the left sub-tree of *p* is the same as *q*, or whether the right sub-tree of *p* is the same as *q*.

In order to implement the first bullet, we need two methods. To better understand why we need two methods, check out the following diagram:

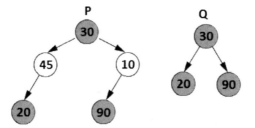

Figure 13.19 – Roots and leaves match but the intermediate nodes don't

If the roots of *p* and *q* match but some of the nodes from the left/right sub-trees don't match, then we have to go back to where we started with *p* and *q* to check whether *q* is a sub-tree of *p*. The first method should check whether the trees are the same once their roots are the same. The second method should handle the case where we find that the trees are not the same but start at a certain node. Pay attention to this aspect, since many candidates don't take it into account.

So, in terms of code, we have the following (for *n* nodes, this runs in O(n) time):

```
public boolean isSubtree(BinaryTree q) {

   return isSubtree(root, q.root);
}

private boolean isSubtree(Node p, Node q) {

   if (p == null) {
     return false;
   }

   // if the roots don't match
   if (!match(p, q)) {
     return (isSubtree(p.left, q) || isSubtree(p.right, q));
   }

   return true;
}

private boolean match(Node p, Node q) {

   if (p == null && q == null) {
     return true;
   }

   if (p == null || q == null) {
     return false;
   }

   return (p.element == q.element
      && match(p.left, q.left)
      && match(p.right, q.right));
}
```

The application is called *BinaryTreeSubtree*.

Coding challenge 5 – Landing reservation system

Amazon, Adobe, Microsoft

Problem: Consider an airport with a single runway. This airport receives landing requests from different airplanes. A landing request contains the landing time (for example, 9:56) and the time in minutes needed to complete the procedure (for example, 5 minutes). We denote it as 9:56 (5). Write a snippet of code that uses a BST to design this reservation system. Since there is a single runway, the code should reject any landing request that overlaps an existing one. The order of requests dictates the order of reservations.

Solution: Let's consider a time screenshot of our landing timeline (the order for the landing requests was 10:10 (3), 10:14 (3), 9:55 (2), 10:18 (1), 9:58 (5), 9:47 (2), 9:41 (2), 10:22 (1), 9:50 (6), and 10:04 (4). This can be seen in the following diagram:

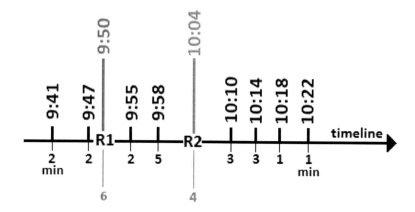

Figure 13.20 – Timeline screenshot

So, we have already done several reservations, as follows: at 9:41, an airplane will land and it will need 2 minutes to complete the procedure; at 9:47 and 9:55, there are two other airplanes that need 2 minutes to complete landing; at 9:58, we have an airplane that needs 5 minutes to complete landing; and so on. Moreover, we also have two new landing requests denoted in the diagram as *R1* and *R2*.

Notice that we cannot approve the *R1* landing request. The landing time is 9:50 and it needs 6 minutes to complete, so it ends at 9:56. However, at 9:56, we already have the airplane from 9:55 on the runway. Since we have a single runway, we reject this landing request. We consider such cases as overlappings.

On the other hand, we approve the *R2* landing request. The request time is 10:04 and it needs 4 minutes to complete, so it ends at 10:08. At 10:08, there is no other airplane on the runway since the next landing is at 10:10.

Notice that we have to use a BST to solve this problem, but using an array (sorted or unsorted) or a linked list (sorted or unsorted) is also a valid approach. Using an unsorted array (or linked list) will need O(1) time for inserting a landing request and O(n) time for checking the potential overlapping. If we were to use a sorted array (or linked list) and the Binary Search algorithm, then we could check the potential overlapping in O(log n). However, to insert a landing request, we will need O(n) because we have to shift all the elements to the right from the position of insertion.

How about using a BST? First, let's represent the preceding timeline screenshot as a BST. Check out the following diagram (the order of the landing requests was 10:10 (3), 10:14 (3), 9:55 (2), 10:18 (1), 9:58 (5), 9:47 (2), 9:41 (2), 10:22 (1), *9:50 (6)*, and 10:04 (4)):

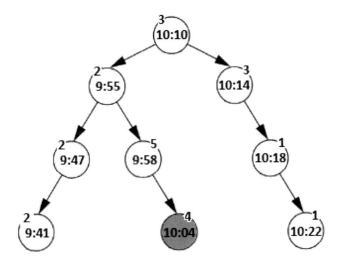

Figure 13.21 – Timeline screenshot as a BST

This time, for each landing request, we only have to scan half of the tree. This is the consequence of using a BST (all the nodes on the left are smaller than all the nodes on the right, so a landing request time can only be in the left or the right sub-tree). For example, the landing request at 10:04 is less than the root (10:10), so it goes in the left sub-tree. If, at any given landing request, we encounter an overlapping, then we just return without inserting the corresponding node into the tree. We can find the potential overlappings in O(h), where *h* is the height of the BST, and we can insert it in O(1) time.

An overlapping is given by the following simple computation (we're using the Java 8 Date-Time API, but you can reduce it to simple integers as well – if you are not familiar with the Java 8 Date-Time API, then I strongly recommend that you buy my book, *Java Coding Problems*, published by Packt (https://www.packtpub.com/programming/java-coding-problems). This book has an astonishing chapter about this topic that is a *must-read* for any candidate:

```
long t1 = Duration.between(current.element.
    plusMinutes(current.time), element).toMinutes();

long t2 = Duration.between(current.element,
    element.plusMinutes(time)).toMinutes();

if (t1 <= 0 && t2 >= 0) {
    // overlapping found
}
```

So, in *t1*, we compute the time between the (*landing time + time needed to complete*) of the current node and the *landing time* of the current request. In *t2*, we compute the time between the *landing time* of the current node and the (*current request landing time + time needed to complete*). If *t1* is less than or equal to *t2*, then we have found an overlapping, so we reject the current landing request. Let's see the complete code:

```
public class BinarySearchTree<Temporal> {

    private Node root = null;

    private class Node {

        private Node left;
        private Node right;

        private final LocalTime element;
        private final int time;

        public Node(LocalTime element, int time) {
            this.time = time;
            this.element = element;
```

```java
      this.left = null;
      this.right = null;
    }

    public Node(Node left, Node right,
          LocalTime element, int time) {
      this.time = time;
      this.element = element;
      this.left = left;
      this.right = right;
    }
  }

  public void insert(LocalTime element, int time) {

    if (element == null) {
      throw new IllegalArgumentException("...");
    }

    root = insert(root, element, time);
  }

  private Node insert(Node current,
        LocalTime element, int time) {

    if (current == null) {
      return new Node(element, time);
    }

    long t1 = Duration.between(current.element.
        plusMinutes(current.time), element).toMinutes();
    long t2 = Duration.between(current.element,
        element.plusMinutes(time)).toMinutes();

    if (t1 <= 0 && t2 >= 0) {
      System.out.println("Cannot reserve the runway at "
```

```
            + element + " for " + time + " minutes !");

      return current;
    }

    if (element.compareTo(current.element) < 0) {
      current.left = insert(current.left, element, time);
    } else {
      current.right = insert(current.right, element, time);
    }

    return current;
  }

  public void printInOrder() {
    printInOrder(root);
  }

  private void printInOrder(Node node) {
    if (node != null) {
      printInOrder(node.left);
      System.out.print(" " + node.element
          + "(" + node.time + ")");
      printInOrder(node.right);
    }
  }
}
```

Notice that we can easily print the timeline by using the In-Order traversal of a BST. The complete application is called *BinaryTreeLandingReservation*.

Coding challenge 6 – Balanced binary tree

Amazon, Microsoft

Problem: Consider you've been given a binary tree. We consider it balanced if the heights of the two sub-trees of any node don't differ by more than one (this is what we call a height-balanced binary tree). Write a snippet of code that returns `true` if the binary tree is balanced.

Solution: So, in order to have a balanced binary tree, for each node, the two sub-trees cannot differ in height by more than one. Conforming to this statement, the image on the right represents a balanced binary tree, while the image on the left represents an unbalanced binary tree:

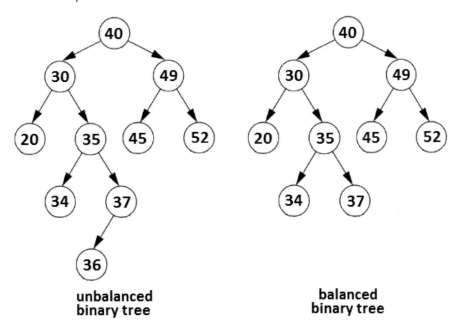

Figure 13.22 – Unbalanced and balanced binary trees

The binary tree on the left is unbalanced since the difference between the heights of the left sub-trees corresponding to nodes 40 (the root) and 30 and the right sub-trees is greater than one (for example, the *left-height*(40) = 4 while the *right-height*(40) = 2).

The right-hand side binary tree is balanced since, for each node, the difference between the height of the left sub-tree and the right sub-tree is not greater than one.

Based on this example, we can intuit that a simple solution consists of a recursive algorithm. We can traverse each node and compute the height of the left and right sub-trees. If the difference between these heights is greater than one, then we return `false`. In terms of code, this is quite straightforward:

```
public boolean isBalanced() {
  return isBalanced(root);
}

private boolean isBalanced(Node root) {
  if (root == null) {
    return true;
  }
  if (Math.abs(height(root.left) - height(root.right)) > 1) {
    return false;
  } else {
    return isBalanced(root.left) && isBalanced(root.right);
  }
}

private int height(Node root) {
  if (root == null) {
    return 0;
  }
  return Math.max(height(root.left), height(root.right)) + 1;
}
```

This approach performs in O(n log n) time because, on each node, we apply the recursion through its entire sub-tree. So, the problem is the number of `height()` calls. At this moment, the `height()` method only computes the heights. But it can be improved to check whether the tree is balanced as well. All we need to do is signal an unbalanced sub-tree via an error code. On the other hand, for a balanced tree, we return the corresponding height. In place of an error code, we can use `Integer.MIN_VALUE`, as follows:

```java
public boolean isBalanced() {
    return checkHeight(root) != Integer.MIN_VALUE;
}

private int checkHeight(Node root) {

    if (root == null) {
        return 0;
    }

    int leftHeight = checkHeight(root.left);
    if (leftHeight == Integer.MIN_VALUE) {
        return Integer.MIN_VALUE; // error
    }

    int rightHeight = checkHeight(root.right);
    if (rightHeight == Integer.MIN_VALUE) {
        return Integer.MIN_VALUE; // error
    }

    if (Math.abs(leftHeight - rightHeight) > 1) {
        return Integer.MIN_VALUE; // pass error back
    } else {
        return Math.max(leftHeight, rightHeight) + 1;
    }
}
```

This code runs in O(n) time and O(h) space, where *h* is the height of the tree. The application is called *BinaryTreeBalanced*.

Coding challenge 7 – Binary tree is a BST

Amazon, Google, Adobe, Microsoft, Flipkart

Problem: Consider you've been given a binary tree that may contain duplicates. Write a snippet of code that returns `true` if this tree is a **Binary Search Tree (BST)**.

Solution: Right from the start, we notice that the problem is explicitly mentioning that the given binary tree may contain duplicates. Why is this important? Because if the binary tree doesn't allow duplicates, then we can rely on a simple In-Order traversal and an array. If we add each traversed element to an array, then the resulting array will be sorted only if the binary tree is a BST. Let's clarify this aspect via the following diagram:

left descendants of n ≤ n < right descendants of n

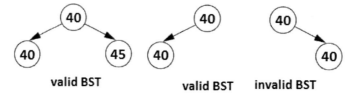

Figure 13.23 – Valid and invalid BSTs

We know that the BST property says that for each node, *n*, of a BST, the *left descendants of n ≤ n < right descendants of n*. This means that the first two binary trees shown in the previous diagram are valid BST, while the last one is not a valid BST. Now, adding the elements of the middle and the last binary tree to the array will result in an array of [40, 40]. This means we cannot validate or invalidate a BST based on this array since we cannot distinguish between the trees. So, in conclusion, you should rely on this simple algorithm if the given binary tree doesn't accept duplicates.

Now, it's time to take this a step further. Let's examine the *left descendants of n ≤ n < right descendants of n* statement shown in the following binary tree:

Left descendants of n ≤ n < right descendants of n

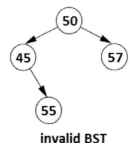

Figure 13.24 – Invalid BST

Check this out! For each node, *n*, we can write that *n.left* ≤ *n* < *n.right*, but it is clear that 55 is in the wrong place. So, let's reinforce that all the left nodes of the current node should be less than or equal to the current node, which must be less than all the right nodes.

In other words, it is not enough to validate the left and right nodes of the current node. We must validate each node against a range of nodes. More precisely, all the nodes of a left or a right sub-tree should be validated against a range bounded by the minimum accepted element, respectively the maximum accepted element (*min, max*). Let's consider the following tree:

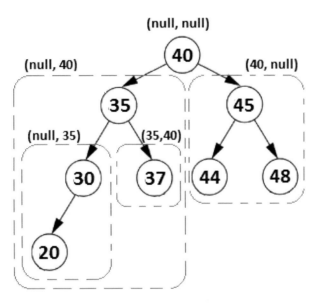

Figure 13.25 – Validating a BST

We start from the root (40) and we consider (*min*=null, *max*=null), so 40 meets the condition since there is no minimum or maximum limit. Next, we go to the left sub-tree (let's denote this sub-tree as 40-left-sub-tree). All the nodes from the 40-left-sub-tree should range between (null, 40). Next, we go to the left again, and we meet the 35-left-sub-tree, which should range between (null, 35). Basically, we continue to go left until there are no nodes left. At this point, we start going to the right, so the 35-right-sub-tree should range between (35, 40), the 40-right-sub-tree should range between (40, null), and so on. So, when we go to the left, the maximum value gets updated. When we go to the right, the minimum gets updated. If anything goes wrong, then we stop and return `false`. Let's see the code based on this algorithm:

```
public boolean isBinarySearchTree() {
    return isBinarySearchTree(root, null, null);
```

```
}

private boolean isBinarySearchTree(Node node,
        T minElement, T maxElement) {

    if (node == null) {
        return true;
    }

    if ((minElement != null &&
        node.element.compareTo(minElement) <= 0)
            || (maxElement != null && node.element.
                compareTo(maxElement) > 0)) {
        return false;
    }

    if (!isBinarySearchTree(node.left, minElement, node.element)
            || !isBinarySearchTree(node.right,
                node.element, maxElement)) {
        return false;
    }

    return true;
}
```

The complete application is called *BinaryTreeIsBST*.

Coding challenge 8 – Successor node

Google, **Microsoft**

Problem: Consider you've been given a **Binary Search Tree** (**BST**) and a node from this tree. Write a snippet of code that prints the successor node of the given node in the context of In-Order traversal.

Solution: So, let's recall the In-Order traversal of a binary tree. This **Depth-first Search (DFS)** flavor traverses the left sub-tree, then the current node, and then the right sub-tree. Now, let's assume that we arbitrarily choose a node from a BST (let's denote it as *n*) and we want to find its successor (let's denote it as *s*) in the context of In-Order traversal.

Let's consider the following diagram as the given BST. We can use it as support for distinguishing between the possible cases:

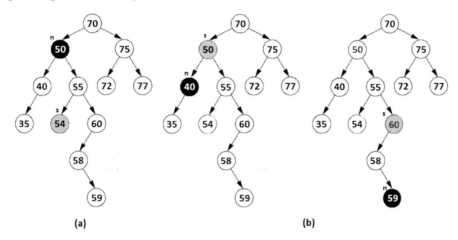

Figure 13.26 – BST sample with start and successor nodes

As shown in the preceding diagram, we denoted two main cases as (a) and (b). In case (a), the node, *n*, has the right sub-tree. In case (b), the node, *n*, doesn't contain the right sub-tree.

Case (a), exemplified in the left-hand side BST, reveals that if the node, *n*, has the right sub-tree, then the successor node, *s*, is the leftmost node of this right sub-tree. For example, for *n*=50, the successor node is 54.

Case (b) has two sub-cases: a simple case and a tricky case. The simple case is exemplified by the middle BST shown in the preceding diagram. When the node, *n*, doesn't contain the right sub-tree and *n* is the left child of its parent, then the successor node is this parent. For example, for *n*=40, the successor node is 50. This is the simple sub-case of (b).

The tricky sub-case of (b) is exemplified by the right-hand side BST shown in the preceding diagram. When the node, *n*, doesn't contain the right sub-tree and *n* is the right child of its parent, then we have to traverse upward until *n* becomes the left child of its parent. Once we've done that, we return this parent. For example, if *n*=59, then the successor node is 60.

Moreover, we must consider that if *n* is the last node in the traversal, then we return the root's parent, which can be null.

If we glue these cases to form some pseudocode, then we get the following:

```
Node inOrderSuccessor(Node n) {
  if (n has a right sub-tree) {
    return the leftmost child of right sub-tree
  }

  while (n is a right child of n.parent) {
    n = n.parent; // traverse upwards
  }

  return n.parent; // parent has not been traversed
}
```

Now, we can translate this pseudocode into code, as follows:

```java
public void inOrderSuccessor() {

  // choose the node
  Node node = ...;

  System.out.println("\n\nIn-Order:");
  System.out.print("Start node: " + node.element);
  node = inOrderSuccessor(node);
  System.out.print(" Successor node: " + node.element);
}

private Node inOrderSuccessor(Node node) {

  if (node == null) {
    return null;
  }

  // case (a)
  if (node.right != null) {
    return findLeftmostNode(node.right);
  }
```

```
  // case (b)
  while (node.parent != null && node.parent.right == node) {
    node = node.parent;
  }

  return node.parent;
}
```

The complete application is called *BinarySearchTreeSuccessor*. This application also contains the same problem, but is resolved via Pre-Order and Post-Order traversal. Before checking the solutions for the Pre-Order and Post-Order contexts, you should challenge yourself by identifying the possible cases and sketching the pseudocode and its implementation.

Coding challenge 9 – Topological sort

Amazon, **Google**, **Adobe**, **Microsoft**, **Flipkart**

Problem: Consider you've been given a **Directed Acyclic Graph** (**DAG**); that is, a directed graph without cycles. Write a snippet of code that returns the linear ordering of vertices such that for every directed edge, *XY*, vertex *X* comes before *Y* in the ordering. In other words, for every edge, the source node comes before the destination. This is also known as topological sort, and it only works for DAGs.

Solution: Let's dive into this problem via the following DAG:

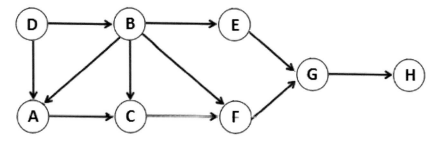

Figure 13.27 – Directed acyclic graph (DAG)

Let's start the topological sort from vertex D. Before vertex D, there is no other vertex (no edge), so we can add D to the result, (D). From D, we can go to B or A. Let's go to vertex A. We cannot add A to the result because we didn't process vertex B of edge BA, so let's go to vertex B. Before B, we have only D, which was added to the result, so we can add B to the result, (D, B). From B, we can go to A, E, C, and F. We cannot go to C since we didn't process AC, and we cannot go to F since we didn't process CF. However, we can go to A since DA and BA have been processed, and we can go to E since before E, there's only B, which is in the result. Notice that the topological sort may provide different results. Let's go to E. Due to this, E is added to the result (D, B, E). Next, we can add A to the result, which allows us to add C, which allows us to add F. So, the result is now (D, B, E, A, C, F). From F, we can go to G. Since EG has been processed, we can add G to the result. Finally, from G, we go to H and we obtain the topological sort result as (D, B, E, A, C, F, G, H).

This traversal is just an arbitrary traversal that we cannot put it into code. However, we know that a graph can be traversed via the BFS and DFS algorithms. If we try to think in the context of DFS, then we start from node D and we traverse B, A, C, F, G, H, and E. While we perform the DFS traversal, we cannot simply add the vertices to the result since we break the problem requirement (for every directed edge, *XY*, vertex *X* comes before *Y* in the ordering). However, we can use a `Stack` and push a vertex into this stack after traversing all its neighbors. This means that H is the first vertex that's pushed into the stack, followed by G, F, C, A, E, B, and D. Now, popping from the stack until it is empty will give us the topological sort as D, B, E, A, C, F, G, and H.

So, topological sort is just a DFS flavor based on a `Stack` that can be implemented as follows:

```java
public Stack<T> topologicalSort(T startElement) {

    Set<T> visited = new HashSet<>();
    Stack<T> stack = new Stack<>();
    topologicalSort(startElement, visited, stack);

    return stack;
}

private void topologicalSort(T currentElement,
        Set<T> visited, Stack<T> stack) {

    visited.add(currentElement);
```

```
        List<T> adjacents = adjacencyList.get(currentElement);
        if (adjacents != null) {
            for (T t : adjacents) {
                if (t != null && !visited.contains(t)) {
                    topologicalSort(t, visited, stack);
                    visited.add(t);
                }
            }
        }

        stack.push(currentElement);
    }
```

The complete application is called *GraphTopologicalSort*.

Coding challenge 10 – Common ancestor

Amazon, Google, Microsoft, Flipkart

Problem: Consider you've been given a binary tree. Write a snippet of code that finds the first common ancestor of two given nodes. You cannot store additional nodes in a data structure.

Solution: The best way to analyze this kind of problem is by taking some paper and a pen and drawing a binary tree with some samples. Notice that the problem doesn't say that this is a BST. Practically, it can be any valid binary tree.

In the following diagram, we have three possible scenarios:

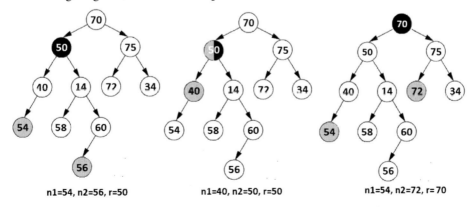

Figure 13.28 – Finding the first common ancestor

Here, we can see that the given nodes can be in different sub-trees (left- and right-hand trees) or in the same sub-tree (middle tree). So, we can traverse the tree starting from the root using a method of the `commonAncestor(Node root, Node n1, Node n2)` type and return it as follows (*n1* and *n2* are the two given nodes):

- Returns *n1* if the root's sub-tree includes *n1* (and doesn't include *n2*)
- Returns *n2* if the root's sub-tree includes *n2* (and doesn't include *n1*)
- Returns `null` if neither *n1* nor *n2* are in the root's sub-tree
- Else, it returns the common ancestor of *n1* and *n2*.

When `commonAncestor(n.left, n1, n2)` and `commonAncestor(n.right, n1, n2)` return non-null values, this means that *n1* and *n2* are in different sub-trees and *n* is the common ancestor. Let's see this in terms of code:

```
public T commonAncestor(T e1, T e2) {

  Node n1 = findNode(e1, root);
  Node n2 = findNode(e2, root);

  if (n1 == null || n2 == null) {
    throw new IllegalArgumentException("Both nodes
        must be present in the tree");
  }

  return commonAncestor(root, n1, n2).element;
}

private Node commonAncestor(Node root, Node n1, Node n2) {

  if (root == null) {
    return null;
  }

  if (root == n1 && root == n2) {
    return root;
  }
```

```
    Node left = commonAncestor(root.left, n1, n2);
    if (left != null && left != n1 && left != n2) {
      return left;
    }

    Node right = commonAncestor(root.right, n1, n2);
    if (right != null && right != n1 && right != n2) {
      return right;
    }

    // n1 and n2 are not in the same sub-tree
    if (left != null && right != null) {
      return root;
    } else if (root == n1 || root == n2) {
      return root;
    } else {
      return left == null ? right : left;
    }
  }
```

The complete application is called *BinaryTreeCommonAncestor*.

Coding challenge 11 – Chess knight

Amazon, Microsoft, Flipkart

Problem: Consider you've been given a chess board and a knight. Initially, the knight is placed in a cell (start cell). Write a snippet of code that computes the minimum number of moves needed to move the knight from the start cell to a given target cell.

Solution: Let's consider an example. The chess board is 8x8 in size and the knight starts from cell (1, 8). The target cell is (8, 1). As the following image reveals, the knight needs to make a minimum of 6 moves to go from cell (1, 8) to cell (8, 1):

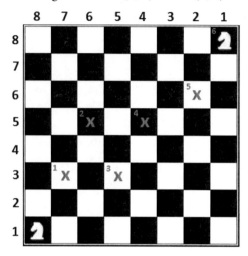

Figure 13.29 – Moving the knight from cell (1, 8) to cell (8, 1)

As this image reveals, a knight can move from an (r, c) cell to eight other valid cells, as follows: ($r+2$, $c+1$), ($r+1$, $c+2$), ($r-1$, $c+2$), ($r-2$, $c+1$), ($r-2$, $c-1$), ($r-1$, $c-2$), ($r+1$, $c-2$), and ($r+2$, $c-1$). So, there are eight possible movements. If we think of these possible movements as directions (edges) and the cells as vertices, then we can visualize this problem in the context of a graph. The edges are the possible moves, while the vertices are the possible cells for the knight. Each move holds the distance from the current cell to the start cell. For each move, the distance is increased by 1. So, in the context of a graph, the problem reduces to finding the shortest path in a graph. Hence, we can use BFS to solve this problem.

The steps for this algorithm are as follows:

1. Create an empty queue.

2. Enqueue the starting cell so that it has a distance of 0 from itself.

3. As long as the queue is not empty, do the following:

    a. Pop the next unvisited cell from the queue.

    b. If the popped cell is the target cell, then return its distance.

    c. If the popped cell is not the target cell, then mark this cell as visited and enqueue each of the eight possible movements into the queue by increasing the distance by 1.

Since we rely on the BFS algorithm, we know that all the cells whose shortest path is 1 are visited first. Next, the visited cells are the adjacent cells whose shortest paths are 1+1=2 and so on; hence any cell whose shortest path is equal to the *shortest path of its parent + 1*. This means that when we traverse the target cell for the first time, it gives us the final result. This is the shortest path. Let's see the code:

```java
private int countknightMoves(Node startCell,
        Node targetCell, int n) {

  // store the visited cells
  Set<Node> visited = new HashSet<>();

  // create a queue and enqueue the start cell
  Queue<Node> queue = new ArrayDeque<>();
  queue.add(startCell);

  while (!queue.isEmpty()) {

    Node cell = queue.poll();

    int r = cell.r;
    int c = cell.c;
    int distance = cell.distance;

    // if destination is reached, return the distance
    if (r == targetCell.r && c == targetCell.c) {
      return distance;
    }

    // the cell was not visited
    if (!visited.contains(cell)) {

      // mark current cell as visited
      visited.add(cell);

      // enqueue each valid movement into the queue
      for (int i = 0; i < 8; ++i) {
```

```
            // get the new valid position of knight from current
            // position on chessboard and enqueue it in the queue
            // with +1 distance
            int rt = r + ROW[i];
            int ct = c + COL[i];

            if (valid(rt, ct, n)) {
                queue.add(new Node(rt, ct, distance + 1));
            }
          }
        }
      }

      // if path is not possible
      return Integer.MAX_VALUE;
    }

    // Check if (r, c) is valid
    private static boolean valid(int r, int c, int n) {
      if (r < 0 || c < 0 || r >= n || c >= n) {
        return false;
      }

      return true;
    }
```

The application is called *ChessKnight*.

Coding challenge 12 – Printing binary tree corners

Amazon, Google

Problem: Consider you've been given a binary tree. Write a snippet of code that prints the corners of this tree at each level.

Solution: Let's consider the following tree:

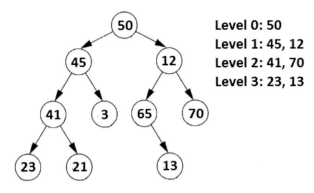

Figure 13.30 – Printing binary tree corners

So, the main idea is to print the leftmost and rightmost nodes at each level. This means that a Level-Order traversal (BFS) can be useful since we can traverse each level. All we have to do is identify the first and the last node on each level. To do this, we need to adjust the classical Level-Order traversal by adding a condition that's meant to determine whether the current node represents a corner. The code speaks for itself:

```
public void printCorners() {

  if (root == null) {
    return;
  }

  Queue<Node> queue = new ArrayDeque<>();
  queue.add(root);

  int level = 0;
  while (!queue.isEmpty()) {

    // get the size of the current level
    int size = queue.size();
    int position = size;

    System.out.print("Level: " + level + ": ");
    level++;

    // process all nodes present in current level
    while (position > 0) {
```

```
            Node node = queue.poll();
            position--;

            // if corner node found, print it
            if (position == (size - 1) || position == 0) {
                System.out.print(node.element + " ");
            }

            // enqueue left and right child of current node
            if (node.left != null) {
                queue.add(node.left);
            }

            if (node.right != null) {
                queue.add(node.right);
            }
        }

        // level done
        System.out.println();
    }
}
```

The application is called *BinaryTreePrintCorners*.

Coding challenge 13 – Max path sum

Amazon, Google, Adobe, Microsoft, Flipkart

Problem: Consider you've been given a non-empty binary tree. Write a snippet of code that computes the maximum path sum. A path is considered any sequence of nodes starting from any node and ending in any node in the tree, along with the parent-child connections. The path must contain at least one node and may or may not go through the root of the tree.

Solution: The following diagram shows three examples of a max path sum:

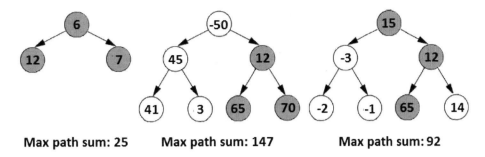

Figure 13.31 – Three examples of a max path sum

Finding a solution to this problem requires us to identify the number of ways in which the current node can be a part of the maximum path. By inspecting the preceding examples, we can isolate four cases, as shown in the following diagram (take your time and look at more examples until you reach the same conclusion):

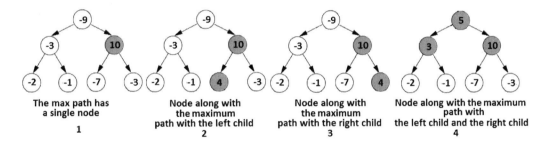

Figure 13.32 – Number of ways the current node can be a part of the maximum path

So, a node that is part of the max path is put into one of the following four cases:

1. The node is the only node in the max path
2. The node is part of the max path next to its left child
3. The node is part of the max path next to its right child
4. The node is part of the max path next to its left and right children

These four steps lead us to a clear conclusion: we must iterate over all the nodes of the tree. A good choice is the DFS algorithm, but, more precisely, the Post-Order tree traversal, which imposes the traversal order as **left sub-tree | right sub-tree | root**. While we traverse the tree, we pass the maximum of the rest of the tree to the parent. The following diagram reveals this algorithm:

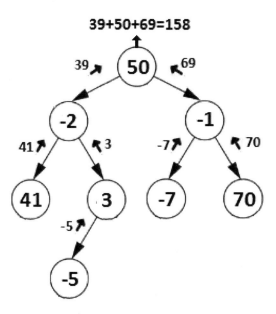

Figure 13.33 – Post-order traversal and passing the maximum in the tree to the parent

So, if we apply this algorithm step by step to the preceding diagram, we get the following (remember that this is a Post-Order traversal):

- 41 does not have children, so 41 is added to max(0, 0), 41+max(0, 0)=41.
- 3 only has the left child, -5, so 3 is added to max(-5, 0), 3+max(-5, 0)=3.
- -2 is added to the max(41, 3) sub-trees, so -2+max(41, 3)=39.
- -7 does not have children, so -7 is added to max(0, 0), -7+max(0, 0)=-7.
- 70 does not have children, so 70 is added to max(0, 0), 70+max(0, 0)=70.
- -1 is added to the max(-7, 70) sub-trees, so -1+70=69.
- 50 is added to the maximum of the left (39) and the right (69) sub-trees, so 39+69+50=158 (this is the max path sum).

The following code reveals the implementation of this algorithm:

```
public int maxPathSum() {
  maxPathSum(root);

  return max;
}

private int maxPathSum(Node root) {

  if (root == null) {
    return 0;
  }

  // maximum of the left child and 0
  int left = Math.max(0, maxPathSum(root.left));

  // maximum of the right child and 0
  int right = Math.max(0, maxPathSum(root.right));

  // maximum at the current node (all four cases 1,2,3 and 4)
  max = Math.max(max, left + right + root.element);

  //return the maximum from left, right along with current
  return Math.max(left, right) + root.element;
}
```

The application is called *BinaryTreeMaxPathSum*.

Coding challenge 14 - Diagonal traversal

Amazon, Adobe, Microsoft

Problem: Consider you've been given a non-empty binary tree. Write a snippet of code that prints all the nodes for each negative diagonal (\). A negative diagonal has a negative slope.

Solution: If you are not familiar with the notion of a binary tree negative diagonal, then ensure you clarify this aspect with the interviewer. They will probably provide you with an example, similar to the one shown in the following diagram:

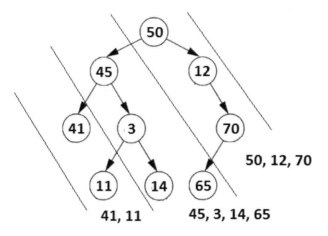

Figure 13.34 – Negative diagonals of a binary tree

In the preceding diagram, we have three diagonals. The first diagonal contains nodes 50, 12, and 70. The second diagonal contains nodes 45, 3, 14, and 65. Finally, the third diagonal contains nodes 41 and 11.

Recursion-based solution

One solution to this problem is to use recursion and *hashing* (if you are not familiar with the concept of hashing, then please read *Chapter 6, Object-Oriented Programming*, the *Hash table* problem). In Java, we can use hashing via the built-in `HashMap` implementation, so there is no need to write a hashing implementation from scratch. But how is this `HashMap` useful? What should we store in an entry (key-value pair) of this map?

We can associate each diagonal in the binary tree with a key in the map. Since each diagonal (key) contains multiple nodes, it is very convenient to represent the value as a `List`. While we traverse the binary tree, we need to add the current node to the proper `List`, so under the proper diagonal. For example, here, we can perform a Pre-Order traversal. Every time we go to the left sub-tree, we increase the diagonal by 1, and every time we go to the right sub-tree, we maintain the current diagonal. This way, we obtain something similar to the following:

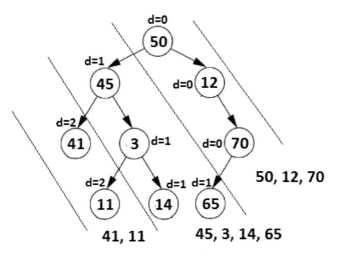

Figure 13.35 – Pre-Order traversal and increasing the diagonal by 1 for the left child

The time complexity of the following solution is O(n log n) with an auxiliary space of O(n), where *n* is the number of nodes in the tree:

```
// print the diagonal elements of given binary tree
public void printDiagonalRecursive() {

  // map of diagonals
  Map<Integer, List<T>> map = new HashMap<>();

  // Pre-Order traversal of the tree and fill up the map
  printDiagonal(root, 0, map);

  // print the current diagonal
  for (int i = 0; i < map.size(); i++) {
    System.out.println(map.get(i));
  }
}

// recursive Pre-Order traversal of the tree
// and put the diagonal elements in the map
private void printDiagonal(Node node,
        int diagonal, Map<Integer, List<T>> map) {
```

```
  if (node == null) {
    return;
  }

  // insert the current node in the diagonal
  if (!map.containsKey(diagonal)) {
    map.put(diagonal, new ArrayList<>());
  }

  map.get(diagonal).add(node.element);

  // increase the diagonal by 1 and go to the left sub-tree
  printDiagonal(node.left, diagonal + 1, map);

  // maintain the current diagonal and go
  // to the right sub-tree
  printDiagonal(node.right, diagonal, map);
}
```

Now, let's look at another solution for this problem.

Iterative-based solution

Solving this problem can be done iteratively as well. This time, we can employ Level-Order traversal and enqueue the nodes of a diagonal using a `Queue`. The main pseudocode for this solution can be written as follows:

```
(first diagonal)
Enqueue the root and all its right children

While the queue is not empty
    Dequeue (let's denote it as A)
    Print A

    (next diagonal)
    If A has a left child then enqueue it
    (let's denote it as B)
        Continue to enqueue all the right children of B
```

When this pseudocode is put into code, we get the following:

```
public void printDiagonalIterative() {

  Queue<Node> queue = new ArrayDeque<>();

  // mark the end of a diagonal via dummy null value
  Node dummy = new Node(null);

  // enqueue all the nodes of the first diagonal
  while (root != null) {
    queue.add(root);
    root = root.right;
  }

  // enqueue the dummy node at the end of each diagonal
  queue.add(dummy);

  // loop while there are more nodes than the dummy
  while (queue.size() != 1) {

    Node front = queue.poll();
    if (front != dummy) {

      // print current node
      System.out.print(front.element + " ");

      // enqueue the nodes of the next diagonal
      Node node = front.left;
      while (node != null) {
        queue.add(node);
        node = node.right;
      }
    } else {
      // at the end of the current diagonal enqueue the dummy
      queue.add(dummy);
```

```
            System.out.println();
        }
    }
}
```

The preceding code runs in O(n) time with an auxiliary space of O(n), where *n* is the number of nodes in the tree. The complete application is called *BinaryTreePrintDiagonal*.

Coding challenge 15 – Handling duplicates in BSTs

Amazon, Microsoft, Flipkart

Problem: Consider you've been given a BST that allows duplicates. Write an implementation that supports the insert and delete operations while handling duplicates.

Solution: We know that the property of a BST claims that for each node, *n*, we know that the *left descendants of n ≤ n < right descendants of n*. Commonly, problems that involve BSTs don't allow duplicates, so duplicates cannot be inserted. However, if duplicates are allowed, then our convention will be to insert the duplicate into the left sub-tree.

However, the interviewer probably expects to see an implementation that allows us to associate a count with each node, as shown in the following diagram:

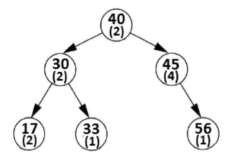

Figure 13.36 – Handling duplicates in a BST

To provide this implementation, we need to modify the structure of a classical BST so that it supports a counter:

```
private class Node {

    private T element;
    private int count;
    private Node left;
```

```
    private Node right;

    private Node(Node left, Node right, T element) {
      this.element = element;
      this.left = left;
      this.right = right;
      this.count = 1;
    }
  }
```

Every time we create a new node (a node that doesn't exist in the tree), the counter will be equal to 1.

When we insert a node, we need to distinguish between a new node and a duplicate node. If we insert a duplicate node, then all we need to do is increase the counter of that node by one, without creating a new node. The relevant part of the insert operation is listed here:

```
private Node insert(Node current, T element) {

  if (current == null) {
    return new Node(null, null, element);
  }

  // START: Handle inserting duplicates
  if (element.compareTo(current.element) == 0) {
    current.count++;

    return current;
  }
  // END: Handle inserting duplicates
  ...
}
```

Deleting a node follows similar logic. If we delete a duplicate node, then we just decrease its counter by one. If the counter is already equal to 1, then we just delete the node. The relevant code is as follows:

```
private Node delete(Node node, T element) {

  if (node == null) {
    return null;
  }

  if (element.compareTo(node.element) < 0) {
    node.left = delete(node.left, element);
  } else if (element.compareTo(node.element) > 0) {
    node.right = delete(node.right, element);
  }

  if (element.compareTo(node.element) == 0) {

    // START: Handle deleting duplicates
    if (node.count > 1) {
      node.count--;
      return node;
    }
    // END: Handle deleting duplicates
    ...
}
```

The complete application is called *BinarySearchTreeDuplicates*. Another solution to this problem consists of using a hash table to keep count of the nodes. This way, you don't modify the tree structure. Challenge yourself and complete this implementation.

Coding challenge 16 – Isomorphism of binary trees

Amazon, Google, Microsoft

Problem: Consider you've been given two binary trees. Write a snippet of code that decides whether these two binary trees are isomorphic to each other.

Solution: If you are not familiar with the term *isomorphic*, then you have to clarify this with the interviewer. This term is very well-defined in mathematics, but the interviewer probably won't give a mathematical explanation/demonstration, and, as you know, mathematicians have their own language that hardly passes for fluent and easy-to-understand English. Moreover, in mathematics, the notion of isomorphism refers to any two structures, not only binary trees. So, the interviewer will probably give you an explanation, as follows (let's denote the trees as *T1* and *T2*):

Definition 1: *T1 and T2 are isomorphic if T1 can be changed to T2 via swapping the children several times. T1 and T2 don't have to be the same physical shape at all.*

Definition 2: *T1 and T2 are isomorphic if you can translate T1 into T2 and T2 into T1 without losing information.*

Definition 3: *Think of two strings, AAB and XXY. If A is transformed into X and B is transformed into Y, then AAB becomes XXY, so these two strings are isomorphic. So, two binary trees are isomorphic if T2 is a structure-wise mirror of T1.*

No matter what definition you get from the interviewer, I am pretty sure that all of them will attempt to give you an example. The following diagram shows a bunch of examples of isomorphic binary trees:

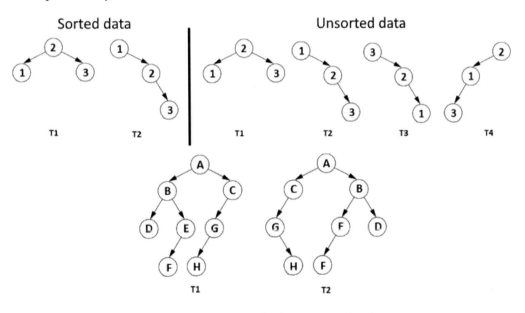

Figure 13.37 – Isomorphic binary tree examples

Based on the preceding definitions and examples, we can shape the following algorithm for determining whether two binary trees are isomorphic:

1. If *T1* and *T2* are `null`, then they are isomorphic, so return `true`.
2. If *T1* or *T2* is `null`, then they are not isomorphic, so return `false`.
3. If *T1.data* is not equal to *T2.data*, then they are not isomorphic, so return `false`.
4. Traverse the left sub-tree of *T1* and the left sub-tree of *T2*.
5. Traverse the right sub-tree of *T1* and the right sub-tree of *T2*:

    a. If the structures of *T1* and *T2* are identical, then return `true`.

    b. If the structures of *T1* and *T2* are not identical, then we check whether one tree (or sub-tree) is mirroring another tree (sub-tree),

6. Traverse the left sub-tree of *T1* and the right sub-tree of *T2*.
7. Traverse the right sub-tree of *T1* and the left sub-tree of *T2*:

    a. If the structures are mirrored, then return `true`; otherwise, return `false`.

Putting this algorithm into code results in the following:

```
private boolean isIsomorphic(Node treeOne, Node treeTwo) {

    // step 1
    if (treeOne == null && treeTwo == null) {
        return true;
    }

    // step 2
    if ((treeOne == null || treeTwo == null)) {
        return false;
    }

    // step 3
    if (!treeOne.element.equals(treeTwo.element)) {
        return false;
    }

    // steps 4, 5, 6 and 7
    return (isIsomorphic(treeOne.left, treeTwo.right)
```

```
            && isIsomorphic(treeOne.right, treeTwo.left)
        || isIsomorphic(treeOne.left, treeTwo.left)
            && isIsomorphic(treeOne.right, treeTwo.right));
}
```

The complete application is called *TwoBinaryTreesAreIsomorphic*.

Coding challenge 17 – Binary tree right view

Amazon, Google, Adobe, Microsoft, Flipkart

Problem: Consider you've been given a binary tree. Write a snippet of code that prints the right view of this tree. Printing the *right view* means printing all the nodes that you can see if you look at the binary tree from its right-hand side.

Solution: If you're unsure what the right view of a binary tree is, then clarify this with the interviewer. For example, the following diagram highlights the nodes that represent the right view of a binary tree:

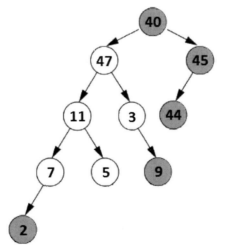

Figure 13.38 – Right view of a binary tree

So, if you are placed in the right-hand side of this tree, you'll only see nodes 40, 45, 44, 9, and 2. If we think about Level-Order traversal (BFS), we obtain the following output:

- **40**, 47, **45**, 11, 3, **44**, 7, 5, **9**, **2**

The highlighted nodes are the ones that represent the right view. However, each of these nodes represents the rightmost node at each level in the tree. This means that we can adjust the BFS algorithm and print the last node of each level.

This is an O(n) complexity time algorithm with an auxiliary O(n) space (represented by the queue), where *n* is the number of nodes in the tree:

```java
private void printRightViewIterative(Node root) {

  if (root == null) {
    return;
  }

  // enqueue root node
  Queue<Node> queue = new ArrayDeque<>();
  queue.add(root);

  Node currentNode;
  while (!queue.isEmpty()) {

    // number of nodes in the current level is the queue size
    int size = queue.size();

    int i = 0;

    // traverse each node of the current level and enqueue its
    // non-empty left and right child
    while (i < size) {

      i++;
      currentNode = queue.poll();

      // if this is last node of current level just print it
      if (i == size) {
        System.out.print(currentNode.element + " ");
      }

      if (currentNode.left != null) {
```

```
            queue.add(currentNode.left);
        }

        if (currentNode.right != null) {
            queue.add(currentNode.right);
        }
      }
    }
  }
```

Here, we can implement a recursive solution as well.

This is an O(n) complexity time algorithm with an auxiliary O(n) space (represented by a map), where *n* is the number of nodes in the tree. You can find the recursive approach in the code bundled with this book in the *BinaryTreeRightView* application. Challenge yourself and implement the binary tree's left view.

Coding challenge 18 – k^{th} largest element

Google, Flipkart

Problem: Consider you've been given a BST. Write a snippet of code that prints the kth largest element without changing the BST.

Solution: Let's consider the following BST:

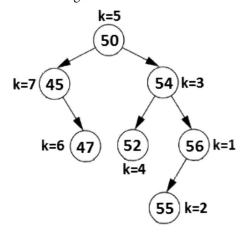

Figure 13.39 – kth largest element in a BST

For $k=1$, we can see that 56 is the first largest element. For $k=2$, we can see that 55 is the second largest element, and so on.

The brute-force solution is quite simple and will run in O(n) time, where *n* is the number of nodes in the tree. All we have to do is extract an array and place it in the In-Order traversal **(left sub-tree | right sub-tree | root)** of the tree: 45, 47, 50, 52, 54, 55, 56. Once we've done that, we can find the kth element as *array[n-k]*. For example, for *k*=3, the third element is *array[7-3]* = *array[4]*=54. You can challenge yourself if you wish and provide this implementation.

However, another approach that runs in O(k+h) complexity time, where *h* is the height of the BST, can be written based on the Reverse-In-Order traversal **(right sub-tree | left sub-tree | root)**, which gives us the elements in descending order: 56, 55, 54, 52, 50, 47, 45.

The code speaks for itself (the c variable counts the visited nodes):

```
public void kthLargest(int k) {
   kthLargest(root, k);
}

private int c;
private void kthLargest(Node root, int k) {

   if (root == null || c >= k) {
      return;
   }

   kthLargest(root.right, k);
   c++;

   // we found the kth largest value
   if (c == k) {
      System.out.println(root.element);
   }

   kthLargest(root.left, k);
}
```

The complete application is called *BinarySearchTreeKthLargestElement*.

Coding challenge 19 – Mirror binary tree

Amazon, **Google**, **Adobe**, **Microsoft**

Problem: Consider you've been given a binary tree. Write a snippet of code that constructs the mirror of this tree.

Solution: A mirrored tree looks as follows (the tree on the right is the mirrored version of the left-hand side tree):

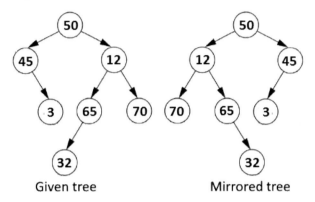

Figure 13.40 – Given tree and the mirrored tree

So, a mirrored tree is like a horizontal flip of the given tree. To create the mirror of a tree, we have to decide whether we will return the mirror tree as a new tree or mirror the given tree in place.

Mirroring the given tree in a new tree

Returning the mirror as a new tree can be done via a recursive algorithm that follows these steps:

1. For each node of the given tree:
    a. Create the corresponding node in the mirror tree
    b. Call the method (recursion) for the child nodes of the mirror tree as:
        i. left child = call the method with the right child of the given tree
        ii. right child = call the method with the left child of the given tree

Figure 13.41 - Recursive Algorithm

In terms of code, we have the following:

```
private Node mirrorTreeInTree(Node root) {

  if (root == null) {
    return null;
  }

  Node node = new Node(root.element);
  node.left = mirrorTreeInTree(root.right);
  node.right = mirrorTreeInTree(root.left);

  return node;
}
```

Now, let's try to mirror the given tree in place.

Mirroring the given tree in place

Mirroring the given tree in place can be done via recursion as well. This time, the algorithm follows these steps:

1. Mirror the left sub-tree of the given tree.
2. Mirror the right sub-tree of the given tree.
3. Swap the left and right sub-trees (swap their pointers).

In terms of code, we have the following:

```
private void mirrorTreeInPlace(Node node) {

  if (node == null) {
    return;
  }

  Node auxNode;

  mirrorTreeInPlace(node.left);
  mirrorTreeInPlace(node.right);
```

```
    auxNode = node.left;
    node.left = node.right;
    node.right = auxNode;
}
```

The complete application is called *MirrorBinaryTree*.

Coding challenge 20 – Spiral-level order traversal of a binary tree

Amazon, **Google**, **Microsoft**

Problem: Consider you've been given a binary tree. Write a snippet of code that prints the spiral-level traversal of this binary tree. More precisely, all the nodes present at level 1 should be printed from left to right, followed by all the nodes present at level 2 printed from right to left, followed by all the nodes present at level 3 printed from left to right, and so on. So, odd levels should be printed from left to right and even levels should be printed from right to left.

Solution: The spiral-level traversal can be formulated in two ways, as follows:

- Odd levels should be printed from left to right and even levels from right to left.
- Odd levels should be printed from right to left and even levels from left to right.

The following diagram represents these statements:

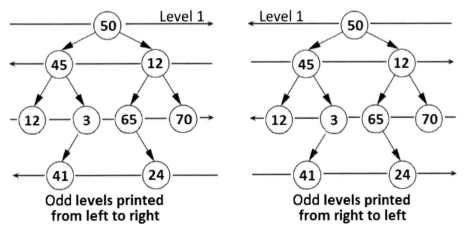

Figure 13.42 – Spiral order traversal

So, on the left-hand side, we obtain 50, 12, 45, 12, 3, 65, 70, 24, and 41. On the other hand, on the right-hand side, we obtain 50, 45, 12, 70, 65, 3, 12, 41, and 24.

Recursive approach

Let's try to implement the spiral order traversal from the left-hand side of the preceding diagram. Notice that the odd levels should be printed from left to right, while the even levels should be printed in reverse order. Basically, we need to adjust the well-known Level-Order traversal by flipping the direction of the even levels. This means that we can use a boolean variable to alternate the printing order. So, if the boolean variable is true (or 1), then we print the current level from left to right; otherwise, we print it from right to left. At each iteration (level), we flip the boolean value.

Applying this via recursion can be done as follows:

```
public void spiralOrderTraversalRecursive() {
   if (root == null) {
      return;
   }

   int level = 1;
   boolean flip = false;

   // as long as printLevel() returns true there
   // are more levels to print
   while (printLevel(root, level++, flip = !flip)) {
      // there is nothing to do
   };
}

// print all nodes of a given level
private boolean printLevel(Node root,
         int level, boolean flip) {

   if (root == null) {
      return false;
   }

   if (level == 1) {
```

```
      System.out.print(root.element + " ");
      return true;
    }

    if (flip) {
      // process left child before right child
      boolean left = printLevel(root.left, level - 1, flip);
      boolean right = printLevel(root.right, level - 1, flip);

      return left || right;
    } else {
      // process right child before left child
      boolean right = printLevel(root.right, level - 1, flip);
      boolean left = printLevel(root.left, level - 1, flip);

      return right || left;
    }
  }
}
```

This code runs in O(n²) time, which is quite inefficient. Can we do this more efficiently? Yes – we can do it in O(n) time with extra space, O(n), via an iterative approach.

Iterative approach

Let's try to implement the spiral order traversal from the right-hand side of the given diagram. We'll do this via an iterative approach this time. Mainly, we can use two stacks (`Stack`) or a double ended queue (`Deque`). Let's learn how we can do this via two stacks.

The main idea of using two stacks is quite straightforward: we use one stack to print the left-to-right nodes and the other stack to print the right-to-left nodes. At each iteration (or level), we have the corresponding nodes in one of the stacks. While we print the nodes from a stack, we push the nodes of the next level into the other stack.

The following code puts these statements into code form:

```
private void printSpiralTwoStacks(Node node) {

  if (node == null) {
    return;
  }
```

```java
    // create two stacks to store alternate levels
    Stack<Node> rl = new Stack<>(); // right to left
    Stack<Node> lr = new Stack<>(); // left to right

    // Push first level to first stack 'rl'
    rl.push(node);

    // print while any of the stacks has nodes
    while (!rl.empty() || !lr.empty()) {

      // print nodes of the current level from 'rl'
      // and push nodes of next level to 'lr'
      while (!rl.empty()) {

        Node temp = rl.peek();
        rl.pop();

        System.out.print(temp.element + " ");

        if (temp.right != null) {
          lr.push(temp.right);
        }

        if (temp.left != null) {
          lr.push(temp.left);
        }
      }

      // print nodes of the current level from 'lr'
      // and push nodes of next level to 'rl'
      while (!lr.empty()) {
        Node temp = lr.peek();
        lr.pop();

        System.out.print(temp.element + " ");
```

```
        if (temp.left != null) {
           rl.push(temp.left);
        }

        if (temp.right != null) {
           rl.push(temp.right);
        }
      }
   }
}
```

The complete application is called *BinaryTreeSpiralTraversal*. In this application, you can also find the implementation based on a `Deque`.

Coding challenge 21 – Nodes at a distance k from leafs

Amazon, Google, Microsoft, Flipkart

Problem: Consider you've been given a binary tree of integers and an integer, *k*. Write a snippet of code that prints all the nodes that are at a distance *k* from a leaf node.

Solution: We can intuit that a distance of *k* from a leaf means *k* levels above the leaf. But to clarify any doubts, let's follow the classical approach and try to visualize an example. The following diagram represents a binary tree; the highlighted nodes (40, 47, and 11) represent the nodes that are at a distance of *k*=2 from a leaf node:

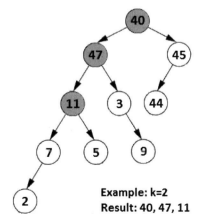

Figure 13.43 – Nodes at a distance of k=2 from a leaf node

From the preceding diagram, we can make the following observations:

- Node 40 is at a distance of 2 from leaf 44.
- Node 47 is at a distance of 2 from leaf 9 and leaf 5.
- Node 11 is at a distance of 2 from leaf 2.

If we look at each level, then we can see the following:

- The nodes at distance 1 from a leaf node are 3, 11, 7, and 45.
- The nodes at distance 2 from a leaf node are 11, 47, and 40.
- The nodes at distance 3 from a leaf node are 40 and 47.
- The node at distance 4 from a leaf node is 40.

So, the root node is the greatest distance away from a leaf, and k doesn't make sense to be greater than the number of levels; that is, 1. If we start from the root and we go down the tree until we find a leaf, then the resulting path should contain a node that it is at a distance of k from that leaf.

For example, a possible path is 40 (the root), 47, 11, 7, and 2 (the leaf). If $k=2$, then node 11 is at a distance of 2 from the leaf. Another possible path is 40 (the root), 47, 11, and 5 (the leaf). If $k=2$, then node 47 is at a distance of 2 from the leaf. Yet another path is 40 (the root), 47, 3, and 9 (the leaf). If $k=2$, then node 47 is at a distance of 2 from the leaf. We already found this node; therefore, we now have to pay attention and remove the duplicates.

The paths that have been listed so far indicate that there's a Pre-Order traversal of the tree (**root | left sub-tree | right sub-tree**). During the traversal, we must keep track of the current path. In other words, the constructed path is made up of the ancestors of the current node in the Pre-Order traversal. When we find a leaf node, we have to print the ancestor that is at a distance k from this leaf.

To eliminate duplicates, we can use a Set (let's denote it as `nodesAtDist`), as shown in the following code:

```
private void leafDistance(Node node,
    List<Node> pathToLeaf, Set<Node> nodesAtDist, int dist) {

  if (node == null) {
    return;
  }
```

```
        // for each leaf node, store the node at distance 'dist'
        if (isLeaf(node) && pathToLeaf.size() >= dist) {
            nodesAtDist.add(pathToLeaf.get(pathToLeaf.size() - dist));

            return;
        }

        // add the current node into the current path
        pathToLeaf.add(node);

        // go to left and right subtree via recursion
        leafDistance(node.left, pathToLeaf, nodesAtDist, dist);
        leafDistance(node.right, pathToLeaf, nodesAtDist, dist);

        // remove the current node from the current path
        pathToLeaf.remove(node);
    }

    private boolean isLeaf(Node node) {
        return (node.left == null && node.right == null);
    }
```

The preceding code runs in O(n) time complexity and auxiliary space O(n), where *n* is the number of nodes in the tree. The complete application is called *BinaryTreeDistanceFromLeaf*.

Coding challenge 22 – Pair for a given sum

Amazon, Google, Adobe, Microsoft, Flipkart

Problem: Consider you've been given a BST and a sum. Write a snippet of code that returns `true` if there is a pair of nodes that have this sum.

Solution: Let's consider the BST shown in the following diagram and *sum=74*:

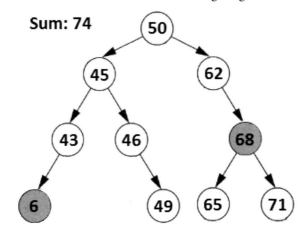

Figure 13.44 – The pair for sum=74 contains nodes 6 and 68

So, for *sum=74*, we can find the pair (6, 68). If *sum=89*, then the pair is (43, 46). If *sum=99*, then the pair is (50, 49). The nodes that form the pair can be from the same sub-tree or different sub-trees and can include the root and leaf nodes as well.

One solution to this problem relies on *hashing* and recursion. Mainly, we traverse the tree using In-Order traversal (**left sub-tree | root | right sub-tree**) and we insert each node's element into a set (for example, into a HashSet). Moreover, before inserting the current node into the set, we check whether (*the given sum - the current node's element*) is present in the set. If it is, then we have found a pair, so we stop the process and return true. Otherwise, we insert the current node into the set and continue this process until we find a pair, or the traversal is done.

The code for this is listed here:

```
public boolean findPairSum(int sum) {

    return findPairSum(root, sum, new HashSet());
}

private static boolean findPairSum(Node node,
        int sum, Set<Integer> set) {

    // base case
    if (node == null) {
        return false;
```

```
      }

      // find the pair in the left subtree
      if (findPairSum(node.left, sum, set)) {
        return true;
      }

      // if pair is formed with current node then print the pair
      if (set.contains(sum - node.element)) {
        System.out.print("Pair (" + (sum - node.element) + ", "
          + node.element + ") = " + sum);
        return true;
      } else {
        set.add(node.element);
      }

      // find the pair in the right subtree
      return findPairSum(node.right, sum, set);
    }
```

The runtime of this code is O(n) with an auxiliary space of O(n). The complete application is called *BinarySearchTreeSum*.

Another solution that you may like to consider and challenge yourself with starts from the fact that a BST, when traversed using In-Order traversal, outputs the nodes in sorted order. This means that if we scan the BST and store the outputs in an array, then the problem is exactly the same as finding the pair for the given sum in an array. But this solution requires two traversals of all the nodes and an auxiliary space of O(n).

Another approach starts from the BST property: *left descendants of n ≤ n < right descendants of n*. In other words, the minimum node in the tree is the leftmost node (in our case, 6) and the maximum node in the tree is the rightmost node (in our case, 71). Now, consider two traversals of the tree:

- A Forward In-Order traversal (the leftmost node is the first visited node)
- A Reverse In-Order traversal (the rightmost node is the first visited node)

Now, let's evaluate the (*minimum* + *maximum*) expression:

- If (*minimum* + *maximum*) < *sum*, then go to the next *minimum* (next node returned by the Forward In-Order traversal).
- If (*minimum* + *maximum*) > *sum*, then go to the next *maximum* (next node returned by the Reverse In-Order traversal).
- If (*minimum* + *maximum*) = *sum*, then return `true`.

The main problem here is that we need to manage these two traversals. An approach can rely on two stacks. In one stack, we store the outputs of the Forward In-Order traversal, while in another stack, we store the outputs of the Reverse In-Order traversal. When we reach the *minimum* (leftmost) and the *maximum* (rightmost) nodes, we must pop the tops of the stacks and perform an equality check against the given *sum*.

This equality check passes through one of the preceding checks (given by the preceding three bullets) and is interpreted as follows:

- If (*minimum* + *maximum*) < *sum*, then we go to the right sub-tree of the popped node via the Forward In-Order traversal. This is how we can find the next greatest element.
- If (*minimum* + *maximum*) > *sum*, then we go to the left sub-tree of the popped node via the Reverse In-Order traversal. This is how we can find the next smallest element.
- If (*minimum* + *maximum*) = *sum*, then we have found a pair that validates the given *sum*.

The algorithm is applied as long as the Forward In-Order and Reverse In-Order traversals do not meet. Let's see the code for this:

```java
public boolean findPairSumTwoStacks(int sum) {

    return findPairSumTwoStacks(root, sum);
}

private static boolean findPairSumTwoStacks(
            Node node, int sum) {

    Stack<Node> fio = new Stack<>(); // fio - Forward In-Order
    Stack<Node> rio = new Stack<>(); // rio - Reverse In-Order
```

```java
    Node minNode = node;
    Node maxNode = node;

    while (!fio.isEmpty() || !rio.isEmpty()
            || minNode != null || maxNode != null) {
      if (minNode != null || maxNode != null) {
        if (minNode != null) {
          fio.push(minNode);
          minNode = minNode.left;
        }

        if (maxNode != null) {
          rio.push(maxNode);
          maxNode = maxNode.right;
        }
      } else {
        int elem1 = fio.peek().element;
        int elem2 = rio.peek().element;

        if (fio.peek() == rio.peek()) {
          break;
        }

        if ((elem1 + elem2) == sum) {
          System.out.print("\nPair (" + elem1 + ", "
              + elem2 + ") = " + sum);
          return true;
        }

        if ((elem1 + elem2) < sum) {
          minNode = fio.pop();
          minNode = minNode.right;
        } else {
          maxNode = rio.pop();
          maxNode = maxNode.left;
        }
      }
```

```
        }
    }

    return false;
}
```

The runtime of this code is O(n) with an auxiliary space of O(n). The complete application is called *BinarySearchTreeSum*.

Coding challenge 23 – Vertical sums in a binary tree

Amazon, Google, Flipkart

Problem: Consider you've been given a binary tree. Write a snippet of code that computes the vertical sums for this binary tree.

Solution: In order to have a clear picture of this problem, it is very important that you sketch a meaningful diagram. It will be quite useful to use a notebook with squares (a math notebook). This is useful because you must draw the edges between the nodes at 45 degrees; otherwise, it is possible that you won't see the vertical axes of the nodes correctly. Commonly, when we draw a binary tree, we don't care about the angle between the nodes, but in this case, this is a vital aspect for understanding the problem and finding a solution to it.

The following diagram is a sketch of the binary tree. It shows some helpful landmarks that will lead us to the solution:

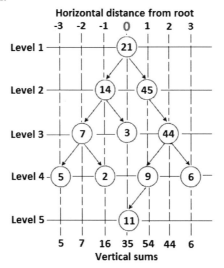

Figure 13.45 – Vertical sums in a binary tree

If we scan the tree from the left-hand side to the right-hand side, we can identify seven vertical axes whose sums are 5, 7, 16, 35, 54, 44, and 6. At the top of the diagram, we've added the horizontal distance of each node from the root node. If we consider the root node as having the distance 0, then we can easily uniquely identify each vertical axis from the left or the right of the root by decreasing, respectively increasing 1 as, -3, -2, -1, 0 (the root), 1, 2, 3.

Each axis is uniquely identified by its distance from the root, and each axis holds the nodes that we have to sum up. If we think about the unique distance of an axis as a key and the sum of the nodes on this axis as a value, then we can intuit that this problem can be solved via *hashing* (if you are not familiar with the concept of hashing, then please take a look at *Chapter 6, Object-Oriented Programming*, the *Hash table* problem). In Java, we can use hashing via the built-in `HashMap` implementation, so there is no need to write a hashing implementation from scratch.

But how can we fill up this map? It is quite obvious that we have to traverse the tree while we are filling up the map. We can start from the root and add the key to the map as 0 (0 corresponds to the axis that contains the root) and the value as the root (21). Next, we can use recursion to go to the left-axis of the root by decreasing the distance from the root by 1. We can also use recursion to go through the right-axis of the root by increasing the distance from the root by 1. At every node, we update the value in the map that corresponds to the key that identifies the current axis. So, if we recursively follow path **root|left sub-tree|right sub-tree**, then we use the Pre-Order traversal of a binary tree.

In the end, our map should contain the following key-value pairs: (-3, 5), (-2, 7), (-1, 16), (0, 35), (1, 54), (2, 44), and (3, 6).

Putting this algorithm into code results in the following (`map` contains the vertical sums):

```
private void verticalSum(Node root,
        Map<Integer, Integer> map, int dist) {

  if (root == null) {
    return;
  }

  if (!map.containsKey(dist)) {
    map.put(dist, 0);
  }

  map.put(dist, map.get(dist) + root.element);
```

```
    // or in functional-style
    /*
    BiFunction <Integer, Integer, Integer> distFunction
       = (distOld, distNew) -> distOld + distNew;
    map.merge(dist, root.element, distFunction);
    */

    // decrease horizontal distance by 1 and go to left
    verticalSum(root.left, map, dist - 1);

    // increase horizontal distance by 1 and go to right
    verticalSum(root.right, map, dist + 1);
}
```

The preceding code runs in O(n log n) time with an auxiliary space of O(n), where *n* is the total number of nodes of the tree. Adding to a map has an O(log n) complexity time and since we make an addition for each node of the tree, this means we get O(n log n). For an interview, the solution presented here should be enough. However, you can challenge yourself and decrease the complexity of time to O(n) by using an additional doubly linked list. Mainly, you need to store each vertical sum in a node of a linked list. First, add the vertical sum corresponding to the axis that contains the root to the linked list. Then, *node.next* and *node.prev* of the linked list should store the vertical sums of the axis from the left and the right of the root axis. Finally, rely on recursion to update the linked list while traversing the tree.

The complete application is called *BinaryTreeVerticalSum*.

Coding challenge 23 – Converting a max heap into a min heap

Amazon, Google, Adobe, Microsoft, Flipkart

Problem: Consider you've been given an array representing a Min Binary Heap. Write a snippet of code that converts the given Min Binary Heap into a Max Binary Heap in linear time and without extra space.

Solution: The solution to this problem is inspired by the *Heap Sort* algorithm (this algorithm is presented in *Chapter 14, Sorting and Searching*).

Initially, this problem may sound complicated, but after a few minutes of reflection, you may come to the conclusion that the problem can be reduced to building a Max Binary Heap from an unsorted array. So, the fact that the given array is, or isn't, a Min Binary Heap is not important. We can build the required Max Binary Heap from any array (sorted or unsorted) by following two steps:

1. Start from the rightmost, bottommost node (last internal node) of the given array.
2. *Heapify* all the nodes via the bottom-up technique.

The code speaks for itself:

```
public static void convertToMinHeap(int[] maxHeap) {

    // build heap from last node to all
    // the way up to the root node
    int p = (maxHeap.length - 2) / 2;
    while (p >= 0) {
        heapifyMin(maxHeap, p--, maxHeap.length);
    }
}

// heapify the node at index p and its two direct children
private static void heapifyMin(int[] maxHeap,
        int p, int size) {

    // get left and right child of node at index p
    int left = leftChild(p);
    int right = rightChild(p);

    int smallest = p;

    // compare maxHeap[p] with its left and
    // right child and find the smallest value
    if ((left < size) && (maxHeap[left] < maxHeap[p])) {
        smallest = left;
    }

    if ((right < size)
```

```
         && (maxHeap[right] < maxHeap[smallest])) {
      smallest = right;
    }

    // swap 'smallest' with 'p' and heapify
    if (smallest != p) {
      swap(maxHeap, p, smallest);
      heapifyMin(maxHeap, smallest, size);
    }
  }

  /* Helper methods */
  private static int leftChild(int parentIndex) {
    return (2 * parentIndex + 1);
  }

  private static int rightChild(int parentIndex) {
    return (2 * parentIndex + 2);
  }

  // utility function to swap two indices in the array
  private static void swap(int heap[], int i, int j) {
    int aux = heap[i];
    heap[i] = heap[j];
    heap[j] = aux;
  }
```

The runtime of this code is O(n) with no extra space needed. The complete application is called *MaxHeapToMinHeap*. It also contains the conversion of a Min Binary Heap into a Max Binary Heap.

Coding challenge 24 – Finding out whether a binary tree is symmetric

Amazon, **Google**, **Adobe**, **Microsoft**, **Flipkart**

Problem: Consider you've been given a binary tree. Write a snippet of code that returns `true` if this binary tree is symmetric (a mirror image of itself or not; the left sub-tree and right sub-tree are mirror images of each other).

Solution: First, let's take a look at a diagram containing symmetric and asymmetric binary trees. The binary trees labeled (a), (b), and (d) are asymmetric, while the binary trees labeled (c), (e), and (f) are symmetric. Notice that a binary tree is symmetric if both the structure and the data are symmetric:

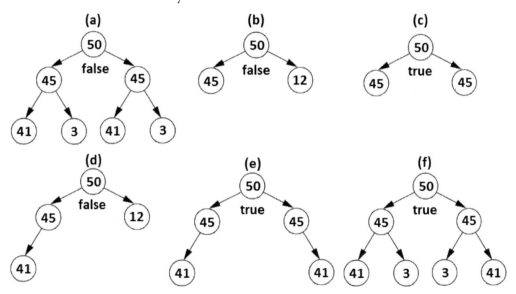

Figure 13.46 – Symmetric and asymmetric binary tree examples

We can think of this problem as mirroring *root.left* and checking whether it is identical to *root.right*. If they are identical, then the binary tree is symmetric. However, we can also express the symmetry of two binary trees via three conditions, as follows (the easiest way to understand these conditions is to take each of them and pass them to the samples shown in the preceding diagram):

1. The root node's elements are the same.
2. The left sub-tree of the left tree and the right sub-tree of the right tree must be mirror images.
3. The right sub-tree of the left tree and the left sub-tree of the right tree must be mirror images.

I think that we have enough experience to recognize that these conditions can be implemented via recursion, as follows:

```java
private boolean isSymmetricRecursive(
       Node leftNode, Node rightNode) {

  boolean result = false;

  // empty trees are symmetric
  if (leftNode == null && rightNode == null) {
    result = true;
  }

  // conditions 1, 2, and 3 from above
  if (leftNode != null && rightNode != null) {
    result = (leftNode.element.equals(rightNode.element))
        && isSymmetricRecursive(leftNode.left, rightNode.right)
        && isSymmetricRecursive(leftNode.right, rightNode.left);
  }

  return result;
}
```

The time complexity of this code is O(n) with O(h) extra space, where h is the height of the tree. How about an iterative implementation? We can provide an iterative implementation via a queue. The following code is the best explanation for this approach:

```java
public boolean isSymmetricIterative() {

  boolean result = false;
  Queue<Node> queue = new LinkedList<>();

  queue.offer(root.left);
  queue.offer(root.right);

  while (!queue.isEmpty()) {
    Node left = queue.poll();
    Node right = queue.poll();

    if (left == null && right == null) {

      result = true;
    } else if (left == null || right == null
                || left.element != right.element) {

      result = false;
      break;
    } else {
      queue.offer(left.left);
      queue.offer(right.right);

      queue.offer(left.right);
      queue.offer(right.left);
    }
  }

  return result;
}
```

The time complexity of this code is O(n) with O(h) extra space, where *h* is the height of the tree. The complete application is called *IsSymmetricBinaryTree*.

Coding challenge 25 – Connecting *n* ropes at the minimum cost

Amazon, Google, Adobe, Microsoft, Flipkart

Problem: Consider you've been given an array containing the lengths of *n* ropes, and we need to connect all these ropes to a single rope. Consider that connecting two ropes has a cost equal to the sum of their lengths. Write a snippet of code that connects all the ropes to a single rope at the minimum cost.

Solution: Let's consider that we have four ropes whose lengths are 1, 3, 4, and 6. Let's connect the shortest two ropes first. This means we need to connect ropes 1 and 3, which has a cost of 1+3=4. Continuing with the same logic, the next two ropes are 4 (the one we just obtained) and 4 in length. The cost is 4+4=8, so the total cost is 4+8=12. We have two ropes left that are 8 and 6 in length. The cost of connecting them is 8+6=14. Hence, the total and final cost is 12+14=26.

Now, let's try another strategy. Let's connect the longest two ropes first. This means we need to connect ropes 4 and 6, which has a cost of 4+6=10. Continuing with the same logic, the next two ropes are 10 (the one we just obtained) and 3 in length. The cost is 10+3=13, so the total cost is 10+13=23. We have two ropes left that are 13 and 1 in length. The cost of connecting them is 13+1=14. Therefore, the total and final cost is 23+14=37.

Since 37>26, it is obvious that the first approach is better than the second one. But what's the catch? Well, in case you haven't noticed yet, the lengths of the ropes that are connected first occur in the rest of the connections. For example, when we connect ropes 1 and 3, we write 1+3=4. So, 4 is the total cost so far. Next, we add 4+4=8, so the new total cost is the previous total cost + 8, which is 4+8, but 4 was obtained from 1+3, so 1+3 occurs again. Finally, we connect 8+6=14. The new total cost is the previous cost + 14, which is 12 + 14, but 12 was obtained from 4+8, and 4 was obtained from 1+3, so 1+3 occurs again.

Analyzing the preceding statement leads us to the conclusion that we can obtain the minimum cost of connecting all the ropes if the repeated added rope is the smallest, then the second smallest, and so on. In other words, we can think of the algorithm for this as follows:

1. Sort the ropes by their lengths in descending order.
2. Connect the first two ropes and update the partial minimum cost.
3. Replace the first two ropes with the resulting one.

4. Repeat from *step 1* until there is a single rope left (the result of connecting all the ropes).

After implementing this algorithm, we should obtain the final minimum cost. If we try to implement this algorithm via a sorting algorithm such as Quick Sort or Merge Sort, then the result will perform in $O(n^2 \log n)$ time. As you know from *Chapter 7, Big O Analysis of Algorithms*, these sorting algorithms perform in $O(n \log n)$ time, but we have to sort the array each time two ropes are connected.

Can we do this better? Yes, we can! At any moment, we only need the two ropes with the smallest lengths; we don't care about the rest of the array. In other words, we need a data structure that gives us efficient access to the minimum element. Hence, the answer is a Min Binary Heap. Adding and removing from a Min Binary Heap is an $O(\log n)$ complexity time operation. The algorithm for this can be expressed as follows:

1. Create the Min Binary Heap from the array of rope lengths ($O(\log n)$).
2. Poll the root of the Min Binary Heap, which will give us the smallest rope ($O(\log n)$).
3. Poll the root again, which will give us the second smallest rope ($O(\log n)$).
4. Connect two ropes (sum up their lengths) and put the result back into the Min Binary Heap.
5. Repeat from *step 2* until there is a single rope left (the result of connecting all the ropes).

So, the algorithm that performs in $O(n \log n)$ complexity time is as follows:

```java
public int minimumCost(int[] ropeLength) {

    if (ropeLength == null) {
        return -1;
    }

    // add the lengths of the ropes to the heap
    for (int i = 0; i < ropeLength.length; i++) {
        add(ropeLength[i]);
    }

    int totalLength = 0;
```

```
while (size() > 1) {
  int l1 = poll();
  int l2 = poll();

  totalLength += (l1 + l2);

  add(l1 + l2);
}

return totalLength;
}
```

The complete application is called *HeapConnectRopes*.

Advanced topics

Right from the start, you should know that the following topics are rarely encountered in technical interviews. First, let me enumerate these topics as a non-exhaustive list:

- AVL trees (a brief description and an implementation are available in the code bundled with this book)
- Red-Black trees (a brief description and an implementation are available in the code bundled with this book)
- Dijkstra's algorithm
- Rabin-Karp substring search
- The Bellman-Ford algorithm
- The Floyd-Warshall algorithm
- Interval trees
- Minimum spanning trees
- B-trees
- Bipartite graph
- Graph coloring
- P, NP, and NP-complete

- Combinatory and probability
- Regular expressions
- A*

If you have mastered all the problems covered in this book, then I strongly recommend that you continue learning by looking into the aforementioned topics. If you don't do this, then please consider all the problems as having a higher priority than these topics.

Most of the topics outlined here may or may not be asked in interviews. They represent complex algorithms that you either know or you don't – the interviewer cannot get a true insight into your logic and thinking capabilities just because you are able to reproduce a famous algorithm. The interviewer wants to see that you are capable of exploiting your knowledge. These algorithms don't reveal your capability to solve a problem that you haven't seen before. It is obvious that you cannot intuit such complex algorithms, so your footprint is almost insignificant. Don't worry if you don't know these algorithms! They don't make you look smarter or stupider! Furthermore, since they are complex, they require a lot of time to implement, and, in an interview, time is limited.

However, it doesn't hurt to study more! That's a rule, so if you have the time, then take a look at these advanced topics as well.

Summary

This was one of the tough chapters of this book and a *must-read* for any technical interview. Trees and graphs are such wide, wonderful, and challenging topics that entire books have been dedicated to them. However, when you have to prepare for an interview, you don't have the time to study tons of books and deep dive into every topic. This is exactly where the magic of this chapter comes into the picture: this chapter (just like the entire book) is totally focused on the fact that you must achieve your goal: ace a technical interview.

In other words, this chapter contained the most popular tree and graph problems that may be encountered in technical interviews, along with meaningful figures, comprehensive explanations, and clear and clean code.

In the next chapter, we'll tackle problems related to sorting and searching.

14
Sorting and Searching

This chapter covers the most popular sorting and searching algorithms that are encountered in technical interviews. We will cover sorting algorithms such as Merge Sort, Quick Sort, Radix Sort, Heap Sort, and Bucket Sort, and searching algorithms such as Binary Search.

By the end of this chapter, you should be able to tackle a wide range of problems that involve sorting and searching algorithms. We'll cover the following topics:

- Sorting algorithms
- Searching algorithms
- Coding challenges

Let's get started!

Technical requirements

You can find all the code files for this chapter on GitHub at `https://github.com/PacktPublishing/The-Complete-Coding-Interview-Guide-in-Java/tree/master/Chapter14`.

Sorting algorithms

Considering the sorting algorithms from the perspective of a person preparing for an interview reveals two main categories: a category containing a lot of relatively simple sorting algorithms that don't occur in interviews, such as Bubble Sort, Insertion Sort, Counting Sort, and so on, and a category containing Heap Sort, Merge Sort, Quick Sort, Bucket Sort, and Radix Sort. These represent the top five sorting algorithms that occur in technical interviews.

If you are not familiar with the simple sorting algorithms, then I strongly recommend that you buy my book, *Java Coding Problems* (`www.packtpub.com/programming/java-coding-problems`), published by Packt. In *Chapter 5, Arrays, Collections, and Data Structures*, of *Java Coding Problems*, you can find detailed coverage of Bubble Sort, Insertion Sort, Counting Sort, and so on.

Furthermore, the application called *SortArraysIn14Ways* contains the implementations of 14 different sorting algorithms that you should know. The complete list is as follows:

- Bubble Sort
- Bubble Sort with a `Comparator`
- Bubble Sort optimized
- Bubble Sort optimized with a `Comparator`
- Pancake Sort
- Exchange Sort
- Selection Sort
- Shell Sort
- Insertion Sort
- Insertion Sort with a `Comparator`
- Counting Sort
- Merge Sort
- Heap Sort
- Heap Sort with a `Comparator`
- Bucket Sort
- Cocktail Sort

- Cycle Sort
- Quick Sort
- Quick Sort with a `Comparator`
- Radix Sort

In the following sections, we will have a brief overview of the main algorithms that are encountered in interviews: Heap Sort, Merge Sort, Quick Sort, Bucket Sort, and Radix Sort. If you are already familiar with these algorithms, then consider jumping directly to the *Searching algorithms* section, or even to the *Coding challenges* section.

Heap Sort

If you are not familiar with the heap concept, then consider reading the *Binary Heaps* section of *Chapter 13, Trees and Graphs*.

Heap Sort is an algorithm that relies on a binary heap (a complete binary tree). The time complexity cases are as follows: best case O(n log n), average case O(n log n), worst case O(n log n). The space complexity case is O(1).

Sorting elements in ascending order can be accomplished via a Max Heap (the parent node is always greater than or equal to the child nodes), and in descending order via a Min Heap (the parent node is always smaller than or equal to the child nodes).

The Heap Sort algorithm has several main steps, as follows:

1. Transform the given array into a Max Binary Heap.
2. Next, the root is swapped with the last element from the heap and the heap's size is reduced by 1 (this is like deleting the root element of the heap). So, the greater element (the heap root) goes to the last position. In other words, the elements that are at the root of the heap come out one by one in sorted order.
3. The final step consists of *heapifying* the remaining heap (apply the recursive process that reconstructs the max heap in a top-down manner).
4. Repeat from *step 2* while the heap size is greater than 1.

The following diagram represents a test case of applying the Heap Sort algorithm:

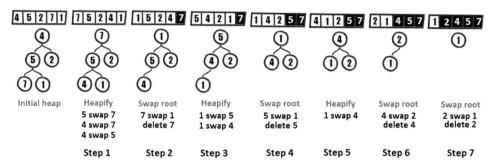

Figure 14.1 – Heap Sort

For example, let's assume the array from the preceding diagram; that is, 4, 5, 2, 7, 1:

1. So, at the first step, we build the Max Heap: 7, 5, 2, 4, 1 (we swapped 5 with 7, 4 with 7, and 4 with 5).

2. Next, swap the root (7) with the last element (1) and delete 7. Result: 1, 5, 2, 4, **7**.

3. Furthermore, we construct the Max Heap again: 5, 4, 2, 1 (we swapped 1 with 5 and 1 with 4).

4. We swap the root (5) with the last element (1) and delete 5. Result: 1, 4, 2, **5, 7**.

5. Next, we construct the Max Heap again: 4, 1, 2 (we swapped 1 with 4).

6. We swap the root (4) with the last element (2) and delete 4. Result: 2, 1, **4, 5, 7**.

7. This is a Max Heap already, so we simply swap the root (2) with the last element (1) and remove 2: 1, **2, 4, 5, 7**.

8. Done! There is a single element left in the heap (1). So, the final result is **1, 2, 4, 5, 7**.

In terms of code, the preceding example can be generalized as follows:

```
public static void sort(int[] arr) {

  int n = arr.length;
  buildHeap(arr, n);
  while (n > 1) {
    swap(arr, 0, n - 1);
    n--;
    heapify(arr, n, 0);
```

```java
    }
  }

  private static void buildHeap(int[] arr, int n) {
    for (int i = arr.length / 2; i >= 0; i--) {
      heapify(arr, n, i);
    }
  }

  private static void heapify(int[] arr, int n, int i) {

    int left = i * 2 + 1;
    int right = i * 2 + 2;
    int greater;

    if (left < n && arr[left] > arr[i]) {
      greater = left;
    } else {
      greater = i;
    }

    if (right < n && arr[right] > arr[greater]) {
      greater = right;
    }

    if (greater != i) {
      swap(arr, i, greater);
      heapify(arr, n, greater);
    }
  }

  private static void swap(int[] arr, int x, int y) {
    int temp = arr[x];
    arr[x] = arr[y];
    arr[y] = temp;
  }
```

Heap Sort is not a stable algorithm. A stable algorithm guarantees the order of duplicate elements. The complete application is called *HeapSort*. This application contains an implementation based on `Comparator` as well – this is useful for sorting objects.

Merge Sort

Now, let's discuss the Merge Sort algorithm. The time complexity cases are as follows: best case O(n log n), average case O(n log n), worst case O(n log n). The space complexity may vary, depending on the chosen data structures (it can be O(n)).

The Merge Sort algorithm is a recursive algorithm based on the famous *divide and conquer* strategy. Considering that you've been given an unsorted array, applying the Merge Sort algorithm requires you to continually split the array in half until we obtain empty sub-arrays or sub-arrays that contains a single element (this is *divide and conquer*). If a sub-array is empty or contains one element, it is sorted by its definition – this is the recursion *base case*.

If we haven't reached the *base case* yet, we divide both these sub-arrays again and attempt to sort them. So, if the array contains more than one element, we split it and we recursively invoke the sort operation on both sub-arrays. The following diagram shows the splitting process for the 52, 28, 91, 19, 76, 33, 43, 57, 20 array:

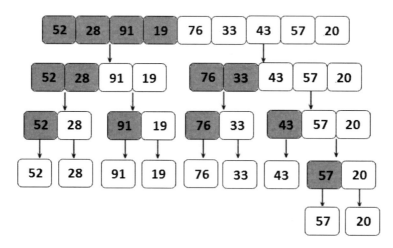

Figure 14.2 – Splitting the given array in the Merge Sort algorithm

Once the splitting is done, we call the fundamental operation of this algorithm: the *merge* operation (also known as the *combine* operation). Merging is the operation of taking two smaller sorted sub-arrays and combining them into a single, sorted, new sub-array. This is done until the entire given array is sorted. The following diagram shows the merging operation for our array:

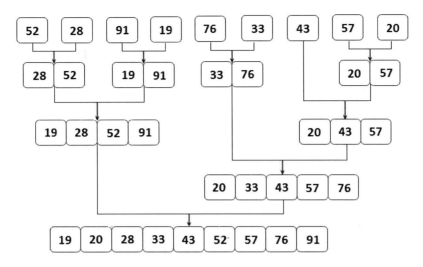

Figure 14.3 – Merging operation for Merge Sort

The following code implements the Merge Sort algorithm. The flow begins from the `sort()` method. Here, we begin by asking the *base case* question. If the size of the array is greater than 1, then we call the `leftHalf()` and `rightHalf()` methods, which will split the given array into two sub-arrays. The rest of the code from `sort()` is responsible for calling the `merge()` method, which sorts two unsorted sub-arrays:

```
public static void sort(int[] arr) {

   if (arr.length > 1) {
     int[] left = leftHalf(arr);
     int[] right = rightHalf(arr);

     sort(left);
     sort(right);

     merge(arr, left, right);
   }
}

private static int[] leftHalf(int[] arr) {

   int size = arr.length / 2;
   int[] left = new int[size];
```

```java
      System.arraycopy(arr, 0, left, 0, size);

   return left;
}

private static int[] rightHalf(int[] arr) {

   int size1 = arr.length / 2;
   int size2 = arr.length - size1;
   int[] right = new int[size2];
   for (int i = 0; i < size2; i++) {
      right[i] = arr[i + size1];
   }

   return right;
}
```

Next, the merge operation places the elements back into the original array one at a time by repeatedly taking the smallest element from the sorted sub-arrays:

```java
private static void merge(int[] result,
      int[] left, int[] right) {

   int t1 = 0;
   int t2 = 0;

   for (int i = 0; i < result.length; i++) {
      if (t2 >= right.length
            || (t1 < left.length && left[t1] <= right[t2])) {
         result[i] = left[t1];
         t1++;
      } else {
         result[i] = right[t2];
         t2++;
      }
   }
}
```

Note that the `left[t1] <= right[t2]` statement guarantees that the algorithm is stable. A stable algorithm guarantees the order of duplicate elements.

The complete application is called *MergeSort*.

Quick Sort

Quick Sort is another recursive sorting algorithm based on the famous *divide and conquer* strategy. The time complexity cases are as follows: best case O(n log n), average case O(n log n), worst case O(n²). The space complexity is O(log n) or O(n).

The Quick Sort algorithm debuts with an important choice. We have to choose one of the elements of the given array as the *pivot*. Next, we partition the given array so that all the elements that are less than the *pivot* come before all the elements that are greater than it. The partitioning operation takes place via a bunch of swaps. This is the *divide* step in *divide and conquer*.

Next, the left and the right sub-arrays are again partitioned using the corresponding pivot. This is achieved by recursively passing the sub-arrays into the algorithm. This is the *conquer* step in *divide and conquer*.

The worst case scenario (O(n²)) takes place when all the elements of the given array are smaller than the chosen pivot or larger than the chosen pivot. Choosing the pivot element can be done in at least four ways, as follows:

- Choose the first element as the pivot.
- Choose the end element as the pivot.
- Choose the median element as the pivot.
- Choose the random element as the pivot.

Consider the array 4, 2, 5, 1, 6, 7, 3. Here, we're going set the pivot as the end element. The following diagram depicts how Quick Sort works:

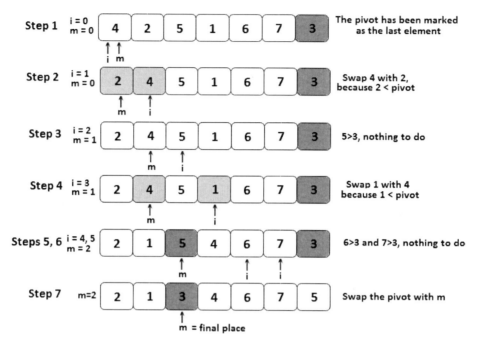

Figure 14.4 – Quick Sort

Step 1: We choose the last element as the pivot, so 3 is the pivot. Partitioning begins by locating two position markers – let's call them *i* and *m*. Initially, both point to the first element of the given array. Next, we compare the element at position *i* with the pivot, so we compare 4 with 3. Since 4 > 3, there is nothing to do, and *i* becomes 1 (*i*++), while *m* remains 0.

Step 2: We compare the element at position *i* with the pivot, so we compare 2 with 3. Since 2<3, we swap the element at position *m* with the element at position *i*, so we swap 4 with 2. Both *m* and *i* are increased by 1, so *m* becomes 1 and *i* becomes 2.

Step 3: We compare the element at position *i* with the pivot, so we compare 5 with 3. Since 5 > 3, there is nothing to do, so *i* becomes 3 (*i*++), while *m* remains as 1.

Step 4: We compare the element on position *i* with the pivot, so we compare 1 with 3. Since 1 < 3, we swap the element at position *m* with the element at position *i*, so we swap 1 with 4. Both *m* and *i* are increased by 1, so *m* becomes 2 and *i* becomes 4.

Step 5 and 6: We continue to compare the element at position *i* with the pivot. Since 6>3 and 7 > 3, there is nothing to do at these two steps. After these steps, *i*=7.

Step 7: The next element for *i* is the pivot itself, so there are no more comparisons to perform. We just swap the element at position *m* with the pivot, so we swap 5 with 3. This brings the pivot to its final position. All the elements from its left are smaller than it, while all the elements from its right are greater than it. Finally, we return *m*.

Furthermore, the algorithm is repeated for the array bounded by 0 (*left*) and *m*-1 and for the array bounded by *m*+1 and the array's end (*right*). The algorithm is repeated as long as *left<right* is true. When this condition is evaluated as false, the array is sorted.

The pseudocode for the quick sort algorithm is as follows:

```
sort(array, left, right)
    if left < right
        m = partition(array, left, right)
        sort(array, left, m-1)
        sort(array, m+1, right)
    end
end

partition(array, left, right)
    pivot = array[right]
    m = left
    for i = m to right-1
        if array[i] <= pivot
            swap array[i] with array[m]
            m=m+1
        end
    end
    swap array[m] with array[right]
    return m
end
```

To sort the entire array, we call `sort(array, 0, array.length-1)`. Let's see its implementation:

```
public static void sort(int[] arr, int left, int right) {

    if (left < right) {
        int m = partition(arr, left, right);
```

```
        sort(arr, left, m - 1);
        sort(arr, m + 1, right);
    }
}

private static int partition(int[] arr, int left, int right) {
    int pivot = arr[right];
    int m = left;
    for (int i = m; i < right; i++) {
        if (arr[i] <= pivot) {
            swap(arr, i, m++);
        }
    }

    swap(arr, right, m);

    return m;
}
```

Quick Sort can swap non-adjacent elements; therefore, it is not stable. The complete application is called *QuickSort*. This application contains an implementation based on `Comparator` as well – this is useful for sorting objects.

Bucket Sort

Bucket Sort (or Bin Sort) is another sorting technique that's encountered in interviews. It is commonly used in computer science and useful when the elements are uniformly distributed over a range. The time complexity cases are as follows: the best and average cases O(n+k), where O(k) is the time for creating the bucket (this will be O(1) for a linked list or hash table), while O(n) is the time needed to put the elements of the given array into the bucket (this will also be O(1) for a linked list or hash table). The worst case is $O(n^2)$. The space complexity is O(n+k).

Its climax relies on dividing the elements of the given array into groups that are called *buckets*. Next, each bucket is sorted individually using a different suitable sorting algorithm or using the bucket sorting algorithm via recursion.

Creating the buckets can be done in several ways. One approach relies on defining a number of buckets and filling each bucket with a specific range of elements from the given array (this is known as *scattering*). Next, each bucket is sorted (via bucket sorting or other sorting algorithms). Finally, the elements are collected from each bucket to obtain the sorted array (this is known as *gathering*). This is also known as the *scatter-sort-gather* technique and is exemplified in the following diagram. Here, we are using bucket sort on the 4, 2, 11, 7, 18, 3, 14, 7, 4, 16 array:

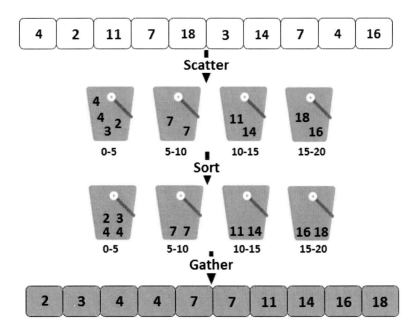

Figure 14.5 – Bucket Sort via the scatter-sort-gather approach

So, as the preceding diagram reveals, we have defined four buckets for the elements in intervals; that is, 0-5, 5-10, 10-15, and 15-20. Each element of the given array fits into a bucket. After distributing all the elements of the given array into buckets, we sort each bucket. The first bucket contains elements 2, 3, 4, and 4. The second bucket contains elements 7, 7, and so on. Finally, we gather the elements from the buckets (from left to right) and we obtain the sorted array; that is, 2, 3, 4, 4, 7, 7, 11, 14, 16, 18.

So, for this, we can write the following pseudocode:

```
sort(array)
    create N buckets each of which can hold a range of elements
    for all the buckets
        initialize each bucket with 0 values
```

```
    for all the buckets
        put elements into buckets matching the range
    for all the buckets
        sort elements in each bucket
        gather elements from each bucket
end
```

An implementation of this pseudocode using lists can be done as follows (the `hash()` methods that are being called in this code are available in the code bundled with this book):

```java
/* Scatter-Sort-Gather approach */
public static void sort(int[] arr) {

    // get the hash codes
    int[] hashes = hash(arr);

    // create and initialize buckets
    List<Integer>[] buckets = new List[hashes[1]];
    for (int i = 0; i < hashes[1]; i++) {
        buckets[i] = new ArrayList();
    }

    // scatter elements into buckets
    for (int e : arr) {
        buckets[hash(e, hashes)].add(e);
    }

    // sort each bucket
    for (List<Integer> bucket : buckets) {
        Collections.sort(bucket);
    }

    // gather elements from the buckets
    int p = 0;
    for (List<Integer> bucket : buckets) {
        for (int j : bucket) {
```

```
            arr[p++] = j;
        }
    }
}
```

Another approach to creating buckets consists of putting a single element into a bucket, as shown in the following diagram (this time, there is no sorting involved):

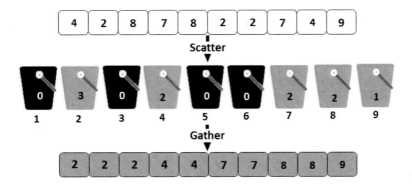

Figure 14.6 – Bucket Sort via the scatter-gather approach

In this *scatter-gather* approach, we store the number of occurrences of an element in each bucket, not the element itself, while the position (the index) of the bucket represents the element value. For example, in bucket number 2, we store the number of occurrences of element 2, which in array 4, 2, 8, 7, 8, 2, 2, 7, 4, 9 occurs three times. Since elements 1, 3, 5, and 6 are not present in the given array, their buckets are empty (have 0s in them). The gathering operation collects the elements from left to right and obtains the sorted array.

So, for this, we can write the following pseudocode:

```
sort(array)
    create N buckets each of which can track a
        counter of a single element
    for all the buckets
        initialize each bucket with 0 values
    for all the buckets
        put elements into buckets matching a single
            element per bucket
    for all the buckets
        gather elements from each bucket
end
```

An implementation of this pseudocode may look as follows:

```java
/* Scatter-Gather approach */
public static void sort(int[] arr) {

  // get the maximum value of the given array
  int max = arr[0];
  for (int i = 1; i < arr.length; i++) {
    if (arr[i] > max) {
      max = arr[i];
    }
  }

  // create max buckets
  int[] bucket = new int[max + 1];

  // the bucket[] is automatically initialized with 0s,
  // therefore this step is redundant
  for (int i = 0; i < bucket.length; i++) {
    bucket[i] = 0;
  }

  // scatter elements in buckets
  for (int i = 0; i < arr.length; i++) {
    bucket[arr[i]]++;
  }

  // gather elements from the buckets
  int p = 0;
  for (int i = 0; i < bucket.length; i++) {
    for (int j = 0; j < bucket[i]; j++) {
      arr[p++] = i;
    }
  }
}
```

Bucket Sort is not a stable algorithm. A stable algorithm guarantees the order of duplicate elements. The complete application is called *BucketSort*.

Radix Sort

Radix Sort is a sorting algorithm that works very well for integers. In Radix Sort, we sort the elements by grouping the individual digits by their positions in the numbers. Next, we sort the elements by sorting the digits at each significant position. Commonly, this is done via Counting Sort (the Counting Sort algorithm is detailed in the book *Java Coding Problems* (www.packtpub.com/programming/java-coding-problems), published by Packt, but you can find an implementation of it in the application called *SortArraysIn14Ways*). Mainly, sorting the digits can be done via any stable sorting algorithm.

A simple approach to understanding the Radix Sort algorithm relies on an example. Let's consider the array 323, 2, 3, 123, 45, 6, 788. The following image reveals the steps of sorting this array by sequentially sorting the units, the tens, and the hundreds:

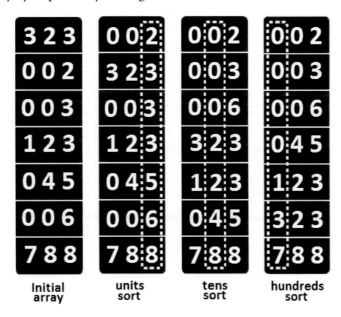

Figure 14.7 – Radix Sort

So, first, we sort the elements based on the digit corresponding to the unit place. Second, we sort the elements based on the digit corresponding to the tenth place. Third, we sort the elements based on the digit corresponding to the hundreds place. Of course, depending on the maximum number from the array, the process continues with thousands, ten thousands, and so on until no more digits are left.

The following code is an implementation of the Radix Sort algorithm:

```java
public static void sort(int[] arr, int radix) {

  int min = arr[0];
  int max = arr[0];
  for (int i = 1; i < arr.length; i++) {
    if (arr[i] < min) {
      min = arr[i];
    } else if (arr[i] > max) {
      max = arr[i];
    }
  }

  int exp = 1;
  while ((max - min) / exp >= 1) {
    countSortByDigit(arr, radix, exp, min);
    exp *= radix;
  }
}

private static void countSortByDigit(
    int[] arr, int radix, int exp, int min) {

  int[] buckets = new int[radix];
  for (int i = 0; i < radix; i++) {
    buckets[i] = 0;
  }

  int bucket;
  for (int i = 0; i < arr.length; i++) {
    bucket = (int) (((arr[i] - min) / exp) % radix);
    buckets[bucket]++;
  }

  for (int i = 1; i < radix; i++) {
    buckets[i] += buckets[i - 1];
```

```java
    }

    int[] out = new int[arr.length];
    for (int i = arr.length - 1; i >= 0; i--) {
        bucket = (int) (((arr[i] - min) / exp) % radix);
        out[--buckets[bucket]] = arr[i];
    }

    System.arraycopy(out, 0, arr, 0, arr.length);
}
```

The time complexity of Radix Sort depends on the algorithm that's used to sort the digits (remember that this can be any stable sorting algorithm). Since we are using the Counting Sort algorithm, the time complexity is O(d(n+b)), where *n* is the number of elements, *d* is the number of digits, and *b* is the radix or base (in our case, the base is 10). The space complexity is O(n+b).

The complete application is called *RadixSort*. Well, so far, we've managed to cover the top five sorting algorithms that occur in technical interviews. Now, let's quickly provide an overview of the searching algorithms.

Searching algorithms

The main searching algorithm that occurs in interviews as a standalone problem or part of another problem is the Binary Search algorithm. The best case time complexity is O(1), while the average and worst case is O(log n). The worst case auxiliary space complexity of Binary Search is O(1) for the iterative implementation and O(log n) for the recursive implementation due to the call stack.

The Binary Search algorithm relies on the *divide and conquer* strategy. Mainly, this algorithm debuts by dividing the given array into two sub-arrays. Furthermore, it discards one of these sub-arrays and operates on the other one iteratively or recursively. In other words, at each step, this algorithm halves the search space (which is initially the whole given array).

So, these algorithms describe the steps for looking for element *x* in an array, *a*. Consider a sorted array, *a*, that contains 16 elements, as shown in the following image:

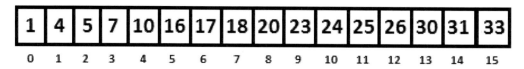

Figure 14.8 – Ordered array containing 16 elements

First, we compare *x* with the midpoint of the array, *p*. If they are equal, we return. If $x > p$, then we search the right-hand side of the array and discard the left-hand side (the search space is the right-hand side of the array). If $x < p$, then we search on the left-hand side of the array and discard the right-hand side (the search space is the left-hand side of the array). The following is a graphical representation of the Binary Search algorithm for finding the number 17:

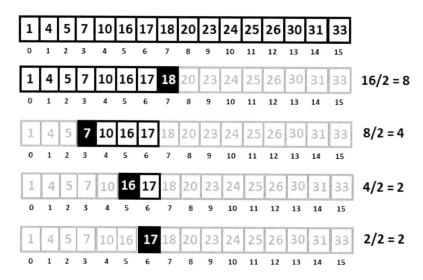

Figure 14.9 – The Binary Search algorithm

Notice that we start with 16 elements and end with 1. After the first step, we are down to 16/2 = 8 elements. At the second step, we are down to 8/2 = 4 elements. At the third step, we are down to 4/2 = 2 elements. And, at the final step, we find the searched number, 17. If we put this algorithm into pseudocode, then we will obtain something similar to the following:

```
search 17 in {1, 4, 5, 7, 10, 16, 17, 18, 20,
              23, 24, 25, 26, 30, 31, 33}
    compare 17 to 18 -> 17 < 18
```

```
search 17 in {1, 4, 5, 7, 10, 16, 17, 18}
    compare 17 to 7 -> 17 > 7
    search 17 in {7, 10, 16, 17}
        compare 17 to 16 -> 17 > 16
        search 17 in {16, 17}
            compare 17 to 17
            return
```

The iterative implementation is listed here:

```
public static int runIterative(int[] arr, int p) {

  // the search space is the whole array
  int left = 0;
  int right = arr.length - 1;

  // while the search space has at least one element
  while (left <= right) {

    // half the search space
    int mid = (left + right) / 2;

    // if domain overflow can happen then use:
    // int mid = left + (right - left) / 2;
    // int mid = right - (right - left) / 2;

    // we found the searched element
    if (p == arr[mid]) {
      return mid;
    } // discard all elements in the right of the
      // search space including 'mid'
    else if (p < arr[mid]) {
      right = mid - 1;
    } // discard all elements in the left of the
      // search space including 'mid'
    else {
      left = mid + 1;
```

```
        }
    }
    // by convention, -1 means element not found into the array
    return -1;
}
```

The complete application is called *BinarySearch*. It also contains the recursive implementation of the Binary Search algorithm. In *Chapter 10, Arrays and Strings*, you can find different coding challenges that take advantage of the Binary Search algorithm.

Coding challenges

So far, we've covered the most popular sorting and searching algorithms that are encountered in technical interviews. It is advised that you practice these algorithms since they may occur as standalone problems that require the pseudocode or the implementation.

That being said, let's tackle 18 problems that are related to sorting and searching algorithms.

Coding challenge 1 – Merging two sorted arrays

Amazon, **Google**, **Adobe**, **Microsoft**, **Flipkart**

Problem: Consider you've been given two sorted arrays, *p* and *q*. The *p* array is large enough to fit *q* at the end of it. Write a snippet of code that merges *p* and *q* in a sorted order.

Solution: It is important to highlight the fact that *p* has enough space at the end to fit *q*. This suggests that the solution shouldn't involve any auxiliary space. The solution should output the result of merging *p* and *q* in a sorted order by inserting the elements from *q* in *p* in order.

Mainly, we should compare the elements from *p* and *q* and insert them into *p* in order until we've processed all the elements in *p* and *q*. Let's take a look at a meaningful diagram that reveals this action (*p* contains elements -1, 3, 8, 0, 0, while *q* contains elements 2, 4):

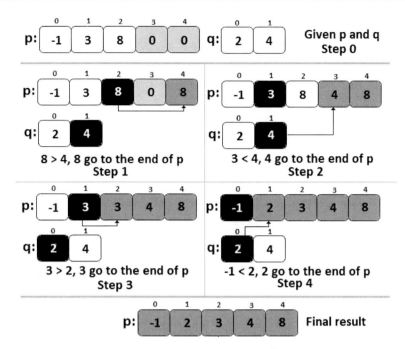

Figure 14.10 – Merging two sorted arrays

Let's see this test case step by step (let's denote the index of the last element from *p* with *pIdx* and the index of the last element from *q* with *qIdx*). In the previous diagram, *pIdx*=2 (corresponding to element 8) and *qIdx*=1 (corresponding to element 4).

Step 1: We compare the last element from *p* (the element at index *pIdx*) with the last element from *q* (the element at index *qIdx*), so we compare 8 with 4. Since 8 > 4, we copy 8 to the end of *p*. Since both arrays are sorted, 8 is the maximum of these arrays, so it must go to the last position (index) in *p*. It will occupy an empty slot in *p* (remember that *p* is large enough to fit *q* at its end). We decrease *pIdx* by 1.

Step 2: We compare the last element from *p* (the element at index *pIdx*) with the last element from *q* (the element at index *qIdx*), so we compare 3 with 4. Since 3 < 4, we copy 4 to the end of *p*. We decrease *qIdx* by 1.

Step 3: We compare the last element from *p* (the element at index *pIdx*) with the last element from *q* (the element at index *qIdx*), so we compare 3 with 2. Since 3 > 2, we copy 3 to the end of *p*. We decrease *pIdx* by 1.

Step 4: We compare the last element from *p* (the element at index *pIdx*) with the last element from *q* (the element at index *qIdx*), so we compare -1 with 2. Since -1 < 2, we copy 2 to the end of *p*. We decrease *qIdx* by 1. There are no more elements to compare and *p* is sorted.

Check this out! After each comparison, we insert the elements at the end of *p*. This way, we don't need to shift any elements. However, if we choose to insert the elements at the beginning of *p*, then we must shift the elements backward to make room for each inserted element. This is not efficient!

Now, it's time to see the implementation of this algorithm:

```
public static void merge(int[] p, int[] q) {

  int pLast = p.length - q.length;
  int qLast = q.length;

  if (pLast < 0) {
    throw new IllegalArgumentException("p cannot fit q");
  }

  int pIdx = pLast - 1;
  int qIdx = qLast - 1;
  int mIdx = pLast + qLast - 1;

  // merge p and q
  // start from the last element in p and q
  while (qIdx >= 0) {

    if (pIdx >= 0 && p[pIdx] > q[qIdx]) {
      p[mIdx] = p[pIdx];
      pIdx--;
    } else {
      p[mIdx] = q[qIdx];
      qIdx--;
    }

    mIdx--;
  }
}
```

The complete application is called *MergeTwoSortedArrays*. If you'd like to check/remember how to merge *k* sorted arrays, then revisit *Chapter 10, Arrays and Strings*, the *Merging k sorted arrays in O(nk log k)* coding challenge.

Coding challenge 2 – Grouping anagrams together
Adobe, Flipkart

Problem: Consider you've been given an array of words (containing characters from 'a' to 'z') representing several mixed anagrams (for example, "calipers", "caret", "slat", "cater", "thickset", "spiracle", "trace", "last", "salt", "bowel", "crate", "loop", "polo", "thickest", "below", "thickets", "pool", "elbow", "replicas"). Write a snippet of code that prints this array so that all the anagrams are grouped together (for example, "calipers", "spiracle", "replicas", "caret", "cater", "trace", "crate", "slat", "last", "salt", "bowel", "below", "elbow", "thickset", "thickest", "thickets", "loop", "polo", "pool").

Solution: First, here's a quick reminder regarding anagrams. Two or more strings (words) are considered to be anagrams if they contain the same characters but in different orders.

Based on the example provided for this problem, let's define the following array of mixed anagrams:

```
String[] words = {
  "calipers", "caret", "slat", "cater", "thickset",
  "spiracle", "trace", "last", "salt", "bowel", "crate",
  "loop", "polo", "thickest", "below", "thickets",
  "pool", "elbow", "replicas"
};
```

Since anagrams contain exactly the same characters, this means that if we sort them, then they will be identical (for example, sorting "slat", "salt" and "last" result in "alst"). So, we can say that two strings (words) are anagrams by comparing their sorted versions. In other words, all we need is a sorting algorithm. The most convenient way to do this is to rely on Java's built-in sorting algorithm, which is Dual-Pivot Quicksort for primitives and TimSort for objects.

The built-in solution is called `sort()` and comes in many different flavors in the `java.util.Arrays` class (15+ flavors). Two of these flavors have the following signatures:

- `void sort(Object[] a)`
- `<T> void sort(T[] a, Comparator<? super T> c)`

If we convert a string (word) into `char[]`, then we can sort its characters and return the new string via the following helper method:

```java
// helper method for sorting the chars of a word
private static String sortWordChars(String word) {

  char[] wordToChar = word.toCharArray();
  Arrays.sort(wordToChar);

  return String.valueOf(wordToChar);
}
```

Next, we just need a `Comparator` that indicates that two strings that are anagrams of each other are equivalent:

```java
public class Anagrams implements Comparator<String> {

  @Override
  public int compare(String s1, String s2) {
    return sortStringChars(s1).compareTo(sortStringChars(s2));
  }
}
```

Finally, we sort the given array of strings (words) via this `compareTo()` method:

```java
Arrays.sort(words, new Anagrams());
```

However, the problem doesn't actually ask us to sort the given array of anagrams; the problem asks us to print the anagrams grouped together. For this, we can rely on *hashing* (if you are not familiar with the concept of hashing, then please read *Chapter 6, Object-Oriented Programming*, the *Hash table* problem). In Java, we can use hashing via the built-in `HashMap` implementation, so there is no need to write a hashing implementation from scratch. But how is this `HashMap` useful? What should we store in an entry (key-value pair) of this map?

Each group of anagrams converges to the same sorted version (for example, the group of anagrams containing the strings (words) "slat", "salt" and "last" have the unique and common sorted version as "alst"). Being unique, the sorted version is a good candidate to be the key in our map. Next, the value represents the list of anagrams. So, the algorithm is quite simple; it contains the following steps:

1. Loop over the given array of words.
2. Sort the characters of each word.
3. Populate the map (add or update the map).
4. Print the result.

In code lines:

```java
/* Group anagrams via hashing (O(nm log m) */
public void printAnagrams(String words[]) {

    Map<String, List<String>> result = new HashMap<>();

    for (int i = 0; i < words.length; i++) {

        // sort the chars of each string
        String word = words[i];
        String sortedWord = sortWordChars(word);

        if (result.containsKey(sortedWord)) {
            result.get(sortedWord).add(word);
        } else {
            // start a new group of anagrams
            List<String> anagrams = new ArrayList<>();
            anagrams.add(word);
            result.put(sortedWord, anagrams);
        }
    }

    // print the result
    System.out.println(result.values());
}
```

If *n* is the number of strings (words) and each string (word) has a maximum of *m* characters, then the time complexity of the preceding two approaches is O(nm log m).

Can we do this better? Well, to do this better, we have to identify the issue of the preceding two approaches. The issue consists of the fact that we sort every string (word) and that this will cost us extra time. However, we can use an additional `char[]` to count up the number of occurrences (frequency) of each character in a string (word). After we build this `char[]`, we convert it into a `String` to obtain the key that we have to search for in `HashMap`. Since Java handles `char` types the same as it does (unsigned) `short`, we can make calculations with `char`. Let's see the code (the `wordToChar` array tracks the frequency of characters from *a* to *z* for each string (word) in the given array):

```java
/* Group anagrams via hashing (O(nm)) */
public void printAnagramsOptimized(String[] words) {

    Map<String, List<String>> result = new HashMap<>();

    for (int i = 0; i < words.length; i++) {

        String word = words[i];
        char[] wordToChar = new char[RANGE_a_z];

        // count up the number of occurrences (frequency)
        // of each letter in 'word'
        for (int j = 0; j < word.length(); j++) {
            wordToChar[word.charAt(j) - 'a']++;
        }

        String computedWord = String.valueOf(wordToChar);

        if (result.containsKey(computedWord)) {
            result.get(computedWord).add(word);
        } else {
            List<String> anagrams = new ArrayList<>();
            anagrams.add(word);
            result.put(computedWord, anagrams);
        }
    }
}
```

```
        System.out.println(result.values());
}
```

If *n* is the number of strings (words) and each string (word) contains a maximum of *m* characters, then the time complexity of the preceding two approaches is O(nm). If you need to support more characters, not just from *a* to *z*, then use an `int[]` array and `codePointAt()` – more details are available in *Chapter 10, Arrays and Strings*, in the *Extracting code points of surrogate pairs* coding challenge. The complete application is called *GroupSortAnagrams*.

Coding challenge 3 – List of unknown size

Problem: Consider you've been given a data structure representing a sorted list of unknown size (this means that there is no `size()` or similar method) containing only positive numbers. The code for this list is as follows:

```
public class SizelessList {

  private final int[] arr;

  public SizelessList(int[] arr) {
    this.arr = arr.clone();
  }

  public int peekAt(int index) {
    if (index >= arr.length) {
      return -1;
    }

    return arr[index];
  }
}
```

However, as you can see, there is a method called `peekAt()` that returns the element at the given index in O(1). If the given index is beyond the bounds of this list, then `peekAt()` returns -1. Write a snippet of code that returns the index at which an element, *p*, occurs.

Solution: When we must search in a sorted data structure (for example, in a sorted array), we know that Binary Search is the proper choice. So, can we use Binary Search in this case? Since the given list is sorted and we can access any element of it in O(1) time, this means that Binary Search should be a good choice. Apart from that, the Binary Search algorithm requires the size of the data structure since we have to halve the search space (for example, `list.size()/2`) to find the middle point. The given data structure (list) doesn't reveal its size.

So, the problem is reduced to finding the size of this list. We know that `peekAt()` returns -1 if the given index is beyond the bounds of this list, so we can loop the list and count the iterations until `peekAt()` returns -1. When `peekAt()` returns -1, we should know the size of the list, so we can apply the Binary Search algorithm. Instead of looping the list element by element (linear algorithm), we can try to do so exponentially. So, instead of looping `peekAt(1)`, `peekAt(2)`, `peekAt(3)`, `peekAt(4)` ..., we loop `peekAt(1)`, `peekAt(2)`, `peekAt(4)`, `peekAt(8)`, ... In other words, instead of doing this in O(n) time, we can do so in O(log n) time, where *n* is the size of the list. We can do this because the given list is sorted!

The following code should clarify this approach and the remaining details:

```
public static int search(SizelessList sl, int element) {

    int index = 1;
    while (sl.peekAt(index) != -1
            && sl.peekAt(index) < element) {
      index *= 2;
    }

    return binarySearch(sl, element, index / 2, index);
}

private static int binarySearch(SizelessList sl,
        int element, int left, int right) {

    int mid;
```

```
    while (left <= right) {

      mid = (left + right) / 2;
      int middle = sl.peekAt(mid);
      if (middle > element || middle == -1) {
        right = mid - 1;
      } else if (middle < element) {
        left = mid + 1;
      } else {
        return mid;
      }
    }

    return -1;
}
```

The complete application is called *UnknownSizeList*.

Coding challenge 4 – Merge sorting a linked list

Amazon, **Google**, **Adobe**, **Microsoft**, **Flipkart**

Problem: Consider you've been given a singly linked list. Write a snippet of code that sorts this linked list via the Merge Sort algorithm.

Solution: Solving this problem requires knowledge of several topics that we've already covered in this book. First, you must be familiar with linked lists. This topic was covered in *Chapter 11, Linked Lists and Maps*. Second, you will need have read the *Merge Sort* section of this chapter.

Conforming to the Merge Sort algorithm, we have to continually split the linked list in half until we obtain empty sub-lists or sub-lists that contain a single element (this is the *divide and conquer* approach). If a sub-list is empty or contains one element, it is sorted by definition – this is known as *base case* recursion. The following diagram reveals this process for the initial linked list 2 → 1 → 4 → 9 → 8 → 3 → 7 → null:

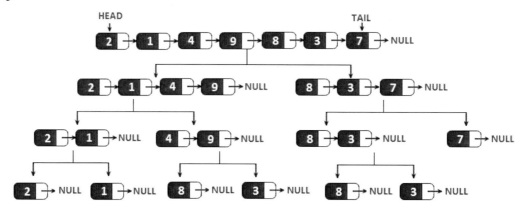

Figure 14.11 – Using divide and conquer on a linked list

Dividing the given linked list like this can be done via the Fast Runner/Slow Runner approach. This approach was detailed in *Chapter 11, Linked Lists and Maps*, in the *The Fast Runner/Slow Runner approach* section. Mainly, when the **Fast Runner** (**FR**) reaches the end of the given linked list, the **Slow Runner** (**SR**) points to the middle of this list, so we can split the list in two. The code for this is listed here:

```
// Divide the given linked list in two equal sub-lists.
// If the length of the given linked list is odd,
// the extra node will go in the first sub-list
private Node[] divide(Node sourceNode) {

  // length is less than 2
  if (sourceNode == null || sourceNode.next == null) {
    return new Node[]{sourceNode, null};
  }

  Node fastRunner = sourceNode.next;
  Node slowRunner = sourceNode;

  // advance 'firstRunner' two nodes,
  // and advance 'secondRunner' one node
```

```
  while (fastRunner != null) {
    fastRunner = fastRunner.next;
    if (fastRunner != null) {
       slowRunner = slowRunner.next;
       fastRunner = fastRunner.next;
    }
  }

  // 'secondRunner' is just before the middle point
  // in the list, so split it in two at that point
  Node[] headsOfSublists = new Node[]{
        sourceNode, slowRunner.next};
  slowRunner.next = null;

  return headsOfSublists;
}
```

The rest of the code is a classical Merge Sort implementation. The sort() method is responsible for recursively sorting the sub-lists. Next, the merge() method places the elements back into the original linked list one at a time by repeatedly taking the smallest element from the sorted sub-lists:

```
// sort the given linked list via the Merge Sort algorithm
public void sort() {

  head = sort(head);
}

private Node sort(Node head) {

  if (head == null || head.next == null) {
    return head;
  }

  // split head into two sublists
  Node[] headsOfSublists = divide(head);
```

```
    Node head1 = headsOfSublists[0];
    Node head2 = headsOfSublists[1];

    // recursively sort the sublists
    head1 = sort(head1);
    head2 = sort(head2);

    // merge the two sorted lists together
    return merge(head1, head2);
}

// takes two lists sorted in increasing order, and merge
// their nodes together (which is returned)
private Node merge(Node head1, Node head2) {

    if (head1 == null) {
      return head2;
    } else if (head2 == null) {
      return head1;
    }

    Node merged;

    // pick either 'head1' or 'head2'
    if (head1.data <= head2.data) {
      merged = head1;
      merged.next = merge(head1.next, head2);
    } else {
      merged = head2;
      merged.next = merge(head1, head2.next);
    }

    return merged;
}
```

The complete application is called *MergeSortSinglyLinkedList*. Sorting a doubly linked list is quite similar. You can find such an implementation in the application called *MergeSortDoublyLinkedList*.

Coding challenge 5 – Strings interspersed with empty strings

Amazon, Google, Adobe, Microsoft, Flipkart

Problem: Consider you've been given a sorted array of strings that is interspersed with empty strings. Write a snippet of code that returns the index of the given non-empty string.

Solution: When we must search in a sorted data structure (for example, in a sorted array), we know that the Binary Search algorithm is the proper choice. So, can we use Binary Search in this case? We have the size of the given array, so we can halve the searching space and locate the middle point. If we denote the index 0 of the array as *left* and the *array.length*-1 as *right*, then we can write *mid* = (*left* + *right*) / 2. So, *mid* is the middle point of the given array.

But what we can do if the *mid* index falls on an empty string? In such a case, we don't know if we should go to the *right* or the *left*. In other words, which half should be discarded, and what half should be used for continuing our search? The answer can be found in the following diagram (the given string is "cat", "", "", "", "", "", "", "rear", ""):

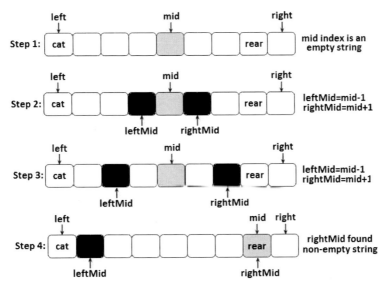

Figure 14.12 – Computing the middle point in the case of an empty string

So, when the middle point (*mid*) falls on an empty string, we must correct its index by moving it to the nearest non-empty string. As shown in *step 2* of the preceding diagram, we choose *leftMid* as *mid*-1 and *rightMid* as *mid*+1. We keep moving away from *mid* until the *leftMid* or *rightMid* index points out a non-empty string (in the preceding diagram, *rightMid* finds the string, "rear", after *steps 3* and *4*). When this happens, we update the *mid* position and continue the classical Binary Search (*step 4*).

In terms of code, this is quite straightforward:

```
public static int search(String[] stringsArr, String str) {

  return search(stringsArr, str, 0, stringsArr.length - 1);
}

private static int search(String[] stringsArr,
    String str, int left, int right) {

  if (left > right) {
    return -1;
  }

  int mid = (left + right) / 2;

  // since mid is empty we try to find the
  // closest non-empty string to mid
  if (stringsArr[mid].isEmpty()) {

    int leftMid = mid - 1;
    int rightMid = mid + 1;

    while (true) {

      if (leftMid < left && rightMid > right) {
        return -1;
      } else if (rightMid <= right
          && !stringsArr[rightMid].isEmpty()) {
        mid = rightMid;
        break;
```

```
      } else if (leftMid >= left
          && !stringsArr[leftMid].isEmpty()) {
        mid = leftMid;
        break;
      }

      rightMid++;
      leftMid--;
    }
  }

  if (str.equals(stringsArr[mid])) {
    // the searched string was found
    return mid;
  } else if (stringsArr[mid].compareTo(str) < 0) {
    // search to the right
    return search(stringsArr, str, mid + 1, right);
  } else {
    // search to the left
    return search(stringsArr, str, left, mid - 1);
  }
}
```

The worst-case time complexity for this approach is O(n). Notice that if the searched string is an empty string, then we return -1, so we treat this case as an error. This is correct since the problem says that the given string that needs to be found is non-empty. If the problem doesn't provide any details about this aspect, then you have to discuss this with the interviewer. This way, you are showing the interviewer that you pay attention to details and corner cases. The complete application is called *InterspersedEmptyStrings*.

Coding challenge 6 – Sorting a queue with the help of another queue

Amazon, Google, Adobe, Microsoft, Flipkart

Problem: Consider you've been given a queue of integers. Write a snippet of code that sorts this queue with the help of another queue (an extra queue).

Solution: The solution to this problem must include an extra queue, so we must think about how to use this extra queue when sorting the given queue. There are different approaches, but a convenient approach for an interview can be summarized as follows:

1. As long as the elements from the given queue are in ascending order (starting from the front of the queue), we dequeue them and enqueue in the extra queue.
2. If an element breaks the preceding statement, then we dequeue and enqueue it back in the given queue, without touching the extra queue.
3. After all the elements have been processed via *step 1* or *2*, we dequeue all the elements from the extra queue and enqueue them back in the given queue.
4. As long as the size of the extra queue is not equal to the initial size of the given queue, we repeat from *step 1* since the queue is not sorted yet.

Let's consider that the given queue contains the following elements: rear → 3 → 9 → 1 → 8 → 5 → 2 → front. The following diagram represents the given queue and the extra queue (initially empty):

Figure 14.13 – The given queue and the extra queue

Applying *step 1* of our algorithm means dequeuing 2, 5, and 8 from the given queue and enqueuing them in the extra queue, as shown in the following diagram:

Figure 14.14 – Enqueuing 2, 5, and 8 in the extra queue

Since the next element in the given queue is smaller than the last element that's added to the extra queue, we apply *step 2* of our algorithm, so we dequeue 1 and enqueue it in the given queue, as shown in the following diagram:

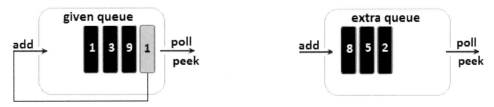

Figure 14.15 – Dequeuing and enqueuing 1 in the given queue

Furthermore, we apply *step 1* again since 9 (the front of the given queue) is bigger than the last element that's added to the extra queue (8). So, 9 goes in the extra queue, as shown in the following diagram:

Figure 14.16 – Enqueuing 9 in the extra queue

Next, 3 is smaller than 9, so we must dequeue and enqueue it back in the given queue, as shown in the following diagram:

Figure 14.17 – Dequeuing and enqueuing 3 in the given queue

At this point, we've processed (visited) all the elements from the given queue, so we apply *step 3* of our algorithm. We dequeue all the elements from the extra queue and enqueue them in the given queue, as shown in the following diagram:

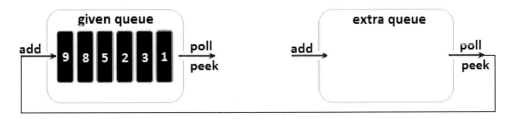

Figure 14.18 – Dequeuing from the extra queue and enqueuing in the given queue

Now, we repeat the whole process until the given queue is sorted in ascending order. Let's see the code:

```java
public static void sort(Queue<Integer> queue) {

  if (queue == null || queue.size() < 2) {
    return;
  }

  // this is the extra queue
  Queue<Integer> extraQueue = new ArrayDeque();

  int count = 0;              // count the processed elements
  boolean sorted = false;     // flag when sorting is done

  int queueSize = queue.size();      // size of the given queue
  int lastElement = queue.peek();    // we start from the front
                                     // of the given queue

  while (!sorted) {
    // Step 1
    if (lastElement <= queue.peek()) {
      lastElement = queue.poll();
      extraQueue.add(lastElement);
    } else { // Step 2
      queue.add(queue.poll());
    }

    // still have elements to process
    count++;
    if (count != queueSize) {
      continue;
    }

    // Step 4
    if (extraQueue.size() == queueSize) {
      sorted = true;
```

```
    }

    // Step 3
    while (extraQueue.size() > 0) {
      queue.add(extraQueue.poll());
      lastElement = queue.peek();
    }

    count = 0;
  }
}
```

This code's runtime is O(n²). The complete application is called *SortQueueViaTempQueue*.

Coding challenge 7 – Sorting a queue without extra space

Amazon, Google, Adobe, Microsoft, Flipkart

Problem: Consider you've been given a queue of integers. Write a snippet of code that sorts this queue without using extra space.

Solution: In the preceding problem, we had to solve the same problem but using an extra queue. This time, we cannot use an extra queue, so we must sort the queue in place.

We can think of sorting as a continuous process of finding the minimum element from the given queue, extracting it from its current position, and adding it to the rear of this queue. Expanding this idea may result in the following algorithm:

1. Consider the current minimum as `Integer.MAX_VALUE`.
2. Dequeue an element from the unsorted part of the queue (initially, the unsorted part is the entire queue).
3. Compare this element with the current minimum.

4. If this element is smaller than the current minimum, then do the following:

   a. If the current minimum is `Integer.MAX_VALUE`, then this element becomes the current minimum and we do not enqueue it back in the queue.

   b. If the current minimum is not `Integer.MAX_VALUE`, then we enqueue the current minimum back in the queue and this element becomes the current minimum.

5. If this element is bigger than the current minimum value, then we enqueue it back in the queue.

6. Repeat from *step 2* until the whole unsorted part is traversed.

7. At this step, the current minimum is the minimum of the entire unsorted part, so we enqueue it back in the queue.

8. Set the new boundary of the unsorted part and repeat from *step 1* until the unsorted part size is 0 (every time we execute this step, the unsorted part's size is decreased by 1).

The following diagram is a snapshot of this algorithm for the queue; that is, rear → 3 → 9 → 1 → 8 → 5 → 2 → front:

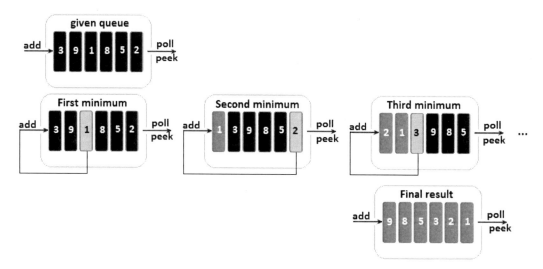

Figure 14.19 – Sorting a queue without extra space

Notice how each minimum of the unsorted part (initially, the whole queue) is added back into the queue and becomes a member of the sorted part of the queue. Let's see the code:

```
public static void sort(Queue<Integer> queue) {

  // traverse the unsorted part of the queue
  for (int i = 1; i <= queue.size(); i++) {

    moveMinToRear(queue, queue.size() - i);
  }
}

// find (in the unsorted part) the minimum
// element and move this element to the rear of the queue
private static void moveMinToRear(Queue<Integer> queue,
        int sortIndex) {

  int minElement = Integer.MAX_VALUE;
  boolean flag = false;

  int queueSize = queue.size();
  for (int i = 0; i < queueSize; i++) {

    int currentElement = queue.peek();

    // dequeue
    queue.poll();

    // avoid traversing the sorted part of the queue
    if (currentElement <= minElement && i <= sortIndex) {

      // if we found earlier a minimum then
      // we put it back into the queue since
      // we just found a new minimum
      if (flag) {
        queue.add(minElement);
      }
```

```
        flag = true;
        minElement = currentElement;
    } else {
        // enqueue the current element which is not the minimum
        queue.add(currentElement);
    }
}

// enqueue the minimum element
queue.add(minElement);
}
```

This code's runtime is O(n²). The complete application is called *SortQueueWithoutExtraSpace*.

Coding challenge 8 – Sorting a stack with the help of another stack

Amazon, Google, Adobe, Microsoft, Flipkart

Problem: Consider you've been given an unsorted stack. Write a snippet of code that sorts the stack in descending or ascending order. You can only use an additional temporary stack.

Solution: If we could use two additional stacks, then we could implement an algorithm that repeatedly searches the minimum value in the given stack and pushes it into the final or resulting stack. A second additional stack will be used as a buffer while searching the given stack. However, the problem requires us to use only one additional temporary stack.

Due to this constraint, we are forced to pop from the given stack (let's denote it as *s1*) and push in order into the additional stack (let's denote it as *s2*). To accomplish this, we use a temporary or auxiliary variable (let's denote it as *t*), as shown in the following diagram (the given stack is top → 1 → 4 → 5 → 3 → 1 → 2):

Coding challenges

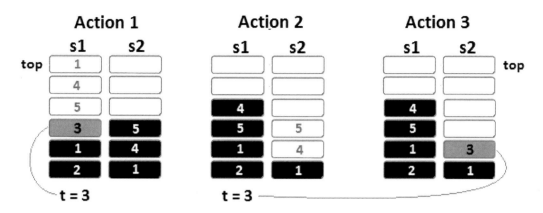

Figure 14.20 – Sorting a stack

The solution consists of two main steps:

1. While *s1* is not empty, do the following:

    a. Pop a value from *s1* and store it in *t* (*action 1* in the previous diagram shows this for value 3).

    b. Pop from *s2* and push it into *s1* as long as what we pop from *s2* is bigger than *t* or *s2* is not empty (*action 2* in the previous diagram).

    c. Push *t* into *s2* (*action 3* in the previous diagram).

2. Once *step 1* is complete, *s1* is empty and *s2* is sorted. The biggest value is at the bottom, so the resulting stack is top → 5 → 4 → 3 → 2 → 1 → 1. The second step consists of copying *s2* into *s1*. This way, *s1* is sorted in the reverse order of *s2*, so the smallest value is at the top of *s1* (top → 1 → 1 → 2 → 3 → 4 → 5).

Let's see the code:

```
public static void sort(Stack<Integer> stack) {

  Stack<Integer> auxStack = new Stack<>();

  // Step 1 (a, b and c)
  while (!stack.isEmpty()) {

    int t = stack.pop();
    while (!auxStack.isEmpty() && auxStack.peek() > t) {
      stack.push(auxStack.pop());
```

```
            }
        auxStack.push(t);
    }

    // Step 2
    while (!auxStack.isEmpty()) {
        stack.push(auxStack.pop());
    }
}
```

The complete code is called *SortStack*.

Coding challenge 9 – Sorting a stack in place

Amazon, Google, Adobe, Microsoft, Flipkart

Problem: Consider you've been given an unsorted stack. Write a snippet of code that sorts the stack in place. Note that a variation of this problem will explicitly mention that you cannot use any repetitive statements, such as `for`, `while`, and so on.

Solution: In the preceding problem, we had to solve the same problem but using an explicit extra stack. This time, we cannot use an explicit extra stack, so we must sort the stack in place.

Let's consider that the given stack is top → 4 → 5 → 3 → 8 → 2 →1. The solution starts by popping the values from the stack until the stack is empty. Afterward, we insert the values from the recursion call stack back into the given stack in sorted position.

Let's try to apply this approach to our stack. The following diagram reveals the process of popping the values from the stack until the stack is empty. On the left-hand side, we have the initial state. On the right-hand side, we have the result:

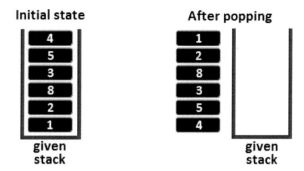

Figure 14.21 – Sorting the stack in place (1)

Next, we push back into the stack as long as the current element to push is smaller than the current top of the stack or the stack is empty. So, we will push 1, 2, and 8. We don't push 3 (the next element to be pushed) since 3 is less than 8 (you can see this statement in the following diagram as *action 1*). At this point, we need to make room to 3, so we must pop the top of the stack, 8 (you can see this statement in the following diagram as *action 2*). Finally, we push 3 and, afterward, we push 8 into the stack (you can see this statement in the following diagram as *action 3*):

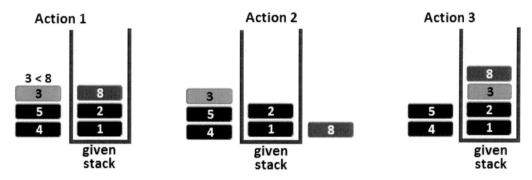

Figure 14.22 – Sorting the stack in place (2)

So far, so good! Next, we must repeat the flow presented in the preceding diagram. So, the next element to be pushed from the recursion call stack into the given stack is 5. But 5 is less than 8, so we cannot push it (you can see this statement in the following diagram as *action 1*). At this point, we need to make room for 5, so we have to pop the top of the stack, which is 8 (you can see this statement in the following diagram as *action 2*). Finally, we push 5 and, afterward, we push 8 into the stack (you can see this statement in the following diagram as *action 3*):

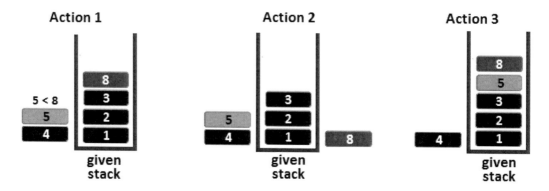

Figure 14.23 – Sorting the stack in place (3)

Finally, the last element that should be pushed from the recursion call stack into the given stack is 4. However, 4 is less than 8, so we cannot push it (you can see this statement in the following diagram as *action 1*). At this point, we need to make room to 4, so we must pop the top of the stack, which is 8 (you can see this statement in the following diagram as *action 2*). However, we still cannot push 4 into the stack because 4 is less than 5 (the new top element after popping 8). We must pop 5 as well (you can see this statement in the following diagram as *action 3*). Now, we can push 4. Next, we push 5 and 8. You can see this in the following diagram as *action 4*:

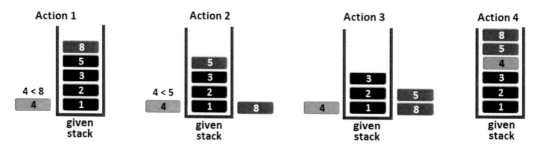

Figure 14.24 – Sorting the stack in place (4)

Done! The given stack has been sorted. Let's see the code:

```java
public static void sort(Stack<Integer> stack) {

  // stack is empty (base case)
  if (stack.isEmpty()) {
    return;
  }

  // remove the top element
  int top = stack.pop();

  // apply recursion for the remaining elements in the stack
  sort(stack);

  // insert the popped element back in the sorted stack
  sortedInsert(stack, top);
}

private static void sortedInsert(
  Stack<Integer> stack, int element) {

  // the stack is empty or the element
  // is greater than all elements in the stack (base case)
  if (stack.isEmpty() || element > stack.peek()) {
    stack.push(element);
    return;
  }

  // the element is smaller than the top element,
  // so remove the top element
  int top = stack.pop();

  // apply recursion for the remaining elements in the stack
  sortedInsert(stack, element);

  // insert the popped element back in the stack
```

```
        stack.push(top);
}
```

The runtime of this code is O(n²) with an auxiliary space of O(n) for the recursion call stack (*n* is the number of elements in the given stack). The complete application is called *SortStackInPlace*.

Coding challenge 10 – Searching in a full sorted matrix

Amazon, Microsoft, Flipkart

Problem: Consider you've been given a matrix of integers of size *rows* x *cols* that is full and sorted in ascending order. A *full sorted matrix* means that the integers in each row are sorted from left to right and that the first integer of each row is greater than the last integer of the previous row. Write a snippet of code that returns true if a given integer is in this matrix.

Solution: The brute-force method is quite inefficient. If we try to iterate the matrix and compare each (*row, col*) integer with the searched one, then this will impose a time complexity of O(mn), where *m* is the number of rows and *n* is the number of columns in the matrix.

Another solution will rely on the Binary Search algorithm. We have enough experience to implement this algorithm for a sorted array, but can we do it for a sorted matrix? Yes, we can, thanks to the fact that this sorted matrix is *fully sorted*. More precisely, since the first integer of each row is greater than the last integer of the previous row, we can look at this matrix as an array of length *rows* x *cols*. The following diagram clarifies this statement:

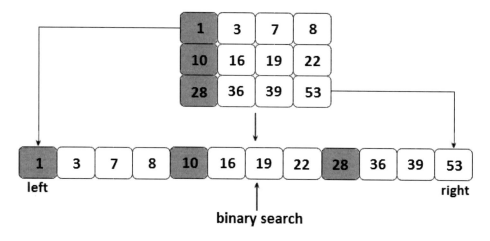

Figure 14.25 – Fully sorted matrix as an array

So, if we see the given matrix as an array, then we can reduce the problem of applying the Binary Search to a sorted array. There is no need to physically transform the matrix into an array. All we need to do is express the Binary Search accordingly using the following statements:

- The left-most integer of the array is at index 0 (let's denote it as *left*).
- The right-most integer of the array is at index (*rows* * *cols*) - 1 (let's denote it as *right*).
- The middle point of the array is at (*left* + *right*) / 2.
- The integer at the middle point of the index is at *matrix*[*mid* / *cols*][*mid* % *cols*], where *cols* is the number of columns in the matrix.

With these statements in place, we can write the following implementation:

```
public static boolean search(int[][] matrix, int element) {

  int rows = matrix.length;      // number of rows
  int cols = matrix[0].length;   // number of columns

  // search space is an array as [0, (rows * cols) - 1]
  int left = 0;
  int right = (rows * cols) - 1;

  // start binary search
  while (left <= right) {

    int mid = (left + right) / 2;
    int midElement = matrix[mid / cols][mid % cols];

    if (element == midElement) {
      return true;
    } else if (element < midElement) {
      right = mid - 1;
    } else {
      left = mid + 1;
    }
  }
}
```

```
        return false;
}
```

The preceding code performs in O(log mn) time, where *m* is the number of rows and *n* is the number of columns in the given matrix. The application is called *SearchInFullSortedMatrix*.

Coding challenge 11 – Searching in a sorted matrix

Amazon, Microsoft, Flipkart

Problem: Consider you've been given a sorted matrix of integers of size *rows* x *cols*. Each row and each column are sorted in ascending order. Write a snippet of code that returns `true` if a given integer is in this matrix.

Solution: Notice that this problem is not like the previous coding challenge since the first integer of each row doesn't have to be greater than the last integer of the previous row. If we apply the Binary Search algorithm (as we did for the previous coding challenge), then we must apply it to every row. Since Binary Search has a complexity time of O(log n) and we have to apply it to every row, this means that this approach will perform in O(m log n) time, where *m* is the number of rows and *n* is the number of columns in the given matrix.

In order to find a solution, let's consider the following diagram (a matrix of 4 x 6):

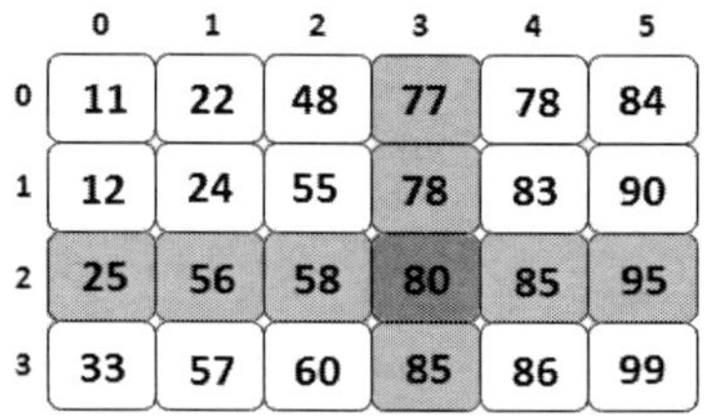

	0	1	2	3	4	5
0	11	22	48	77	78	84
1	12	24	55	78	83	90
2	25	56	58	80	85	95
3	33	57	60	85	86	99

Figure 14.26 – Searching in a sorted matrix

Let's assume that we search for the element 80, which can be found at (2, 3). Let's try to deduce this position. The climax of this deduction orbits the fact that the matrix has sorted rows and columns. Let's analyze the start of the columns: if the start of a column is greater than 80 (for example, column 4), then we know that 80 cannot be in that column, since the start of the column is the minimum element in that column. Moreover, 80 cannot be found in any of the columns to the right of that column since the start element of each column must increase in size from left to right. Furthermore, we can apply the same logic to rows. If the start of a row is greater than 80, then we know that 80 cannot be in that row or subsequent (downward) rows.

Now, if we look at the end of the columns and rows, we can deduce some similar conclusions (mirrored conclusions). If the end of a column is less than 80 (for example, column 2), then we know that 80 cannot be in that column since the end of the column is the maximum element in that column. Moreover, 80 cannot be found in any of the columns to the left of that column since the start element of each column must decrease in size from right to left. Furthermore, we can apply the same logic to rows. If the end of a row is less than 80, then we know that 80 cannot be in that row or subsequent (upward) rows.

If we join, synthesize, and generalize these conclusions for an element, p, then we can deduce the following:

- If the start of a column is greater than p, then p must be to the left of that column.
- If the start of a row is greater than p, then p must be above that row.
- If the end of a column is less than p, then p must be to the right of that column.
- If the end of a row is less than p, then p must be below that row.

This is already starting to look like an algorithm. There is one more thing that we must decide, though. Where do we start from? From which row and column? Fortunately, we have several options. For example, we can start with the greatest column (0, *last column*) and work to the left of the same row, or with the greatest row (*last row*, 0) and work up on the same column.

Let's assume that we choose to start with the greatest column (0, *last column*) and work to the left to find the element, p. This means that our flow will be as follows (let's denote $i=0$ and $j=cols$-1):

1. If *matrix*[i][j] > p, then move left in the same row. The elements in this column are definitely greater than *matrix*[i][j] and hence, by extension, greater than p. So, we discard the current column, decrease j by 1, and repeat.

2. If *matrix*[i][j] < p, then move down in the same column. The elements in this row are definitely less than *matrix*[i][j] and hence, by extension, less than p. So, we discard the current row, increase i by 1, and repeat.

3. If p is equal to *matrix*[i][j], return `true`.

If we apply this algorithm to find element 80 in our 4 x 6 matrix, then the path from (0, 5) to (2, 3) will be as follows:

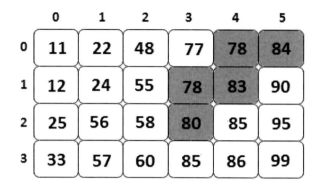

Figure 14.27 – Path to the solution

If we put this algorithm into code, then we get the following:

```
public static boolean search(int[][] matrix, int element) {

    int row = 0;
    int col = matrix[0].length - 1;

    while (row < matrix.length && col >= 0) {

        if (matrix[row][col] == element) {
            return true;
        } else if (matrix[row][col] > element) {
            col--;
        } else {
            row++;
        }
    }

    return false;
}
```

The time complexity of this algorithm is O(m+n), where *m* is the number of rows and *n* is the number of columns. The complete application is called *SearchInSortedMatrix*. It also contains a recursive implementation of this algorithm.

Coding challenge 12 – First position of first one

Amazon, Google, Adobe

Problem: Consider you've been given an array that contains only values of 0 and 1. There is at least a 0 and a 1. All 0s comes first, followed by 1s. Write a snippet of code that returns the index of the first 1 in this array.

Solution: Consider the array *arr*=[0, 0, 0, 1, 1, 1, 1]. The searched index is 3 since *arr*[3] is 1, and this is the first 1.

Since 0s comes first, followed by 1s, the array is sorted.

> **Note**
> Since this is a very common topic in interviews, I'll say it again: when we have to find something in a sorted array, we have to consider the Binary Search algorithm.

In this case, the Binary Search algorithm can be implemented quite easily. The middle point that's computed in Binary Search can fall on 0 or 1. Since the array is sorted, if the middle point falls on 0, then we know for sure that the first value of 1 must be on the right-hand side of the middle point, so we discard the left-hand side of the middle point. On the other hand, if the middle point falls on 1, then we know that the first value of 1 must on the left-hand side of the middle point, so we discard the right-hand side of the middle point. The following code clarifies this:

```java
public static int firstOneIndex(int[] arr) {

    if (arr == null) {
        return -1;
    }

    int left = 0;
    int right = arr.length - 1;

    while (left <= right) {

        int middle = 1 + (right - left) / 2;

        if (arr[middle] == 0) {
            left = middle + 1;
```

```
        } else {
            right = middle - 1;
        }

        if (arr[left] == 1) {
            return left;
        }
    }

    return -1;
}
```

The complete application is called *PositionOfFirstOne*.

Coding challenge 13 – Maximum difference between two elements

Problem: Consider you've been given an array of integers, *arr*. Write a snippet of code that return the maximum difference between two elements when the larger integer appears after the smaller integer.

Solution: Let's consider several examples.

If the given array is 1, 34, 21, 7, 4, 8, 10, then the maximum difference is 33 (computed as 34 (index 1) - 1 (index 0)). If the given arrays is 17, 9, 2, 26, 32, 27, 3, then the maximum difference is 30 (computed as 32 (index 4) - 2 (index 2)).

How about an array sorted in ascending order, such as 3, 7, 9, 11? In this case, the maximum difference is 11 - 3 = 8, so this is the difference between the maximum and the minimum element. How about an array sorted in descending order such as 11, 9, 7, 6? In this case, the maximum difference is 6 - 7 = -1, so the maximum difference is the difference closest to 0.

Based on these examples, we can think of several solutions. For example, we can start by computing the minimum and maximum of the array. Next, if the index of the maximum is greater than the index of the minimum, then the maximum difference is the difference between the maximum and the minimum of the array. Otherwise, we need to compute the next minimum and maximum of the array and repeat this process. This can lead to a complexity time of $O(n^2)$.

Another approach can start by sorting the array. Afterward, the maximum difference will be the difference between the maximum and the minimum elements (the difference between the last and the first elements). This can be implemented via a sorting algorithm in O(n log n) runtime.

How about doing it in O(n) time? Instead of sorting the array or computing its maximum or minimum, we try another approach. Note that if we consider that p is the first element from the array, we can compute the difference between every successive element and p. While we are doing this, we are tracking the maximum difference and updating it accordingly. For example, if the array is 3, 5, 2, 1, 7, 4 and $p=3$, then the maximum difference is $7-p=7-3=4$. However, if we look carefully, the real maximum difference is $7-1=6$ and 1 is smaller than p. This leads us to the conclusion that, while traversing the elements successive to p, if the current traversed element is smaller than p, then p should become that element. Subsequent differences are computed between the successors of this p until the array is completely traversed or we find another element smaller than p. In such a case, we repeat this process.

Let's see the code:

```
public static int maxDiff(int arr[]) {

  int len = arr.length;
  int maxDiff = arr[1] - arr[0];
  int marker = arr[0];

  for (int i = 1; i < len; i++) {

    if (arr[i] - marker > maxDiff) {
      maxDiff = arr[i] - marker;
    }

    if (arr[i] < marker) {
      marker = arr[i];
    }
  }

  return maxDiff;
}
```

This code runs in O(n) time. The complete application is called *MaxDiffBetweenTwoElements*.

Coding challenge 14 – Stream ranking

Problem: Consider you've been given a stream of integers (such as a continuous flux of integer values). Periodically, we want to inspect the rank of a given integer, *p*. By rank, we understand the number of values less than or equal to *p*. Implement the data structure and algorithm that supports this operation.

Solution: Let's consider the following stream: 40, 30, 45, 15, 33, 42, 56, 5, 17, 41, 67. The rank of 45 is 8, the rank of 5 is 0, the rank of 17 is 2, and so on.

The brute-force approach may work on a sorted array. Each time a new integer is generated, we add it to this array. While this will be very convenient for returning the rank of a given integer, this approach has an important drawback: each time we insert an element, we have to shift the elements greater than the new integer to make room for it. This is needed to maintain the array when it's sorted in ascending order.

A much better choice consists of a **Binary Search Tree** (**BST**). A BST maintains a relative order and inserting a new integer will update the tree accordingly. Let's add the integers from our stream to a Binary Search Tree, as follows:

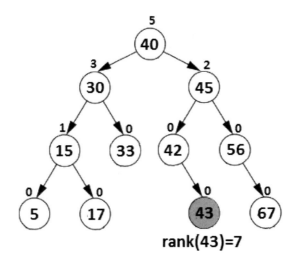

Figure 14.28 – BST for stream ranking

Let's suppose that we want to find rank 43. First, we compare 43 with the root and we conclude that 43 must be in the right sub-tree of the root, 40. However, the root has 5 nodes in its left sub-tree (obviously, all of them are smaller than the root), so the rank of 43 is at least 6 (5 nodes of the left sub-tree of the root, plus the root). Next, we compare 43 with 45 and we conclude that 43 must be to the left of 45, so the rank remains 5. Finally, we compare 43 with 42, and we conclude that 43 must be in the right sub-tree of 42. The rank must be increased by 1, so the rank of 43 is 7.

So, how can we generalize this example with an algorithm? Here, we noticed that, for each node, we already know the rank of its left sub-tree. This doesn't need to be computed each time the rank is required since this will be quite inefficient. We can track and update the rank of the left sub-tree each time a new element is generated and inserted into the tree. In the preceding diagram, each node has its sub-tree rank highlighted above the node. When the rank of a node is required, we already know the rank of its left sub-tree. Next, we have to consider the following recursive steps, which are applied via `int getRank(Node node, int element)`:

1. If `element` is equal to `node.element`, then return `node.leftTreeSize`.
2. If `element` is on the left of `node`, then return `getRank(node.left, element)`.
3. If `element` is on the right of `node`, then return `node.leftTreeSize + 1 + getRank(node.right, element)`.

If the given integer is not found, then we return -1. The relevant code is listed here:

```
public class Stream {

  private Node root = null;

  private class Node {

    private final int element;
    private int leftTreeSize;
    private Node left;
    private Node right;

    private Node(int element) {
      this.element = element;
      this.left = null;
```

```java
            this.right = null;
        }
    }

    /* add a new node into the tree */
    public void generate(int element) {

        if (root == null) {
            root = new Node(element);
        } else {
            insert(root, element);
        }
    }


    private void insert(Node node, int element) {

        if (element <= node.element) {
            if (node.left != null) {
                insert(node.left, element);
            } else {
                node.left = new Node(element);
            }
            node.leftTreeSize++;
        } else {
            if (node.right != null) {
                insert(node.right, element);
            } else {
                node.right = new Node(element);
            }
        }
    }

    /* return rank of 'element' */
    public int getRank(int element) {
        return getRank(root, element);
    }
```

```
    private int getRank(Node node, int element) {

  if (element == node.element) {
    return node.leftTreeSize;
  } else if (element < node.element) {
    if (node.left == null) {
      return -1;
    } else {
      return getRank(node.left, element);
    }
  } else {
    int rightTreeRank = node.right == null
      ? -1 : getRank(node.right, element);

    if (rightTreeRank == -1) {
      return -1;
    } else {
      return node.leftTreeSize + 1 + rightTreeRank;
    }
  }
 }
}
```

The preceding code will run in O(log n) time on a balanced tree and O(n) time on an unbalanced tree, where *n* is the number of nodes in the tree. The complete application is called *RankInStream*.

Coding challenge 15 – Peaks and valleys

Amazon, Google, Adobe, Microsoft, Flipkart

Problem: Consider you've been given an array of positive integers representing terrain elevations. If an integer from this array is greater than or equal to its neighbors (adjacent integers), then this integer is called a *peak*. On the other hand, if an integer from this array is smaller than or equal to its neighbors (adjacent integers), then this integer is called a *valley*. For example, for array 4, 5, 8, 3, 2, 1, 7, 8, 5, 9, we can see that 8 (both) and 9 are peaks, while 4, 1, and 5 (except the last one) are valleys. Write a snippet of code that sorts the given array into an alternating sequence of peaks and valleys.

Solution: At first sight, a handy solution would be to start by sorting the array in ascending order. Once the array is sorted as $l1 \leq l2 \leq l3 \leq l4 \leq l5 ...$, we can see each triplet of numbers as $large(l1) \leq larger(l2) \leq largest(l3)$. If we swap $l2$ with $l3$, then $l1 \leq l3 \geq l2$, so $l3$ becomes a peak. For the next triplet, $l2 \leq l4 \leq l5$, we swap $l4$ with $l5$ to obtain $l2 \leq l5 \geq l4$, so $l5$ is a peak. For the next triplet, $l4 \leq l6 \leq l7$, we swap $l6$ with $l7$ to obtain $l4 \leq l7 \geq l6$, so $l7$ is a peak. If we continue these swaps, then we obtain something like this: $l1 \leq l3 \geq l2 \leq l5 \geq l4 \leq l7 \geq l6$ .... But is this efficient? Since we have to sort the array, we can say that the time complexity of this solution is O(n log n). Can we do better than this? Yes, we can! Let's assume that we represent our array as follows:

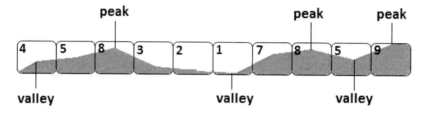

Figure 14.29 – Given array of terrain elevations

Now, we can clearly see the peaks and valleys of the given array. If we focus on the first triplet (4, 5, 8) and try to obtain a peak, then we have to swap the value from the middle (5) with the maximum between its neighbors (adjacent integers). So, by swapping 5 with max(4, 8), we obtain (4, 8, 5). Therefore, 8 is a peak and can be represented as follows:

Figure 14.30 – Swapping 5 with 8

Next, let's focus on the next triplet (5, 3, 2). We can obtain a peak by swapping 3 with max(5, 2), so by swapping 3 with 5. The result is (3, 5, 2), as shown here:

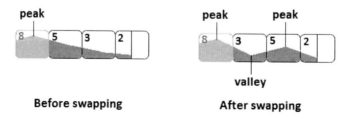

Figure 14.31 – Swapping 3 with 5

Now, 5 is a peak and 3 is a valley. We should continue with the triplet (2, 1, 7) and swap 1 with 7 to obtain the peak (2, 7, 1). The next triplet will be (1, 8, 5) and have 8 as a peak (there is nothing to swap). In the end, we obtain the final result, as can be seen in the following diagram:

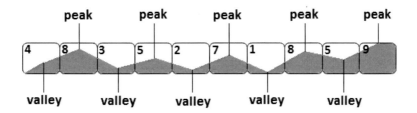

Figure 14.32 – Final result

The interviewer will want you to pay attention to details and mention them. For example, when we swap the middle value with the left value, can we break the already processed terrain? Can we break a valley or a peak? The answer is no, we cannot break anything. This is because when we swap the middle with the left, we already know that the middle value is smaller than the left value and that the left value is a valley. Therefore, we just create a deeper valley by adding an even smaller value to that place.

Based on these statements, the implementation is quite simple. The following code will clarify any remaining details:

```
public static void sort(int[] arr) {

    for (int i = 1; i < arr.length; i += 2) {

        int maxFoundIndex = maxElementIndex(arr, i - 1, i, i + 1);
        if (i != maxFoundIndex) {
            swap(arr, i, maxFoundIndex);
        }
    }
}

private static int maxElementIndex(int[] arr,
  int left, int middle, int right) {

    int arrLength = arr.length;
    int leftElement = left >= 0 && left < arrLength
```

```
            ? arr[left] : Integer.MIN_VALUE;
    int middleElement = middle >= 0 && middle < arrLength
            ? arr[middle] : Integer.MIN_VALUE;
    int rightElement = right >= 0 && right < arrLength
            ? arr[right] : Integer.MIN_VALUE;

    int maxElement = Math.max(leftElement,
        Math.max(middleElement, rightElement));

    if (leftElement == maxElement) {
        return left;
    } else if (middleElement == maxElement) {
        return middle;
    } else {
        return right;
    }
}
```

This code performs in O(n) complexity time. The complete application is called *PeaksAndValleys*.

Coding challenge 16 – Nearest left smaller number

Amazon, Google, Adobe, Microsoft, Flipkart

Problem: Consider you've been given an array of integers, *arr*. Write a snippet of code that finds and prints the nearest smaller number for every element so that the smaller element is on left-hand side.

Solution: Let's consider the given array; that is, 4, 1, 8, 3, 8, 2, 6, 7, 4, 9. The expected result is _, _, 1, 1, 3, 1, 2, 6, 2, 4. From left to right, we have the following:

- *arr*[0]=4 and in its left there is no element, so we print _.
- *arr*[1]=1 and in its left there is no element smaller than it, so we print _.
- *arr*[2]=8 and the nearest smallest element in its left is 1, so we print 1.
- *arr*[3]=3 and the nearest smallest element in its left is 1, so we print 1.
- *arr*[4]=8 and the nearest smallest element in its left is 3, so we print 3.
- *arr*[5]=2 and the nearest smallest element in its left is 1, so we print 1.

- *arr*[6]=6 and the nearest smallest element in its left is 2, so we print 2
- *arr*[7]=7 and the nearest smallest element in its left is 6, so we print 6
- *arr*[8]=4 and the nearest smallest element in its left is 2, so we print 2
- *arr*[9]=9 and the nearest smallest element in its left is 4, so we print 4

A simple but inefficient solution relies on two loops. The outer loop can start from the second element (index 1) and go to the length of the array (*arr.length*-1), while the inner loop traverses all the elements on the left-hand side of the element picked by the outer loop. As soon as it finds an element smaller, it stops the process. Such an algorithm is very easy to implement, but it runs in $O(n^2)$ complexity time.

However, we can reduce the time complexity to $O(n)$ via a Stack. Mainly, we can traverse the given array from 0 to *arr.length*-1 and rely on a Stack to track the subsequence of elements that have been traversed so far that are smaller than any later element that has already been traversed. While this statement may sound complicated, let's clarify it by looking at this algorithm's steps:

1. Create a new, empty stack.
2. For every element of *arr*, (*i* = 0 to *arr.length*-1), we do the following:

    a. While the stack is not empty and the top element is greater than or equal to *arr*[*i*], we pop from the stack.

    b. If the stack is empty, then there is no element in the left of *arr*[*i*]. We can print a symbol representing no element found (for example, -1 or _).

    c. If the stack is not empty, then the nearest smaller value to *arr*[*i*] is the top element of the stack. We can peek and print this element.

    d. Push *arr*[*i*] into the stack.

In terms of code, we have the following:

```
public static void leftSmaller(int arr[]) {

  Stack<Integer> stack = new Stack<>();

  // While the top element of the stack is greater than
  // equal to arr[i] remove it from the stack
  for (int i = 0; i < arr.length; i++) {
    while (!stack.empty() && stack.peek() >= arr[i]) {
      stack.pop();
```

```
    }

    // if stack is empty there is no left smaller element
    if (stack.empty()) {
      System.out.print("_, ");
    } else {
      // the top of the stack is the left smaller element
      System.out.print(stack.peek() + ", ");
    }

    // push arr[i] into the stack
    stack.push(arr[i]);
  }
}
```

This code has a runtime of O(n), where *n* is the number of elements in the given array. The complete application is called *FindNearestMinimum*.

Coding challenge 17 – Word search

Amazon, Google

Problem: Consider you've been given a 2D board (a matrix) and a word. Each cell of the board contains a letter. You can construct a word by concatenating the letters from cells that are horizontally or vertically neighboring. Write a snippet of code that returns `true` if the given word is present on the board. The same letter cell may not be used more than once.

Solution: Let's consider that we have the following board:

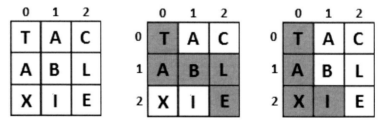

Figure 14.33 – Board sample

Remember that this is not the first time where we need to solve a problem that requires us to find a certain path in a grid. In *Chapter 8, Recursion and Dynamic Programming*, we had the *Robot grid* problems, including *Color spots, Five Towers, The falling ball,* and *Knight tour*. In *Chapter 12, Stacks and Queues*, we had *Islands*. Finally, in *Chapter 13, Trees and Graphs*, we had *Chess knight*.

Based on the experience you've accumulated from these problems, challenge yourself to write an implementation for this problem without having any further instructions. The complete application is called *WordSearch*. If *k* is the length of the given word and the board has a size of *m* x *n*, then this application runs in O(m * n * 4^k) time.

Coding challenge 18 – Sorting an array based on another array

Amazon, **Google**, **Microsoft**

Problem: Consider you've been given two arrays. Write a snippet of code that reorders the elements of the first array according to the order defined by the second array.

Solution: Let's consider we've been given the following two arrays:

```
int[] firstArr = {4, 1, 8, 1, 3, 8, 6, 7, 4, 9, 8, 2, 5, 3};
int[] secondArr = {7, 4, 8, 11, 2};
```

The expected result is {7, 4, 4, 8, 8, 8, 2, 1, 1, 3, 3, 5, 6, 9}.

The solution to this problem relies on *hashing*. More precisely, we can employ the following algorithm:

1. Count and store the frequency of each element from the first array in a map.
2. For each element of the second array, check if the current element from the second array is present in the map or not.

   Then, do the following:

   a. If so, then set it *n* times in the first array (*n* is the frequency of the current element from the second array in the first array).

   b. Remove the current element from the map so that, in the end, the map will contain only the elements that are present in the first array but are not present in the second array.

3. Append the elements from the map to the end of the first array (these are already sorted since we used a `TreeSet`).

Let's see the code:

```java
public static void custom(int[] firstArr, int[] secondArr) {

    // store the frequency of each element of first array
    // using a TreeMap stores the data sorted
    Map<Integer, Integer> frequencyMap = new TreeMap<>();

    for (int i = 0; i < firstArr.length; i++) {
      frequencyMap.putIfAbsent(firstArr[i], 0);
      frequencyMap.put(firstArr[i],
            frequencyMap.get(firstArr[i]) + 1);
    }

    // overwrite elements of first array
    int index = 0;

    for (int i = 0; i < secondArr.length; i++) {

        // if the current element is present in the 'frequencyMap'
        // then set it n times (n is the frequency of
        // that element in the first array)
        int n = frequencyMap.getOrDefault(secondArr[i], 0);
        while (n-- > 0) {
           firstArr[index++] = secondArr[i];
        }

        // remove the element from map
        frequencyMap.remove(secondArr[i]);
    }

    // copy the remaining elements (the elements that are
    // present in the first array but not present
    // in the second array)
    for (Map.Entry<Integer, Integer> entry :
          frequencyMap.entrySet() {
```

```
      int count = entry.getValue();
      while (count-- > 0) {
         firstArr[index++] = entry.getKey();
      }
   }
}
```

The runtime of this code is O(m log m + n), where *m* is the number of elements in the first array and *n* is the number of elements in the second array. The complete application is called *SortArrayBasedOnAnotherArray*.

Well, this was the last problem in this chapter. Now, it's time to summarize our work!

Summary

This was a comprehensive chapter that covered sorting and searching algorithms. You saw the implementations of Merge Sort, Quick Sort, Radix Sort, Heap Sort, Bucket Sort, and Binary Search. Moreover, in the code bundled with this book, there's an application called *SortArraysIn14Ways* that contains the implementations of 14 sorting algorithms.

In the next chapter, we will cover a suite of problems categorized as mathematical and puzzle problems.

15
Mathematics and Puzzles

This chapter covers a controversial topic that's faced in interviews: mathematics and puzzle problems. A significant number of companies consider that these kinds of problems should not be part of a technical interview, while other companies still consider this topic relevant.

The problems included in this topic are brain-teasing and may require a decent level of knowledge in mathematics and logic. You should expect such problems if you plan to apply to a company that works in academic fields (mathematics, physics, chemistry, and so on). However, big companies such as Amazon and Google are also willing to rely on such problems.

In this chapter, we will cover the following topics:

- Tips and suggestions
- Coding challenges

By the end of this chapter, you should be familiar with these kinds of problems and be able to explore more such problems.

Technical requirements

All the code files present in this chapter are available on GitHub at `https://github.com/PacktPublishing/The-Complete-Coding-Interview-Guide-in-Java/tree/master/Chapter15`.

Tips and suggestions

When you get a brain-teaser problem, the most important aspect is to not panic. Read the problem several times and write down your conclusions in a systematic approach. It is mandatory to clearly identify what input, output, and constraints it should obey.

Try to take several examples (input data samples), make some sketches, and keep talking with the interviewer while analyzing the problem. The interviewer doesn't expect you to have the solution immediately, but they are expecting to hear you talking while trying to solve the problem. This way, the interviewer can track the logic of your ideas and understand how you approach the problem.

Also, it is very important to write down any rules or patterns that you noticed while developing the solution. With every statement you write down, you are closer to the solution. Commonly, if you look from the solution perspective (you know the solution), such problems are not extremely hard; they just require a high level of observation and increased attention.

Let's try a simple example. Two fathers and two sons sit down and eat eggs. They eat exactly three eggs; each person has an egg. How is this possible?

If this is the first time you've seen such a problem, you may think that it is illogical or impossible to solve. It is normal to think that there is some mistake in the text (there was probably four eggs, not three) and read it again and again. These are the most common reactions to brain-teaser problems. Once you see the solution, it looks quite simple.

Now, let's act as a candidate in the presence of the interviewer. The following paragraphs follow a *thinking aloud approach*.

It may seem obvious that if each person has an egg and there are three eggs, then one of them doesn't have any egg. So, you may think that the answer is that three people eat an egg (each of them eats an egg) and that the fourth person doesn't eat anything. But the problem says that two fathers and two sons sit down and eat eggs, so all four of them eat eggs.

How about thinking like this: each person has an egg and they (four people) eat exactly three eggs, so it doesn't say that each person *eats* an egg; they only *have* an egg. Maybe one of them shares their egg with another person. Hmmm, this doesn't seem too logical!

Is it possible to have only three people? If one of the fathers is also a grandfather, this means that the other father is a son and a father at the same time. This way, we have two fathers and two sons via three people. They eat three eggs and each of them has an egg. Problem solved!

As you can see, the solution is the result of a cascade of reasoning that eliminates the wrong solutions one by one. Trying to solve the problem by eliminating the wrong solutions via logical deduction is one of the approaches to solving these kinds of problems. Other problems are just about computing. Most of the time, there are no complicated computations or a lot of computations, but they require mathematical knowledge and/or deductions.

It is quite hard to claim that there are some tricks and tips that will help you solve math and logical puzzle problems in seconds. The best approach is to practice as much as possible. With that, let's proceed with the *Coding challenges* section.

Coding challenges

In the following 15 coding challenges, we will focus on the most popular problems from the math and logical puzzles category. Let's get started!

Coding challenge 1 – FizzBuzz

Adobe, **Microsoft**

Problem: Consider you've been given a positive integer, *n*. Write a problem that prints the numbers from 1 to *n*. For multiples of five, print *fizz*, for multiples of seven, print *buzz*, and for multiples of five and seven, print *fizzbuzz*. Print a new line after each string or number.

Solution: This is a simple problem that relies on your knowledge of division and the Java modulus (%) operator. When we divide two numbers, the *dividend* and the *divisor*, we get a *quotient* and the *remainder*. In Java, we can obtain the remainder of a division via the modulus (%) operator. In other words, if *X* is the dividend and *Y* is the divisor, then *X* modulus *Y* (written in Java as *X* % *Y*) returns the remainder of dividing *X* by *Y*. For example, 11(dividend) / 2(divisor) = 5(quotient) 1(remainder), so 11 % 2 = 1.

Put another way, if the remainder is 0, then the dividend is a multiple of the divisor; otherwise, it's not. So, a multiple of five must respect that $X \% 5 = 0$, while a multiple of seven must respect that $X \% 7 = 0$. Based on these relations, we can write the solution to this problem as follows:

```
public static void print(int n) {

  for (int i = 1; i <= n; i++) {
    if (((i % 5) == 0) && ((i % 7) == 0)) { // multiple of 5&7
      System.out.println("fizzbuzz");
    } else if ((i % 5) == 0) { // multiple of 5
      System.out.println("fizz");
    } else if ((i % 7) == 0) { // multiple of 7
      System.out.println("buzz");
    } else {
      System.out.println(i); // not a multiple of 5 or 7
    }
  }
}
```

The complete application is called *FizzBuzz*.

Coding challenge 2 – Roman numerals

Amazon, Google, Adobe, Microsoft, Flipkart

Problem: Consider you've been given a positive integer, *n*. Write a snippet of code that converts this number into its Roman number representation. For example, if *n*=34, then the Roman number is XXXIV. You've been given the following constants, which contain the Roman number symbols:

SYMBOL	VALUE
I	1
IV	4
V	5
IX	9
X	10
XL	40
L	50
XC	90
C	100
CD	400
D	500
CM	900
M	1000

Figure 15.1 – Roman numbers

Solution: This problem relies on the fact that Roman numbers are common knowledge. If you've never heard about Roman numbers, then it is advisable to mention this to the interviewer. They will probably agree to give you another coding challenge in place of this one. But if you do know what the Roman numbers are, then great – let's see how we can write an application that solves this problem.

The algorithm for this problem can be deduced from several examples. Let's look at several use cases:

- $n = 73 = 50+10+10+1+1+1 = L+X+X+I+I+I = LXXIII$
- $n = 558 = 500+50+5+1+1+1 = D+L+V+I+I+I = DLVIII$
- $n = 145 = 100+(50-10)+5 = C+(L-X)+V = C+XL+V = CXLV$
- $n = 34 = 10+10+10+(5-1) = X+X+X+(V-I) = X+X+X+IV = XXXIV$
- $n = 49 = (50-10)+(10-1) = (L-X)+(X-I) = XL+IX = XLIX$

Roughly, we take the given number and try to find the Roman symbols corresponding to ones, tens, hundreds, or thousands. This algorithm can be expressed as follows:

1. Start from the thousand's place and print the corresponding Roman number. For example, if the digit at thousand's place is 4, then print the Roman equivalent of 4,000, which is MMMM.

2. Continue by dividing the number using digits at hundred's place and print the corresponding Roman number.

3. Continue by dividing the number using digits at ten's place and print the corresponding Roman number.

4. Continue by dividing the number using digits at one's place and print the corresponding Roman number.

In terms of code, this algorithm works as follows:

```java
private static final String HUNDREDTHS[]
  = {"", "C", "CC", "CCC", "CD", "D",
     "DC", "DCC", "DCCC", "CM"};
private static final String TENS[]
  = {"", "X", "XX", "XXX",
     "XL", "L", "LX", "LXX", "LXXX", "XC"};
private static final String ONES[]
  = {"", "I", "II", "III", "IV", "V",
     "VI", "VII", "VIII", "IX"};

public static String convert(int n) {

  String roman = "";

  // Step 1
  while (n >= 1000) {
    roman = roman + 'M';
    n -= 1000;
  }

  // Step 2
  roman = roman + HUNDREDTHS[n / 100];
  n = n % 100;

  // Step 3
  roman = roman + TENS[n / 10];
  n = n % 10;

  // Step 4
  roman = roman + ONES[n];
```

```
    return roman;
}
```

The complete application is called *RomanNumbers*. Another approach relies on successive subtractions instead of division. The *RomanNumbers* application contains this implementation as well.

Coding challenge 3 – Visiting and toggling 100 doors

Adobe, Microsoft, Flipkart

Problem: Consider you've been given 100 doors in a row that are initially closed. You have to visit these doors 100 times and each time you do, you start from the first door. For each visited door, you toggle it (if it is closed, then you open it, and vice versa). At the first visit, you visit all 100 doors. At the second visit, you visit every second door (#2, #4, #6 ...). At the third visit, you visit every third door (#3, #6, #9, ...). You follow this pattern until you visit only the 100th door. Write a snippet of code that reveals the state of the doors (closed or opened) after 100 visits.

Solution: The solution to this problem can be intuited by traversing several steps. At the initial state, all 100 doors are closed (in the following image, each 0 is a closed door and each 1 is an opened door):

0000000000000000000000000000000000000000000000000000000000000000000000000000000000000000000000000000

Figure 15.2 – All the doors are closed (initial state)

Now, let's see what we can observe and conclude at each of the following steps:

At the first pass, we open every door (we visit each door, #1, #2, #3, #4, ..., #100):

1111111111111111111111111111111111111111111111111111111111111111111111111111111111111111111111111111

Figure 15.3 – All the doors are opened (step 1)

At the second pass, we only visit the even doors (#2, #4, #6, #8, #10, #12 ...), so the even doors are closed and the odd ones are opened:

1010101010101010101010101010101010101010101010101010101010101010101010101010101010101010101010101010

Figure 15.4 – The even doors are closed and the odd ones are opened (step 2)

At the third pass, we only visit doors #3, #6, #9, #12, …. This time, we close door #3, which we opened on our first visit, open door #6, which was closed on our second visit, and so on and forth:

1000111000111000111000111000111000111000111000111000111000111000111000111000111000111000111000111000111000

Figure 15.5 – The result of applying the third visit (step 3)

At the fourth visit, we only visit doors #4, #8, #12 …. If we continue like this, then at the 100th visit, we will get the following result:

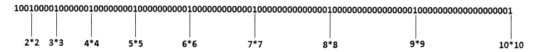

Figure 15.6 – The opened doors are all perfect squares (last visit)

So, at the last visit (the 100th visit), the opened doors are all perfect squares, while the rest of the doors are closed. Obviously, even if we observe this, we don't have the necessary time in an interview to traverse 100 visits. But maybe we don't even need to do all 100 visits to observe this result. Let's assume that we do only 15 steps and we try to see what's happening to a certain door. For example, the following image reveals the state of door #12 over 15 steps:

```
Step 1   11111111111  [1]  111111111 …
Step 2   10101010101  [0]  101010101 …
Step 3   10001110001  [1]  100011100 …
Step 4   10011111001  [0]  100111110 …
         10010111011   0   101111100 …
Step 6   10010011011  [1]  101110100 …
         10010001011   1   111110101 …
         10010000011   1   111010101 …
         10010000111   1   111011101 …
         10010000101   1   111011111 …
         10010000100   1   111011111 …
Step 12  10010000100  [0]  111011111 …
         10010000100   0   011011111 …
         10010000100   0   001011111 …
         10010000100   0   000011111 …
```

Figure 15.7 – Door #12 after 15 steps

Check out the steps highlighted in the preceding image. The state of door #12 has changed at *steps 1, 2, 3, 4, 6,* and *12*. All these steps are divisors of 12. Moreover, *step 1* opens the door, *step 2* closes the door, *step 3* opens the door, *step 4* closes the door, *step 6* opens the door, and *step 12* closes the door. Starting from this observation, we can conclude that for every pair of divisors, the door will just end up back in its initial state, which is closed. In other words, each door that has an even number of divisors remains closed in the end.

Let's see whether this is true for a perfect square, such as 9. The reason for choosing a perfect square relies on the fact that a perfect square always has an odd number of positive divisors. For example, the divisors of 9 are 1, 3, and 9. This means that door #9 remains open.

Based on these two paragraphs, we can conclude that, after 100 visits, the doors that remain opened are those that are perfect squares (#1, #4, #9, #16, ..., #100), while the rest of the doors remain closed.

Once you understand the preceding process, it is quite straightforward to write an application that confirms the final result:

```java
private static final int DOORS = 100;

public static int[] visitToggle() {

    // 0 - closed door
    // 1 - opened door
    int[] doors = new int[DOORS];

    for (int i = 0; i <= (DOORS - 1); i++) {
        doors[i] = 0;
    }

    for (int i = 0; i <= (DOORS - 1); i++) {
        for (int j = 0; j <= (DOORS - 1); j++) {

            if ((j + 1) % (i + 1) == 0) {

                if (doors[j] == 0) {
                    doors[j] = 1;
                } else {
                    doors[j] = 0;
```

```
            }
          }
        }
      }

    return doors;
}
```

The complete application is called *VisitToggle100Doors*.

Coding challenge 4 – 8 teams

Amazon, Google, Adobe

Problem: Consider there's a contest where there's 8 teams. Each team plays twice with other teams. From all these teams, only 4 go to the semi-finals. How many matches should a team win to go through to the semi-finals?

Solution: Let's denote the teams as T1, T2, T3, T4, T5, T6, T7, and T8. If T1 plays with T2...T8, they will play 7 matches. Since each team must play with the other teams twice, we have 8*7=56 matches. If, at each match, a team can win a point, then we have 56 points that are distributed between 8 teams.

Let's consider the worst-case scenario. T0 loses all their games. This means that T0 gets 0 points. On the other hand, T1 wins 2 points against T0 and loses all their other matches, T2 wins 4 points against T0 and T1 and loses all their other matches, T3 wins 6 points against T0, T1, and T2 and loses all their other matches, and so on. T4 wins 8 points, T5 wins 10 points, T6 wins 12 points, and T7 wins 14 points. So, a team that wins all their matches wins 14 points. The last four teams (those that go through to the semi-finals) have won 8+10+12+14=44 points. So, a team can be sure that they go through to the semi-finals if they obtain a minimum of 44/4=11 points.

Coding challenge 5 – Finding the kth number with the prime factors 3, 5, and 7

Adobe, Microsoft

Problem: Design an algorithm to find the kth number where the only prime factors are 3, 5, and 7.

Solution: Having a list of numbers whose only prime factors are 3, 5, and 7 means a list that looks as follows: 1, 3, 5, 7, 9, 15, 21, 25, and so on. Or, to be more suggestive, it can be written as follows: 1, 1*3, 1*5, 1*7, 3*3, 3*5, 3*7, 5*5, 3*3*3, 5*7, 3*3*5, 7*7, and so on.

With this suggestive representation, we can see that we can initially insert the value 1 into a list, while the rest of the elements must be computed. The simplest way to understand the algorithm for determining the rest of the elements is to look at the implementation itself, so let's see it:

```
public static int kth(int k) {

    int count3 = 0;
    int count5 = 0;
    int count7 = 0;

    List<Integer> list = new ArrayList<>();
    list.add(1);

    while (list.size() <= k + 1) {

        int m = min(min(list.get(count3) * 3,
            list.get(count5) * 5), list.get(count7) * 7);

        list.add(m);
        if (m == list.get(count3) * 3) {
            count3++;
        }

        if (m == list.get(count5) * 5) {
            count5++;
        }
```

```
        if (m == list.get(count7) * 7) {
            count7++;
        }
    }

    return list.get(k - 1);
}
```

We can provide an implementation via three queues as well. The steps of this algorithm are as follows:

1. Initialize an integer, *minElem*=1.
2. Initialize three queues; that is, *queue3*, *queue5*, and *queue7*.
3. Loop from 1 to the given *k*-1:
   a. Insert *minElem**3, *minElem**5, and *minElem**7 into *queue3*, *queue5*, and *queue7*, respectively.
   b. Update *minElem* as min(*queue3*.peek, *queue5*.peek, *queue7*.peek).
   c. If *minElem* is *queue3*.peek, then do *queue3*.poll.
   d. If *minElem* is *queue5*.peek, then do *queue5*.poll.
   e. If *minElem* is *queue7*.peek, then do *queue7*.poll.
4. Return *minElem*.

The complete application is called *KthNumber357*. It contains both solutions presented in this section.

Coding challenge 6 – Count decoding a digit's sequence

Amazon, Microsoft, Flipkart

Problem: Consider that *A* is 1, *B* is 2, *C* is 3, ... *Z* is 26. For any given sequence of digits, write a snippet of code that counts the number of possible decodings (for example, 1234 can be decoded as 1 2 3 4, 12 3 4, and 1 23 4, which means as ABCD, LCD, and AWD). The given sequence of digits is valid if it contains digits from 0 to 9. No leading 0s, no extra trailing 0s, and no two or more consecutive 0s are allowed.

Solution: This problem can be solved via recursion or via dynamic programming. Both techniques were covered in *Chapter 8, Recursion and Dynamic Programming*. So, let's look at the recursive algorithm for a sequence of *n* digits:

1. Initialize the total number of decodings with 0.
2. Start from the end of the given sequence of digits.
3. If the last digit is not 0, then apply recursion for the (*n*-1) digits and use the result to update the total number of decodings.
4. If the last two digits represent a number less than 27 (therefore, a valid character), then apply recursion to the (*n*-2) digits and use the result to update the total number of decodings.

In terms of code, we have the following:

```java
public static int decoding(char[] digits, int n) {

    // base cases
    if (n == 0 || n == 1) {
        return 1;
    }

    // if the digits[] starts with 0 (for example, '0212')
    if (digits == null || digits[0] == '0') {
        return 0;
    }

    int count = 0;

    // If the last digit is not 0 then last
    // digit must add to the number of words
    if (digits[n - 1] > '0') {
        count = decoding(digits, n - 1);
    }

    // If the last two digits represents a number smaller
    // than or equal to 26 then consider last two digits
    // and call decoding()
```

```
    if (digits[n - 2] == '1'
        || (digits[n - 2] == '2' && digits[n - 1] < '7')) {
      count += decoding(digits, n - 2);
    }

    return count;
}
```

This code runs in an exponential time. But we can apply dynamic programming to reduce the runtime to O(n) via a similar non-recursive algorithm, as follows:

```
public static int decoding(char digits[]) {

    // if the digits[] starts with 0 (for example, '0212')
    if (digits == null || digits[0] == '0') {
      return 0;
    }

    int n = digits.length;

    // store results of sub-problems
    int count[] = new int[n + 1];

    count[0] = 1;
    count[1] = 1;

    for (int i = 2; i <= n; i++) {
      count[i] = 0;

      // If the last digit is not 0 then last digit must
      // add to the number of words
      if (digits[i - 1] > '0') {
        count[i] = count[i - 1];
      }

      // If the second last digit is smaller than 2 and
      // the last digit is smaller than 7, then last
```

```
        // two digits represent a valid character
        if (digits[i - 2] == '1' || (digits[i - 2] == '2'
            && digits[i - 1] < '7')) {
          count[i] += count[i - 2];
        }
      }

      return count[n];
    }
```

This code runs in O(n) time. The complete application is called *DecodingDigitSequence*.

Coding challenge 7 – ABCD

Problem: Find a number of types, ABCD, such that when multiplied by 4, it gives us DCBA.

Solution: These kinds of problems are usually quite hard. In this case, we have to use some math to solve it.

Let's start with some simple inequalities:

- $1 <= A <= 9$ (A cannot be zero because ABCD is a four-digit number)
- $0 <= B <= 9$
- $0 <= C <= 9$
- $4 <= D <= 9$ (D must be at least 4*A, so it should be at least 4)

Next, we can assume that our number, ABCD, is written as 1000A + 100B + 10C + D. Following the problem statement, we can multiply ABCD by 4 to obtain DCBA, which can be written as 1000D + 100C + 10B + A.

Conforming to divisibility by 4, BA is a two-digit number divisible by 4. Now, the larger ABCD is 2499, because a number greater than 2499 multiplied by 4 will result in a five-digit number.

Next, A can be 1 and 2. However, if BA is a two-digit number divisible by 4, then A must be even, so it must be 2.

Continuing with this logic, this means that D is either 8 or 9. However, since D times 4 would end in 2, D must be 8.

Moreover, 4000A + 400B + 40C + 4D = 1000D + 100C + 10B + A. Since A=2 and D=8, this can be written as 2C-13B=1. B and C can only be a single digit integer in [1, 7], but B must be odd since BA is a two-digit number divisible by 4. Since the greatest possible number is 2499, this means that B can be 1 or 3.

So, the result is 2178 because 2178*4=8712, so ABCD*4=DCBA.

We can use the brute-force approach to find this number as well. The following code speaks for itself:

```java
public static void find() {

  for (int i = 1000; i < 2499; i++) {

    int p = i;
    int q = i * 4;

    String m = String.valueOf(p);
    String n = new StringBuilder(String.valueOf(q))
      .reverse().toString();

    p = Integer.parseInt(m);
    q = Integer.parseInt(n);

    if (p == q) {
      System.out.println("\n\nFound: " + p + " : " + (q * 4));
      break;
    }
  }
}
```

The complete application is called *Abcd*.

Coding challenge 8 – Rectangles overlapping

Amazon, Google, Microsoft

Problem: Consider you've been given two rectangles. Write a snippet of code that returns `true` if these rectangles overlap (also referred to as colliding or intersecting).

Solution: This problem sounds a little bit vague. It is important to discuss this with the interviewer and agree about two important aspects:

The two rectangles are parallel to each other and form an angle of 0 degrees with the horizontal plane (they are parallel to the coordinate axes) or can they be rotated under an angle?

Most of the time, the given rectangles are parallel to each other and to the coordinate axes. If rotation is involved, then the solution requires some geometry knowledge that is not so obvious during an interview. Most probably, the interviewer wants to test your logic, not your knowledge of geometry, but challenge yourself and implement the problem for non-parallel rectangles as well.

Are the coordinates of the rectangles given in the Cartesian plane? The answer should be affirmative since this is a common coordinates system used in mathematics. This means that a rectangle increases its size from left to right and from bottom to top.

So, let's denote the rectangles as *r1* and *r2*. Each of them is given via the coordinates of the top-left corner and bottom-right corner. The top-left corner of *r1* has the coordinates *r1lt.x* and *r1lt.y*, while the bottom-right corner has the coordinates *r2rb.x* and *r2rb.y*, as shown in the following diagram:

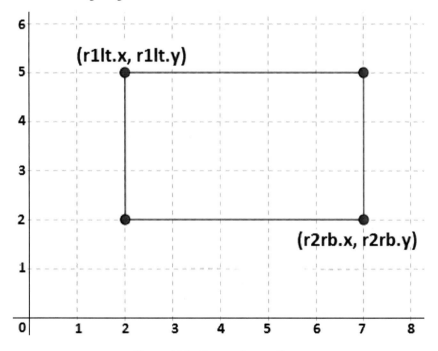

Figure 15.8 – Rectangle coordinates

We might say that two rectangles are overlapping if they *touch* each other (they at least have a common point). In other words, the five pairs of rectangles shown in the following diagram overlap:

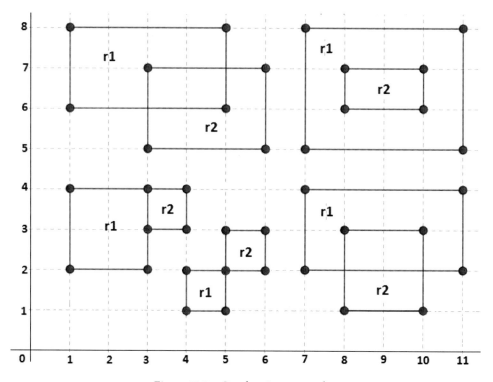

Figure 15.9 – Overlapping rectangles

From the preceding diagram, we can conclude that two rectangles that don't overlap can be in one of the following four cases:

- *r1* is totally to the right of *r2*.
- *r1* is totally to the left of *r2*.
- *r1* is totally above *r2*.
- *r1* is totally below *r2*.

The following diagram reveals these four cases:

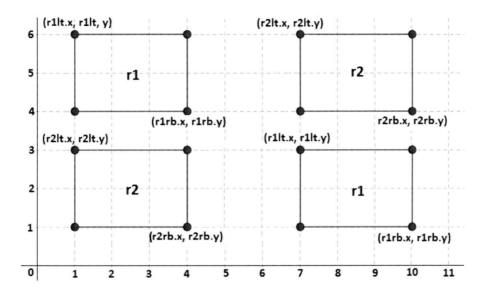

Figure 15.10 – Non-overlapping rectangles

We can express the preceding four bullets in terms of coordinates, as follows:

- *r1* is totally to the right of *r2* →*r1lt.x>r2rb.x*
- *r1* is totally to the left of *r2* →*r2lt.x>r1rb.x*
- *r1* is totally above *r2* →*r1rb.y>r2lt.y*
- *r1* is totally below *r2* →*r2rb.y>r1lt.y*

So, if we group these conditions into code, we get the following:

```
public static boolean overlap(Point r1lt, Point r1rb,
      Point r2lt, Point r2rb) {

  // r1 is totally to the right of r2 or vice versa
  if (r1lt.x > r2rb.x || r2lt.x > r1rb.x) {
    return false;
  }

  // r1 is totally above r2 or vice versa
  if (r1rb.y > r2lt.y || r2rb.y > r1lt.y) {
    return false;
  }
```

```
        return true;
}
```

This code runs in O(1) time. Alternatively, we can condense these two conditions into a single one, as follows:

```
public static boolean overlap(Point r1lt, Point r1rb,
        Point r2lt, Point r2rb) {

  return (r1lt.x <= r2rb.x && r1rb.x >= r2lt.x
        && r1lt.y >= r2rb.y && r1rb.y <= r2lt.y);
}
```

The complete applications is called *RectangleOverlap*. Note that the interviewer may define *overlapping* in different ways. Based on this problem, you should be able to adapt the code accordingly.

Coding challenge 9 – Multiplying large numbers

Amazon, Microsoft

Problem: Consider you've been given two positive large numbers as strings, *a* and *b*. These numbers don't fit in `int` or `long` domains. Write a snippet of code that computes *a*b*.

Solution: Let's consider that *a*=4145775 and *b*=771467. Then, *a*b*=3198328601925. Solving this problem relies on mathematics. The following image depicts the *a*b* solution that can be applied on paper and coded as well:

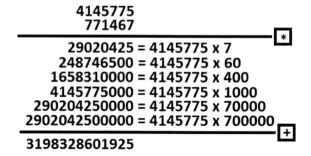

Figure 15.11 – Multiplying two large numbers

Mainly, we rely on the fact that multiplication can be written as a suite of additions. So, we can write 771467 as 7+60+400+1000+70000+700000 and we multiply each of these numbers by 4145775. Finally, we add the results to obtain the final result, 3198328601925. Taking this logic one step further, we can take the last digit of the first number (5) and multiply it by all the digits of the second number (7, 6, 4, 1, 7, 7). Then, we take the second digit of the first number (7) and multiply it by all the digits of the second number (7, 6, 4, 1, 7, 7). Then, we take the third digit of the first number (7) and multiply it by all the digits of the second number (7, 6, 4, 1, 7, 7). We continue this process until we've multiplied all the digits of the first number by all the digits of the second number. While adding the results, we state that the tth multiplication shifted.

In terms of code, we have the following:

```
public static String multiply(String a, String b) {

  int lenA = a.length();
  int lenB = b.length();

  if (lenA == 0 || lenB == 0) {
    return "0";
  }

  // the result of multiplication is stored in reverse order
  int c[] = new int[lenA + lenB];

  // indexes to find positions in result
  int idx1 = 0;
  int idx2 = 0;

  // loop 'a' right to left
  for (int i = lenA - 1; i >= 0; i--) {

    int carry = 0;
    int n1 = a.charAt(i) - '0';

    // used to shift position to left after every
    // multiplication of a digit in 'b'
    idx2 = 0;
```

```java
      // loop 'b' from right to left
      for (int j = lenB - 1; j >= 0; j--) {

        // current digit of second number
        int n2 = b.charAt(j) - '0';

        // multiply with current digit of first number
        int sum = n1 * n2 + c[idx1 + idx2] + carry;

        // carry of the next iteration
        carry = sum / 10;

        c[idx1 + idx2] = sum % 10;
        idx2++;
      }

      // store carry
      if (carry > 0) {
        c[idx1 + idx2] += carry;
      }

      // shift position to left after every
      // multiplication of a digit in 'a'
      idx1++;
    }

    // ignore '0's from the right
    int i = c.length - 1;
    while (i >= 0 && c[i] == 0) {
      i--;
    }

    // If all were '0's - means either both or
    // one of 'a' or 'b' were '0'
    if (i == -1) {
```

```
      return "0";
   }
```

```
   String result = "";
   while (i >= 0) {
      result += (c[i--]);
   }
```

```
   return result;
}
```

The complete application is called *MultiplyLargeNumbers*.

Coding challenge 10 – Next greatest number with the same digits

Amazon, Google, Microsoft

Problem: Consider you've been given a positive integer. Write a snippet of code that returns the next greatest number with the same digits.

Solution: The solution to this problem can be observed via several examples. Let's consider the following examples:

- Example 1: 6   → Not possible
- Example 2: 1234   → 1243
- Example 3: 1232   → 1322
- Example 4: 321   → Not possible
- Example 5: 621873   → 623178

From the preceding examples we can intuit that the solution can be obtained by rearranging the digits of the given number. So, if we can find the set of rules for swapping the digits that leads us to the searched number, then we can attempt an implementation.

Let's try several observations:

- From examples 1 and 4, we can see that if the digits of the given number are in descending order, then it is impossible to find a greater number. Every swap will lead to a smaller number.
- From example 2, we can see that if the digits of the given number are in ascending order, then the next greater number that has the same digits can be obtained by swapping the last two digits.
- From examples 3 and 5, we can see that we need to find the smallest of all the greater numbers. For this, we have to process the number from the right-most side. The following algorithm clarifies this statement.

Based on these three observations, we can elaborate the following algorithm, which has been exemplified on the number 621873:

1. We start by traversing the number digit by digit from the right-most side. We keep traversing until we find a digit that is smaller than the previously traversed digit. For example, if the given number is 621873, then we traverse the number until digit 1 in 621873. Digit 1 is the first digit that's smaller than the previously traversed digit, 8.
2. Next, we focus on the digits from the right-hand side of the digit that we found at step 1. We want to find the smallest digit among these digits (let's denote it as *t*). Since these digits are sorted in descending order, the smallest digit is at the last position. For example, 3 is the smallest digit among the digits from the right-hand side of 1, 621873.
3. We swap these two digits (1 with 3) and we obtain 62**3**87**1**.
4. Finally, we sort all the digits to the right-hand side of *t* in ascending order. But since we know that all the digits from the right-hand side of *t* are sorted in descending order, except for the last digit, we can apply a linear reverse. This means that the result is 623**178**. This is the searched number.

This algorithm can be easily implemented, as follows:

```
public static void findNextGreater(int arr[]) {

    int min = -1;
    int len = arr.length;

    int prevDigit = arr[arr.length - 1];
```

```java
    int currentDigit;

    // Step 1: Start from the rightmost digit and find the
    // first digit that is smaller than the digit next to it.
    for (int i = len - 2; i >= 0; i--) {
      currentDigit = arr[i];
      if (currentDigit < prevDigit) {
        min = i;
        break;
      }
    }

    // If 'min' is -1 then there is no such digit.
    // This means that the digits are in descending order.
    // There is no greater number with same set of digits
    // as the given one.
    if (min == -1) {
      System.out.println("There is no greater number with "
        + "same set of digits as the given one.");
    } else {
      // Steps 2 and 3: Swap 'min' with 'len-1'
      swap(arr, min, len - 1);

      // Step 4: Sort in ascending order all the digits
      // to the right side of the swapped 'len-1'
      reverse(arr, min + 1, len - 1);

      // print the result
      System.out.print("The next greater number is: ");
      for (int i : arr) {
        System.out.print(i);
      }
    }
  }

  private static void reverse(int[] arr, int start, int end) {
```

```
    while (start < end) {
        swap(arr, start, end);
        start++;
        end--;
    }
}

private static void swap(int[] arr, int i, int j) {
    int aux = arr[i];
    arr[i] = arr[j];
    arr[j] = aux;
}
```

This code runs in O(n) time. The complete application is called *NextElementSameDigits*.

Coding challenge 11 – A number divisible by its digits

Amazon, Google, Adobe, Microsoft

Problem: Consider you've been given an integer, *n*. Write a program that returns `true` if the given number is divisible by its digits.

Solution: Let's consider that *n*=412. The output should be `true` since 412 is divisible by 2, 1, and 4. On the other hand, if *n*=143, then the output should be `false` since 143 is not divisible by 3 and 4.

If you think that this problem is simple, then you're absolutely right. These kinds of problems are used as *warm-up* problems and are useful to quickly filter a lot of candidates. Most of the time, you should solve it in a given time (for example, 2-3 minutes).

> **Important note**
> It is advisable to treat these simple problems with the same degree of seriousness as any other problem. A little mistake can prematurely eliminate you from the race.

So, for this problem, the algorithm is comprised of the following steps:

1. Fetch all the digits of the given number.
2. For each digit, check whether the *given number % digit* is 0 (this means divisible).

3. If any of them are non-zero, return `false`.
4. If, for all the digits the *given number % digit* is 0, return `true`.

In terms of code, we have the following:

```
public static boolean isDivisible(int n) {

  int t = n;

  while (n > 0) {

    int k = n % 10;
    if (k != 0 && t % k != 0) {
      return false;
    }

    n /= 10;
  }

  return true;
}
```

The complete application is called *NumberDivisibleDigits*.

Coding challenge 12 – Breaking chocolate

Amazon, Google, Adobe, Microsoft, Flipkart

Problem: Consider you've been a given rectangular bar of chocolate of size *width* x *height* and a number of tiles. As usual, the chocolate consists of a number of little tiles, so the *width* and *height* give us the number of tiles (for example, the chocolate is 4 x 3 in size and contains 12 tiles). Write a snippet of code that computes the number of breaks (cuts) we need to apply to the given chocolate to obtain a piece that has exactly the required number of tiles. You can break (cut) the given chocolate into two rectangular pieces via a single vertical or horizontal break (cut) along the tile edges.

Solution: Let's consider the chocolate shown in the following image (a 3 x 6 bar of chocolate that has 18 tiles):

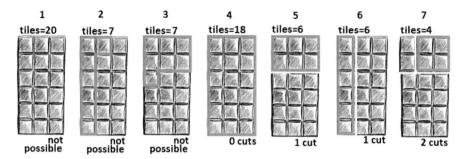

Figure 15.12 – A 3 x 6 chocolate bar

The preceding image reveals seven cases that can lead us to the solution, as follows:

- Cases 1, 2, and 3: If the number of given tiles is greater than 3 x 6 or we cannot arrange the tiles along with the chocolate's *width* or *height*, then it is not possible to attain a solution. For no solution, we return -1.

- Case 4: If the number of given tiles is equal to 3 x 6 = 18, then this is the solution, so we have 0 cuts. We'll return 0.

- Case 5: If the number of given tiles can be arranged along with the chocolate bar's *width*, then there is a single cut. We'll return 1.

- Case 6: If the number of given tiles can be arranged along with the chocolate bar's *height*, then there is a single cut. We'll return 1.

- Case 7: In all other cases, we need 2 cuts. We'll return 2.

Let's see the code:

```
public static int breakit(int width, int height, int nTiles) {

if (width <= 0 || height <= 0 || nTiles <= 0) {
   return -1;
}

// case 1
if (width * height < nTiles) {
   return -1;
}
```

```
// case 4
if (width * height == nTiles) {
  return 0;
}

// cases 5 and 6
if ((nTiles % width == 0 && (nTiles / width) < height)
    || (nTiles % height == 0 && (nTiles / height) < width)) {
  return 1;
}

// case 7
for (int i = 1; i <= Math.sqrt(nTiles); i++) {
  if (nTiles % i == 0) {
    int a = i;
    int b = nTiles / i;
    if ((a <= width && b <= height)
        || (a <= height && b <= width)) {
      return 2;
    }
  }
}

// cases 2 and 3
return -1;
}
```

The complete application is called *BreakChocolate*.

Coding challenge 13 – Clock angle

Google, Microsoft

Problem: Consider you've been given the time in *h:m* format. Write a snippet of code that calculates the shorter angle between the hour and the minute hand on an analog clock.

Solution: Right from the start, we have to take into account several formulas that will help us come up with a solution.

First of all, a clock is divided into 12 equal hours (or 12 equals parts) and since it is a complete circle, it has 360°. So, 1 hour has 360°/12 = 30°. So, at 1:00, the hour hand forms an angle of 30⁰ with the minute hand. At 2:00, the hour hand forms an angle of 60° with the minute hand, and so on and so forth. The following image clarifies this aspect:

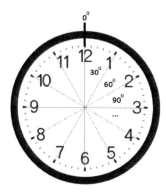

Figure 15.13 – 360 degree split at 12 hours

Taking this logic further, an hour has 60 minutes and 30°, so a minute has 30/60 = 0.5°. So, if we refer only to the hour hand, then at 1:10, we have an angle of 30° + 10*0.5° = 30° + 5° = 35°. Or, at 4:17, we have an angle of 4*30° + 17*0.5° = 120° + 8.5° = 128.5°.

So far, we know that we can compute the angle of the hour hand for a given *h:m* time as $h*30^0 + m*0.5°$. For computing the angle of the minute hand, we can think that, in 1 hour, the minute hand takes a complete 360° tour, so 360°/ 60 minutes = 6° for each minute. So, at *h*:24, the minute hand forms an angle of 24 * 6° = 144°. At *h*:35, the minute hand forms an angle of 35 * 6° = 210°, and so on and so forth.

So, the angle between the hour and the minute hand is the abs(($h*30° + m*0.5°$) - $m*6°$). If the returned *result* is greater than 180°, then we have to return (360° - *result*) since the problem requires us to calculate the shorter angle between the hour and the minute hand.

Now, let's try to calculate the required angle for the clocks shown in the following image:

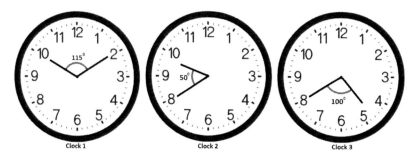

Figure 15.14 – Three clocks

Clock 1, 10:10:

- Hour hand: 10*30° + 10*0.5° = 300° + 5° = 305°
- Minute hand: 10 * 6° = 60°
- Result: abs(305° - 60°) = abs(245°) = 245° > 180°, so return 360° - 245° = 115°

Clock 2, 9:40:

- Hour hand: 9*30° + 40*0.5° = 270° + 20° = 290°
- Minute hand: 40 * 6° = 240°
- Result: abs(290° - 240°) = abs(50°) = 50°

Clock 3, 4:40:

- Hour hand: 4*30° + 40*0.5° = 120° + 20° = 140°
- Minute hand: 40 * 6° = 240°
- Result: abs(140° - 240°) = abs(-100°) = 100°

Based on these statements, we can write the following code:

```
public static float findAngle(int hour, int min) {

  float angle = (float) Math.abs(((30f * hour)
      + (0.5f * min)) - (6f * min));

  return angle > 180f ? (360f - angle) : angle;
}
```

The complete application is called *HourMinuteAngle*.

Coding challenge 14 – Pythagorean triplets

Google, Adobe, Microsoft

Problem: A Pythagorean triplet is a set of three positive integers {a, b, c} such that $a^2 = b^2 + c^2$. Consider you've been given an array of positive integers, *arr*. Write a snippet of code that prints all the Pythagorean triplets of this array.

Solution: The brute-force approach can be implemented via three loops that can try all the possible triples in the given array. But this will work in O(n³) complexity time. Obviously, the brute-force approach (commonly known as the *naive* approach) will not impress the interviewer, so we must do better than this.

We can, in fact, solve the problem in O(n²) time. Let's see the algorithm's steps:

1. Square every element in the input array (O(n)). This means that we can write $a^2 = b^2 + c^2$ as $a = b + c$.
2. Sort the given array in ascending order (O(n log n)).
3. If $a = b + c$, then a is always the largest value between a, b, and c. So, we fix a so that it becomes the last element of this sorted array.
4. Fix b so that it becomes the first element of this sorted array.
5. Fix c so that it becomes the element right before element a.
6. So far, $b<a$ and $c<a$. To find the Pythagorean triplets, execute a loop that increases b from 1 to n and decreases c from n to 1. The loop stops when b and c meet:

    a. Increase the index of b if $b + c < a$.

    b. Decrease the index of c if $b + c > a$.

    c. If $b + c$ is equal to a, then print the found triplet. Increment the index of b and decrement the index of c.

7. Repeat from *step 3* for the next a.

Let's consider that arr={3, 6, 8, 5, 10, 4, 12, 14}. After the first two steps, arr={9, 16, 25, 36, 64, 100, 144, 196}. After *steps 3, 4,* and *5*, we have $a=196$, $b=9$, and $c=144$, as follows:

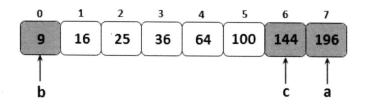

Figure 15.15 – Setting a, b, and c

Since 9+144 < 196, the index of b is increased by 1, conforming to *step 6a*. The same step applies for 16+144, 25+144, and 36+144. Since 64+144 > 196, the index of c is decreased by 1, conforming to *step 6b*.

Since 64 +100 < 196, the index of b is increased by 1, conforming to *step 6a*. The loop stops here since b and c have met, as follows:

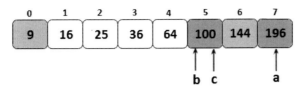

Figure 15.16 – b and c at the end of the loop

Next, conforming to *step 7*, we set *a*=144, *b*=9, and *c*=100. This process is repeated for each *a*. When *a* becomes 100, we find the first Pythagorean triplet; that is, *a*=100, *b*=36, and *c*=64, as shown here:

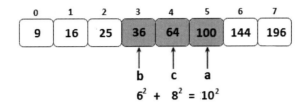

Figure 15.17 – A Pythagorean triplet

Let's put this algorithm into code:

```
public static void triplet(int arr[]) {

  int len = arr.length;

  // Step1
  for (int i = 0; i < len; i++) {
    arr[i] = arr[i] * arr[i];
  }

  // Step 2
  Arrays.sort(arr);

  // Steps 3, 4, and 5
  for (int i = len - 1; i >= 2; i--) {

    int b = 0;
    int c = i - 1;

    // Step 6
```

```java
        while (b < c) {

            // Step 6c
            if (arr[b] + arr[c] == arr[i]) {
                System.out.println("Triplet: " + Math.sqrt(arr[b])
                    + ", " + Math.sqrt(arr[c]) + ", "
                    + Math.sqrt(arr[i]));
                b++;
                c--;
            }

            // Steps 6a and 6b
            if (arr[b] + arr[c] < arr[i]) {
                b++;
            } else {
                c--;
            }
        }
    }
}
```

The complete application is called *PythagoreanTriplets*.

Coding challenge 15 – Scheduling one elevator

Amazon, Google, Adobe, Microsoft, Flipkart

Problem: Consider you've been given an array representing the destination floors of *n* people. The elevator has a capacity of the given *k*. Initially, the elevator and all the people are on floor 0 (ground floor). It takes 1 unit of time for the elevator to reach any consecutive floor (up or down) from the current floor. Write a snippet of code that will schedule the elevator in such a way that we obtain the minimum total time needed to get all the people to their destination floors and then return to the ground floor.

Solution: Let's consider that the given array of destinations is *floors* = {4, 2, 1, 2, 4} and *k*=3. So, we have five people: one person for the first floor, two people for the second floor, and two people for the fourth floor. The elevator can take three people at a time. So, how can we schedule the elevator to take these five people to their floors in the shortest amount of time?

The solution consists of getting the people to their respective floors in descending order. Let's tackle this scenario based on the following image:

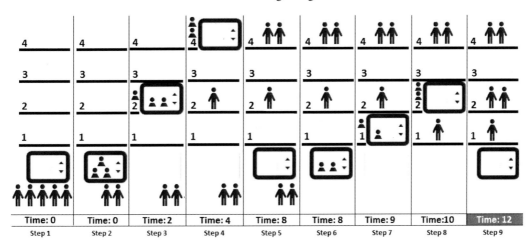

Figure 15.18 – Scheduling an elevator example

Let's traverse the steps of this scenario:

1. This is the initial state. The elevator is on the ground floor and five people are ready to take it. Let's consider that the minimum time is 0 (so, 0 units of time).

2. In the elevator, we take the people who are going to the 4th floor and the one person who is going to the 2nd floor. Remember that we can take a maximum of three people at a time. So far, the minimum time is 0.

3. The elevator goes up and stops at the 2nd floor. One person gets off. Since each floor represents a unit of time, we have a minimum time of 2.

4. The elevator goes up and stops at the 4th floor. The remaining two people get off. The minimum time becomes equal to 4.

5. At this step, the elevator is empty. It must go down to the ground floor to pick up more people. Since it goes down four floors, the minimum time becomes 8.

6. We pick up the remaining two people. The minimum time remains as 8.

7. The elevator goes up and stops at the 1st floor. One person gets off. The minimum time becomes 9.

8. The elevator goes up and stops at the 2nd floor. One person gets off. The minimum time becomes 10.

9. At this step, the elevator is empty. It must go down to the ground floor. Since it goes down two floors, the minimum time becomes 12.

So, the total minimum time is 12. Based on this scenario, we can elaborate the following algorithm:

1. Sort the given array in descending order of destinations.
2. Create groups of *k* persons. The time needed for each group will be 2 * *floors*[*group*].

So, sorting our testing data will result in *floors* = {4, 4, 2, 2, 1}. We have two groups. One group contains three people (4, 4, 2), while the other group contains two people (2, 1). The total minimum time is (2 * *floors*[0]) + (2 * *floors*[3]) = (2 * 4) + (2 * 2) = 8 + 4 = 12.

In terms of code, we have the following:

```
public static int time(int k, int floors[]) {

    int aux;
    for (int i = 0; i < floors.length - 1; i++) {
      for (int j = i + 1; j < floors.length; j++) {
        if (floors[i] < floors[j]) {
          aux = floors[i];
          floors[i] = floors[j];
          floors[j] = aux;
        }
      }
    }

    // iterate the groups and update
    // the time needed for each group
    int time = 0;
    for (int i = 0; i < floors.length; i += k) {
      time += (2 * floors[i]);
    }

    return time;
}
```

Of course, you may end up choosing a better sorting algorithm. The complete application is called *ScheduleOneElevator*. This was the last coding challenge of this chapter.

Scheduling multiple elevators

But how do we schedule multiple elevators with an arbitrary number of floors? Well, most probably, in an interview, you won't need to implement a solution for more than one elevator, but you could be asked how you'd design a solution for more.

The problem of scheduling multiple elevators and the algorithm are famous and difficult. There is no best algorithm for this problem. In other words, creating an algorithm that can be applied to the real-world scheduling of elevators is really difficult, and apparently, it is patented.

The Elevator algorithm (https://en.wikipedia.org/wiki/Elevator_algorithm) is a good place to start. Before thinking about how to design a solution for multi-elevators, you must make a list of all the assumptions or constraints that you want to consider. Every available solution/algorithm has a list of assumptions or constraints referring to the number of floors, number of elevators, capacity of each elevator, number of average people, rush hour times, elevator speed, load and unload times, and so on. Mainly, there are three solutions, as follows:

- **Sectors**: Each elevator is allocated to a sector (it services a subset of floors).
- **Nearest elevator**: Each person is assigned to the nearest elevator (it does this based on the elevator's position, the direction of call, and the current direction of the elevator).
- **Nearest elevator with capacity considerations**: This is similar to the nearest elevator option, but it takes the load in each elevator into account.

Sectors

For example, a building that has eight floors and three elevators can be serviced like this:

- Elevator 1 serves floors 1, 2, and 3.
- Elevator 2 serves floors 1, 4, and 5.
- Elevator 3 serves floors 1, 6, 7, and 8.

Each elevator services the ground floor since the ground floor has the highest arrival rate.

Nearest elevator

Allocate a score to each elevator. This score represents the suitability score for an elevator when a new person arrives:

- *Toward the call, same direction*: $FS = (N + 2) - d$
- *Toward the call, opposite direction*: $FS = (N + 1) - d$
- *Away from the call*: $FS = 1$

Where, N = #Floors – 1, and d = distance between elevator and call.

Nearest elevator with capacity considerations

This is exactly the same as the nearest elevator situation, but it takes into account the excess capacity of the elevator:

- *Toward the call, same direction*: $FS = (N + 2) - d + C$
- *Toward the call, opposite direction*: $FS = (N + 1) - d + C$
- *Away from the call*: $FS = 1 + C$

Here, N is #Floors – 1, d is the distance between the elevator and the call, and C is the excess capacity.

I strongly recommend that you search and study different implementations for this problem and try to learn the one that you find the most suitable for you. I suggest that you start from here:

- `https://github.com/topics/elevator-simulation`
- `https://austingwalters.com/everyday-algorithms-elevator-allocation/`.

Now, let's summarize this chapter.

Summary

In this chapter, we covered the most popular problems that fit into the mathematics and puzzles categories. While many companies avoid such problems, there are still major players such as Google and Amazon that rely on these kinds of problems in their interviews.

Practicing such problems represents a good exercise for our brains. Besides the math knowledge, these problems sustain analytical thinking based on deductions and intuition, which means they are great support for any programmer.

In the next chapter, we'll tackle a hot topic in interviews: concurrency (multithreading).

Section 4: Bonus – Concurrency and Functional Programming

Companies are very sensitive to topics such as concurrency and functional programming. This chapter covers the most popular questions surrounding these two topics. These four chapters are bonus chapters; the approach of which is not similar to the chapters you've read so far. Owing to the nature of the topics, we will touch upon them briefly, elaborating on the questions asked in interviews on the respective topics. You can find the codes used in the chapter on the GitHub repository, link to which is shared in the technical requirements section of the chapter.

This section comprises the following chapters:

- *Chapter 16, Concurrency*
- *Chapter 17, Functional-Style Programming*
- *Chapter 18, Unit Testing*
- *Chapter 19, System Scalability*

16
Concurrency

Developing single-threaded Java applications is rarely feasible. Therefore, most of your projects will be multithreaded (that is, they will run in a multithreaded environment). This means that, sooner or later, you'll have to tackle certain multithreading problems. In other words, at some point, you'll have to get your hands dirty with code that manipulates Java threads directly or via dedicated APIs.

This chapter covers the most popular questions about Java concurrency (multithreading) that occur in general interviews about the Java language. As usual, we will start with a brief introduction that covers the main aspects of Java concurrency. Therefore, our agenda is straightforward, covering the following topics:

- Java concurrency (multithreading) in a nutshell
- Questions and coding challenges

Let's begin with the fundamental knowledge of our topic, Java concurrency. Use the following nutshell section to extract answers to some basic questions about concurrency, such as *What is concurrency?*, *What is a Java thread?*, *What is multithreading?*, and more.

Technical Requirements

The codes used in this chapter can be found on GitHub on: `https://github.com/PacktPublishing/The-Complete-Coding-Interview-Guide-in-Java/tree/master/Chapter16`

Java concurrency (multithreading) in a nutshell

Our computers can run multiple *programs* or *applications* at the same time (for example, we can listen to music on a media player and navigate the internet at the same time). A *process* is an executing instance of a program or application (for example, by double-clicking on the NetBeans icon on your computer, you start a process that will run the NetBeans program). Additionally, a *thread* is a *lightweight subprocess* that represents the smallest executable unit of work of a process. A Java thread has relatively low overhead, and it shares common memory space with other threads. A process can have multiple threads with one *main thread*.

> **Important note**
> The main difference between processes and threads is the fact that threads share common memory space while processes don't. By sharing memory, threads shave off lots of overhead.

Concurrency is the ability of an application to handle the multiple tasks it works on. The program or application can process one task at a time (*sequential processing*) or process multiple tasks at the same time (*concurrent processing*).

Do not confuse concurrency with *parallelism*. *Parallelism* is the ability of an application to handle each individual task. The application can process each task serially, or it can split the task up into subtasks that can be processed in parallel.

> **Important note**
> Concurrency is about **handling** (not doing) lots of things at once, while parallelism is about **doing** lots of things at once.

Concurrency is achieved via *multithreading*. *Multithreading* is a technique that enables a program or application to handle more than one task at a time and to also synchronize those tasks. This means that multithreading allows the maximum utilization of a CPU by executing two or more tasks virtually at the same time. We say *virtually at the same time* here because the tasks only look like they are running simultaneously; however, essentially, they cannot do that. They take advantage of CPU *context switching* or the *time slicing* feature of the operating system. In other words, CPU time is shared across all running tasks, and each task is scheduled to run for a certain period of time. Hence, multithreading is the key to *multitasking*.

> **Important note**
> With a single-core CPU, we may achieve concurrency but *not* parallelism.

In conclusion, threads can create the illusion of multitasking; however, at any given point in time, the CPU is executing only one thread. The CPU switches control between the threads so quickly that it creates the illusion that the tasks are executed (or advance) in parallel. Actually, they are executed concurrently. Nevertheless, with advances in hardware technology, it is now common to have multi-core machines and computers. This means that applications can take advantage of these architectures and have a dedicated CPU running each thread.

The following diagram clarifies the confusion between concurrency and parallelism via four threads (**T1**, **T2**, **T3**, and **T4**):

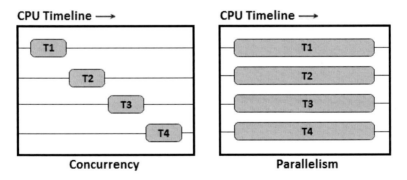

16.1 – Concurrency versus parallelism

So, an application can be one of the following:

- **Concurrent but not parallel**: It executes more than one task at the same time, but no two tasks are executed at the same time.

- **Parallel but not concurrent**: It executes multiple subtasks of a task in a multi-core CPU at the same time.
- **Neither parallel nor concurrent**: It executes all of the tasks one at a time (sequential execution).
- **Both parallel and concurrent**: It executes multiple tasks concurrently in a multi-core CPU at the same time.

A set of homogenous worker threads that are assigned to execute tasks is called a *thread pool*. A worker thread that finishes a task is returned to the pool. Typically, thread pools are bound to a queue of tasks and can be tuned to the size of the threads they hold. Commonly, for optimal performance, the size of a thread pool is equal to the number of CPU cores.

The *synchronization* of a multithreaded environment is achieved via *locking*. Locking is used to orchestrate and limit access to a resource in a multithreaded environment.

If multiple threads can access the same resource without causing errors or unpredictable behaviors/results, then we are in a *thread-safe context*. *Thread safety* can be achieved via various synchronization techniques (for example, the Java `synchronized` keyword).

Next, let's tackle several questions and coding challenges regarding concurrency in Java.

Questions and coding challenges

In this section, we will cover 20 concurrency questions and coding challenges that are very popular in interviews.

You should be aware that Java concurrency is a wide and complex topic that needs to be covered in great detail by any Java developer. Having fundamental insights about Java concurrency should be enough to pass a general Java language interview, but it is not enough for specific interviews (for example, if you apply for a job that will imply developing a concurrency API, then you must deep dive into this topic and learn advanced concepts – most probably, the interview will be concurrency-centric).

Coding challenge 1 – Thread life cycle states

Problem: Enumerate and explain, in a few sentences, the states of a Java `Thread`.

Solution: The states of a Java thread are available via the `Thread.State` enumeration. The possible states of a Java thread can be seen in the following diagram:

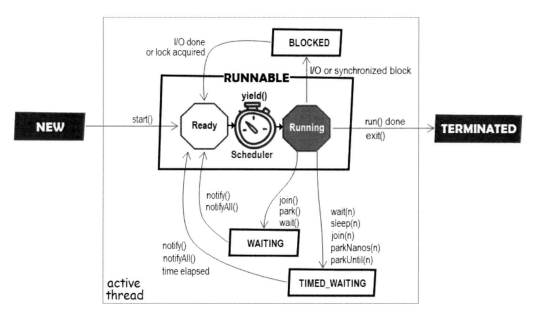

16.2 – Java thread states

The different lifecycle states of a Java Thread are as follows:

- **The NEW state**: A thread that is created but not started (this is the state until the Thread#start() method is invoked).

- **The RUNNABLE state**: By calling the Thread#start() method, the thread passes from NEW to RUNNABLE. In the RUNNABLE state, a thread can be running or ready to run. A thread that is waiting for the **JVM (Java Virtual Machine)** thread scheduler to allocate the necessary resources and time to run is ready to run, but it is not running yet. As soon as the CPU is available, the thread scheduler will run the thread.

- **The BLOCKED state**: A thread that executes synchronized blocks or I/O tasks may enter the BLOCKED state. For example, if a thread, *t1*, attempts to enter into a synchronized block of code (for example, a block of code marked synchronized) that is already being accessed by another thread, *t2*, then *t1* is held in the BLOCKED state until it can acquire the required lock.

- **The WAITING state**: A thread, *t1*, that waits (without having set an explicit timeout period) for another thread, *t2*, to finish its job is in the WAITING state.

- **The TIMED_WAITING state**: A thread, *t1*, that waits for an explicit period of time (typically, this is specified in milliseconds or seconds) for another thread, *t2*, to finish its job is in the TIMED_WAITING state.

- **The `TERMINATED` state**: A Java thread that is abnormally interrupted or successfully finishes its job is in the `TERMINATE` state.

Besides describing the possible states of a Java thread, the interviewer might ask you to code an example for each state. This is why I highly recommended that you take your time and analyze the application named *ThreadLifecycleState* (for brevity, the code is not listed in the book). The application is structured in a very intuitive way, and the leading comments explain each scenario/state.

Coding challenge 2 – Deadlocks

Problem: Explain deadlock to us and we'll hire you!

Solution: Hire me, and I'll explain it to you.

Here, we've just described a deadlock.

A deadlock can be explained like this: thread *T1* holds the lock, *P*, and is trying to acquire the lock, *Q*. At the same time, there is thread *T2* that holds the lock, *Q*, and is trying to acquire the lock, *P*. This kind of deadlock is known as *circular wait* or *deadly embrace*.

Java doesn't provide deadlock detection and/or a resolving mechanism (like databases have, for example). This means that a deadlock can be very embarrassing for an application. A deadlock can partially or completely block an application. This leads to significant performance penalties, unexpected behaviors/results, and more. Commonly, deadlocks are hard to find and debug, and they force you to restart the application.

The best way to avoid race deadlocks is to avoid using nested locks or unnecessary locks. Nested locks are quite prone to deadlocks.

A common problem of simulating a deadlock is **The Dining Philosophers** problem. You can find a detailed explanation and implementation of this problem in the *Java Coding Problems* book (`https://www.packtpub.com/programming/java-coding-problems`). *Java Coding Problems* contains two chapters that are dedicated to Java concurrency and are meant to dive deep into this topic using specific problems.

In the code bundle for this book, you can find a simple example of causing a deadlock named *Deadlock*.

Coding challenge 3 – Race conditions

Problem: Explain what *race conditions* are.

Solution: First of all, we must mention that a snippet/block of code that can be executed by multiple threads (that is, executed concurrently) and exposes shared resources (for example, shared data) is known as a *critical section*.

Race conditions occur when threads pass through such critical sections without thread synchronization. The threads *race* through the critical section attempting to read/write shared resources. Depending on the order in which threads finish this race, the application's output changes (two runs of the application may produce different outputs). This leads to inconsistent behavior in the application.

The best way to avoid race conditions involves the proper synchronization of critical sections by using locks, synchronized blocks, atomic/volatile variables, synchronizers, and/or message passing.

Coding challenge 4 – reentrant locking

Problem: Explain what is the *reentrant locking* concept.

Solution: Generally speaking, *reentrant locking* refers to a process that can acquire a lock multiple times without deadlocking itself. If a lock is not reentrant, then the process can still acquire it. However, when the process tries to acquire the lock again, it will be blocked (deadlock). A reentrant lock can be acquired by another thread or recursively by the same thread.

A reentrant lock can be used for a piece of code that doesn't contain updates that could break it. If the code contains a shared state that can be updated, then acquiring the lock again will corrupt the shared state since the code is called while it is executing.

In Java, a reentrant lock is implemented via the `ReentrantLock` class. A reentrant lock acts like this: when the thread enters the lock for the first time, a hold count is set to one. Before unlocking, the thread can re-enter the lock causing the hold count to be incremented by one for each entry. Each unlock request decrements the hold count by one, and, when the hold count is zero, the locked resource is opened.

Coding challenge 5 – Executor and ExecutorService

Problem: What are `Executor` and `ExecutorService`?

Solution: In the `java.util.concurrent` package, there are a number of interfaces that are dedicated to executing tasks. The simplest one is named `Executor`. This interface exposes a single method named `execute (Runnable command)`.

A more complex and comprehensive interface, which provides many additional methods, is `ExecutorService`. This is an enriched version of `Executor`. Java comes with a full-fledged implementation of `ExecutorService`, named `ThreadPoolExecutor`.

In the code bundle for this book, you can find simple examples of using `Executor` and `ThreadPoolExecutor` in the application named *ExecutorAndExecutorService*.

Coding challenge 6 – Runnable versus Callable

Problem: What is the difference between the `Callable` interface and the `Runnable` interface?

Solution: The `Runnable` interface is a functional interface that contains a single method named `run()`. The `run()` method doesn't take any parameters and returns `void`. Moreover, it cannot throw checked exceptions (only `RuntimeException`). These statements make `Runnable` suitable in scenarios where we are not looking for the result of the thread execution. The `run()` signature is as follows:

```
void run()
```

On the other hand, the `Callable` interface is a functional interface that contains a single method named `call()`. The `call()` method returns a generic value and can throw checked exceptions. Typically, `Callable` is used in `ExecutorService` instances. It is useful for starting an asynchronous task and then calling the returned `Future` instance to get its value. The `Future` interface defines methods for obtaining the result generated by a `Callable` object and for managing its state. The `call()` signature is as follows:

```
V call() throws Exception
```

Notice that both of these interfaces represent a task that is intended to be executed concurrently by a separate thread.

In the code bundle for this book, you can find simple examples of using `Runnable` and `Callable` in the application named *RunnableAndCallable*.

Coding challenge 7 – Starvation

Problem: Explain what thread *starvation* is.

Solution: A thread that never (or very rarely) gets CPU time or access to the shared resources is a thread that experiences *starvation*. Since it cannot obtain regular access to shared resources, this thread cannot progress its job. This happens because other threads (so-called *greedy* threads) get access before this thread and make the resources unavailable for long periods of time.

The best way to avoid thread starvation is to use *fair* locks, such as Java `ReentrantLock`. A *fair* lock grants access to the thread that has been waiting the longest. Having multiple threads run at once while preventing starvation can be accomplished via Java `Semaphore`. A *fair* `Semaphore` guarantees the granting of permits under contention using FIFO.

Coding challenge 8 – Livelocks

Problem: Explain what thread *livelock* is.

Solution: A livelock takes place when two threads keep taking actions in response to another thread. The threads don't make any progress with their own jobs. Notice that the threads are not blocked; both of them are too busy responding to each other to resume work.

Here is an example of a livelock: imagine two people trying to cross each other in a hallway. Mark moves to his right to let Oliver pass, and Oliver moves to his left to let Mark pass. Both are now blocking each other. Mark sees that he's blocking Oliver and moves to his left, and Oliver moves to his right after seeing that he's blocking Mark. They never manage to cross each other and keep blocking each other.

We can avoid livelocks via `ReentrantLock`. This way, we can determine which thread has been waiting the longest and assign it a lock. If a thread can't acquire a lock, it should release the previously acquired locks and try again later.

Coding challenge 9 – Start() versus run()

Problem: Explain the main differences between the `start()` method and the `run()` method in a Java `Thread`.

Solution: The main difference between `start()` and `run()` is the fact that the `start()` method creates a new thread while the `run()` method doesn't. The `start()` method creates a new thread and calls the block of code written inside the `run()` method of this new thread. The `run()` method executes that code on the same thread (that is, the calling thread) without creating a new thread.

Another difference is that calling `start()` twice on the thread object will throw an `IllegalStateException`. On the other hand, calling the `run()` method twice doesn't lead to an exception.

Typically, novices ignore these differences, and, since the `start()` method eventually calls the `run()` method, they believe there is no reason to call the `start()` method. Therefore, they call the `run()` method directly.

Coding challenge 10 – Thread versus Runnable

Problem: To implement a thread, should we extend `Thread` or implement `Runnable`?

Solution: As the question suggests, implementing a Java thread can be accomplished by extending `java.lang.Thread` or by implementing `java.lang.Runnable`. The preferred way to go is to implement `Runnable`.

Most of the time, we implement a thread just to give it something to run, not to overwrite the behavior of the `Thread`. As long as all we want is to give something to run to a thread, we definitely should stick to implementing `Runnable`. In fact, using `Callable` or `FutureTask` is an even better choice.

In addition to this, by implementing `Runnable`, you can still extend another class. By extending `Thread`, you cannot extend another class since Java doesn't support multiple inheritances.

Finally, by implementing `Runnable`, we separate the task definition from the task execution.

Coding challenge 11 – CountDownLatch versus CyclicBarrier

Problem: Explain the main differences between `CountDownLatch` and `CyclicBarrier`.

Solution: `CountDownLatch` and `CyclicBarrier` are two of the five Java *synchronizers* next to `Exchanger`, `Semaphore`, and `Phaser`.

The main difference between `CountDownLatch` and `CyclicBarrier` is the fact that a `CountDownLatch` instance cannot be reused once the countdown reaches zero. On the other hand, a `CyclicBarrier` instance is reusable. A `CyclicBarrier` instance is cyclical because it can be reset and reused. To do this, call the `reset()` method after all of the threads waiting at the barrier are released; otherwise, `BrokenBarrierException` will be thrown.

Coding challenge 12 – wait() versus sleep()

Problem: Explain the main differences between the `wait()` method and the `sleep()` method.

Solution: The main difference between the `wait()` method and the `sleep()` method is that `wait()` must be called from a synchronized context (for example, from a `synchronized` method), while the `sleep()` method doesn't need a synchronized context. Calling `wait()` from a non-synchronized context will throw an `IllegalMonitorStateException`.

Additionally, it is important to mention that `wait()` works on `Object`, while `sleep()` works on the current thread. Essentially, `wait()` is a non-`static` method defined in `java.lang.Object`, while `sleep()` is a `static` method defined in `java.lang.Thread`.

Moreover, the `wait()` method releases the lock, while the `sleep()` method doesn't release the lock. The `sleep()` method only pauses the current thread for a certain period of time. Both of them throw `IntrupptedException` and can be interrupted.

Finally, the `wait()` method should be called in a loop that decides when the lock should be released. On the other hand, it is not recommended that you call the `sleep()` method in a loop.

Coding challenge 13 – ConcurrentHashMap versus Hashtable

Problem: Why is `ConcurrentHashMap` faster than `Hashtable`?

Solution: `ConcurrentHashMap` is faster than `Hashtable` because of its special internal design. `ConcurrentHashMap` internally divides a map into segments (or buckets), and it locks only a particular segment during an update operation. On the other hand, `Hashtable` locks the whole map during an update operation. So, `Hashtable` uses a single lock for the whole data, while `ConcurrentHashMap` uses multiple locks on different segments (buckets).

Moreover, reading from a `ConcurrentHashMap` using `get()` is lock-free (no locks), while all the `Hashtable` operations are simply `synchronized`.

Coding challenge 14 – ThreadLocal

Problem: What is Java `ThreadLocal`?

Solution: Java threads share the same memory. However, sometimes, we need to have dedicated memory for each thread. Java provides `ThreadLocal` as a means to store and retrieve values for each thread separately. A single instance of `ThreadLocal` can store and retrieve the values of multiple threads. If thread *A* stores the *x* value and thread *B* stores the *y* value in the same instance of `ThreadLocal`, then, later on, thread *A* retrieves the *x* value, and thread *B* retrieves the *y* value. Java `ThreadLocal` is typically used in the following two scenarios:

1. To provide per-thread instances (thread safety and memory efficiency)
2. To provide per-thread context

Coding challenge 15 – submit() versus execute()

Problem: Explain the main differences between the `ExecutorService#submit()` and `Executor#execute()` methods.

Solution: While both of these methods are used to submit a `Runnable` task for execution, they are not the same. The main difference can be observed by simply checking their signatures. Notice that `submit()` returns a result (that is, a `Future` object representing the task), while `execute()` returns `void`. The returned `Future` object can be used to programmatically cancel the running thread later on (prematurely). Moreover, by using the `Future#get()` method, we can wait for the task to complete. If we submit a `Callable`, then the `Future#get()` method will return the result of calling the `Callable#call()` method.

Coding challenge 16 – interrupted() and isInterrupted()

Problem: Explain the main differences between the `interrupted()` and `isInterrupted()` methods.

Solution: The Java multithreading interrupt technique uses an internal flag known as the *interrupt status*. The `Thread.interrupt()` method interrupts the current thread and sets this flag to `true`.

The main difference between the `interrupted()` and `isInterrupted()` methods is the fact that the `interrupted()` method clears the interrupt status while `isInterrupted()` doesn't.

If the thread was interrupted, then Thread.interrupted() will return true. However, besides testing, if the current thread was interrupted, Thread.interrupted() clears the interrupted status of the thread (that is, sets it to false).

The non-static isInterrupted() method doesn't change the interrupt status flag.

As a rule of thumb, after catching InterruptedException, don't forget to restore the interrupt by calling Thread.currentThread().interrupt(). This way, the caller of our code will be aware of the interruption.

Coding challenge 17 – Canceling a thread

Problem: How can we stop or cancel a thread?

Solution: Java doesn't provide a preemptive way of stopping a thread. Therefore, to cancel a task, a common practice is to rely on a loop that uses a flag condition. The task's responsibility is to check this flag periodically, and when it finds the flag set, then it should stop as quickly as possible. Notice that this flag is commonly declared as volatile (also known as the lightweight synchronization mechanism). Being a volatile flag, it is not cached by threads, and operations on it are not reordered in memory; therefore, a thread cannot see an old value. Any thread that reads a volatile field will see the most recently written value. This is exactly what we need in order to communicate the cancellation action to all running threads that are interested in this action. The following diagram illustrates this:

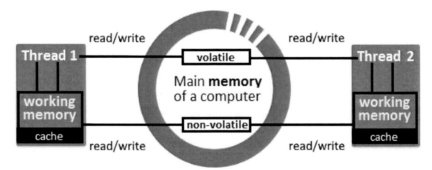

16.3 – Volatile flag read/write

Notice that the volatile variables are not a good fit for read-modify-write scenarios. For such scenarios, we will rely on atomic variables (for example, AtomicBoolean, AtomicInteger, and AtomicReference).

In the code bundle for this book, you can find an example of canceling a thread. The application is named *CancelThread*.

Coding challenge 18 – sharing data between threads

Problem: How can we share data between two threads?

Solution: Sharing data between two (or more) threads can be done via thread-safe shared objects or data structures. Java comes with a built-in set of thread-safe data structures such as `BlockingQueue`, `LinkedBlockingQueue`, and `ConcurrentLinkedDeque`. It is very convenient to rely on these data structures to share data between threads because you don't have to bother about thread safety and inter-thread communication.

Coding challenge 19 – ReadWriteLock

Problem: Explain what `ReadWriteLock` is in Java.

Solution: The main purpose of `ReadWriteLock` is to sustain the efficiency and thread safety of reading and writing operations in a concurrent environment. It accomplishes this goal via the *lock striping* concept. In other words, `ReadWriteLock` uses separate locks for reads and writes. More precisely, `ReadWriteLock` keeps a pair of locks: one for read-only operations and one for writing operations. As long as there are no writer threads, multiple reader threads can hold the read lock simultaneously (shared pessimistic lock). A single writer can write at a time (exclusive/pessimistic locking). So, `ReadWriteLock` can significantly improve the performance of the application.

Besides `ReadWriteLock`, Java comes with `ReentrantReadWriteLock` and `StampedLock`. The `ReentrantReadWriteLock` class adds the *reentrant locking* concept (refer to *Coding challenge 4*) to `ReadWriteLock`. On the other hand, `StampedLock` performs better than `ReentrantReadWriteLock` and supports optimistic reads. But it is not *reentrant*; therefore, it is prone to deadlocks.

Coding challenge 20 – Producer-Consumer

Problem: Provide an implementation for the famous Producer-Consumer problem.

> **Note**
> This is a favorite problem during any Java multithreading interview!

Solution: The Producer-Consumer problem is a design pattern that can be represented as follows:

16.4 – Producer-Consumer design pattern

Most commonly, in this pattern, the producer thread and the consumer thread communicate via a queue (the producer enqueues data and the consumer dequeues data) and a set of rules specific to the modeled business. This queue is known as the *data buffer*. Of course, depending on the process design, other data structures can play the role of data buffer as well.

Now, let's assume the following scenario (set of rules):

- If the data buffer is empty, then the producer produces one product (by adding it to the data buffer).
- If the data buffer is not empty, then the consumer consumes one product (by removing it from the data buffer).
- As long as the data buffer is not empty, the producer waits.
- As long as the data buffer is empty, the consumer waits.

Next, let's solve this scenario via two common approaches. We will start with a solution that is based on the `wait()` and `notify()` methods.

Producer-Consumer via wait() and notify()

Some interviewers may ask you to implement a **Producer-Consumer** application using the `wait()` and `notify()` methods. In other words, they don't allow you to use a built-in thread-safe queue such as `BlockingQueue`.

For example, let's consider that the data buffer (`queue`) is represented by a `LinkedList`, that is, a non-thread-safe data structure. To ensure that this shared `LinkedList` is accessible in a thread-safe manner by the producer and the consumer, we rely on the `synchronized` keyword.

The producer

If the queue is not empty, then the producer waits until the consumer finishes. To do this, the producer relies on the `wait()` method, as follows:

```java
synchronized (queue) {
  while (!queue.isEmpty()) {
    logger.info("Queue is not empty ...");
    queue.wait();
  }
}
```

On the other hand, if the queue is empty, then the producer enqueues one product and notifies the consumer thread via `notify()`, as follows:

```java
synchronized (queue) {
  String product = "product-" + rnd.nextInt(1000);
  
  // simulate the production time
  Thread.sleep(rnd.nextInt(MAX_PROD_TIME_MS));
  
  queue.add(product);
  logger.info(() -> "Produced: " + product);
  
  queue.notify();
}
```

After adding a product to the queue, the consumer should be ready to consume it.

The consumer

If the queue is empty, then the consumer waits until the producer finishes. For this, the producer relies on the `wait()` method, as follows:

```java
synchronized (queue) {
  while (queue.isEmpty()) {
    logger.info("Queue is empty ...");
    queue.wait();
  }
}
```

On the other hand, if the queue is not empty, then the consumer dequeues one product and notifies the producer thread via `notify()`, as follows:

```
synchronized (queue) {
  String product = queue.remove(0);

  if (product != null) {
    // simulate consuming time
    Thread.sleep(rnd.nextInt(MAX_CONS_TIME_MS));
    logger.info(() -> "Consumed: " + product);

    queue.notify();
  }
}
```

The complete code is available in the bundled code, *ProducerConsumerWaitNotify*.

Producer-Consumer via built-in blocking queues

If you can use a built-in blocking queue, then you can choose a `BlockingQueue` or even a `TransferQueue`. Both of them are thread-safe. In the following code, we use a `TransferQueue` or, more precisely, a `LinkedTransferQueue`.

The producer

The producer waits for the consumer to be available via `hasWaitingConsumer()`:

```
while (queue.hasWaitingConsumer()) {

  String product = "product-" + rnd.nextInt(1000);

  // simulate the production time
  Thread.sleep(rnd.nextInt(MAX_PROD_TIME_MS));
  queue.add(product);
  logger.info(() -> "Produced: " + product);
}
```

After adding a product to the queue, the consumer should be ready to consume it.

The consumer

The consumer uses the `poll()` method with a timeout to extract the product:

```
// MAX_PROD_TIME_MS * 2, just give enough time to the producer
String product = queue.poll(
  MAX_PROD_TIME_MS * 2, TimeUnit.MILLISECONDS);

if (product != null) {
  // simulate consuming time
  Thread.sleep(rnd.nextInt(MAX_CONS_TIME_MS));

  logger.info(() -> "Consumed: " + product);
}
```

The complete code is available in the bundled code, *ProducerConsumerQueue*

Summary

In this chapter, we covered the most popular questions that occur in Java multithreading interviews. Nevertheless, Java concurrency is a vast topic, and it is very important to deep dive into it. I strongly suggest that you read *Java Concurrency in Practice* by Brian Goetz. This is a must-read for any Java developer.

In the next chapter, we will cover a hot topic: Java functional-style programming.

17
Functional-Style Programming

As you probably know, Java is not a purely functional programming language like Haskell, but starting with version 8, Java has added some functional-style support. The effort of adding this support was a success and functional-style code was widely adopted by developers and companies. Functional-style programming sustains code that is more understandable, maintainable, and testable. However, writing Java code in the functional style requires serious knowledge of lambdas, the stream API, `Optional`, functional interfaces, and so on. All these functional programming topics can be interview topics as well and, in this chapter, we will cover some of the hot questions that are mandatory to know for passing a regular Java interview. Our agenda contains the following topics:

- Java functional-style programming in a nutshell
- Questions and coding challenges

Let's get started!

Java functional-style programming in a nutshell

As usual, this section is meant to highlight and refresh the main concepts of our topic and to provide a comprehensive resource for answering the fundamental questions that may occur in a technical interview.

Key concepts of functional-style programming

So, the key concepts of functional programming include the following:

- Functions as first-class objects
- Pure functions
- Higher-order functions

Let's briefly dive into each of these concepts.

Functions as first-class objects

Saying that functions are first-class objects means that we can create an *instance* of a function as having a variable referencing that function instance. This is like referencing a `String`, `List`, or any other object. Moreover, functions can be passed as parameters to other functions. However, Java methods are not first-class objects. The best we can do is to rely on Java lambda expressions.

Pure functions

A *pure* function is a function whose execution has no *side effects* and the return value depends only on its input parameters. The following Java method is a pure function:

```
public class Calculator {

  public int sum(int x, int y) {
    return x + y;
  }
}
```

If a method uses member variables or mutates the states of a member variable, then it is not a *pure* function.

Higher-order functions

A higher-order function takes one or more functions as parameters and/or returns another function as a result. Java emulates higher-order functions via lambda expressions. In other words, in Java, a higher-order function is a method that gets one (or more) lambda expressions as arguments and/or returns another lambda expression.

For example, the `Collections.sort()` method, which takes a `Comparator` as parameter, is a higher-order function:

```
Collections.sort(list, (String x, String y) -> {
   return x.compareTo(y);
});
```

The first parameter of `Collections.sort()` is a `List` and the second parameter is a lambda expression. This lambda expression parameter is what makes `Collections.sort()` a higher-order function.

Pure functional programming rules

Now, let's briefly discuss pure functional programming rules. Pure functional programming has a set of rules to follow too. These are as follows:

- No state
- No side effects
- Immutable variables
- Favoring recursion over looping

Let's briefly dive into each of these rules.

No state

By *no state*, we do not mean that functional programming eliminates state. Commonly, no state means that there is no external state to the function. In other words, a function may work with local variables that contain temporary states internally, but it cannot reference any member variables of the class/object it belongs to.

No side effects

By *no side effects*, we should understand that a function cannot change (mutate) any state outside of the function (outside of its functional scope). State outside of a function includes the following:

- The member variables in the class/object that contain that function
- The member variables that are passed as parameters to the function
- Or the state in external systems (for example, databases or files).

Immutable variables

Functional programming encourages and sustains the usage of immutable variables. Relying on immutable variables helps us to avoid *side effects* in a much easier and more intuitive way.

Favoring recursion over looping

Since recursion relies on repeated function calls to emulate looping, the code becomes more functional. This means that the following iterative approach for calculating factorials is not encouraged by functional programming:

```
static long factorial(long n) {

  long result = 1;
  for (; n > 0; n--) {
    result *= n;
  }

  return result;
}
```

Functional programming encourages the following recursive approach:

```
static long factorial(long n) {
  return n == 1 ? 1 : n * factorial(n - 1);
}
```

We use *tail recursion* to improve the performance penalty caused by the fact that, in the preceding example, every function call is saved as a frame in the recursion stack. Tail recursion is preferred when there are many recursive calls. In tail recursion, the function executes the recursive call as the last thing to do, so the compiler doesn't need to save the function call as a frame in the recursion stack. Most compilers will optimize tail recursion, hence avoiding the performance penalty:

```
static long factorialTail(long n) {
   return factorial(1, n);
}

static long factorial(long acc, long v) {
   return v == 1 ? acc : factorial(acc * v, v - 1);
}
```

Alternatively, looping can be achieved via the Java Stream API, which is functionally inspired:

```
static long factorial(long n) {

   return LongStream.rangeClosed(1, n)
        .reduce(1, (n1, n2) -> n1 * n2);
}
```

Now, it is time to practice some questions and coding challenges.

Questions and coding challenges

In this section, we cover 21 questions and coding challenges that are very popular in interviews. Let's begin!

Coding challenge 1 – Lambda parts

Problem: Describe the parts of a lambda expression in Java. In addition, what characterizes a lambda expression?

Solution: As the following diagram reveals, a lambda has three main parts:

Figure 17.1 – Lambda parts

The parts of a lambda expression are as follows:

- On the left of the arrow, there are the parameters of this lambda that are used in the lambda body. In this example, these are the parameters of the `FilenameFilter.accept(File folder, String fileName)` method.

- On the right of the arrow, there is the lambda body. In this example, the lambda body checks whether the folder (`folder`) in which the file (`fileName`) was found can be read and whether the name of this file is suffixed with the *.pdf* string.

- The arrow that sits between the list of parameters and the body of a lambda acts as a separator.

Next, let's talk about the characteristics of a lambda expression. So, if we write the anonymous class version of the lambda from the preceding diagram, then it will be as follows:

```
FilenameFilter filter = new FilenameFilter() {

  @Override
  public boolean accept(File folder, String fileName) {
    return folder.canRead() && fileName.endsWith(".pdf");
  }
};
```

Now, if we compare the anonymous version and the lambda expression, then we notice that the lambda expression is a concise anonymous function that can be passed as a parameter to a method or be held in a variable.

The four words shown in the following diagram characterize a lambda expression:

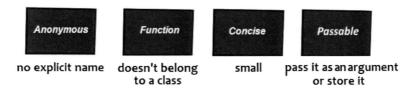

Figure 17.2 – Lambda characteristics

As a rule of thumb, keep in mind that lambdas sustain the Behavior Parameterization design pattern (a behavior is passed as parameter of a function) and it can be used only in the context of a functional interface.

Coding challenge 2 – Functional interface

Problem: What is a functional interface?

Solution: In Java, a functional interface is an interface that contains only one abstract method. In other words, a functional interface contains only one method that is not implemented. So, a functional interface wraps a function as an interface and the function is represented by a single abstract method on the interface.

Optionally, besides this abstract method, a functional interface can have default and/or static methods as well. Commonly, a functional interface is annotated with @FunctionalInterface. This is just an informative annotation type that's used to mark a functional interface.

Here is an example of a functional interface:

```
@FunctionalInterface
public interface Callable<V> {

   V call() throws Exception;
}
```

As a rule of thumb, if an interface has more methods without implementation (that is, abstract methods), then it is no longer a functional interface. This means that such an interface cannot be implemented by a Java lambda expression.

Coding challenge 3 – Collections versus streams

Problem: What are the main differences between collections and streams?

Solution: Collections and streams are quite different. Some of the differences are as follows:

- **Conceptual differences**: The main difference between collections and streams consists of the fact that they are conceptually two different things. While collections are meant to store data (for example, `List`, `Set`, and `Map`), streams are meant to apply operations (for example, *filtering*, *mapping*, and *matching*) on that data. In other words, streams apply complex operations on a view/source represented by data stored on a collection. Moreover, any modification/change performed on a stream is not reflected in the original collection.

- **Data modification**: While we can add/remove elements from a collection, we cannot add/remove elements from a stream. Practically, a stream consumes a view/source, performs operations on it, and returns a result without modifying the view/source.

- **Iteration**: While a stream consumes a view/source, it automatically and internally performs the iteration of that view/source. The iteration takes place depending on the chosen operations that should be applied to the view/source. On the other hand, collections must be iterated externally.

- **Traversal**: While collections can be traversed multiple times, streams can be traversed only once. So, by default, Java streams cannot be reused. Attempting to traverse a stream twice will lead to an error reading *Stream has already been operated on or closed*.

- **Construction**: Collections are eagerly constructed (all the elements are present right from the beginning). On the other hand, streams are lazily constructed (the so-called *intermediate* operations are not evaluated until a *terminal* operation is invoked).

Coding challenge 4 – The map() function

Problem: What does the `map()` function do and why would you use it?

Solution: The `map()` function is an intermediate operation named *mapping* and available via the `Stream` API. It is used to transform a type of object to other type by simply applying the given function. So, `map()` traverses the given stream and transforms each element in a new version of it by applying the given function and accumulating the results in a new `Stream`. The given `Stream` is not modified. For example, transforming a `List<String>` into a `List<Integer>` via `Stream#map()` can be done as follows:

```
List<String> strList = Arrays.asList("1", "2", "3");
List<Integer> intList = strList.stream()
   .map(Integer::parseInt)
   .collect(Collectors.toList());
```

Challenge yourself to practice more examples. Try to apply `map()` to transform an array into another array.

Coding challenge 5 – The flatMap() function

Problem: What does the `flatMap()` function do and why would you use it?

Solution: The `flatMap()` function is an intermediate operation named *flattening* and is available via the `Stream` API. This function is an extension of `map()`, meaning that apart from transforming the given object into another type of object, it can also flatten it. For example, having a `List<List<Object>>`, we can turn it into a `List<Object>` via `Stream#flatMap()` as follows:

```
List<List<Object>> list = ...
List<Object> flatList = list.stream()
   .flatMap(List::stream)
   .collect(Collectors.toList());
```

The next coding challenge is related to this one, so consider this as well.

Coding challenge 6 – map() versus flatMap()

Problem: What's the difference between `map()` and `flatMap()` functions?

Solution: Both of these functions are intermediate operations capable of transforming a given type of object into another type of object by applying the given function. In addition, the `flatMap()` function is capable of flattening the given object as well. In other words, `flatMap()` can also flatten a `Stream` object.

Why does this matter? Well, `map()` knows how to wrap a sequence of elements in a `Stream`, right? This means that `map()` can produce streams such as `Stream<String[]>`, `Stream<List<String>>`, `Stream<Set<String>>`, or even `Stream<Stream<R>>`. But the problem is that these kinds of streams cannot be manipulated successfully (that is, as we expected) by stream operations such as `sum()`, `distinct()`, and `filter()`.

For example, let's consider the following `List`:

```
List<List<String>> melonLists = Arrays.asList(
  Arrays.asList("Gac", "Cantaloupe"),
  Arrays.asList("Hemi", "Gac", "Apollo"),
  Arrays.asList("Gac", "Hemi", "Cantaloupe"));
```

We try to obtain the distinct names of melons from this list. If wrapping an array into a stream can be done via `Arrays.stream()`, for a collection, we have `Collection.stream()`. Therefore, the first attempt may look as follows:

```
melonLists.stream()
  .map(Collection::stream)  // Stream<Stream<String>>
  .distinct();
```

But this will not work because `map()` will return `Stream<Stream<String>>`. The solution is provided by `flatMap()`, as follows:

```
List<String> distinctNames = melonLists.stream()
  .flatMap(Collection::stream)  // Stream<String>
  .distinct()
  .collect(Collectors.toList());
```

The output is as follows: `Gac`, `Cantaloupe`, `Hemi`, `Apollo`.

Moreover, if you find trouble understanding these functional programming methods, then I strongly recommend you to read my other book, *Java Coding Problems*, available from Packt (https://www.packtpub.com/programming/java-coding-problems). That book contains two comprehensive chapters about Java functional-style programming that provide detailed explanations, diagrams, and applications useful for deep diving into this topic.

Coding challenge 7 – The filter() function

Problem: What does the `filter()` function do and why would you use it?

Solution: The `filter()` function is an intermediate operation named *filtering* available via the `Stream` API. It is used to filter the elements of a `Stream` that satisfy a certain condition. The condition is specified via the `java.util.function.Predicate` function. This predicate function is nothing but a function that takes as a parameter an `Object` and returns a `boolean`.

Let's assume that we have the following `List` of integers:

```
List<Integer> ints
  = Arrays.asList(1, 2, -4, 0, 2, 0, -1, 14, 0, -1);
```

Streaming this list and extracting only non-zero elements can be accomplished as follows:

```
List<Integer> result = ints.stream()
   .filter(i -> i != 0)
   .collect(Collectors.toList());
```

The resulting list will contain the following elements: 1, 2, -4, 2, -1, 14, -1.

Notice that, for several common operations, the Java `Stream` API already provides out-of-the-box intermediate operations. For example, there is no need to use `filter()` and define a `Predicate` for operations such as the following:

- `distinct()`: Removes duplicates from the stream
- `skip(n)`: Discards the first n elements
- `limit(s)`: Truncates the stream to be no longer than s in length
- `sorted()`: Sorts the stream according to the natural order
- `sorted(Comparator<? super T> comparator)`: Sorts the stream according to the given `Comparator`

All these functions are built into the `Stream` API.

Coding challenge 8 – Intermediate versus terminal operations

Problem: What is the main difference between intermediate and terminal operations?

Solution: Intermediate operations return another `Stream`, while the terminal operations produce a result other than `Stream` (for example, a collection or a scalar value). In other words, intermediate operations allow us to chain/call multiple operations in a type of query named a *pipeline*.

Intermediate operations are not executed until a terminal operation is invoked. This means that intermediate operations are lazy. Mainly, they are executed at the moment when a result of some given processing is actually needed. A terminal operation triggers the traversal of the `Stream` and the pipeline is executed.

Among the intermediate operations, we have `map()`, `flatMap()`, `filter()`, `limit()`, and `skip()`. Among the terminal operations, we have `sum()`, `min()`, `max()`, `count()`, and `collect()`.

Coding challenge 9 – The peek() function

Problem: What does the `peek()` function do and why would you use it?

Solution: The `peek()` function is an intermediate operation named *peeking* available via the `Stream` API. It allows us to see through a `Stream` pipeline. Mainly, `peek()` should execute a certain *non-interfering* action on the current element and forward the element to the next operation in the pipeline. Typically, this action consists of printing a meaningful message on the console. In other words, `peek()` is a good choice for debugging issues related to streams and lambda expression processing. For example, imagine that we had the following list of addresses:

```
addresses.stream()
    .peek(p -> System.out.println("\tstream(): " + p))
    .filter(s -> s.startsWith("c"))
    .sorted()
    .peek(p -> System.out.println("\tsorted(): " + p))
    .collect(Collectors.toList());
```

It is important to mention that, even if `peek()` can be used to mutate state (to modify the data source of the stream), it stands for *look, but don't touch*. Mutating state via `peek()` can become a real problem in case of parallel stream pipelines because the mutating action may be called at whatever time and in whatever thread the element is made available by the upstream operation. So, if the action modifies the shared state, it is responsible for providing the required synchronization.

As a rule of thumb, think twice before using `peek()` to mutate the state. Also, be aware that this practice is a point of contention among developers and can be categorized as bad practice or even anti-pattern umbrellas.

Coding challenge 10 – Lazy streams

Problem: What does it mean to say that a stream is lazy?

Solution: Saying that a stream is lazy means that a stream defines a pipeline of intermediate operations that are executed only when the pipeline encounters a terminal operation. This question is related to *Coding challenge 8* of this chapter.

Coding challenge 11 – Functional interfaces versus regular interfaces

Problem: What is the main difference between a functional interface and a regular interface?

Solution: The main difference between a functional interface and a regular interface consists of the fact that a regular interface can contain any number of abstract methods, while a functional interface can have only one abstract method.

You can consult *Coding challenge 2* of this book for a deeper understanding.

Coding challenge 12 – Supplier versus Consumer

Problem: What are the main differences between `Supplier` and `Consumer`?

Solution: `Supplier` and `Consumer` are two built-in functional interfaces. `Supplier` acts as a factory method or as the `new` keyword. In other words, `Supplier` defines a method named `get()` that doesn't take arguments and returns an object of type T. So, a `Supplier` is useful to *supply* some value.

On the other hand, `Consumer` defines a method named `void accept(T t)`. This method accepts a single argument and returns `void`. The `Consumer` interface *consumes* the given value and applies some operations to it. Unlike other functional interfaces, `Consumer` may cause *side effects*. For example, `Consumer` can be used as a setter method.

Coding challenge 13 – Predicates

Problem: What is `Predicate`?

Solution: `Predicate` is a built-in functional interface that contains an abstract method whose signature is `boolean test(T object)`:

```
@FunctionalInterface
public interface Predicate<T> {

  boolean test(T t);

  // default and static methods omitted for brevity
}
```

The `test()` method tests a condition and returns `true` if that condition is met, otherwise it returns `false`. A common usage of a `Predicate` is in conjunction with the `Stream<T> filter(Predicate<? super T> predicate)` method for filtering unwanted elements of a stream.

Coding challenge 14 – findFirst() versus findAny()

Problem: What are the main differences between `findFirst()` and `findAny()`?

Solution: The `findFirst()` method returns the first element from the stream and is especially useful in obtaining the first element from a sequence. It returns the first element from the stream as long as the stream has a defined order. If there is no encounter order, then `findFirst()` returns any element from the stream.

On the other hand, the `findAny()` method returns any element from the stream. In other words, it returns an arbitrary (non-deterministic) element from the stream. The `findAny()` method ignores the encountered order, and, in a non-parallel operation, it will most likely return the first element, but there is no guarantee of this. In order to maximize performance, the result cannot be reliably determined in parallel operations.

Notice that, depending on the stream's source and the intermediate operations, streams may or may not have a defined encounter order.

Coding challenge 15 – Converting arrays to streams

Problem: How would you convert an array to a stream?

Solution: Converting an array of objects into a stream can be done in at least three ways, as follows:

1. The first is via `Arrays#stream()`:

```
public static <T> Stream<T> toStream(T[] arr) {
   return Arrays.stream(arr);
}
```

2. Second, we can use `Stream#of()`:

```
public static <T> Stream<T> toStream(T[] arr) {
   return Stream.of(arr);
}
```

3. The last technique is via `List#stream()`:

```
public static <T> Stream<T> toStream(T[] arr) {
   return Arrays.asList(arr).stream();
}
```

Converting an array of primitives (for example, integers) into a stream can be done in at least two ways, as follows:

1. Firstly, via `Arrays#stream()`:

```
public static IntStream toStream(int[] arr) {
   return Arrays.stream(arr);
}
```

2. Secondly, by using `IntStream#of()`:

```
public static IntStream toStream(int[] arr) {
  return IntStream.of(arr);
}
```

Of course, for longs, you can use `LongStream`, and for doubles, you can use `DoubleStream`.

Coding challenge 16 – Parallel streams

Problem: What is a parallel stream?

Solution: A parallel stream is a stream that can parallelize the execution using multiple threads. For example, you may need to filter a stream of 10 million integers to find the integers smaller than a certain value. Instead of using a single thread to traverse the stream sequentially, you can employ a parallel stream. This means that multiple threads will concurrently search for those integers in different parts of the stream and then combine the result.

Coding challenge 17 – The method reference

Problem: What is a method reference?

Solution: In a nutshell, *method references* are shortcuts for lambda expressions. Mainly, the method reference is a technique that's used to call a method by name rather than by a description of how to call it. The main benefit is readability. A method reference is written by placing the target reference before the delimiter, `::`, and the name of the method is provided after it. We have the following references:

- A method reference to a static method: *Class::staticMethod* (for example, `Math::max` is equivalent to `Math.max(x, y)`)

- A method reference to a constructor: *Class::new* (for example, `AtomicInteger::new` is equivalent to `new AtomicInteger(x)`)

- A method reference to an instance method from instance: *object::instanceMethod* (`System.out::println` equivalent to `System.out.println(foo)`)

- A method reference to an instance method from class type: *Class::instanceMethod* (`String::length` equivalent to `str.length()`)

Coding challenge 18 – The default method

Problem: What is a default method?

Solution: Default methods were added to Java 8 mainly to provide support for interfaces so that they can evolve beyond an abstract contract (that is, containing only abstract methods). This facility is very useful for people who write libraries and want to evolve APIs in a compatible way. Via default methods, an interface can be enriched without disrupting existing implementations.

A default method is implemented directly in the interface and is recognized by the `default` keyword. For example, the following interface defines an abstract method called `area()` and a default method called `perimeter()`:

```
public interface Polygon {

  public double area();

  default double perimeter(double... segments) {
    return Arrays.stream(segments)
      .sum();
  }
}
```

Since `Polygon` has a single abstract method, it is a functional interface as well. So, it can be annotated with `@FunctionalInterface`.

Coding challenge 19 – Iterator versus Spliterator

Problem: What are the main differences between `Iterator` and `Spliterator`?

Solution: `Iterator` was created for the `Collection` API, while `Spliterator` was created for the `Stream` API.

By analyzing their names, we notice that *Spliterator = Splittable Iterator*. Hence, a `Spliterator` can split a given source and it can iterate it, too. Splitting is needed for parallel processing. In other words, an `Iterator` can sequentially iterate the elements in `Collection`, while a `Spliterator` can iterate the elements of a stream in parallel or sequential order.

An `Iterator` can traverse the elements of a collection only via `hasNext()`/`next()` because it doesn't have a size. On the other hand, a `Spliterator` can provide the size of the collection either by approximating it via `estimateSize()` or exactly via `getExactSizeIfKnown()`.

A `Spliterator` can use several flags for internally disabling unnecessary operations (for example, `CONCURRENT`, `DISTINCT`, and `IMMUTABLE`). An `Iterator` doesn't have such flags.

Finally, you can create a `Spliterator` around an `Iterator` as follows:

```
Spliterators.spliteratorUnknownSize(
  your_Iterator, your_Properties);
```

In the book *Java Coding Problems* (https://www.amazon.com/gp/product/B07Y9BPV4W/), you can find more details on this topic, including a complete guide for writing a custom `Spliterator`.

Coding challenge 20 – Optional

Problem: What is the `Optional` class?

Solution: Inspired by Haskell and Scala, the `Optional` class was introduced in Java 8 with the main purpose of mitigating/avoiding `NullPointerException`. The Java language architect Brian Goetz's definition is as follows:

Optional is intended to provide a limited mechanism for library method return types where there needed to be a clear way to represent no result, and using null for such was overwhelmingly likely to cause errors.

In a nutshell, you can think of `Optional` as a single value container that contains either a value or is empty. For example, an empty `Optional` looks like this:

```
Optional<User> userOptional = Optional.empty();
```

And a non-empty `Optional` looks like this:

```
User user = new User();
Optional<User> userOptional = Optional.of(user);
```

In *Java Coding Problems* (https://www.amazon.com/gp/product/B07Y9BPV4W/), you can find a complete chapter dedicated to best practices for using `Optional`. This is a must-read chapter for any Java developer.

Coding challenge 21 – String::valueOf

Problem: What does `String::valueOf` mean?

Solution: `String::valueOf` is a method reference to the `valueOf` static method of the `String` class. Consider reading *Coding challenge 17* as well for more information on this.

Summary

In this chapter, we've covered several hot topics regarding functional-style programming in Java. While this topic is quite extensive, with many books dedicated to it, the questions covered here should be enough to pass a regular Java interview that covers the main features of the Java 8 language.

In the next chapter, we will discuss scaling-related questions.

18
Unit Testing

As a developer (or software engineer), you must have skills in the testing field as well. For example, developers are responsible for writing the unit tests of their code (for example, using JUnit or TestNG). Most probably, a pull request that doesn't contain unit tests as well won't be accepted.

In this chapter, we will cover unit testing interview problems that you may encounter if you apply for a position such as developer or software engineer. Of course, if you are looking for a tester (manual/automation) position, then this chapter may represent just another perspective of testing, so do not expect to see questions specific to manual/automation tester positions here. In this chapter, we'll cover the following topics:

- Unit testing in a nutshell
- Questions and coding problems

Let's begin!

Technical Requirements

The codes used in this chapter can be found on GitHub on: `https://github.com/PacktPublishing/The-Complete-Coding-Interview-Guide-in-Java/tree/master/Chapter18`

Unit testing in a nutshell

The process of testing an application contains several layers of testing. One of these layers is the *unit testing* layer.

Mainly, an application is built by small functional parts called units (for example, a regular Java method can be considered a unit). Testing the functionality and correctness of these units under specific inputs/conditions/constraints is called unit testing.

These unit tests are written by developers using the source code and the test plan. Ideally, every developer should be capable of writing unit tests that test/validate their code. Unit tests should be meaningful and provide accepted code coverage.

If the unit tests fails, then the developer is responsible for fixing the issues and executing the unit tests again. The following diagram depicts this statement:

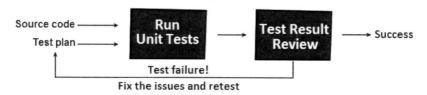

Figure 18.1 – Unit testing flow

Unit testing uses **unit test cases**. A *unit test case* is a pair of input data and expected output meant to shape a test for a certain functionality.

If you are in an interview where you are expected to know unit testing, don't be surprised if you are asked questions on functional testing and/or integration testing. Hence, it is advisable to be prepared with answers to these questions as well.

Functional testing is about testing functional requirements based on the given input and a produced output (behavior) that needs to be compared with the expected output (behavior). Each functional test uses the functional specification to verify the correctness of the component (or a group of components) that represents the implementation of that functional requirement. This is explained in the following diagram:

Figure 18.2 – Functional testing

The goal of **integration testing** is to find out the defects in the software components while they are being integrated in an iteratively incremental manner. In other words, the modules that have been unit tested are integrated (grouped together or aggregated) and tested by following the integration plan. This has been depicted in the following diagram:

Unit testing in a nutshell

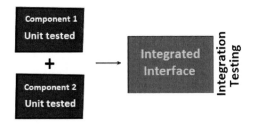

Figure 18.3 – Integration testing

A question regarding unit and integration testing that is frequently put to interview candidates is about highlighting the main differences between these two. The following table will help you prepare an answer to this question:

Unit test	Integration test
Typically, useful to developers.	Useful to QA, DevOps, and Help Desk as well
Results depend only on Java code.	Results may depend on external systems.
Fairly easy to write.	May be quite complicated to set up
Units are tested in isolation.	One or more components are tested.
Can use mocking for dependencies.	Mocking should be avoided.
Only test the implementation of code.	Test the implementation of the components and the interconnection behavior between them
Uses JUnit/TestNG.	Uses real environments via tools such as Arquillian and DbUnit.
A failed test is a regression problem.	A failed test can be caused by changes in the environment
Such tests shouldn't take too long to run.	Such tests can take quite a long time (for example, 1 hour)

Figure 18.4 – Comparison between unit tests and integration tests

A good tester is capable of stressing and abusing the subject of testing without making any kinds of assumptions or constraints regarding the input. This applies to unit tests as well. Now that we have touched on unit testing, let's have a look at some coding challenges and questions on unit testing.

Questions and coding challenges

In this section, we'll cover 15 questions and coding challenges related to unit testing that are very popular in interviews. Let's begin!

Coding challenge 1 – AAA

Problem: What is AAA in unit testing?

Solution: The **AAA** acronym stands for [A]rrange, [A]ct, [A]ssert, and it represents an approach to structuring tests to sustain clean code and readability. Today, AAA is a testing pattern that's almost a standard across the industry. The following snippet of code speaks for itself:

```
@Test
public void givenStreamWhenSumThenEquals6() {

    // Arrange
    Stream<Integer> theStream = Stream.of(1, 2, 3);

    // Act
    int sum = theStream.mapToInt(i -> i).sum();

    // Assert
    assertEquals(6, sum);
}
```

Arrange section: In this section, we prepare or set up the test. For example, in the preceding code, we prepared a stream of integers where the elements are 1, 2, and 3.

Act section: In this section, we perform the necessary actions to obtain the result of the test. For example, in the preceding code, we sum the elements of the stream and store the result in an integer variable.

Assert section: In this section, we check whether the unit test's result matches the expected results. This is done via assertions. For example, in the preceding code, we checked that the sum of the elements is equal to 6.

You can find this code in the application called *junit5/ArrangeActAssert*.

Coding challenge 2 – FIRST

Problem: What is **FIRST** in unit testing?

Solution: Good testers use FIRST to avoid many of the pitfalls encountered in unit tests. The **FIRST** acronym stands for [**F**]ast, [**I**]solated, [**R**]epeatable, [**S**]elf-validating, [**T**]imely. Let's see what each of them mean:

Fast: It is advisable to write unit tests that run fast. Fast is an arbitrary notion that depends on how many unit tests you have, how often you run them, and how long you are willing to wait for them to run. For example, if each unit test has an average completion time of 200 ms and you run 5,000 unit tests, then you'll wait ~17 minutes. Commonly, unit tests are slow because they access external resources (for example, databases and files).

Isolated: Ideally, you should be able to run any test at any time, in any order. This is possible if your unit tests are isolated and they focus on small snippets of code. Good unit tests don't depend on other unit tests, but this is not always achievable. Nevertheless, strive to avoid chains of dependencies since they are evil when things go wrong, and you'll have to debug.

Repeatable: A unit test should be repeatable. This means that the unit test's assertions should produce the same result every time you run it. In other words, the unit tests should not depend on anything that may introduce variable results to assertions.

Self-validating: Unit tests should be self-validating. This means that you shouldn't manually verify the results of the tests. This is time-consuming and reveals that the assertions are not doing their job. Strive to write assertions so that they work as expected.

Timely: It is important to not postpone writing unit tests. The more you postpone, the more defects you'll face. You'll find out that you cannot find time to come back and write unit tests. Think of what's happening if we constantly postpone taking out the trash. The more we postpone, the harder it will be to take it on, and we risk our health. Did I say anything about the smell? So, write the unit tests in a timely fashion. This is a good habit!

Coding challenge 3 – Test fixtures

Problem: What are test fixtures?

Solution: By test fixtures, we mean any test data that lives outside that test and is used to set up the application so that it's in a fixed state. Having a fixed state for the application allows the tests to be run against a constant and known environment.

Coding challenge 4 – Exception testing

Problem: What are the common approaches for testing exceptions in JUnit?

Solution: In JUnit 4, we commonly test exceptions via the `try/catch` idiom, the `expected` element of `@Test`, and via the `ExpectedException` rule.

The `try/catch` idiom prevailed in JUnit 3.x and can be used as follows:

```
@Test
public void givenStreamWhenGetThenException() {

  Stream<Integer> theStream = Stream.of();

  try {
    theStream.findAny().get();
    fail("Expected a NoSuchElementException to be thrown");
  } catch (NoSuchElementException ex) {
    assertThat(ex.getMessage(), is("No value present"));
  }
}
```

Since `fail()` throws an `AssertionError`, it cannot be used to test this error type.

Starting with JUnit 4, we can use the `expected` element of the `@Test` annotation. The value of this element is the type of the expected exception (subclasses of `Throwable`). Check out the following example, which was written using `expected`:

```
@Test(expected = NoSuchElementException.class)
public void givenStreamWhenGetThenException() {

  Stream<Integer> theStream = Stream.of();
  theStream.findAny().get();
}
```

This approach is alright as long as you don't want to test the value of the exception message. Moreover, pay attention that the test passes if a `NoSuchElementException` is thrown by any line of code. You may expect this exception to be caused by a particular line of code, while it can, in fact, be caused by other code.

Another approach relies on the `ExpectedException` rule. This approach was deprecated starting with JUnit 4.13. Let's take a look at the code:

```
@Rule
public ExpectedException thrown = ExpectedException.none();

@Test
public void givenStreamWhenGetThenException()
    throws NoSuchElementException {

  Stream<Integer> theStream = Stream.of();

  thrown.expect(NoSuchElementException.class);
  thrown.expectMessage("No value present");

  theStream.findAny().get();
}
```

Via this approach, you can test the value of the exception message. These examples have been grouped into an application called *junit4/TestingExceptions*.

Starting with JUnit5, there are two approaches we can use to test exceptions. Both of them rely on the `assertThrows()` method. This method allows us to assert that a given function call (passed in as a lambda expression or even as a method reference) results in the expected type of exception being thrown. The following example speaks for itself:

```
@Test
public void givenStreamWhenGetThenException() {

  assertThrows(NoSuchElementException.class, () -> {
    Stream<Integer> theStream = Stream.of();
    theStream.findAny().get();
  });
}
```

This example just validates the type of exception. However, since the exception has been thrown, we can assert more details of the thrown exception. For example, we can assert the value of the exception message as follows:

```java
@Test
public void givenStreamWhenGetThenException() {

  Throwable ex = assertThrows(
    NoSuchElementException.class, () -> {
      Stream<Integer> theStream = Stream.of();
      theStream.findAny().get();
    });

  assertEquals(ex.getMessage(), "No value present");
}
```

Simply use the `ex` object to assert anything you consider useful from `Throwable`. Whenever you don't need to assert details about the exception, rely on `assertThrows()`, without capturing the return. These two examples have been grouped into an application called *junit5/TestingExceptions*.

Coding challenge 5 – Developer or tester

Problem: Who should use JUnit – the developer or the tester?

Solution: Commonly, JUnit is used by developers for writing unit tests in Java. Writing unit tests is a coding process that tests the application code. JUnit is not a testing process. However, many testers are open to learn and use JUnit for unit testing.

Coding challenge 6 – JUnit extensions

Problem: What useful JUnit extensions do you know/use?

Solution: The most widely used JUnit extensions are JWebUnit (a Java-based testing framework for web applications), XMLUnit (a single JUnit extension class for testing XML), Cactus (a simple testing framework for testing server-side Java code), and MockObject (a mocking framework). You will need to say a few words about each of these.

Coding challenge 7 – @Before* and @After* annotations

Problem: What `@Before*`/`@After*` annotation do you know about/use?

Solution: In JUnit 4, we have `@Before`, `@BeforeClass`, `@After`, and `@AfterClass`.

When executing a method before each test, we annotate it with the `@Before` annotation. This is useful for executing a common snippet of code before running a test (for example, we may need to perform some reinitializations before each test). To clean up the stage after each test, we annotate a method with the `@After` annotation.

When executing a method only once before all tests, we annotate it with the `@BeforeClass` annotation. The method must be `static`. This is useful for global and expensive settings, such as opening a connection to a database. To clean up the stage after all the tests are done, we annotate a `static` method with the `@AfterClass` annotation; for example, closing a database connection.

You can find a simple example under the name *junit4/BeforeAfterAnnotations*.

Starting with JUnit5, we have `@BeforeEach` as the equivalent of `@Before` and `@BeforeAll` as the equivalent of `@BeforeClass`. Practically, `@Before` and `@BeforeClass` were renamed with more suggestive names to avoid confusion.

You can find a simple example of this under the name *junit5/BeforeAfterAnnotations*.

Coding challenge 8 – Mocking and stubbing

Problem: What is mocking and stubbing?

Solution: Mocking is a technique that's used to create objects that emulate/mimic real objects. These objects can be pre-programmed (or preset or pre-configured) with expectations and we can check whether they have been called. Among the most widely used mocking frameworks available, we have Mockito and EasyMock.

Stubbing is like mocking, except that we cannot check whether they have been called. Stubs are pre-configured to respond to particular inputs with particular outputs.

Coding challenge 9 – Test suite

Problem: What is a test suite?

Solution: A test suite is the concept of aggregating multiple tests divided among multiple test classes and packages so that they run together.

In JUnit4, we can define a test suite via the `org.junit.runners.Suite` runner and the `@SuiteClasses(...)` annotation. For example, the following snippet of code is a test suite that aggregates three tests (`TestConnect.class`, `TestHeartbeat.class`, and `TestDisconnect.class`):

```
@RunWith(Suite.class)
@Suite.SuiteClasses({
   TestConnect.class,
   TestHeartbeat.class,
   TestDisconnect.class
})
public class TestSuite {
    // this class was intentionally left empty
}
```

The complete code is called *junit4/TestSuite*.

In JUnit5, we can define a test suite via the `@SelectPackages` and `@SelectClasses` annotations.

The `@SelectPackages` annotation is useful for aggregating tests from different packages. All we have to do is specify the names of the packages, as shown in the following example:

```
@RunWith(JUnitPlatform.class)
@SuiteDisplayName("TEST LOGIN AND CONNECTION")
@SelectPackages({
   "coding.challenge.connection.test",
   "coding.challenge.login.test"
})
public class TestLoginSuite {
   // this class was intentionally left empty
}
```

The `@SelectClasses` annotation is useful for aggregating tests via the names of their classes:

```
@RunWith(JUnitPlatform.class)
@SuiteDisplayName("TEST CONNECTION")
@SelectClasses({
   TestConnect.class,
   TestHeartbeat.class,
   TestDisconnect.class
})
public class TestConnectionSuite {
   // this class was intentionally left empty
}
```

The complete code is called *junit5/TestSuite*.

Additionally, filtering test packages, test classes, and test methods can be done via the following annotations:

- Filter packages: `@IncludePackages` and `@ExcludePackages`
- Filter test classes: `@IncludeClassNamePatterns` and `@ExcludeClassNamePatterns`
- Filter test methods: `@IncludeTags` and `@ExcludeTags`

Coding challenge 10 – Ignoring test methods

Problem: How can we ignore a test?

Solution: In JUnit4, we can ignore a test method by annotating it with the `@Ignore` annotation. In JUnit5, we can do the same thing via the `@Disable` annotation.

Ignoring test methods can be useful when we have written some tests in advance and we want to run the current tests without running these particular tests.

Coding challenge 11 – Assumptions

Problem: What are assumptions?

Solution: Assumptions are used to execute tests if the specified conditions have been met. They are commonly used to handle external conditions that are required for the test to execute properly, but that are not under our control and/or are not directly related to what is being tested.

In JUnit4, assumptions are `static` methods that can be found in the `org.junit.Assume` package. Among these assumptions, we have `assumeThat()`, `assumeTrue()`, and `assumeFalse()`. The following snippet of code exemplifies the usage of `assumeThat()`:

```java
@Test
public void givenFolderWhenGetAbsolutePathThenSuccess() {

  assumeThat(File.separatorChar, is('/'));
  assertThat(new File(".").getAbsolutePath(),
    is("C:/SBPBP/GitHub/Chapter18/junit4"));
}
```

If `assumeThat()` doesn't meet the given condition, then the test is skipped. The complete application is called *junit4/Assumptions*.

In JUnit5, assumptions are `static` methods that can be found in the `org.junit.jupiter.api.Assumptions` package. Among these assumptions, we have `assumeThat()`, `assumeTrue()`, and `assumeFalse()`. All three come in different flavors. The following snippet of code exemplifies the usage of `assumeThat()`:

```java
@Test
public void givenFolderWhenGetAbsolutePathThenSuccess() {

  assumingThat(File.separatorChar == '/',
    () -> {
      assertThat(new File(".").getAbsolutePath(),
        is("C:/SBPBP/GitHub/Chapter18/junit5"));
  });

  // run these assertions always, just like normal test
  assertTrue(true);
}
```

Notice that the test method (`assertThat()`) will only execute if the assumption is met. Everything after the lambda will be executed, irrespective of the assumption's validity. The complete application is called *junit5/Assumptions*.

Coding challenge 12 – @Rule

Problem: What is `@Rule`?

Solution: JUnit provides a high degree of flexibility via so-called *rules*. Rules allows us to create and isolate objects (code) and reuse this code in multiple test classes. Mainly, we enhance tests with reusable rules. JUnit comes with built-in rules and with an API that can be used to write custom rules.

Coding challenge 13 – Method test return type

Problem: Can we return something other than `void` from a JUnit test method?

Solution: Yes, we can change the return of a test method from `void` to something else, but JUnit will not recognize it as a test method, so it will be ignored during the test's execution.

Coding challenge 14 – Dynamic tests

Problem: Can we write dynamic tests (tests generated at runtime) in JUnit?

Solution: Up until JUnit5, all tests were static. In other words, all the tests annotated with `@Test` were static tests that were fully defined at compile time. JUnit5 introduced dynamic tests – a dynamic test is generated at runtime.

Dynamic tests are generated via a factory method, which is a method annotated with the `@TestFactory` annotation. Such a method can return `Iterator`, `Iterable`, `Collection`, or `Stream` of `DynamicTest` instances. A factory method is not annotated with `@Test`, and is not `private` or `static`. Moreover, dynamic tests cannot take advantage of life cycle callbacks (for example, `@BeforeEach` and `@AfterEach` are ignored).

Let's look at a simple example:

```
1:  @TestFactory
2:  Stream<DynamicTest> dynamicTestsExample() {
3:
4:      List<Integer> items = Arrays.asList(1, 2, 3, 4, 5);
5:
6:      List<DynamicTest> dynamicTests = new ArrayList<>();
7:
8:      for (int item : items) {
9:          DynamicTest dynamicTest = dynamicTest(
```

```
10:            "pow(" + item + ", 2):", () -> {
11:                assertEquals(item * item, Math.pow(item, 2));
12:            });
13:         dynamicTests.add(dynamicTest);
14:     }
15:
16:     return dynamicTests.stream();
17: }
```

Now, let's point out the main lines of code:

1: At line 1, we use the `@TestFactory` annotation to instruct JUnit5 that this is a factory method for dynamic tests.

2: The factory method returns a `Stream<DynamicTest>`.

4: The input for our tests is a list of integers. For each integer, we generate a dynamic test.

6: We define a `List<DynamicTest>`. In this list, we add each generated test.

8-12: We generate a test for each integer. Each test has a name and a lambda expression containing the requisite assertion(s).

13: We store the generated test in the proper list.

16: We return the `Stream` of tests.

Running this test factory will produce five tests. The complete example is called *junit5/TestFactory*.

Coding challenge 15 – Nested tests

Problem: Can we write nested tests in JUnit5?

Solution: Yes, we can! JUnit 5 supports nested tests via the `@Nested` annotation. Practically, we create a nested test class hierarchy. This hierarchy may contain the setup, teardown, and test methods. Nevertheless, there are some rules that we must respect, as follows:

- Nested test classes are annotated with the `@Nested` annotation.
- Nested test classes are non-`static` inner classes.
- A nested test class can contain one `@BeforeEach` method, one `@AfterEach` method, and test methods.

- The `static` members are not allowed in inner classes, which means that the `@BeforeAll` and `@AfterAll` methods cannot be used in nested tests.
- The depth of the class hierarchy is unlimited.

Some sample code for a nested test can be seen here:

```
@RunWith(JUnitPlatform.class)
public class NestedTest {

  private static final Logger log
    = Logger.getLogger(NestedTest.class.getName());

  @DisplayName("Test 1 - not nested")
  @Test
  void test1() {
    log.info("Execute test1() ...");
  }

  @Nested
  @DisplayName("Running tests nested in class A")
  class A {

    @BeforeEach
    void beforeEach() {
      System.out.println("Before each test
        method of the A class");
    }

    @AfterEach
    void afterEach() {
      System.out.println("After each test
        method of the A class");
    }

    @Test
    @DisplayName("Test2 - nested in class A")
    void test2() {
```

```
            log.info("Execute test2() ...");
        }
    }
}
```

The complete example is called *junit5/NestedTests*.

Summary

In this chapter, we covered several hot questions and coding challenges about unit testing via JUnit4 and JUnit5. It is important to not neglect this topic. Most likely, in the last part of an interview for a Java developer or software engineer position, you'll get several questions related to testing. Moreover, those questions will be related to unit testing and JUnit.

In the next chapter, we will discuss scaling and scaling-related interview questions.

19
System Scalability

Scalability is, for sure, one of the most critical demands for the success of a web application. An application's capacity to scale depends on the whole system architecture, and building a project while having scalability in mind is the best way to go. You'll be very thankful later when the success of the business may require the application to be highly scalable due to heavy loads of traffic.

So, as the web grows, designing and building scalable applications is also becoming more important. In this chapter, we cover all the scalability interview questions you may be asked during a junior/middle-level interview for a position such as a web application software architect, Java architect, or software engineer. If you are looking for a position that doesn't involve tasks related to software architecture and design, then most probably scalability will not be an interview topic.

Our agenda for this chapter includes the following:

- Scalability in a nutshell
- Questions and coding challenges

Let's get started!

Scalability in a nutshell

The most predictable yet important question your interviewer will ask you is: What is scalability? Scalability is the capability and ability of a process (system, network, application) to cope with an increase in workload (by workload, we understand anything that pushes the system to the limit, such as traffic, storage capacity, a maximum number of transactions, and so on) when adding resources (typically hardware). Scalability can be expressed as the ratio between the increase in system performance and the rise in resources used. Moreover, scalability also means the ability to add extra resources without affecting/modifying the structure of the main nodes.

If adding more resources results in a slight increase in performance, or even worse, boosting the resources has no effect on performance, then you are facing so-called *poor scalability*.

How can you achieve scalability? During an interview that involves scalability questions, you will most probably be asked this question as well. Giving a general, comprehensive, and not too time-consuming answer is the best choice. The main points that should be touched upon are the following:

- **Leverage 12factor** (`https://12factor.net/`): This methodology is independent of the programming language and can be really helpful for delivering flexible and scalable applications.

- **Implement persistence wisely**: From choosing the proper database for your application and developing the most optimized schema, to mastering techniques for scaling the persistence layer (for example, clustering, replicas, sharding, and so on), this is one of the key aspects that deserve your entire attention.

- **Don't underestimate queries**: Database queries are a key factor in acquiring short transactions. Tune your connection pool and queries for scalability. For example, pay attention to cross-node joins, which can quickly downgrade performance.

- **Choose hosting and tools**: Scaling is not only about the code! The infrastructure counts a lot as well. Today, many cloud players (for example, Amazon) provide autoscaling and dedicated tools (Docker, Kubernetes, and so on).

- **Consider load balancing and reverse proxying**: One day, you have to switch from a single server to a multi-server architecture. Running under a cloud infrastructure (for example, Amazon) will easily provide these facilities with just several configurations (for most cloud providers, load balancing and reverse proxying are part of the *ready-to-go* offer). Otherwise, you have to be prepared for this significant change.

- **Caching**: While scaling your application, consider new caching strategies, topologies, and tools.
- **Relieve the backend**: Move as many computations as possible from the backend to the frontend. This way, you take some work from your backend shoulders.
- **Test and monitor**: Testing and monitoring your code will help you to discover issues as soon as possible.

There are many other aspects to discuss, but at this point, the interviewer should be ready to advance the interview to the next step.

Questions and coding challenges

In this section, we cover 13 questions and coding challenges that represent *must-knows* in junior/middle-level scalability interviews. Let's begin!

Coding challenge 1 – Scaling types

Problem: What do scaling up and scaling out mean?

Solution: Scaling up (or vertical scaling) is achieved by adding more resources to an existing system to achieve better performance and successfully face a greater workload. By resources, we can understand more storage, more memory, more network, more threads, more connections, more powerful hosts, more caching, and so on. Once the new resources are added, the application should be capable of respecting the SLAs. Today, scaling up in the cloud is very efficient and fast. Clouds such as AWS, Azure, Oracle, Heroku, Google Cloud, and so on can automatically allocate more resources based on the threshold plan in just a couple of minutes. When the traffic decreases, AWS can disable these extra resources. This way, you pay only for what you use.

Scaling out (or horizontal scaling) is typically related to distributed architectures. There are two basic forms of scaling out:

- Add more infrastructure capacity in pre-packaged blocks of infrastructure/nodes (for example, hyper-converged).
- Use an independent distributed service that can harvest information about customers.

Typically, scaling out is done by adding more servers or CPUs that are the same type as those that are currently used or any compatible kind. Scaling out makes it easy for service providers to offer customers a *pay-as-you-grow* infrastructure and services. Scaling out happens quite fast since nothing has to be imported or rebuilt. Nevertheless, scale-out speed is limited by the speed with which the servers can communicate.

Clouds such as AWS can automatically allocate more infrastructure based on the threshold plan in just a couple of minutes. When the traffic is low, AWS can disable these extra infrastructures. This way, you pay only for what you use.

Typically, scaling up offers better performance than scaling out.

Coding challenge 2 – High availability

Problem: What is high availability?

Solution: High availability and low latency are mission-critical for tons of businesses.

Typically expressed as a percentage of uptime in a given year, high availability is achieved when an application is available to its users without interruption (99.9% of the time during a year).

Achieving high availability is commonly done via clustering.

Coding challenge 3 – Low latency

Problem: What is low latency?

Solution: Low latency is a term used in relation to computer networks that are optimized to handle and process an extremely high volume of data with minimal delay or latency. Such networks are designed and built to handle operations that attempt to achieve near real-time data processing capabilities.

Coding challenge 4 – Clustering

Problem: What is a cluster and why do we need clustering?

Solution: A cluster is a group of machines that can individually run an application. We can have an application server cluster, a database server cluster, and so on.

Having a cluster significantly reduces the chances of our service becoming unavailable in the event that one of the machines from the cluster fails. In other words, clustering's main purpose consists of achieving 100% availability or zero downtime in service (high availability – see *Coding challenge 2*). Of course, there is still be a small chance of all the cluster machines failing at the same time, but that is typically mitigated by having the machines located at different locations or supported by their own resources.

Coding challenge 5 – Latency, bandwidth, and throughput

Problem: What are latency, bandwidth, and throughput?

Solution: The best way to explain these notions during an interview relies on a simple analogy with a tube as in the following figure:

Figure 19.1 – Latency versus bandwidth versus throughput

Latency is the amount of time it takes to travel through the tube, not the tube length. It is, however, measured as a function of the tube length.

Bandwidth is how wide the tube is.

Throughput is the amount of water flowing through the tube.

Coding challenge 6 – Load balancing

Problem: What is load balancing?

Solution: Load balancing is a technique used for distributing workloads across multiple machines or clusters. Among the algorithms used by load balancing, we have Round Robin, sticky session (or session affinity), and IP address affinity. A common and simple algorithm is Round Robin, which divides the workload in a circular order, ensuring that all the available machines get an equal number of requests and none of them is overloaded or underloaded.

For example, the following figure marks the place of a load balancer in a typical master-slave architecture:

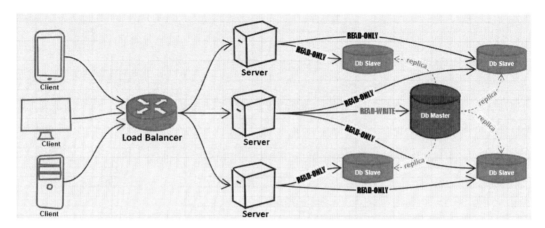

Figure 19.2 – Load balancer in a master-slave architecture

By dividing the work across the machines, load balancing strives to achieve maximum throughput and response time.

Coding challenge 7 – Sticky session

Problem: What is sticky session (or session affinity)?

Solution: Sticky session (or session affinity) is a notion encountered in a load balancer. Typically, the user information is stored in the session, and the session is replicated on all the machines from the cluster. But session replication (see *Coding challenge 11*) can be avoided by serving a particular user session requests from the same machine.

For this, the session is associated with a machine. This happens when the sessions are created. All the incoming requests for this session are always redirected to the associated machine. The user data is only on that machine.

In Java, sticky session is typically done via the `jsessionid` cookie. At the first request, the cookie is sent to the client. For each subsequent request, the client request contains the cookie as well. This way, the cookie identifies the session.

The main drawback of the sticky session approach consists of the fact that if the machine fails then the user information is lost, and that session is unrecoverable. If the client browser doesn't support cookies or cookies are disabled, then sticky session via cookies cannot be achieved.

Coding challenge 8 – Sharding

Problem: What is sharding?

Solution: Sharding is an architectural technique for distributing a single logical database system across a cluster of machines. The following figure depicts this statement:

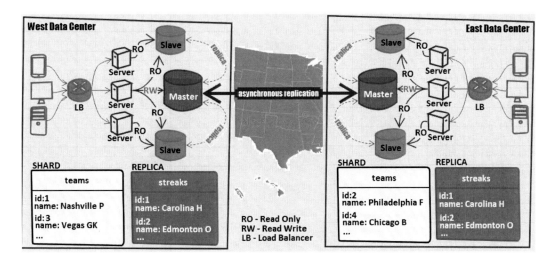

Figure 19.3 – Sharding

As you can see in the preceding figure, sharding is about the horizontal partitioning of the database scheme. Mainly, the rows of a database table (for example, `teams`) are stored separately (West Data Center holds odd rows, while East Data Center holds even rows), instead of splitting the table into columns (splitting into columns is known as normalization and vertical partitioning).

Each partition is called a *shard*. As you can see from the preceding figure, each shard can be independently located on a physical location or on a separate database server.

The sharding goal is to make a database system highly scalable. The small number of rows in each shard reduces the index size and improves the read/search operations' performance.

The drawbacks of sharding are the following:

- The application must be aware of the data location.
- Adding/removing nodes from the system requires rebalancing the system.
- The cross-node join queries come with performance penalties.

Coding challenge 9 – Shared-nothing architecture

Problem: What is shared-nothing architecture?

Solution: Shared-nothing architecture (denoted as **SN**) is a distributed computing technique that holds that each node is independent and contains everything it needs to have autonomy. Moreover, there is no single point of contention required across the system. The main aspects of an SN architecture are the following:

- The nodes work independently.
- No resources (memory, files, and so on) are shared between the nodes.
- If a node fails, then it affects only its users (other nodes continue to work).

Having a linear and theoretically infinite scalability, the SN architecture is quite popular. Google is one of the major players that relies on SN.

Coding challenge 10 – Failover

Problem: What is failover?

Solution: Failover is a technique used for achieving high availability by switching to another machine from the cluster when one of the machines fails. Commonly, failover is applied automatically by a load balancer via a heartbeat check mechanism. Mainly, the load balancer checks the machines' availability by ensuring that they respond. If a heartbeat of a machine fails (the machine doesn't respond), then the load balancer doesn't send any requests to it and redirects the requests to another machine from the cluster.

Coding challenge 11 – Session replication

Problem: What is session replication?

Solution: Session replication is commonly encountered in application server clusters with the main goal of achieving session failover.

Session replication is applied every time a user changes their current session. Mainly, the user session is automatically replicated to other machines from the cluster. This way, if a machine fails, the load balancer sends the incoming requests to another machine from the cluster. Since every machine in the cluster has a copy of the user session, the load balancer can choose any of those machines.

While session replication sustains session failover, it may have extra cost in terms of memory and network bandwidth.

Coding challenge 12 – The CAP theorem

Problem: What is the CAP theorem?

Solution: The CAP theorem was published by Eric Brewer and is specific to distributed computing. Conforming to this theorem, a distributed computer system can simultaneously provide only two of the following three things:

- **Consistency**: Concurrent updates are available to all nodes.
- **Availability**: Every request receives a response of success or fail.
- **Partition tolerance**: The system continues to operate despite a partial failure.

The following figure depicts the CAP theorem:

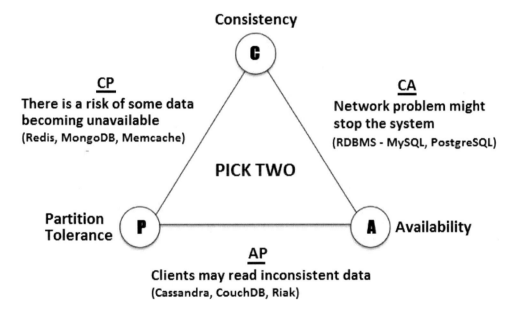

Figure 19.4 – The CAP theorem

Companies such as Google, Facebook, and Amazon use the CAP theorem to decide their application architecture.

Coding challenge 13 – Social networks

Problem: How would you design the data structures for a social network like Facebook? Describe the algorithm to show the shortest path between two people (for example, Tom → Alice → Mary → Kely).

Solution: Commonly, social networks are designed using graphs. The result is a huge graph such as those in the next figure (this figure was gathered via Google Image via the *social network graph* keywords):

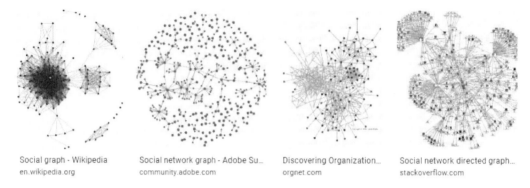

Figure 19.5 – Social network graph

So, finding a path between two people means finding a path in such a graph. In this case, the problem reduces to how to efficiently find a path between two nodes in such a huge graph.

We can start with one person and traverse the graph to find the other person. Traversing a graph can be done using **BFS** (**Breadth-first Search**) or **DFS** (**Depth-first Search**). For more details about these algorithms, check out *Chapter 13, Trees and Graphs*.

DFS will be very inefficient! Two persons might be only one degree of separation apart, but DFS may traverse millions of nodes (persons) before finding this relatively immediate connection.

Hence, the winner is BFS. More precisely, we can employ bidirectional BFS. Like two trains that come from opposite directions and intersect at some moment in time, we use one BFS that starts from person *A* (the source) and one BFS that starts from person *B* (the destination). When the searches collide, we have found a path between *A* and *B*.

Why not unidirectional BFS? Because going from *A* to *B* will traverse $p+p*p$ people. Mainly, unidirectional BFS will traverse *A*'s p friends, and then each of their p friends. This means that for a path of length q, the unidirectional BFS will perform in $O(p^q)$ runtime. On the other hand, the bidirectional BFS traverses $2p$ nodes: each of *A*'s p friends and each of *B*'s p friends. This means that for a path of length q, the bidirectional BFS performs in $O(p^{q/2} + p^{q/2}) = O(p^{q/2})$. Obviously, $O(p^{q/2})$ is better than $O(p^q)$.

Let's consider a path such as Ana -> Bob -> Carla -> Dan -> Elvira, where each person has 100 friends. A unidirectional BFS will traverse 100 million (100^4) nodes. A bidirectional BFS will traverse only 20,000 nodes (2×100^2).

Finding an efficient way to connect *A* and *B* is just one of the problems. Another problem is caused by the high number of persons, when the amount of data is so huge it cannot be stored on a single machine. This means that our graph will use multiple machines (for example, a cluster). If we represent the list of users as a list of IDs, then we can use sharding and store ranges of IDs on each machine. This way, we go to the next person in the path by going first onto the machine that contains the person's ID.

In order to mitigate a lot of random jumps between machines, which will downgrade performance, we can distribute the users across machines by taking into account country, city, state, and so on. It is more likely that users from the same country will be friends.

Further questions that need an answer refer to caching usage, when to stop a search with no results, what to do if a machine fails, and so on.

It is clear that tackling problems such as the preceding one is not an easy task. It requires addressing a lot of questions and issues, therefore reading and practicing as much as possible is a must.

Practicing is the key to success

The topic of this short chapter deserves an entire book. But, challenging yourself to solve the following top 10 problems will boost your insights about scalability and your chances of becoming a software engineer.

Designing bitly, TinyURL, and goo.gl (a service for shorting URLs)

Questions to address:

- How do you assign a unique identifier (ID) for each given URL?
- Having thousands of URLs per second, how do you generate unique identifiers (IDs) at scale?
- How do you handle redirects?
- How do you deal with custom short URLs?
- How do you deal with the expired URLs (delete them)?
- How do you track statistics (for example, click stats)?

Designing Netflix, Twitch, and YouTube (a global video streaming service)

Questions to address:

- How do you store and distribute data in a way that accommodates a large number of simultaneous users (the users can watch and share data)?
- How do you track statistics (for example, the total number of views, voting, and so on)?
- How do you allow users to add comments on videos (preferably, in real time)?

Designing WhatsApp and Facebook Messenger (a global chat service)

Questions to address:

- How do you design one-on-one conversations/meetings between users?
- How do you design group chats/meetings?
- How do you deal with offline users (not connected to the internet)?
- When should you send push notifications?
- How do you support end-to-end encryption?

Designing Reddit, HackerNews, Quora, and Voat (a message board service and social network)

Questions to address:

- How do you track the stats of each answer (the total number of views, voting, and so on)?
- How do you allow users to follow other users or topics?
- How do you design the timeline consisting of a user's top questions (similar to newsfeed generation)?

Designing Google Drive, Google Photos, and Dropbox (a global file storage and sharing service)

Questions to address:

- How do you design user features such as upload, search, view, and share files/photos?
- How do you track permissions for file sharing?
- How do you allow a group of users to edit the same document?

Designing Twitter, Facebook, and Instagram (an extremely large social media service)

Questions to address:

- How do you efficiently store and search for posts/tweets?
- How do you implement newsfeed generation?
- How do you tackle the social graph (see *Coding challenge 13*)?

Designing Lyft, Uber, and RideAustin (a ride-sharing service)

Questions to address:

- How do you match a ride request with nearby drivers?
- How do you store millions of locations (geographical coordinates) for riders and drivers that are continuously moving?
- How do you update the driver/rider locations (updates every second)?

Designing a type-ahead and web crawler (a search engine related service)

Questions to address:

- How do you refresh data?
- How do you store the previous search queries?
- How do you detect the best matches for the already typed string?

- How do you tackle a case when the user is typing too fast?
- How do you find new pages (web pages)?
- How do you assign priorities to web pages that are changing dynamically?
- How do you guarantee that the crawler is not stuck on the same domain forever?

Designing an API rate limiter (for example, GitHub or Firebase)

Questions to address:

- How do you limit the number of requests within a time window (for example, 30 requests per second)?
- How do you implement rate-limiting to work in a cluster of servers?
- How do you tackle throttling (soft and hard)?

Designing nearby places/friends and Yelp (a proximity server)

Questions to address:

- How do you search for nearby friends or places?
- How do you rank places?
- How do you store location data according to the population density?

Answering these challenges is not an easy task and requires significant experience. However, if you are a junior/middle-level programmer and you have read this introductory chapter about scalability, then you should be able to decide whether your career path should go in this direction or not. However, keep in mind that designing large-scale distributed systems is a very demanding area in software engineering interviews.

Summary

This is the last chapter of this book. We've just covered a bunch of problems that fit into the scalability topic.

Congratulations on coming this far! Now, at the end of this book, remember to practice as much as possible, have confidence in your judgment, and never give up! I really hope that your next Java position will bring you the job of your dreams and that this book makes a contribution to your success.

Other Books You May Enjoy

If you enjoyed this book, you may be interested in these other books by Packt:

Java Coding Problems

Anghel Leonard

ISBN: 9781789801415

- Adopt the latest JDK 11 and JDK 12 features in your applications
- Solve cutting-edge problems relating to collections and data structures
- Get to grips with functional-style programming using lambdas
- Perform asynchronous communication and parallel data processing
- Solve strings and number problems using the latest Java APIs
- Become familiar with different aspects of object immutability in Java
- Implement the correct practices and clean code techniques

Learn Java 12 Programming

Nick Samoylov

ISBN: 9781789957051

- Learn and apply object-oriented principles
- Gain insights into data structures and understand how they are used in Java
- Explore multithreaded, asynchronous, functional, and reactive programming
- Add a user-friendly graphic interface to your application
- Find out what streams are and how they can help in data processing
- Discover the importance of microservices and use them to make your apps robust and scalable
- Explore Java design patterns and best practices to solve everyday problems
- Learn techniques and idioms for writing high-quality Java code

Leave a review - let other readers know what you think

Please share your thoughts on this book with others by leaving a review on the site that you bought it from. If you purchased the book from Amazon, please leave us an honest review on this book's Amazon page. This is vital so that other potential readers can see and use your unbiased opinion to make purchasing decisions, we can understand what our customers think about our products, and our authors can see your feedback on the title that they have worked with Packt to create. It will only take a few minutes of your time, but is valuable to other potential customers, our authors, and Packt. Thank you!

Index

A

Abcd application 643, 644
abstract class
  about 115
  versus interfaces 115
  without abstract method 115
Abstract Data Type (ADT) 380
abstraction 67, 69
Abstraction/AbstractionViaInterface 69
acyclic graph 481
adapter patterns
  versus bridge patterns 122
adjacency list 483
adjacency matrix 482
aggregation 81-83
algorithms, efficiency
  best case 154
  expected case 154
  worst case 154
Amazon interview 28
arrays 290
ASCII characters 290
association 79-81
AVLTreeImpl application 476

B

balanced binary tree 474
base case recursion 590
best online practices, for gaining experience
  about 12
  certifications 17
  GitHub account, starting 13
  Learn->Code practice 17
  open source projects, contributing to 13
  rules 12
  Stack Overflow account, starting 14
  technical articles, posting 15
  technical blog, starting 15
  work (portfolio), promoting 15
  YouTube channel, starting 14
BestTimeToBuySellStock application
  about 356, 367
  scenarios 356-366
BiggestColorSpot application 193-196
Big O cheat sheet
  reference link 154
Big O examples
  Big O expressions, reducing 170
  digits 175
  factorial Big O 173

half of array, looping 170
half of matrix, looping 168, 169
in-order traversal, of binary tree 164
log n runtimes 161-163
looping, with O(log n) 171
memoization 166-168
n may vary 165, 166
n notation, using 174
non-dominant terms, dropping 158, 159
number of iteration counts, in Big O 175
O(1) loops, identifying 169, 170
O(n), dropping constants 156-158
O(n), linear time algorithms 155
recursive runtimes 163, 164
sorting 176, 177
string comparison 172
sum, and count 174, 175
binary heap 479-481
binary search algorithm 324
BinarySearch application 580
binary search tree (BST) 473, 502, 616
BinarySearchTreeDuplicates
    application 526
BinarySearchTreeKthLargestElement
    application 532
BinarySearchTreeSuccessor
    application 507
BinarySearchTreeSum
    application 543, 546
BinarySearchTreeTraversal
    application 473
binary tree 469, 470
BinaryTreeBalanced application 501
BinaryTreeCommonAncestor
    application 511
BinaryTreeDistanceFromLeaf
    application 541
BinaryTreeIsBST application 504

BinaryTreeLandingReservation
    application 498
BinaryTreeMaxPathSum application 519
BinaryTreePrintCorners application 516
BinaryTreePrintDiagonal application 524
BinaryTreeRightView application 531
BinaryTreeSpiralTraversal application 539
BinaryTreeSubtree application 493
binary tree traversal 470
BinaryTreeTraversal application 472
BinaryTreeVerticalSum application 548
binding operation 116
bin sort algorithm. *See also*
    bucket sort algorithm
bit manipulation
    about 236
    binary representation, obtaining
        of Java integer 236, 237
    bit shift operators, using 239
    bitwise operators, using 237, 238
    coding challenges 242
    tips and tricks 241, 242
bit shift operators
    negative integers, in Java 239, 240
    Signed Left Shift [<<] 239
    Signed Right Shift [>>] 240
    Unsigned Right Shift [>>>] 241
    using 239
Bitwise AND [&] 237, 238
Bitwise Exclusive OR (XOR) [^] 238
bitwise operators
    Bitwise AND [&] 237
    Bitwise Exclusive OR (XOR) [^] 238
    Bitwise OR [|] 238
    unary bitwise complement
        operator [~] 237
    using, for bit manipulation 237, 238
Bitwise OR [|] 238

Blogger
  URL 15
bottom-up dynamic programming.
      See also tabulation
Braces application 217-219
breadth-first search (BFS)
  about 470, 484
  for trees 470
BreakChocolate application 655, 657
brute-force approach. *See also*
      naive approach
buckets 570
bucket sort algorithm 570-574
BucketSort application 575
builder pattern
  versus factory pattern 121

C

Camtasia Studio
  reference link 14
CAP theorem
  about 733
  availability 733
  consistency 733
  partition tolerance 733
CareerBuilder
  URL 22
certifications
  reference link 17
ChessKnight application 514
circular doubly linked list 378
circular singly linked list 378
class 66
ClearBits application 245, 246
clustering 728
code 11
code points 290

CodersRank
  about 16, 17
  reference link 16
coding challenge
  interviewer's presence 52, 53
  paper-pen, versus computer
      approach 53
  tackling 52
  tackling, process 54
coding challenge, tackling
  about 54
  algorithm(s), selecting 55, 56
  blockage, handling 58
  example, building 55
  process 54
  skeleton, coding 56, 57
  solution, coding 57
coding challenges, for OOP
  about 50, 123
  CircularByteBuffer application 150
  DeckOfCards application 129-133
  FileSystem application 149
  HashTable application 145-149
  Jukebox application 123-126
  MovieTicketBooking application 149
  online reader system
      application 139-145
  ParkingLot application 133-139
  specific problems 50, 51
  Tuple application 149
  VendingMachine application 126-129
coding challenges, for
      functional-style programming
  arrays, converting to streams 703, 704
  collections, versus streams 696
  default method 705
  filter() function 699

findFirst() method, versus
    findAny() method 702, 703
flatMap() function 697
functional interface 695
functional interface, versus
    regular interface 701
intermediate operations, versus
    terminal operations 700
Iterator, versus Spliterator 705
lambda expression 693-695
lazy streams 701
map() functions, versus flatMap()
    functions 696-698
method reference 704
Optional class 706
parallel streams 704
peek() function 700
Predicates 702
String::valueOf 707
Supplier, versus Consumer 701
coding challenges, for Java
    concurrency (multithreading)
    about 674
    ConcurrentHashMap, versus
        Hashtable 681
    CountDownLatch, versus
        CyclicBarrier 680
    data, sharing between threads 683
    deadlocks 675
    ExecutorAndExecutorService
        application 677
    interrupted() method 682
    isInterrupted() method 682
    livelocks 679
    Producer-Consumer
        application 684, 685
    race conditions 676
    ReadWriteLock application 684
    reentrant locking 677
    RunnableAndCallable application 678
    start() method, versus run() method 679
    starvation 678
    submit() method, versus
        execute() method 682
    thread, canceling 682, 683
    ThreadLifecycleStates
        application 674, 675
    ThreadLocal 681
    Thread, versus Runnable 679
    wait() method, versus sleep()
        method 680, 681
coding challenges, for recursion
    and dynamic programming
    BiggestColorSpot application 193-196
    Braces application 217-219
    Coins application 196-198
    FiveTowers application 198-201
    HanoiTowers 188-191
    HighestColoredTower
        application 206-208
    Josephus application 191-193
    KnightTour application 214-216
    MagicIndex application 202, 203
    Permutations application 208-213
    RobotGridMaze application 186, 188
    Staircase application 219, 220
    SubsetSum application 220
    TheFallingBall application 204, 205
    WordBreak application 228
coding challenges, for
    scalability interviews
    about 727
    bandwidth 729, 730
    CAP theorem 733
    clustering 728, 729

failover 732
high availability 728
latency 729
low latency 728
scaling types 727, 728
session replication 732
sharding 731
shared-nothing architecture (SN) 732
social networks 733-735
sticky session 730
throughput 729
coding challenges, for solving math and logical puzzle problems
  8 teams 638
  Abcd application 643, 644
  about 631
  BreakChocolate application 655, 656
  DecodingDigitSequence application 640, 642
  FizzBuzz application 631
  HourMinuteAngle application 657, 659
  KthNumber357 application 639, 640
  MultiplyLargeNumbers application 648, 649
  NextElementSameDigits application 651, 652
  NumberDivisibleDigits application 654, 655
  PythagoreanTriplets application 659-661
  RectangleOverlap application 644-648
  RomanNumbers application 632-634
  ScheduleOneElevator application 662-664
  VisitToggle100Doors application 635, 637
coding challenges, for sorting and searching algorithms
  about 580

FindNearestMinimum application 622, 623
GroupSortAnagrams application 583-587
InterspersedEmptyStrings application 593-595
MaxDiffBetweenTwoElements application 614, 615
MergeSortDoublyLinkedList application 589, 591
MergeSortSinglyLinkedList application 589, 591
MergeTwoSortedArrays application 580-582
PeaksAndValleys application 619-621
PositionOfFirstOne application 613
RankInStream application 616, 617
SearchInFullSortedMatrix application 608, 609
SearchInSortedMatrix application 610-612
SortArrayBasedOnAnotherArray application 625
SortQueueViaTempQueue application 595-597
SortQueueWithoutExtraSpace application 599-601
SortStack application 602, 603
SortStackInPlace application 604-606
UnknownSizeList application 587, 588
WordSearch application 624
coding challenges, for strings and arrays
  about 290, 291
  BestTimeToBuySellStock application 356
  ContainerMostWater application 334-338

CountDistinctAbsoluteSortedArray application 375
CountDistinctInSubarray application 375
CountScore3510 application 369, 370
DuplicatesInArray application 370-373
EncodedString application 296
ExtractIntegers application 301
ExtractSurrogatePairs application 302-304
FindPairsSumEqualK application 318-320
LongestConsecutiveSequence application 367, 368
LongestDistinctSubstring application 374
MatrixWithZeros application 309-312
MaxMatrixOfOne application 330-332
MedianOfSortedArrays application 324-328
MergeIntervals application 342-346
MergeKSortedArr application 321, 322
OneEditAway application 297
PetrolBunks application 348-350
ReplaceElementWithRank application 374
RotateArrayKTimes application 375
RotateMatrix application 306, 309
RotateString application 305
SearchInCircularArray application 339, 340
StringShrinker application 299
ThreeStacksInOneArrayFixed application 313-318
TrapRainWater application 351-355
unique characters application 292

UniqueCharactersAZ application 294, 295
coding challenges, for bit manipulations
  about 242
  binaries, dividing on paper 254-256
  binaries, multiplying on paper 249, 250
  binaries, subtracting on paper 252, 253
  binaries, summing on paper 246, 247
  ClearBits application 245, 246
  Conversion application 266, 267
  DividingBinaries application 256, 257
  expressions, maximizing 267, 268
  FindDuplicates application 277
  FloatToBinaryAndBack application 284
  GetBitValue application 242
  LongestSequence application 259-262
  MultiplyingBinaries application 250, 251
  NextNumber application 262-266
  NumberWithOneInLR application 272, 273
  OnceTwiceThrice application 273-276
  PositionOfFirstBitOfOne application 283
  PowerSetOfSet application 281, 282
  ReplaceBits application 257, 259
  RotateBits application 270, 272
  SetBitValue application 243, 244
  SubtractingBinaries application 253, 254
  SummingBinaries application 247-249
  SwapOddEven application 269, 270
  TwoNonRepeating application 278-280
coding challenges, of maps and linked lists 380
  DoublyLinkedListReverse application 417, 418
  LinkedListLoopDetection application 393

LinkedListMergeTwoSortedRecursion
    application 406-410
LinkedListMoveLastToFront
    application 413, 414
LinkedListNthToLastNode
    application 391, 392
LinkedListPairwiseSwap
    application 403-406
LinkedListPalindrome
    application 397-399
LinkedListRearranging
    application 389-391
 LinkedListRemoveDuplicates
    application 387-389
LinkedListRemoveRedundantPath
    application 411, 412
LinkedListsIntersection
    application 401-403
LinkedListSum application 399, 400
LRUCache application 418-420, 423
Map application 381-385
NutsAndBolts application 385, 386
ReverseLinkedListInGroups
    application 415-417
coding challenges, of stacks and queues
  about 432
  MinStackConstantTimeAndSpace
    application 442-446
  QueueIslands application 457-461
  QueueViaStack application 446, 448
  ShortestSafeRoute application 461-464
  SmallestNumber application 455-457
  StackBraces application 433-435
  StackHistogramAre application 452-455
  StackOfPlates application 435-438
  StackReverseString application 432, 433
  StackViaQueue application 448-452

StockSpan application 438-440, 442
coding challenges, of unit testing
  @Rule 721
  about 712
  developer or tester 716
  dynamic tests 721, 722
  FIRST 713
  junit4/Assumptions application 719, 720
  junit4/TestSuite application 717-719
  junit5/ArrangeActAssert
    application 712
  junit5/BeforeAfterAnnotations
    application 717
  junit5/NestedTests application 722-724
  junit5/TestingExceptions
    application 714-716
  JUnit extensions 716
  method test return type 721
  mocking 717
  stubbing 717
  test methods, ignoring 719
  text fixtures 713
coding challenges, trees and graphs
  about 486
  balanced binary tree 499-501
  binary search tree (BST) 502
  binary tree corners, printing 514-516
  binary tree is symmetry, finding 551-554
  binary tree right view 529-531
  chess knight 511-514
  common ancestor 509, 511
  diagonal traversal 519
  duplicates, handling in BSTs 524-526
  isomorphism, of binary
    trees 526, 528, 529
  k^{th} largest element 531, 532
  landing reservation system 494-498

list per level 489, 490
max heap, converting into
 min heap 548, 550
max path sum 516-519
mirror binary tree 533
nodes at distance k, from
 leaf nodes 539-541
n ropes, connecting with
 minimum cost 554, 555
pair, for given sum 541-546
paths, between two nodes 486
sorted array, to minimal BST 487, 488
spiral Level-Order traversal,
 of binary tree 535, 536
sub-tree 491, 492
successor node 504-507
topological sort 507, 508
vertical sums, in binary tree 546-548
Coins application 196-198
collections
 versus streams 696
combine operation 564
Compile-Time Polymorphism 75, 115
complete binary tree 477
composition 83-85
ConcurrentHashMap
 versus Hashtable 681
Consumer
 versus Supplier 701
ContainerMostWater application 334, 338
Conversion application 266, 267
CountDistinctAbsoluteSortedArray
 application 375
CountDistinctInSubarray application 375
CountDownLatch
 versus CyclicBarrier 680
CountScore3510 application 369, 370

covariant method overriding
 in Java 108
Criteria Cognitive Aptitude
 Test (CCAT) 30
Crossover interview 30, 31

D

data
 sharing, between threads 683
 data-hiding mechanism 70
deadlocks 675, 676
DeckOfCards application 129-133
DecodingDigitSequence
 application 640-643
decorator design pattern
 composition 119
default method 705
Dependency Inversion Principle (DIP)
 about 102
 breaking 103
 following 103, 104
depth-first search (DFS)
 about 470, 484
 for graphs 485
 for trees 471, 472
depth-first search (DFS), for graphs
 iterative implementation 485
 via recursion 485
diagonal traversal
 iterative-based solution 522, 524
 recursion-based solution 520-522
Dice
 URL 22
digital tree 481
directed acyclic graph (DAG) 507
DirectedGraphPath application 487
Divide and Conquer (D&C) 171

DividingBinaries application 256, 257
Don't Repeat Yourself (DRY) 56
doubly linked list 378
DoublyLinkedListReverse
    application 417, 418
DuplicatesInArray application 370, 374
Dynamic Method Dispatch 76
dynamic programming
  about 181, 182
  memoization 182
  tabulation 184, 185
DZone
  URL 15

E

Elevator algorithm
  URL 665
encapsulation. *See also*
    data-hiding mechanism 70, 72
EncodedString application 296, 297
entries 380
enqueue (rear) operation 429
execute() method
  versus submit() method 682
ExecutorAndExecutorService
    application 677
experience
  gaining 11
ExtractIntegers application 301, 302
ExtractSurrogatePairs
    application 302, 305

F

facade pattern
  versus decorator patterns 120

Facebook interview 29, 30
failover 732
failure, handling
  about 42
  company obsession, avoiding 44
  confidence, building up 44
Fast, Isolated, Repeatable,
    Self-Validating, Timely (FIRST) 713
Fast Runner (FR) 590
Fast Runner/Slow Runner
    approach 393-397
FileSystem application 149
filter() function 699
final class 115
findAny() method
  versus findFirst() method 702
FindDuplicates application 277
findAny() method
  versus findFirst() method 702
FindNearestMinimum
    application 622, 624
FindPairsSumEqualK application 318, 321
first-in-first-out (FIFO) principle 429
FiveTowers application 198-201
FizzBuzz application 631, 632
flatMap() function
  about 697
  versus map() functions 697, 698
FlexJobs
  URL 22
FloatToBinaryAndBack application 284
Free2X Webcam Recorder
  reference link 14
front (dequeue or poll) operation 429
full binary tree 478
functional interface
  about 695

versus regular interface 701
functional-style programming,
    key concepts
  about 690
  as first-class objects 690
  higher-order functions 691
  immutable variables 692
  no-side effects 692
  no state 691
  pure functional programming, rules 691
  pure functions 690
  recursion over looping, favoring 693
functional testing 710

G

gathering 571
general tree 469
GetBitValue application 242
Glassdoor
  URL 22
Google interview 28
Google Sites
  reference link 16
graph
  about 481
  adjacency list 483
  adjacency matrix 482
  edge 481
  vertex 481
GraphAdjacencyListTraversal 485
GraphAdjacencyMatrixTraversal 485
GraphTopologicalSort application 509
graph traversal 484
GroupSortAnagrams application 583, 587

H

HanoiTowers application 188
Hashtable
  versus ConcurrentHashMap 681
HashTable application 145-149
HeapConnectRopes application 556
heapify-down operation 481
heapify-up operation 480
heap sort algorithm 561, 562, 564
HeapSort application 564
high availability 728
HighestColoredTower
    application 206-208
Hiring Committee (HC) 28
histogram class interval 452
HourMinuteAngle application 657, 659

I

Indeed
  URL 22
infix expressions 464
InfoQ
  URL 15
InformIT
  URL 15
inheritance. *See* also IS-A relationship
(parent-child relationship) 73-75
In-Order traversal 472
integration testing 710, 711
Interface Segregation Principle (ISP)
  about 98, 99
  breaking 99, 100
  following 101, 102

interfaces, with default methods
versus interfaces, with
abstract classes 114
intermediate operations
versus terminal operations 700
InterspersedEmptyStrings
application 593, 595
interview preparations
  about 23
  in-person interviews 24
  mistakes, avoiding 24, 25
  phone screening stage 23
interviews
  at Amazon 28
  at Crossover 30, 31
  at Facebook 29, 30
  at Google 28
  at Microsoft 29
  key hints 177
IS-A relationship (parentchild relationship) 73-75
IsSymmetricBinaryTree application 554
Iterator
  versus Spliterator 705

J

Java
  covariant method overriding 107, 108
  method hiding 116, 117
  virtual methods, writing 118
Java Code Geeks
  URL 15
Java concurrency (multithreading) 672-674
Java functional-style programming 690
Java integer

binary representation, obtaining 236, 237
Java interface
non-abstract method 111-14
Java interview
  feedback, obtaining 43
  marketable skills, developing 8-11
  preparations 4-8
  roadmap 4
Java surveys
  URLs 5, 9
Java Virtual Machine (JVM) 675
job application process
  about 22
  hiring companies, searching for 22
  resume, submitting 23
Josephus application 191-193
Jukebox application 123-126
junit4/Assumptions application 719, 720
junit4/TestSuite application 717-719
junit5/ArrangeActAssert application 712
junit5/BeforeAfterAnnotations application 717
junit5/NestedTests application 722-724
junit5/TestingExceptions application 714-716

K

key 379
key-value pair 379
KnightTour application 214-216
KthNumber357 application 639, 640

L

lambda expression 693-695
last-in-first-out (LIFO) principle 426

latency 729
lazy streams 701
Least Recently Used Cache (LRU) 418
Least Significant Bit (LSB) 240
LinkedIn
  URL 22
LinkedIn resume 21
LinkedListLoopDetection application
  about 393
  Fast Runner/Slow Runner
    approach 393-397
LinkedListMergeTwoSorted
    application 410
LinkedListMergeTwoSortedRecursion
    application 406-410
LinkedListMoveLastToFront
    application 413, 414
LinkedListNthToLastNode
    application 391, 392
LinkedListPairwiseSwap
    application 403-406
LinkedListPalindrome
    application 397-399
LinkedListRearranging
    application 389-391
LinkedListRemoveRedundantPath
    application 411, 412
linked lists
  about 378, 379
  head 378
  tail 378
LinkedListsIntersection
    application 401-403
LinkedListSum application 399, 400
LinkeListMergeNSortedRecursion
    application 410
Liskovs Substitution Principle (LSP)
  about 93

  breaking 94-96
  following 96-98
ListPerBinaryTreeLevel application 491
livelocks 679
load balancing 729
LongestConsecutiveSequence
    application 367, 369
LongestDistinctSubstring application 374
LongestSequence application 260-262
low latency 728
LRUCache application 418-420, 423

M

MagicIndex application 201-203
main() method
  overloading 110
  overriding 110
Map application 381-85
map capacity 381
map() functions
  versus flatMap() functions 697, 698
maps 379, 380
math and logical puzzle problems
  solving, suggestions 630, 631
  solving, tips 630, 631
MatrixWithZeros application 309, 312
MaxDiffBetweenTwoElements
    application 614, 616
MaxHeap application 481
MaxHeapToMinHeap application 550
MaxMatrixOfOne application 330, 333
MedianOfSortedArrays
    application 324, 330
Medium
  URL 15
memoization 182-84
MergeIntervals application 342, 347

MergeKSortedArr application 321, 323
merge operation 564
merge sort algorithm 564-566
MergeSort application 567
MergeSortDoublyLinkedList
    application 590, 593
MergeSortSinglyLinkedList
    application 590, 593
MergeTwoSortedArrays
    application 580, 583
method
  hiding, in Java 116, 117
  overloading, in OOP (Java) 106
  overriding, in OOP (Java) 106
  reference 704
Microsoft interview 29
MinStackConstantTimeAndSpace
    application 442-446
MirrorBinaryTree application 535
mismatches
  eliminating 44
  identifying 44
Mkyong
  URL 15
Most Significant Bit (MSB) 240
MovieTicketBooking application 149
MultiplyingBinaries application 250, 251
MultiplyLargeNumbers
    application 648, 651
MyQueue application 432
MyStack application 429

N

naive approach 660
negative integers, in Java 239, 240
NextElementSameDigits
    application 651, 654

NextNumber application 262-266
non-binary tree 469
non-static method, Java
    overriding, as static 110
non-technical interview questions 35-40
normalization 731
NumberDivisibleDigits
    application 654, 655
NumberWithOneInLR
    application 272, 273
NutsAndBolts application 385, 386

O

object 65
Object-Oriented Programming (OOP) 28
offer
  accepting 42
  rejecting 42
OnceTwiceThrice application 273-276
OneEditAway application 297, 299
online reader system application 139-145
OOP concepts
  about 64, 65
  abstraction 67-69
  aggregation 81-83
  association 79-81
  class 66
  composition 83-85
  encapsulation 70, 72
  inheritance 73-75
  object 65
  polymorphism 75, 76
OOP (Java)
  method overloading 106, 107
  method overriding 105, 106
Open Closed Principle (OCP)
  about 89

breaking 90, 91
following 91-93
Optional class 706
overloading
  polymorphism, implementing with 118
overloading methods
  exceptions, working with 109
overriding methods
  exceptions, working with 109

P

parallel stream 704
ParkingLot application 133-139
peak 619
PeaksAndValleys application 619, 622
peek() function 700, 701
perfect binary tree 478
Permutations application 208, 210-213
personal website (portfolio)
  about 16
  building, reference link 16
  reference link 16
PetrolBunks application 348, 350
PluralSight
  URL 15
polymorphism
  about 75, 76
  implementing, via method overloading
    (compile time) 76, 77
  implementing, via method
    overriding (runtime) 77, 78
  implementing, with overloading 118
  versus abstraction 118
pop operation 426
PositionOfFirstBitOfOne application 283
PositionOfFirstOne application 613, 614
postfix expressions 464

Post-Order traversal 472
PowerSetOfSet application 281, 282
Predicates 702
prefix expressions 464
Pre-Order traversal 471
Producer-Consumer application
  about 684, 685
  solving, via built-in blocking queues 687
  solving, via notify() method 685, 686
  solving, via wait() method 685, 686
proxy design pattern
  versus decorator patterns 120
push operation 426
PythagoreanTriplets application 659, 662

Q

QueueIslands application 457-461
queues
  about 429-432
  operations 429
QueueViaStack application 446, 448
quick sort algorithm 567-569
QuickSort application 570

R

race conditions 676
radix sort algorithm 575, 577
RadixSort application 577
RankInStream application 616, 619
ReadWriteLock application 684
RectangleOverlap application 644, 648
recursion 180
recursive method 180
recursive problem
  recognizing 180, 181
Red-Black tree 474, 475

RedBlackTreeImpl application 475
reentrant locking 677
regular interface
    versus functional interface 701
rejection reasons 43
ReplaceBits application 257, 259
ReplaceElementWithRank
        application 374
resume preparation
    best practices 18-21
    technical skills section, do's
        and don'ts 20, 21
ReverseLinkedListInGroups
        application 415-417
RobotGridMaze application 186-188
RomanNumbers application 632, 635
RotateArrayKTimes application 375
RotateBits application 270-272
RotateMatrix application 306, 309
RotateMatrix application, code
        challenges solutions
    matrix, rotating ring by ring 308
    matrix transpose, using 306-308
RotateString application 305, 306
run() method
    versus start() method 679
Runnable
    versus Thread 679
RunnableAndCallable application 678
Runtime Polymorphism 75, 76, 115

S

scalability 726, 727
scalable applications
    designing, practicing 735-738
scaling out (horizontal scaling) 727, 728
scaling up (vertical scaling) 727

scattering 571
scatter-sort-gather technique 571
ScheduleOneElevator application 662, 664
scheduling multiple elevators problem
    about 665
    solutions 665
SearchInCircularArray
        application 339, 342
SearchInFullSortedMatrix
        application 608, 610
searching algorithms 578
SearchInSortedMatrix
        application 610, 612
session replication 732
SetBitValue application 243, 244
shard 731
sharding
    about 731
    drawbacks 731
shared-nothing architecture (SN) 732
ShortestSafeRoute application 461-464
Signed Left Shift [<<] 239
Single responsibility, Open-closed, Liskov
        substitution, Interface segregation,
        Dependency inversion (SOLID) 56
Single Responsibility Principle (SRP)
    about 86
    breaking 87
    following 88, 89
Singleton design pattern
    using 119
singly linked list 378
SitePoint
    URL 15
Situation|Action|Result (SAR)
        approach 25
sleep() method
    versus wait() method 680

Sliding Window Technique
  reference link 375
Slow Runner (SR) 590
SmallestNumber application 455-457
social network profiles 16
social networks 733-735
SOLID principles
  about 86
  Dependency Inversion
    Principle (DIP) 102
  Interface Segregation
    Principle (ISP) 98, 99
  Liskovs Substitution Principle (LSP) 93
  Open Closed Principle (OCP) 89
  references 105
  Single Responsibility Principle (SRP) 86
solutions, for scheduling multiple
elevators problem
  nearest elevator 665, 666
  nearest elevator with capacity
    considerations 665, 666
  sectors 665
SortArrayBasedOnAnotherArray
    application 625, 627
SortArraysIn14Ways application 560, 575
SortedArrayToMinBinarySearchTree
    application 489
sorting algorithms
  about 560, 561
  bucket sort algorithm 570-574
  heap sort algorithm 561-564
  merge sort algorithm 564-566
  quick sort algorithm 567-569
  radix sort algorithm 575, 577
SortQueueViaTempQueue
    application 595, 599
SortQueueWithoutExtraSpace
    application 599, 602

SortStack application 602, 604
SortStackInPlace application 604, 608
spiral Level-Order traversal, of binary tree
  iterative approach 537, 539
  recursive approach 536, 537
Spliterator
  versus Iterator 705
StackBraces application 433-435
StackHistogramAre application 452-455
StackOfPlates application 435- 437
Stack Overflow
  URL 22
StackReverseString application 433
stacks
  about 426-429
  operations 426
StackViaQueue application 448, 449, 452
Staircase application 219, 220
start() method
  versus run() method 679
starvation 678
static binding
  versus dynamic binding 116
sticky session 730
StockSpan application 438-440, 442
strategy design pattern
  versus state design patterns 119, 120
streams
  arrays, converting to 703, 704
  versus collections 696
String::valueOf 707
strings 290
StringShrinker application 299, 301
subclass overriding method
  superclass overridden method,
    calling from 110
submit() method
  versus execute() method 682

SubsetSum application
  about 220
  dynamic programming
    approach, using 222-226
  recursive approach, using 221, 222
SubtractingBinaries application 253, 254
SummingBinaries application 248, 249
Supplier
  versus Consumer 701
surrogate pair 303
SwapOddEven application 269, 270

T

tabulation 184, 185
technical quiz
  about 48, 49
  answering approaches 48, 49
  approaches 49
template method
  versus strategy pattern 121
terminal operations
  versus intermediate operations 700
text fixtures 713
TheFallingBall application 204, 205
thread
  canceling 682, 683
  versus Runnable 679
ThreadLifecycleState application 675
ThreadLocal 681
ThreeStacksInOneArrayFixed
    application 313-318
throughput 729
top-down dynamic programming.
    See also memoization
top operation 426
Tower of Hanoi challenge 189-191
transaction 356

TrapRainWater application 351, 356
trees
  about 468
  advanced topics 556, 557
  child node 468
  depth 468
  edge 468
  general tree 469
  height 468
  leaf node 468
  mirroring, in place 534
  mirroring, in tree 533, 534
  parent node 468
  root 468
Trie 481
Tuple application 149
TwoBinaryTreesAreIsomorphic
    application 529
two-head doubly linked list 379
two-head singly linked list 379
TwoNonRepeating application 278-280
two-pointers 319
two's complement 239, 240

U

Udemy
  URL 15
unary bitwise complement
    operator [~] 237
unbalanced binary tree 474
Unicode characters 290
unique characters application 292, 293
UniqueCharactersAZ application 294, 295
units 710
unit test case 710
unit testing

about 710, 711
coding challenges 712
functional testing 710
integration testing 710, 711
unit testing layer 710
UnknownSizeList application 587, 589
Unsigned Right Shift [>>>] 241
Upwork
  URL 22

V

valley 619
value 379
VendingMachine application 126-129
vertical partitioning 731
virtual methods
  writing, in Java 118
VisitToggle100Doors application 635, 638

W

wait() method
versus sleep() method 680
Wix
  reference link 16
WordBreak application
  about 227
  bottom-up solution 229, 230
  plain recursion-based solution 228, 229
  trie-based solution 230, 232
WordPress
  URL 15
WordSearch application 624, 625

Made in United States
North Haven, CT
11 October 2021